# The
# Bourbon
# Restoration

# THE
# BOURBON
# RESTORATION

*by*

Guillaume de Bertier de Sauvigny

*Institut Catholique de Paris*
and
*University of Notre Dame*

*Translated from the French by*
LYNN M. CASE
*University of Pennsylvania*

PHILADELPHIA
THE UNIVERSITY OF PENNSYLVANIA PRESS

# *Preface*

IN every society at any particular period there are conservatives and reformers. The conservatives benefit by the status quo, and try to preserve it; the reformers either suffer from the status quo or dream of something better, and try to change it. If the conservatives are wise enough to make a few concessions, and if the reformers are patient enough to be momentarily satisfied with such concessions, then a wholesome social compromise of gradual reform ensues. This represents in its general course what we might call success in human relations.

On the other hand, if the conservatives stubbornly refuse to make any concessions, and if the reformers in their impatience then make excessive demands, the resulting impasse may explode into a violent revolution which destroys the accepted traditions and institutions of that society. Uprooted from their past, the people of this torn society usually fall into a nervous frenzy and a regime of terror. However, after a few months or years of this wandering in an uncharted wilderness, the majority begins to seek a return to the old status quo; a reaction or restoration sets in. The revolutionary approach, with its disturbances and human suffering, with its violent oscillations from right to left and back again, represents a failure in human relations. But reactionary restorations almost inevitably do follow revolutions. The great tragedy of the twentieth century is that nearly half of the world is now dedicated to the belief in disruptive revolution as the norm in human relations when reforms are required.

History has taught us over and over again these lessons of successes and failures in human relations. What causes the recurrence of the revolutionary approach is that some conservatives and reformers do not read or heed history. Santayana once said that "those who cannot remember the past are condemned to repeat it." Most of those who read the

v

history of the French Revolution either do not discern the lesson it contains or forget it. Indeed, everyone who reads the history of the French Revolution should also read that of the Bourbon Restoration, for they are two parts of the same human and social episode. One does not have the total historical lesson without both the high tide and the low, both the fever and the chill. Yet the tendency is always to be absorbed in the more exciting revolutionary half of the total episode. The quieter slump back into the familiar groove of an old regime is never as interesting. Thus the readers of the history of the French Revolution and Empire were legion, those of the Restoration were few. One result of this was that the demand affected the supply. The production of works on the Revolution and Empire has been voluminous; that concerned with the Restoration has been scanty.

A few rough comparisons can be made of the relative amount of bibliography devoted to the two periods. Looking only at works on the internal history of France we would find that the bibliography of the old *Cambridge Modern History* devoted thirty-two pages to the Revolution and Empire and only nine to the Restoration; the bibliographies in the three pertinent volumes of the Langer series (by Brinton, Bruun, and Artz) devote about twenty-two pages to the earlier periods and only about two to the Restoration; while the new *Guide to Historical Literature* (1961) lists 229 works for the Revolution and Empire and only twenty-four for the Restoration. Even though the Restoration period is a little shorter than that of the Revolution and Empire, the disparity in historical coverage is striking. Likewise, much less has been written in English or translated from the French on the Restoration period, as will appear in the bibliography at the end of this work.

Not only has there been a quantitative historiographical neglect of the Restoration, but there have also been widespread interpretative distortions in the historical literature dealing with the period. Most of the nineteenth-century works concerned with the Restoration were not by professional historians but rather by journalists and politicians. For them the archives were closed, and many of the printed source collections had not yet been published. Consequently their histories were clearly biased: a few favorable to the regime (Nettement, Dareste de la Chavanne, and Ernest Daudet); most of them hostile (Duvergier de Hauranne, Vaulabelle, and Viel-Castel); and that of Hamel perhaps the nearest to impartial.

In the twentieth century, the sources are more available and the works of the professionally trained historians predominate. And yet even in this period we find lingering hostile prejudices during the Third Republic reflected in the works of such respectable historians as Charléty and Weill. While the republican and democratic historians of our century tried to be unbiased, they were still too much influenced by the political philosophy of their time to see much good in the Restoration in spite of its parliamentary progress and economic development.

Finally in the second third of the twentieth century more sympathetic and understanding studies began to appear. The weakness of the democratic and republican regimes made the mid-century historians more critical of their own republican institutions and more impartial toward the earlier monarchical periods. One of the first works in the new trend was a short topical study by an American, Frederick B. Artz. This was followed in France by the brief and accurate account of Ponteil and the Sorbonne lectures of Pouthas. More recently the most extensive and thorough one-volume study to appear was that of De Bertier de Sauvigny in Flammarion's "Collection 'L'Histoire'" in 1955. Here was a unique effort at impartiality. Instead of a republican historian trying to see the good aspects of the Restoration, we had a clerical historian, sympathetic to the monarchical ideal, trying to be both appreciative and critical of an earlier monarchical regime—one in which his ancestor, Ferdinand de Bertier, had played an active role. So successful was he in meeting the requirements of scholarship and literary style that his work was recognized as the standard one-volume account of the period.

For British and American readers, however, nothing was available except Artz's topical treatment and Lucas-Dubreton's popular account, both now thirty-five years old. While both of these older works have their merits, it was felt that a translation of de Bertier's more recent study was needed for the English-reading public. It was not surprising, therefore, that this book (as revised in 1963) should be one of the few chosen for translation by the Society for French Historical Studies upon the unanimous recommendation of its Committee on Translations.

It was a privilege and a pleasure to be permitted by the author and the Society to present this valuable work in the English language. It has enabled me to probe more deeply into the facts and significance of Restoration history and to discover more fully the thoughts and appreciations of the author. Indeed, at every step in the process of translating, the author has generously cooperated in reviewing the English text to assure a faithful rendering of his original French version. The task has been an education in itself and has contributed to a revision of some earlier prejudices stemming from my own milieu and training. As a democratic American, a layman, and a Protestant, I cannot but have a feeling of appreciation for the lofty impartiality, the sincerity, and the

sly wit of an author whose nationality, native language, political background, religion, and clerical status are so different from my own. It is
therefore to be hoped that this effort at translation may also reflect three
noticeable trends of our times: the international community of scholarship, the mutual understanding of differing religious communities, and the
historical revisionism which emerges from open archives and open minds.

LYNN M. CASE

University of Pennsylvania
November 22, 1966

# Contents

## PART II

## *The Reign of Louis XVIII*

## PART III

### French Life During the Restoration

## PART IV

### The Reign of Charles X

*The First Restoration and the Hundred Days*

# France in Early 1814

## Europe Strikes Back

1814—France, exhausted by twenty years of revolutionary and crusading fever, encountered the recoil of the forces that she had unleashed. She had been the first to experience the intoxication and enthusiasm of that national feeling which unites all classes and all people in a country into a community of free association. This new nationalist energy, utilized and directed by a popular leader, had enabled the French nation to spill across its linguistic and natural frontiers; the French flag had been raised on the shores of the Baltic and Adriatic, on the banks of the Vistula and the Danube; it had been unfurled over Vienna, Berlin, and even Moscow. Under the humiliation of defeat and the stimulus of foreign occupation, all these formerly quiescent peoples, who had known no other patriotism than their loyalty to their sovereign, these people of continental Europe, had finally had their own reawakening of national consciousness. The fire which had stirred the French volunteers now burned in the hearts of Spaniards, Austrians, Prussians, and Russians. The Valmys and Jemappes of 1812 and 1813 now bore the names of Malo-Jaroslavetz, Vittoria, Dennwitz, and Leipzig.

France had also introduced armies of a new type; based upon national conscription, they had overrun and beaten up the old machine-like mercenary armies. Napoleon had taken over this new metal, had tempered it in the white heat of his forge, and had wielded this new sword in a novel and disconcerting way: no more of those slow and cautious maneuvers of fancy wars, those fortifications taken like pieces in a game of chess. Now quick lightning strokes intended less for obtaining diplomatic hostages than for annihilating one's adversary and handing him over, bleeding and prostrate, to the mercy of his conqueror. In this department too, Europe, at first stunned, had learned its lesson. Jominis,

Moreaux, and Bernadottes had, for the instruction of their generals, taken apart the mechanism of Napoleonic tactics; Prussia and Austria had organized their own systems of conscription, and for their support the reservoir of men from Muscovy, whose flood-gates were heedlessly opened, poured forth an endless stream of docile and husky cannon-fodder.

So it was, at the beginning of 1814, that the hour of retribution had struck, and on all the borders of France the enemy hosts, more than a million strong, unleashed their attacks. Under the command of the cautious Schwartzenberg and the impetuous Blücher the first wave of 250,000 men crossed the Rhine in the beginning of January and began to overrun the northeast provinces. On their right Holland rose up against French domination and welcomed the Prince of Orange with enthusiasm; she was protected by the Army of the North, commanded by Bernadotte, prince-royal of Sweden, who lingered in Belgium but threatened with the weight of his 159,000 men. Switzerland had abrogated on December 29 the act of mediation which bound her to the emperor; while in Italy, Murat, the brother-in-law of Napoleon, betrayed him without a blush in the hope of saving his kingdom of Naples, and joined his forces with those of the Austrians under Bellegarde, who were pushing back the loyal Eugène de Beauharnais toward the Alps. On the Pyrenees border Wellington, with an army of less than a hundred thousand, but compact, war-hardened, heavily equipped, and well disciplined, had, since October 1813, forced the crossing of the Bidassoa. Now, slowly and relentlessly, he nibbled at French home territory in spite of the resistence of Soult, who was just as clever a maneuverer as himself.

Napoleon could meet this flood with only the wreckage of his Grand Army, new conscripts hastily called up, and the dregs from the army depots. This might amount to 400,000 on paper; but only sixty thousand of them could be mustered for the real campaign, and it was these who performed the famous miracles of those weeks. But his surest trump was, and should have been expected to be, the presence of the enemy on French soil. With an invader, all the patriotism, the instinct of self-preservation, the spirit of national defence, should have been on the French side. Then, too, the material resources should have permitted him to keep up a resistence long enough to wear down his adversary, if not to repulse him.

However, contrary to its reaction in 1793, the nation remained inert. The imperial cult had undermined and weakened French patriotism. Yet, danger would at least draw Frenchmen around their chief whom they had so often acclaimed. "If France should abandon me, I could

do nothing," Napoleon had said at the end of 1813. The doubt revealed
by this conditional phrase was already his own answer. Louis XIV,
on the eve of the battle of Denain, did not think, did not write: "If my
people should abandon me"; nor did Francis II when Napoleon camped
at Schönbrunn, nor Frederick-William III in flight at Königsberg.

What was there different about Napoleon's situation? Was his military
defeat to compass the fall of his regime? If one wants to understand
the why and wherefore of the restoration of the Bourbons to the throne,
one must probe the feelings of the French nation at this decisive hour
of its destiny.

## The Attitudes of the Social Classes

What did France think and want in 1814? No one asked her at
that time by any electoral consultation or referendum. Without such
indications one is too easily inclined to base one's opinions upon fallacious samplings of individual testimonies whose arbitrary choice is more
indicative of the opinion of the searcher than of the country as a whole.
By their variety these testimonials give us at least one sure fact: the
nation was not unanimously behind the emperor.

Yet one should try to be a little more precise. And to do that,
instead of speaking of France, let us speak of Frenchmen, of Frenchmen
who are divided into classes by very different conditions and interests.
Although idealism may inspire the conduct of some individuals, the
reactions of the masses are primarily determined by their interests,
and it is relatively easy to discern where these interests lay, at the
beginning of 1814, for the different categories of Frenchmen.

Let us first remember that more than half of the nation was illiterate,
ignorant of politics, profoundly indifferent to anything beyond the bounds
of their immediate material cares. For this mass of people any government is good provided it assures order and their economic security; it is
not in the habit of expressing an opinion and is not asked for one.
Essentially passive, it is ready to follow with docility or resignation any
prompting from above.

Yet the peasantry, which represented about four-fifths of the nation,
contained elements which were already politically conscious and which
carried the others along. It accepted the Empire with satisfaction because
it consolidated the principal results of the Revolution without the excesses
of anarchy or the menaces of reaction: such revolutionary results as the
abolition of feudal rights, the tithe, the corvées, the absurd and vexatious financial system, and the redistribution of the lands of the church

and nobility. On the other hand they had seen the local customs duties and salt tax revived under new names: the administration of the combined indirect taxes (*droits réunis*), established in 1804, had penalized the French citizen at his most sensitive spot by taxing beverages at all their stages from production to consumption; the tax on salt had been re-established in 1806 and the tobacco monopoly in 1810. Worst of all, the longer the war continued and the farther it spread, the more demanding conscription became. The sons of the peasants had been scarcely old enough to plow when the sturdier among them were called up and disappeared forever or returned crippled and disabled. In 1813 in several provinces the women and children were the only ones left to work in the fields. And then when the war moved back nearer home, the army, accustomed to living bountifully in conquered countries, fell back upon the French countryside and began an unending requisition of horses, cattle, fodder, grain, wine—the insatiable and pitiless supply service was always demanding more. In the Landes one prefect wrote in November 1813: "Our resources have been devoured to such an extent that no more animals are left for field work, nor forage to feed them, nor corn for sowing or food." And yet Marshal Soult wrote this official: "You should help us . . . indeed even if the army consumed the last grain of corn and the last bit of hay in the department."

Is it difficult to imagine what would be the reactions of Jacques Bonhomme under these conditions? There was no open revolt, not even concealed resistance, but a growing disaffection, using the same force of inertia and the same guile that they had used in earlier times against the salt tax and land tax collectors. Rather than put on a uniform, the young fellows would take to the hills, or blow off their trigger fingers, or pull out their teeth used for biting cartridges, or cut deep wounds in their legs, or sometimes, as a less painful expedient, hurry out and get married. But at the end of 1813 this last expedient no longer worked. The emperor then insisted on putting all able-bodied men into the national guard. Of course at first the authorities said it was only for the defence of their homes, but once the men were organized into units, they marched them off like the conscripts. This was just too much. Here and there there were open revolts, and the prefects were forced to ease or suspend, under various pretexts, the execution of imperial orders. By the end of January 1814 they had scarcely twenty thousand national guards ready for combat duty.

The working class was much less numerous and did not count in public life. It did not have much reason to be pleased with the imperial regime. The Napoleonic laws concerning this class were largely police regulations. Workers were forbidden to organize or to change their residence or employer. Discipline required that the master should always be in the right. Poverty, even when unavoidable, was considered a crime; anyone who was destitute must go to a *dépôt de mendicité,* patterned upon the hideous English workhouse. However, during the Empire the workers showed no discontent. Right up until near the end the prospering industries and the great public works programs employed to the full all labor left over from conscription, and wages went up faster than the cost of living. More so than the peasant, isolated in the country, the city worker was exposed to the manifestations of military glory. His simple patriotism was easily aroused by military parades and victory celebrations, and he gladly shouted "Long live the Emperor!" Yet, at the end of 1813, industrial prosperity was only a memory. Permanent unemployment had arrived and with it misery and discontent.

The economic crisis also hit the industrial and commercial bourgeoisie. To be sure this class suffered less than the working class, but its disillusionment was more dangerous for the future of the regime. The continental system and the sumptuous expenditures of the imperial court and the thousands of newly rich at first gave a wonderful burst of activity to industry. But at the end of 1810 and during 1811 a deep crisis shook the whole structure; there was a lack of raw materials, markets, and credit. All attempts to ease the situation were foiled by poor harvests in 1812. Crops were better in 1813, but the loss of European markets prevented industrial recovery. Capitalists lost confidence in the face of military reverses. Early in 1814 the five-per-cent consolidateds, "barometer of the bourse" (stock market), fell to fifty francs from eighty at the beginning of 1813, and the quotations of the shares of the Bank of France went down at the same time from 1,480 to 690 francs.

The merchants and shipbuilders of the seaports were hit hardest because of the blockade and the war on the sea interrupted commerce. Marseilles saw her population decline from 101,000 to 96,000 in ten years; Bordeaux in twenty years had lost thirty thousand souls, a third of her houses were empty; the price of a barrel (906 liters) of red wine fell from 2,850 francs in 1801 to 850 francs in 1813. Need we say more?

Besides, the vocal and thinking classes suffered from military despotism and police surveillance, which stifled every inclination toward independent expression and censored even the lines of Corneille and Racine.

The clergy also had its grievances which hardly need elaboration. The "new Constantine," restorer of worship, had conducted himself since 1809 more like a new Constantius. The pope had been imprisoned and dragged from Rome to Savona and from Savona to Fontainebleau; and cardinals, bishops, and priests had been thrown into prison for having shown more attachment to the head of the church than to the head of the state. At the end of January 1814 the emperor decided to free Pius VII and restore him to his states, but this tardy atonement could not wipe out the memory of past injuries, and the odious "organic articles" of the Concordat hardly eased the clergy's yoke very much.

At the top of the social ladder the new nobility of handsomely paid, active, and powerful higher government officials should have been that much more faithful to the emperor because its fortune was closely tied to his. But even here were hidden weaknesses which would become betrayals in the succeeding months. There were, on the one hand, the former republicans who had been very willing to accept senatorial stipends and other emoluments which the emperor had offered them in return for their support or their silence, but who had not forgotten the days when they had been able to speak up, when generals had trembled before the representatives of the people. There was, on the other hand, that whole segment of the old nobility which Napoleon had succeeded in attaching to himself, especially since he had entered, by his marriage, the family of legitimate kings. There was no doubt that these prefects, councillors of state, and chamberlains with high-sounding titles would be faithful; "they know how to serve," their new master exclaimed with satisfaction. But their rather recent fidelity should not be put to the test by the competition of that atavistic devotion to the older dynasty; between the two there would be little doubt about their choice.

And then all of them—whether ennobled former commoners, or degraded old nobles, or new men coming from out of the bourgeoisie or the common people—were troubled with the same concern: their position was good but how long would it last? What sense was there to these endless wars and these gigantic and far-away expeditions, "that game that's always won and always gambled away again" (Chateaubriand)? Even as far back as 1809 Decrès, the minister of the navy, was telling Marmont: "Do you want me to tell you the truth? The emperor is crazy, completely crazy, and will throw us all out, just as we are, head over heels, and it will all end up with an awful catastrophe." And what would happen when the emperor was gone? Was it reasonable to suppose that so many vested interests would remain, as they say, hanging by so slender a thread? The astounding experience of a certain General Malet, who had plotted Napoleon's overthrow in October 1812, caused sober second thoughts for everybody. Already the more astute, such as Talleyrand and Fouché, had partially disengaged themselves from the system. Was not this a somewhat disturbing indication of its stability?

Then there was the army, the origin and the underpinning of the imperial dictatorship. No doubt the plain draftee, who had just recently left home, could easily become a deserter, but the devotion of the elite corps and the lower cadres knew no bounds. As a devotion to a man rather than to a political system, it resembled more the feeling, a thousand years before, of the "antrustions" (Frankish vassals) toward the Merovingian kings, and more recently that of the émigrés toward the king in exile. But there was not exactly the same feeling on the part of the older marshals and generals who remembered having rubbed elbows with the little general Bonaparte and called him by his first name. And their fidelity was rotting just to the same extent that they had been heaped with honors. Old Lefebvre, a faithful marshal who had risen from the ranks, expressed it rather brutally right after Napoleon's abdication: "Did he think we would die for him once we had titles, palatial residences, and estates? It's partly his fault, he took our begger's sacks off our backs too soon."

## Parliament Demands Peace

The France of 1814, then, was no longer like the France of 1804. Yet Frenchmen still followed their leader, impelled by fear or habit, but not with enthusiasm or confidence. The wishes of the man were no longer entirely those of the nation. What did the people want? Just one thing: peace, immediate peace, peace at any price. This was proclaimed, as if with one voice, by the great state bodies which were supposed to represent them in Paris; it was also repeated in different ways by the commissioners sent out by the emperor into the departments.

In December 1813 Napoleon had thought it necessary to appeal to the senate and legislative body to obtain their approval of his attitude toward peace proposals made to him by the coalition and not accepted. "Peace," the senate had replied, "is the wish of France and the need of humanity." "Sire, obtain peace by a final effort worthy of you and the French people." The address of the legislative body was still more remarkable. To see the full significance of its reply, one must remember that this house was constituted of men carefully chosen by the administration for their devotion to the Empire during more fortunate days and that its voice was raised at a time when the required tone was one of slavish adulation. "Our suffering is overwhelming," it said. "Our country is threatened on all its borders; we sense a destitution unexampled in the history of the state. Business is at a standstill. . . . Industry is

dead. . . . What are the causes of these unutterable miseries? A vexatious administration, exorbitant taxes, deplorable methods for their collection, and still more cruel excesses in the system used for raising
troops for the armies. Conscription has become a dreadful scourge for
all France because this measure has always been carried to extremes in its enforcement. For the past two years they have been harvesting men every four months. A barbarous and purposeless war has
regularly swallowed up our young men who have thereby been taken
away from education, farming, business, and the trades. What we must
do now is return within our own territories and bridle our ambitious
impulses and activities, which have been, for the past twenty years, so
disastrous for all the people of Europe."

The author of this audacious indictment was Joachim Lainé, a deputy
from Bordeaux since 1810, and we know that that city had more reason
than others for being hostile to the Empire. Yet, what was of more
ominous importance was that this report was approved by his colleagues
by a vote of 223 to fifty-one. Napoleon could, and did, exile the rash
deputy, adjourn the legislative body, and forbid the printing of the
condemnatory document; but it nevertheless remained the most impressive evidence of the widening gulf between him and the nation as a
whole.

## Discontent in the Provinces

There was other concurring evidence which could be suspected of
actually understating the real truth. This was given by the twenty-three
special commissioners sent by Napoleon at the end of December 1813
into all the provinces to coordinate and stimulate the work of the local
authorities. Their correspondence has been published in full and gives
us an opportunity to perceive the shades of opinion and attitudes manifested from province to province.

The Nord and the Pas-de-Calais had a large number of draft-dodgers
who formed armed bands in several districts. At Lille the national guard
was completely apathetic and lacked any military spirit. Nor was there the
least patriotic impulse in either Picardy or Normandy. At Caen the
special commissioner even had to halt the organization of the national
guard. "Peace," he said, "is the greatest boon that the emperor could
grant to the people, and I doubt not that all the commissioners of
His Majesty say the same thing: it is a universal demand."

Alsace, Lorraine, and Champagne were better disposed, but material
was lacking for organizing an effective resistance. In contrast Franche-

Comté and Burgundy were very slow in their responses. The Dijon national guard said openly that it would surrender the city without a fight in order to prevent pillage. In the area between Chaumont and Langres an "inconceivable apathy and deep discouragement" was noted. At Lyons, where all factories were closed down, the local officials were hard put to hold down and feed the thousands of unemployed. The mountain people of Auvergne sat on the fence and awaited events, while the cities were hesitant and timorous. The Savoyards looked forward to the return of the King of Sardinia; here and there they hoisted the cross of St. Maurice. In Dauphiné, on the other hand, all classes of citizens joined energetically to organize the defence against the invader.

South of the Durance, however, was quite the contrary to the Dauphiné: from the Leberon to the Sainte-Baume the whole mountain region was crammed with the "maquis" of draft-dodgers who engaged in raids and sudden attacks up to the very outskirts of Marseilles. It was the same in the Ardèche, the Gard, and the Hérault where the resistance to the authorities became bolder day by day. In the whole area of Aquitaine, particularly at Toulouse and Bordeaux, the disaffection from the imperial regime was at its height. Taxes were no longer paid, the draft-dodgers amounted to a third or a half of those called up; the people were exasperated by the pitiless requisitions of Soult's army. "People talk only peace," wrote Senator Lapparent, the commissioner to Périgord and Quercy, "it is a general cry coming from every direction."

The Limousin and Berry were calm but exhausted, their economic life was paralyzed. The region of the old Vendée was uneasy; north and south of the Loire the royalist organizations began to reform; bands of draft-dodgers were stealing local governmental funds, raiding weapons depots, and terrorizing public officials. To prevent a general uprising, Commissioner Boissy d'Anglas was forced to discontinue conscription. In Brittany, too, rebellion was making frightful progress, except along the coasts, where the old hatred for England kept the people in line.

Such was the disturbing picture of France in 1814 as seen through the eyes of the imperial administration. The Allies knew about these difficulties and their astute diplomacy was able to exploit them to the hilt to assure the success of their campaign. Yet, no matter how tired France was of war or how willing she was to exchange defeat for peace, that did not mean that she was desirous in the same degree for a change of regime. "The mass of the population think only of the Empire and the emperor," Mollien wrote. Even in 1812, if we are to believe Joseph de Maistre, the name Bourbon was just as unknown as the Heraclides or the Ptolemies, at least among the younger generation. In fact, in the lycées (secondary schools) history studies were very summary; they talked a little about Henry IV and Louis XIV, but they were forbidden to call them Bourbons or to say that their legitimate heirs were living in England. In 1814, nevertheless, the situation had changed. By that time in France a small royalist party began to appear. It was still almost invisible but it was passionate and enterprising. Since its activity was to become decisive in the political crisis arising from the upcoming military defeat, it is important to know about its early beginnings and activities.

## The Revival of the Royalist Idea

Since Napoleon's coup d'état of 18 Brumaire (November 8, 1799) and until about 1810, the idea of the old royalism (loyalty to the ancient Bourbon house) had continued to lose ground in the nation. The principles of social order and authority, which the old royalism embodied, as against republican anarchy, were achieved just as well by the new imperial monarchy of Napoleon I. After all, this had not been the first time in French history when a worn-out dynasty had been replaced by a new one. The difference between usurpation and legitimacy was just a matter of time.

For most of the original royalists, who would also be royalists after 1815, the sentimental longing for an old out-of-date dynasty did not exclude a practical loyalty to the new Napoleonic state. Pure royalism had been found only among a small number of individuals who spurned any compromise with the new regime or any political office which required taking an oath of fealty to the "usurper." Among these were some noble families of the Faubourg Saint-Germain (aristocratic quarter of Paris), some writers like Chateaubriand, some manor lords who voluntarily retired from Paris to stay on their estates, a few priests of the "Little Church" who did not recognize Napoleon's Concordat of 1802 with the pope, and some former insurrectionist Chouans.

But from 1810 on, especially from 1812 on, this little nucleus of faithful began to snowball into a much larger group. It was partly the result of the religious policy of the emperor, which caused him to lose ground among the Catholics who had previously been won over by the Concordat. The church, persecuted in the person of its head, and the exiled Most Christian King now found themselves suffering a common adversity. Napoleon was astounded to find in 1809 a little group of young people, organized by the Congregation, daring to conspire in favor of the pope. In the opposite direction, allies for royalism were found among those antagonized by the excesses of imperial despotism. From 1790 to 1800 there had always been some sincere liberals whose ideal was constitutional monarchy, combining monarchical stability with the virtues of a liberty judiciously limited by laws, as in England. They remembered that *"le gros Monsieur"* (the fat prince royal), who was now calling himself Louis XVIII, had formerly shown some sympathy for constitutional ideas. Would they not be better off with him than with the tyrant who tried to rule France like a Turk? This idea inspired two illustrious exiles who had sought, by going to a foreign country, the opportunity for free expression denied to their friends who stayed in France. These were Benjamin Constant, who published in November 1813 his work *On the spirit of conquest and usurpation in its relation to European civilization,* and Madame Germaine de Staël.

Yet, royalism could not become a party or qualify as a real danger to the Empire as long as it remained just an academic opinion. To emerge from this nebulous state, it needed organization and a program of action. One certainly cannot consider as early beginnings of a party those "business agents" of the princes who had operated in Paris under the revolutionary regimes of the Directory and Consulate, nor even the Vendean royalist organizations, which were purely military and limited to the western provinces. Here, nevertheless, was a whole system of hierarchical relations, from parish captain to army commander, a system which was momentarily inactive but which could be easily reactivated at the right time. What, in the past, had come closer to being a royalist party in the modern sense of the term was the strange secret organization called the Philanthropic Institute, founded in 1796 by Chevalier Despomelles, to restore monarchy in France by making use of the existing machinery. By using his committees of loyal members, active in most departments, the Institute had succeeded in packing the councils of the Directory with a monarchist majority. But it was broken up by the coup d'état of Fructidor (September 1797). The Philanthropic Institute, discouraged by this setback and disorganized by the arrest of most of its leaders, managed to survive in the south of France where, in the year VII (1798–1799) it had tried to incite a very dangerous insurrection in the region around Toulouse. After 1800 this group also became inactive, but even here was a region of faithful and committed men who could eventually be reawakened.

## The Knights of the Faith

However, a new spur was needed to revive and federate these earlier organizations, to give a rallying point and a program of action to the

Parisian and provincial royalists. This stimulation should have come from
the princes themselves, but Fouché's police had exposed and snuffed out
all the secret avenues by which they could have passed along their instructions. The revival and the spur were going to come finally, in 1810,
from inside the country.

Ferdinand de Bertier, the youngest son of the last intendant of the
generality of Paris, was one of a small number of intransigents who had
never bowed their heads before the usurper and had repulsed all his advances. The atrocious lynching of his father, on July 22, 1789 as an after-
math of the fall of the Bastille, had kindled in his heart an unqualified
hatred of the Revolution, and from that day on he had lived only to
conspire. The Congregation of the Virgin (an aristocratic lay order of
piety) had admitted him in 1807, and in 1809 he participated, along with
his friends Mathieu de Montmorency and Alexis de Noailles, in the circulation of the bull of excommunication issued by Pius VII against Napoleon.
For a long time he had been trying, along with his brother Bénigne-
Louis, as incorrigible a conspirator as himself, to find a way to organize
all the royalist forces into one solid bloc of resistance. The idea came to
them to imitate, for the benefit of the church and king, the Masonic organization which had been the principal instrument for the success of the
revolutionary idea—at least such had been the opinion held among
émigrés (upper-class refugees) from reading Abbé Barruel's *Mémoires
pour servir à l'histoire du jacobinisme* (Hamburg, 1798; Paris, 1803).
The two brothers did not even hesitate to join a Masonic lodge temporarily to study its way of operating. In 1807 Bénigne-Louis had been imprisoned by the imperial police, just managing to escape the firing squad. It
was left to Ferdinand de Bertier to formulate and carry out alone their
original designs.

The institution of the Order of the Chevaliers de la Foi (Knights of
the Faith), as he created it in the middle of 1810, was derived from
Masonry and the military and knightly orders of the Middle Ages. From
the former it took the secret hierarchy which kept the lower grades from
knowing of the existence of higher grades or the real designs of the
leaders; from the latter it drew the titles and the Christian and monarchical ideal which put it to the service of throne and altar.

The first grade of the order was that of Associates of Charity who contributed, by their prayer and subscriptions, to what they thought was only
a pious association for good works and the propagation of Christian and
monarchical ideas. The second grade was that of squire to whom was revealed the secret of the restoration of knighthood. The knight (the third
grade) was initiated in a simple and impressive ceremony: on his knees

before a crucifix surrounded by lights, he swore himself, on the Bible, to secrecy, obedience, fidelity to God, honor, king, and country. Then he received the tap of a sword on his shoulder and the accolade from all the knights present; a blessed ring, with an interior inscription of the word *caritas*, was put on his finger; and he was given the passwords and secret signs. Then came the grade of Knight Hospitaler devoted especially to work in prisons and hospitals. His insignia were a rosary with a pendant ebony cross. The highest rank was that of the Knights of the Faith, who alone knew the whole extent of the order and double purpose, both political and religious. Their outward insignia were a rosary and silver cross. They governed the society by a high council of nine members which gave instructions to seneschals, each responsible for a military division; the smallest subdivision was a banner, the counterpart of a Masonic lodge, whose territorial jurisdiction was usually a department (principal French territorial subdivision).

The first members recruited by Bertier were his brothers Anne-Pierre and Bénigne-Louis and his friends in the Congregation and the Faubourg Saint-Germain: Alexis de Noailles, Armand and Jules de Polignac, Eugène and Mathieu de Montmorency, Victor de Vibraye, and Fitz-James. Almost immediately Bertier, who was only twenty-eight years of age, felt obliged to surrender the post of "grand master" of the order to Mathieu de Montmorency, who, by his age, the prestige of his name, his qualities, and his connections, was more likely to inspire confidence and give official directives. There seem to be significant indications that Chateaubriand was also a member of the order.

At the end of 1813 the Paris "banner" was headed by Count Clermont-Mont-Saint-Jean, and his very active secretary was Louis de Gobineau, the father of the famous author of the *Essai sur l'inégalité des races humaines*. Gobineau was even supposed to have enrolled people from among the husky porters of the grain market. The order expanded into the provinces during the intervening years, obviously with uneven success. In the west and southwest all it had had to do was to revive the old organizations and bring them together through their leaders. It had also found fertile soil in Franche-Comté (eastern France), in the former provinces of Flanders and Artois in the north, and in Auvergne, the Rhone valley, Provence, and Aquitaine in the south. In Toulouse a large number of the common people were serving the local "banner" whose membership list carried the names of Mac-Carthy, Villèle, Monbel, Saint-Géry, and Cantalause. Among these important groups, and here and there in the castles and parsonages, was a thin network of members whose principal job was to transmit orders and news. All these communications were oral; so much had experience inculcated a fear of the imperial police that nothing, absolutely nothing, was to be put in writing. The lines of the information network were organized in such a way that no messenger had to travel more than ten or twelve leagues. As soon as one messenger arrived, another knight mounted his own horse and was off to the next station with the message. This explains why on several occasions the Empire officials noted with amazement that news of Allied victories and events in Paris spread to the cities in distant provinces long before the official couriers arrived.

What could such an organization do with a membership weighted so heavily on the aristocratic side? A liberal royalist, Bruno de Boisgelin, who joined early in 1814, was right in considering that its resources did not give it sufficient "strength for action or resistance," but that it was perfectly equipped, with its little groups of correspondents in all the provinces, "to spread on the surface of things a thin cloud . . . a veneer of royalism, which could become dominant in time of need." In other words, as long as the Empire lasted, an insurrection or a forceful overthrow "like the Malet attempt" was out of the question. But, while waiting for circumstances to create the right occasion, the order could devote itself to useful propaganda work: recall the existence of legitimate princes, stir up and rekindle loyalties by conversations, group elements of good will, take advantage of all occasions to sow discontent with the imperial regime and to underline its weaknesses. The result of this undermining effort could already be seen at the beginning of 1814. While, two years earlier, the existence of the Bourbons had been practically unknown and the idea of their recall had seemed like "an untenable sophism," the reports of the prefects and the special commissioners now began to mention "activities of the Bourbon party."

So it was that right when the imperial structure was beginning to crack, and when the French nation—from weariness or from an instinct for self-preservation—was turning away from its leader which it had chosen a few years before, right when the Allies were wondering what political advantages they should take from their military victories, the royalist card could be played, not only by the isolated princes without prestige, but also by an organized minority acting from within the nation. No doubt, in these revived organizations was to be found, in the early months of 1814, the best possibility of a Bourbon restoration.

# 2

❧ ❧ ❧ ❧ ❧

# *"The Force of Circumstances"*

## Peace, the Trump Card

The emperor's own brother, Joseph Bonaparte, who was serving as head of the council of regency, remarked significantly on March 4, after one of the meetings of the council:

> They were generally agreed in thinking that the necessity of France being reduced to the territory she held in 1792 should be accepted rather than to expose the capital [to the devastation of war]. Every effort therefore . . . should be made to sign a definitive treaty restricting France to the boundaries of the last Bourbon monarch, but delivering her immediately from enemy occupation. . . . An early peace is indispensable, no matter what kind; but good or bad, we must have peace.

While this imperial brother may have sounded defeatist, even treasonable, he was only expressing the opinion of the highest-ranking officials of the Empire. Again on March 11 he relapsed into the same mood with a prescience even more remarkable than the position he held:

> The day when the people are convinced [he wrote the emperor] that Your Majesty prefers the prolongation of the war to even a disadvantageous peace, there is no doubt but what weariness will turn opinion to the other side. I cannot be mistaken because my views coincide with those of everyone else. We are on the eve of a total dissolution; there is no way out except to make peace.

If we keep these words in mind, they will give us a clear realization of the complicated card game, in its hundreds of different plays, which we must relive in the telling. In this game, it cannot be said too often, peace is the main trump card. It was peace which the French nation wanted desperately—peace with Napoleon if possible; without him if he

17

refused to agree to it. The Allies also wanted peace—with Napoleon if he accepted their conditions; without him if he rejected them. If the emperor had been able, had dared, to play this trump card right at the beginning and with decisiveness, all indications seem to point to the possibility that he might have kept his throne. But he also had the war card in his hand, and unfortunately he had too often played it and won to withhold it this time. Louis XVIII, the Bourbon claimant to the throne, had only one possible card to play, but fortunately for him it was the right one. Neither France nor the Allies at first seemed inclined to be on the watch for it; but finally the card showed up—an immediate peace desired by the former, an advantageous and stable peace sought by the latter, were to be found in the weak hands of the Hartwell exile (Louis XVIII).

This history of the spring crisis of 1814 was, then, the story of the gradual recognition of the value of this main trump card. But, in the meantime, there were many hesitations and trials and errors.

## The Allied Position

First we must look at the position of the Allies as they confronted the political problem raised by the invasion of France. They realized rather soon the value, for the success of their military campaign, of detaching the French nation from its ruler by gambling on its desire for peace. Metternich, the Austrian chancellor, had begun this maneuver at the beginning of November 1813 by offering peace terms at Frankfort to the French diplomat, Saint-Aignan. The Allies, he said, were ready to negotiate a treaty which would leave France with her Revolutionary conquests—that is, her natural frontiers. Because Napoleon had hesitated to reply promptly and positively and because his military position had worsened in the intervening month, these terms were considered out-of-date by December. Nevertheless, the Allies were careful not to say so in so many words and, instead, pursued the splitting maneuver by a manifesto on December 1, twenty thousand copies of which were distributed throughout France.

> The Allied Sovereigns declare that they are not waging war against France, whom they desire to see strong and happy . . . and whose territory may comprise a larger area than her [previous] kings had ever known. . . . They are only warring against the emperor, or rather against that preponderance which he has too long exercised beyond his empire to the detriment of France and Europe.

In all this it is evident that they were not talking about a change of dynasty. They were warring against the emperor, but they were ready to come to an agreement with him if he were willing to renounce his hegemony. This did not mean they had forgotten about the Bourbons, because Louis XVIII had repeatedly appealed to the Allied rulers; but his dynasty seemed so foreign to France, his cause so unpopular, that they were afraid of arousing national feeling against themselves if they showed it any favor.

In practice the Allied attitude toward the Bourbons was to be the one expressed by the tsar on January 18, 1815:

> The powers will not decide in favor of the Bourbons, but they will leave the initiative on this question to the French. . . . They will keep to their passive role. They will not prevent the Bourbons from acting beyond the lines occupied by their troops, but will not encourage them and will avoid even the appearance of taking the least part in their activities.

Along with this common approach, however, each of the Allies harbored individual designs which must be noticed in order to understand the disagreements which arose as events unfolded.

Austria was condescending enough to look ahead to a conquered France, kept under her influence through a regency of Marie-Louise (wife of Napoleon) in the name of the King of Rome (his son). Austria had just the right man, Talleyrand, on the spot, who was supposed to prefer this solution to all others. Alexander, the Tsar of Russia, being personally opposed to the Bourbons, saw himself entering Paris as liberator, convoking a representative assembly which would place on a national and liberal throne a former French soldier, his protegé, Bernadotte of Sweden. As for the Prussian king, always ready to follow the tsar's ideas, he only burned with the desire of taking revenge on Paris and on Napoleon.

As for England, her policy had been defined by Pitt as early as 1800: "I consider the restoration of the French monarchy as a most desirable goal, because I think it would guarantee to our country and to Europe the best, the firmest security . . . but for us to take an initiative in that direction, it would be necessary that, after great successes by the Allies, a strong and prevailing disposition for the return of the Monarch appear in France itself." This was to be exactly the position of the British foreign secretary, Castlereagh, when he joined with his colleagues on the continent in January 1814 in order to keep a closer watch on developments. "The Bourbons," he wrote on December 30, 1813 on board the ship taking him to Hamburg, "will have to play their own game, at their own risk and peril, and in their own way. As for us we won't oppose them."

Indeed, he would work indirectly for them as he tried to sidetrack the solutions proposed by the Russians and Austrians. It was easy enough to line up Russia and Prussia against the Austrian idea of a regency. Nor was it less difficult to excite Austria against Bernadotte, because she did not want to see a Russian hegemony substituted for Napoleon's; and besides, Bernadotte did not seem to have many advocates in France anyway. These two solutions having neutralized each other, the way seemed open for the solution England secretly preferred. Yet, in order to persuade her partners to accept this last solution, two conditions had to be fulfilled over which the British government had no control: it had to be shown that it was impossible to negotiate an acceptable peace with Napoleon, and a spontaneous movement for the Bourbons must appear within the French nation. The first of these conditions would arise by the failure of the negotiations at Châtillon from February 4 to March 19, the sorry history of which need not be discussed here. How would the second, quite as indispensable condition (French approval of the Bourbons) be achieved? That is something that now should engage our attention.

### Schemes of the Princes

Count François des Cars, one of the followers in England of the Count of Artois (brother of Louis XVIII), wrote to his friend Semallé in December 1813, "Our salvation can only come from France." At that time, in fact, Louis XVIII had become convinced, by the kind of reception given to his emissaries, that the Allies would not lift a finger for his cause. Therefore some royalist demonstrations must be stirred up at all costs at some point on French territory. Unfortunately, communications between the king and his supporters in France were terribly uncertain. However, he learned from Alexis de Noailles, who arrived in England in the spring of 1812, that the secret organization of the Knights of the Faith existed. In October 1813, after Napoleon's defeat at Leipzig, Louis XVIII had had his instructions transmitted to them in purposely vague terms: "The time has come to be more effective." And he gave them free rein to carry them out as they pleased. The high council of the order, meeting on October 9 at the home of Mathieu de Montmorency, immediately drew up a plan of action which lacked a certain imagination. It asked for an Anglo-Royalist invasion of Brittany and boasted of strong support for it from the interior. This ignored completely the real attitude of England without whose active aid such an operation was impossible. Besides, the plan was never to get to the king because the messenger was arrested near Auray when he tried to embark for England.

The princes, however, could not remain inactive. After considerable urging they were able to obtain England's permission in mid-January (1814) to make a try. The Count of Artois, brother of the king, sailed for Holland from whence he was to go to Switzerland and Franche-Comté behind the Austrian army. His older son, the Duke of Angoulême, was authorized to join Wellington in the south of France. Finally, the Duke of Berry, the most ardent and audacious of them all, went to the island of Jersey. From there he hoped to jump to the Normandy coast where his arrival, it was thought, could be the signal for a general uprising of the western provinces.

What a disillusionment! Scarcely arrived in Jersey, on February 6, the prince received an old soldier of Frotté, Michelot Moulin, who assured him that lower Normandy was not at all ready to take up arms. The Duke of Berry hesitated, but agreed that one of his companions, Chevalier de Bruslart, should go back to the continent with Michelot to survey the situation. The two men left on February 11, and in the midst of endless dangers, did establish some disappointing contacts. On his return Bruslart concluded: "On the coasts there is really no one to receive the Duke of Berry except gendarmes!" And the fuming Charles-Ferdinand had to champ at the bit, useless and helpless on his island, while he waited for things to be decided without him.

His father was not to be much luckier in the eastern provinces. His chances had seemed better, however, during the first days of the invasion. The royalists had spread the rumor that the Allies had decided to return the Bourbons to the throne. This ought to encourage the people, they thought, to show at least an interest in royalism, which in turn might impress the invaders and persuade them to adopt in fact the attitude which had been attributed to them. It was a Machiavellian scheme, or perhaps even a naive illusion, and because of it the Restoration for many years was to bear the weight of the damning legend of the "foreign baggage train" which had its beginning here.

At first everything seemed to go well. The Austrians were greeted as liberators in Franche-Comté. Lieutenant Colonel Thurn wrote on January 1, 1814 to Generalissimo Schwarzenberg: "The attitude of the people surprises me and surpasses our hopes. Weary of a shameful and detested government, the inhabitants admit that they have been waiting impatiently for their hour of deliverance." The Russian armies encountered the same state of mind in Lorraine. From Vesoul, on January 20, the foreign minister, Nesselrode, wrote to his wife: "The people . . . are very well disposed toward us, and here, as everywhere else, we are received with open arms." Not a trace of national resistance: Epinal surrendered to fifty Cossacks; Rheims to a squadron of troops; Chaumont to one cavalryman; Langres capitulated after the second cannon shot, and Dijon to the second bearer of a flag of truce.

But the royalist cause was not advanced by all this, because the Allied leaders obeyed to the letter the instructions they had been given to ignore the Bourbons. In Franche-Comté, where the latter counted more supporters, the Austrians appointed a military governor who did all he could to encourage a separatist movement in favor of the Austrian dynasty and specifically forbade the mention of the Bourbon name. At Dijon the local "banner," made up of about sixty members, tried wearing the white (Bourbon) emblem, but the Austrian commander reprimanded them severely and even arrested one of their ringleaders.

Alexis de Noailles, backed by a small group of faithful, went to a great deal of trouble, and all in vain, to see Russian and Austrian higher authorities and have them take a more sympathetic attitude. With the help of the émigré Rochechouart, now a Russian general, an approach was made to Tsar Alexander by a small group of "knights." "How does it happen," he replied coldly, "that after having occupied a third of France, we find that the people are not acclaiming the old dynasty?" A few days later, at Troyes, he was to refuse outright to receive two "knights," the Marquis de Widranges and Chevalier de Gouault, who had succeeded in organizing a royalist demonstration on the arrival of Prussian troops in their town.

Besides, by this time, the relations between the Allied troops and the French people had completely changed. It did not take the invader long to show his true colors. Requisitions and exactions began to be imposed on the towns. Why should they have hesitated? The French had done the same thing in their own occupied territory in the last few years, even in recent months. Troyes, for example, was required by Prince Hohenlohe to pay 150,000 francs and had to furnish the Prussians 18,000 hundredweights of flour, 1,000 oxen, 334,000 oat rations, 3,000 bottles of brandy, and 12,000 bottles of wine. In the rural areas it was worse; there the barrack-room attitude of the troops, especially of the Cossacks, far from the watchful eyes of superior officers, led them to engage in the most brutal pillage. And the peasant of course then recovered his will to fight. As long as it had only involved the fate of the emperor, the big consumer of men and taxes, the farmer had remained uninterested; but when he saw his home burned and his wife and daughters violated, then a change came. The peasant thereupon took his gun, joined with other equally determined men, and began to hunt the Cossack down. This was the "blue overall war" (*guerre des blouses bleues*) so feared by the enemy. And when suddenly, as if by miracle, Napoleon began to win victories and the enemy began to flee, they started to shout more lustily than ever before, "Long live the emperor!" By then they were ready to rally around him and fight for him.

The extraordinary military recovery achieved by Napoleon in February 1814 also had the effect of cooling the ardor of the royalists and lessening their hopes of Allied help. When the emperor retook Troyes on February 27, he had the imprudent Gouault shot and from Fismes, on March 5, had a decree issued threatening death to anyone wearing the white cockade. At Châtillon the Allies were very upset and divided in counsel. After all, maybe it was better to come to terms with Napoleon, let him have more than they had intended originally. Even Castlereagh seemed resigned to the idea and brusquely snapped at the prince-regent in England for publicly favoring the Bourbons. Nesselrode wrote on March 10: "I fear there is no more hope for the poor royalists. I don't find any real party favoring them, and we would only be plunging ourselves into an endless war by espousing the Bourbon cause."

It was under these unfortunate conditions that the Count of Artois arrived in this theater of operations—at Basel on February 6 and at Vesoul on the 21st. And what a reception he received! The Austrian commander of the department sent a lower ranking officer to demand his passport. When he claimed the right to enter his own country without Allied consent, some talked of sending him back. However, they let him stay on condition that neither he nor the members of his party would wear the white emblem, put on a uniform, bear arms, or stir up any public demonstration. Everywhere around him there seemed to be a veritable blockade, a determination to humiliate him.

Yet from Paris and from different provinces, emissaries arrived with conflicting suggestions. Some urged the prince forward, others begged him to go back. Sometimes there were those who wanted him to go into Auvergne or even into the more dangerous Vendée; at other times they appealed to Augereau at Lyons, who had seemed to be softening toward them and had aroused the anger of the emperor as well as the hopes of the royalists. Again they tried to soften up Bernadotte, who had made some sort of promises. But to whom had he not offered some deal?

Finally Monsieur (title of address of the heir to the throne) set up his headquarters in Nancy, where a handful of royalists had succeeded in giving him a meager welcome. However, the Russian governor, Alopeus, would not permit the posting of proclamations, the wearing of the white emblem, or any act of government.

Obviously something else had to be done to soften the Allies. Talleyrand sent Baron Vitrolles from Paris. When he arrived in Troyes on March 12, all his southern eloquence could not melt the wall of ice of the Allied ministers. "Let France speak out," said Metternich, "it's her business, not ours."

## The Bordeaux Revolution

Yet it was on this very day of March 12 that France, or at least one of her big cities, did speak out, and so dramatically that it gave the Bourbon cause just the support and push which had been lacking before.

To understand the origins of this important event, one must go back a bit. The region around the Garonne river in southwestern France was a favored spot for the Knights of the Faith. Late in November 1813 the high council of the order had sent Ferdinand de Bertier there to take over the direction of the movement, and he had established his head-quarters in the home of his sister, Madame de Solages, in the Château de Mezens, on the border between the departments of Tarn and Haute-Garonne. From here he gave quite a strong impetus to the propaganda work designed to undermine the morale of the imperial authorities and to prepare the people for a change of regime. The attitude of the English army gave special help to this propaganda. Wellington had been able to maintain a strict discipline over his troops. Not only was there no pillaging, but he paid immediately and generously for all requisitioned food supplies. This clever and generous conduct on the part of the English general contrasted with that of the French soldiers under Soult, his opponent. These home soldiers, a contemporary said, were "brave, but undisciplined brigands" who had bled the country white by requisitions and pillaged and brutalized without restraint the very people they were supposed to defend. The result was not hard to foresee; everywhere in the south the English were hailed as true liberators.

Yet, no more than the Prussians, Russians, and Austrians, were they to take the side of the Bourbons openly. No doubt Wellington was personally favorable to them; but he had the same instructions mentioned above, and he adhered to them firmly and loyally.

Furthermore Bertier had seen that a royalist movement, to have a convincing appearance, should develop independently of any foreign intervention and in the midst of the area still under the imperial government. He resolved, therefore, to attempt an uprising in Rodez, a rather isolated town where the authorities had only a few gendarmes and some unreliable national guard troops. Toward the end of February, by the mountain paths which converged on this little capital of Aveyron, little groups of "knights" and draft-dodgers enlisted by them moved on the town. The assembly point was the Château de la Goudalie a few miles north of the city. When Ferdinand de Bertier and his brother, Bénigne, arrived, all was ready to make the attempt on the night of February 16. However, at the last moment the directors of the *"sénéchaussée"* of Toulouse, which was supposed to join the affair, got cold feet and recalled their contingents who were already on the march. On the other hand, it was learned that the authorities at Rodez had heard of the plot and were on the alert. Bertier did not dare risk the lives of the two hundred men under his control, and so he dispersed them quickly. This was a fatal faltering in which one sees a parlor conspirator who had not been trained in the hard knocks of the Chouanerie (the revolts in Normandy of fifteen years before). No doubt even if the white flag of the Bourbons had been raised over Rodez, the movement could not have spread, and just a few battalions from Soult's army could have crushed the insurrection. But the incident could have had a symbolic value.

After this the royalists in the South could not hope to succeed except under the protection of English bayonets. Everything was ready at Bordeaux for such an eventuality. Nowhere were all classes more hostile to the empire. As always happens in the darkness of underground activities, three organizations had developed simultaneously among the royalists of Bordeaux: the old *Institut philanthropique,* led by Count de Lur-Saluces; a "banner" of the Knights of the Faith, headed by Chevalier de Gombault; and finally the "Royal Guard," created in 1813 by a certain Taffard who called himself "de Saint-Germain." This latter was the only one who could boast of receiving proper authorization from Louis XVIII, through the latter's friend, Rollac, a Bordeaux merchant sent from England. Ferdinand de Bertier, when he had visited Bordeaux in the middle of November 1813, had succeeded in federating the three organizations by forming a committee of two members from each.

The Knights of the Faith had also succeeded in obtaining the complicity of the city government. The mayor of Bordeaux, Jean-Baptiste Lynch, former counsellor of the *parlement* of Bordeaux, had come to Paris at the end of 1813. His compatriot, Louis de Gobineau, obtained an interview for him with the Polignacs, members of the higher council of the secret order. After his return in January, Lynch contacted the local "banner" and promised that, when the first occasion came, he would don the white emblem along with three of his assistants.

This occasion would be the arrival of the prince royal (Duke of Augoulême) coinciding with the invasion of the English. It should be remembered that this eldest son of the Count of Artois had gone to join Wellington's army in February. The English general, following instructions, had received him rather coolly, and would tolerate him only if he would stay in Saint-Jean-de-Luz and remain quiet. The poor prince, timid and uncertain by nature and disappointed by his cool reception at headquarters, was thinking of returning to England, when there came to him simultaneously two "knights" sent by Bertier from Toulouse and Louis de la Rochejaquelein, representing the Bordeaux "banner." The description they brought of the secret organizations and their means of action in the two big cities was enough to revive hope. For the time being nothing could be done in Toulouse where Soult had his base of operations and where his troops swarmed all over the place. But Bordeaux was denuded of troops by their withdrawal toward upper Languedoc after the bloody battle of Orthez (February 27). Wellington decided to send a small corps of ten thousand English and Portuguese to Bordeaux under the command of General Beresford. His instructions reflected the desire of the commander-in-chief to avoid later criticism that he had taken any step contrary to the policy of his government; but at the same time they set down the real French and national character of the move.

> In detaching these troops for Bordeaux, I intend to take this city from the enemy and become master of the navigation of the Gironde, a great advantage to our army. . . . If they ask your consent to proclaim Louis XVIII . . . reply that wherever our troops are, as long as public peace is not disturbed, we will intervene in no way to stop this party from doing what it considers useful and appropriate to its interests, . . . that nevertheless the aim of the Allies in this war is above all else . . . peace, and that it is well known that they are engaged at this time in negotiating a treaty with Bonaparte, and that however disposed I might be to give aid and assistance to whatever group might be opposed to Bonaparte, this assistance would cease at the very instant when peace should be concluded; and I beg the inhabitants to weigh this point carefully before raising the standard of revolt against the Bonaparte government. . . . If the city government claims to proclaim Louis XVIII only by virtue of your orders, you are thereupon to refuse to give them.

Beresford started out at once, on March 8. Some distance behind him came the Duke of Angoulême. The imperial officials at Bordeaux, becoming panic-stricken at the approach of the English, evacuated the city and took shelter on the right bank of the Gironde River. The way was now open for the royalists. Some were afraid to cross the Rubicon; but Gombault and La Rochejaquelein, who had secretly returned to Bordeaux, stirred them to action by saying that the "banner" would act by itself if necessary.

On the morning of March 12, while Lynch convoked the city council, the English advance guard arrived at the gates of the city and was loudly acclaimed by the people. At about ten o'clock Lynch entered his carriage and went out to meet the English general with an escort of young royalists and a big crowd of curious onlookers, carefully infiltrated by royalist supporters. He exchanged the usual courtesies with Beresford and received from him the assurance that the English entered the city as friends. Lynch then jumped up in his open carriage and with a theatrical gesture tore off his tricolored ribbon of office and revealed underneath a white ribbon. He then put the white cockade on his hat and shouted "Long live the king! Long live the Bourbons!" The gesture and the shout were imitated by those around him, and the crowd was caught up in the excitement. "There was a roar from what seemed a tremendous crowd of people, with mingled cries of 'Long live the king!' rending the heavens," one unenthusiastic witness reported. A big white flag was unfurled atop the Saint-Michel tower.

Then they all went back into town and held an improvised reception at the city hall. Lynch and Lur-Saluces asked Beresford's authorization to replace all the imperial insignia with those of the king. These ill-advised men did not seem to realize that this inappropriate request seemed merely to confirm the old canard that the Restoration was being unloaded from "the wagon-train of foreigners." Fortunately for them Beresford knew his business; florid and haughty, he gave them a withering look from his one eye and said: "The English have come to Bordeaux to protect the *people,* their property, and their free opinions. I neither authorize nor forbid; do as you please." The mayor was therefore thrown back upon his own responsibility, and he signed orders to have the national guard assume the white cockade and to have the imperial insignia removed.

At about three o'clock in the afternoon the Duke of Angoulême finally arrived, and received a delirious welcome from what appeared to be a unanimously enthusiastic crowd. On the square before the cathedral he was awaited by the old archbishop, d'Aviau du Bois de Sanzay, one of those who had dared to raise objections in the presence of the emperor at the time of the unfortunate church council of 1811. During the next few days the prince set up a semblance of royal government with the help of Lainé and the archbishop, and he claimed to extend his authority over the whole region.

It seems proper to stress this episode somewhat more than others because its significance has been too often overlooked by French historians as they became hypnotized by what was going on in Paris. The English historians were not similarly misled, and they generally saw this as one of the most decisive events for the restoration of the Bourbons. Nor did Louis XVIII minimize its importance, because it was in memory of the "miracle" of March 12, 1814, that he was later to give the heir to the crown, the "miracle child" of 1820, the title of Duke of Bordeaux.

## Allied Acceptance of the Bourbons

The news of the Bordeaux events of March 12 caused from the beginning an electrifying agitation throughout the whole region. From all over the area the imperial officials were writing to express dismay at the popular excitement. The Vendée came alive and planned a general uprising for April 11.

But still more the Bordeaux revolution was going to exert an influence on developments north of the Loire. If it was known in Paris by March 18 at the latest, arousing hopes for some and concern others, the Allies, at the time they broke up their Châtillon discussions, seemed still to be ignorant of it on March 19. London received the news on March 22, and the prime minister, Lord Liverpool, not yet knowing of the failure of negotiations at Châtillon, immediately wrote to Castlereagh that, even if he had already signed some protocol, he should refuse to ratify it and should get in contact with the Count of Artois. At Dijon, where the Allied ministers were meeting on March 26, the news of the events in Bordeaux caused the same sensation. Even before Castlereagh received Liverpool's dispatch, he was moving far in the same direction. Metternich, at the English minister's persuasion, was recognizing that the Bourbons were now inevitable, and he sent an invitation to the Count of Artois to come and confer with the Allied ministers. Two days later they were confirmed in their new line of policy by the arrival of a delegate from the Paris "banner," Gain-Montagnac, who finally brought them detailed information on the royalist strength and plans in Paris, something that Vitrolles had not been able to do. On that very evening,

March 28, all the diplomats gathered at Castlereagh's residence—Hardenberg, Metternich, Razumowski, and lesser lords—and drank for the first time to the success of the Bourbons.

But that was all they could do for them at that time, because the final decision was not in their hands but in those of the tsar, who had left them and was marching on Paris with Schwarzenberg. What would he do? What would he decide? Could the military developments and the attitude of the capital put an end to his hesitation? When he had left, he had been determined on only one point: not to negotiate with Napoleon. Besides, he was still trying to find a solution which would set aside those disagreeable Bourbons. Then what? Bernadotte of Sweden? Eugène de Beauharnais, Napoleon's stepson? The Duke of Orleans of the younger branch of the Bourbons? Perhaps even a republic "prudently organized." Such were the hypotheses which he was still pondering as he journeyed with Vitrolles on March 14.

In Paris the royalists were feverishly preparing their own "March 12." Their situation was obviously less favorable than that at Bordeaux. The central administration of the imperial government was in Paris as well as the terrifying proximity of the emperor and his army. Besides, there were only a handful of royalists in the midst of a hostile and indifferent population. The high council of the Order of the Knights of the Faith had been weakened by the departure of its most energetic members to stir up the provinces. On top of this, the movement had been hampered by an ill-conceived intervention. The Count of Semallé, an upstanding royalist, enterprising and devoted, but extremely naive and muddleheaded, had thrown himself athwart the prudent maneuvers of the Knights of the Faith. He had succeeded in joining up with the Count of Artois at Vesoul and in obtaining from him official powers to act. He arrived back in Paris on March 16 and claimed the right to take over operations. Montmorency had no other alternative than to go himself to the prince in an effort to clarify the situation, but this was the very thing which made him absent from Paris at the decisive moment.

Just as at Bordeaux, the success of the political operations presupposed the complicity of local authorities. They were certain of a royalist majority in the general council of the Seine department. The prefect of police, Pasquier, and the prefect of the Seine, Chabrol, both of them members of old *parlement* families (holders of hereditary judgeships in the pre-Revolutionary Paris high court), promised nothing, but their sympathy could not be doubted. The national guard had been carefully infiltrated: the Duke of Fitz-James and other determined conspirators had been able to get themselves chosen to head some legions and companies. Finally, too, contact had been made with the senatorial opposition. Secret advances and promises had been made by the king to a certain number of people, and especially Talleyrand had been worked upon, the only man who would be in a position to play the role of mediator and catalyzer between the Allies and the great state deliberative bodies. In truth it was not easy to nail Talleyrand down. "You don't know that monkey," his friend Dalberg said of him, "he would never take a chance of burning his paws, even if the chestnuts were all for him." So they had assigned an intriguing woman, Aimée de Coigny, to contact him, and she had elicited from him assurances of devotion which he authorized them to pass on to the Pretender. He himself took over the job of dangling before the eyes of the senate opposition glittering prospects of a constitutional monarchy and of winning over "these patriarchs of revolution who know how to overturn thrones so easily with the words *country, tyranny, liberty*. If they utter these words, we are saved."

By a strange irony of Providence, Napoleon himself was the best accomplice of the royalists. In fact the launching of another operation analogous to the one in Bordeaux depended on several prior conditions which only the emperor could determine. First, the Allies must stop threatening royalist plans with the terrifying prospect of making a desperate deal with the tyrant, a deal which would leave any imprudent royalists at the mercy of his vengeance. It was especially to obtain assurances on this point that Talleyrand had sent Vitrolles to the Allied sovereigns and that the higher council of the Knights of the Faith had, on their part, dispatched Gain-Montagnac to them. Their wishes had been fulfilled in advance by the breaking off of the Châtillon negotiations because of Napoleon's equivocating attitude. However, before the royalists could throw off their mask, it was still necessary that the Allied forces take Paris and that the imperial government no longer be in power there. Here again Napoleon hastened his own downfall because his push westward to interrupt his enemies' lines of communications, even though militarily justifiable, opened the road to Paris to the Allies. The latter, after a brief hesitation, were going to commit themselves resolutely to an attempt against the city on the morning of March 25, even with a chance of disaster if Paris held out long enough to allow Napoleon to get through and attack them from the rear. But they knew from intercepted dispatches of Napoleon's ministers that Paris was in no condition or mood to resist very long.

Still a third condition had to be fulfilled before the way was open for royalist activity. The government of Marie Louise's regency would have to be set aside. But this condition, too, depended on Napoleon's decision. On the evening of March 28 there took place the last meeting of the council of regency with all the ministers and all the great dignitaries present, including Talleyrand. They were almost all agreed that the empress and the little King of Rome should stay in Paris. They would have nothing to fear from the Allies (the empress had been an Austrian archduchess), and they might help to spur a weakening resistance. What they did not say to each other, but what they were certainly thinking, was that—in case of defeat and the flight of the emperor—the presence of the empress in Paris might save the imperial regime. Around her could rally all those who were weary of imperial tyranny and military adventures but who had something to fear from a return of the Bourbons. This last chance was lost, however. After all the others had spoken out in the discussion, Joseph presented a letter from Napoleon, dated March 16:

> Dear brother [he wrote], in conformity with the verbal instructions I gave you and in line with the spirit of all my letters, you must not permit the empress and the King of Rome to fall into the hands of the enemy. If the enemy advances on Paris with so much force as to make resistance impossible, have them all depart in the direction of the Loire—the regent, my son, the great dignitaries, the officers of the senate, the presidents of the council of state, the grand officers of the crown, and Baron de la Bouillerie and the treasury. Do not leave my son's side and remember that I would prefer to see him drowned in the Seine than to be in the hands of the enemies of France. . . .

Those present were stunned and looked at each other in silence. The habit of passive obedience paralyzed their reflexes; no one dared to raise any objection. The die had been cast; the empress was to leave Paris the next day, taking with her the last hope of the regime.

On leaving this memorable council at two in the morning, Talleyrand went over to Savary and said: "Well, this means the end of all this, isn't that your opinion? Good gracious, it's throwing away the game. . . . Now what shall we do? No one wants to be crushed beneath the ruins of the edifice. Come, let's see what's going to happen. Let's see." Talleyrand obviously had definitely made up his mind by that time, and he was henceforth calling the plays.

While complicated in appearance, his game was going to be played out over a whole week and through so many secondary episodes that its main lines were to become blurred and its results, although inevitable, were to appear uncertain right up to the last. But it was like the ball in the roulette wheel: To watchers its path seems uncertain; but that is an illusion. From the moment the wheel is spun, the spot where the ball will stop is determined by the law of physics with its weight, speed, and friction. When these multiple outside forces were through with their actions and counteractions, they would mostly cancel each other out by their very number.

So it only remains to record day-by-day, hour-by-hour, the unwinding of the film. History here can resort to the style of newspaper headlines.

*March 30.* At dawn, a hundred thousand Allied soldiers attacked the suburbs of Paris, which were defended by Marshals Marmont and Mortier with 39,000 men and 154 cannon. A fierce and indecisive battle.

—12:00 NOON. King Joseph authorized the marshals to parlay with the enemy. Soon after, he left the capital.

—4:00 P.M. Marmont stopped the fighting and started negotiations with Colonel Orloff, the tsar's aide-de-camp.

—5:00 P.M. Talleyrand, who had been ordered to go to Rambouillet, arranged to have himself stopped at the Enfer toll-gate and returned to his residence on Saint-Florentin Street.

*March 31.* 2:00 A.M. The surrender of Paris was signed while French troops were already evacuating the capital and withdrawing toward Fontainebleau.

Their advance columns met Napoleon near Juvisy as he was hurrying back to Paris. "What treachery! Surrendering! Joseph has lost the whole thing! Four hours sooner and all would have been saved!"

—5:00 A.M. Napoleon, deciding not to attack immediately, sent Caulaincourt to negotiate, and went on to set up his headquarters at Fontainebleau.

—6:00 A.M. At Boudy, Tsar Alexander received the Paris city council, headed by Chabrol and Pasquier. Schwartzenberg issued this proclamation:

> The Allied sovereigns sincerely seek a salutary authority in France which will be able to cement the union of all nations and governments with her. It is for the city of Paris under the present circumstances to hasten world peace. Her wish is awaited with the interest that such an immense result might be expected to arouse. . . . Parisians, you know the situation your country is in, the conduct of Bordeaux, the friendly occupation of Lyons, the evils brought down upon France and the real feelings of your fellow-citizens.

—10:00 A.M. Paris streets were crowded with people. On the boulevards a small group of Knights of the Faith tried to stir up a royalist demonstration without much success.

—11:00 A.M. The Allied sovereigns and their troops entered the Saint-Denis gate and moved up the boulevards. As they advanced, the shouts of welcome and cries of "Long Live the King" became more numerous. The parade ended with a great military review on the Champs-Elysées.

—5:00 P.M. Alexander arrived at Talleyrand's home, where he decided to take up his residence. In the large reception room there were assembled around him the King of Prussia, Schwartzenberg, Nesselrode, Pozzo di Borgo, and a few others. The tsar was saying that he saw only three possible solutions: 1) make peace with Napoleon after obtaining from him every possible guarantee; 2) establish a regency with Empress Marie Louise; or 3) re-establish the Bourbons. Talleyrand rejected the first two: no peace was possible with Napoleon; the regency was, as Nesselrode said, "the Empire with the emperor behind the scenes." "To find a durable solution . . . one must follow a principle, and there is only one principle: Louis XVIII is a principle, the legitimate King of France."

"How do I know," the tsar replied, "that France wants the house of Bourbon?"

"By a deliberation, Sire, which I will call for in the senate. . . ."

"You're sure of it?"

"On my word, Sire."

The King of Prussia and Schwartzenberg also came out for the Bourbons. "All right," Alexander concluded, "I now state that I will no longer deal with Emperor Napoleon . . . nor with any member of his family." Without further ado a proclamation was drawn up, printed, and posted in the city: The Allies declared that they would no longer negotiate with Napoleon and that "they would respect the territorial integrity of pre-war France as it had existed under her legitimate kings. . . . They would recognize whatever constitution the French nation chose. Consequently, they invited the senate to designate immediately a provisional government which could provide for administrative needs and prepare a constitution pleasing to the French people."

—7:00 P.M. The royalists held an exciting meeting at the home of Lepelletier de Mortefontaine. They decided to send to the tsar a deputation made up of Ferrand, César de Choiseul, Chateaubriand, and Sosthènes de la Rochefoucauld. Nesselrode promised them that the tsar would favor the return of the Bourbons.

*April 1.* The Paris newspapers, having come under royalist control, published pro-Bourbon articles. A poster in big capital letters announced the imminent publication of a work entitled *On Bonaparte, on the Bourbons, and on the Necessity of Rallying to Our Legitimate Princes, for the Happiness of France and of Europe,* by Fr.-Aug. Chateaubriand, author of *The Genius of Christianity,* etc.

"The general council of the department of the Seine, the city council of Paris, spontaneously assembled in a joint meeting, declare by unanimous vote of their members present that they formally renounce all obedience to Napoleon Bonaparte.

"Express the most ardent wish that a monarchical government be re-established in the person of Louis XVIII and his legitimate successors.

"Decree that the present declaration and the proclamation which explains it be printed and posted up in Paris, notified to all authorities remaining in Paris and in the departments, and sent to all the general councils in the departments."

—5:00 P.M. The senators still in Paris—64 out of 140—met under the presidency of Talleyrand, vice-grand-elector. They appointed a provisional government of five members: "M. de Talleyrand, Prince of Benevento, Senator Count of Beurnonville, Senator Count of Jaucourt, the Duke of Dalberg, Councillor of State, M. de Montesquiou, former member of the Constitutional Assembly."

—The provisional government appointed "commissioner delegates" to the administration of the various ministries, General Dessolles, former chief of staff of Moreau, was put in command of the Paris national guard.

—At Fontainebleau, Napoleon concentrated his troops for a counter-offensive.

*April 2.* The provisional government addressed a proclamation to the army: "You are no longer soldiers of Napoleon. The senate, and indeed all France, absolves you from your oaths of allegience to him."

—Alexander told Caulaincourt that he could still accept a regency of Marie Louise if Napoleon decided to abdicate without delay. This offer was immediately delivered to the emperor.

—The senate, on a motion by Lambrechts, decided to proclaim the deposing of Napoleon. It went in a body to present this resoluiton to Tsar Alexander.

*April 3.* Marshal Marmont received an emissary from the provisional government and from the Allied generalissimo, Schwartzenberg. He declared he was ready to withdraw his troops from Napoleon's army to "avoid any chance of civil war and to stop any shedding of French blood," provided he would be permitted to withdraw freely to Normandy and that a suitable position be assured to Napoleon.

—The senate adopted the final text of the deposition, with a long series of reasons, constituting an accusation against the government of the emperor.

—The legislative body supported the senate by approving Napoleon's deposition by a vote of seventy-seven out of seventy-nine present.

—Vitrolles, arriving from Nancy during the previous night, furnished with power from the Count of Artois, made contact with Talleyrand and the royalists in Paris.

—In the evening Talleyrand brought together the principal leaders of the senate and the members of the provisional government to discuss the bases of a new constitution.

*April 4.* Vitrolles arranged with Talleyrand the conditions by which the brother of the king, the lieutenant general of the realm, would be received in Paris.

—A senate committee was working on the new constitution.

—The provisional government learned of Marmont's decision with a feeling of great relief. The Allied generals took steps to assist the agreed movement of this French corps which had stood athwart the road to Fontainebleau.

—The marshals declared to Napoleon that they refused to expose Paris to the fate of a new battle. They hoped he would abdicate in favor of his son. Napoleon gave in and agreed. He decided to send Ney, Coulaincourt, and Macdonald to Paris with the following declaration:

> The foreign powers having declared that Emperor Napoleon was an obstacle to the re-establishment of peace and the integrity of French territory, faithful to his principles and his oaths to do everything for the welfare and glory of the French people, Emperor Napoleon declares that he is ready to abdicate in favor of his son and to deposit this act in due form with the senate by a message as soon as Napoleon II is recognized by the powers as well as the constitutional regency of the empress. On this condition the emperor will immediately retire to an agreed place.

—4:00 P.M. At Essonnes the emperor's three emissaries met Marmont, who had just arranged his defection with his division commanders. The marshal admitted to them his agreement with Schwartzenberg. But the abdication of Napoleon changed his mind, and he promised them that he would go back on his agreement and decided to return with them to Paris to obtain the recognition of the King of Rome.

*April 5,* 3:00 A.M.—Napoleon's plenipotentiaries were received by Alexander. The tsar was uncertain: "I hold no brief for the Bourbons. I don't even know them. It will be impossible, I fear, to get a regency. Austria is the most opposed to it. As for myself, I would accept it willingly, but I must act in concert with my allies. Well—I'll let my allies know your proposals and I'll support them. Also I'd like to get this question settled once and for all. Come back at nine and we'll finish it."

—4:00 A.M. The tsar conferred with the members of the provisional government and suggested that they accept the King of Rome. They protested that it was impossible to reverse the action taken, after the events in Bordeaux and Paris. Too many people had compromised themselves by relying on the previous declarations by the Allies.

—At this same time, Marmont's corps commanders had begun marching their troops over into enemy lines. They arrived at Versailles in the morning.

—Upon awakening, the tsar learned this news. "You see," he said to Pozzo di Borgo, "it's the hand of Providence . . . no more need for doubt or hesitation." He received the marshals at nine and told them the regency was definitely impossible. The restoration of the Bourbons was "a necessary consequence, imposed by the force of circumstances." The emperor would have to abdicate unconditionally. They would see that he was provided for. And, in the meantime, he arranged with the marshals a twenty-four-hour armistice.

—At Versailles Marmont's troops mutinied in favor of the emperor. The marshal, at first dumbfounded to learn of their action, decided, at the urging of Talleyrand, to resign himself to the inevitable. He rushed to Versailles, calmed the soldiers, and brought them again under his control.

—At Fontainebleau, Napoleon was stunned to learn of Marmont's defection. He regrouped his army with the intention of moving it to the Loire.

—11:00 P.M. The marshals, back from Paris, awakened the emperor to tell him of the failure of their mission. He declared that he would then continue the fighting.

*April 6,* 6:00 A.M. Napoleon confided to Caulaincourt that he was resigned to the idea of abdication.

—The marshals, for their part, were determined to force the emperor's hand, and they enjoined Major General Berthier not to transmit any more orders from Napoleon.

—Napoleon tried one last time to bring his marshals around to the idea of continuing the fight. In the face of their stubborn refusal he decided to give Coulaincourt his unconditional abdication and furnished him detailed instructions for settling the questions of his personal interests and those of his family. Ney immediately sent the news to Talleyrand.

—8:00 P.M. The senate adopted unanimously the constitution drawn up and proposed by the committee:

"*Article 1.* The French government is monarchical and hereditary from male to male by order of primogeniture.

"*Article 2.* The French people, by their own free will, call to the throne of France, Louis-Stanislas-Xavier of France, brother of the last king and after him the other members of the House of Bourbon, in the ancient order. . . ."

There is no need to quote further. The big decision had been made. Just a glance, however, at the financial page—

Quotations from the Paris Bourse (stock market):

Five per cent consolidated government bonds

March 29: 45 fr.
April 1: 49 fr.
April 4: 58 fr.
April 6: 66 fr.

Bank of France shares:

March 29: 550–520 fr.
April 1: 640–680 fr.
April 4: 760–787 fr.
April 6: 980–920 fr.

## To Whom the Credit?

Is it possible now to determine to whom to attribute the responsibility or honor for the Bourbon Restoration? Were the Bourbons recalled "by the free will" of the French people as the senate resolution claimed? Or instead, as the enemies of the monarchy were to repeat over and over again, were they imposed by the Allies?

Certainly the intervention of foreigners was needed to break the Napoleonic regime, and no less necessary was their consent to Louis

XVIII's succession. They gave their consent to it because they finally saw that it was the solution most likely to guarantee to them that there would be no repetition of the conquests of revolutionary and imperial France, but, instead, the stability of thrones and the peace of Europe. But it is just as certain that they had not planned it at the outset of their invasion and that they had not intended to impose it on a protesting nation. Such an attempt would have been condemned to failure from the start and would most surely have compromised the very interests which they were defending.

Nor was the French nation, at the beginning of 1814, thinking of a change in regime. To overcome its habits, its ignorance, and its suspiciousness, this solution had to be presented to it by the persistent urging of a bold and determined minority which was aided by circumstances. Napoleon's stubbornness was needed to make the French people recognize that there was no other way to achieve, with independence and dignity, their supreme desire of the moment—peace.

But again, in this series of obscure or conspicuous, heroic or abject acts by which this decision eventually emerged, what were the decisive events? Were they the secret meetings of the early conspirators? The efforts of the princes? The Bordeaux revolution? The maneuverings of Talleyrand? The senate's decision? Marmont's betrayal? The marshals' defections? These were all interesting questions for discussion in 1814 when so many wanted to claim credit and were seeking compensation for their services. However, today one is more inclined to admit that the effort to find the answer is pointless because the problem is insoluble. One may as well admit that each of these developments, taken alone, was not decisive, that it was their combination and the order in which they occurred which tipped the scales. A better conclusion would be that the outcome transcended the men involved, that the Bourbon Restoration was, as Tsar Alexander put it unenthusiastically, "a necessary result of the force of circumstances."

# 3

# *Louis, by the Grace of God, King of France and Navarre*

### *The Senatorial Consitution*

HOWEVER necessary and sensible the solution was which led to the re-establishment of the ancient dynasty, far from solving all the problems of the moment, it actually raised some new ones. The most serious one was what the nature of the royal power would be, once it was restored. Louis XVIII could not be expected "to sleep in Napoleon's bed," or in other words to adopt purely and simply the style and methods of the imperial despotism. "Natural liberties," wrote Chateaubriand, "reviving with the disappearance of the restraining hand, would have resumed their uninterrupted course." In the light of recent events, the Revolution and Empire appeared as an unfortunate parenthesis in the historical evolution of the nation. This parenthetical phase had been closed, and it was now a question of picking things up again from the point where the deviation had begun. But just where was this point—1789 or 1792? Was it the absolute, divine-right monarchy or the contractual, constitutional monarchy based on popular sovereignty?

These two concepts had already collided, even before the abdication of the emperor, in the claims of the French groups which had cooperated in the restoration of the Bourbons. One was made up of the "pure" royalists who had never accepted the Revolution and the Empire, the other consisted of the higher officials of the fallen regime who had sponsored the legal revolution. The former thought that the king ought to take in his firm grasp "the scepter of the Louis' and Henrys," except for a few necessary concessions to the evil of the times. This was an attitude entirely unacceptable to the men of the Revolution who had deposed and guillotined a king and made and unmade an emperor. They now had a chance to found a constitutional monarchy in the style of the English, to make "a legitimate 1688," as Mounier, the son of a Constituent of 1789, called it; and they thought they could benefit by it. They advocated this solution less, indeed, from love of liberty, which they had so indifferently sacrificed, than from concern for safeguarding their privileged positions. "Constitutional guarantees," Barante said, "were claimed by them as safety zones against a hostile authority and not as means for establishing a free and sound government."

Everything at first seemed to work in favor of their plans. The king was far away, and his brother, appointed by him as "lieutenant general of the realm," was moping around in Nancy without authority. In Paris the pure royalists, represented by the Knights of the Faith and the phantom government of Semallé, had no authority to interfere, and Talleyrand had easily bypassed them with a few sweet words. The senatorial party was strongly supported by Tsar Alexander especially. Disappointed at having seen his own plans foiled by the rapidity of events, this autocrat intended at least to give France, as he said, "strong and liberal institutions in line with present ideas." Louis XVIII was not to take the throne without having signed a good and proper surrender, tying his hands for all future time.

This group would have to work fast. While the events in Paris and Fontainebleau had been taking place, a senatorial committee had been hastily drawing up the constitution favored by Alexander. Unanimously adopted by the senators on the evening of April 6, also unanimously ratified on the following day by the legislative body (lower house), this text was the best proof that these beneficiaries of the Revolution, later transformed into imperial dignitaries, had been able to furnish of their aspirations and fears. The organization of the government was so hastily sketched out in it that it only seemed to be a pretext for a series of articles intended to guarantee, pell-mell, every interest and every situation arising from the Revolution and Empire: nationalized property, titles of nobility, decorations, ranks, pensions, bonds. The keystone of the governmental system was the subordination of the king to the nation, that is, to the senate, which arrogated to itself the right to speak in its name, and all the phrases were chosen so as to assert this idea. "The French people *freely* called to the throne"; they did not call Louis XVIII, but *Louis-Stanislas-Xavier, brother of the last king; brother,* and not *uncle,* because Louis XVII did not exist in the eyes of the people who had deposed Louis XVI just as freely and legally as they today recalled his brother. The twenty-ninth and last article again asserted the contractual nature of the monarchy: "The present constitution will be submitted to the French people for ratification by a procedure to be determined. Louis-Stanislas-Xavier shall be proclaimed King of the French as soon as he shall have taken and signed the following oath: 'I accept the Constitution; I swear to obey it and enforce it.' This oath shall be reiterated in a solemn ceremony in which he shall likewise receive the fealty of Frenchmen."

That was a lot to ask of a descendant of Louis XIV. How could anyone think that he would have submitted to such legalistic requirements? "Monsieur de Talleyrand," Louis XVIII was to say later, "if I had taken an oath to that constitution, you would be sitting and I would be standing." However, Louis XVIII might have been obliged to accept it if the senate had been able to obtain, in addition to the tsar's approval, the unanimous support of a public opinion ready to accept any regime that guaranteed foreign peace and domestic stability. Fortunately for the king, the senators had been so blinded by their own egotism that they had gone too far. Article 6 of their constitution read: "There shall be at least fifty senators and not more than two hundred. They are irremovable and hereditary. The present senators . . . continue to hold their seats and are a part of this number. The present endowment of the senate and its members shall still belong to them. The incomes from it shall be equally distributed among them and shall be passed on to their successors. . . . The senators appointed in the future shall not share this endowment." This passage needs no comment.

Public opinion, led by the pure royalists, reacted vigorously. "A constitution? What do you mean?" they exclaimed. "It's a constitution dealing with dividends!" Without the support of public opinion, the senate only spoke for itself. This was to be its weakness in the tight game played in the lobbies, while the attention of the people was to be fixed on the various manifestations accompanying the return of the Bourbons.

## Artois' Arrival in Paris

In the initial phase of this game, Talleyrand was to find opposite him a first-rate player in the person of Vitrolles. This little Provençal gentleman, whom he had sent early in March to contact the Allies to find out their attitudes, had acquired almost overnight an unrivaled position with the Count of Artois. By April 4 he was back in

Paris as the representative of the prince and negotiating with the provisional government the terms for Monsieur's entrance into Paris. They had agreed then that Talleyrand would use his influence to prevent the senate from publishing a constitution which might compromise the king's authority, that Monsieur would enter Paris in the uniform of the national guard, and that the letters patent of the king, appointing him as lieutenant general of the realm, would be taken to the senate the following day for their registration.

When Vitrolles returned to Nancy, the Count of Artois had just received an invitation from the Emperor of Austria to go to Langres for a conference with the ministers of the coalition. It was not difficult for Vitrolles to convince the count that it was more important to go to Paris while the situation was still fluid. But was it not already too late? At Vitry-le-François a courier brought them an envelope containing the text of the senatorial constitution passed in spite of Talleyrand's promises, with a letter from him insisting on the adoption of the tricolor cockade (of the Revolution and Empire). Vitrolles was stupified by this news. From the moment the senate subordinated the recall of Louis XVIII to his acceptance of the constitution, the powers of the Count of Artois were automatically invalidated. However, it was impossible to turn back. Vitrolles contented himself with confirming the arrival of the prince while leaving his intentions vague. Then, leaving Monsieur at Meaux, he hurried on to Paris in an effort to find a compromise. Talleyrand was willing to give in on everything, but the senators stiffened in their attitude, saying that Louis XVIII would not be king unless he took an oath to the constitution and, until then, they could not recognize a lieutenant general sent by him. In the end the provisional government proposed that the senate appoint the prince as head of the government on his arrival. They would thus avoid a clash over the title of lieutenant general. This message reached the Count of Artois at Livry where he was to spend the night before his joyous entry into Paris. Already a swarm of gentlemen and dignitaries had come to surround him along with the mounted national guard. The enthusiasm of the Paris crowds, of which they brought him the first intoxicating whiffs, would take care, he thought, of the senate pretensions.

Indeed, his journey of April 12 was a triumphal one. A radiant spring sun was shining in a blue sky when the procession set out at 11:00 A.M. On both sides of the road the country people lined up, admiring and applauding this cavalcade of gaily bedecked uniforms which moved along in picturesque disorder. And the prince! How attractive he looked on his white horse with its red saddleblanket decorated with golden fleurs de lys! Thin-waisted and young looking even beneath his white hair, he radiated joy and kept bowing untiringly with unequalled graciousness. As agreed, he wore the uniform of the national guard: a blue jacket with red facings, white knee-breeches, gold epaulettes, and a cocked hat with a plume and a white cockade.

At the Bondy barrier he was welcomed by the provisional government and the Paris city authorities, but the senate stayed away. Talleyrand came up and, leaning nonchalantly on the prince's horse, addressed him with a short and insignificant speech. The Count of Artois, unable entirely to control his emotions, replied in a voice choked with sobs: "Monsieur de Talleyrand, gentlemen, I thank you . . . I am too happy . . . let's go on . . . let's get along . . . I am too overcome." From here they moved toward Notre Dame by Rue Saint-Denis. All the house fronts were decked out with flags, bunting, tapestries, and flowers; waving handkerchiefs fluttered at windows, accompanied by shouts; the national guard was the escort without the aid of any foreign troops; it had a hard time holding back the crowd, which, at some points, broke through the line to rush toward the prince to touch him and kiss his hand. At the cathedral, filled to the point of bursting, they sang the *Te Deum* and *Domine, salvum fac Regem,* while Monsieur, on his knees, prayed fervently, his face lighted by a ray of sunlight coming through the upper windows. When he came out amid tumultuous acclamation, Marshal Ney, whose scowling looks had been noticed earlier, could not conceal his astonishment: "How can you explain such enthusiasm?" he asked Vitrolles. "Who could have believed it?" Even the most hardened and cynical were caught up in this wild manifestation of the old monarchical religion.

At the Tuileries, the prince, overcome with emotion, came very near fainting as he began to climb the great stairway, and had to lean on the marshals surrounding him. Beugnot showed him to his apartments and apologized for tiring him by asking his orders. "What do you mean tiring me?" he replied. "This is the first day of happiness I've had in thirty years! Ah, Monsieur! What a wonderful day! Tell them I am happy and pleased with everybody. Those are my orders for today."

## Agreement with the Senate

But the next day they faced the same dilemma. By its absence the senate had indicated that it did not intend to recognize an authority which did not emanate from itself. On the other hand the triumphal welcome he had received more than ever encouraged the Count of Artois not to make concessions. During the day of the thirteenth, while the prince was busying himself with receptions, Vitrolles took up again his discussions with the provisional government. Could not the latter just simply transfer its authority to the prince? Impossible, they argued, because the government received its authority from the senate and it could not transfer it without the senate's consent. Just then a man whom Vitrolles did not know but who had been so far following the discussion in silence, broke in sharply: "What you are saying does not make sense."

"Can you think of anything better?"

"Why, sure. There is only one way to get around the difficulty and that is to have the senate itself confer on the Count of Artois the lieutenancy general of the realm."

The man was Fouché, recently arrived from Illyria.

"But who could guarantee that they would agree to do it?" Vitrolles asked.

"I will," Fouché replied with vigor, "if the Count of Artois will consent to make a declaration of principle that will satisfy opinion."

"But, what kind of a declaration?"

Fouché at this point took up a piece of paper and began to write on a nearby stand. According to his plan the prince would say that, having read the constitutional act recalling his brother, he did not fear being disavowed by swearing to obey and enforce its bases. The principal guarantees included in the constitution were then enumerated.

At first the Count of Artois refused to accept this plan which meant tying the king's hands. But what else could he do? Attempt a coup d'état, as Vitrolles suggested, or, perchance, retire to a city in the provinces? Certainly public opinion did not support the senate's pretensions but, on the other hand, the senate had at its disposal the force of the Allied armies. Alexander I let it be clearly understood that, if necessary, "all foreign bayonets in France would join in supporting the senate and its constitution, come what may." It was necessary to bow to this. But Vitrolles cleverly revised the wording of the proposed declaration to eliminate any expressions which could undermine the king's freedom or rights.

On April 14, on Talleyrand's motion, warmly seconded by Fouché, the senate passed the following decree: "The senate confers the provisional government of France upon His Royal Highness, the Count of Artois, under the title of lieutenant general of the realm, until

Louis-Stanislas-Xavier of France, called to the throne of the French, may have accepted the constitutional charter." At 8:00 P.M. the senate went to the Tuileries Palace in a body to present the decree officially to the prince. The Count of Artois, concealing the disappointment which the wording of the text had caused him, replied: "Gentlemen, I have acquainted myself with the act recalling the king, my august brother, to the throne. I have not been authorized by him to accept a constitution; but I know his sentiments and his principles, and I do not fear being disavowed in giving you assurances in my name that he will admit its bases." Whereupon he enumerated briefly those bases found in the Fouché plan.

In general, then, each of the two opposing sides had gained a point: the senate by obliging the king's representative to accept his power from its hands; and the Count of Artois in taking this power without compromising by a single word or by a specific commitment the principle of the pre-existing divine right of the monarchy. But, in substance, the conflict remained unresolved, and they would have to await the return of Louis XVIII before finding a definitive solution.

## The People Accept the Restoration

On the following day, April 15, the provisional government came to hand over its powers to the lieutenant general; and no really big change was made because its members were asked to form a governmental council and the provisional commissioners whom they had appointed remained in charge of the ministerial departments. However, to enlist the support of the army, they added to the government council Marshals Moncey and Oudinot, who had been the first to rally to the new regime, as well as General Dessolles, commander of the Paris national guard.

One of the first acts of the lieutenant general was to send into the provinces royal commissioners with broad powers for getting the new order recognized and reactivating the local administrative machinery. As a matter of fact their job was, above all, to inform the local authorities of exactly what direction events were taking and to reassure those who might have feared some reprisals from the restored monarchy, especially the holders of national lands. "There will be neither victors nor vanquished." According to their instructions, such was to be the tone of their approach.

As to the fact itself of a change in regime, its acceptance had been general, allowing for some necessary delays—sometimes rather long—before the official news arrived. Nothing better illustrated the delayed communications than the battle unleashed by Wellington in front of Toulouse against the solidly entrenched troops of Soult in the improvised fortifications, a battle costing almost twelve thousand human lives. Yet, this terrible hecatomb, bloodier than all the rest of the campaigns in France, took place on April 10, four days after Napoleon's abdication! Two days later, when Wellington made his triumphant entry into Toulouse, they still did not know about the events in Paris. As in Bordeaux a month earlier, the royalists, organized by the Knights of the Faith, carried out their local revolution under their own responsibility. It was only on the evening of April 12 that Wellington, having received the official news, felt authorized to abandon the reserve he had religiously observed and associate himself with the people's outbursts of delirious joy.

Except in the south, where the fall of the imperial regime occasioned a few noisy but not bloody demonstrations, the change in regime was carried out almost everywhere quietly and with the cooperation of the local authorities. Fifteen years of passive submission had accustomed everybody to following without question the decisions of Paris. Only one prefect, and not one military commander, is known to have refused his collaboration. Everyone jumped on the bandwagon, and soon they would be seen almost standing in line to proclaim their devotion to the king. The columns of the official *Moniteur* were full of these declarations in which they exhausted, in favor of the new rising sun, the whole arsenal of laudatory expressions previously reserved for emperor worship—and created some new ones as well.

The press, unmuzzled for the first time in many years, gave free rein to its repressed rancor and unleashed a number of unchivalrous attacks upon the fallen emperor. One could get some idea of their tone from Chateaubriand's denunciations of "the son of the Ajaccio process server" and of "his semi-African family" of whose regime he wrote: "Crimes, oppression, slavery marched in step with madness." By the press of the pamphleteers Napoleon became Nicholas, Jupiter-Seapin, Attila, and Ghengis Khan. The good royalists called him *Bonaparte, Buonaparte, Buona-parte,* and even, as a pun, *Buon'a parte.*

The only manifestations of fidelity to Napoleon came naturally from the military—not so much from the ordinary soldier, who was so happy to see the end of the hostilities that 180,000 deserted in two months, but more from the company officers and noncommissioned officers, who were exasperated at France's defeats and the fall of their idol. For example, at Clermont on April 11 and 12, elements of the eighth regiment of the line manhandled the prefect to the cries of *Long Live the Emperor!* Some officers rode their horses into the cathedral, broke down the door leading to the belltower, hauled down the white flag, stamped on it, and dragged it through the mud.

The most delicate job was to get the military to wear the white cockade. The Count of Artois insisted on it as a requirement: it was the emblem under which so many brave men had bled for the royal cause in the wars of the West, and, in recent events, the white cockade had been the rallying sign for Bourbon supporters. Public opinion, at least that opinion allowed to express itself, had also come out on this side. Even Benjamin Constant cautioned the Bourbons "not to commit the immoral act of abandoning the historic oriflamme of their fathers in favor of a flag bloody with crimes and bereft of the aureole of success." However, the army, especially, remained strongly attached to their glorious (tricolored) cockade, and even in the prince's procession on April 12 the two cockades were both represented. With our present perspective of history we may be somewhat puzzled by the fact that the men in responsible positions in those days had not tried at all costs to work out a compromise which would have deprived the enemies of the monarchy of a powerful sentimental lever. But how could they have measured the seriousness of this flag question before the events of the succeeding years which were later to load it with all its explosive force? The man whom all agreed was the most far-sighted of his day, Talleyrand, was the very one who persuaded the army to abandon its colors. He had them write falsely to Marshal Jourdan, in command of the 15th military division at Rouen, that Marshal Marmont had just had his corps assume the white cockade. The honest Jourdan, thinking he was following his example, adopted it, and since no one doubted the patriotism of the victor of Fleurus, all the generals little by little succeeded in having the white flag accepted by their troops.

Among all the mistakes committed by the Restoration during its early days, this mediocre tricky success seemed to be the most irritating because it could have been so easily avoided.

## The Armistice Agreement

"Until the king arrives," Talleyrand wrote on April 17, "only the very indispensable things should be done, and nothing more." And, in fact, the provisional government of the lieutenant general was to limit itself, for the most part, to setting the wheels of government in motion again and to dealing with routine affairs. Only on two points was it to make commitments for the future: one was to deal with the provisions for Napoleon and the other was the making of peace preliminaries with the Allies.

In truth, as to Napoleon, the provisional government only had to ratify the decision of the Allies, or more exactly that of Tsar Alexander. It was more particularly he who determined the former emperor's exile to the island of Elba in spite of England's and Austria's well-founded apprehensions over this. The treaty signed on April 11 provided, among other things, for the payment by France of an annuity of two million francs ($400,000) for Napoleon and of 3,500,000 francs ($700,000) for various members of his family, who in addition were to be allowed to keep all their personal property. Besides, the French treasury was to pay the emperor's debts and to make two million francs ($400,000) available to him for use as gifts to his former servants and followers. He could take with him four hundred volunteers for his imperial guard. Frenchmen who accompanied him would lose their citizenship after three years except by special permission from the new government.

Talleyrand, in the name of the provisional government, signed a declaration in which he agreed to the treaty as far as it was necessary and guaranteed to fulfill it as far as France was concerned. England's approval of the territorial clauses, to which she restricted herself, was held up until April 17, and it was only on the twentieth that Napoleon could leave Fontainebleau. There is no need to go into detail about his trip out of France, marked as it was at times by demonstrations of loyalty on the part of some units of troops whom he met and at other times by hostile receptions from royalist civilians in the South. It was with the greatest relief that the provisional government learned that he had finally embarked on April 27 for his new kingdom. Should one believe that they had once contemplated a more radical method of getting rid of Napoleon? The strange affair of Maubreuil raises the question. This adventurer, in order to conceal an act of brigandage committed against Queen Catherine of Westphalia, claimed he had been engaged by Talleyrand to assassinate the emperor. This murky affair has never been cleared up and would take us too far afield. It did, however, illustrate what curious disorder reigned at that time in the councils of the provisional government.

The most important act of the government of the lieutenant general was its signature, on April 23, of an armistice agreement which brought to an end hostilities between France and the Allies. Here are its main provisions:

*Article 2.* To confirm the re-establishment of friendly relations between the Allied powers and France and to have the advantages of peace enjoyed in advance, as much as possible, the Allied powers will have each of their armies evacuate French territory back to the boundary of January 1, 1792 as fast as the places occupied by French troops beyond these limits are evacuated by them and returned to the Allies.

*Article 3.* The lieutenant general of the realm of France will so order the commanders of these places to hand them over that the transfers will all be accomplished by next June 1.

*Article 7.* On both sides, prisoners, officers, soldiers, and hostages will be released and returned to their respective countries without payment of ransom or exchange arrangements.

*Article 8.* The administration of the departments and cities presently occupied by the Allied forces will be turned over to magistrates appointed by His Royal Highness the Lieutenant General of the Kingdom of France as soon as the present act is signed. The royal authorities will provide for the supplies and needs of these troops until the moment when they evacuate French territory. Because of their new friendly relations with France the Allied powers wish to end their military requisitions as soon as the transfer of authority to the legitimate officials can be effected.

Most historians, when they mention this armistice, feel constrained to brand it as an irreparable mistake, revealing the Count of Artois' indifference, or his lack of patriotism. In fact, the man who was responsible was Talleyrand, in whose hands the prince had naturally left the entire matter. This paternity requires a closer look. Talleyrand came to his own defense on this armistice. The charge that the armistice was conceived in too great haste, he countered with the argument of the urgent need to put an end to the fighting in the invaded regions of France. The provisional government not only could not take over authority in these occupied departments, but the Allied commanders were actually collecting taxes there for their own use, emptying the state supply depots, crushing the inhabitants with requisitions and forced contributions, and giving themselves over without restraint to every kind of act which an arbitrary military regime could think of. This violence had to be stopped at all costs, and French officials had to recover the legal means to protect those under their jurisdiction. But was it not paying too much for this deliverance to give up, at a stroke of the pen, the fifty-three fortresses which French troops still held outside France's old boundaries—fortresses which could still have been used for bargaining in the coming peace negotiations? To that argument it could be replied that these fortified places actually did not represent real strength. Their scattered and besieged garrisons were militarily powerless and just as useless to the king as they had been to the emperor. On the contrary, once returned to France and regrouped, the troops could furnish, along with the prisoners of war released by the same agreement, quite a formidable force. Bargaining money? Perhaps, but it was soft money whose value was going down with every day's continuance of the blockade. So it was wise to bargain with it at its highest quotation.

The most serious reproach that could be leveled at Talleyrand, and one from which it is difficult to exonerate him, is his prejudicing the territorial conditions of the future treaty by agreeing without argument to the boundaries of January 1792 and making no claim to the natural frontiers which had been so dearly bought. But were not the Allies, occupying the capital and a large part of the country, in a position to impose their will anyway? And this determination to push France back to her former limits had been firmly fixed and clearly expressed. Defeated France could only hope to obtain a few concessions in the territorial clauses of the future treaty, a few advantages in other clauses, some immediate relief, largely by gaining the confidence of the Allies, by encouraging Tsar Alexander's evident goodwill and generosity. For all these reasons Talleyrand felt justified in sacrificing illusory hopes in return for modest but tangible benefits.

Nevertheless, public opinion, more given to feeling than to reason, reacted unfavorably to this. A police report said: "The armistice conditions have seemed harsh, they satisfy no one."

Other matters of discontent helped cloud the joyful glow of the early days: the unemployment of the destitute working classes, the discontent in the army, the inertia and confusion within the government, the industrialists' fear of English competition, and finally the explosion in the press of antirevolutionary sentiments and aristocratic claims which caused former Jacobins to fear an era of reaction and reprisals. In the Vendée, especially, the old royalist organizations began to go back on a war footing. "The countryside," wrote the prefect of Loire-Inférieure, "is in full revolt. Against whom? They don't know, but to shoulder a gun is one way of expressing their thoughts in the Vendée." The old "blues," terrorized, took refuge in the cities and complained of not being protected.

It was high time for the king to arrive.

### Louis XVIII's Return to France

When the Marquis of La Maisonfort came to give his master the news of the events in Paris, he cried out joyously: "Sire, you are King of France!" Louis XVIII replied coldly: "Have I ever ceased to be?" His unshakeable conviction of his rights, his awareness of his dignity were second nature to him. "Louis XVIII," said Chateaubriand, "was king everywhere, as God is God everywhere, in a cradle or in a temple, at a golden or a silver altar. Never did his misfortune lead him to make the slightest concession; the lower he fell, the higher he stood; his name was his diadem." While he was uncompromising on questions of principle, Louis XVIII was no less disposed to make allowances for national aspirations as long as they did not undermine his authority. As early as 1799 he wrote: "A wise government ought to consult the wishes of the people and defer to them when they are reasonable, but it should always act on its own decision [*proprio motu*]—that is the secret of combining love with respect." This was to be exactly his line of conduct in 1814.

In spite of Vitrolles' affirmation, even though he was not at Louis' side, it is difficult to believe that Louis XVIII was on the point of countersigning the senatorial constitution and that the Count of Bruges, sent by the Count of Artois after April 12, had arrived just in time to prevent him from doing it. In any case the story he heard of the enthusiastic reception of his brother in France could only have encouraged him in his resistance to the senate's pretensions, and it was easy for him to answer Talleyrand's epistolary promptings by saying that he did not want to commit the future of the monarchy before he himself had a chance to size up the situation.

It was not until April 19 that Louis XVIII left Hartwell House, which had sheltered the morose tranquillity of the last eight years of his exile; he was accompanied by the Duchess of Angoulême, daughter of Louis XVI, the aged Condé and his son the Duke of Bourbon, and various people at his little court. The Prince-Regent of England wanted very much to make amends for all the irritating slights which his ministry may have shown toward his illustrious guest, and so gave him a truly royal reception. The people of London deliriously acclaimed Louis XVIII as the symbol of restored peace.

To the congratulations and good wishes of the prince, the king replied: "It is to the counsels of Your Royal Highness, to this glorious
country, and to the confidence of its citizens that I attribute, along
with Providence, the re-establishment of our house upon the throne
of our ancestors." Whatever was exaggerated or even false in these
words can certainly be explained by his excitement over the unexpected warmth of the greeting he received, but a deeper design can
also be seen in it: by saying he was obligated to England, Louis
XVIII reduced by just that much the gratitude he would owe to the
Tsar of All the Russians and guarded himself in advance from his
counsels.

The prince-regent then insisted on accompanying the king all
the way to Dover, from whence the king sailed on April 24 on the
"Royal Sovereign." As the ship sailed away, escorted by eight ships
of the line, in the midst of a vast farewell throng waving the white
flag, the shore guns thundered in response to the salutes of the guns
of the ships. The "Royal Sovereign" was scarcely out of earshot of
the English shore when it began to hear in the distance the French
artillery at Calais welcoming the returning king. When the ship was
about to dock, Louis XVIII standing on the bridge, raised his hat,
extended his arms towards his country, and then placed one hand
on his heart. In the midst of sobs and shouts the old monarch, with
his niece strongly supporting his arm, finally set foot on his native
soil. In a loud voice he cried out: "After an absence of ten years,
Heaven returns my children to me, Heaven returns me to my children! Let us go to His temple and render thanks to God!" That evening, after the *Te Deum* and a reception by the local authorities, the
people were admitted, according to custom, into the dining room
where they could see with their own eyes that the earlier emotions
had not spoiled the royal appetite.

In the next few days, going through Boulogne, Abbéville, and
Amiens on his way to the capital, Louis XVIII experienced a hero's
welcome of triumphal arches, speeches of greeting, singing, salvoes,
and *Te Deum*'s. On April 29, at about six in the evening, he
arrived at Compiègne where politics was awaiting him. Almost immediately the marshals paid their respects; to the speech of the
Prince of Neuchâtel, the king replied with a dignity and elegance
which made a profound impression; and the compliments that he
phrased so adroitly in his later remarks to individuals completed
his captivation of those around him. Deep down, these old warriors,
most of whom were of plebian origin, were very much impressed at

being treated so familiarly by a king when their childhood memories had left them with the idea that he was very inaccessible. The calm majesty and refined language of the sovereign retained their respect more than the ranting and railing of the emperor's army-camp language.

After the marshals, came a delegation from the legislative body, but no one from the senate! This absence was a reminder of the conflict of principles which remained unresolved. However, the spontaneous homage and the unconditional submission of the army chiefs and the elected representatives of the nation were already a considerable success for the legitimist thesis.

On the following day the king chalked up new gains in dealing with two persons on whom the senatorial party counted still more— Talleyrand and Tsar Alexander. Talleyrand was received after Mass and not without having to wait a long time in the midst of a crowd of courtiers. Since no one was present at their first meeting, we only know what Talleyrand deigned to tell Beugnot: "My dear Prince of Benevento," so the king was reported to have said in greeting him, "I am very happy to see you again." "A lot has happened since the last time we met. You see we [the Bourbons] have come out on top. If you had, you would have said to me 'Let's sit down and talk,' but I say 'Sit down and let's talk.'" By this subtle turn of phrase of Louis XVIII let his guest know who was boss. As to the main question, Talleyrand did not recall what was said, but subsequent events showed that the king had not allowed himself to be convinced by the prince's arguments. Nor was he moved from his stand on the following day by the urging of the tsar, who came all the way out from Paris for this purpose. The tsar's ugly mood was not improved by the etiquette of the court, which let him know that it was not for a younger branch of the Holstein royal house to lecture to a descendant of Saint Louis and Louis XIV on the question of royal authority. When Louis XVIII entered the dining room, he calmly went ahead of his guest and sat in a high-backed chair while the tsar was assigned a regular chair.

Having become convinced of the king's obstinacy and of the impossibility of getting him to back down, the senate decided to compromise: they would not insist on his accepting the constitution before they would recognize him, and, in return the sovereign would solemnly promise to give without delay a constitution on the bases acknowledged by the Count of Artois.

At Saint-Ouen, where the king went on May 2, he finally received the representatives of the senate, but without giving them anything other than polite words. That night Blacas, Vitrolles, and La Maison-fort revised the proposed royal declaration, which Talleyrand had gotten the senators to accept, by eliminating certain expressions offensive to the king. By two o'clock in the morning the final text was approved, sent to Paris, and printed. At seven it was posted on the walls of the capital.

Louis, by the grace of God, King of France and of Navarre, to all those who see these present declarations, greetings.

Recalled by the love of our people to the throne of our fathers, fully informed of the misfortunes of the nation which we are destined to govern, our first thought is to evoke that mutual confidence so necessary to our repose and to its welfare.

After having carefully read the plan of a constitution proposed by the senate in its session of last April sixth, we have recognized that its bases are good, but that a great number of articles, carrying the imprint of the haste with which they were drawn up, cannot in their present form become the fundamental laws of the state.

Resolved to adopt a liberal constitution, wanting it to be properly put together, and not being able to accept one which required revision, we convoke upon next June tenth the senate and legislative body and promise to submit for their examination a text which we will have had prepared by a committee chosen from the membership of the two houses and which will be based upon the following guarantees:

Representative government shall be continued such as it is today, divided into two houses: a senate and a chamber composed of deputies from the departments.

Taxes are to be approved by the representatives;

Civil and personal liberty is assured;

Freedom of the press is to be respected, except for necessary precautions to preserve the peace;

Religious freedom is guaranteed;

Private property is inviolable and sacred; the [previous] sale of national [confiscated] lands shall remain irrevocable.

The responsible ministers can be impeached by one chamber and tried for impeachment by the other.

Judgeships shall be for life and the judicial power shall be independent.

The public debt is recognized; pensions, ranks, and military honors are retained, as well as the old and new nobility.

The Legion of Honor, whose investiture we shall determine, shall be continued.

All Frenchmen are eligible for consideration for civil and military appointments.

Finally, no individual shall be disturbed because of his [previous] opinions or votes.

In other words, although the senate had succeeded in preventing the return of outright absolute monarchy, the principle of divine right remained intact. Louis XVIII asked for nothing more as, with his head high, he made his entry into the capital.

The ceremony had been prepared down to the last detail, and, for that reason, there was not the informal spontaneity and the explosive enthusiasm which had marked the joyous entry of the Count of Artois. The king's own person and his retinue indeed inspired more curiosity than sympathy. What did the people see? First of all, they saw, far back in a carriage drawn by eight horses, a fat man, looking sick and weary, dressed in a blue overcoat with gold epaulettes and with a huge cocked hat on his head, apparently unimpressed by the joyous cries filling the air as he passed. At his side, the Duchess of Angoulême, straight and stiff in her new corset, wore a naturally sad look on her face. Old Condé, with his hair curled and powdered in the old style, was seated beside his son, facing the king, living symbols of the awful impression left in the minds of the people by the earlier emigration (flight from the Revolution). The Count of Artois rode his horse near the royal carriage, accompanied by his two sons, the Duke of Berry and Duke of Angoulême. The latter, not having had time to find a new uniform, wore an English one. The soldiers of the old imperial guard, lined up along the parade route or marching in front of the procession, showed by their expressions their humiliation and their rage at having to participate in the triumph of a shameful cause.

In spite of all this, popular acclaim was not lacking. The king, as usual, played his role to perfection. The daughter of Louis XVI (the Duchess of Angoulême) could not conceal her emotions as well as could the king. When she arrived at the Tuileries, which she had not seen since that fatal day of August 10, 1792, she fell in a faint. Yet Louis XVIII compelled her to appear with him on the balcony and, in a disgusting theatrical scene smacking of the pastoral games of the Trianon hamlet [le Hameau], he placed a crown of flowers on her head. It is also said—but the witness who originated the story is suspected of malice—that, while throwing kisses to the crowd, the king muttered under his breath: "You scoundrels, you Jacobins, you monsters!"

# 4

✤ ✤ ✤ ✤ ✤

# King, Charter, and Peace

## Initial Difficulties

OF all the details of the ceremony of May 3, the one of which Beugnot, its grand arranger, was proudest was the inscription which he had composed for the statue of Henry IV, put in place again on the Pont Neuf for this occasion: *Ludovico reduce, Henricus redivivus* (By Louis' return, Henry lives again). It was no more than natural that the Bourbons were pleased at that time to put their return under the popular aegis of the first king of their line, who had been in his time a restorer of the kingdom and a conciliator of parties. But could Louis XVIII really claim to be a second Henri IV? Alas, he could not, no more than the painted plaster statue, hastily erected by Beugnot, could replace the bronze one by Jean Boulogne, which had been broken in August 1792. Henry IV had won his kingdom from within by his own efforts; he was king by sword as well as by birth. Louis XVIII, on the other hand, was king by defeat, and he followed the most glorious leader who had ever led French armies. Henry IV's authority also had been greatly enhanced by the tremendous need for peace and quiet after so many years of bloody anarchy; while in 1814 the country, weary of Napoleonic despotism, hoped to regain its liberty. Last, but not least, Henry had never abandoned his people, and his years of doughty combat had given him a chance to know them more intimately than any other French monarch; while Louis XVIII was a fugitive king, cut off from the nation by twenty years of exile, a period in which France had passed through the most rapid transformations in all her history.

To bind up the wounds of war; to rebuild the house of France from the ruins of the great European Empire; to fit the old monarchical, patriarchal, theocratic, and feudal institution into the new

56

Napoleonic, national, secular, and administrative state; to balance the new society emerging from the Revolution with the old privileged classes who intended to reoccupy their places along with the king— all of this was a superhuman and infinitely delicate task, which would have required, for lack of a brilliant monarch, a council of exceptional ministers. The misfortune of the Restoration was that it had to undertake this work with mediocre princes and a weak and heterogeneous governmental team.

## *The King and the Princes*

Louis XVIII was, however, not without certain kingly qualities. Glued to his chair by an excessive corpulence and uneven hips, which would have made walking difficult under any circumstances, he had been able to make a majestic trait out of his idol-like immobility. His head was completely royal with a forehead both wide and high beneath his powdered hair; his blue eyes could charm a person or make him squirm; and his ruddy face was full and regular. He could make his voice either low or loud—his bell-tower voice, he called it. After Louis XIV, he was undoubtedly of all the kings of France, the one best able to play the role of monarch. "People in our position," he once said, "should always remember their rank and never let others forget it." He loved magnificence in ceremonies, he looked upon etiquette as a way of reigning, and he required the most minute observance of its rules. Cuvillier-Fleury tells the story of how he one day fell heavily to the ground, and M. de Nogent, an officer of the guards, came rushing to help him up. "M. de Nogent!" the king shouted angrily as he rejected his assistance. And there the king stayed flat on his back until the captain of the guards, the only proper person, could arrive on the scene and help him up.

Very early in life he had sought in mental gymnastics a substitute for his physical handicaps which deprived him of more active recreation. He had acquired a sort of pigeonhole erudition, which supplied him with anecdotes and quotations for every situation. Unfortunately his authors were not just Horace and Racine, but also the third-rate poets Baculard and Arnaud. His carefully chosen words often approached affectation or sentimental effusiveness, "political madrigals" Molé called them. Nor did he refrain from unnecessarily caustic witticisms, or at times even downright dirty jokes.

The king was able to command respect but not inspire love. Behind a facade of paternal kindness, which he was fond of displaying, one could sense a basic Olympian selfishness. Even that tyrannical tenderness he showed toward his favorites had a false ring; it was like a sort of comedy role which the monarch reserved for himself. It was difficult to forget the sly and inexorable ambition which had characterized his conduct as Count of Provence in the reign of Louis XVI. Having attained the objective of his aspirations, he firmly intended to hold onto it, and that was why, no matter how jealous he was of his authority, he was ready to make certain necessary concessions. However, there seems to be no evidence that his stay in England had given him the least esteem for the role of a constitutional monarch. On the contrary, every fibre of his being clung to the Old Regime. While rather realistic and prudent in wanting to reassure the new France and to adjust himself to her, at heart he could not really understand her or love her.

The Count of Artois, the brother of the king, did not even try to conceal his dislike for anything connected with the Revolution. He who was to become Charles X will be described later on. Suffice it to note here what his position was in relation to Louis XVIII. According to Beugnot, he is said to have declared on his arrival in Paris: "The king has a fine head on his shoulders, as keen as that of a man of thirty, but he is as helpless as a cripple, or nearly so. He will do the thinking for us, and we will take action for him." In this the count was to be greatly mistaken. Louis XVIII had never taken his brother into his confidence and in an aloof sort of way thought of him as a narrow-minded and rash muddlehead. If one adds to this the secret jealousy of a gouty old man because of his younger brother's handsome appearance and the fact that the younger man had children to assure the continuance of the dynasty while nature had deprived the elder one of such a satisfaction, one can understand why the king did all he could to relegate his brother to a purely honorific position. "Monsieur" had too noble a character to show any resentment; and he had too much respect for the crown and too much realization of his older brother's intellectual superiority to come out in open opposition to him in the beginning. However, he continued his practice from his exile days of gathering around himself all the most fanatical and reactionary elements of the royalist party, who realized they could obtain nothing from the king. Just the same he could hardly fail to have some interest in the fate of the kingdom he was eventually to inherit, and, lacking a definite place in the administrative machinery, he tried to have his views prevail by using oblique and secret maneuvers to which he had become accustomed by his twenty years or more of futile and childish intrigue.

The count's oldest son, the Duke of Angoulême, then twenty-nine years old, was far from sharing his father's preference for the old order of things, an order which he himself had not known. Simple in his tastes, and just as charitable and honest as he was pious and loyal, he was very careful at first to model his conduct on the prescriptions of the king. Unfortunately these sterling qualities were spoiled by an inferiority complex, stemming from a physical degeneracy, including stunted growth, nearsightedness, nervous and embarrassing twitchings of the face, hesitant speech, and, worst of all, impotence.

The Duke of Berry, his younger brother, was by this very fact the last and only hope of the dynasty, and they could rest assured that he would do a good job at furnishing offspring. He had hardly arrived in Paris when his amorous escapades were the topic of public malicious gossip. In fact they were more amused than scandalized by it; in a way it was refreshing to have at least one black sheep in an otherwise prudish flock, which was said to be steeped in piety. Besides being a lusty young fellow, the Duke of Berry also had physical courage and a quick wit in repartee. On one occasion, when he was reviewing troops, a grenadier cried out as he passed: "Long Live the Emperor!" "So you liked him a lot?" said the prince without any visible anger. "He led us to victory." "Why shouldn't he with soldiers like you?" He was the only one among the princes who had some success in winning goodwill among the people and the military by his spontaneity, his coarse familiarity, and his inexhaustible generosity. His appearance matched his manners; he was a common-looking man with a heavy body on short legs, a head barely emerging from massive shoulders, a ruddy complexion, and black, curly hair.

The daughter of Louis XVI, who became the Duchess of Angoulême by her marriage to her cousin, should have deserved, more than any other member of the royal family, the belated sympathy of the French people because of her tragic misfortunes, her high courage, and her great character. Unfortunately the blond and frail orphan of the Temple (her prison during the Revolution) had become a quarrelsome woman with a blotchy complexion, hard lines in her face, and a grating voice. From her father she inherited bluntness, but without his good nature; from her mother came her pride, without her mother's charm. Motherhood might have dimmed the memory of her misfortunes and softened a heart hardened by adversity, but she was denied that joy. Henceforth she sought consolation in fervent, but somewhat narrow and morose, religious worship and in works of charity. The natural horror she felt for anything concerning the Revolution put her politically on the side of her father-in-law, the Count of Artois, and she tried to influence Louis XVIII in that direction. Without being disrespectful, she could still argue her point of view with him. One little incident illustrates this trait in her character. It happened early in 1796, soon after her liberation. Louis XVIII, then in exile, and always quick to utilize incidents for propaganda purposes, wanted her to write a letter of thanks to Father Edgeworth, Louis XVI's confessor, giving it the date of her liberation and then making it public. The young princess replied: "That is the sort of thing older people could do, especially when it was urgently needed. But my age [18 years old] and my character require that I be as plain and precise as truth itself."

## The Ministers

Princely deficiencies were not to cause too serious inconveniences in the early days of the Restoration. Indeed France was used to such handicaps among the Napoleonic princes. But more serious were the deficiencies of those appointed to the various cabinet posts. With two exceptions all of them came from the personnel of the provisional government, which the Count of Artois himself had continued in his stopgap cabinet. When Talleyrand gave up the presidency of the provisional government, he naturally chose to keep the portfolio of foreign affairs. Either from indolence or caution, he was going to stick to this post and was quite happy not to get involved in the imbroglio of domestic affairs. With the absence of Talleyrand in internal matters, the principal influence should have been that of Father de Montesquiou. A man of the Old Regime, and a priest who frequented court and salon, he could not forget that he had once presided over the National Constituent Assembly (the second Revolutionary legislature). His convictions and his associations made him favor constitutional monarchy, but in his handling of administrative affairs he showed such impetuosity, changeableness, and fickleness that he soon earned the dislike of his colleagues and the disgust of his subordinates.

In contrast, the ministry of finance could not have been in better hands than those of Baron Louis. He was, like his patron Talleyrand, a former clergyman, who was to show unusual foresight in his choice of methods to restore France's fiscal stability and exemplary energy in getting them accepted by his colleagues and subordinates. At the same time he was hotheaded and blunt, refusing to consider other factors outside the field of finance.

To officiate at the abolition of what remained of the navy, they disinterred a half-decomposed former Constituent, old Malouet. He completed his decomposition in September 1814 and was succeeded by Beugnot who had been director of police and before that, under the provisional government, minister of the interior. The latter was a good administrator, but somewhat lacking in character and prestige.

A still more deplorable choice was General Dupont as minister of war. No doubt, in the first uncertain days of the provisional government, the leaders, in looking around for a general who would be sure not to make a deal with Napoleon, turned to Dupont as a last resort because he had been so unfairly treated by the emperor as a result of his defeat at Baylen. But now that the whole army had clearly rallied to the Bourbon regime, there was no good reason for humiliating it by putting it under the direction of a man who reminded them of an earlier misfortune. Besides, the unfortunate Dupont, as a former division commander, had had no training or experience for a so much higher responsibility. He would very soon prove his complete incapacity for the job.

Only two of the new ministers were to be entirely the king's choices: Chancellor Dambray and the Count of Blacas, Minister of the Royal Household. The former had previously been an advocate general in the *parlement* of Paris, and, for twenty years had lived on his estates in Normandy. No doubt he was a fine and honorable gentleman; but his clock had stopped in 1789, and he knew absolutely nothing of the people, institutions, and laws of the new France. The only reason for his appointment was the fact that he was the son-in-law of Barentin, the last keeper of the seal of Louis XVI. The king had thus wanted to restore the Old Regime custom of having high state offices become hereditary possessions, especially those held by the nobility of the robe (nobility derived from judicial or administrative office).

The Count of Blacas d'Aulps had come back from England with the king. After the departure of the Count of Avaray, in 1810, he was Louis XVIII's indispensable man, his confidant on all occasions, his eyes, his ears, his legs—in other words, his favorite. The favor of the king and his title of grand master of the wardrobe would have permitted him in any case to rule over the court of the Tuileries much as he had done over the little court at Hartwell. It was therefore felt that it would be better to regularize his position of influence in the eyes of the public by assigning him to a ministerial post. Just the fact that he was the "favorite" was enough to make him unpopular; his haughty manner and his noble and émigré prejudices were to make him the scapegoat for all the mistakes of the First Restoration. However, beneath this grim exterior was hidden a tender heart, a solid and moderate judgment, and a devotion of feudal magnitude that no shock or ingratitude could alter.

What unity of action could one expect from such a widely differing team? Not one of the principal ministers had such preponderance of right or personal authority which would have made him a council president or "premier" in the English sense. The king claimed to be the head of the council; but his age, his infirmities, and his habits were poor preparation for this task. Indeed, it soon became apparent that administrative details wearied and bored him. In the early council meetings over which he presided, and at which the princes of the blood and the ministers of state were present, there was a lot of discussion without much accomplishment. This provided the occasion for one of Talleyrand's witticisms. When he was asked what went on during the three-hour council meeting presided over by the king, he replied, "Three hours." The ministers henceforth decided to deal directly with the king on the affairs of their department which required his signature, and these occasions became much too numerous for him to give proper attention to each question.

In the absence of the king or a prime minister, the job of coordination could have been done by the secretary of state who played such a commanding role under Napoleon. Vitrolles, put in this key position by the Count of Artois, planned to exercise a great influence through it, but the open hostility of Montesquiou and of other ministers reduced him to the role of writer of the council minutes and of editor of the *Moniteur*. The resurrection of the High Council, by the Ordinance of June 29, 1814, as well as that of the Council of Parties, in no way helped the situation, because, according to ancient custom, the ministers did not automatically sit on these councils but had to be invited individually each time. In short it was a return to the paternal anarchy of the time of Louis XVI.

## The First Peace of Paris

It is highly significant in regard to this cabinet relationship that the two most important acts of this period—the First Treaty of Paris and the Charter—were not even discussed in the council.

The peace terms were negotiated directly between Talleyrand and the Allied foreign ministers. The agreements, rather quickly formulated, were drawn up in four identical treaties signed on May 30,

1814 with the four great powers, Austria, Great Britain, Prussia, and Russia. Each of these documents contained some special clauses. The secondary Allies were also to have their separate treaties, Sweden's on June 8, Portugal's on June 12, and Spain's on July 20.

The preamble declared that these treaties were "to bring to an end the prolonged disturbances in Europe and the misfortunes of its peoples by establishing a sound peace on a fair distribution of power among the states." They no longer wished to "require from France the conditions they had demanded from her under her previous government, now that, having put herself under the paternal government of her king, she thus assured to Europe conditions of stability and security." This passage harked back to a proclamation issued by Alexander I on March 31, when he entered Paris. He had said that the Allies "would respect the integrity of the old France as she had existed under her legitimate kings." "They can even do more," he continued, "because they still profess the same principle that for the welfare of Europe there must be a France both great and strong."

This phrase had caused some to hope that the powers would let France keep her natural frontiers on the Rhine and in the Alps which had been conquered before Napoleon's time. The disappointment caused by the armistice of April 23 was therefore all the more bitter. Louis XVIII and Talleyrand had insisted in vain on obtaining this extra that they had been promised along the Belgian border, but England was inflexible. France had to be satisfied on the northern border with some very small frontier concessions: four cantons of the department of Jemmapes, and four in the department of Sambre-et-Meuse. On the northeast side France retained Saarlouis, Philippeville, Marienbourg, and Landau, plus the old enclaves which previously had been dependencies of the Holy Roman Empire, especially the towns of Monbéliard and Mulhouse. The most sizable acquisition was taken from Savoy: the arrondissements of Chambéry and Annecy which would form the department of Mont-Blanc. Finally the Allies recognized, over the protests of the pope, the Revolutionary annexation in 1791 of Avignon and the Comtat-Venaissin. In all, France emerged with 636,000 more people than before the war. Certainly this was slight comfort if one considered the loss of all the territories then considered French after twenty years of possession. But the Allies claimed that they were very generous when it was remembered how brutally Napoleon had dismembered their territories after each of his victories over them. Six "separate and secret" articles provided that the disposition of the territories taken from France would be determined in a congress and "on bases drawn up by the Allies among themselves." But even this distribution was hinted at in broad terms.

England restored to France all the French colonies taken during the war, except Tobago and Saint Lucia in the West Indies and Mauritius in the Indian Ocean. Sweden restored Guadeloupe, and Portugal handed back French Guiana. On the other hand, France retroceded to Spain part of the island of Santo Domingo which had been surrendered to her by the Treaty of Basel of 1795. As to the other half of the island, which had always belonged to France but had been temporarily lost after the Negro insurrection, England promised not to oppose any eventual attempts to restore France's authority. Except for one instance favoring Holland, the arsenal equipment and warships in places surrendered by France were to be distributed on the basis of two-thirds for France and one-third to the previous Allied owners. In short, England felt sure enough of her naval supremacy so that she did not need to take excessive advantage of her victory.

The financial terms of the treaty were particularly generous. In spite of the demands of Prussia, France was not compelled to pay any war indemnity. The powers, "wishing to give to the King of France a new proof of their desire to have disappear, as much as possible, the consequences of an unfortunate period, *renounced* all their claims against France from contracts, supply requisitions, or military fines and impositions exacted by the French government in the wars since 1792." The French government, however, promised to arrange for the payment of debts owed to individuals arising from contracts, requisitions, and loans.

The treaty also contained certain articles guaranteeing the freedom of choice and the possession of property for people who were to be transferred under new rulers. Thus the sale of nationalized property in territories temporarily annexed by France were declared to be irrevocable. Finally, at Talleyrand's demand—and in this he seemed singularly ahead of his times—an article provided for freedom of navigation on the Rhine and the extension of an international control to all the international rivers in Europe. He saw this as a compensation for the loss of Belgium. "Do you know where my Belgium is? It is in the freedom of river navigation!"

Such was the First Treaty of Paris. Its principal author, Talleyrand, always claimed that it was impossible to obtain more under the circumstances. One must admit that at least the Allies showed themselves to be more generous in victory than France had been toward them previously. Talleyrand and Louis XVIII, by accepting inevitable sacrifices with good grace and by clearly repudiating the spirit of conquest represented by Napoleon, re-established France's foreign policy on the bases defined by Vergennes. After having too readily succumbed to the intoxication of military power, France could still regain her prestige and her standing as a great nation if she could become a factor favorable to peace and stability instead of to disturbances and war. All the small nations threatened by the appetites of their powerful neighbors would again look to France, and she would become once more the arbiter of a continent in the name of right and justice. This great and promising policy Talleyrand was going to try to develop at the Congress of Vienna, until the unfortunate adventure of the Hundred Days relegated it to the melancholy museum of great opportunities lost.

## The Constitutional Charter

Almost at the same time that peace was concluded between France and Europe, Louis XVIII was able to proclaim still another treaty whose high contracting parties were none other than the monarchy of St. Louis (King Louis IX) and the French Revolution. Actually, if the constitutional charter was indeed really a compromise, it was offered as a unilateral act of the crown and constituted a victory for the crown by that fact alone. We have already seen how Louis XVIII had succeeded in setting aside the senate's pretension of imposing on him, as a prior condition of his investiture, a constitution which would have subordinated his authority to that of the nation. Perhaps it would have been wiser just the same to have had the country participate in the elaboration of the constitutional documents by summoning a more representative assembly than the imperial senate and legislative body. This idea never seemed to have entered the head of Louis XVIII or his advisors. They were in a hurry to get the job done, and the Allies themselves had let it be understood that they would not evacuate France until they saw a French government firmly established on a constitutional base. But the king was especially insistent on avoiding a repetition of 1789; he intended himself to fix the limits to his own power.

Still, he had promised to seek the advice of a committee composed of senators and deputies, and this was formed on May 18. Along with eight members from each house there were three royal commissioners: Montesquiou, Beugnot, and Ferrand. The latter was an old, experienced parliamentarian, much heeded by the king and much overrated as a political thinker. Chancellor Dambray presided over the deliberations. When these finally got under way on May 22, the royal commissioners presented a draft constitution already prepared by Montesquiou, and the discussion could begin at once on the articles. Because the Allies were impatient to leave Paris by June 3, most of the original draft was to be adopted almost without discussion. As to those articles encountering objections, as well as those requiring additions or omissions, the king also had to have the last word, because every evening the chancellor reported to him what had been done during the day and nothing was adopted without his formal approval. The Charter of 1814 was definitely the creation of Louis XVIII.

One must examine this important documentary text closely. At first sight the lapidary and limpid style of its seventy-four articles and their distribution into seven parts gives the impression of a carefully constructed monument. But if it is examined more closely, incongruities appear and questions are raised.

The first part, entitled *Civil Rights of Frenchmen,* invoked again the great principles of liberty and equality first enunciated by the *Declaration of the Rights of Man* of 1789, but one can also see other articles in it which apply very concretely to the various concerns of those who engineered the Restoration in the spring of 1814.

"*Article 5.* Everyone may profess his own religion with equal liberty and receive the same protection for his religious worship." This was to reassure Protestants who could not very easily forget the intolerance to which they had been subjected since the end of the eighteenth century.

"*Article 6.* However, the apostolic Roman Catholic religion is the state religion." Thus the "very Christian" king rejected the principle of state religious neutrality, and he eliminated the previous formula of "the religion of the great majority of Frenchmen"—set by the First Consul in the Concordat of 1801.

"*Article 8.* All Frenchmen have the right to publish and have printed their opinions provided they comply with the laws intended to prohibit abuses of this liberty." One senses here a desire to find a happy medium between the total liberty of the press tried at the beginning of the Revolution and the total control imposed by the Empire. One suspects that it would only be possible to achieve that happy medium by feeling their way, and that that was why they cautiously tried to avoid tying their hands in advance. But certainly nobody foresaw that the Restoration was going to wear itself out for fifteen long years trying to solve this problem, and that it would finally fall in the attempt.

"*Article 9.* All property is inviolable and no exception is made for what is called *national* property. The law will make no distinction as to properties." Perhaps the law would not, but would public opinion? This was just another one of the tough problems not yet solved. Even before his return Louis XVIII had understood the necessity of reassuring the purchasers of national property (confiscated from the anti-Revoluntionary refugees). But could he prevent the former owners from demanding the return of their possessions after they had followed him into exile? And here was another clause which recalled those tragic years:

"*Article 11.* Any search back into opinions held, or votes cast, prior to the Restoration is forbidden. The same oblivion is required of citizens and courts alike."

Then followed the important articles on the executive and legislative branches of the government, a few of which are reproduced here. Those concerning the executive were:

"*Article 13.* The person of the king is inviolate and sacred. His ministers are accountable to him. To the king alone belongs the executive power."

"*Article 14.* The king is the supreme head of the state. He commands the land and sea forces, declares war, makes treaties of peace, alliance, and commerce, appoints all public officials, and makes all regulations and ordinances for the execution of the laws and the security of the state."

Those concerning the legislative branch were:

"*Article 15.* The legislative power is exercised collectively by the king, the chamber of peers, and the chamber of deputies chosen from the departments."

"*Article 16.* The king proposes the laws."

"*Article 17.* The bills [proposed laws] may be presented to either chamber as the king may decide, except that tax bills must be presented first to the chamber of deputies."

"*Article 19.* The chambers have the right to petition the king to propose a law on any subject and to indicate what they think the law should contain."

"*Article 20.* The king alone sanctions and promulgates the laws."

"*Article 24.* The chamber of peers is an essential part of the legislative power."

"*Article 27.* The appointment of the peers belongs to the king.

Their number is unlimited. He can by his own pleasure transfer them to other offices, appoint them for life, or make their appointment hereditary."

"*Article 28*. The peers may take their seats in the chamber at the age of twenty-five and may not debate or vote until the age of thirty."

"*Article 33*. The chamber of peers shall try all cases involving high treason and attempts against the security of the state as defined by law."

"*Article 35*. The chamber of deputies shall be composed of deputies elected by electoral colleges whose organization shall be determined by law."

"*Article 37*. The deputies will be elected for five years, one fifth every year."

"*Article 38*. No deputy may take his seat in the chamber until he is forty years old and unless he pays a direct tax of a thousand francs [two hundred dollars]."

"*Article 40*. The electors [voters] who select the deputies may not vote unless they are at least thirty years old and pay a direct tax of three hundred francs [sixty dollars]."

"*Article 46*. No bill may be amended unless the amendment is proposed or accepted by the king and only after being referred to the bureaux [standing committees] and considered by them."

"*Article 48*. No tax may be instituted or collected unless voted by both the chambers and sanctioned by the king."

"*Article 49*. The land tax may be voted only for one year at a time. Indirect taxes may be imposed for a period of several years."

"*Article 50*. Once a year the king will call the two chambers into session. He may also prorogue them and even dissolve the chamber of deputies. In the latter case he must call a new one into session within three months."

"*Article 54*. Ministers may be members of either chamber and have access to both chambers. At their request they have a right to be heard in them."

"*Article 55*. The chamber of deputies has the right to impeach ministers and to present such impeachments before the chamber of peers, which alone has the right to try such cases."

"*Article 56*. Ministers may be impeached only in cases of treason and peculation."

How should one characterize a regime as defined by these articles? First of all it is seen that there was no such thing as a separation of powers as in 1789. Like the first consul in the Constitution of the

Year VII [1800], the king, while possessing full executive power, also shared a good part of the legislative power. What power exactly did the legislature retain, squeezed as it was between the initiative and the sanction of the king? In spite of its apparent weakness it still possessed the means of effectively intervening in the executive realm. In fact, if the chambers had the right each year to approve or withhold taxes, did they not have the means of exercising an irresistible pressure on the administration? Besides, the right of initiative, denied to them by Article 16, is given to them obliquely by Article 19, which was obviously a late addition to the original constitutional text.

In case of an eventual conflict between the legislature and executive it was not clear what would happen. Article 13 said the ministers were responsible, but this did not mean parliamentary responsibility, that is, parliament's right to overthrow ministers they did not like. Indeed, Article 56 was specific in saying that only criminal responsibility involved parliament. The ministers were the agents of the king, and a parliamentary adverse vote was a refusal to collaborate with the king. Any political conflict thus, of necessity, involved the crown. This was a situation fraught with danger. Certainly the king's authority was well fortified. His person was inviolate; he could change the majority in the chamber of peers by appointments; and he could dissolve the chamber of deputies. But in spite of that, he would still have an empty treasury. How could he govern without collecting taxes and passing laws? Article 14 on the ordinance power, by which Charles X was to try to find a solution, was far from authorizing a royal dictatorship, in the opinion of the authors of the Charter. Beugnot said it was simply a formula borrowed from previous constitutional precedents without much thought given to it. It never occurred to these constitution-makers that this would be used to give independent legislative power to the king. This kind of interpretation was directly contradicted by the articles which followed.

It is hardly necessary to underline the undemocratic character of the representative system. The creation of a chamber of peers caused no debate. The advisability of an upper house seemed to be justified by the Revolutionary experience and by the English example; it offered a practical way of satisfying the old dignitaries of the Empire. As to the chamber of deputies, it represented only a very small minority of citizens; the three hundred franc [sixty-dollar] tax requirement for voting disfranchised about ninety-nine percent of adult Frenchmen, and only about ten thousand would be eligible to vote. These restrictions, it was thought, would make it easier to have a docile and well-behaved electorate; but in fact it turned the political influence over to the upper bourgeoisie, which was, of all the classes, the least disposed to tolerate a strong executive and the revival of the nobility. The power of money was replacing the privileges of birth. Was the nobility necessary any more? In any case such a chamber could not pretend to be the voice of the nation.

Part VI of the Charter dealt with the judiciary and assured its independence by providing for the life-term of judges (Art. 58), the retention of the judicial system of the Consulate (Arts. 59–61), the suppression of special courts (Art. 63), public court sessions (Art. 64), and jury trial (Art. 65). Article 68 provided that the Napoleonic Civil Code and all existing laws not contrary to the new Charter would remain in force unless or until they were legally abrogated. By these three lines the restored monarchy perpetuated the entire social and administrative structure of the Revolution and the Empire.

The last part of the Charter, called *Guaranteed Individual Rights,* was a sort of catchall section without much semblance to a constitutional document in which were reaffirmed the promises made by the Count of Artois and those made by the king in his declaration of Saint-Ouen: the continuance of the ranks, honors, and pensions of the armed services and the Legion of Honor granted by the previous government; and the acknowledgement of the bonds and other obligations of the state.

Here then was the Charter, a compromise hastily thrown together which was to last for a considerable time. "It was only little by little," Barante said, "after discussions and reflections about it, that one could finally have any systematic idea about it or find in it some kind of fundamental principle. But at first everybody thought of it as a formality required by circumstances and not expected to last very long." No doubt this paradoxical good fortune of survival is explained by certain outside influences, such as the fact that to some men of the Revolution the Charter appeared like their Edict of Nantes (Henry IV's earlier guarantee to the Protestants), their assurance against a return of the political and social Old Regime. But the Charter itself had many commendable aspects. Precisely because it was a compromise growing out of the existing situation, it was more likely to translate the real prevailing political forces into constitutional formulas. Its very vagueness gave it a certain flexibility. Also it should be observed that its authors, as master politicians, somewhat disillusioned but realistic, were quite well qualified for the job of explaining in plain and practical terms the better part of the remaining political thought of the eighteenth century after it had passed through the crucible of experience.

For the moment the king could be proud of his masterpiece. The principal demands of public opinion had been satisfied, and yet his divine-right authority, his principle of legitimacy, remained intact. But was he not wrong in wanting to emphasize too strongly his victory on that point? Was it really necessary to include that long preamble where he explained laboriously, with constant reference to historical examples, how his concessions could in no way alter the ancient constitution according to which the authority in France resided completely in the person of her kings? Did he have to go into the baneful deviations of the Revolution? And at the end did he have to make use of outworn and offensive formulas in order to emphasize the gracious character of the document, with such words as: "We have voluntarily, and by the free exercise of our royal authority, granted and do grant, concede, and accord to our subjects. . . ." And then came the last slap to all those who had recognized and served another sovereign— "Given in Paris, in the year of Our Lord 1814, and of our reign the nineteenth." It is easy to understand how Louis XVIII could not, without contradicting himself, give any other date for the beginning of his reign than that of the death of his little imprisoned nephew, Louis XVII, in the Temple; but could he not have just omitted the second date?

In those days a caricature was handed on from cloak to cloak in secrecy, showing the king radiant with joy, receiving from a half-starved writer a beautifully bound dedicatory copy of a book with the title *Histoire des dix neuf glorieuses années du règne de Louis XVIII* (*History of the nineteen glorious years of the reign of Louis XVIII*). The book was very thick, but the pages were blank. So it was that offended common sense avenged itself with irony. It would have been better not to have furnished such an occasion.

On June 4 the king went to the Bourbon Palace (the legislative hall) in full ceremonial regalia. There he found assembled the members of the senate, the members of Napoleon's old legislative body which became automatically the chamber of deputies of the new regime, the representatives of the great state bodies, the members of the king's court, the princes, and the foreign ambassadors, etc. The king, having seated himself on the throne, read a short speech which he had written himself. Well-phrased and effectively delivered, the speech was greeted with great enthusiasm. Chancellor Dambray then threw a slight dash of cold water on the occasion by explaining the spirit which inspired the formulators of the Charter, the fact that they put a heavy emphasis on royal authority. Then the dean of the royal commissioners, Count Ferrand, read the Charter itself. The greater number of the audience, not having known what the commission had prepared, were pleasantly surprised to find included most of the liberal guarantees suggested by the senatorial constitution. Thus the favorable reception appeared to be sincere and general.

After this, the chancellor read out a list of new peers. On it were twenty-nine old ecclesiastical and lay peers of the Old Regime to which the king had added seventeen others of the ancient nobility. Men from the Revolution and Empire had the lion's share with ninety-three former senators to whom were added ten marshals. Among the fifty-one former senators not included, twenty belonged to the territories taken from France, twelve were former members of the Convention (Revolutionary legislature, 1792–1795)—Fouché, Siéyès, Grégoire, Garat, Roederer, etc., and eight were members of the imperial family or of the immediate entourage of the emperor, Cambacérès for example. The "victims" of the purge did not have too much to complain about for they kept their salaries of 36,000 francs ($7,200) as life pensions. Louis XVIII could very well play the role of a generous prince: was this not his great day of victory?

# 5

❧ ❧ ❧ ❧ ❧

# *Early Blunders*

## *Military and Administrative Reductions*

WITH the promulgation of the Charter and the Treaty of May 30, 1814, Louis XVIII had successfully liquidated the two big problems arising from the fall of the Empire. But once having gotten over these major obstacles, his government was besieged by a swarm of minor difficulties which were to trip it up and quickly exhaust its good standing with the nation.

One of the principal difficulties at that time was aptly described in the witticism of Madame de Staël when she said: "The first article of the rights of man in France is the right of every Frenchman to a government job." On this question of jobs the royal government seemed to be faced with an insoluble problem of having twice as many applicants for half as many jobs. The collapse of the imperial European edifice had thrown back on France a whole crowd of exported government civilian officials who thought themselves eligible for corresponding positions back home. At the same time the returning émigrés, now without income, who had refused to serve under Napoleon and had, in one way or another, helped in the restoration of the Bourbons, thought that the time had come to compensate them for their loyalty, and all of them were besieging the princes and the ministers for government positions. How could all of these be satisfied? Should new jobs be created? The critical financial situation would not permit it. Indeed, Baron Louis, the finance minister, had just abolished fifteen thousand government jobs. Still another expedient would be to dismiss the avowed supporters of the Empire and the former Jacobins (radical revolutionists) in order to appoint loyal men to these vacant posts. Louis XVIII did not want to move in this direction. "Unite, Forget, and Forgive" was his motto, and Blacas himself, although accused of being the pillar of reaction, once declared that "whoever served Bonaparte in the interest of France, has served the king."

Of all the changes in regime which took place in the nineteenth century, the one in 1814 was perhaps the only one not accompanied by massive purges. During the Hundred Days, Napoleon tried to prove that the first Restoration had been the rule of the émigrés and assembled the statistics on the personnel in the prefectures (corresponding to American state government employees). Surprisingly the result was an impressive testimony to the moderation of the royal government. Of the forty-three prefect appointments up to March 1815 there were only seven from among former émigrés and declared royalists, as against twenty-nine former imperial employees and two personal friends of Guizot.* The position of Guizot is interesting because, although a Protestant, he was secretary general of the interior ministry. Of the 147 new subprefects and secretaries general of prefectures, there were only twenty-five émigrés, and most of these had returned to France under the Consulate and had served under the Empire. In all, only thirty-five per cent of the prefectorial personnel had been replaced. The same policy was followed in the other ministries. According to Barante, Chancellor Dambray had such a repugnance for dismissals that at the end of nine months he had not been able to bring himself to dismiss one justice of the peace.

Unfortunately the army was handled with much less consideration. Certainly no one thought of keeping 500,000 men on a war footing right after signing a peace treaty. But the inevitable reduction of army strength was aggravated by the haste and clumsiness with which General Dupont carried it out. By a series of ordinances, issued in June 1814, more than 300,000 men were sent home. The reorganized standing army was made up of 105 regiments of infantry, eight of artillery, and three of engineers, making a total of 223,000 men. They pensioned off all those officers who came within the categories stipulated by the ordinances, but there still remained a large quota of unassigned officers. These were put on inactive duty with half pay; captains received seventy-three francs ($14.60) a month and lieutenants forty-four francs ($8.80). What else could these eleven thousand to twelve thousand officers on half-pay do except to curse the king and dream of the Little Corporal's (Napoleon's) return? As to the imperial guard, Napoleon had given this warning: "If I were Louis XVIII, I would not keep my guard. I am the only

* In his recently published book, *The French prefectural corps, 1814-1830* (1966), Mr. Nicholas Richardson challenges the accuracy of the figures compiled by the Napoleonic administration. According to his own careful tabulation, the proportion of former émigrés among the new prefects was somewhat higher than that given by the official document.

one who can handle it. . . . . I would dismiss it and give good pensions
to the non-coms and privates and promotions and transfers to the regular
army for those who wanted to stay in the service." The king could have
appealed to their pride and loyalty by making them the royal guard.
He did neither of these and made the worst decision by humiliating
them without disarming them. The regiments of the imperial guard,
renamed grenadiers and chasseurs of France, were scattered among the
provincial garrisons; and the officers were allowed to keep a rank higher
than their assignments provided but were put on one-third pay.

Other economies, which hurt the army's pride as much as its welfare,
came with deep budgetary cuts for the Legion of Honor and the Invalides (veterans' home and hospital) and the closing of the military
schools of Saint-Cyr, Saint-Germain, and La Flèche. In their place the
king re-established a single military school at Paris "in order to let the
nobles of our kingdom enjoy the advantages granted to them by the
edict of our ancestor in January 1751." These unfortunate expressions
were well contrived to confirm the officers of the imperial army in the
belief that the real reason for these economies was to reward men of
the Old Regime at their expense.

## Military and Court Extravangances

Indeed, right at the same time when they were demobilizing some
officers, General Dupont, desirous of courting favor with the princes, was
integrating into the army units a large number of Old Regime officers
who had fought in the royal armies of the Vendée insurrection, in
Condé's émigré army, and even under enemy flags. And all these
fine people claimed the right to be appointed to a rank corresponding
to their seniority. Vitrolles told the story of the minister of the navy,
Malouet, presenting to the council the petition of a royal naval officer
who had not been on active duty since 1789, when he was a cadet,
but who now asked for at least the rank of a rear-admiral because that
would have been his rank if he had been allowed to continue his career
without interruption. "When you answer him," Vitrolles said, "admit the
logic of his reasoning, but add that he overlooked one essential fact—
that he was killed in the Battle of Trafalgar."

There was also another rather insignificant reason for a rush for
military rank among the courtiers, a reason often overlooked by historians. In re-establishing the old royal court they had not required the
old French style of knee-breeches and powdered hair. To these courtiers
the long trousers worn in town were too middle-class (bourgeois) and
consequently they all wanted to appear in the more dazzling and

flattering military uniforms worn by the princes and made popular by the previous imperial court. This meant that they all wanted commissions in order to be qualified to wear a uniform, and naturally none was satisfied with the insignia of second lieutenant. So, in less than a year, the Restoration created 387 general officers, many of whom had never commanded troops. It is true that most of these newly commissioned generals had only honorary titles, to give them rank, but later several of them received their corresponding salaries.

While these honorary military titles were more ridiculous than expensive, the re-establishment of the royal military household had more serious results. Louis XVIII and many other royalists were obsessed with the idea that the monarchy would never have fallen during the Revolution if Louis XVI had taken the precaution to surround himself with a strong and faithful guard. Since they had done away with the old imperial guard, they felt it was necessary to set up a new royal guard. Although this was decided upon, it was not carried out, and, in the meantime, they revived the former ceremonial units of the royal household with many different names and gaudy uniforms. This had the practical advantage of recognizing the services of thousands of favor-seekers who hounded the princes and ministers without disturbing too much the regular army units and the civil administration. Thus it was that one saw re-established in rapid succession four old companies of bodyguards, to which were added two extra companies to satisfy the vanity of Marshals Berthier and Marmont: the guards of the door, four red companies (light horse, gray and black musketeers, constable guard), the provost guards of the palace, the Swiss Hundred, and the body guard of Monsieur (heir to the throne). At the end of September 1814 a treaty was signed with the Bern authorities to enlist five Swiss regiments. Altogether these constituted a little privileged army of six thousand men, all receiving the rank and pay of officers, to the tune of 20,390,000 francs ($4,078,000).

Alongside the military household Louis XVIII was re-establishing his civil household and those of the princes, with their traditional subdivisions and their anachronistic names: captain of the mule teams, the arquebus bearer, the chair pusher, masters of the horse, masters of the tennis court, page masters, etc. The food service alone required 140 officials. All these positions were reserved for the Old Regime nobility, and those who had followed the king into exile had priority. They even reinstalled in their old positions those who had survived. Such a one was the old Marquis of Dreux-Brézé who, with the aid of Blacas, was going to try to revive the Versailles etiquette in all its minute details.

It was only natural that all this high society would try to make the new nobles of the imperial court, when they were bold enough to go to the Tuileries or to the drawing rooms of the Faubourg Saint-Germain, feel the huge gulf separating the noble by birth from the Bonapartist noble. And one can guess to what extremes of cattiness the court ladies could go in these matters. The wife of Marshal Ney, they say, was one victim of this, to the point of weeping from humiliation.

The provincial nobles did not wait for the example of Paris before they tried to regain their privileges. As early as April 23, 1814, Barante, prefect of Loire-Inférieure (now Loire-Maritime), wrote to Montlosier: "There is not one self-styled gentleman but thinks the King of France returned for his own particular benefit. They must have all the positions, pensions, and decorations. Everything was for them, their time had arrived. . . ." There was nothing that would irritate and worry the bourgeoisie more than this disgusting revival of the Old Regime society. Barante again explains: "When a country gentleman with an income of two or three thousand francs (four hundred to six hundred dollars a year), without a knowledge of proper spelling, without an agreeable disposition, and even without an army commission, looks down on landowners, lawyers, and physicians, they react against him and add a seething rage to their proverbial aversion."

## The Religious Restoration

The return of the Old Regime was also felt in religious matters. The king did not think it was enough just to restore Catholicism to its predominant position as the state religion, he intended to annul the effect of the Concordat of 1801 against which he had made a solemn protest at the time of its promulgation. The direction of ecclesiastical affairs was taken away from the minister of the interior and was turned over to an ecclesiastical commission of nine men, a majority of whom were hostile to the Concordat. At the same time Mgr. Cortois de Pressigny, former Bishop of Saint-Malo, was sent to Rome to obtain the restitution of the Concordat of 1516. While awaiting the results of these negotiations, which promised big changes for the position for the clergy, the government increased clerical salaries, restored liberty to religious orders, and freed ecclesiastical schools from University control. Indeed the latter itself was to be split up into seventeen local universities, and the board of directors of the University was replaced by a "Royal Council of Public Instruction" with a bishop as president. This last measure, decreed by an ordinance of February 17, 1815, was not to be carried out.

This new tendency of the government was accentuated by the ill-advised zeal of Beugnot, director of police. On June 7, on his own authority, he prohibited anyone to work or cause someone to work on Sunday under penalty of a fine; all shops were to be closed, and even the cafés were to be closed on Sunday forenoons. Another police order required all householders to decorate residences for the passage of the procession of the Blessed Sacrament, an order which evoked complaints from Protestants. The processions of the festival of Corpus Christi, indeed, returned to the streets of Paris where they had not been seen for a long time. The city police accompanied the processions and asked men to remove their hats. August 15, a day which Napoleon had tried to set aside in his own honor, was now to be the day reserved for the old procession of the Vow of Louis XIII when all the members of the royal family and the great state assemblies walked down the street, carrying candles.

Also there were numerous politico-religious funeral or expiatory ceremonies as Revolutionary anniversaries came around—in memory of Louis XVI, Marie Antoinette, Mme Elizabeth, Louis XVII, the Duke of Enghien, and other victims of the Revolution. There were even commemorations for Pichegru, Cadoudal, and Moreau. It was certainly laudable to honor the dead, but the publicity of all these commemorations seemed to contradict the king's official promises to throw a veil over the sad past. It disturbed all those who had directly or indirectly participated in the Revolution. The most striking demonstration along these lines was the ceremony held on the occasion of the transfer of the mortal remains of Louis XVI and Marie Antoinette from the Madeleine Cemetery to the Basilica of Saint-Denis. This transfer took place on January 21, 1815, anniversary of the execution of the former king, which was declared to be a day of national mourning. All the civil and military pomp was displayed; in the gloomy atmosphere of a dark and chilly day, the monumental funeral hearse, covered with all sorts of emblems, went slowly down the narrow streets. At one point, when the decorative emblems became caught in the cords of a street-lamp, one impish onlooker could not let this delightful opportunity pass without bellowing the mob cry of the Revolution: "String him to the lamp-post." Thus we see that they had succeeded only too well in reviving Revolutionary memories.

## The Question of Confiscated Estates

A more general and more lasting concern was the question of national confiscated lands. The Charter had certainly guaranteed the validity of the sales of these lands, but the former owners would have had to be inspired by a spirit of heroic abnegation to have accepted this spoliation in silence. In newspapers and pamphlets they were loudly demanding justice. Here and there some intimidated purchasers of these disputed lands acquiesced in settlements.

In September, the question was finally brought up in parliament by the government itself. Louis XVIII could not remain indifferent to the unhappy fate of those émigrés who had lost all by serving him. Although he had felt it necessary to approve the sales already transacted, he could at least return to their former owners those lands not yet sold to individuals. Napoleon had already done this to those nobles who returned to France under the Consulate, but at that time he had not included the woods and forests which now made up the great mass of unsold national lands—about 350,000 hectares (864,850 acres). A bill was proposed on September 13 which provided for the return of all unsold national lands to their former owners. Count Ferrand, the minister of state, assigned to defend the bill in the chamber of deputies, envenomed the debate, defending the emigration movement in a provocative tone by comparing those who had remained loyal émigrés with those who had been persuaded to adjust themselves more or less to each successive Revolutionary phase. This unfavorable comparison applied to the majority of deputies, and they reacted angrily. In the end the law barely managed to pass.

The question of the church lands was connected with that of the émigrés' lands. Many clergymen and even laymen, like Bonald, would not admit to the legality of their confiscation, even though it had been ratified by the pope when he agreed to the Concordat of 1801. In their eyes even the Concordat was null and void. In many places the parish priests, in their statements, made no distinction between holders of stolen property and those holding the church's lands ("black lands") and sometimes refused them absolution. This question also came up before the chamber of deputies, but obliquely through the budget.

## Baron Louis' Financial Policy

At the end of July, Baron Louis presented both his budget of 1814 and that of 1815 to the chamber of deputies. In contrast to those of the Empire these budgets represented an honest and complete picture of all the expenses and incomes of the government without concealing anything under special or extraordinary accounts. The budget of 1815 was to be clearly balanced, but that of 1814 would have a deficit of 307 million francs to which would have to be added the Empire's arrears in payments, which might go as high as seven hundred million. The minister of finance in fact insisted on the principle that all debts be recognized without distinction: that was the necessary condition for a quick restoration of the government's credit.

The balancing of the ordinary budget was to be obtained by the retention of existing taxes and their rigorous collection. As to the past indebtedness, Baron Louis thought it should be liquidated by borrowing. However, this loan was not to take the form of a new issue of long-term government bonds at five per cent; the quotations of these issues (at sixty-five francs on one hundred) was too far below their real value and the value they would soon have again. By paying the government creditors with these five per cent bonds at their current value, they would have made too high a profit at the expense of the treasury and put too heavy a burden on future budgets to pay the accrued interest. So Baron Louis proposed to issue new short-term liquidation bonds at eight per cent interest. The rapid amortizing of this issue would be assured by the sale of the 300,000 hectares of national forests previously held by the clergy.

This proposal to sell the confiscated church forests raised a storm of protest from the royalists. Nevertheless, on the whole, Baron Louis' proposals were adopted by parliament with only slight changes in small details. Soon thereafter the five per cent bonds had risen to seventy-eight francs ($15.60), an indubitable sign that the state's credit had been restored.

Such a clear-cut success should not obscure the weaknesses in Baron Louis' system, and it is all the more necessary to emphasize them because it has been the habit to shout the praises of the finance minister's ability in order to contrast it with the ineptitude of his colleagues. In fact the good and bad were bound together, and nowhere does one see better than here how the Restoration was entangled by circumstances: it could not eliminate one cause of discontent and controversy without thereby stirring up several others.

This was the case when it tried to satisfy the excessive claims of the former army contractors of the Empire period, for which it then had to increase the tax rate, deprive the local communities of their additional centimes, and disappoint the general public who had hoped that the return of the monarchy would ease their tax burdens. In this connection nothing was more unpopular than the continuation of the excise taxes (*droits réunis*), especially on alcoholic beverages, whose abolition had been promised by the Count of Artois and the Duke of Angoulême when they arrived in France. "No more conscription, no more excise taxes" had been their rallying cry. But the minister of finance insisted on their retention, arguing that the government could not forego a source of revenue estimated at 86 million francs ($17,200,000). Yet, on the other hand, how much did the cause of the monarchy lose in popularity when it so deeply disappointed the people by immediately violating its tax reduction promise? By this decision there began, to use Beugnot's phrase, "a tavern war against the administration," and there were at that time from 260,000 to 280,000 taverns or bars. And in those days public opinion was formed in the taverns rather than in the fashionable salons or by the newspapers. It did no good for the prefect of Bouches-du-Rhône to make this silly defence: "The term excise taxes had become odious because of previous abuses, but now it is again in good odor when Louis XVIII uses it." As a matter of fact when these extremely unpopular taxes were reimposed, there were disorders in many places and in some even bloody uprisings.

So, when people admire the system of severe retrenchment imposed on the government by Baron Louis, they forget the reduction in public work projects and the resulting unemployment among the working classes. And, above all, they likewise overlook the fact that this same penny-pinching policy served as an excuse for violating the financial clauses of the Fontainebleau Treaty by which Napoleon and some of his followers were to receive incomes amounting to 5,500,000 francs ($1,100,000) a year and then this grievance was one of the reasons which led the emperor to attempt his unfortunate return to France.

## The Alienation of Public Opinion

Whatever may have been the reasons, public opinion became more and more hostile during the last months of 1814, and gave actual cause for alarm by the beginning of 1815. The press, once freed from the imperial despotism, quickly became a dangerous disturber of the peace. The early violent attacks by the royalists against the remaining vestiges of Revolution and Empire only stirred up equally bitter rebuttals. As the press did not dare attack the king, it made the nobility and its pretensions the first victims of its ridicule in pamphlets and cartoons. The adventures of M. de la Jobardière (Lord Gullible), of M. de la Rodomontade (Lord Bluster), of M. de la Fiérenville (Lord City-Snob), and other "musketeers of Louis XIV," fed the popular imagination. Then, with the opening of parliament, certain questions were brought up in debate: constitutional theories, national lands, excise taxes, peace terms, etc.

All the old antagonisms, stifled by Napoleon when he was First Consul, came violently to the fore.

The administration tried to limit the damage to its position by legislative restrictions on the freedom of the press as permitted by the Charter. Such a bill, proposed early in August, unleashed a torrent of passionate debates. Not until the end of the month did it pass by a slim majority, but only after the administration had agreed to several amendments and had specifically limited it to the end of the 1816 session. Thus censorship was reimposed on all publications of less than twenty printed pages.

This did not put an end to public debate, which could still go on by padding the arguments beyond twenty pages or by getting around certain form requirements. Carnot published, under a fictitious Brussels imprint, a *Mémoire adressé au Roi en juillet 1814* (*Petition to the King in July 1814*), and it is said he sold over sixty thousand copies. It was in fact a violent and audacious indictment of all that the Restoration had done.

> If today [it read] you want to be received with distinction at the king's court, be careful not to say that you are one of the twenty-five million citizens who defended their country with considerable courage against enemy invasions, because they will tell you that these twenty-five millions of so-called citizens are twenty-five million rebels, and that these so-called enemies are and were always our friends. Rather, you should say that you had the good fortune to be Chouans and Vendeans [insurrectionists in Brittany], or deserters, or Cossacks [Russians], or English, or that, having stayed in France, you did not ask for a position in the transitory governments before the Restoration so that you could effectively betray them and bring them down to ruin. . . . One stroke of the pen was enough to move us out of these superb regions [Belgium] from which all the forces of Europe had been unable to dislodge us for ten years. . . . They particularly demanded that we turn over all our conquests for fear that we might leave some trace of our glory that we had achieved before the Restoration.

The Bonapartists, recovering their courage by January 1815, issued a small paper called the *Nain Jaune* (*Yellow Dwarf*). With a sly and humorous editorial approach, it tried, for example, to ridicule the men in power by awarding them with the decoration of the Order of the Weathercock and the followers of the clergy with the decoration of the Order of the Candle-Snuffer. This kind of humorous ridicule was so successful that it was to reappear under the Second Restoration.

One general had declared to Blacas that the inactivity of the army was like taking a "rest-stop in the mud." The natural hostility of the military element spread into the cafés and among some of the lower classes. In imitation of the soldiers, many workmen enjoyed shouting: "Long live the King . . . of Rome and his papa!" (the King of Rome was Napoleon's son). In these verbal demonstrations there were quite a few denunciations of the clergy as well as of the regime. For example, in Nancy early in August, there was a popular demonstration with cries of "Down with excise taxes! Down with priests!" In July a sign was posted on the door of the Church of Saint-Etienne reading "House for an auctioning, priest for a hanging, Louis 18 three days, Napoleon always."

Two serious incidents in early January 1815 revealed the exasperation of public opinion. The king had sent an investigation committee to Rennes to verify the claims of veteran fighters in the western revolts (Vendeans and Chouans) for pensions and decorations. The president of this committee, Piquet de Boisguy, a former Chouan, was loudly denounced by a furious crowd, and, to avoid a bloody encounter, he had to flee by night. A few days later an outbreak of another kind was aimed at the parish priest of Saint-Roch in Paris, who had refused funeral rites for an actress named Raucourt. A crowd of several hundred people took possession of the coffin with the cry of "Hang the priests!" (literally "Priests to the lamp-post!"). They forced open the doors of the church, and the priest, to avoid any more serious disturbances, had to authorize his vicar to go through with a quick ceremony.

The king had on one occasion sent his brother and his nephews on a tour of the country, but all that the public remembered about their visits were the inappropriate remarks they had made. The administration, alarmed and discouraged, was at a loss to find a way to win back opinion. On the one hand the liberals, like Benjamin Constant, Mme de Staël, La Fayette, and Lanjuinais, exhorted it to take a stand resolutely for constitutional government so that the public would forget the military glory and material progress of the Empire by the enjoyment of liberty. Yet, on the other hand, the absolutists, like Bonald and Fiévée, encouraged by Monsieur (the Count of Artois), urged it to go back to an authoritative administration and to let the Charter lapse. Their influence gained support in the council by early December when General Dupont was replaced in the war ministry by Marshal Soult, who had taken on the appearance of an energetic leader by showing excessive royalist zeal. At the same time Beugnot, transferring to the naval ministry, was replaced as police director by Dandré, a former conspirator under the Consulate, who only returned to France when the king came. His inability left a free field for republican, Bonapartist, and Orleanist conspirators.

At the center of all these intrigues Fouché, focus of the discontented, was weaving his web. But this did not prevent him from having warnings passed on to the ministers and princes. Feeling instinctively that a Bonapartist coup was coming, he wanted to prevent it by a military proclamation which would overthrow Louis XVIII in favor of the King of Rome (Napoleon's son) or the Duke of Orleans (head of a younger branch of the Bourbons), and he obtained the help of General Drouet d'Erlon, commander of the 16th Military Division at Lille. As soon as Fouché learned of Napoleon's landing (on the latter's return from Elba), he had Drouet d'Erlon tipped off by General Lallemand. The troops at Lille began to move on March 7. At the same time General Lefebvre-Desnouettes brought his infantry from Cambrai and General Lallemand his troops scattered in the Aisne. Soult learned of these movements taken without his orders, and Marshal Mortier was hastily sent to meet them. He easily brought the officers back into line, since they had been misled about the reason for this maneuver; they even sent the king an address, protesting their loyalty. The conspiratorial generals had to flee.

This strange episode, never fully elucidated because of the confused circumstances, proved at least two things: first, that in the spring of 1815 the internal situation was tense enough for certain hostile elements to believe that the moment had arrived to prepare to move from verbal opposition to direct action. Its pitiful collapse showed, on the other hand, that such attempts had very little chance of success. Thus is confirmed the present conclusion, after a detailed study of the internal history of the first Restoration (April 1814 to March 1815), that in spite of all the blunders of the royal government, in spite of all the efforts of the opposition, the regime at first could have maintained itself no matter what happened and then could have even consolidated itself, thanks to the experience acquired by its supporters and the discouragement of its opposition, if the audacious action of Napoleon had not compassed its fall.

# 6

❦ ❦ ❦ ❦ ❦

# *The Congress of Vienna*

## *The Hopes and Aims of Talleyrand*

THE return of Napoleon also compromised the advantages achieved by the patient maneuvers of Talleyrand at the Congress of Vienna. As a matter of fact these advantages were a lot less brilliant than the minister thought or than he succeeded in convincing his contemporaries and posterity that they were. There is a legend about the Congress of Vienna, piously circulated among French diplomats and accorded a too-willing acceptance by many historians following the lead of Albert Sorel. Since this story has been told over and over again, it only requires a very brief account here.

Right after the signing of the Treaty of Paris, Talleyrand entertained great hopes. France's position, he thought, was more favorable than it seemed. The other powers would need her to help organize a more stable order in Europe. Since she was not called upon—and for good reason—to take part in the redistribution of contested territories, she could all the more easily play the role of arbiter; her disinterestedness would make it possible for her to gather around her the little states threatened by the appetites of the Big Four. These trumps would give her an advantage in getting her own interests considered in the territorial rearrangements, and, in any case, in reassuming her rightful and equal place in the European concert.

The *Instructions* given to him by the king, and actually composed by Talleyrand himself, contained these optimistic views and the means for their attainment. This document has rightly been considered as one of the masterpieces of French diplomacy, which continued to draw inspiration from its principles not only until the end of the Restoration in 1830 but until the end of the Orleans Monarchy in 1848. The nations of Europe, Talleyrand argued, should conform, in their international

85

relations, to international public law consecrated by customary usage and by the numerous conventions previously agreed upon.

> Now there are in this law two fundamental principles: one is that sovereignty may not be acquired by the simple fact of conquest, nor be transferred to a conqueror unless the sovereign cedes it; the other is that no title of sovereignty, and consequently the right which goes with it, exists for the other states except to the extent that they have recognized it.

The European balance of power cannot be just a balance of material forces, it must rest on moral principles, on right and justice. "France is in the fortunate position of not needing to make a distinction between justice and gain or to seek her own gain elsewhere than in that justice which is the boon of all peoples."

As to the concrete and immediate objectives to be sought by the representative of Louis XVIII, they were summarized as follows: 1) that Austria or her archdukes should not be allowed to acquire territory belonging to the King of Sardinia; 2) that Naples should be restored to Ferdinand IV (later known as Ferdinand I of the Two Sicilies); 3) that all Polish territory should not, and could not, be transferred to Russia; and 4) that Prussia should not be allowed to have Saxony, at least not all of it, nor Mainz.

The last two points were to become the crux of the difficulties which were to paralyze the work of the congress for a long time. Indeed, Tsar Alexander was intending to re-establish the Kingdom of Poland under himself, and Prussia was claiming Saxony, whose king had for too long remained loyal to Napoleon and therefore did not deserve any special consideration from the Allies. He could be compensated in part by some of the former ecclesiastical territories on the west bank of the Rhine. The two sovereigns would have easily come to an agreement along these lines, since the acquisition of Saxony would have amply compensated Prussia for her surrender of her Polish possessions to Russia. But neither Austria nor England saw it that way. Austria feared any increase in Prussian territory because it threatened her security and hegemony in Germany; nor was she disposed to give up her Polish territories which she had received from earlier partitions in the late eighteenth century. Besides, she had designs on Italy, and here she was to encounter an unfavorable British attitude. And England, too, was not inclined to foster any increase in Russia's influence in central Europe by a disguised annexation of Poland. England did not mind having Austria menaced by Prussia in Saxony, but she did not like the part of this scheme which would put a weak monarch along the Rhine where he would come under a French protectorate. It was her plan to put Prussia beyond the Rhine where, as a watchful policeman, the latter could counter any French attempts to recover her Rhine boundaries.

These opposing points of view were apparent in the earliest conversations that the Allied sovereigns and ministers had in Paris in May 1814 and later in London. Being unable to come to an understanding, they agreed on June 20 to adjourn the forthcoming congress until October 1. They were, however, in accord on one point: not to let France participate in the settlement of important questions. On June 29 they had reaffirmed the Treaty of Chaumont, which stipulated the military contingents that they would furnish in enforcing the future arrangements.

How was Talleyrand to crack this solid and hostile bloc? He could no longer count on the tsar, who was very much disappointed by the circumstances surrounding the restoration in France. Consequently he turned hopefully to England, and, when Castlereagh went through Paris at the end of August, he tried to convince him of the common interest their two countries had in the Polish and Italian questions. The English minister, however, let him understand that he should not expect him to disagree with his allies.

As a matter of fact the representatives of the four great powers were meeting unofficially in Vienna in the month of September in order to resume their own previous conversations of Paris and London. Since their ever more accentuated disagreements did not give them much hope of coming to an understanding before the official opening of the congress, they decided on September 23, in a protocol on the procedure to be followed, that France should be excluded from the preliminary conversations on "the larger interests of Europe." Yet, at the insistence of Castlereagh, it was agreed that France and Spain should be "invited to express their opinions and wishes." It was not very much, but, by this little crack, Talleyrand was to succeed in reopening the door which they had slammed in his face.

## Allied Dissensions

Prince Talleyrand arrived in Vienna on this same September 23. Anyone else would have been appalled by the difficulties of his position and by the cool reception which he received. But he was not one to let himself be treated as a negligible quantity; and the diplomats who had had friendly relations with him for so long could not very well exclude him entirely without appearing to be insulting him personally. So on September 30 they invited him and Labrador, the Spanish representative, to a preliminary conference at Metternich's residence. Here they communicated to him the text of the protocol of September 23. As soon as they came to the words "Allied Powers," Talleyrand immediately protested: "Allied?" "Allied against whom?" "You are no longer allied against Napoleon; he is on the island of Elba. You are certainly not allied against the King of France; he is the guarantor of a durable peace. Gentlemen, let me speak frankly, if there is still such a thing as Allied Powers, then this is no place for me!" The others, embarrassed by these remarks, remained silent. But the French representative went on:

> And yet if I were not here, you would miss me very much. I am perhaps the only one who is not asking for anything. Consideration and respect is all I want for France. . . . I repeat, I am not asking for anything, but I can bring you a lot. The presence here of a minister of Louis XVIII lends support to the principle on which rests the whole social order. Europe's first need is to banish forever the idea that rights can be acquired by conquest alone and to revive the sacred principle of legitimacy from which springs order and stability. . . . If, as some rumors are already saying, some privileged powers wanted to exercise dictatorial authority over the congress, I must say that I cannot agree to recognize, in this meeting, any supreme power in questions coming within the jurisdiction of the congress and I would not consider any proposal on such a basis.

The embarrassed diplomats ended up by saying that they did not insist on the protocol and that they would be willing to set it aside. A few days later they decided to adjourn the opening of the congress until November 1; in the meantime the solutions to controversial questions would be prepared "by free and confidential communications" among the representatives of the great powers. When this decision was presented to Talleyrand on October 8, it furnished him the occasion for another big scene. On accepting the principle of an adjournment, he asked that they add that the opening of the congress should be carried out "in conformity with the principles of public law." "What does public law have to do with us here?" Humboldt, the Prussian representative, blurted out. "It has to do with your being here at all," Talleyrand replied. Another Prussian delegate, Hardenberg, was furious at this remark and continued the argument: "Why say that we are acting according to public law? That goes without saying." "If it goes without saying," retorted Talleyrand, "then it will go even better by saying it." And so here again he won the argument.

By his well-timed interventions and his smashing retorts, the French representative had thrust himself upon the scene like a rough jouster, but the Allies adopted procedures which were purposely designed to avoid any subsequent frontal encounter. Talleyrand could well boast that he had forced open the door to the European congress, but actually he was to find himself in an empty room while the meaningful conversations took place in the lobbies. In vain would he submit notes, suggestions, and memoranda; the Allies went right on making important decisions without him.

However, the lack of compromise and the ever-growing disagreement among the Allies themselves was going to give him a chance to reappear on the scene. By the end of December things had come to such a pass that Hardenberg of Prussia, supported by Russia, was saying that Austria's persistent rejection of his demands to annex Saxony was tantamount to a declaration of war. Seeing this impasse, Castlereagh suddenly decided, on January 2, to respond to the advances that Talleyrand had been making to him for some time. He now proposed a triple military alliance composed of England, Austria, and France. Talleyrand was so delighted that he agreed immediately, and they signed an alliance treaty the next day. The three powers promised to give each other mutual support in case they were attacked "because of proposals that they thought it their duty to make and support in common" for the complete execution of the Treaty of Paris. In such a war they would each furnish 150,000 men, and they would invite Bavaria, Hanover, and Holland to join them.

Talleyrand was exultant. His letter of January 4 to Louis XVIII was a veritable hymn of triumph:

> Sire, the coalition is now and forever dissolved. Not only is France no longer isolated in Europe, but Your Majesty already has a federative system which did not seem a possibility for another fifty years. . . . You will be practically the leader and soul of this union, formed to defend principles that you were the first to proclaim. . . . Such an important and favorable change can only be attributed to the protection of Divine Providence, so evident before in the return of Your Majesty!

In fact, this was all far from the mark. In the estimation of the English foreign secretary this famous treaty was nothing but an expedient, a sort of blackmail, to force Prussia and Russia to give up their intransigent attitude. To this extent the treaty was a great success. The spreading rumor of a secret agreement between England, Austria, and France, even more disconcerting because its terms were not known, brought about an early compromise. The tsar contented himself with a smaller Poland, with some Polish territories remaining with Prussia and Austria, while Prussia agreed to let the King of Saxony keep the southern part of his kingdom in return for Prussia's annexation of Rhine territories which had been held in reserve for bargaining purposes. Once the principle of territorial compensations was accepted, all there was left to do was to parcel out the territories and peoples. That was the work of the "Statistical Committee" on which France was represented. From that time on nothing was heard of the alliance treaty of the three. While Talleyrand thought he had dissolved the coalition, he had actually helped it to overcome a crisis which could have otherwise been fatal to it. What was more, he had promoted the designs of England that were the most harmful to the real interests of France. He had helped her place the Prussians, France's most rabid enemy, along the Rhine instead of the compliant King of Saxony, a kinsman and ally of the King of France. His only consolation was that he had prevented the complete spoliation of the King of Saxony and thus had safeguarded, although not without some damage, the principle of legitimacy.

## The Last Days of the Congress

Once the affairs of central Europe were settled, Talleyrand turned all his energies to the solution of the question of Naples. There was nothing that Louis XVIII wanted more than to dethrone Murat and restore the Bourbon dynasty there, and all he asked of the powers was that he be left free to take action against him. Prussia and Russia were quite willing to let him do it. "That rascal who betrayed us" was Alexander's opinion of Murat. England also would have been happy to eliminate this dangerous Napoleonic minion from the Italian scene. Certainly Metternich had no particular fondness for Murat, but his hands were tied by a treaty signed on January 11, 1814, a treaty of alliance and friendship which guaranteed to Napoleon's brother-in-law the integrity of his kingdom. Moreover, it was against the permanent policy of Austria to permit France to intervene actively in the Italian peninsula. Metternich therefore indicated to Talleyrand on February 25, 1815 that he would not tolerate the passage of French troops into Italy. If Murat was to fall, he should fall of his own weight. As soon as Murat heard of Napoleon's return from Elba, he called on all Italy to fight for independence and invaded the Papal States. This action gave Austria a good pretext for abrogating her treaty obligations, and she mounted an offensive against him. In a few weeks the Austrians had the upper hand, dethroned Murat, and restored Ferdinand IV (in 1816 called Ferdinand I). France did profit by this change of fate, but Talleyrand did not have anything to do with it.

After Napoleon's return to Paris, Talleyrand represented only a phantom government which had fled to a Belgian city. What weight did his voice then have in the congress? As soon as the emperor's landing in France had been announced, this representative of Louis XVIII had taken the initiative to issue a virulent declaration outlawing "this disturber of world peace." At that moment the Allies still thought that the royal government had the energy to hold its own. But when the Bourbon monarchy collapsed and they found themselves in the same situation as in the spring of 1814, the Allies put their quarrels behind them and again made common cause against France. On March 25 the Treaty of Chaumont was renewed with a promise that the Allies would not lay down their arms until Napoleon was rendered incapable of causing further trouble. They were particularly irritated at the Bourbons, whom they accused of having helped the "flight of the Eagle" by their bungling policies. For that reason they refused to promise anything definite in favor of Louis XVIII in spite of the pleas of Talleyrand.

However, Talleyrand was permitted to sign the Final Act of the Congress on June 9, 1815. This is no place for a complete description of how this important document, with the help of the cannon of Waterloo, was to set up a new European order which would last for nearly a half a century. It will suffice here to draw up the balance sheet of the results for France and to notice how far they still were from the great ambitions Talleyrand enunciated in September 1814. In the profit column we can put a negative advantage: the continuation of a fragmented Germany and Italy. In the peninsula Naples was returned to a Bourbon, and an independent Sardinia had been restored; but, on the other hand, the ambitions of Austria, moving from her Lombardo-Venetian kingdom and from her vassal principalities of Parma, Tuscany, Lucca, and Modena, could expand dangerously. The re-establishment of Switzerland protected the French boundary from this direction. Prussia was not allowed to swallow all of Saxony or to take Mainz, but we have already seen how she had been granted the Rhineland. The formation of the Kingdom of the Netherlands was likewise directed against France. Thus the territorial results of the Congress of Vienna were more detrimental to France than those of the Treaty of Paris because they erected around her some solid barriers against her later attempts to expand toward her natural frontiers.

From the point of view of prestige Talleyrand had won a few moral victories. England's appeal to France, in order to intimidate Russia and Prussia, was in itself an acknowledgement of the force that she still represented. But this advantage had been only temporary, and after this, as before, the hostile combination of the four powers stood guard over France. Talleyrand was not even able, as he had hoped, to become the leader of the group of little states, since everything was decided in the lobbies by the "Big Four." In fact the real winner at the congress was not Talleyrand, but Castlereagh.

Nevertheless, if we consider these deliberations from the point of view of pure diplomatic art in which the final results are often more beautiful when less profitable, then we can not help admiring Talleyrand's clever game at the Congress of Vienna as a remarkable example of what the tenacity and skill of one statesman can accomplish in the face of an overwhelming accumulation of unfavorable circumstances.

# 7

⚜ ⚜ ⚜ ⚜ ⚜

# *The Hundred Days*

### *First Reactions to Napoleon's Landing*

IT was only on Sunday, March 5, late in the afternoon, that the news of Napoleon's landing reached Paris. When one realizes that the emperor had already been in France since March first and that he was going to enter the city of Grenoble on the sixth, one can easily understand how much his success was due to slow communications. The telegraph line (a system of signal towers) only began at Lyons; up to here they had to depend on couriers who went around by way of Marseilles. Because of this, by the time the government was in a position to take action, Napoleon had already surmounted the most difficult part of his enterprise. Before this delay, the government would have only needed a handful of determined men and a few blown-up bridges to nip his plans in the bud. But now he was master of one of the strongest fortified towns, and several regiments had rallied to his cause. The royalist authorities in the little Alpine towns through which he passed were so disconcerted and dumbfounded that all they could do was flee before him. The troops of the Marseilles garrison, ordered to go in pursuit only after considerable delay by Messena, commander of the military region, had done nothing to catch up with him before it was too late.

The king received the bad news with great composure. From the distance of Paris the return of Napoleon could look like a mad escapade; the ministers, too, were full of confidence, and several of them congratulated themselves for now having the opportunity to have it out, once and for all, with the threat that had always hung over them from the island of Elba. "Really, Sire," Dandré exclaimed, "this rogue of a Bonaparte must have been out of his mind to make such a landing. Thanks be to God; we will shoot him down, and that will be the last we'll hear of him."

During the night of March 5, the Count of Artois left for Lyons where he would be joined by Macdonald. They went to take command of the troops stationed there and of those being moved in. Other plans were made on the following day so as to surround Napoleon within a perimeter bordered by the Rhone, Saône, Doubs, and the Alpine frontier. The troops of the Eastern Region would concentrate in Franche-Comté under the command of the Duke of Berry, while his brother, the Duke of Angoulême, who at that moment was making an official visit to Bordeaux, was ordered into the Rhone valley to organize the forces in the royalist south.

A royal proclamation, announcing the event, called the two legislative houses back from their winter vacation into an urgent special session. The king was hoping in this manner to counter the fascination of the imperial glories with the prestige of constitutional institutions and the moral support of the representatives of the nation, the very same ones who a year ago had proclaimed the overthrow of the emperor. Another ordinance declared Napoleon Bonaparte to be "a rebel and traitor" and enjoined all officials to go in hot pursuit of him and, as soon as he was identified, to impose on him the full penalties of the law. All his followers who did not abandon him within a week were to suffer the same punishments. The violence of these measures and the antiquated terms in which they were expressed reminded one more of the ravings of a senile and helpless anger than of calm strength or confidence in one's right.

In reply to this appeal came forth, in the same high-flown rhetoric, thousands of addresses, proclamations, and resolutions from the cities, the departmental general councils, the courts, all sorts of deliberative bodies, military leaders, countless individuals, and even from those officers who previously had been put on half pay, renewing their oaths of fidelity to the king and rivaling each other in their expressions of hate for the "usurper." Never was there more talk about honor and loyalty than at this very moment when honor and loyalty were to receive such a staggering blow. Day after day crowds gathered beneath the windows of the Tuileries Palace, seeking the latest news, watching the comings and goings, loudly acclaiming the king whenever he appeared. It was, observed Vitrolles, like a chorus of an ancient tragedy whose moans and movements were in rhythm with the inexorable working out of fate. Numerous volunteers signed up to join in the defense of the throne, but the only use they could make of them was to tire them out with endless and purposeless rallies because arms and capable leaders were lacking. Even a goodly number of sincere opposition liberals were seen to come over to the support of the government. La Fayette himself appeared at the Tuileries wearing the white cockade; and Benjamin Constant thundered, in his *Journal des Débats,* against the new Attila, adding that "I will never, Oh Miserable Deserter, drag myself from one authority to another or justify infamy with sophistry." Fifteen days later he was to offer his services to Napoleon to help in the preparation of a new constitution.

## Reverses and Consternation

All of this was only sound and fury. The real action would take place elsewhere. The Count of Artois arrived at Lyons on the morning of March 8, but the thirty thousand men Soult was sending there had not yet arrived. The garrison, composed of two regiments of regulars and a regiment of dragoons, seemed uneasy and uncertain. The National Guard, which could supply, at the most, fifteen hundred guns, was just as hesitant. The prince had occasion to observe this uncertainty: when he asked volunteers to sign up, most of them said they were ready to go on duty if they were given a fixed time and place for assembling, but they refused to sign their names for fear they might be punished if the other side won. They already knew about what had happened in Grenoble, and the general impression was that the same thing would take place in Lyons.

The Count of Artois revealed the secret of Napoleon's extraordinary success in a letter to his brother: "Bonaparte's peaceful pose disarms the bellicose spirit. No one could be expected to go out and fight against something that does him no harm." The emperor was acting like an animal-trainer who knew that any quick movement might bring the lions down upon him. With his eyes fixed upon the eyes of his adversaries, he charmed them into submission; every day, every hour, every minute gained without a shot fired rallied more supporters to him, created a sort of moral trend in his favor, and made the outbreak of civil war ever more difficult.

On the ninth of March, Marshal Macdonald joined the Count of Artois at Lyons and had the garrison assemble at Bellecour Square for a military review. To the officers crowding around the marshal, he depicted what harm would come to France if Napoleon were to succeed and then he begged them to remain faithful to their oaths of loyalty. At the end of his talk, when he asked them to make a public show of their sentiments by shouting *Long Live the King!,* there was only a deathly silence. The Count of Artois, who came over to the group a few minutes later, had no better success. Under such conditions resistance was impossible. Each hour brought news of Napoleon's approach and of the defection of all the troops in the region. The working classes were coming to a boil. The marshal begged the prince to leave town, and the Count of Artois, easily persuaded, departed in a coach at five o'clock on the morning of the tenth. With remarkable courage and firmness Macdonald stayed on until the last moment, even trying to defend alone with gun in hand the access to the Guillotière Bridge. Finally overwhelmed, he jumped on his horse just in time to avoid being run through as the Bonapartist troops began to swarm into the city. Napoleon himself did not arrive until seven in the evening, when a delirious crowd accompanied him in a torchlight parade, shouting "Long Live the Emperor! Down with Priests! Death to Royalists! Hang the Bourbons!" To this reawakening of old revolutionary passions, Napoleon was to reply with a series of decrees proscribing the émigrés, abolishing the old titles of nobility, re-establishing the old privileges of the army, and dissolving parliament.

The news of the events in Lyons naturally aroused the greatest consternation in Paris, and at first they tried to delay the circulation of the reports. The overconfidence of the Bourbon leaders and supporters now changed abruptly into extreme panic. The miraculous success of Napoleon, combined with the news of the attempted revolt of Generals Drouet d'Erlon and Lefebvre-Desnouettes, made it seem as if there was a widespread plot throughout the army. Soult was accused of having a hand in it, and all the measures that he had taken, on orders from the king, to move troops to cut off Napoleon's forward march were interpreted as proof of his treason. Blacas spoke of forcing his resignation at the point of a gun, but Soult, sensing that he could do nothing more, resigned of his own volition. He was replaced by General Clarke, Duke of Feltre, who was far from enjoying the same prestige among the military leaders. Shortly thereafter Dandré, director of police, was replaced by Bourrienne, Napoleon's former secretary but now his personal enemy. One of his first acts was to order Fouché's arrest; but with unbelievable audacity, Fouché tricked those who came to seize him and disappeared almost before their eyes by a secret door.

As if reeling from shock, the government seemed to want to make up for the ineffectiveness of its measures by multiplying them endlessly: orders to all officers and soldiers to rejoin their units; orders to all departments to form reserve battalions; orders calling up all national guard units; orders for the creation of councils of war to prevent troop subversion or desertion, etc. But the last hope of the royal cause was

Marshal Ney, who had been put in command of the troops assembled in Franche-Comté, which had previously been destined to be under the command of the Duke of Berry. A quick move by these units against Napoleon's flank could have stopped him cold, and the first shots could have been the unleashing of a civil war. It is known that when Ney took leave of the king, he promised to bring back Napoleon in a cage. "We don't insist that you go that far," Louis XVIII grumbled. We also know the dramatic outcome of the story. Ney arrived at Lons-le-Saunier late on March 11 firmly resolved to keep his promise. During the night of the thirteenth, emissaries arrived bearing letters from Napoleon and General Bertrand. The next morning, having made up his mind to go over to the other side, he announced it himself to his troops drawn up for a review. Later the historian, Houssaye, was to say that Ney "hurled himself into the abyss just as he used to hurl himself into the jaws of the cannon."

However, in Paris the two houses had opened their sessions. On the sixteenth they met in royal session to hear a speech from the king. "I do not fear for myself," Louis XVIII told them, "but I do fear for France"; and he asked them to unite around him for the defence of the Charter. This speech electrified the audience, especially the passage in which the old monarch, after having recalled what he had done for the country, asked them "Could I, now in my sixtieth year, end my career in any better way than by dying for its defence?" From the legislative hall the enthusiasm spread to all the town, and in the next few days was to be seen a renewal of the declarations of loyalty.

### Exile Again

Alas, on this same March 16, in the evening, the news came of Ney's defection, and it became clear that Napoleon would soon arrive in Paris. What now should be done? Blacas proposed that the king, accompanied by all his officials, go out to meet Napoleon and demand to know just what he was doing here. "In that fine procession," Vitrolles remarked sarcastically, "you forgot to include the Archbishop of Paris with the Blessed Sacrament." And who could be sure Napoleon would agree to such a meeting? All he would have to do would be to change his route and send over a squadron of hussars to surround the royal carriage. Chateaubriand would have preferred that the king stay in the Tuileries, with the two legislative houses and the military officers of the court around him. Marmont argued strongly for transforming the palace into a fortress which Napoleon would be able to take only after a long and bloody battle; the heroism of the old king would arouse the enthusiasm of France and of all Europe. "Let Napoleon's last exploit be cutting the throat of an old man; Louis XVIII, by sacrificing his life, would win the only battle he had ever fought." If one can believe Chateaubriand, this plan for a moment appealed to Louis XVIII because of its majestic Louis XIV overtones; but his ministers and court officials, called upon to play their roles in this holocaust, were much less enthusiastic. Why should we leave such a hostage, they asked, in the hands of the Usurper? Then, too, the king, like his brother Louis XVI, hesitated to expose his loyal followers and the city of Paris to the horrors of civil war. So he forgot his brave declarations before the chamber and decided on flight. But flight to where?

Ever since the beginning of this crisis Vitrolles had regained great influence in the cabinet by his audacious activity and the originality of his planning. He now devised a plan for organizing resistance in the provinces. The king would set up his headquarters in the fortified city of La Rochelle, from which, in case of necessity, he could embark for Spain. Here he would be the center of a vast call-up of men which was now under way under the direction of the Duke of Bourbon, who had been sent earlier into the Vendée, and under the Duke and Duchess of Angoulême in Languedoc and the region of Bordeaux. Montesquiou was violently opposed to this idea; by this plan, he said, Louis XVIII would become merely the king of the Vendée. Vitrolles' apt reply to this was that it was better to be king of the Vendée than to be king of foreigners. It was finally on the advice of Marshal Macdonald that Louis XVIII decided to flee toward the north, where he would find just as trusty royalist people as in the west. Here he could take up his position behind the fortresses of Lille and receive more easily the military support of the English.

Once the decision was made, they tried to keep it as secret as possible. At noon on March 19 the king had another review of the royal house guards on the Champ de Mars. At about midnight a small silent crowd of faithful began to gather on the landing and along the great staircase of the Tuileries; sorrow and anguish wrung their hearts, they were reminded of the sixth of October, 1789, of the return from Varennes, of the tenth of August, 1792. The door of the small apartments opened, and there, behind a page with a torch, the king appeared, leaning on the arms of the Dukes of Blacas and Duras. Those present fell to their knees weeping. "I knew it would be this way," Louis XVIII remarked, "I didn't want to see them." "They should have spared me all this emotion." Then wending his way through the crowd and descending the stairs with difficulty, he spoke a few words: "My children, I am touched by your loving concern. But I have need to harbor my strength. Please spare me this. . . . Return to your homes. . . . I will see you again soon." Outside, the rain was coming down in great gusts, dousing the lights. The great royal coach disappeared into the night, followed by a few horsemen.

Elsewhere, Marshal Macdonald and the Duke of Berry had ordered the royal house guard and a few battalions of Paris volunteers to start marching northward. It was a forlorn sight to follow this painful three-day flight through interminable rain and over roads heavy with mud. As might have been predicted, the attitude of the garrison of Lille, where the king arrived almost alone on March 22, did not permit a long stopover, and on the next afternoon he crossed the frontier, heading for Ostend, with the intention of going on to Dunkirk, where he had arranged a rendezvous with the Count of Artois and his nephew and whatever troops they still had under their command. Monsieur learned of the king's departure before he received this order, and he also decided to cross the frontier, releasing his faithful followers from any further obligations. Henceforth Louis XVIII resigned himself to what he hoped would be a short exile, and he finally settled in Ghent on March 30.

Napoleon's return to the Tuileries did not immediately put an end to attempts at royalist resistance. As we have seen, the Duke of Bourbon had already been sent into the Vendée. Here he was torn between two hard choices. On the one hand he could provoke uprisings among the rural royalist organizations and thereby alienate the sympathies of the old Revolutionaries of the cities, who, carried away by their old defensive reflex and supported by the regular troops, would rally all the sooner to the cause of the emperor. Or, on the other hand, he could make his appeal to the local authorities and the regular troops, in which case he could not arouse the zeal of the peasants nor obtain from the region any greater resources for the royal cause than elsewhere. The prince lost a lot of time in useless consultations, first at Angers and later at Beaupreau. The outcome was that he secretly embarked for England on March 31 on the advice of the Vendean leaders, who told him it was impossible to carry out an immediate mobilization of their old organizations.

In the end the family's honor may have been saved by the Duchess of Angoulême and her husband, with the assistance of Vitrolles. The latter had received from the king, just a few moments before his departure from Paris, the order to go into the south with full powers to organize the resistance there. With unbelievable courage and energy Vitrolles went at the job. First he went to Toulouse, where he tried unsuccessfully to centralize the correspondence and resources of the departments of that region. While he was in Bordeaux, he concerted his plans with those of the Duchess of Angoulême.

This princess and her husband had been in the city since the fifth of March to join in its celebration of the first anniversary of March 12, 1814, when the city had opened its gates to the Bourbons and the Allies. They were at the height of the festivities when the fatal news had arrived, along with orders to the prince to go and take command of the royalist forces in the region of the Rhone. The duchess elected to stay on in Bordeaux where her presence could rally sentiment favorable to the royalist side. But, there as elsewhere, if the great majority of the people were full of enthusiasm for the royalist cause, the regular troops were from the first on the side of the emperor. Only the respect inspired by this daughter of Louis XVI could still sustain the hopes of the leaders. The approach of General Clausel, commissioned by Napoleon to take over the command of the region, precipitated the crisis. The princess summoned General Decaen, commander of the regular troops in Bordeaux, and asked him, yes or no, whether his men were ready to obey her. Since the general refused to commit himself, she decided to go and find out for herself what their sentiments were. Decaen strongly advised against it because of the dangers involved. "I am not compelling anyone to go with me," she said, "no more arguments, those are my orders, carry them out." She then went out to the three barracks where the garrison regiments had been confined in an ugly mood. Each one of her appeals encountered an embarrasing silence or hostile shouts. In her final attempt, at Château-Trompette, the commander would not even allow her escort to enter, and she went alone before the troops drawn up in battle formation. As her words became insulting on seeing their stubbornness, they drowned her out with their angry cries. Decaen then tried to persuade her to leave, but she resisted and stood motionless and haughty facing the stormy demonstration until the men, impressed by her firmness and ashamed of having threatened a woman, quieted down. Only then did she retire slowly while a long roll of the drums saluted her luckless courage.

As she left the barracks, she said to Martignac: "It's all over, the troops have definitely refused to fight. I thank God for that, because, if they had promised me their loyalty, they would not have kept their word, and Bordeaux would have been the victim of my mistaken confidence." Then she ordered the National Guard to turn in their arms and soon after left Bordeaux for Pauillac, where she embarked on an English ship which took her first to Spain and thence to England.

"She's the only man in the family," Napoleon was said to have remarked on learning the details of this incident. But he was not being exactly fair because at this time the Duke of Angoulême was showing a determination and courage quite out of line with his weak and puny appearance. He had left Bordeaux on the night of March 9, and had established his headquarters at Nîmes. But fifteen precious days had been lost before he had succeeded in assembling sufficient forces. At the head of a small corps of four thousand men he went on the offensive toward the north, while another corps, under the command of General Ernouf, moved toward Gap and Grenoble. Inspired by the presence of the prince, who was putting himself so tirelessly into the campaign, this little royalist army repulsed the Bonapartist forces commanded by General Debelle, took Montélimar on March 30, forced a crossing of the Durance River at Loriol, entered Valence on April 3, and seized the Romans bridge which opened the way to Lyons. Then on the night of the fourth came a whole series of catastrophic news reports: the troops under General Ernouf had rallied to the emperor and were marching against the royalists by the valley of the Isère; another army commanded by Grouchy was coming at them for a frontal assault from Lyons; and finally, to top it all off, the troops they had left back in Nîmes had mutinied at the call of General Gilly and were trying to cross the Rhone and to cut off their retreat; and at the same time the prince learned of Napoleon's arrival in Paris and of the end of resistance in Bordeaux and Toulouse. There was only one thing to do, to try to move down to Marseilles, where the white flag was still flying. Upon his arrival at Montélimar on April 8 the prince learned that General Gilly had crossed the Rhone at Pont-Saint-Esprit and that he was thereby cutting off his route of escape. At this point the Duke of Angoulême, now especially concerned for the safety of his devoted supporters, decided to negotiate surrender terms with Gilly. A capitulation agreement was signed that very evening at La Palud, a small town about four miles north of Pont-Saint-Esprit; the prince was to embark at Sète; his royal volunteers were to be disbanded, and sent home without incurring any punitive action; and lastly, the regular troops would submit to the authority of the new government, and the conduct of their officers would be overlooked.

Some of these terms were to be later violated. A certain number of royalist volunteers who went home unarmed were horribly massacred by the fanatical Protestants in the Cevennes region. The Duke of Angoulême himself was in danger when Grouchy suspended the terms of surrender which applied to him. After having toyed with the idea of holding Angoulême as a hostage, Napoleon finally decided to have him escorted to Sète. Once in Spain, this prince, under orders from the king, was to try to organize volunteers among French refugees to be ready, with the help of the Spanish, to resume the offensive on the first favorable occasion.

In the meantime, at Ghent, Louis XVIII was calmly reassuming his role of exiled sovereign, at which he was such an experienced player, and maintaining as much as possible the unchanging etiquette of the Tuileries and the daily rounds of his court schedule. Soon most of his ministers rejoined him, except Montesquiou, who had gone to live in London. In his place the king had appointed Chateaubriand as interim minister of the interior. His principal job was to edit the *Journal Universel,* published in Ghent as a substitute for the *Moniteur Universel* in order to counter the official publications of the imperial government in Paris. One item of note which he published on May 12 was a long *Report to the King,* drawn up in the name of all the ministers. Composed in the incomparable style of Chateaubriand, it was not only a defence of the cause of the royal government and a virulent attack against the emperor, but also an important political event in itself. Its theme was that the government of the king, by taking a firm stand in favor of liberal and constitutional institutions, had refuted the allegations of Napoleon who was claiming that he had had to return to restore liberty. This report also dissociated the king's policy from the ideas of a little circle in Ghent which, inspired and encouraged by the heir to the throne, the Count of Artois, was insisting that the experiment in constitutional government had failed, and that it would be advisable, when they took over France again, to abolish the Charter or to amend it in an authoritarian direction.

## Napoleon's Internal Difficulties

The news coming from France was such as to warm the hearts of the exiles. After the early days of ecstatic enthusiasm were over, Napoleon discovered that he was faced with a very unusual situation with which his temperament was unprepared to cope. After a year of constitutional government he had an entirely different nation on his hands. Chateaubriand put it this way: "He had left France dumb and prostrate, he now found it standing up and talking back." For a while he himself had thought that he should have recourse to the use of revolutionary language, but the passions he had thus aroused then got out of control and he found he could no longer restrain them. He therefore became resigned to playing the role of a constitutional monarch, for the time being, and to having Benjamin Constant throw together a sort of liberal constitution for him. Under the misleading title of *Acte additionnel aux constitutions de l'Empire,* it was nothing more than a carbon copy of the Charter of Louis XVIII. It was to displease the pure Bonapartists as well as the republicans. When the new regime opened the registers for the popular ratification of the constitution, it obtained only a little over a million votes out of five or six million registered voters, and almost a quarter of these votes came from the army. In the later elections for the new chamber, the voters stayed away from the polls in very large numbers. In Marseilles, for example, four deputies were elected by a total of thirteen voters. This chamber, in the end, found itself composed of an overwhelming majority of liberals, for whom La Fayette was the spokesman and standard-bearer. The new chamber was obviously going to be an embarrassment and a danger for the emperor. In vain did he try to arouse enthusiasm by a big Champ-de-Mai demonstration (copying an ancient Carolingian custom) which was also supposed to be a new Federation Festival (recalling the Revolutionary one held on July 14, 1790); this hollow and theatrical ceremony fell flat.

Indeed treason was installed within the very precincts of his cabinet in the person of Fouché. This Duke of Otranto, now reappointed minister of police, shrewdly and cynically sized up the emperor's shaky position. "He's very active right now," he told Pasquier, "but he won't last three months. . . ." "I concede that he may win one or two battles, but he'll lose the third one, and that's when we shall have to go to work." In the meantime he was trying to make friends in all quarters. To republicans and liberals he tried to appear as the defender of liberty; on the other hand he did what he could to protect royalists and did save Vitrolles, whom Napoleon was said to have wanted to execute. On leaving the emperor's room, he would correspond with Metternich and Talleyrand in Vienna, with the Duke of Orleans in London, and with the Count of Artois in Ghent. He carefully chose some of the replies in this correspondence and showed them to the emperor, and thus concealed his treason by openly acknowledging the existence of the correspondence and by giving it a laudable motive.

The royalists, encouraged by this self-seeking toleration, began to renew their activity. Here and there the secret organizations of 1814 were coming to life and using the same tactics: no open resistance, but an undercover war to gain public opinion by posters, songs, cartoons, and the circulation of false or alarming news. They urged passive resistance to the army draft, tax evasion, and abstention from public functions. In the provinces of the south the supporters of the imperial regime and the former Jacobins, discovering that they were a minority in the midst of a hostile population, had recourse to violence and arbitrary action, thus inviting bloody reprisals in the future.

The western provinces, which had remained quiet at the time of the downfall of the king, finally came to life in mid-April when Napoleon tried to carry out conscription there. Some fifty thousand insurgents were to seal off the region from the north of Brittany to the Vendean marshes. Napoleon, who had at first underestimated the danger, finally had had to detach twenty thousand men, under the command of General Lamarque, to go against them—twenty thousand men who were urgently needed on the battlefields of Belgium. Yet, this Bourbonist uprising of 1815 was to be, from a military point of view, a fiasco for the royalists. In contrast to the great Chouan movement of 1793, there was now no religious controversy involved; the wise moderation of the imperialist leaders prevented as much as possible the usual civil war atrocities; from Paris, Fouché saw that the royalist leaders were given peaceful assurances, which paralyzed their will to fight; arms were lacking in spite of all the efforts which were exerted at Ghent to get the English to land guns and munitions; lastly the royalist leaders were hamstrung by quarrels among themselves. General Lamarque succeeded in exploiting this situation and in defeating isolated royalist groups in several separate engagements where the objectives were generally to obtain possession of some arms cargoes coming from England. The commanding general of the royalist armies, Louis de La Rochejaquelein, was killed on June 4. Lamarque then offered to suspend hostilities. "I am not ashamed to ask you to agree to peace," he wrote, "because the only glory that can be gained in a civil war is in ending it." Finally on June 26 a peace agreement was to be signed at Cholet. Fighting was to be fiercer and to last longer in lower Brittany, where the old Chouan leader, Desol de Grisolles, faced General Bigarré, an officer as able as Lamarque but less patient.

In fact this royalist uprising in the West, even if it had been better led and better supported, would not have enabled the king, as he was hoping, to recover his throne without the help of foreign armies. Louis XVIII had not hesitated a moment to accede to the Allied invitation to sign the treaty of March 25, which had been concluded by them against Napoleon. But, while the powers made it clear that his signature did not impose on them an unconditional obligation to restore him to his throne, still Louis XVIII used this fiction of an alliance to try to make the Allied armies appear as liberators rather than as enemy invaders and to have them follow Wellington's example of 1814.

It was like talking to the deaf. The Allies, especially the Prussians, were determined to make the French people regret their espousal of the Bonaparte cause. If that had the effect of hurting the prospects of Louis XVIII, they cared not a whit. After all, was it not his own fault if Napoleon had been able so easily to regain his power? And they had another possible king in reserve—the Duke of Orleans. The latter had disassociated himself from the head of the family by taking refuge in London without Louis' permission and had not hesitated to say publicly that "if they had listened to him, they would not have committed so many foolish blunders." The tsar even went so far as to ask the Congress of Vienna to give serious consideration to the advantages of this solution.

In a situation like this, the defeat or even the abdication of Napoleon did not mean the automatic restoration of Louis XVIII, any more than in 1814. Leaving aside the choice of a republic, which no one took seriously, there were two other solutions: the son of Napoleon (later spoken of as Napoleon II) and the above-mentioned Duke of Orleans. The former had the support of a large number of the old imperial civil servants and officials, those who had openly rallied to the government of the Hundred Days and who could no longer keep their jobs in case of the restoration of Louis XVIII. Napoleon's son also had the enthusiastic support of the army and of part of the Paris common people, who were loud in their acclaim of the imperial dynasty. The accession of the Duke of Orleans would have been more popular with the liberal majority of the representative chamber, which was just as apprehensive of the continuation of the imperial despotism, under the cloak of a regency for Napoleon II, as they were of the return of the legitimate king. The Orleans cause, as we have seen, encountered some sympathy in the Allied camp, and the intrigues of Fouché, as far as it is possible to discern his inclinations, seemed at first to be leaning in that same direction.

Louis XVIII was, nevertheless, to carry the day, because he had in his favor the advantage of one year of possession, and it must not be forgotten that his supporters were numerous and active enough to create difficulties for any other government. In the end, Wellington, to whom the fortunes of war had given the role of commander of the coalition forces in France, came out firmly for re-establishing the king.

## *Fouché at the Helm of Transition*

However, no one knows at what cost of violent clashes and bloody encounters this inevitable solution of Louis' restoration would have been accomplished, if there had not been at the center of the drama the one necessary man to guide the events into the proper channel for a peaceful solution. This man was Fouché, who with his incomparable grasp of the situation was able to recognize in a moment the solution which had the most chance of success. And from that time forward, his aim was to act in such a way as to make it appear that it was his efforts which turned the trick. Thereby he could make sure that he would become the minister of the restored king, and at the same time he could persuade the king to follow policies most favorable to the interests that he represented. During the whole three weeks of the critical transition, from June 20 to July 8, Fouché played the greatest political game of his whole life with a perspicacity, a cool composure, and a Machiavellian ingenuity which makes one of the most thrilling spectacles in French history—but not one of the most edifying.

His first job was to eliminate the emperor. To accomplish that, Fouché made use of two opposing parties—the liberals and the imperialists. He alarmed the former by making them think that Napoleon would like to get rid of the chamber and to go back to a military dictatorship which the critical situation would seem to justify. He insinuated that to prevent this despotism it was up to the chamber to assume responsibilities and to show itself worthy of the great revolutionary legislatures. To the latter, the imperialists, especially to the Minister of State Regnault de Saint-Jean-d'Angely, who was the emperor's spokesman in the assemblies, he conceded that Napoleon could save the dynasty by a spontaneous abdication in favor of his son. To nail this down more tightly, he also implied that he had information from the Allied camp which made it seem certain that they favored Napoleon II.

The mine was planted and ready when the emperor returned to Paris at eight in the morning of June 21, after his defeat at Waterloo. Since Napoleon was physically exhausted, his ability to make decisions was greatly weakened during the next few hours. The chamber at once showed a hostile attitude and, after twenty-four hours of negotiation, let it be known that it was going to dethrone the emperor if he did not abdicate. His brother, Lucien, urged him to carry out another 18 Brumaire by breaking up the legislature with popular support. Napoleon rejected this idea because he did not want to unleash a civil war. "I do not want to be the king of the mob," he said. His more faithful followers—

Regnault, Caulaincourt, his brother Joseph—urged him to save the crown for his son, the King of Rome. Finally on June 22, shortly after noon, he signed his second abdication.

Fouché immediately carried this document to the chamber and proposed the nomination of an executive committee of five members. Then by his own maneuvers in the lobbies he succeeded in eliminating La Fayette, and the provisional government turned out to be composed of himself, Carnot, Caulaincourt, an obscure general named Grenier, and a former regicide (one who voted for Louis XVI's death), Quinette. Then by another sleight-of-hand trick he won the presidency by beating Carnot, and from then on he acted as head of the executive authority, slighting his colleagues on the committee.

The game, however, was far from won. The majority of the deputies in the chamber were violently opposed to the Bourbons, and they had the support of the army and the people of Paris. In the government committee itself Fouché was the only one even to consider the return of Louis XVIII; Carnot and Quinette, both of them former Conventionals and regicides, would have preferred the Duke of Orleans, while Caulaincourt and Grenier remained faithful to the imperial dynasty.

To keep the chambers occupied, Fouché asked them to draw up a new liberal constitution to be imposed on the new sovereign whoever he might be. He very cleverly got rid of La Fayette and the principal liberal leaders by having them sent on a mission to negotiate with the Allies on an armistice and the recognition of Napoleon II. La Fayette believed naïvely that he was going to play the glorious role of mediator between Europe and France, when, in fact, as Fouché foresaw, he would be sent from general to general without accomplishing anything.

Then Fouché succeeded in getting rid of Napoleon, who at Malmaison could have gone back on his abdication if the Allies refused to recognize his son. On June 29 he had offered to resume the command of the armies just as a general. "What kind of a joke is this?" was Fouché's reaction. Then pretending that he was concerned lest the emperor be captured by the enemy, he persuaded him to move on to Rochefort on the coast, where Fouché put two frigates at his disposal.

In the meantime Fouché had already started negotiations with the royalists through Vitrolles whom he had had released from prison. He used him both to give Louis XVIII assurances of his devotion and also to restrain the Parisian royalists from starting a premature revolt in the capital and proclaiming the restoration before the arrival of the Allies. That was one eventuality which our Duke of Otranto wanted least of all. In fact if the revolt succeeded, the restoration would be achieved without him and against him; if it failed, he would be forced to take the lead in its repression and would be thereby disqualified for a role in the future government of the king.

However, the Anglo-Prussian armies arrived outside of Paris. Davout had under his command 117,000 men and 600 cannon—strength enough to inflict a bloody setback for the invaders—and the army was burning to take its revenge on Waterloo. But what good would a victory be that obviously would bring no lasting advantage? Would they not be running the risk of submitting Paris to the fury of an exasperated enemy? For this reason Davout seconded Fouché's efforts to obtain an armistice or, failing that, a military surrender of Paris without a fight. On July 3 the French negotiators met Wellington and Blücher at the Château of Saint-Cloud and signed an agreement providing that the French army would retire behind the Loire within a week. Article 10 stipulated that the Allied leaders would respect the present authorities in France "as long as they remained in office"; and Article 12 promised that no one would be molested because of his office or his political opinions. In Wellington's mind these clauses obligated only the military leaders who had signed them, and then only until the royal authority had been re-established. Fouché presented them as unconditional guarantees to the chambers and to his colleagues on the executive committee. The people of Paris welcomed with great relief this agreement which spared them the horrors of war. But the army, spoiling for a fight, was threatening to shoot the government traitors and refusing to leave Paris. It required all the authority and prestige of Davout, Carnot, and other respected leaders like Drouot to persuade it to start its march southward. If finally complied during the fifth and sixth of July. By this army retirement Fouché finally came to dominate the scene. Deprived of army support, the chambers now could no longer put up any effective resistance to his intrigues.

The final scene was now going to be acted out between the Duke of Otranto (Fouché) and the king. Louis XVIII had not been losing time either. His swift return to France confronted the Allies with a *fait accompli* and helped to thwart the Orleanist intrigue. By June 22 he had started back and had arrived at Mons on French soil. Talleyrand arrived there that same evening from Vienna with all the prestige of a man enjoying the full confidence of Europe. Louis XVIII had had to let Blacas go because he had been made the scapegoat for the mistakes of the first year of the reign. Therefore, whether he liked it or not, he had to rely completely on Talleyrand for the conduct of affairs. In order to show clearly that he was master of the situation, the minister refused to go to the king immediately, as Chateaubriand had advised him; perhaps he recalled how the king had humiliated him the year before at Compiègne by making him wait for the audience.

"I am never in a hurry; tomorrow will be time enough."

"But are you sure the king won't be moving on?"

"He won't dare."

At three o'clock the next morning they came and woke him up. The king was about to depart. Talleyrand, furious, hurriedly dressed and running on foot as fast as his deformed foot would allow, he arrived at the king's rooms. The royal carriage was just at that moment driving away from the entrance, but with a wave the prince stopped the driver. The king rather reluctantly sent the carriage back and returned to his apartment with Talleyrand. The minister, very angry, began to explain his views: the king should interrupt his voyage, he must not give the appearance of returning to his capital under the protection of foreign bayonets; he ought to go to Lyons where he could negotiate in all freedom the conditions of his return. Then Talleyrand implied that he would resign if his advice was not followed. Louis XVIII heard him without saying a word. At the end he replied crisply: "My prince, you are leaving us? The waters of Carlsbad are excellent. They will do you a lot of good, and you can write us from there." Without another word he got up and again entered his carriage, leaving Talleyrand stupefied by his superior air of composure. "He [Talleyrand] was foaming with rage," Chateaubriand related. However, the disagreement did not last long; Wellington reconciled them again soon after; and the prince rejoined the king at Cambrai, where the latter, on the twenty-fifth, was hailed by joyous popular demonstrations.

The first act of Louis XVIII was to issue a proclamation whose terms had been carefully weighed to give reassurance to Paris opinion. "My government was bound to make mistakes, and perhaps made some. There are times when the purest intentions are not enough for directing affairs, when sometimes they even misguide those in authority. Experience alone can give a warning which will have its good effect." The king promised to add to the Charter any guarantees which could assure its full enjoyment. "Ministerial solidarity is the strongest guarantee that I can offer; I understand that it already exists and that the frank and confident action of my council guarantees all interests and calms all anxieties." Louis XVIII then made the further promise to forget and forgive "those Frenchmen who had gone astray," but he added, "I must, however, for the dignity of my throne, the welfare of my people, and the peace of Europe, exempt from pardon those instigators and authors of that horrible plot. They will be designated for punishment by laws to be passed by the two chambers, which I propose to call into early session."

As soon as the capitulation of July 3 was known, the king went on to take up quarters in the Legion of Honor house in Saint-Denis. During this same time Fouché was negotiating with Talleyrand and, in order to increase the value of his assistance, he greatly exaggerated the remaining difficulties to be overcome. Louis XVIII, urged on by his ministers, by Wellington, and even by the Count of Artois himself, finally accepted Fouché as minister of police. On July 6, in the evening, Talleyrand came to present him to the king. "It was vice leaning on the arm of crime," wrote Chateaubriand; "the trusty regicide, on his knees, put his hands, which had pushed Louis XVI's head under the knife, into the hands of the brother of the martyred king; the apostate bishop was guarantor of the oath."

The next day Fouché called together the committee of the provisional government and blandly stated to his colleagues that the only thing left for them to do was to disband because the Allies had decided to restore the king. Carnot protested: "We should not thus betray the authority given to us by the chambers; rather we should go down and take our stand with the army of the Loire. . . ." But a detachment of Prussian troops came along and put an end to the session. Before they broke up, however, the committee members addressed a message to the chambers, the army, and the national guard in which they said they were giving up only in the face of force and the firm determination of the Allied sovereigns to re-establish Louis XVIII on the throne. This was Fouché's final lie and final treason, because no more now than in 1814, did the Allies intend to impose on France a regime contrary to the wishes of the nation. Thus the Restoration was besmirched with an initial stain that it was never able to wash away. Our fine Duke of Otranto had thus worthily crowned his work by succeeding, in one single act, in betraying the cause of the Revolution out of which he had come, the cause of the Empire which had brought him his highest honors, and the cause of the monarchy where he hoped to find a dominant place for himself.

Louis XVIII finally returned to the capital on the afternoon of July 8. Because Fouché wanted to avoid royalist demonstrations, he had pretended the most touching concern about the kind of welcome the king might encounter in the working quarters of the city and had begged him to enter by the Etoile tollgate. The king, however, did well to reject this advice with scorn because the Empire supporters did not make a hostile demonstration and, on the other hand, the long pent-up royalists came out openly in the streets and gave him a warm reception. As he entered the city, Chabrol, the prefect of the Seine, addressed the sovereign with a short speech of welcome which began with words which were destined to remain in French history as the title of one of its most dramatic chapters: "A hundred days have passed since that fatal moment when Your Majesty left his capital. . . ." Louis XVIII listened with a grave and stern countenance and then merely replied: "It was only with the deepest grief that I left my good city of Paris. I come back to her with feelings of great emotion. I had foreseen the evils which were threatening her. I desire to prevent them and to make reparation for them." The task which awaited him was indeed full of difficulties and dangers.

PART

II

❧ ❧ ❧ ❧ ❧

*The Reign of Louis XVIII*

# 8

✤ ✤ ✤ ✤ ✤

# The Talleyrand-Fouché Ministry

## The Difficult Early Days

THE Second Restoration took place under much worse conditions, from every point of view, than the earlier one of April 1814. In the previous year the Allies, glad to have eliminated Napoleon and put France back to her former boundaries, had tried to show some consideration for French national feeling. They had quickly withdrawn their troops without imposing a war indemnity and without damaging the country too much. Now, a year later, their exasperated armies moved into France determined to crush the insolent nation under the weight of their victory. The Allied sovereigns, who had previously given Louis XVIII the credit for the establishment of a stable order, had now lost all confidence in his discretion and were in a mood to demand much stronger guarantees. France, instead of being admitted as an equal in the European concert, was to be treated like a dangerous madman in need of the strait-jacket treatment. The peace terms would be much more difficult to make, and they would leave much deeper resentments on both sides.

No less venomous was the internal situation. In 1814 the Bourbons had been restored, in spite of the ill will of the Allies, by the authorized representatives of the nation, and the people in general had rallied to them without mental reservation. Now to all appearances it seemed as if they had a government imposed by foreigners. It could no longer be said, as in 1814, "neither victor nor vanquished." Some were the vanquished: all of those who had abandoned the Bourbons in favor of Napoleon, and they were now marked with an indelible stigma which was to make them irreconcilable enemies of the monarchy. The victors, those who had remained faithful to the

115

king, now loudly demanded the punishment of the others. Napoleon, by arousing the Jacobin passions against the nobility and the clergy, had laid the foundations for a fearful and unnatural alliance between two ideologies—republicans and Bonapartists, democrats and war-mongers. These passions could no longer be calmed, and by reaction they exasperated the royalists who had broken with the liberals of 1814. For many long years France would be divided into two hostile groups.

Soon after his return the king carried out his promise of cabinet solidarity by assembling a veritable governmental team under the direction of a prime minister (president of the council). All laws, all appointments of high government officials, all important policies were to be discussed in the cabinet (council of ministers). The royal princes would no longer be members of it. Talleyrand, retaining the portfolio of foreign affairs, was the obvious choice as head of the government. The old senatorial party was back in power with Fouché as minister of police, Marshal Gouvion-Saint-Cyr as minister of war, Baron Louis as minister of finance, Pasquier as minister of justice and interior, and Jaucourt as naval minister. The pure royalists, completely excluded from the cabinet, were to become very indignant at seeing the monarchy thus turned over to the old revolutionary and imperial personnel.

One of the first preoccupations of the ministry was to obtain the submission of Davout's army beyond the Loire, which was still hostile to the king and the foreign invader. The Allies themselves were no less desirous to see this potential threat disappear, since royalist leaders in the West were already starting negotiations with Davout with the purpose of joining in a common action against the invaders. Talleyrand was fearful of both groups and never for an instant thought of using the strength of such a national coalition to support his peace negotiations. At first Davout agreed to adopt the white cockade for his troops on two conditions: (1) no reprisals against those who had been compromised; (2) no dissolution of the army while the enemy was still on French soil. They tried to persuade him that an unconditional submission would be the best way to make sure that his officers would receive generous treatment. He finally consented, on July 14, to the raising of the white flag (the Bourbon banner—not a flag of truce). A few days later the minister of war notified him that it was necessary to begin the "reorganization" of the army by a reassignment of his units. Further, when Davout had read the new ordinance of proscription of July 24, he saw clearly that he had been tricked. He then turned in his resignation, and Marshal Macdonald took over his command. The latter was to carry out the actual dissolution of the remaining units of the Army of the Loire as well as the early steps of army reorganization, which indeed had been very well planned by Gouvion-Saint-Cyr.

This ordinance of July 24 which caused Davout's resignation had not only been contrary to the promises made to the army but was also in violation of the king's solemn engagements, given in his Proclamation of Cambrai, that he would leave it to the legislature to decide who should be punished. But the Allies demanded immediate punitive action; and besides, so many people were being accused, so many people felt themselves threatened, that it seemed wise to lance the abscess without delay and thus reassure the greater number by taking action against a few. Fouché was given the job of preparing the lists, and the first one he presented to the cabinet contained such an incongruous medley of names that it almost seemed as if he had deliberately drawn it up in a way to discredit the whole project. "We must give the Duke of Otranto credit for one thing," remarked Talleyrand sarcastically, "he did not forget any of his friends in drawing up the list." Some of the ministers and some other influential people managed to strike off some names. The final proscription list contained fifty-seven names, among which were nineteen officers who, having violated their oaths of loyalty, were to be court-martialed. The others were put under house arrest outside of Paris until the legislature could determine their fate. Carnot, a member of this latter group, wrote Fouché: "Where do you want me to go, traitor?" "Wherever you wish, idiot," replied the Duke of Otranto.

The minister of police, in accepting the odious task of proscribing his former friends and collaborators, nevertheless did all he could secretly to help them escape. Not only did he warn them early enough to help them evade arrest, but he also furnished passports and money to make possible their flight from France. The only ones who were arrested were those who really wanted to be. Such a one was Colonel La Bédoyère who had been the first one to deliver his regiment over to Napoleon. Everything had been done to get him out to the United States, but he made the mistake of returning to Paris to bid his wife good-bye. Recognized and arrested, the poor man was condemned to death by court-martial and executed on August 19, the first victim of the legal repression.

## White Terror and Allied Occupation

Unfortunately he was not the first one to lose his life, because, in addition to governmental action and quite contrary to the wishes of the king, the reactionaries had already done some killing on their own in the southern provinces where what came to be called the "White Terror" was raging. It is easier today, after the events of 1944 in the same area, to understand the unleashing of such a movement; the analogy is in fact very striking. A people had been repressed by the armed supporters in the service of an execrated dictatorial authority—the "federates" in 1815, like the militia in 1944; foreign intervention had struck off the yoke; and the clandestine resistance committees came out in the open—royalist committees of 1815, resistance committees in 1944. They took over the local governments; the irregular popular militias—*miquelets* and *verdets* in 1815 and the F.T.P. and others in 1944—dominated the country, settling personal grudges as well as committing acts of pillage. Not even conflicting ideologies were exempted from a share in the movements: Catholics against Protestants in 1815, Communists against Fascists in 1944. Again, at the same time the central government in Paris, just barely reinstated and hesitant about taking rigorous action against those who claimed to be its warmest supporters, found itself for a time to be completely powerless to control the situation. The Duke of Angoulême had arrived from Spain, and, acting by virtue of the authority given him by the king, had appointed, throughout the region of Languedoc, prefects chosen from among the leaders of the local secret organizations. On the other hand, Talleyrand's government in Paris had also designated its own prefects in this area. Naturally there were then conflicts of authority, and in many places several weeks were to go by before the Paris appointees could effectively take over their duties. Thus for more than a month all the south found itself handed over to the arbitrary anarchical rule of royalist committees and gang leaders.

The people of Marseilles had risen in revolt on June 25, and the imperial troops had withdrawn from the city, losing about a hundred men. Delirious over their victory, the "tough boys" ("*nervis*") massacred all the Jacobins and Federates they could lay hands on as well as some Egyptians whom Napoleon had set up in Marseilles after his expedition of 1798. Marshal Brune, in command at Toulon, had at first refused to recognize the king's authority and had said something about going to punish the Marseillais. On his way back to Paris after having surrendered his command, he was imprudent enough to stop over in Avignon, which had come completely under the control of a gang of royalist volunteers. Here he was recognized and his hotel, to which he had fled, was besieged by a howling mob. The prefect and the military commander risked their lives in vain to try to rescue him. Brune was killed by a bullet through the back of his head, and his body was ignominiously dragged through the streets and thrown into the Rhone river.

At Nîmes, the imperial troops who had refused their submission were decimated as at Marseilles. Both the city and the region witnessed many murders to avenge the deaths of royalist volunteers of the preceding April. It was about this region particularly that later disputes arose from the charges of liberals and Protestants, who, under the influence of a persecution complex, exaggerated the losses which were bad enough at any figure. The number of three hundred victims often quoted is too high; a careful study of the sources points to less than one hundred, but the number of people thrown in prison, assaulted, and robbed was evidently a great deal larger.

In Toulouse, where there was indeed a large number of very aroused royalists, there were no murders, because the officials had the good idea to throw into prison all those who might have been the objects of reprisals. The only casualty was General Ramel, the king's military commander in the department. He was a sincere and moderate royalist, but he had the misfortune of wanting to bring the *"verdet"* irregular militia to heel. The *"verdets"* got their name from their white and green cockade, the colors of the Count of Artois and symbol of "pure" royalism. They assassinated General Ramel under the most revolting circumstances. Respectable people were so shocked at this stupid and atrocious crime that it brought about a salutary reaction. The king hurried the Duke of Angoulême to Toulouse, and his popularity succeeded in calming the public and imposing the Paris government's authority in the whole region.

In the West the situation was more quiet. The popular mood was less explosive, and the leaders kept their people under better control. In fact at Vannes there was a parade and a reconciliation banquet between two groups who had begun by challenging each other to armed combat.

The rest of the country was spared the worst excesses of the reactionaries by the presence of the Allied armies in sixty-one departments. But the inhabitants of these departments were to pay dearly for this advantage. The victory at Waterloo and the return of the king had not halted the march of the soldiers from all parts of Europe who converged on France, eager now for vengeance and booty; 310,000 Prussians, 320,000 Austrians, 126,000 Bavarians, Badeners, Wurtembergers, as well as contingents from all the small German states, Sardinia, Spain, and even Switzerland. By the beginning of September there would be in France over 1,200,000 foreign soldiers, roaring, drinking, pillaging, ransacking, and raping, with utter disregard as to who was on which side. "We have conquered France" Canning told Madame de Staël in brutal terms, "France is our prey, and we want so to weaken her that she will not be able to move for another ten years." The Allied leaders requisitioned right and left, seized the public funds, and interfered in all the subdivisions of local government. Officials who tried to object were maltreated; several prefects were removed and sent away to Prussia. If the English were restrained by the severe discipline which Wellington was able to impose, and the Russians by the will of the still sympathetic Tsar Alexander, the Austrians and especially the Prussians showed no restraint whatever. When someone complained to Blücher (the Prussian commander), he replied: "What? Is that all they did? They should have done a lot more!"

This sort of violence was attempted even in Paris right under the very nose of the king. Blücher wanted to blow up the Iéna Bridge over the Seine to wipe out this commemoration of the Prussian defeat in 1806. On this occasion, when Louis XVIII wrote to the King of Prussia that he would go over himself and sit on the bridge, Blücher had to give up his scheme. A little later the Allies demanded the restitution of the works of art which had been taken from them during the wars of the Revolution and Empire. The royal government refused to give them up. Wellington was insistent; the Allies, he said, "should not let this occasion go by without teaching the French a good lesson in morals." The removal of paintings and statues from the Louvre Museum took place by military force before the eyes of a humiliated and irritated population.

## The Elections and the Fall of the Ministry

Fouché, spurned by those whom he had betrayed as well as by the royalists, thought he could strengthen his position by becoming the spokesman and champion of all those who suffered from the Allied invasion and the White Terror. From the information he received from the provinces, he wrote two reports to the king which he read in cabinet meetings early in August. In the first he described the Allied requisitions and ended with a threat to cause a national uprising against the invaders. In the second report he portrayed two domestic foes at each other's throats, brandished the threat of national uprising, and tried to create a fear that in such a case the royalists would be crushed. "One can find among Frenchmen scarcely one-tenth who want to go back to the Old Regime and hardly a fifth who are frankly devoted to royal authority." He advised that they quickly win over the support of the former republicans by a decided and unreserved adherence to the principles of 1789.

The other ministers were astounded at such audacity. The king merely said: "Just as soon as the situation appears this way to the Duke of Otranto, he has done well to present it to me as he sees it. Besides, this frankness can cause no embarrassment, because nothing said here under the seal of secrecy can leak to the outside." Nevertheless, a few days later these explosive documents were widely circulated and discussed in public. Louis XVIII wanted to dismiss his minister of police immediately, but the latter got Wellington to intervene in his favor. The king had too much need of the English supreme commander to obtain better peace and occupation conditions, so once more he swallowed his humiliation.

The final blow was to fall on Fouché when the new chamber of deputies assembled after the August elections. The king had promised to call the two houses at the earliest possible moment. There was no difficulty about doing this for the chamber of peers because the king appointed them. As early as July 24 an ordinance had excluded twenty-nine men who had sat in the upper house during the Hundred Days. Another ordinance of August 17 appointed ninety-four new members, bringing the total number up to two hundred in contrast to the 150 in 1814. In this new batch could be seen some courtiers like Blacas and Jules de Polignac, some "pure" royalists like Chateaubriand, some loyal military leaders like Marshal Victor, sitting side by side with a large number of friends of Talleyrand and Fouché. The latter had even been able to reinstate two of those removed by the ordinance of July 24—that is, Boissy d'Anglas and Lanjuinais. They claimed that Lanjuinais had not taken his seat in the upper house during the Hundred Days. Actually he had not been in the upper house because he had been presiding over the lower house—a strange alibi! To assure the permanence of his influence in the upper house, Talleyrand persuaded the king to make the peers hereditary, for which the Charter did not provide. The liberals, who were to fight so hard against the principle of the hereditary peerage fifteen years later, were at this time very happy with it.

In the case of the elective house they could not think of calling into session the House of the Hundred Days, which had been chosen by 7,669 voters under the pressure of imperial officials. But what could be done? The First Restoration had not had time to pass an election law. They therefore resorted to a royal ordinance which continued the use of departmental and arrondissement electoral colleges of the empire. However, in 1815 the prefects were allowed to add ten members to the arrondissement colleges and twenty to the departmental colleges. Each arrondissement college was to nominate a number equal to the final departmental delegation; then the departmental college was to choose the final delegation, at least half of which would have to come from the arrondissement lists. It was a two-stage indirect election with the departmental notables having the final voice. In two other ways the Charter was also modified: the voting age was reduced from thirty to twenty-one and the age of candidates from forty to twenty-five; and the size of the lower house was increased from 262 to 402.

The two stages of the indirect elections took place on August 14 and 22. Talleyrand, Fouché, and Pasquier felt sure they would obtain a house reflecting their views of monarchism tinted with liberalism. Had they not chosen liberal presidents of the electoral colleges for whom the royal appointment made them seem, in a sense, like official candidates? Did not the prefects, whom they had appointed, have the means to tip the scales both by their personal influence and by the pressure they were allowed to exert? But the result was that "Unexpected House" (*Chambre Introuvable*) in which the royalists were to win an overwhelming majority. One attempted explanation of the result was said to be the wholesale abstention by the liberal voters. In fact only 48,000 voted out of 72,000. This difference is considerable; but there were seven times more voters than in the elections of the Hundred Days, and there is no way to prove that all nonvoters were liberals. Were the voters terrorized? Yes, certainly, in some cities of the south; but one should not forget that in the sixty-one departments occupied by the Allies the freedom to vote was completely guaranteed. Perhaps one must see in the election results some influence by the royalist secret societies, especially that of the *Chevaliers de la Foi* (Knights of the Faith), who were so strong in the south. The simplest explanation is that an irresistible conservative movement impelled the upper classes toward the monarchy in the very same regions where Fouché claimed that there were not twenty per cent of the citizens devoted to the king.

Certainly there were not that many who were devoted to the Duke of Otranto! The first deputies arriving in Paris declared emphatically that they would not stand for the presence of a regicide on the ministerial benches. Talleyrand easily resigned himself to dumping that dead weight; they got rid of Fouché by appointing him as diplomatic minister to Dresden. Treason and double-dealing just do not pay, and Louis XVIII must have regretted having tarnished his honor for a man whom France spewed out.

Talleyrand was not to survive much longer himself. The deputies did not feel any more kindly toward the apostate bishop than they did toward the regicide. And, besides, the prime minister, since his big deal at Vienna, was no longer *persona grata* with the tsar, and this made the peace negotiations more difficult.

In 1814 it only required three weeks to compose a peace arrangement, while in 1815 it took there months to conclude the second treaty. To a large extent this delay is explained by the deliberate intention of the Allies—and especially the military leaders—to take advantage of the situation to exploit France more easily, and to some extent by their own disagreements among themselves. The Prussians, supported by all the German princes, wanted a drastic revision of the 1814 territorial provisions. The French, they said, had shown that they would never be resigned to the loss of the Rhine frontier; there was no reason now to be considerate of their feelings. Indeed, prudence would dictate weakening them as much as possible and taking enough of their northern and eastern provinces to set up a large buffer state. The tsar was agreeable to imposing a heavy indemnity on France and a temporary occupation, but he wanted to retain the boundaries of 1814. England and Austria mediated the disagreement, and finally, on September 20, a draft treaty, drawn up by all the victors, was submitted to the royal government.

It came just in time to give Talleyrand an honorable way out. On the previous evening, in the course of a conversation with Louis XVIII, he had gained the impression that the king was about to replace him. So he immediately, on September 21, replied to the Allies by a haughty note rejecting the treaty—thus obviously giving himself the halo of a patriotic martyr in the eyes of public opinion. On the following day he presented the king with his resignation and that of the whole cabinet. One wonders whether he would have so lightly surrendered his power if he could have foreseen that he would never again return to that high office.

# 9

❧ ❧ ❧ ❧ ❧

# The "*Chambre Introuvable*"*

## The Richelieu Cabinet

THE situation required a cabinet which could collaborate with the new lower house (chamber of deputies) and obtain from Europe the best possible peace terms. This last consideration was especially in the king's mind when he authorized the Duke of Richelieu to form a new government.

Armand-Emmanuel du Plessis, Duke of Richelieu, was the grandson of the famous Marshal of Richelieu. Born in 1767, he had emigrated after the October days of 1789 (when the mobs had compelled Louis XVI to remove his residence from Versailles to Paris), and, to avoid idleness, had enrolled in Russia's military service. His gallantry and fine character had won him the friendship of Grand Duke Alexander. When the latter mounted the Russian throne in 1801, he assigned the young duke the job of governing the immense southern territory recently conquered from the Turks. Richelieu worked miracles there and in just a few years transformed this area into a prosperous province. In 1814 he had come back to offer his allegiance to the new king, Louis XVIII, who appointed him as first gentleman of the privy chamber and peer of France. On the king's return from Ghent in 1815, when he was offered the ministry of the royal household, left vacant by the departure of Blacas, he refused, saying he did not intend to sit beside Fouché, did not think he was cut out for the life of a courtier, and longed only to go back to his dear Odessa. Now it took all the persuasive efforts of the tsar to get him to accept

* This is an almost untranslatable expression used by Louis XVIII on hearing of the election returns. In a sense it means such a freakish chamber that it could never be matched or "Unexpected Chamber."

the presidency of the council (the office of prime minister) when the king made him the offer. "Be the link of a sincere alliance between our two countries," Alexander told him, "I insist on it in the name of the welfare of France."

In many personal respects Richelieu seemed unprepared for such an assignment. "The one man in France who knows most about the Crimea," sneered Talleyrand. In fact he did feel like a foreigner in France; he had not even met his fellow-members in the cabinet. The swirl of passions and intrigues which prevailed in domestic politics left him completely bewildered; "What an awful country!" he often moaned. In a legislature which was just learning the ways of a parliamentary regime he was unable to overcome his fear of public speaking. He did not know how to extemporize or to give quick rebuttal in debate or to control the direction of discussions. In a position where he would have to expect to take a lot of criticism, this hypersensitive man was so easily offended that he was driven to despair or fury by the least setback or slight. Following after one of the most cunning of diplomats, he could not conceal his thoughts or impressions. His modesty and excessive lack of self-confidence made it impossible to come to quick and firm decisions. Moreover, he did not let himself be influenced by others, because he had been so often and so easily misled that he almost always suspected ulterior motives of those with whom he was dealing. Molé compared him to a frisky horse which you must approach from a distance and tame down gradually.

However, in the long run his shortcomings were to be just as useful to him as his strong points. Never having engaged in party fights, he could more easily control and arbitrate them. Especially, his great Christian gentlemanliness won everybody's respect. In no way did he seek selfish advantage; and even at the height of his power he continued to live the simple life of an officer in the field. When he took over the ministry, he broke off all negotiations with the purchasers of his estates, confiscated during the Revolution, for fear that his new position would tend to give him an unfair advantage in drawing up the terms of settlement. His chivalrous sense of honor, his absolute trustworthiness were to do more to bring France back into the good graces of Europe than all the trickiness of Talleyrand. Alexander said, "He is the only friend who will tell me the truth to my face." And Wellington remarked that "his word is as good as a treaty."

Richelieu's inexperience accounts for the weakness of his cabinet team. To the justice ministry came Barbé-Marbois, a former minister of Napoleon, an austere and rough man in appearance, but basically

rather weak, a filmsy reed with an iron disguise. In the finance ministry was the Genoese Corvetto, another former official of the Empire,
a good technician without political affiliations. As minister of war
General (soon to be marshal) Clarke, Duke of Feltre, was chosen.
The military men called him the "Ink Marshal" (*maréchal d'Encre*)
because for many years his only battlefield had been some ministerial office.[1] "Under the king he was right where he had been under
the emperor," said Molé, "adoring despotism and arbitrary decisions
because they did not require him to give reasons or have ideas." In
the naval ministry appeared the old Viscount Dubouchage, a former
minister of Louis XVI, who had been out of public life for over a
quarter of a century. The minister of interior, the Count of Vaublanc,
was at least a man who had had a lot of experience in public office;
deputy in the Legislative Assembly of 1791, in the Council of Five
Hundred during the Directory, in the Legislative Body of the Consulate, he had likewise been prefect of Moselle from 1805 to 1814 and
prefect of Bouches-du-Rhône in July 1815. He was also energetic and
indefatigable, but his vanity exceeded by far even the ridiculous and
extended to cutting remarks, roaring speeches, and emphatic circulars. By this excess of Ultra-Royalist zeal he tried to cover up the
fact that he had once been in the service of Napoleon. His convictions
as well as his official duties were soon to bring him into conflict with
the new minister of police, Elie Decazes.

Son of a notary of Libourne, Decazes had been attached to the
household of Madame Mère (mother of Napoleon I) and later appointed as councillor to the imperial court in Paris. During the Hundred Days he had courageously refused to swear allegiance to the
emperor. At the time of the organization of the Talleyrand cabinet,
there had been some difficulty in finding the right man to be Paris
prefect of police. Baron Louis proposed Decazes, and Fouché consented disdainfully. The young twenty-five-year-old prefect of police
obtained permission to communicate directly with the king; Louis
XVIII delighted in the little pieces of gossip brought to him by the
police and the secret service, but he objected to hearing these things
from Fouché. To gain his sovereign's favor, Decazes played the role
of a naive, very devoted young man, who wanted to learn about
government and men by instruction from the wisest and most experienced of princes. For example, if the king tried to teach him

[1] There was also a double meaning to this nickname because it reminded people
of the notorious Concini, favorite of Marie de Médicis, who had been given the
title of *maréchal d'Ancre*.

English, Decazes studied diligently and secretly with another professor so that the king could marvel at the rapid progress of his pupil and also at his own teaching ability. This strategem worked so well that Louis XVIII soon considered his young prefect of police as his disciple, his creation, his spiritual son. He became attached to him with a senile passion. Here is an example of one of many daily notes the king wrote to him: "My Elie, I love you, I bless you with all my soul, I hold you close to my heart. Come and receive the tenderest kisses of your friend, your father, your Louis." The king's affection extended to all the family of his favorite; Decazes' sister, Mme Princeteau, had a whole brood of children whom the king treated like grandchildren, asking anxiously about their colds and colics, spending his royal leisure time making cones of candy for them. "By these attentions," said Frénilly with a tinge of cruelty, "he acquired a little barnyard family which was not one of the least concerns of his empire." Later on the king was to negotiate the marriage of his favorite with a rich heiress, Mlle de Saint-Aulaire, and he had the young bride brought to him to teach her in detail how to please her husband.

This extraordinary favor shown to Decazes was, for the next four years, to make him the pivot around which would revolve all the political combinations. So we must take a closer look at his personality. None has set it down with a more trenchant pen than his colleague Molé:

> His features were regular and handsome but lacked charm or nobility. His hawk eyes were large, round, clear, and piercing; his nose also resembled the beak of a bird of prey. However, the turned-down corners of his mouth, his thin lips, his low and prominent forehead deprived his face of any appearance of expressive or moral beauty. His glance was always vague and uncertain, and he never looked steadily at anyone except behind his back as if he wanted to see without being seen. He was tall but fat, round, and effeminate; and his manners, while easy, friendly, and unrestrained, could be ridiculously vulgar; and, when he took thought of his conduct, he acted like a parvenu. So much for his outward appearance. As for his character, I must say that I have been studying it for three years and I still fear that I may be wrong. . . . The most difficult question to solve is whether M. Decazes is sincere or false. If I can trust my impression and his face, I would say he was the most dishonest man alive. . . . He considered the science of government to be one of ingratiating one's self. . . . He won over the great by appealing to their baseness, and he gained the small people by raising them to his level. . . . He had neither wide knowledge nor

general ideas, he had read perhaps only five hundred pages in his whole life. As to history he only knew his own. . . . Without doctrines or principles, he governed only by expedients. But he was neither discouraged nor dismayed, and his strong point was always knowing how to get out of a tight spot. Although the principal agent for human affairs . . . M. Decazes absolutely lacked continuity. . . . There was nothing more difficult than to try to carry on a conversation with him and nothing more rare than for him to pursue his idea to the end. His mind seemed vague and wandering, as if his glance needed some distraction in order to fix it on something. He always was doing several things at the same time; he was always reading while he talked and talking while he wrote. If he had nothing else to do, he would trim his fingernails or look at his beautiful hands to which he was attracted. In ordinary times he would have been only a provincial fop who had extended his field of success from Libourne to Saint-Denis Street, but circumstances had opened to him the road to fortune. . . . It is the only example in history up to now of a royal favorite who became popular, and that among a people who would allow their king twenty mistresses rather than one favorite.

## The Second Treaty of Paris and the So-Called Holy Alliance

The peace treaty was to be the first and principal objective of Richlieu's efforts. The tsar had promised to help him obtain some attenuation in the terms presented by the Allies on September 2. To carry this out, it was agreed that Louis XVIII would write Alexander a letter saying that he would rather abdicate than accept them. Armed with this document the tsar would force some concession from his allies: in the Ardennes, France would keep Givet, Condé, and Charlemont; and in the Jura, the forts of Joux and the Ecluse; the indemnity was reduced by a hundred million francs (twenty million dollars) and the period of occupation from seven to five years. On these bases the preliminaries were signed on October 2; the various texts of the final treaty (as in 1814, there was one for each of the four great powers) and the three technical conventions accompanying them were still subject to discussion on details. It was not until November 20 that they signed this collection of documents called the Second Treaty of Paris. Barante, who saw Richelieu soon after the signing, told how upset the latter was over the ordeal:

> He came into the room, his face was distraught. He threw down his hat and, falling into a chair, buried his head in his hands in the deep-

est despair. "Well, it's over now. The king ordered me to do it. A Frenchman should be hanged for signing such a treaty!" M. de Marbois tried to console him . . . but nothing could calm the Duke of Richelieu. He wept from pain and anger.

France's territorial boundaries would be those of January 1, 1790 rather than those of 1792—that is, she had to cede Philippeville, Marienbourg, and the duchy of Bouillon to the Low Countries; Saarlouis and Saarbrucken to Prussia; Landau and the territory north of the Lauter to Austria, who was to turn them over to Bavaria and Hesse respectively; and Savoy to Sardinia. The departments along the northern and eastern frontiers were to be occupied by 150,000 foreign troops for from three to five years. France had to pay the costs of occupation to the tune of 150 million francs (thirty million dollars) a year and an indemnity of 700 million (140 million dollars). And finally the royal government promised to settle every sort of debt and obligation contracted by previous French governments with individual citizens in the Allied countries.

These conditions were harsh, much more severe than those of 1814. Alas, the king could do no more than liquidate a situation for which he was not responsible. Was it too astonishing that the first ones to criticize him were the very ones who had done the most to plunge their country into this misfortune by supporting Napoleon on his return?

When, later on, critics were to blame the Restoration for the humiliation of the treaties of 1815, they were alluding not only to the Second Treaty of Paris but also to the system of alliances concluded at the same time by the four great powers to guarantee its fulfillment. The so-called Holy Alliance Treaty, signed on September 26 at the urging of Alexander, was in itself nothing but a general statement of principles, inspired by a lofty ideal; and England was to refuse to sign it. But much more important was the treaty of November 20, 1815 concluded among the four Allies and called the Quadruple Alliance, which renewed the previous military pact signed at Chaumont in 1814. The significant new clause contained in it was Article VI, which read: "To guarantee and facilitate the execution of the present [alliance] treaty and to solidify the close relations uniting the four powers . . . the high contracting parties agree to renew at certain periods . . . their meetings to consider their important common interests and to examine what measures might be judged most salutary for the tranquility and prosperity of peoples and for the preservation of peace in Europe." This was the first seed of international organizations which recur, alas, after every great war.

It is not necessary to point out the humiliating character of this alliance for France, how, in a sense, it put her under constant great power surveillance. The temporary coalition, created to oppose Napoleon, was becoming a permanent feature in international politics.

## The "Chambre Introuvable" and its Repressive Laws

France's internal situation, by its uneasiness, could very well justify precautionary measures in the eyes of the Allies. The new parliamentary session opened on October 7, and the new lower house soon showed its intention of intervening directly in the management of government. The liberal historical school has imposed the legend of a "Chambre Introuvable" almost entirely composed of nobles and old unreconstructed émigrés, hoping to turn France back to the Old Regime. All one needs to do is to call the roll—but pay attention to the noble sound of their elongated names with which the upper bourgeoisie liked to decorate themselves in those days. Of the 381 deputies in the chamber at the beginning of 1816 we find 197 of bourgeois origin and eight who were made nobles during the Empire, as contrasted with 176 Old Regime nobles. Of the seventy-three former émigrés, most of them had accepted military or government appointments under the Empire. Among the bourgeois members ninety-one were lawyers, judges, and barristers and twenty-five were merchants or industrialists. Another interesting characteristic of this chamber was the low average age of its members compared to other legislatures of those times. Only forty-five were in their sixties, and 130 deputies were under forty-five, that is they had been less than twenty years old at the beginning of the Revolution and could not have enjoyed the privileges of the Old Regime. Their royalism consisted of hopes and not of resentments. Another remarkable thing was that there was not one clergyman in a chamber which seemed so concerned about religious interests. Lastly, most of the members were new in politics; only sixty-one had ever sat in a previous legislature. Because of this and because of the youth of its members, it is understandable that this chamber should have been, like that of 1789, nervous, impulsive, passionate, and often blundering.

Its first act, an address in reply to the speech from the throne, expressed its desire to punish those who had brought on the evils from which the country now suffered. The ease with which Napoleon had been able to take over the country on his return was largely due to the fact that the first Restoration had continued in office practically all the military and administrative staffs of the Empire. To these royalists the inevitable defections to Napoleon, due to excitement, weakness, or force of habit, appeared to be a premeditated conspiracy. The guilty, now unmasked, should now be punished; the questionable officeholders should be purged; it was a question of life or death for the monarchy. The cabinet members were all inclined to accept these views. One must not forget that Decazes at that time appeared to be an Ultra-Royalist and that he was to have a large share in the preparation and execution of the punitive measures. It must also be pointed out that these bills had as reporters and defenders on the floor such men as Pasquier and Royer-Collard, who were later to abandon the majority and go over to the Moderates. The gentle Fontanes said in those days: "You must strike fear into their hearts if you want to avoid worse evils."

One after another four laws were voted which made up what could be called the legal weaponry of the second White Terror: the Law of General Security (October 29); the Law on Seditious Speech and Publications (November 9); the re-establishment of the Provost Courts (December 27); and the Amnesty Law (January 12, 1816).

The first, proposed by Decazes, permitted arrest without trial of anyone plotting against the royal family or against the security of the state, but these exceptional provisions were supposed to end with the close of the following session. The law on sedition provided for two categories of offences. First, it applied to those words or demonstrations which were aimed at the overthrow of a legitimate government or constituted a threat against the life of the king or of members of the royal family. Such acts would bring the offenders before the Court of Assizes, until the Provost Courts were organized, and would carry a punishment of deportation. Second, it applied to other acts or seditious manifestations which only weakened respect for the authority of the king, such as songs, cries of *Long Live the Emperor,* the showing of the tricolor flag, etc. All these less serious misdemeanors would be dealt with by the correctional courts and could be punished by imprisonment from a month to five years and by a fine of up to twenty thousand francs (four thousand dollars).

The Provost Courts, re-established by the law of December 27, were not a new institution. The Old Regime had used them, and Napoleon had revived them to put an end to the brigandage resulting from the Chouannerie (insurrections in the northwest). The new

Provost Courts, set up in each department, were composed of four civilian judges, but the roles of accuser and prosecutor were assigned to a military provost. Their jurisdiction covered political crimes involving public violence openly apprehended, such as seditious meetings, armed rebellion, and threats against the government and the royal family. There was to be no jury and no appeal, and the punishment was to be carried out within twenty-four hours.

The debate on the Amnesty Bill was the occasion for the first disagreement between the government and the majority in the chamber, and here for the first time appeared a governmental minority party opposed to the Ultra-Royalist majority. This legislative majority thought that the Ordinance of July 24 did not annul the chamber's jurisdiction over seeking out and punishing those guilty of involvement in the Hundred Days' regime. Making use of its right of indirect proposal of legislation, the chamber considered in secret committee several proposals to submit to the king. The one brought forward by the deputy of Maine-et-Loire, the Count of La Bourdonnaye, has remained famous. He asked that several large categories be exempted from amnesty: "To stop their criminal conspiracies," he said, "we must use irons, executioners, and torture." "Death, and only death, can frighten their accomplices and put an end to their plots. . . . As defenders of humanity, we must be ready to spill a few drops of blood in order to avoid having it run in torrents." This sounded just like Saint-Just at the height of the Revolutionary Terror.

The rumors of these debates, leaking to the public outside, aroused even more fear because of the secret deliberations. The liberals exaggerated La Bourdonnaye's "categories," according to them thousands of people were going to be subject to punishment. A popular refrain went the rounds of the cafés:

> It isn't fair now to lament
> This good and royal government,
> Whose loyal generosity
> And unexampled clemency
> Accords to all full pardon,
> Except to not one citizen.

Richelieu now became alarmed. He asked the chamber to limit itself to banishing the thirty-eight listed in the Ordinance of July 24, adding only the members of the Bonaparte family. The chamber's committee objected to this because several men on the list were guilty enough not just to be banished but actually to be tried in the courts. On the other hand some on the list were more deserving of clemency than those, like Fouché, who were not listed at all. Lastly the committee insisted on perpetual banishment for those regicides who had gone over to the Hundred Days' regime and had thus lost all claim to the amnesty granted in Article 11 of the Charter.

The course of the debates was to be influenced by events outside the confines of parliament. It was at this same time that the trial of Marshal Ney was drawing to a close. The Ordinance of July 24 had naturally listed him among those to be court-martialed, but the government had given him every opportunity to escape to a foreign country. For some unknown reason Ney would not take advantage of this and was arrested in the department of Lot on August 5 by some overzealous subordinate officials. Louis XVIII was much upset about this: "He is doing us more harm by letting us catch him than he did when he betrayed us." It was impossible to avoid punishing him; his was the most notorious defection of all; they could not have punished anyone if they had acquitted him. Ney challenged the jurisdiction of the court-martial, and, because he was a peer, he insisted on the right to be tried by the upper house. The authorities could not dodge this issue without admitting their helplessness, and the Allies were letting it be known that they would judge the ability of the royal government to control the domestic situation by the way this affair was handled. Consequently Richelieu went in person to ask the peers to undertake the great trial. The solemn judicial proceedings went on from November 21 to December 6, and the peers declared Ney to be guilty of high treason by one vote short of unanimity. On the penalty the vote was 139 for death, seventeen for deportation, and five abstentions. The king could have pardoned him, and today one is surprised that he did not do it. But the friends of the condemned man had really hurt Ney's cause by challenging the government to lay a hand on this glorious soldier; and the Ultra-Royalists and the Allies were taunting the government on being weak-kneed. Louis XVIII would have had to have the genius and authority which he did not possess to have been discerning enough by himself at that time to impose a solution whose appropriateness would only have been appreciated by history at a later date. So it was that Ney went to his death on December 7, compensating for the errors of his life by the courageous grandeur of his end.

Richelieu counted on the reaction to Ney's execution to win the debate on the amnesty bill. The day after the execution he mounted

the rostrum with the words: "A great example has just been given."
He then presented in the name of the government a new bill which
would refer back to the famous Ordinance of July 24 and incorporate
its provisions, with a few additions, into a law. The chamber insisted
on its own bill, and an incident redoubled its ugly mood. Lavalette,
director of the postal service during the Hundred Days, had also been
condemned to die, but on the eve of his execution his wife helped him
escape by substituting herself for him during their last interview. This
stratagem was so audacious that the authorities suspected a wide complicity in the plot. Indeed, Decazes was wrongly suspected of having
a hand in it. Therefore the final debate on the amnesty bill took
place in an atmosphere poisoned by suspicion and hatred. In the end
the government succeeded in having the exceptions proposed by the
committee of the chamber voted down, but it had to accept the exile
of the regicides.

### The Legal White Terror

By the passage of this law the arsenal of repression was completed.
Because its enforcement depended to a large extent on local officials,
there was considerable variation from department to department. In
contrast to the popular excesses of the summer of 1815 it is now
possible in general to obtain exact figures for the legal and governmental White Terror which now took place. Researches recently carried out by a young American historian (Daniel Resnick) in the
records of seventy per cent of the ordinary courts find that 3,746
political condemnations were made during the period between July
1815 and June 1816. The total then would come to around five
thousand. The arrests and the confinements to domicile carried out
by virtue of the law of exception increased, up to December 1816,
to the number of 3,382. As to the provosts' courts, to which the
historian Houssaye boldly attributed eight thousand condemnations,
out of the 2,280 cases tried during their entire existence, only 237
were purely political, 1,560 were cases involving common law, and
the rest were mixed in character. Of the 237 political cases, the majority ended in either light sentences or acquittal for lack of sufficient
evidence.

However, another aspect of the White Terror was the wave of
purges which took place in all the government's ministerial and departmental administrations. The royal government, like all regimes
established on the ruins of a fallen government, had only two choices:

either retain the officeholders of the previous regime and run the risk of being paralyzed or betrayed by these holdover agents, or else dismiss them and make them irreconcilable enemies and, in addition, cause a temporary disruption of the governmental services. It was quite understandable that it chose the second solution after it had tried the first one in 1814 with the results we now know. The ministers, the directors of services, and the prefects then instituted severe purges in their respective domains with differing methods and degrees of severity. Naturally they had to gather information on the conduct of each official during the Hundred Days. Had he sworn fealty to the Usurper? That was the touchstone. Royal committees became purge and accusation committees; royalist secret societies were also involved in these activities. On these purges we do not have reliable statistics to measure how extensive they were. It is likely that as many as fifty to eighty thousand were purged, from a fourth to a third of the government employees. Those who lost their positions protested loudly, but they were to carry out the same policy of mass dismissals when they returned to power in 1830.

## The Chamber Versus the Government

During the debate on the Amnesty Law, the ministry was only able to wrest concessions from the majority in the chamber by falling back on the wishes of the king in every instance. The deputies of the Ultra majority, who had believed that the king's will was absolute, now on the contrary invoked the will of the nation and shouted "Long Live the King Just the Same!" In the last days of the debates there appeared a strange reversal of positions. The liberals became the defenders of the royal prerogative, and the Ultra-Royalists became the champions of parliamentary authority. Royer-Collard, the liberal and leader of the ministerial minority, argued dogmatically that the chamber existed only by virtue of the Charter and that it was not representative of the nation. It could not have any powers not conceded to it by the king, who was the one and only repository of authority. In rebuttal, Vitrolles, in his pamphlet *Du ministère dans le gouvernment représentatif* (*On the Ministry in a Representative Government*), argued that "in representative governments, opinion is sovereign and the ministry [cabinet] should necessarily be selected from among those designated by the chambers if they were called upon to chose it directly."

The latter part of the session was taken up with a fierce struggle between the ministry and the Ultra majority over the electoral law and the budget. The minister of the interior, Vaublanc, had presented an electoral bill which smacked too much of Napoleonic precedents. The publicist Fiévée put it this way: "The ministers appoint the electors, who in turn elect the deputies." Likewise the bill provided for the renewal of the chamber, according to Article 37 of the Charter, by one-fifth each year. The Ultra majority, anxious to stay in power, wanted an electoral system which would provide for indirect elections by two separate steps and thus would extend the vote at the lowest level to all citizens paying fifty francs (ten dollars) or even twenty-five francs (five dollars) in direct taxes. It was their idea to drown the liberal bourgeoisie in a flood of more popular votes. "Cancel out the middle class, the only one you have to fear," said Villèle, their parliamentary leader. Here again, the Ultra-Royalists were led, by the tactical necessities of their cause, to take a more democratic stand than their liberal opponents. The government succeeded in getting the chamber of peers to reject the total election every five years as voted by the lower chamber over government opposition, and the electoral law remained in suspense.

The budget, that year, presented some extraordinary difficulties. The liquidation of the arrears bequeathed by the Empire, worked out, as we have seen, by Baron Louis, had hardly begun to be put into effect when the Hundred Days came on to augment still further the state debts. Now the arrears amounted to 695 million francs (139 million dollars), to which must be added the first installment of the war indemnity—140 million francs (twenty-eight million dollars)—and the occupation costs—135 million francs (27 million dollars)—and the regular budget of 525 million francs (105 million dollars). In all it was a sum of 1,495 million francs (299 million dollars) which had to be provided. Corvetto proposed that the regular budget be taken care of by increased taxes and by reductions in government salaries. As to the latter, the king set the example by foregoing ten million francs (two million dollars) of his civil list of thirty-five million (seven million dollars). As to the arrears, Corvetto, adopting his predecessor's (Louis') method, proposed to liquidate them by eight per cent government bonds backed by the sale of one million acres of national forests. The Ultra majority absolutely refused to alienate this property which had belonged to the church and which it intended to restore as it had already restored the unsold confiscated private property to the returning émigrés. The Ultras said that it was immoral to have the monarchy pay the debts contracted by the rebels in their effort to overthrow the king. Indeed, it would be treating them too kindly to reimburse them even partially in paying them in bonds listed at one hundred francs (twenty dollars) in value when in fact they only had a market value of sixty francs (twelve dollars).

In spite of all its efforts the government did not succeed in obtaining a majority. It had to resort to a compromise. It gave up the sale of national forests, and the Ultra majority accepted the principle of the total refinancing of the state debts by a special issue bearing five per cent interest until 1820, to which date they would put off the question of how they would liquidate the principal. The budget was then voted on April 27. The government hastened to rid itself of this ungovernable chamber by declaring the session closed on April 29.

A few days before, the king had had it reported to the leaders of the Right that he had no intention of calling for new elections immediately, even for a renewal of one-fifth, and that he planned to recall the chamber, just as it was, for a new session in October. One must believe he was sincere at the time. Richelieu, in spite of his dissatisfaction with the chamber, was of the same opinion and continued to humor the Right. After closing the session, he felt he should remove Vaublanc from the cabinet. The minister of the interior had made himself unbearable to his colleagues by his haughtiness and by his devotion to the Ultra majority. A short time before, Decazes had told him in full cabinet meeting: "You are nothing more than the minister of the Count of Artois, and you would like to be more powerful than the king's ministers." "If I were more powerful than you," retorted Vaublanc, "I should use my power to have you indicted for treason, because you are, M. Decazes, a traitor to king and country." Richelieu, having replaced Vaublanc with Lainé, the president of the chamber and a Moderate Royalist like himself, felt obliged to make some concession to the Ultra-Royalists by also dismissing Barbé-Marbois and his secretary general Guizot, both of whom were unacceptable to the Ultra majority, and by returning the ministry of justice to the old chancellor, Dambray.

The contrivers of the chamber's dissolution were Decazes and the Allied representatives. Decazes had, of course, become intolerable to the Right; the Ultra majority did not conceal its intention of getting him out of the cabinet when the chamber resumed its sessions. So the young minister began a deft campaign to influence both the king and the prime minister against the chamber. By submitting to them carefully chosen items of information, he made it appear to them that the country was exasperated with the chamber and that the Ultra-

Royalists were determined to pursue their reaction to its extreme limits, to impose their will upon the king, and to bring him under the control of Artois.

At the same time the representatives of the Allies in Paris, notably Wellington and Pozzo di Borgo, had become worried over the attitude of the chamber on the budget question, an attitude which seemed to compromise the payment of the war indemnities. They also feared that the laws passed at the beginning of the session, whose full effects were being felt early in the summer, might meet some desperate resistance like that which had caused bloodshed in Grenoble in the month of May. Consequently they brought the strongest kind of pressure to bear on Louis XVIII to persuade him to rid himself of this troublesome chamber. At first Richelieu had shown resentment against this foreign interference in French domestic politics. He had exclaimed: "I should rather die at the hands of Frenchmen than survive with foreign protection!" Decazes brought him around to his own point of view by the only argument that could appeal to his patriotism: he convinced him of the fact that the continuance of the "Chambre Introuvable," so distrusted by the Allies, would be an obstacle in the negotiations by which the prime minister hoped to obtain an earlier liberation of the territory from Allied occupation. Once the king and Richelieu had been won over, the other ministers reluctantly fell into line. The decision to dissolve the chamber was taken in the middle of August, and the dissolution ordinance was signed on September 5, 1816.

The reason given for the dissolution was very astute. The king said he saw the need to go back to the letter of the Charter by bringing the number of deputies down to 262 and their age back up to forty. This would require new elections, and these would be carried out under the provisions laid down by the Ordinance of July 21, 1815. This last statement was rather astonishing because it would mean relying on the same voters who had elected the "Chambre Introuvable"; but there was no other way out, since the government had not succeeded in getting a new electoral law passed.

The foreign governments unreservedly approved this step which they had urged. In France the constitutionalists and liberals were delighted. Royer-Collard said a statue should be erected in honor of Decazes, and there were even scenes where former Jacobins were insulting Ultra-Royalists by shouting *Long Live the King!* In the Ultra camp and around the Count of Artois there was consternation and fury. Chateaubriand succeeded in publishing his book *De la Monarchie selon la Charte* (*On Monarchy According to the Charter*), in which he boldly developed the theory and program of parliamentary government by a royalist majority. To this he added a venomous postscript in which he insinuated that the king had had to give in to the pressure of his ministers: "We have often admired, in the most difficult decisions, the perspicacity of his views and the profoundness of his thoughts. Perhaps he thought that a contented France would send back these same deputies . . . and that after that it would no longer be possible to doubt what was the real opinion of France." Louis XVIII was deeply wounded by the irony in this passage. Decazes ordered the seizure of the work, and its author caused a small scandal by opposing the seizure in person. In the end Chateaubriand was punished by losing his title of minister of state and the pension which went with it. Such a petty revenge deeply embittered this great writer, without really hurting the success of his book at all; indeed it made it even more in demand.

What must one think of this sort of coup d'etat which the dissolution of the "Chambre Introuvable" appeared to be? History considers it to be a commendable act on the part of Decazes and the king; it is often thought of as a good attempt to dissociate the monarchy from reactionary elements and to bring it closer to that larger segment of the nation which was attached to the accomplishments of the Revolution. But it has not been sufficiently noticed that the Ordinance of September 5, 1816 at the same time thwarted the establishment in France of a real parliamentary government. The royalist majority, according to Chateaubriand's way of thinking, was about to found a regime where the authority of parliament was to be imposed on the cabinet and the sovereign himself, and it would have done it with every precaution not to lower the position of the crown. The same thing was to be done fifteen years later, but only by a revolution which was to strike a mortal blow against the monarchical principle. Besides, Decazes, by crushing an elective chamber in the name of royal authority, set a precedent for the fatal July Ordinances of 1830. Were they going to succeed at least in finding outside the Right the elements for a monarchist and liberal government? Were they going to succeed in reconciling men who had, up to then, been hostile to the monarchy? Decazes was going to try in the course of the next few years, but events were to thwart his hopes, and he was to learn that these leftist elements, far from rallying to an accommodating monarchy, would take advantage of the government's tolerance to prepare to overthrow it with more determination than ever. Then it would be necessary to have recourse again to that Right which they had con-

tinuously denounced before the public, which they had helped discredit and portrayed in the most exaggerated terms; indeed, in the
end they would have to hand over the monarchy itself to that party
and have the crown suffer too from its unpopularity.

Did Louis XVIII save or undermine the monarchy by signing the
Ordinance of September 5? It is an insoluble question, no doubt, but
it is also one that we are forced to think about.

# 10

⚜ ⚜ ⚜ ⚜ ⚜

# Richelieu and the Liberation
# of the Territory

## The Election of 1816 and the Parties

To have new elections under the same system and with the same electoral colleges that had chosen the "Chambre Introuvable" the year before could appear to be a risky gamble. Decazes jumped into the campaign with great zeal, and with no qualms about encroaching upon the functions of his colleague Lainé, the minister of the interior, who was too timorous and too upright to engage in such a dubious undertaking. The presidents of the departmental colleges, appointed by the king and by this very designation recommended to the voters as suitable candidates, were all deputies who had supported the moderate cabinet. Decazes encouraged all those who had not voted in 1815 to come out and vote, even those who were declared enemies of the monarchy and who had felt the severity of the Law of General Safety. The prefects and all government officials received orders to put pressure on the voters to vote against the "extreme" candidates in favor of men who are "pure but moderate, who do not belong to any party, to any secret society . . . who do not believe that loving the king and serving him well exempts them from obeying the laws." The tightly controlled press was used to spread the most sinister accusations against the Ultras, such as their desire to reimpose the church tithe and feudal rights.

The pure royalists (Ultras) reacted vigorously with the support of the Count of Artois and powerful organizations (to be discussed later). A large number of prefects were on their side and did not hesitate to campaign against the ministry.

In general the departments of the south and west returned the same deputies, while those of the north and east supported the government. In certain electoral colleges where the Ultras foresaw defeat they had recourse to obstructive tactics by withdrawing en masse to make the voting impossible for a lack of a legal quorum. That is why only 238 deputies were elected out of 262 seats to be filled. Of this number elected the Ultras had only ninety-two, the other 146 supported the Moderate cabinet. Among these supporters were at least a dozen who were at heart opposed to the dynasty but whose fear of reaction would make them secondhand ministerial supporters. Under these new conditions the representative system set up by the Charter could function normally because the three authorities —king, cabinet, and parliamentary majorities—were in agreement.

It is at this point that we can see the political parties become more clearly distinguished and more positively associated with certain men, ideas, newspapers, and organizations. This differentiation was to appear more often as a result of the pressure of events than as an outgrowth of preconceived ideas, more through opposition or defense reactions than by positive programs. In other words, it was by opposing each other that the parties were to take their stands, and this explains how they emerged from their early nebulous state by a sort of biological process of cell division.

The first to take shape was the Ultra-Royalist Party, as it was called by its adversaries; its supporters simply called the group "royalists" or "pure royalists." By this they meant to contrast their unqualified loyalty with the questionable devotion of the men of the Revolution and Empire, who were only recent converts to the monarchy and, the royalists claimed, were adapting it to the new ideas. The Hundred Days having proved to the Ultra-Royalists the evils of a compromise policy, they intended, not to go back to the old Regime, of which they were so often accused, but rather to establish a new monarchical and religious regime based on the ideas which had matured in émigré circles and had even developed in France in the Catholic and romantic revival.

> France [wrote Chateaubriand] wants every liberty, every institution which comes in the course of time, changes in customs, new ideas, but all this along with the survival of the old monarchy, with the internal principles of justice and morality. . . . France wants the political and material interests created by the times and consecrated by the Charter, but she does not want the principles nor the men who have been responsible for our misfortunes.

Yet the party considered Viscount Bonald to be their real spokesman, and he considered the Charter to be "a work of folly and darkness." The party's newspapers were the *Gazette de France* and the *Quotidienne,* edited by Michaud, intransigent defender of the union of throne and altar. "We, on our side, shoot from the windows of the sacristy," he said. The *Journal des Débats,* belonging to the Bertin brothers and influenced by Chateaubriand, was the most influential paper of the period with its 27,000 subscribers. In 1819 it would take over Martainville's *Drapeau blanc,* which was famous for its excessive demagogic violence. To avoid legal interference, the Ultras were also to make use of some publications issued irregularly but qualifying as real magazines, such as the *Correspondance politique et administrative,* edited by Fiévée, a man who had an extremely brillant mind but whose widely known unusual morals put him out on the fringe of good society, and one other, the *Conservateur,* which, between October 1818 and March 1820, had a short but dazzling career under the direction of Chateaubriand.

The main trump card in the party's hand, its hope and its chief, was the very brother of the king, the Count of Artois. When they wanted to refer to his influence without calling him by name, they would speak of the "Marsan Pavilion," which was the part of the Louvre assigned as his residence. His small group of confidential advisors—Baron Vitrolles, the Count of Bruges, and Jules de Polignac—formed a sort of backroom government and was sometimes also called "the green cabinet" because green was the count's color. The Count of Artois, having been appointed colonel general of the national guards of the entire kingdom, with the right to choose all officers, his loyal followers took advantage of this to eliminate from the militia all who disagreed with their ideas and to make it a regular domestic army in the service of the party. Lastly the secret society of the Knights of the Faith (*Chevaliers de la Foi*), organized to combat the Empire and becoming almost inactive under the First Restoration, had sprung to life again, after the second return of the king, to combat the Talleyrand-Fouché ministry and the Orleanist schemes. Another Ultra society was the Regenerated Free-Masons (*Francs-Régénérés*), which had at this time broken away from Masonry and competed with it briefly until the end of its short existence. A considerable part of the clergy was favorable to the ideas of Artois' party and worked in its behalf. One can easily guess the power and means of influence that this support could bring to its cause.

The cohesion of this party in the chamber of deputies was remarkable. "It was seen to rise, sit, speak, and remain silent as one man," remarked Molé. This discipline was the work of the Knights of the Faith through the "banner" it founded in the chamber at the opening of the session of 1815. They agreed upon tactics in a secret committee, and thereafter passed the word along to nonmembers in the meetings held in the home of deputy Piet, a man so unimportant that he caused no jealousy to arise. The real parliamentary party leader was Count Joseph de Villèle, ex-mayor of Toulouse, who turned out to be, in the "Chambre Introuvable," a tireless debater and a smart tactician. With his friend Corbière, deputy from Ille-et-Vilaine and a sharp orator, he was to become the pivot of the Ultra-Royalist party in the chamber in the course of its years of tough fighting. In the chamber of peers, where the pure royalists also found themselves in a minority, the leaders were naturally Chateaubriand, Mathieu de Montmorency, and Jules de Polignac. The last two, like Villèle, were members of the national council of the Knights of the Faith.

The "Constitutional" party traced its birth to a reaction against the extreme positions held by the Ultra-Royalist party, just as the latter developed from its opposition to the policy of compromise of the First Restoration and to the regime of the Hundred Days. It began to emerge from the royalist majority in the later days of the parliamentary session of 1815–1816; and the elections of October 1816 gave it consistency by rallying behind the cabinet all those who repudiated the methods and doctrines of the Ultra-Royalist party. Such a negative policy obviously led to many gradations of attitudes, and in consequence this party was never to have the same tactical cohesion or doctrinal unity as its adversaries. Left and right wings were to appear; the latter, represented in the cabinet by Richelieu and Lainé, were less distant in theory than in method from the Ultra-Royalists; the left wing, represented in the cabinet by Decazes and Gouvion-Saint-Cyr, stood for a political system opposed to that of the Ultras. The development of its views was the work of a small group of intellectuals, known as the "doctrinaires": Camille Jordan, Guizot, Barante, the Count of Serre, the young Duke of Broglie, and later Charles de Rémusat. They recognized Royer-Collard as their master, whose speeches in the chamber were real treatises on political philosophy. Their influence was disproportionate to their numbers. "There are four of them," a leftist journal said mockingly, "and they sometimes boast that there are only three because it seems to them impossible to have four heads to such a force, but at other times they claim there are five of them when they want to frighten their opponents by their large numbers." Decazes showed much favor toward them because they seemed useful to him. They were just the ones to furnish him with high-sounding theoretical reasons to dress up the political attitudes growing out of his tactical requirements. Their official paper at that time was an uninspiring magazine called the *Archives philosophiques, politiques et littéraires.* As for the ministerial party as a whole, it had, besides the *Moniteur,* which was always a governmental paper, the *Journal général de France,* whose political line was taken from Royer-Collard.

The last one to take shape, the party of the Independents, separated from the Constitutional (or Moderate) party during the summer of 1817. Under this name were hidden all the enemies of the regime who did not dare avow their real connections: republicans, Bonapartists, and Orleanists. At first they had mixed their votes with those of the constitutional royalists; but, as soon as they felt strong enough —that is, after the elections of October 1817—they formed, at the extreme left of the chamber, a distinct antiministerial group under the leadership of Casimir Périer, Dupont de l'Eure, the banker Laffitte, and in October 1818 La Fayette and Manuel, and later in 1819 Benjamin Constant. The more important members of the group held regular meetings at one or another of their homes, constituting thereby an "executive committee," in opposition to the Marsan Pavilion and to the national council of the Knights of the Faith, and corresponding with its members and election committees in all the provinces. It is suspected that the Free Masons, most of whom were honorary members, played a role in it, as they did formerly in the organization of the "patriot" party in 1789. In any case its doctrines were just the same as those of Free Masonry of the eighteenth century: popular sovereignty, individual liberty, and hatred of the Catholic Church. When the Bonapartists joined this Independent group and took over more and more control, they added military nationalism and the idea of revenge against the treaties of 1815, as well as a tendency to have recourse to violent methods, somewhat foreign to the liberal spirit. Benjamin Constant was the brains of the party, La Fayette its flag, and Laffitte its moneylender. Because its papers were constantly hit by censorship, they only survived by making themselves infinitely variable, the same team of editors publishing successively a series of papers with different names, suppressed almost as soon as published. Thus, in the one year of 1818, there were fifty-six different Independent newspapers. The best known, because they lasted longest, were the *Constitutionnel* and the *Journal du Commerce.* Benjamin

Constant furnished the prototype which set the example for the Ultras to publish the *Conservateur,* with the *Minerve,* an irregularly published magazine appearing from January 1818 on.

## The New Chambers and the Electoral Law

The principal affair in the session of 1816–1817 was the debate over the electoral law, which had remained tabled during the preceding year. Proposed by Lainé as minister of the interior, it was in fact the work of the doctrinaires. It had the advantage of proposing a simple system quite in accord with the Charter: permitting the vote only to citizens attaining the age of thirty and paying a direct tax of three hundred francs (sixty dollars); providing for elections by a meeting of all voters in the chief town of the department; stating that the president of the electoral college would be appointed by the king and would choose his own secretary and tellers; lastly, assuming that the elections of one-fifth of the chamber would be held each year as provided in the Charter.

The bill favored the constitutional and ministerial party in that it permitted the government to act upon the voters by the combined influence of the prefect and the office of the electoral college; it worked against the Ultra-Royalists, first of all, because it thwarted their hope of influencing the primary assemblies in the cantons and arrondissements, assemblies where the weight of the local nobles and the clergy could be felt; second, because, since the election procedure took place over a period of several days, it required a long and costly absence from home for the landholders, usually Ultra-Royalist voters, while the townsmen, from among whom came most of the liberals, were living right where it all took place.

Naturally, it was not these selfish party interests, but rather great principles, which were invoked on both sides in the hot debate lasting almost two months. The new electoral system, passed in the chamber of deputies by a vote of 132 to one hundred and in the chamber of peers by a vote of ninety-five to seventy-seven, was promulgated on February 8, 1817. The government then had the Law of General Safety renewed for another year, reserving arrests and detentions without trial only for the ministers themselves. Another law kept the press in its straitjacket by forcing newspapers to obtain prior authorization.

The rest of the session was taken up mainly with the budget. The payments on the war indemnity and the occupation caused the

unavoidable expenditures to increase to 1,069 million francs ($213,800,-
000) while the possible tax receipts were only 774 million ($154,800,-
000). This steep deficit of 295 million francs (59 million dollars) therefore had to be provided for by extraordinary means. A serious famine
had hit the country during the winter of 1816 to 1817 and had required
unforeseen expenditures, reduced tax collections, and immobilized available funds of French capitalists, so that it was impossible to launch
a domestic loan. The government had to appeal to foreign investors,
and, as we shall see below, at Draconian rates of interest. In addition, it
wanted to sell 375,000 acres of national forests. As in the previous year,
and for the same reasons (former church ownership of these forests),
the Right vigorously opposed it, and, not being able to eliminate this
section, voted against the whole budget. This attitude, which would today
appear entirely normal, was then considered revolutionary. It created
a precedent which could make it impossible for the king's government to
function if faced with a hostile majority.

The chasm between the ministry and the Ultra minority became
wider because of a reorganizing of the cabinet. Already in January
1815, Chancellor Dambray had again given up the ministry of justice
in favor of Pasquier. Decazes insisted also on eliminating the minister
of the navy, Dubouchage (June 1817), and Marshal Clarke (September 12), since they were both Ultras. The ministry of war was given
to Gouvion-Saint-Cyr and that of the navy to Molé, formerly Napoleon's minister of justice, who had even accepted a position during
the Hundred Days.

The first partial elections, provided for in the new law, took place
on September 20, 1817. The Right lost a dozen seats to the ministerial
party, but the latter lost as many to the Independents of the Left, who
now found themselves strong enough (twenty-five) to make demands.
Their opposition, combined with that of the Right, first of all defeated,
early in the session, a new press law. They then reconciled themselves
briefly with the cabinet to join in passing the important military law prepared by Marshal Gouvion-Saint-Cyr.

Three principal points characterized this bill. In the first place,
the army was to be recruited partly by voluntary enlistments and
partly by an annual draft selected by lot. The size of the standing
army was fixed at 240,000 men, and the number called up by the
draft would be at least forty thousand a year. Those who drew the
unlucky numbers would be allowed to provide substitutes. The Right
objected that the law was reinstituting the detested conscription in
violation of the solemn promises of the king and the Charter.

In the second place, active service lasted six years after which the released servicemen would still be subject, in case of need, to a home guard service of six years. It was a sort of army reserve composed of veterans. The Right said that if they applied this section immediately, it would mean the recall of the old imperial army, whose attitude was only too well known.

The strongest attacks were against the third point. To become an officer, one had to have served two years as a noncommissioned officer or to have been graduated from a military school. To be promoted to a higher rank, one had to serve four years in the next lower rank. Two-thirds of those in officer ranks, up to and including that of lieutenant colonel, would be promoted by seniority, the rest by the choice of the king. These provisions raised a storm of protest from the nobility which had been accustomed, under the Old Regime, to reserve for itself practically all the officer appointments. But the principal objection that the Right brought forward was that the king could not give up a prerogative which had already been reserved for him by the Charter in his position as head of the executive power and which had always belonged to him. They also stressed that this system of automatic promotion could bring a large number into the officer corps who would be politically unreliable.

The discussion in the chamber was often very heated, for the orators of the Left and the minister of war himself took occasion to give warm praise to the soldiers of the Empire. The alarm aroused by the bill was such that the vote in the chamber of peers was obtained by only a very small margin and thanks to a stratagem of the king's. At the very hour that the vote was being taken in the upper house he prolonged his daily drive in such a way as to detain the dukes of Havré, Avaray, and La Châtre, whose votes would have been enough to defeat the law. In fact the veteran reserves were never set up, and, after the departure of Gouvion-Saint-Cyr, promotion by the king's choice was re-established under cover of various stratagems. The only lasting result of the memorable parliamentary battle was the raising of the standing army from 150,000 to 240,000.

Richelieu, in spite of his own dislikes, had, in the debate on the military law, supported Decazes and Gouvion-Saint-Cyr in the hope of softening up the Left on another important question, that of a new concordat with the pope negotiated in 1817. This will be dealt with later. All we need to note here is that his hope was dashed and that this affair, conducted with unexampled clumsiness, ended in a pitiful failure.

The session of 1818, however, closed with more reassuring perspectives. Richelieu had just obtained a diplomatic success which would soon end the foreign occupation of France; and the budget of that year was approved without any difficulty.

The parliamentary sessions lasted only four or five months, but during that time the controversies were very sharp because the government could not prevent the publication of the debates in full in the newspapers. But whether or not the quarrels showed up in the press, the fight went on endlessly and bitterly among the political parties. Since the Ordinance of September 5, 1816 dissolving the "Chambre Introuvable," Decazes had been the target of the hostility of the Ultra-Royalist party, which heaped on him endless insulting accusations. The tone of the salons is revealed by this reply to him by a great lady of that day. "But Madame," Decazes asked her, "do you know to what party I belong and to what party you belong?" "I certainly do," she replied, "I belong to the party they guillotine; you belong to the one they hang." In October 1816 people circulated a cartoon showing Decazes putting a red bonnet on the king's head, while the minister of the interior was taking off his outer trousers. "You see I am a sans-culotte too," the monarch was saying. One strange circumstance was that the candidate of the ministerial or Moderate party was that same Talleyrand whom it had ejected in 1815. This skillful intriguer had made his peace with the Ultra party because it was the only one to help him get back into power, and because he had had a very notorious falling out with Decazes after having insulted him in public. "M. Pasquier," he once shouted in a loud voice in a salon, "believe me in what I just told you a while ago, that a minister of police is nothing but a pimp and that a chamber, without lowering itself, can have no relations with him."

At the end of April 1817 the former royal favorite, Blacas, made an unexpected return to Paris from his embassy in Rome. It was thought that he was going to get back his influence over the king and overthrow Decazes, but Louis XVIII received him very coolly and forced him to go back faster than he had come. The Count of Artois had no better luck when he tried to intervene directly with the king early in 1818. Using his fanciest style—that is, the style of his brain-trust—he wrote to the king, "Sire, my brother and lord, a longer silence on my part, in present circumstances, would seem to me contrary to my duty . . ." and he asked a shake-up of his cabinet for the good of the dynasty and the country. They had a stormy interview in which both brothers wept. Artois threatened to retire to

Fontainebleau, then to Spain. "No," replied the king, "you will not imitate the miserable brother of Louis XIII." Finally the king drew up a long reply, carefully composed, in which he defended point by point the policies of his cabinet. "The system I have adopted and which my cabinet is carrying out unflinchingly is founded on the maxim that I must not be a king of two peoples, and that all the efforts of my government should tend to make these two peoples, and they are too much split in two, united once again. . . . The crown belongs to all . . . but the older brother wears it, that is, he is the only one who exercises the rights under it and he is the only judge and responsible one on how to exercise them. The closer the rank of a prince brings him to the throne [Artois was the heir], the more his duty and interest require him to strengthen and have respected the authority of him who wears it [the crown]. I cannot, without a shudder, look ahead to the time when I shall close my eyes. You will then find yourself caught between two parties, one of which feels it is oppressed by me and the other of which fears it will be by you. . . ." These royal and prophetic words were unfortunately to fall upon deaf ears.

Decazes, for his part, counterattacked with an unscrupulous vigor, using all the resources of the police to discredit his adversaries in the eyes of the king and public opinion. He used his spy system to lift from private correspondence uncomplimentary remarks about the king and then revealed them to him. The police reports, written to be shown to the king, imputed all sorts of intrigues and disorders to the Ultras. Louis XVIII became convinced that everything would run smoothly if it were not for them. Decazes paid for news service abroad and sent to the London *Times* and to papers in Germany articles written in his own offices, as if they were written by the Paris correspondents of these papers and thus less suspected of partiality. Then the ministerial papers would quote these articles without comment. It was in this way that they were able to attack the Count of Artois and his friends without being discovered. Sometimes they were represented as fomenting trouble by frightening the country with the ghosts of Jacobinism and Bonapartism; at other times they were portrayed as organizing for a civil war to overthrow the legal government and replace Louis XVIII with his brother. And finally the most telling argument, because it hit the sensitive patriotic nerve made raw by the defeat and the presence of foreign troops, these articles seemed to lend credence to the idea that the Ultras were so fearful of a liberal come-back that they really wanted an indefinite prolonging of the Allied occupation. Several other affairs, still unfathomed even to-day, added to the campaign.

## Disturbances in the Provinces

On June 8, 1817 an insurrection took place in the city of Lyons. In eleven surrounding communes, armed groups began to gather and march toward the city, flying the tricolored flag. At the same time attacks were being directed against the government authorities in Lyons itself. These officials, being on their guard, easily put the movement down and proceeded to make numerous arrests. The provost courts went into action and eleven of those indicted were guillotined. The central government also approved the repression. But the prosecution charges revealed that the police had played some part in the plot through provocative agents, and on second thought the security measures taken by the local officials did seem excessive. The government finally decided to send Marshal Marmont down there with special investigative powers. He was accompanied by Colonel Fabvier, his chief of staff, a hot-headed liberal. The latter thought he had found evidence to prove that the whole affair from beginning to end was gotten up by the prefect of the Rhone, the Count of Chabrol, and General Canuel, the regional military commander, all of this in order to win honors and rewards for themselves. Marmont stopped the trials and brought charges against General Canuel. To tell the truth the general was a rascal, but Prefect Chabrol was an upright man, incapable of having collaborated in such an infamous plan. The central government was so embarrassed that it decided to dismiss Chabrol and Canuel, but give them new and better positions. However, the affair was not to end there: Fabvier and Marmont brought it all out in the open in pamphlets against which the interested parties replied with vigor. Decazes was happy to let this dispute go on because it helped to throw the blame on the whole Ultra-Royalist party for the suspected activities of Canuel and to make it seem that the Ultras were lending themselves to provoking uprisings in order to undermine the cabinet's policy of reconciliation and pacification.

Early in the summer of 1818 two other affairs, more or less connected, gave Decazes a chance to compromise his adversaries still further. The Count of Artois had asked Vitrolles to draw up a note on the domestic situation in France which would be communicated to the Allied sovereigns before the Congress of Aix-la-Chapelle. Vitrolles, pressed for time, drew up a hasty report without consulting anyone. A copy of this document fell into the hands of Decazes, who had parts of it published under the title of *Secret Note,* which left the impression that the original note was an appeal to the Allies to prolong the occupation of France. In fact, what Vitrolles was asking was their intervention to change the present ministry, and if he thought at all about the prolongation of the occupation, it was to reject it as a wrong and impractical idea. The real danger in his line of argument was that he represented the internal situation as critical, leading to a new explosion of Jacobinism because of the cabinet's policy. If this danger was possible, the Allies might very well hesitate to evacuate France in the near future. The leaders of the Ultra-Royalist party, with Villèle at their head, highly disapproved this published note when they read it. Vitrolles was punished by being deprived of his title of minister of state. But Decazes and the liberals seized upon this incident to denounce the antipatriotic attitude of their opponents.

The so-called affair of "the Conspiracy at the Water's Edge" is even more fantastic. At the end of June 1818 the cabinet was tipped off to a conspiracy which had been supposedly uncovered by the police. It was said to be a plan to seize the ministers with the aid of a segment of the royal guard, to impose a new cabinet on Louis XVIII, and, in case he refused them, to depose him, indeed to give him the "Paul I" treatment (assassination). The leaders were supposed to be General Canuel and General Donnadieu; and Chateaubriand and other persons in the Ultra-Royalist party were said to be involved. Decazes hurried to publicize it through the anonymous news items in the London *Times,* which even connected the brother of the king with it. Richelieu, without believing in the story of the plot, let the authorities make some arrests in the hope that they would help clear up the rumors. It all proved to be nothing but some wild gossip by disgruntled people, who may have stirred up these ideas without any intention of carrying them out. This wild talk had been overheard and exaggerated by some minor police agents with the hope of making an impression on their superior. The liberals themselves emphasized the enormity of the police trickiness. But the affair was useful to Decazes in helping to cause dissension between Louis XVIII and his brother.

On the following September 30 an ordinance took away from Artois all his powers over the national guard, whose central office was abolished. Henceforth it was supposed to be a purely local force, entirely under the orders of mayors and prefects. The latter were requested to reorganize it by eliminating the elements too favorable to the Ultra-Royalists.

This sudden action was designed to prevent Artois' party from using national guard units to give directions in the October elections of another fifth of the chamber of deputies. The Ultra voters, by then discouraged, stayed away from the election meetings in large numbers, and their candidates lost almost everywhere, a loss of fifteen seats in the chamber. But the government party was not much more successful, losing four seats. The big winners were the Independents of the extreme Left, who won about twenty more seats. La Fayette and Manuel, declared enemies of the dynasty, reappeared on the political scene.

This result, coinciding with Richelieu's diplomatic effort, was to bring on a ministerial crisis.

## Aix-la-Chapelle and the End of Occupation

The liberation of the territory from foreign occupation had been for two years the main objective of all Richelieu's efforts, and only the realization that he was the best man to accomplish this gave him the courage to endure the disgusting and bothersome situations of domestic politics.

From the month of April 1816 on, he had been bringing up the idea of a reduction in the size of the occupation forces by arguing that the cost of their upkeep—130 million francs a year (26 million dollars)—was an unbearable burden on the French budget. The Allied sovereigns tended to pass the responsibility on this question back to Wellington, the commander of the occupation troops. He, on the other hand, needed a lot of persuasion—a commander never likes to see a reduction in his command. After some direct and urgent intervention by the tsar, the Iron Duke finally softened and gave his consent in February 1817, but absolved himself of any responsibility for the awful consequences which, according to him, could not fail to happen. After April 1, 1817 the occupation force was to be reduced by thirty thousand men (one-fifth) which eased considerably this burden on the budget.

Still this was not enough to allow the treasury to face the due-date of the war indemnity of 700 million francs (140 million dollars), which was supposed to be paid in installments of forty-five million (nine million dollars) every four months. Richelieu was determined to set everything in motion to meet these installments. It was a question of his and the king's word of honor, and this was the only lever he had to hold the Allies faithful to their own signatures. Because of the impossibility of borrowing money in France, he had to go to the banking houses of Hope (in Amsterdam) and Baring (in London). Yet the insecurity of the French economy, where state bonds had fallen to forty francs (eight dollars)—on one hundred (twenty dollars) face-value—at the end of 1816, gave an excuse to foreign bankers to impose harsh terms. In brief, without entering into technical financial details, this meant that France had to borrow a nominal capital of 384 million francs ($76,800,000) in order to obtain as money in hand a real capital of 187 million ($37,400,000) on which she would have to pay an annual interest of seventeen million ($3,400,000). In other words Hope and Baring would be realizing a profit of a hundred per cent on the capital loaned if the state bonds went back up to par, and, until that day, they would also receive interest of nine-and-a-half per cent of the sums involved!

This costly operation at least gave France the means for living up to her financial obligations. But there was another kind of obligation imposed by the Treaty of Paris which also had to be fulfilled before she could hope to achieve the end of the occupation. This was the payment of the debts contracted by previous French governments toward individuals in the countries occupied by French armies. Richelieu, in signing this convention, and the Allies themselves, had estimated that the total sum of this would run around two hundred million francs (forty million dollars). However, once the claims were all in—over 135,000—the sum was up to 1,600 million francs (320 million dollars). These individuals had included the oldest and most absurd sort of debts: for example, the Duke of Anhalt-Bernburg claimed the settlement of a contract for furnishing mercenary troops by one of his ancestors to Henry IV!

Honest Richelieu was flabbergasted at such extravagant claims. "That extinguishes," he groaned, "the last glimmer of hope that we could see in the distance." Nevertheless, the Allies themselves were to realize that the enormous size of the sum was way beyond France's ability to pay. After many conversations and efforts, Richelieu accepted the proposal, offered by the tsar, to submit it to Wellington's arbitration. Richelieu had declared in September 1817 that France could not pay more than 200 million (forty million dollars). Wellington, after a minute examination of the documents, came up in April 1818 with a sum of 240 million (48 million dollars) and would not make any concessions beyond that. On April 15, the final convention was signed whereby France added 12,040,000 francs ($2,408,000) of *rentes* (dividend payments on bonds) to the great book of public debts, corresponding to a nominal capital of 240 million francs (48 million dollars). The distribution was determined in detail: for example, the Prussian creditors, who received the largest share, obtained two million francs ($400,000) in annual income.

To meet this added obligation, the French minister of finance, Corvetto, decided to float a bond issue in France itself; at the same time the chamber authorized him to make a new appeal to foreign capital in order to pay the remaining indemnity installments in one lump sum. This loan was also made through the banks of Hope and Baring. In 1817 they had taken the French bonds at the quotation of fifty-five francs (eleven dollars) on one hundred, but now in 1818 they were willing to take them at the rate of sixty-seven—a recognition of the improvement in French financial credit. As to the domestic part of the loan, it was offered to the public in May 1818, with the government asking for 14,500,000 francs ($2,900,000) of subscriptions. The public response was a subscription of 163 million ($32,600,000), twelve times what the government had asked. This had a big moral effect, with the government bonds rising to eighty in August 1818. The Allies were sorry that they had been so easy on France; and perhaps the royal government also regretted that it had underestimated the country's wealth and had thereby permitted the foreign capitalists to make such favorable deals for themselves at the expense of France. In any case Richelieu now had the means of obtaining the end of the occupation.

From the beginning of 1818 the Allies had realized that they had no interest in prolonging the military occupation of France beyond the minimum period of three years as provided in the Treaty of Paris. Even though the occupation had been intended to help the consolidation of the royal government, it had only weakened it by arousing national sentiment against it. If it did help put pressure on France to fulfill the financial clauses of the treaty, yet, when these had been carried out, there seemed to be no good reason for keeping an occupation force. So the Allies announced, in May 1818, their intention to call a congress at Aix-la-Chapelle in September, and Louis XVIII was invited to send a representative there. Naturally Richelieu went as that representative.

The congress was opened on September 30, 1818, and by October 9 an agreement had been signed. Foreign troops would be withdrawn from France by November 30, and the sum which France promised to pay immediately as indemnity was fixed at 265 million francs (53 million dollars) instead of 286 million ($57,200,000).

Having done this, the Allies considered what guarantees they should seek for the future. No doubt, as long as Richelieu was in power, they could have confidence in his good judgment and reliability, but the attacks leveled at his government made them wonder how long he would be staying in office. So the Allies decided to renew the Quadruple Alliance in the form of a secret treaty, to make it less humiliating to France. On the other hand France was publicly invited to take part in the international meetings provided for in Article VI of the Treaty of November 25, 1815. Consequently the following note was handed to Richelieu:

> The August Sovereigns have seen with satisfaction that the order of things so happily established in France by the restoration of the legitimate and constitutional monarchy and the success which has crowned up to now the paternal efforts of His Most Christian Majesty fully justify the hope of a progressive strengthening of that order of things so essential for the repose and prosperity of France. . . . [Therefore they invite the king] to unite his efforts and counsels with theirs and take part in their present and future deliberations, devoted to the maintenance of peace, of the treaties upon which it depends, and of the rights and mutual relations established or confirmed by their treaties. . . .

Richelieu, after having received instructions from the king, thereafter sat in the sessions with the four great powers and signed with them, on November 15, the protocols at the close of the congress. "The job will be short and favorable, I hope," Richelieu had written at the moment of his departure for Aix-la-Chapelle, "and France, left now to herself, will re-enter the European community." And now his hope was fulfilled. The people commemorated this liberation in this way: the vintage of the year 1818 having been exceptionally good, the wine-growers in the East called their wine of that year "the departure wine," for the departure of foreign troops.

Richelieu came back to Paris on November 28 and found a full cabinet crisis on his hands. The minister of interior, Lainé, had been very much impressed by the results of the recent elections. His theory was that there was no longer a danger to the government from the Right, but rather from the Left. It was now necessary, he thought, to effect a reconciliation with the Ultras, against whom they had fought too exclusively, so they could present a common front of all sincere royalists against the rising tide of "jacobinism." Decazes did not look at the situation in the same light; he had fought too hard against the Right to ever consent to collaborate with it; such a change in approach would imply his leaving office. Richelieu entirely agreed with Lainé. While at Aix-la-Chapelle he had gained the impression that the Allies no longer feared, as in 1816, any reactionary excesses, but now rather they apprehended a revival of the Revolutionary spirit of which certain symptoms had begun to appear in Germany and Italy as well as in France.

But how could a government keep going without the king's favorite? Richelieu did not care whether he himself stayed in power or not, and he considered his job done with the liberation of the territory. So he submitted his resignation to the king on December 21. Louis XVIII, who could see no alternative other than a Talleyrand cabinet, which he would avoid at any price, begged Richelieu to form a new cabinet. Richelieu insisted as a first condition the dropping of the favorite. There followed several days of feverish and chaotic discussions, of tearful scenes and unforeseen reversals, a real "week of dupes," Decazes playing the comedy role in public of being the sacrificial lamb and behind the scenes doing all he could to wreck any plans which left him out. Richelieu, disheartened and sick with nervous exhaustion, finally realized that the king would not forgive him if he dropped his favorite and so he submitted his unconditional resignation on December 26.

At the beginning of the next session the two chambers decided to vote the Duke of Richelieu a national recompense in the form of a life income of fifty thousand francs (ten thousand dollars). However, he hastened to reply to the president of the chamber of deputies: "I can not bring myself to see myself as the cause for adding anything to the burdens of the nation. . . . Too many calamities have come to it, too many of its citizens have suffered misfortune, there are too many losses to be repaired for me to be able to see my fortune increased in these times. The esteem of my country, the kindness of the king, and the satisfaction of my conscience is all that I crave." When the chamber insisted on awarding the pension, Richelieu gave the money to the hospitals of Bordeaux—a noble gesture which had more admirers than imitators.

# 11

✤ ✤ ✤ ✤ ✤

# Decazes and the Liberal Experiment

## The Policy of the New Ministry

AT the time of his resignation, Richelieu had suggested Marshals Marmont and Macdonald to the king as possible presidents of the council. But these two men were not pleasing to Decazes; both of them had minds of their own and would not have allowed him much freedom of action. So the king's favorite suggested General Dessolles, who, in April 1814, had accepted the command of the Paris national guard in a critical moment and who had received from Louis XVIII a title of nobility as a reward for his services. He had a shrewd and cultivated mind but a weak personality without political appeal. With him at the head Decazes would be the real leader in the government because he controlled the ministries of interior and police. Dessolles himself took over the ministry of foreign affairs, in which his ignorance of Europe was to confine him to a prudent do-nothing policy. Baron Louis came back into the finance ministry to replace Corvetto, and Marshal Gouvion-Saint-Cyr stayed on in the war ministry. Two new men arrived on the political scene: Portal as minister of the navy and the Count of Serre as keeper of the seal (minister of justice). The former was a Bordeaux merchant who had been a member of the council of state under Napoleon and a deputy since 1816; as a Protestant he represented an assurance of toleration on the part of the new ministry. Hercule de Serre was one of the most engaging personalities of this period, and his premature death was to be a real misfortune for the monarchy. As a former officer and émigré, he had come back to accept a judgeship under the Empire. The first Restoration had appointed him as president of the royal court of Colmar, and he had proudly refused to serve Napoleon during the Hundred Days. The department of Haut-Rhin had elected him to the "Chambre Introuvable," where he had split from the Ultras during the debate on the Amnesty Law. His judicial mind and his naturally generous temperament would not allow him to go along with the Ultras' twisted interpretations of the Charter, nor with the spirit of revenge which so colored their speeches. He therefore came more and more under the influence of Royer-Collard until he was considered practically a member of the doctrinaire group. Like Richelieu he came from the old pre-Revolutionary aristocracy, but did not share its prejudices; and again like him he had a lofty outlook. The strong feeling he showed for the causes he supported, the brilliant and warm eloquence with which he defended them, were to make him a political force of the first order.

What was the policy of this new ministry? Gouvion-Saint-Cyr explained it to Molé with typical military bluntness: "All our troubles go back to the reaction in 1815. Now we must reassure the nation by showering it with all the guarantees it demands and launching ourselves frankly into the liberal stream while at the same time reserving to ourselves the possibility of suspending the Charter and substituting bayonets if it takes too much advantage of our concessions." Decazes himself expressed it this way: "Monarchize the nation, and nationalize the monarchy"—a nice way to put it, but as imprecise as it was dangerous. It was fine if they intended by this phrase to adjust the old monarchy to the society emerging from the Revolution; but, if they meant the word "nation" to be a synonym for the French people, it would imply a distortion of facts. A large segment, numerically a majority of the French people had no need to be "monarchized"; on the other hand the patriotism of most of the pure royalists (Ultras) was no less sincere and no less susceptible than that boasted of by the liberals. Was it wise for a king's minister to accept the point of view of the enemies of the regime who claimed to see a conflict between national sentiment and monarchical sentiment?

At any rate, this new policy was imposed on the ministry by the parliamentary situation. Richelieu had governed with a Center party, opposing equally the ever-dwindling Ultra-Royalists on the right and the ever-increasing antidynastic left. Even this Center was itself split in two directions: the Right-Center led by Lainé and the Left-Center of the doctrinaires. The only assured point of support for the Dessolles-Decazes ministry (cabinet) was the Left-Center; to this they added the Right-Center which still refused to think of collaborating with the Ultra extreme Right. But these two groups were not enough to make a majority. Consequently the survival of the ministry depended upon the goodwill of the independent Left, and the latter would be tempted to take advantage of it. "The nation," wrote Paul-Louis Courier in those days, "will make the government follow its route like a hired coachman who has to take you, not where and as he wishes, but where we intend to go and by the road we choose."

## Controlling the Peers and Freeing the Press

The first measures taken by the ministry were in the direction of satisfying the left. Within the short space of a few days Decazes replaced sixteen prefects and forty subprefects: "a slaughter of prefects," Barante called it. The council of state was overhauled to get rid of the Ultra members; stuffed with doctrinaires it became a handy laboratory for the legislative and administrative reforms required by the new political orientation. Gouvion-Saint-Cyr, for his part, put many émigré officers on the inactive list and turned their commands over to former general officers who had been compromised by the Hundred Days—General Foy was one of them. Lastly, Decazes issued authorizations for the return of fifty-two regicides and a number of other people who had been exiled in 1815.

But before it could begin to pass its legislative program, the cabinet had to break the unexpected opposition arising in the chamber of peers. The Right-Center was stronger there than in the chamber of deputies. It was called the "Cardinal group" because it planned its tactics at the residence of Cardinal Bausset. Richelieu's resignation caused it to go over to the opposition. This group, in agreement with the Ultra-Royalist Right, decided to go on the offensive immediately. On February 20, 1819 old Barthélemy, the former negotiator of the treaties of 1795, submitted to his colleagues a proposed resolution: "The king will be humbly supplicated to present to the chambers a law which may realize, in the organization of the electoral colleges, whatever urgent changes may seem necessary." In fact it involved, as everybody well understood, changes in the Electoral Law of 1817 so as to bring an end to liberal electoral victories. Excitement ran high in the press and in the two chambers. The executive committee of the Paris liberals tried to arouse public opinion against it. The government and the king himself used every method it could to bring pressure on individual peers. All was of no avail: the upper house on March 2 passed the Barthélemy proposal by a vote of ninety-eight to fifty-five. A few days later it rejected a government finance bill.

Louis XVIII finally decided to take action in line with what Decazes had been proposing since Richelieu's departure—that is, to change the majority in the upper house by packing it with a lot of new appointments.

Since the ministry had been beaten by a majority of forty-three, it seemed necessary to have a good margin. So the new appointments contained fifty-nine names of those who were, naturally, friends of the king's favorite. It is said that the king made a somewhat bitter remark to Decazes: "At least let me put my cousin d'Esclignac on the list so that somebody of mine will be there along with yours." This was a grave decision, a sort of coup d'état against the chamber of peers, resembling the coup d'état of September 5 against the "Chambre Introuvable." The Ultra-Royalists were exasperated by all this and even considered at one time withdrawing en masse from the parliament. The Duke of Berry dared to say before the king that he would no longer wear his peer's uniform "because it is dirty."

This action in the chamber of peers made it possible for the government to have a press law passed, which turned out to be the major piece of legislation of that session. The bill was prepared by a committee controlled by the doctrinaires: Royer-Collard, Guizot, Barante, and Broglie. The resulting system of press administration was one of the most ingenious and practical that could be imagined up to that time in reconciling freedom of expression with laws on morals and the requirements of public order. It was presented in the form of three distinct laws on, respectively, the definition of press violations and the penalties therefor, the procedure for enforcement, and the requirements for maintaining periodical publications. The first law was based on the principle that the press was only one way among several by which a misdemeanor, as provided by the code, could be committed: "An opinion, whatever it may be, does not become a crime by becoming public." There was therefore no reason to apply special restraints on publicity in itself, but only on misdemeanors in common law of which it may have been the vehicle, such as provocations of crimes, offenses against the person of the king, outrages against public morals and good behavior, libel and insults.

In the second law, dealing with procedures, the great innovation was removing such offenses from the cognizance of the correctional tribunals—which, however, still did retain jurisdiction over libel and insults against individuals—and transferring the rest to jury trial in the criminal courts. Most of the press misdemeanors consisted of attacks against government officials, and the judges, representing the government officials, needed to avoid the appearance of being at the same time judges and parties in the case.

The third law, dealing with newspapers, subjected them to a special set of rules because of their wide circulation. "The owner of a newspaper, in the present state of society, exercises a real power, and society has the right to be assured that this function will be faithfully carried out." Freedom would be real because the formerly required prior authorization to publish a journal and censorship would be abolished; but, in order to prevent violation by legal action, they had to know whom to indict and that no imposed fine would be evaded by the bankruptcy of the guilty. So every prospective newspaper had to furnish an advance declaration by two responsible editors and a deposit of ten thousand francs (two thousand dollars) in government bonds.

The Left opposed these bills as insufficient, while the Right remained silent, not wanting either to defend the liberal principles that it disavowed or to renounce the use of the facilities that it expected to obtain from the press. Only once did it intervene, to add the word "religious" to the phrase "public morals." The Keeper of the Seal, the Count of Serre, undertook almost single-handed the job of defending this legislation in debate, and his eloquence eventually carried the day in both chambers for this new press regime.

There followed naturally a big to-do in the press. The principal influence moved from pamphlets and irregularly published miscellanies to daily newspapers. From the Right and the Left the attacks became sharper against the ministry. To come to its defense, the doctrinaires started their own daily, the *Courier*—with one "r" as in English. But it was too high-class to make an impression on popular opinion, which is more easily influenced by invective than by reason. The government was given no credit for its meritorious and remarkable effort to give a new impulse to the economic life and to improve the administration of public assistance and prisons. "Public antipathy is such," wrote a public prosecutor at that time, "that no one dares to support the government or defend its ministers lest he expose himself to the most offensive of all outrages—that of being a ministerial backer."

Foreign governments were watching with concern the rising radical temperature in France, seemingly connected with the movement in Germany since early in 1819, which had moved Metternich to call a congress at Carlsbad in the month of August. The ambassador of Alexander I, Pozzo di Borgo, the very one who had urged the dissolution of the "Chambre Introuvable," wrote home to his master, "France has been entirely turned over to the people, interests, and spirit of the old army and to the ideological or anarchical doctrinaires. . . . This state of things . . . tends toward the fall of the legitimate dynasty . . . and an inevitable war in Europe."

## Grégoire's Election and the Reaction to It

Decazes counted on the election of the next annual fifth to bring a rise in his political stock, and he prepared assiduously for it. But the electoral committees of the Independents made even more careful preparations, helped as they were by the rancor and discouragement of the Ultras. Out of the fifty-five seats to be filled the Independents won thirty-five, winning twenty-five more votes in the chamber; the right lost ten seats and the ministry fifteen. Still more important than the returns was the symbolic meaning of the election in Grenoble of the constitutional bishop, Grégoire, the former member of the Revolutionary Convention and a regicide. He had not actually voted for the death of Louis XVI because he was absent from that session, but he took pains to write in to the Convention and associate himself with the act, following up on his earlier support of the indictment which had been expressed in these words: "Kings belong to a class of purulent creatures who were always the leprosy of governments and of the human race." His election was a clumsy enough liberal insult to the throne, but how is one to term the gesture of part of the Ultra voters in the Isère department (88 out of 220) who also voted for Grégoire rather than help the ministerial candidate? It was even more unpardonable because all they had had to do was abstain from voting to arrive at the same result.

The Ultra press broke out in strong expressions of indignation. Louis XVIII was himself much upset. "My brother," the Count of Artois remarked to him, "you see where they are trying to lead you." "Yes, my brother," he replied, "I'll take care of that."

To fulfill the king's expectations as well as to reassure foreign governments, Decazes resolved then and there to make a sharp turn to the Right. He began to make plans to change the electoral law in exactly the same direction that the chamber of peers had wanted it earlier in the year. Louis XVIII and Decazes sent an emissary to seek out Richelieu, then travelling in Holland, to beg him to become again the head of the government. When he positively refused, Decazes had to accept the presidency of the council and the full responsibility for the policy he intended to carry out. Dessolles was replaced in foreign affairs by Pasquier, always ready to do anything so long as he could remain a minister; General Latour-Maubourg replaced Gouvion-Saint-Cyr in the war ministry; and finance received the banker Roy, a deputy of the Right-Center. The Count of Serre and Portal, who approved the new political orientation, kept their portfolios (November 19) of justice and navy.

The opening of the parliamentary session was taken up with a hot debate on the case of Grégoire. The Left did not dare go down the line in defending him, and he was flatly denied his seat. After that, interest turned to the electoral law that the king had asked for in vague terms in his opening speech from the throne. Support from the Right was indispensable to obtain passage of such a law over the opposition of the Left and the Left-Center doctrinaires, who now turned against Decazes. "With Decazes there is no salvation," Royer-Collard was saying—the same man who in 1816 had wanted to raise a statue in Decazes' honor. The leaders of the royalist Right (the Ultras) were now very hesitant and divided on the tactics to be followed. Some of them, like Chateaubriand and La Bourdonnaye, wanted to take advantage of the situation to force the immediate resignation of Decazes by voting with the Left—they were called "the impatient ones." Others, like Villèle and Corbière, thought it more politic to let Decazes go through with his change in direction and make himself odious to his former political allies—the publicist, Fiévée dubbed them "the circumspect ones." When the government asked for a vote on the provisional six-twelfths of the budget, in the interim before the passage of the budget as a whole, the Right went along with it in spite of its repugnance. "We have given M. Decazes enough rations for six months," one deputy said.

But they never got around to the promised electoral law because an unexpected situation developed. The Count of Serre, who had prepared the bill and intended to present it and defend it, had to go south for his health. Decazes, much upset, at first did not know who could possibly replace him; he lost a lot of time in indefinite consultations with representatives of the Right, who were very demanding because they knew that they had the minister at their mercy. The Left, on the other hand, did all they could to counter the blow by arousing opinion against the "liberty-killing" plans of the ministry. The whole month of January resulted in nothing but growing impatience in all parties. Finally, Decazes succeeded in making a deal with Villèle, and he could announce that a new electoral bill would be sent to the chamber on February 14.

Then at the last moment an unforeseen catastrophe ruined all of these efforts: on February 13, at eleven o'clock in the evening, the Duke of Berry, son of the Count of Artois and third in line for the throne, was assassinated.

## The Death of Berry and the Fall of Decazes

This assassination was the work of a lone fanatic, a journeyman saddler, Louvel. His purpose—he was to admit it without questioning— was to extinguish the royal line of the Bourbons, and that was the reason he had attacked the Duke of Berry who, it was known, was the only one of the royal family who could provide future descendants. The prince, in 1816, had married a daughter of the King of Naples, Marie-Caroline, a likeable young lady, of a childlike character, and up to 1820 had only had one child, a daughter, who later would become the Duchess of Parma.

The details of the drama are only too well known. The prince was struck down as he left the Opera, at the moment when he was ac-companying his wife as she withdrew before the end of the performance. The dagger had pierced his chest on the right side up to the hilt; it was the prince himself who pulled it out and realized immediately that it was a mortal blow. They carried him into the business office of the Opera. The seven hours elapsing there before his death were, for those attending, a scene of unforgettable horror and tragic greatness. Surrounded by the members of the royal family who, one by one, hastened to his side, and by the doctors whose only treatment seemed to be to add their blood-letting to his bleeding, the prince displayed a nobility of soul, a courage, a Christian resignation, a presence of mind, a tenderness for his dear ones, which redeemed in those few hours all the wildness and thoughtlessness of his dissipated life. It seemed that in the face of death the blood of Saint Louis regained its virtue. He wanted to con-fess his sins and to ask publicly for forgiveness of the scandals he had caused. His last concern was to obtain the pardon of his assassin: "At least may I take with me the thought that the blood of a man will not be shed for me after my death!" At 6:35 the next morning the king himself closed the prince's eyes.

This event profoundly stirred the country. The very next morning, on February 14, an Ultra deputy, Clausel de Coussergues, proposed the impeachment of the minister of the interior, who, according to him, was guilty of being an accomplice in the crime. It was arrant nonsense, and Clausel had acted without consulting his friends, but it could be easily claimed that the atmosphere of revolutionary agitation, encouraged by the policy of Decazes, might have contributed to hatching the idea of the assassination in the mind of Louvel. "I saw Louvel's dagger, and it was a liberal idea," wrote Nodier in the *Journal des Débats*;

and Chateaubriand said in his own way, "The hand that struck the blow does not bear the heaviest guilt."

But by thus accusing Decazes, they were indirectly attacking the king who had supported his policy. As much out of affection as out of wounded pride Louis XVIII did not intend to abandon his favorite to the clamors of his enemies. Decazes, at first overwhelmed and on the point of bowing out, took courage again. He thought he could extricate himself by presenting, along with the new election law, two exceptional laws re-establishing censorship of the press and arbitrary arrests. However, the Right and Right-Center absolutely refused to grant him these additional powers. They were afraid, and not without some justification, that he would use these powers as much against his rightist opponents as against those of the Left. "What is this?" asked the *Journal des Débats,* "Instead of repenting, M. Decazes threatens; instead of running and hiding his regrets and sorrows by retiring from the political scene, he wants to be a dictator! Does this antechamber Bonaparte take us to be people who neither take heed nor remember?"

Some young hotheads talked of laying hands on the favorite and of "stopping" him as was done to the Duke of Guise (who in 1588 had been assailed and killed by the king's bodyguard). The grave and dignified Lainé himself said: "The minister found a scoundrel to stab the Duke of Berry, and no one can find an honest man to kill M. Decazes!" The Count of Artois and the Duchess of Angoulême threw themselves at the king's feet to urge him to dismiss his favorite. Louis XVIII rejected their pleas with such a loud voice that he could be heard in the antechamber. The solution that everybody considered obvious and necessary was the return to power of the Duke of Richelieu; but he fell ill at the very thought of returning to office. Talleyrand was actively intriguing, thinking his hour had come, but the king took advantage of this situation to continue his recalcitrance.

Finally the Count of Artois, by an urgent appeal, obtained Richelieu's consent by promising him his support and that of his friends: "Your policy will be mine. On the faith of a gentleman, I will be your most loyal soldier!" Finally Louis XVIII gave in; with great outward manifestations of ineffable grief, he bade his "dear son" farewell: "Come gaze upon an ungrateful prince who was powerless to defend thee; come mingle thy tears with those of thy most miserable father!" Upon his head he heaped untold honors: minister of state, duke and peer, ambassador to London. On the day he left, the king gave as the watchword *Elie,* the first name of his favorite, and for the password *Chartres,* the city where he would end the first stage of his journey. On receiving

the Count of Saint-Aulaire, he pointed to the painting of Decazes replacing that of Francis I: "That's all I have left; they can take him from
me but they can't pluck him from my heart. . . . I only let him go to
save him!"

The assassination of the Duke of Berry was not the initial cause
of the change in orientation of French internal politics. Already, three
months before, Decazes had had to acknowledge the failure of his
policy of reconciliation, of which the Left took advantage only to prepare
more easily the downfall of the government. But events did hasten this
outcome. By the exceptional measures which he proposed, it took on
the aspect of a brutal reaction. In the end it brought on the dissolution
in parliament of this centrist "third force" which had thought it possible
to reconcile monarchical traditions with revolutionary ideology. Then,
the two factions of this Center each moving toward the two extremes,
there were only two parties left—royalists and liberals; and in the
country, as Louis XVIII had feared, there were now two hostile peoples,
victims of their own fratricidal hatreds. This explains why that ill-starred
date of February 14, 1820 is a dividing line in the history of the
Restoration.

# 12

❧ ❧ ❧ ❧ ❧

# Richelieu and the Trend Toward the Right

## Legislative Reaction to the Assassination

DECAZES had tried a policy in line with the formula of the Left-Center by depending on leftist support; and that policy, as has been shown, led inevitably to the domination of the extreme Left. Richelieu, once more in office, was to try to put together a policy of the Right-Center, by depending on the support of the Right; and, by taking this opposite direction, he ended with the domination of the extreme Right. His ministry never did achieve its parliamentary equilibrium, and, in spite of lasting almost two years, it was only a stopgap team.

The power take-over by the Right came about in three steps. Up to the month of September 1820, the new government's situation being precarious, the Right supported its reactionary program without demanding much for itself. It let Richelieu keep in office the same ministers who had served under Decazes. Then later, when the new electoral law had assured the defeat of the Left, the Right asked to have some of its members brought into the cabinet. Finally, in August 1821, it demanded all the cabinet posts and withdrew its members from the coalition ministry, leaving it so unbalanced that it fell in December 1821.

Villèle, the Ultra leader, would have preferred that the ministry not propose the exceptional laws prepared by Decazes; it was embarrassing for the Right to abandon its position of defending the liberties that it had adopted as a tactical necessity since 1816. But the king insisted on these laws because, if they withdrew them now, people would be justified in saying that Decazes had wanted them less for the safety of the state than for the perpetuation of his own position.

To move faster, the chamber of peers took up the press bill while the chamber of deputies was considering the bill on individual freedom. It appeared right away that the upper house would go along with Richelieu without any difficulty, so the struggle would be in the chamber of deputies. The speakers on the left—Constant, La Fayette, Manuel, General Foy—gave vent to their feelings in violent language and issued scarcely disguised appeals to insurrection. La Fayette said that the bills violated the Charter, and he concluded with the words: "To violate the Charter is to dissolve the mutual guarantees of the nation and the throne, to free us from our obligations, and return us to our original independence in rights and duties." These declamations only succeeded in rallying around the government the previously reticent Right and even some moderate elements of the Left-Center. The two bills were finally passed, but by small majorities, which proves that, if the Left had adopted more prudent tactics, it could have defeated them.

The Law of General Security permitted the government to arrest and detain for three months any person charged with plotting against the person of the king or against the security of the state. The order for arrest should be considered in the council of ministers and bear the signature of three ministers. As for the Press Law, all papers and magazines must obtain prior authorization to publish; political articles would be reviewed by a censorship committee of twelve in Paris and a committee of three in each department. In case of a violation and a court trial, the government could suspend the publication immediately, even before a verdict, and for as long as six months thereafter. These two exceptional laws, however, were enforceable only for one year, until the end of the session of 1821.

The Press Law was to cause the early disapperance of many papers which had sprung up under the liberal regime of the Count of Serre's laws. Chateaubriand himself had to close down the *Conservateur* because he objected to being submitted to censorship. The liberal papers which tried to survive, like the *Constitutionnel,* attempted to get around the censorship in various ways, such as leaving significant blank spaces where passages had been censored, changing the typing arrangement of accepted article so as to give certain words a meaning which the censors had not noticed, publishing forbidden articles in pamphlet form under the title of "censorship rejects," and issuing miscellanies as continuations of suppressed newspapers. But the courts put an end to all these subterfuges and, little by little, eliminated all the opposition's means of expression by imposing fines and prison sentences.

Under these conditions the Left had only one remaining recourse to reach public opinion, that of the debates in the chamber whose publication in the press could not be prohibited. The leftist speakers therefore contrived to produce a sort of violent and aggressive spoken newspaper on the floor of the chamber, which instituted a kind of filibuster with many irrelevant subjects of discussion.

It was for this reason that the proposed electoral law required not less than twenty-three daily sessions from May 15 to June 12, 1820. The minister of justice, the Count of Serre, returned from his convalescence in the south to lead in the promotion of the bill, and, in spite of his weak condition, he manifested an eloquence and a tenacity rarely surpassed in debate. On the Left, too, there was no scarcity of valiant champions: every parliamentary delaying tactic was contrived, and the most violent words that highly exasperated passions could muster were spoken to hold up the vote on the electoral bill. Everybody had the feeling that the fate of the throne or of liberty hung on the outcome, and the fierceness of the struggle became more intense as this outcome, one way or the other, became more uncertain. In contrast to present-day practices when parties which are solidly constituted can count on their votes in advance, the situation in 1820 found a floating mass of centrist deputies between Right and Left who could be pulled in one direction or the other by some speech or maneuver.

One remarkable characteristic of this agitated period was the interest that the parliamentary discussions aroused in the public at large. Every day, when the offices closed about four or five o'clock in the afternoon, crowds of students and employees would gather around the Bourbon Palace (meeting place of the chamber of deputies) and show their fury or enthusiasm according to what their messengers brought them from the discussions inside. They would shout "Long Live the Charter!," they would acclaim the virtuous defenders of liberty, and they would jeer the lackeys of reaction when rightists left the palace. By their speeches at the rostrum the leftist deputies aroused the disturbances in the street, and then they would take advantage of these street clashes to create new incidents in the chamber. The royalist supporters reacted to these taunts: organized by some officers of the royal guard dressed in civilian clothes, they would fall upon the liberal students with their canes. The government took

special security precautions and gave Marshal Macdonald the over-
all command of the troops in Paris. On June 3 a student named
Lallemand was killed during a scuffle with the royal guard. The disturbances reached their peak on June 5 when he was buried. Five
or six hundred young people, wearing black arm-bands, marched behind
his bier. Then, when the ceremonies were over, they called out the workers
of the Saint-Antoine quarter, and they all marched on the Bourbon
Palace from two directions. Fortunately a violent rainstorm broke up
the demonstration, and the cavalry of the royal guard had no difficulty
in dispersing the rest of the assembling columns. It is almost certain
that without that providential shower the violent demonstrations would
have resulted in loss of life and many injured, because the troops were
very much aroused.

Finally, by a deal made with the Left-Center party, which removed the original provision in the bill for indirect, two-stage elections, the bill as a whole was passed by a vote of 154 to ninety-three.
The chamber would have 430 members instead of 258. The original
258 seats, which had previously been elected by single departmental
colleges, would henceforth be chosen in arrondissement colleges
(smaller subdivisions within departments), made up of all single residents paying three hundred francs a year in direct taxes. The 172 new
seats would be filled by the departmental "higher colleges," made up
of the top twenty-five per cent of the taxpayers. As these richer voters
also voted in their arrondissement colleges, they then had the right to
vote twice—from which comes the name of the "Law of the Double
Vote."

## A Conspiracy and a Miracle Child

Between the end of the parliamentary session and the elections
under this new system two events were to take place which were to
have a big influence on those new elections: one was the Bazar Conspiracy and the other was the birth of the Duke of Bordeaux.

The passage of the exceptional laws and the electoral law destroyed the hopes of the Left to win power by legal means. Therefore it went over to an insurrectionary approach. The coalition of
revolutionary elements was made up of several organizations: the
executive committee of the parliamentary liberal party under La
Fayette, d'Argenson, Manuel, Dupont de l'Eure, and the lawyers de
Corcelles and Mérilhou, etc.; the secret society of the "Union,"
founded in 1818 by a lawyer in Grenoble, Joseph Rey, who had

extended his activities into several departments; the lodge of the "Friends of Truth," which included republican students; and finally a group of Bonapartist military men, some pensioned and some active officers who met in Paris on the Rue Cadet in a building called the "French Bazar." These various organizations made contact early in the summer of 1820, and, through the intermediary of La Fayette, agreed on common action. The insurrectionary movement was to break out on August 19 in Paris, Lyons, Colmar, and several other cities under the tricolor banner so dear to republicans and Bonapartists alike. Once the Bourbons were overthrown, the nation would be called upon by a really popular vote to choose what new regime it preferred.

The government learned of the plot from a few loyal officers whom the conspirators had tried to enlist. Mounier, director of police, wanted to let the insurrection break out so as to discover all the conspirators, but Richelieu, out of a sense of humaneness, decided to forestall the insurrection by taking certain preventive measures. Then the leaders, frightened, called off the plan and ran for cover to the country, La Fayette in the lead. Only a few lower-rank leaders were caught by the police. Seventy-five in number, they were haled before the chamber of peers for trial on the charge of attempts against the security of the state. The upper house, afraid to carry the affair up to the real authors of the plot, took a soft attitude toward these lesser confederates on trial. Only six of them were given light prison sentences.

The discovery of this conspiracy was a clear-cut refutation of the assurances of the liberal deputies, like Benjamin Constant, who, not being privy to the secret plans, were honestly insisting that their party restricted itself to legal activity. It was a help to the government by rallying to its support sincere liberal elements, friendly to law and order and opposed to collusion with Bonapartists, those henchmen of a tyranny as hateful to them as that of the Bourbons.

In contrast, the birth of the Duke of Bordeaux to the widowed Duchess of Berry brought to the dynasty and the Bourbon regime that glow of good fortune, that aura of magic, and those hopes for the future that attract the undecided and stir the hearts of the common people.

The happy event, which occurred on September 29—more than seven months after the father's assassination—was to appear as somewhat of a miracle. It seemed as if Providence had wanted to manifest its desire to protect the dynasty by permitting it to revive in spite of

Louvel's crime. Looking toward this birth which might thwart their hopes, the liberals and Orleanists had not failed to insinuate that a lot must have been going on to assure that there would be a Bourbon heir (a Dauphin). The Duchess of Berry countered these rumors with astonishing presence of mind. At the complete sacrifice of her modesty she made sure that there were unimpeachable witnesses in the delivery room. The joy of the royalists was delirious and resounded in all classes of the nation. There were many and repeated manifestations of loyalty. Victor Hugo and Lamartine, along with many other writers, acclaimed the birth of this "miracle child."

## The Elections of 1820 and Their Aftermath

The new elections took place on November 4 and 13 in this atmosphere of joy and almost mystical exaltation. The government had prepared for them by the underhanded practice of reducing the direct taxes of 14,500 opposition voters so as to disfranchise them because their taxes fell below the required three hundred francs. Up for election were not only fifty-one deputies to fill the seats of the one-fifth outgoing ones, as in the preceding years, but in addition the 172 new representatives of the "big colleges." The elections turned out to be a defeat for the Left, which, out of 430 deputies in the new chamber, had only eighty; on the other hand, the Ultras went up to 160, among whom were seventy-five former members of the "Chambre Introuvable." As for the government itself, it had reason to be satisfied if it considered the number of its supporters (190), but the unusual success of the Right went somewhat beyond its hopes. Louis XVIII expressed this idea in his own inimitable way: "Here we are in the situation not unlike that of the poor horseman who lacked the dexterity to mount his horse. He prayed so hard to Saint George that the gallant saint gave him more bounce than he needed, and he fell off on the other side."

Logically, since more than half of the parliamentary majority were now men on the Right, they should have been allowed a corresponding share of cabinet seats, but none of the ministers wanted to give up their portfolios. So they hit upon the following arrangement: Villèle, Corbière, and Lainé—the latter representing the Right-Center —would sit in the cabinet as ministers without portfolios; Corbière would also have the presidency of the royal council on public instruction, where he would replace Royer-Collard. Villèle only consented to this on the condition that he would receive no salary or any other material advantage. This would underline the temporary nature of the situation. At the same time, Chateaubriand, whose opposition could be so dangerous, accepted an appointment as ambassador to Berlin.

Nevertheless, some of the Right remained opposed to the ministry. The lodge of the Knights of the Faith, which supported Villèle's policy in the chamber, were not quite half the rightist deputies; and at the extreme Right, the "impatient faction," led by the clumsy La Bourdonnaye, refused its support to Richelieu. Villèle and Corbière therefore found themselves in a very uncomfortable position. Having only a remote role in governmental affairs, whose details were naturally unknown to them, they nonetheless shared the responsibility for them in the eyes of their party. Obliged to be disagreeable toward their colleagues if they wanted to retain the confidence of their party followers, and forced to disprove the accusations of weakness hurled at them from the extreme Right, they found themselves becoming distrusted by most of the government people.

Among the measures likely to rally the Right to the support of the government—in addition to the inevitable dismissal of high officials—it is necessary to note especially those which tended to strengthen the influence of the Catholic clergy. The most significant one was the ordinance of February 27, 1821 which put the secondary schools under the supervision of the bishops. The university monopoly also received a twist in favor of the religious schools which could then obtain the title and privileges of "fully operating colleges," thus permitting them to compete with royal colleges. In fact, this privilege was to be granted very rarely.

The session of 1821 had gone on without much excitement. But right before adjournment an incident embroiled the ministry with the Right. The government was asking for the continuation of press censorship for one more year, until July 1822. The extreme Right fought furiously against it, and the Villèle faction itself remained reticent. One of the debaters expressed himself this way: "The ministry—which is in favor of a little religion, a little monarchism, a little fidelity, but not too much—must understand that the royalists in their turn have only a little confidence in it and not too much." Nevertheless, the continuation of the censorship was granted, but only for three months after the opening of the next session.

Villèle and Corbière, scolded by the king because of the way their friends voted, saw that their position was untenable. They decided that they would have either to resign or obtain three ministerial portfolios, which would give them an influence corresponding to their parliamentary position. Richelieu thought that their demands were excessive. Consequently the two representatives of the Right withdrew from the cabinet, and Chateaubriand took his stand with them by giving up his Berlin embassy.

The partial elections of October 1821 did not change appreciably the lineup of parliamentary forces. The ministry lost only seven seats in favor of the Left. Yet Richelieu still insisted on following his policy of governing without the Right, but with the support of its votes, in order to follow the line of the Right-Center with a ministry of the Left-Center. Under these circumstances the "impatient faction" made gains, and Villèle had to withdraw into an attitude of reserve without trying any longer to direct the rightist parliamentary group.

## A Hesitant Foreign Policy and the Fall of the Ministry

The foreign policy of the government was to furnish the opposition its grounds for attack for which it was looking at the opening of the next session.

Around the year 1820 Europe seemed to be suffering from a case of a very high fever: liberal agitation in the German universities, a revolutionary coup in Spain (January 1820), a liberal revolution in Naples (July 1820), a national uprising in Greece (March 1821), and a liberal and national insurrection in northern Italy (March 1821); even staid old England had some popular outbreaks herself. Against all this effervescence, the conservative alliance*—directed by Metternich and by Tsar Alexander I, who had repudiated his liberal sympathies of 1814—tried to erect a dam of police and military forces. Great Britain looked upon this action with the greatest suspicion because it would permit Russia and Austria to extend their protectorate over regions (Spain and southern Italy) where she herself aimed at extending her economic and political influence.

What would France's attitude be? Two entirely opposite positions were theoretically conceivable, both involving risks but also the possibilities of considerable gain: either join England in supporting liberal movements abroad and put herself at the head of a popular crusade against absolute monarchs, or, quite to the contrary, join resolutely the conservative alliance camp and thus put France on a really equal rather than a theoretically equal footing with her recent enemies. But

* Some authors and Metternich preferred to call this grouping the conservative alliance. Other authors and popular tradition referred to it as the Holy Alliance.

in fact, the internal political situation in France, no less than the mediocrity of her statesmen, were not to permit her to come to a clearcut decision, and she fell, as the phrase goes, between two stools. On the one hand the French Bourbons could not take sides with the revolutionaries who were attacking the Bourbons of Naples and Spain; but on the other hand the moderate governments of Decazes and Richelieu feared that by supporting the conservative alliance they would exasperate the French liberals. In the end, French foreign policy, instead of being directed solely by considerations of the great political and economic interests of the country, found itself buffeted by every wind of partisan passion: the Ultras, haunted by revolutionary dangers, saw no salvation except in the conservative alliance, and the liberals hoped that the revolutionary movements abroad would lead to a similar movement in France.

Richelieu and Pasquier, his minister of foreign affairs, were to search at home and abroad for some middle way, which really meant retreating into a prudent do-nothing policy which displeased everybody. At the congresses of Troppau and Laibach, which met during the winter of 1820–1821 to settle the affairs in Italy, France did not dare oppose the military intervention desired by Austria, but she did not give her consent to it until after so many hesitations that the tsar could sum up the general impression with the words: "It's too bad for France if she can neither strike fear in her enemies nor inspire confidence in her friends."

So it is easy to understand how, at the opening of the parliamentary session, the government found itself the target of the converging fire of both oppositions: on the Left it was accused of sacrificing France's traditional position by letting Austria crush the Italian liberals, and on the Right they bitterly accused it of timidity by refusing to side unreservedly with the conservative alliance. On the question of the address to the king, the two oppositions combined their votes to pass the following paragraph: "We congratulate you, Sire, on your continuously friendly relations with foreign powers, in the just confidence that such a valued peace is not purchased by sacrifices incompatible with the honor of the nation and the dignity of the crown."

The king was deeply hurt by this obvious insinuation. When the president of the chamber brought him the address, he refused to hear it read, as was customary, and, laying it on his desk, he said in a severe tone:

I am familiar with this address you are presenting. During my exile and persecution I defended my rights, the honor of my family, and that of the good name of France; now that I hold the throne and am surrounded by my people, I become indignant at the very thought that I could ever sacrifice the honor of the nation and the dignity of the crown. I should like to think that those who voted this address had not weighed all its passages. If they had had time to analyze them, they would not have tolerated these expressions which, as king, I do not want to characterize, and, as father, I should like to forget.

At one point it was thought that the chamber would be dissolved, but Richelieu did not dare bring out a new version of the coup d'état of September 5, 1816. The king, in spite of the spasm of indignation he had at the address, was not in a mood to undergo another electoral fight. Physically declining, he would sometimes doze off in the course of his audiences with his ministers, and an intimate influence was now being exercised on him, making him more favorably disposed toward the men on the Right. A lady favorite now replaced the gentleman favorite. The first meeting Louis XVIII had with Mme du Cayla went back to the time when Decazes still ruled his heart. Countess du Cayla, the former Zoé Talon, had needed royal protection in an unfortunate suit with her worthless husband for the custody of her children. The king was so charmed by her grace and intelligence that he invited her to come back to see him. It goes without saying that Mme du Cayla obeyed—and that she won her suit. When Decazes disappeared from the scene, she had already been brought in and was on hand to take his place. One of her friends, Sosthènes de la Rochefoucauld, who was also one of the most active intriguers of Artois' party, encouraged her to work her way further into the confidence of the king in order to break down the prejudices that Decazes had built up against his adversaries. She took on the job and succeeded beyond their wildest dreams. A witty and beautiful brunette, Mme du Cayla, in the somewhat buxom bloom of her thirty-seven years, had all the outward appearance of a royal mistress; but considering the age and infirmities of the king, it obviously could only be a platonic affection—or almost. However, public gossip enjoyed discussing the role of the greybeard lover that the king was playing: daily love notes, tender attentions, assorted delicate or sumptuous gifts. Like the king's whole schedule, his love affairs were strictly regulated and timed: Once a week on Wednesdays the favorite lady would come to the Tuileries to play a game of chess with the king—so she said; this lasted exactly two hours while his door was closely guarded. But every day Mme du Cayla was expected to write him letters on current affairs. Sosthènes de la Rochefoucauld worked out with Villèle what should be written and helped his feminine friend compose her little daily bulletins. And this went on right up to the king's death.

By the end of 1821 Louis XVIII was therefore ready to admit that a ministry of the Right, in line with his brother's wishes, would assure him peace in his old age. Richelieu, however, now hung on to his job with all the stubbornness which he had previously shown in refusing it. He tried to regroup the Right by a proposal to tighten the control of the press; and once more the opposition, combined with the "impatients" of the Left, thwarted him. The president of the council then had recourse to Artois and insisted that he live up to his word by assuring him of his support and that of his followers. "Ah, my dear Duke," the embarrassed prince replied, "you have taken my words too literally. And besides, the circumstances back there were so difficult!" Richelieu, indignant, left him without saying a word and hastened over to see Pasquier and unburden his irritation: "He has broken his word, his word of a gentleman!" Later, on December 12, Richelieu handed in his resignation. Louis XVIII, who knew that Artois had already at hand a substitute ministry, accepted it with indifference, which deeply wounded our excellent duke.

Yet, however great and upright Richelieu was, he had actually lacked a sense of realism. Since he knew that the welfare of the monarchy as well as the parliamentary situation required the union of the Center and the Right, he would have been well advised to invite immediately into the ministry the more moderate and more capable men of the Right and thus give them a chance to sober down with the weight of responsibilities. The Left also lacked political good sense; by joining in the overthrow of Richelieu it was adopting the policy of deliberately making things worse. By dint of repeating up and down the scale that the Right was made up of a bunch of inept and incompetent fanatics, and that the only ones capable of governing the new France were men forged in the Revolution and Empire, the men on the Left finally ended by being convinced that a purely royalist ministry would quickly demonstrate its incapacity and then it would be necessary to have recourse to themselves again. Without realizing it, they were turning the government over to a party which would not let itself be dislodged from its captured fortress.

# 13

❧ ❧ ❧ ❧ ❧

# Villèle and the Triumph of the Right

## Rightist Domestic Policy

THE first idea of Artois, the main architect of the new ministry, had been to bring back into the government the Count of Blacas, the former favorite of the king, by appointing him as president of the council and foreign minister. But Villèle and Corbière objected that he was too unpopular and reminded the public of the mistakes of the First Restoration. Instead, they proposed Viscount Mathieu de Montmorency, grand master of the secret society of the Knights of the Faith. He was a saintly man, a pillar of the Congregation and all its charities, a noble character, a perfect gentleman of handsome appearance and agreeable and distinguished manners. A former pupil of Abbé Sieyès, he had been one of the most ardent of that group of young liberal nobles who, in 1789, had supported the ideas of the Revolution. The Terror's excesses had disgusted him and brought him back again to respect for religion. He was highly regarded at court and in high society, but he possessed only a very mediocre intelligence, a weak will, and no experience in public affairs. Villèle won out to the extent that it was decided to give Montmorency only the foreign ministry, leaving the office of presidency of the council vacant. Perhaps he hoped to bring back Richelieu as prime minister after the noble duke had digested his illhumor; but the latter was to die in the following May, leaving as Talleyrand said, "a bigger void in dying than he had occupied while living."

The rightists had also hoped to retain the financier, Roy, and the keeper of the seal, the Count of Serre, but these two gentlemen refused to identify themselves with a team which they thought could not last. So Villèle took the ministry of finance and Corbière the interior. The latter concealed under the hide of a Danubian peasant a great deal of finesse and a training in the liberal arts; but he was to conduct the affairs of his department with a happy-go-lucky neglect which put the main work on his bureau chiefs. For the ministry of justice the choice fell quite by chance on a new man, Peyronnet, formerly a Bordeaux lawyer who had gained fame as the government's advocate general in the conspiracy trials of August 1820 in the chamber of peers. He was a sort of southern swashbuckler, with a husky physique, proud of his feminine conquests, of his stentorian voice, and of his knack of improvising smashing tirades in the Ciceronian style. Indeed, that was why they chose him: the government had to have a spokesman whose loquacity and lung power could overwhelm that of the opposition. In the war ministry they put Marshal Victor, Duke of Bellune, a former soldier of the Revolution and Empire who had earned his promotions in combat. He was certainly not a military genius, but he was a man of experience and character, and the Ultras held him in high esteem because he had followed Louis XVIII into his Ghent exile. The naval ministry was assigned to the Marquis of Clermont-Tonnerre, a peer of the Right-Center. His diploma from the Ecole Polytechnique seemed—already!—to give him the seal of universal competence. Lastly, General de Lauriston, a man who enjoyed the good things of life but had no particular political affiliation, was made minister of the royal household.

The real head of the government was Villèle, although he did not have the title, and the low rank of the finance ministry did not warrant it. Joseph de Villèle, coming from a family of the lower nobility in the Toulousain, was a young naval officer on overseas duty when the Revolution broke out. For a while he settled down, and married advantageously in the Île Bourbon. Going back to his native province in 1807, he was soon appointed to the departmental council of the Haute-Garonne. He was mayor of Toulouse at the time he was elected to the "Chambre Introuvable" where, little by little, he was to take over the parliamentary leadership of the Ultra party. His contemporaries described him as a short, thin, weak man, with a wizened face made more ugly by a big nose and smallpox scars and with a shrill and nasal voice. But his lively and practical intelligence and his capacity for exhausting work made it possible for him to assimilate rapidly all political questions, and especially those dealing with finance. He was able to explain them with clarity and in great detail. "He was a great light shining with little effort," was what Canning said of him. He was also known for pursuing his objectives stubbornly and against all difficulties. Although personally he was a man of great integrity and was not lacking in moral courage, he had a tendency to approach men on their weak side and preferred to use trickery rather than make a frontal assault on obstacles in his path. Too often he made government consist of a long series of small expedients, of little deals, and petty revenges. Pasquier said, "He never saw any affair from a lofty point of view," and Frénilly, one of his strongest supporters once remarked, "This man, of meticulous character, strict behavior, and mathematical mind, spends his time counting his cash on hand." Metternich criticized him for not acting more like a Frenchman—a rather amusing comment, coming from a foreigner; and Pozzo di Borgo wrote that "he would be a great minister if he had a boss." But that was just it, Villèle wanted no master over himself other than the king, to whom he was most loyally devoted. The susceptible vanity of this small provincial noble could not tolerate around him any men who could outshine him by their talent, character, or birth. As a result, his whole ministry and all the people and accomplishments associated with it, were to bear the hallmarks of that sly trickiness in his nature. Instead of remaining a man of second rank, he wanted to climb to the top and stay there, come what might. With the makings of a very great clerk, he was to become only a second-rate statesman.

The ministry had the unqualified support of the Count of Artois, who was moving closer to the throne every day with the progressive decline in the king's health. Louis XVIII seemed now to have only one concern and that was to end his days in peace. The rigorous observance of etiquette, the composition of short verses, correspondence with Mme du Cayla, the care of his health, these were his main preoccupations. He left the direction of affairs entirely to his brother and Villèle. Some people were saying, "Monsieur [the heir apparent] is already anticipating his royal inheritance."

## The Charbonnerie

The first months of the rightist government were marked, especially in domestic affairs, by a great revolutionary effort by the enemies of the regime. Two young men involved in the conspiracy of August 1820, Joubert and Dugied, had fled to Italy and made contact with the secret society of the *Carbonari,* which had carried out the revolution of July 1820 in Naples and which they found admirably adapted for underground activities. When they returned to France in the spring of 1821, they persuaded their friends to found a French *Charbonnerie.* The smallest unit was the local or communal "sale," composed of ten members; each separate sale sent a delegate up to a cantonal sale; and by the same system of progressive representation they formed a pyramid of departmental, federal, and sectional sales, with a final central (Parisian) sale. The members of different sales did not know each other and had no contacts except by their delegates; and compartmentalization was a good precaution against police infiltration. Each member made four promises: to keep the secret, to pay monthly dues of one franc, always to have a gun and 25 cartridges ready, and to obey the orders of the next higher sale. The political program of the society was definitely liberal and republican, which did not prevent the adherence of many Bonapartist military groups. Napoleon's death on May 5, 1821 helped this fusion by putting off, for some, any hope of an early imperial restoration and by reassuring others that there would be no such restoration. The charter members, most of whom were young men without prominence, approached the members of the old executive committee of the liberal party, and almost all of these became members of the central sale: deputies La Fayette, Voyer d'Argenson, Manuel, de Corcelles; de Schonen, counselor to the Royal Court in Paris; lawyers Barthe, Mauguin, and Mérilhou; the Alsatian industrialist, Koechlin; and Colonel Fabvier. The association spread rapidly in Paris and the provinces; in the west it took over in one fell swoop the fifteen thousand members of the secret society of the Knights of Liberty, which had been organized by liberal officers in 1820. Altogether the Charbonnerie had perhaps thirty to forty thousand members, although it is hard to say exactly. It is known, nevertheless, that it did not reach down to the lower classes and that it did enlist especially students, the smaller units of the army, and the lower (petty) bourgeoisie.

The momentary success of the revolutions in Spain and Italy stirred the Charbonnerie in France to overthrow the Bourbon regime by a similar coup. Grandiose plans were drawn up: the insurrection was to break out simultaneously in the West, with Saumur as its center, and in Alsace, where the garrisons of Belfort and Neuf-Brisach would take over Colmar and raise the tricolor flag. From there they hoped the movement would win over Lyons and Marseilles. La Fayette, d'Argenson, and Koechlin were to set up a provisional government in Alsace. Because of poor co-ordination and the irresolution of the archons of the central sale, the movements happened haphazardly instead of in unison. At Belfort, La Fayette and d'Argenson were not on hand by the agreed date of December 30, 1821; the outbreak was adjourned for forty-eight hours. However, the open gathering of the plotters alerted the authorities, who arrested several of them, and others took flight. La Fayette, already on his way to Alsace, having been warned, quickly started back to Paris, burning his compromising papers and the uniform he was to have worn.

At Saumur, too, the plot had to be put off because of the arrest of some of the conspirators on December 23. But, because the government did not seem to suspect the extensiveness of the plans, they decided to go ahead with the revolts. The leader in this sector was General Berton, who had been put on the inactive list for having expressed strong Bonapartist sentiments. On February 24, 1822 he took over the small town of Thouars, whose garrison consisted of only five gendarmes. On the following day, with a force of a hundred men, he marched on Saumur where he counted on the help of Charbonnerie groups in the cavalry school. The mayor, alerted in time, called up the national guard and closed the gates of the city. Berton did not dare take the city by assault, tried in vain to negotiate a surrender of the town, and, failing this, withdrew. In the meantime the local authorities in Thouars had gotten back control and prepared the city's defenses. All Berton could do then was to dismiss his small force and disappear. In order to capture him, the police accepted the offer of a noncommissioned officer who gained the confidence of the general by promising to win over a cavalry squadron for his command; a trap was set for him and he was caught. By similar, but less laudable methods the government seized Colonel Caron, one of the Colmar plotters. Here tricks and provocations were pushed to unusual lengths. They assigned to Caron two squadrons infiltrated with officers disguised as plain cavalry troopers. When Caron came to take over command of them and the crime had been well established, he was arrested. Both he and Berton were convicted and executed early in October 1822.

Other less important plots, a dozen in all, were uncovered or discouraged. The one of the four sergeants of La Rochelle is the best-known episode, less because of the seriousness of the enterprise than because of the excitement aroused over their trial. These four young men—Bories, Pommier, Raoulx, and Goubin—sergeants of the forty-fifth regiment of the line, garrisoned in Paris, had founded a military sale in their unit. The colonel, suspecting something was up, decided as a precaution to have his regiment transferred to La Rochelle in February 1822. Along the whole route Bories and his friends made contacts with the local sales; their idea was to support Berton's enterprise in Saumur by an uprising in the regiment. In short, they were so active that some of their comrades became fearful and reported them. Their first confessions, after being arrested, had revealed the existence of a central sale and the whole wide network of the conspiracy, of which the government had only a confused idea at that time. But when they were transferred to Paris for trial, their lawyers, members of the central sale, persuaded them to remain silent and retract their previous confessions in order to save the Charbonnerie movement which could take revenge for them and go on with its work. These brave young men accepted the role of martyrs and resisted all offers of royal judicial officials to spare their lives if they would identify the real guilty ones, their leaders. On their execution day the Charbonnerie of Paris had all its forces on the alert, but nothing was done to liberate the condemned men. The "lords of the Upper Sale," as Prosecutor General Marchangy called them, had taken a great interest in seeing them silenced for good. "They will die bravely," Manuel said with obvious relief. At least, after it was all over, nothing was spared to glorify their memory and exalt them as heroes of liberty.

All these setbacks ruined the Charbonnerie. The supreme or central sale complained that it had not been properly obeyed; and the local sales accused the "Gentlemen of Paris" of being very willing to egg on their luckless comrades and then themselves evade the danger of open revolt. Some of the more fanatical or more compromised ones, like Armand Carrel, sought safety in Spain to aid the revolutionists there; others, like Fabvier, were to offer their services to the Greeks; and still others took refuge in Saint-Simonism. Those in parliament decided to limit themselves to a legal opposition and use the rostrum to advance their ideas; this was what Benjamin Constant and Casimir Périer had always advocated. The latter, alluding to La Fayette and d'Argenson, was known to have said at the time, "How can we have anything to do with people, who, after leading us to the edge of the precipice without our realizing it, skip out and leave us in the lurch?" By having surmounted this crisis victoriously, the government came out of it with a stronger position in public opinion, both at home and abroad.

At the same time, the ministers, each in his own department, were working to weed out the liberal and Bonapartist personnel appointed or retained by Decazes and to replace them by people they could rely on. Naturally the royalist secret societies and the clergy found opportunities to make their influence felt by the information they could furnish and the recommendations they could suggest. It was at this time that people began to speak of the influence of the "Congregation" on the ministry and on the administrative departments. One should mention at least the names of Franchet d'Esperey and of Delavau, named respectively director general of police and Paris prefect of police; both were Congregationists, and very probably, Knights of the Faith. The use of the "darkroom" made the postal service a fine instrument for thwarting conspiracies and watching opinion. Nevertheless, some were a little shocked to see a great lord like the Duke of Doudeauville accept such a lowly position: "Mr. de Doudeauville is postal director?" they would ask. "Then who will be Duke of Doudeauville?" Chateaubriand, who could expect a ministry, received instead as compensation the most important of embassies, the one at London. Here he succeeded his sworn enemy, Decazes, and this turn of fortune gave him sweet revenge.

In March 1822 the government obtained the passage of two laws further restricting the press. New offenses were defined: outrages against the state religion and other recognized cults, attacks against the right of succession (aimed at Orleanist intrigues), disloyalty as shown in the minutes of parliamentary debates and court proceedings, and especially the crime of tendency, something entirely new, which the law defined in these terms: "The attitude of a journal or periodical as portrayed by a succession of articles . . . tending to disturb the peace or to undermine the proper respect for the state religion or for other legally recognized religions, or for the king's authority, or for the stability of constitutional institutions, etc." Jurisdiction over press offenses was taken away from juries and turned over to summary correctional courts and royal courts. Prior authorization was to be required of all newspapers founded after January 1, 1822. Lastly, the government could impose censorship by simple decree between sessions of parliament.

By carrying out this legislation without letup or exception, the government succeeded in gradually stifling the liberal press. It had recourse to a rather original method, dreamed up by Sosthènes de la Rochefoucauld; a sort of "amortization fund," supplied by theater and lottery benefits, was used by intermediaries to buy up stocks of the opposition papers. Then, when the government finally obtained control of these papers, they gradually and imperceptibly changed their tone without alienating their regular subscribers. But the readers were not as dumb as they thought, and this wonderful trick only drove the subscribers over to a few big opposition papers like the *Constitutionnel* and the *Journal des Débats* whose financial situation was firm enough to give them the luxury of independence.

The government also took a number of measures, aimed at strengthening the influence of religion, which the Knights of the Faith thought were essential for the inauguration of a truly royalist social order. The Pantheon (used by the Revolution as a patriotic hall of fame) was restored to use for religious services after the remains of Voltaire and Rosseau had been removed. Nineteen archbishops and bishops were appointed as ecclesiastical peers in the upper house, and the decree on Sabbath observance was strictly enforced. Education, especially, was to be placed under the control of the clergy: on June 1 the office of Grand Master of the University was re-established and filled by the appointment of Monseigneur Frayssinous, bishop *"in partibus"* of Herm-opolis. He had earned a wide reputation as a preacher during the Empire, attracting large crowds of young people to his lectures at the Saint-Sulpice Church. He had full authority to appoint the personnel of the royal colleges and determine their curricula. Later, in April 1824, the rectors of the academies were to lose the right to issue teachers certificates to elementary school teachers, a job to be taken over by the bishops.

## The Foreign Policy of the Right

The new trend of the government was also seen in its foreign policy, and this, taking on again an activity and an importance not seen for a long time, became, by counteraction, an important factor in its domestic policy as well.

The conservative powers had repressed the revolution in Italy with-out France and even partly in spite of her. Here Austria was doing the job. But the geographic location of Spain prevented Europe from intervening without French co-operation. Ever since the declaration of early 1820, the Spanish liberals had imposed on Ferdinand VII a con-stitutional regime which was functioning more or less successfully with England's blessing. Yet the situation suddenly became worse in July 1822. The absolutist factions attempted, with the complicity of the king, a military coup to overthrow the liberal government. Their bloody defeat in Madrid led to the opposite result of bringing into power the extrem-ists of the Left. The provinces of the north—Catalonia, Aragon, and Navarre—then rose in open rebellion against Madrid and established at Seo d'Urgel a "regency" in the name of the king, who had become virtually a prisoner in liberal hands; and their forces, under the name of "Army of the Faith," launched a civil war.

These events no longer permitted France to evade her responsibilities. Ever since the preceding year it had been agreed that a European con-gress would meet in Verona at the end of 1822. The dramatic develop-ments in Spanish affairs naturally was to cause the powers to give them priority over other questions listed on the agenda, such as Italy, the Eastern question, revolts of the Spanish colonies in America, and the slave trade. Tsar Alexander and Metternich were very determined to put out this revolutionary fire at any cost. France had an equal interest in its repression because she herself was a house filled with inflammable materials and threatened by any fire breaking out next door. The head of the house of Bourbon likewise could not stand idly by in the face of the danger threatening the freedom, and perhaps the very life, of his cousin without endangering his own crown. But intervention, in whatever form it might take, with or without the active assistance of the armies of the conservative alliance, involved risks almost as frightening as the nonintervention naturally advocated by the liberal party.

Even though a royalist ministry, it was hesitant and divided over what course to follow. On the one hand, Montmorency—supported, it seems, by the rightist majority—considered that the only possible decision which would assure at one and the same time the security and dignity of France would be that she boldly undertake to re-establish order in Spain, even by a military expedition if need be, and to obtain the consent and the eventual support of the conservative powers. In the meantime the French government secretly gave all possible aid to the insurgents in the northern part of the peninsula. Villèle, on the other hand, wanted to avoid a large-scale military campaign at any cost, and he had some good reasons for this. The recent Charbonniere plots gave occasion to distrust the loyalty of the military in case they were asked to bear arms against the Spanish liberals; in this regard it should be remembered that the Spanish revolution had broken out in 1820 precisely among the troops assembled at Cadiz to embark for the repression of the insurrections in the Spanish-American colonies. The more remote remembrance of the fate of Napoleon's armies in Spain made even the boldest ones hesitate, and, as in that earlier episode, they could fear that the Spanish enemy might again receive English support. As Wellington went through Paris on his way to Vienna and Verona, he did not conceal his country's intention of opposing any French military intervention in the peninsula. As a last consideration, Villèle, as minister of finance, feared that a big military effort might unsettle that nice balance that he had worked so hard to establish in the budget.

The king and Artois, persuaded by his arguments, supported his cautious policy. But it was a different matter to try to insist on this point of view with the minister of foreign affairs, who would have the duty of representing France at the Congress of Verona. Villèle obtained the momentary co-operation of Chateaubriand; but this great writer was consumed by a desire to play a big role on the international scene and thus to qualify himself to be foreign minister, the goal of his ambitions. The *Journal des Débats,* which was under his influence, therefore supported Villèle's policy; and Montmorency, urged by the king and worked on by Chateaubriand's active friends in the salons, ended by agreeing to let the latter represent France at Verona. Nevertheless, Villèle could not overlook the fact that the responsible minister could not be absent from Vienna, where the preliminary conversations were to take place. The Allied sovereigns were to be there, and the other powers were to be represented by their leading statesmen. The King of France could not be an exception by sending a mere ambassador. Villèle at least took his precautions. The written instructions, prepared for Montmorency in consultation with the king, provided that he should avoid taking the initiative in bringing up the Spanish question, and, in any case, he should state that France had decided to take independent action at a time and by a means of her own choosing. Nevertheless, he was to assure himself of the assistance which the continental powers could bring to her in case of complications. Besides, a few days after Montmorency's departure, Villèle was appointed president of the council and thus was given the authority to control his foreign minister's actions. In the aristocratic salons of the suburb of Saint-Germain, they winced at this appointment: How is it, they were saying, that the king dared put the heir of one of the greatest names in France, the highest Christian baron, under the control of a lowly Gascon gentleman, who was, besides, ignobly competent in financial matters? And what a way to act— to wait until Montmorency's departure before going ahead with this little inside coup d'état! Montmorency's feelings were hurt by this maneuver, and the previous opposing views of these two men were now complicated by the additional factor of offended self-esteem.

As soon as the French representative arrived in Vienna, he had very cordial conversations with the tsar; their generous and mystical characters found themselves in perfect harmony. These interviews easily inclined Montmorency to go beyond the literal terms of his instructions. Besides, he could have legitimately thought that the best way for France to retain her freedom of maneuver, on which the king insisted, was to take the initiative of intervention plans and not to leave it to someone else to take over the direction of the movement. And how would France find out the intentions of the other powers without raising the question with them? Villèle's policy was timid and tortuous, like that of Pasquier; Montmorency's could be called imprudent, but it had the merits of clarity and dignity. He decided to explain his point of view in a note in which he considered the clear possibility of French intervention and asked the powers to indicate clearly their intentions. Then, as the plenipotentiaries went on to Verona, he decided to go on with them, much to the disappointment of Chateaubriand, who had counted on being France's highest delegate at the congress.

In spite of England's opposition, the congress deliberated on the manner of breaking off relations with the Spanish liberal government. Montmorency, in order to safeguard France's freedom of action, at least in appearance, had them agree that the step would take place not by a joint note but by similar separate but simultaneous notes. The terms, drawn up in concert, made the notes veritable ultimatums demanding the release of King Ferdinand VII. Montmorency asked for still another delay to obtain the king's approval of the French note, and he left for Paris on November 12, giving Chateaubriand the job of defending the French point of view in the other questions taken up in the congress.

Montmorency, once back in the capital, received the title of duke from the hands of Louis XVIII. Villèle concealed his discontent at having seen the duke go beyond his instructions, but he still tried to avoid any positive action. On December 5 he had the council of ministers agree to ask the Allies to hold up the sending of their notes and to leave it to their ambassadors in Paris to decide, in agreement with the French government, on the most favorable time for such action. Russia, Prussia, and Austria agreed to wait a few days, but they let it be clearly understood that they would not allow France to depart from the line of action decided upon at Verona in consultation with the French representative.

As soon as Chateaubriand returned on December 20, Villèle called a meeting of the council. Montmorency strongly defended his point of view: that a war was inevitable, better to have it now before the Spanish monarchist forces were crushed. He had succeeded in getting the co-operation of the other powers; but, if France now refused to join in their common action, she would risk having to face England alone when circumstances might finally compel intervention. All the ministers came over to his support, except Villèle, who closed the meeting abruptly by saying that the final decision rested with the king. Finally, on December 25, the definitive council meeting took place in the presence of Louis XVIII. Villèle again found himself alone in thinking they should not join in the action decided upon by the three powers of the alliance. To everyone's surprise the king came out strongly in favor of the opinion of the prime minister. Immediately Montmorency handed in his resignation; he could not, he said, support a policy contrary to the engagements he had made with the European powers.

Villèle had won, but it was a Pyrrhic victory, because in the end it only helped the more surely to bring about the success of the policy he had been opposing. Montmorency's position in the Ultra party and at the court was such that his eviction threatened to create a deep split in the majority's ranks. The only way to quiet the excitement was to replace him by a person capable of rallying and reassuring the Ultra party. Chateaubriand resisted offers just enough to save face and then gleefully accepted the foreign portfolio which he had been coveting for a long time, and Montmorency was enough of a good loser to give his support and solicit that of his friends.

With this backing and Villèle's need to avoid a domestic crisis, Chateaubriand followed the same policy as his predecessor and got it approved in spite of England's threats from abroad and the angry opposition of the liberals from within. Very soon, the French representative in Madrid was recalled. On January 28, 1823 the king, in his opening speech to parliament, declared:

> Madrid's deafness to our appeals leaves little hope of preserving peace. I have ordered the recall of our minister; and 100,000 French troops commanded by a prince of my family . . . calling on the God of Saint Louis, are ready to go into action to save the throne of Spain for a grandson of Henry IV, to spare this fine kingdom from ruin, and to reconcile it with Europe.

For several weeks thereafter the chambers debated the appropriations for the expedition. This caused a violent interparty conflict. General Foy, with all the influence of his experience in the Napoleonic campaigns in Spain, predicted a military disaster. Deputy Manuel raised an unprecedented storm of violent reaction by calling the execution of Louis XVI (in 1793) a measure of public safety justified by the earlier foreign invasion of France. "Do I need to remind you," he asked, "that the dangers of the royal family had become more menacing when revolutionary France had felt that she had to defend herself by a new form of government and by an entirely new surge of energy?" On hearing these words, the Right lost all control of itself and demanded the speaker's expulsion. This was voted in the next sitting, and, since Manuel refused to leave and remained glued to his seat, he had to be ousted by force. The liberal deputies stood by their colleague and refused to take their seats for the rest of the session. Manuel became transformed into a national hero.

All of this legislative noise did not stop the expedition nor prevent its success. Several months earlier France had been stationing troops along the Spanish border, calling them a "protective buffer" (*cordon sanitaire*), and later an "observation corps." By early April 1823, a hundred thousand men were drawn up and ready, divided into five army corps under the supreme command of the Duke of Angoulême. The prince was aided by General Guilleminot, a former Empire officer, as indeed were most of the commanders of the larger units. Marshal Victor, the minister of war, had very much wanted to have for himself the assignment of major-general in the place of Guilleminot, but the Duke of Angoulême would not consent. The latter was afraid that, with this veteran at his side, he would look like a little boy in leading-strings.

The secret societies and the liberals did their utmost to get the soldiers to desert and to provoke incidents. Béranger, for example, composed a song whose refrain was: "Brave soldiers, about face!" But the idea of having a chance to fight, to get out of their barracks, to try out the theories they had learned, to have a chance to win distinction, aroused such spirit among men and officers up and down the chain of command that soldiers whose enlistments were ending were seen signing up again—and that meant for seven more years!

Yet some refugee French officers in Spain gathered about two hundred men at Bidassoa. Dressed in French uniforms, flying the tricolor flag, and singing the *Marseillaise,* they marched out to bar the way of the royalist troops as they crossed the Spanish border. General Vallin, a former Empire officer, had his men fire three volleys of grapeshot, and, with a cry of *Long live the King!* this token resistance was quashed. As a matter of fact there was no sign of disloyalty on the part of the army during the entire Spanish campaign. Indeed, this problem of loyalty, which liberal propaganda had come to convince Villèle would be serious, evaporated into thin air at the first encounter.

Yet another difficulty, on the supply side, came very near up-setting everything at the last minute. The army supply service had assembled large quantities of food and forage but had neglected to furnish enough transportation to move it along with the advancing armies. Of course, French supplies were absolutely essential because the French had to go into Spain as allies of the legitimate government of the Spanish king. They had to avoid arbitrary requisitioning or pillaging which had characterized the earlier Napoleonic invasions and which would have antagonized the inhabitants. So the Duke of Angoulême ac-cepted the services of Ouvrard, the great army supplier and the big profiteer during the wars of the Directory and Empire. He came on the scene at just the right moment like a bolt out of the blue and outdid himself in setting things straight. It is even suspected that this sly fox may have had something to do with the original predicament which later required his intervention. In any case he took care of everything, paying cash to the Spanish for all supplies, and the army never lacked a thing, while the Spanish peasants, far from suffering from the French occupation, actually turned a good penny.

Nowhere did they encounter serious resistance. A few places which were defended by the Spanish liberals were quickly overrun. The people in the North, mostly royalist, welcomed the French as liberators. This time there was no resemblance to the old days of the invading soldiers of the Empire. Back then a straggler could not have avoided capture and would have suffered indescribable cruelties ending in having his throat slit. Now the limping straggler was taken in with kindness and gently sent on his way in a cart or on mule-back. This time the French had come to defend the same cause as the *guerrilleros* of 1808—that of legitimate king and holy religion.

On May 24, the Duke of Angoulême entered Madrid amid a shower of flowers, beneath triumphal arches, and to the cries of *"mueron los negros!"* (death to all liberals!). But King Ferdinand was not to be found. At the end of March the liberal Spanish government had thought it more prudent to withdraw toward Seville, taking the sovereign with them as a hostage. From there they fled to Cadiz. This fortified place, behind natural defences, was hard to take by main force. During Napoleon's time the French had besieged it for three years without reducing it to submission. On August 30 an assault column, swimming across a channel, by a bold move captured the fortified position of the Trocadero dominating the city. At this point the liberals decided to surrender. Ferdinand VII, finally freed, was welcomed on October 1 by his cousin, Angoulême, in the midst of a great display of military pomp. During the next few weeks the fortified cities still holding out capitulated one by one, and the vestiges of the constitutional armies either surrendered or disbanded. From the military point of view the campaign was a great success. But Spanish domestic policy was not as fortunate. In spite of all the efforts of the Duke of Angoulême, he could not prevent the absolutist triumph from becoming one of the most cruel and bloody reactions. In great distress of mind, he hurried home to France and refused the honors and titles which Ferdinand VII wished to shower upon him. Later, in February 1824, a treaty was signed between France and Spain, which provided that Louis XVIII would furnish Ferdinand VII an army of occupation of 45,000 men. They would be paid by France, but Spain would pay for the difference between the cost of their maintenance in time of peace with that of being on a war

footing. Spain also recognized her debt of thirty-four million francs, resulting from French treasury advances in 1823. Finally the Catholic
King promised an amnesty which, in fact, was not put into effect until
after all the acts of vengeance had been carried out. The French occupation in Spain was to last until September 1828.

In France itself, the success of the undertaking contributed considerably to the consolidation of the rightist regime and government
which had assumed the responsibility for it. The few weeks of a
successful campaign had restored the morale within the army, had dissipated the noxious atmosphere arising from the plots of the preceding
year, and had succeeded in fusing the old and new elements within
the ranks. Henceforth the army would be loyal to the white flag without
any mental reservation. The collapse of the Spanish liberals discouraged
the domestic enemies of the regime and deprived them of a support
and an example. And, what is more, the French liberals found they had
lost prestige in public opinion. Because their predictions had been so
gloomy, the outcome of the campaign was to be all the more of a disaster for them. By holding themselves aloof from this enterprise which
stimulated national pride, by first opposing it and then begrudging the
victory, they lost the right to their claim since 1815 of being the heralds
of patriotism.

And how are we to estimate the prestige France gained abroad?
Canning himself, who had opposed the expedition with everything within
his power, was obliged to admit that "never had an army done so
little harm and prevented so much of it." Chateaubriand could well be
proud of his work and boasted that "eight years of peace had done
less to strengthen the legitimate throne than had twenty days of war."
And Stendhal, not exactly a friend of the regime, declared that "it
cannot be said that the Bourbons were really restored in France until
after the recent war in Spain."

## Royalist Factions

The government hastened to capitalize on its success in the political
sphere. On December 24, 1823 the chamber was dissolved and general
elections were held on the following February 26 and March 6. The
ministry did not fail to use all the sly tricks for which they had previously criticized Decazes: tampering with the voting lists, pressure on
government officeholders, etc. And they won a crushing victory: out of
the 110 liberal seats in the previous lower house only nineteen remained
and many of the most eminent liberal members—such as La Fayette,

Manuel, and d'Argenson—were left lying on the field. Louis XVIII described the result as "the Rediscovered Chamber" (*La Chambre Retrouvée*).

The victorious party intended gradually and quietly to take up the program which had been interrupted in September 1816, and one of the first things the new chamber did was to pass a law which abolished the annual elections of one-fifth of its members and gave all members a term of seven years. This last provision, however, was not to apply to the present chamber.

But at the very hour of this triumph there began to appear in the royalist party some irremediable fissures which were to bring on its own ruin. It has already been pointed out above that in the preceding years there had been a group on the extreme Right, "the impatient ones," who were now called "the edgies" and who were constantly accusing the ministry of moderation and compromise. No doubt it would have been possible to silence some of the most troublesome voices by a judicious distribution of jobs, but Villèle could not bring himself to overcome his resentments. Anyone who criticized him was considered an enemy of the king and was driven into the outer darkness. Previously it had been necessary to close ranks and limit the influence of disagreements in the face of leftist attacks. But the elections of 1824 strengthened this extreme rightist group to the number of seventy seats, and the fact that there was no longer a threat from the Left seemed to permit it more freedom of action. Villèle predicted as much when he remarked: "The absence, in the chamber, of deputies representing revolutionary principles is going to break royalist solidarity. . . . We are going to begin firing on ourselves and lose the fight."

It was even more inexcusable for the council president to give the royalist counteropposition, in addition to reasons for discontent on matters of policy, still other personal reasons for dissatisfaction. We have already seen how he supplanted and then eliminated his minister, Mathieu de Montmorency, thus antagonizing opinion in the aristocratic salons, in the religious party, and among numerous Knights of the Faith. No doubt the virtuous Mathieu, practicing the forgiveness of offenses, had persuaded his friends to continue to give their support to the ministry, but, as Polignac put it, "duty rather than confidence made the donation." In October 1823 it was Marshal Victor's turn to be unhorsed. In fact his disgrace was due principally to the Duke of Angoulême, who blamed him for almost compromising the success of the Spanish expedition by not tending closely enough to the matter of supplies. Villèle did nothing to calm the exaggerated prejudices of the prince, and for this negligence he was criticized by his own party. Chateaubriand saw to it that the marshal was replaced by Baron Maxence de Damas, a very mediocre individual but an honest man, and royalist to the core.

But Villèle's big mistake was to get rid of Chateaubriand himself and in a way which was to make him a mortal enemy. Certainly it was not always easy to get along with this great man; the superiority of his genius eclipsed the solid, down-to-earth qualities of the council president. The success of the Spanish affair had somewhat intoxicated Chateaubriand, and he now tried to be the master in conducting foreign relations by disdainfully relegating Villèle to the domestic kitchen. The king did not like the foreign minister either, whose attitude in 1816 he could never forget. The occasion for the break was the foreign minister's stand during the debate on the bill for the conversion of government bonds as presented by Villèle in May 1824. The bill, barely passing in the chamber of deputies, encountered strong opposition in the chamber of peers. Chateaubriand could perhaps have saved it by giving strong support; but personally he was opposed to it, and he saw no way of balancing his convictions and ministerial solidarity except by taking refuge in a passive attitude. The bill was defeated, and Villèle resented his abstention very much as, still more, did the king, who gave vent to senile fury. "Chateaubriand has betrayed us like a scamp. I won't see him again!" Forthwith the ordinance dismissing him from office was drawn up and signed. On Sunday morning, June 6, Chateaubriand, not yet suspecting anything, went to the Tuileries to make his usual courtesy call on the king, and it was here that his secretary brought him the document with a letter from Villèle—"such a letter," the recipient said, "as one would blush to write to a delinquent valet who was being kicked out into the street." Chateaubriand left the palace immediately, and in two hours he had moved out of his ministerial apartments. Villèle offered to restore his pension as minister of state, of which he had been deprived in 1816; but the great writer scorned this contemptible charity dole with the words "I did not intend to become the pensionary of the council president." He was, in his own words "mortally offended," and Villèle was not to have to wait long to feel the effects of his revenge. A few days later Chateaubriand, pointing to his inkstand, told Berryer, "With this I'll smash that little whippersnapper!" Immediately he brought over to the opposition the *Journal des Débats,* the most influential newspaper of the day, which began to denounce violently all the vices of the government: "A timid, colorless administration, full of deception and power-hungry; a political system incompatible with the genius of France and contrary to the spirit of the Charter; a shady despotism, equating effrontery with strength; corruption raised to a system," etc.

Today one can look back and realize how serious a mistake it was when Villèle drove Chateaubriand into opposition. Lacking general culture and too exclusively preoccupied with material accomplishments, Villèle did not realize the power of ideas; and he had no conception of the fact that a balanced budget was not enough to satisfy the imagination and the sensitivity of a public influenced by the winds of romanticism. On the other hand Chateaubriand was the very man who could masterfully strike these dominant cords. He was also sincerely attached to freedom of expression and to the parliamentary regime, and, if there was anyone who could rally the generous impulses of the younger generation to the cause of the old monarchy, he was the one who could do it. The fall of Chateaubriand was no less fatal in the realm of foreign affairs. He had inaugurated a lofty policy which could raise France's prestige in Europe and monarchy's prestige in France. He had already set in motion a grandiose project for the Spanish colonies in America. His idea was to guarantee the recognition of their autonomy, provided they accepted Spanish royal princes as sovereigns, as was done for Brazil with Dom Pedro, son of the King of Portugal. France would thereby have been assured in this area of a preponderant influence, opening a new outlet to her commerce which England had tried to keep exclusively for herself. Chateaubriand even began looking toward the Rhine frontier. With Villèle, France's foreign policy began to fall back into mediocrity and immobility, and that would be harmful to the regime.

In other words, the dismissal of Chateaubriand appears as Villèle's greatest mistake. By setting this talented writer against him, he also turned against himself the irresistible force of a whole generation of public opinion and prepared not only his own downfall but that of the monarchy.

## The Death of the King

The dismissal of Chateaubriand was the last important act of Louis XVIII, and this unpardonable mistake would certainly bring into question that political good sense generally attributed to him when comparing him too casually with the supposed ineptitude of Charles X. Yet, the latter had criticized this dismissal, at least in the way it was done. He also disapproved the reimposition of censorship on August 15. "Oh Villèle, what foolishness!" he cried out. The prime minister had given as reason for this measure the king's health, which was rapidly getting worse. Gangrene in his legs was spreading, and he was literally wasting away. His head now hung down, resting on his chest, and his ministers, in order to understand his orders, had to bend down to the legs of his armchair. Except for periods of prostration, which were becoming longer and more frequent, Louis XVIII showed his usual firmness and lucidity, insisting on fulfilling his duties to the end. "A king is allowed to die," he remarked, "but he is never permitted to be sick." He also still retained the same inflexible regard for his dignity. After one of his sinking-spells his physician, Dr. Portal, was supervising the difficult operation of putting the king to bed. In an impatient tone he spoke to the valets: "Come on, finish your job, take off his shirt." Whereupon the king opened his eyes and said: "M. Portal, my name is Louis XVIII, you should say: take off His Majesty's shirt." Nor did his bent for bad puns entirely disappear. When he gave the watchword and password for one of his latter days, he murmured: "St. Denis—Givet." (Saint-Denis was the burial place of kings, and Givet could also be rendered *J'y vais* [that's where I'm going].) Mme du Cayla, alerted by Artois, persuaded Louis to receive the last rites on September 13. He lingered on for three more days. Finally on September 16, at exactly four in the morning, he breathed his last. He was to be the last king of France to die while occupying his throne.

The people of Paris, who suspended all their activities, showed by their spontaneous grief how grateful they were to the old monarch whose reign, opening among the worst convulsions and the most frightful disasters, ended in peace and dignity, in a pacified, independent, and prosperous France.

*French Life During the Restoration*

# 14

✣ ✣ ✣ ✣ ✣

# *Economic Life*

## French Roads

THE France of Louis XVIII and Charles X was appreciably smaller than it is today: 203,587 square miles instead of the present 212,660 square miles, and eighty-six departments instead of the present ninety. On the southeast the boundary separating France from Piedmont-Sardinia ran along the lower course of the river Var, then the eastern side of the departments of the Basses-Alpes and Alpes-Maritimes; to the north of these departments the line did not include the present departments of Savoie and Haute-Savoie, and from the confluence of the Guiers up to the territory of Geneva it was the swift and greenish waters of the river Rhone which served as a national boundary. The boundaries of the northeast and north were the same as today except for slight variations.

But if France was smaller then geographically, she was much larger if we count distances by the time it took to travel them. This is an important fact which must be stressed because it lies behind and explains most of the differences between that older world and our own. The similarity of the geographic map, the familiar sound of the place names, the uninterrupted continuity of the human bonds which link us with our forebears, the permanence of certain spiritual values, all of these make it difficult to recognize those differences. It requires a real effort to rediscover that France which is so close to us and yet so far away. Between these two Frances stand the industrial and transportation revolutions, and the latter is perhaps more important than the former. A civilization is not only identified by its means of production, but maybe even more it is a function of its rhythm of exchange. In the period with which we are concerned, it is hard to imagine the slowness and difficulty of travel and trade. This applies to persons, to goods, and even to new ideas, to the extent that they needed material conveyance.

So, if one wishes to understand Restoration France in her concrete reality, it is well to describe at the outset the state of her internal communications. The coastal trade was certainly more active then than now; thus most Mediterranean products arrived in Paris by passing through the Straits of Gibraltar. But this coastal transportation could only serve the coastal regions, and it too had to depend on inland transportation. For this there were only two means at hand—roads and waterways.

In those earlier days roads were very different from those of our century, built now for the needs of automobile traffic. A royal road during the Restoration, including the borders on each side, was from ten to fourteen yards wide, usually lined with trees and built as straight as possible without much regard for unevenness of terrain. In the middle of this cleared roadway was the road itself, about four to six yards wide, either paved with large stones or, more often, surfaced with crushed stone. The wide dirt shoulders on each side were transformed into mudholes most of the year by the heavy wagons and bad weather. When the road in the center was paved—only about one-third of the royal roads were thus constructed—they were so bumpy that postilions were allowed to drive their coaches and carriages on the wide shoulders wherever possible. This paved part of the roadway was so narrow and sometimes so steeply sloped to the sides and so raised above the shoulders that the carriages could not go off on the shoulders or come back on the road without risk of overturning, and passing an oncoming vehicle required very dangerous maneuvering. In some places roads were so full of holes from side to side that the wagons went out around them as best they could in the adjacent fields. It was not unusual for horses to die on the road, and their half-decomposed bodies sprawled dangerously across the most heavily travelled routes.

The engineers of the Bridge and Road Service (*Ponts et Chaussées*), however, tried to improve the technique of stone surfacing (macadamizing), which they had gone to study in McAdam's school in England, and after 1824 the system of paid road-repair crews had been introduced on all royal roads. They also tried to protect the roads from misuse by detailed and vexatious rules on the width of wheel rims, the length of axles, the weight of vehicles, the arrangement of the horses, and their gait—no galloping allowed. But it was all in vain because it was practically impossible to enforce them; and the roads, receiving more and more traffic and more and more abuse, bore mute and ever-increasing testimony to their inadequacy for the tasks imposed upon them by the growth of the French economy.

Henri Sée in his *Histoire économique* asserted that the Restoration paid little attention to roads. It is true that it added very little mileage to the some 19,000 miles of royal roads inherited from the previous regimes, but that does not mean that the Restoration neglected the roads. On the contrary, it carried out a program in this respect which, while not spectacular, was nonetheless considerable. Neither the Revolution nor the Empire had found a practical substitute for the compulsory farm labor on roads (*corvée*), of such odious memory, which had nevertheless permitted the Old Regime to create a whole system of main highways, the envy of foreign travellers. Napoleon reserved his efforts for the construction of strategic roads running from Paris to the northern and eastern frontiers, and he had completed, with heavy outlays, the first roads through the Alps. But in the rest of the country, he allowed the highways to fall into a lamentable state of neglect. In 1811 only thirty-six per cent of the highways were in a "maintained condition"—that is, in a good state of repair. The events between 1813 and 1815 had only made the situation worse. Under such conditions it is understandable that, before thinking of adding new mileage to a highway system already sufficient for an emergency, the government should have preferred to use its limited resources for the repair and improvement of the existing roads.

The Bridge and Road Service, directed between 1816 and 1830 by an excellent administrator, Louis Becquey, was reorganized from top to bottom. The roads were divided into three categories: royal roads of general use, departmental roads, and local roads. The construction and maintenance of the first category devolved entirely upon the national government, and each year its budget provided a regular appropriation which amounted to three or four per cent of the total national expenditures, that is, a higher percentage than present budgets allot to the maintenance of 48,000 miles of national highways. The bridges destroyed during the wars were rebuilt and others were constructed. At Roche-Guyon, on the Seine, in 1819, and on the Rhone at Tournon in 1823, the engineer Marc Seguin introduced the technique of suspension bridges. Slowly the situation improved; the proportion of royal roads in "maintained condition" rose to 44.5 per cent in 1824, and to fifty-two per cent in 1830. But they were still way behind. In 1828 Pasquier, reporting for the parliamentary committee assigned to study the problem, estimated that 198 million francs ($39,600,000) was a required special expenditure to complete the repair of the royal highway system—that is, a sum larger than all that had been spent on the main royal roads in the past ten years.

The departmental roads were in principle maintained by local budgets voted by the general (departmental) councils. So the repair work on these varied from one department to another, and accurate overall statistics are lacking for these. The few local studies which have been made lead one to believe that, under the prodding of a certain number of energetic and enlightened prefects, the mileage of these secondary roads increased considerably more than that of the royal roads. As to the small local roads, whose construction and maintenance fell to the communes (townships), little was done to remedy their notorious disrepair, one of the big obstacles to agricultural progress. The specter of the old hated forced labor prevented for a long time recourse to contributions in kind, the only practical way to get around it. Finally a law of July 28, 1824 allowed the communes to have recourse to this expedient, and after that some improvements were made, but their usefulness was limited by a lack of co-ordination with neighboring communes.

## Passengers and Freight

On these inadequate roads the movement of people and goods was provided by the combined efforts of the government and private enterprise. First of all, the government furnished the post horses—that is, the big post routes had relay service stations about every six or twelve miles apart depending on the difficult conditions along the line. The first duty of the postmasters was to provide teams of horses for official vehicles and mounts for dispatch-riders, but they were also supposed to furnish horses, if they were available, to stagecoach companies and to individuals on presentation of their passports. In return for the cost of upkeep of the horses, some of which were often not in use, they were given important advantages, such as the monopoly of furnishing horses for everyone using the post roads, the right to organize transport services themselves and thus have first call on their own horses, and the right to collect from road users having their own horses a fee of twenty-five centimes (five cents) per horse for every post zone (about every four miles). Thus the Paris postmaster, an important person with two hundred horses in his stables earned about 112,000 francs ($22,400) a year.[1] Indeed, this did not

[1] We would have liked to translate the prices given in the franc of Charles X into present franc prices. In our first edition we had thought to suggest a coefficient of 160 (=1.60 new francs), by basing it on the current price of gold. This evaluation has been thought generally to be too modest. Not only should we take into account the fluctuations in gold quotation, but also the buying power of money, itself a function of the cost of essential commodities. The resultant coefficient would then be somewhere between 2 and 3, but it is impossible to be more precise.

prevent concessionaires from complaining bitterly about the competition they had to face from private relay services.

The postmasters ruled over the turbulent crowd of team-drivers (postilions) who wore a traditional uniform: a royal blue jacket with cuffs, turned-back facings, and vests of red cloth, silver buttons, knee-breeches of yellow leather, and a hat of polished leather in the shape of the lower half of a cone perched on a massive knot of powdered hair. Their job was to drive the teams furnished by the post station to which they are attached and then to return them to the stables. They had the reputation for being particularly fond of the bottle, and this accusation seems to be supported by an official regulation: Article 33 of the ordinance of September 23, 1827 required the postmaster himself "to inspect the postilions, lined up for departure, to make sure that they were not drunk."

The vehicles which made use of this omnipresent force of post horses represented a wide variety. First there was the mail-coach, the express of those days, which had absolute priority over all other users. Owned by the letter post service, it was a solid four-wheel, leather-topped coach drawn by four horses. It was made primarily for courier service, and only carried a maximum of four passengers. Every evening, around six o'clock, the Paris mail-coaches took off in eleven different directions and stopped only long enough to change horses. This was the conveyance for people in a hurry and for government officials on mission. Thanks to various improvements the average speed of mail-coaches increased from 8.5 minutes per kilometer to 5.75 minutes by 1830. Thus the trip from Paris to Bordeaux then took 45 hours instead of 86, to Lyons 47 hours instead of 68, to Toulouse 72 hours instead of 110. They called this "traveling with lightening speed." But the fare was high: 1.5 francs (thirty cents) from post to post, plus .75 francs (fifteen cents) for "guide money" (tips to the postilions). The total fare from Paris to Bordeaux was 181 francs ($36.20), not including meals and incidental expenses.

Wealthier people preferred to travel with their own carriages or by a berlin rented for a particular trip, but they also used post relays unless they wanted to make frequent stopovers. But these means of travel were very expensive: 1.5 francs (thirty cents) per horse per post, plus 1.5 francs tips, plus a double fare for the first post out of Paris. For example, a trip from Paris to Bordeaux by a four-horse berlin would come to thirteen hundred francs ($260) for just the teams of horses. It is therefore easily understood why the large stage-coach (*diligence*) became more and more popular and more numerous as arranged by the coach companies (*messageries*). The finance bill of 1817 abolished the monopoly held by the powerful Royal Messageries Company, successor to the old Régie Générale (government-controlled services). Yet, it was not until after 1826 that it began to face serious competition from the Compagnie des Messageries générales de France, founded by Laffitte, Caillard and Company. For a brief period there was a rate war which soon ended in an understanding by which the two companies agreed to uniform rates and exclusive territories. These two companies alone took care of about one-third of the traffic. In the south their services did not go beyond Lyons, Bordeaux, and Toulouse. This allowed smaller companies to survive and prosper in the south, such as Dotézac of Bordeaux, and Galline and Company of Lyons. Elsewhere there was a swarm of little companies—2,132 in 1827—some of which only owned one coach.

Engravings and pictures have made familiar to all the silhouettes of those heavy and majestic stagecoaches called diligences owned by the big coach companies. They seated from sixteen to twenty travellers in addition to the postilions and the conductor, the company representative who had the job of taking care of every travel detail for the entire run. The stagecoach travelled more slowly than the mailcoach. If, as was usual, they made a night trip on leaving Paris and other large cities, they had to make rest-stops somewhere along this night run. Thus by stagecoach it took two days from Paris to Lille, three days to Dijon, four to Lyons, Rennes, or Nantes, five to Bordeaux, and eight to Toulouse. It is more difficult to determine the exact fares because they often varied depending on competition. Besides, in the same coach, the fare varied up to a double fare depending on the location of the seats—the most expensive were in the forward compartment, the cheapest were on top. In 1830, when a rate war had depressed prices to a low point, it still cost forty francs (eight dollars) to go from Paris to Bordeaux in a second-class seat, and this cost was practically doubled by the extra expenses of rooms, meals, and tips.

When we realize that such an expense represented a whole month's wages for a skilled worker or small employee, we can understand how such coach trips were practically out of the reach of the low-income group. The travelling journeymen workers (*compagnons*) made their proverbial tour of France on foot; as did also the Limousins who came to Paris in groups to work in the building trades. Now and then, toward the end of his trip, a journeyman might hire a stagecart (*patache*), a sort of third-class mode of travel in those days. Perdiguier says it was "a free, proletarian rig, without rules or regulations, and belonging entirely to its own driver." It bumped along without springs or cushions, stopping at every watering trough to rest its single horse and at every inn to wet the raucous gullet of the "*patacheux.*" In the South you could also hire for a few pennies a little donkey which would take you at a tiny trot to a certain station down the line where he would automatically stop. It was useless for you to beat him, he would not move a foot farther, and no sooner had you dismounted than he would take off at a run for his stable.

Such were the costly and uncomfortable facilities at the disposal of the highway traveller, and so can we well understand why they did so much less travelling then than today. "Next to a famine," a contemporary said, "what Parisians fear most are journeys. For them a foreign land begins a few fathom's beyond their city's tollgates." From 1815 to 1824 the Paris Police Prefecture issued an average of 38,000 passports a year, and of course these were required for all travellers within France. In 1824, nevertheless, it seems that three hundred coaches left Paris every day, with a capacity for some three thousand passengers, and the demand for space was such that they had to make reservations well in advance. In the course of the fifteen years of the Restoration passenger travel doubled, as can be seen by the tax collected on fares paid for public conveyances: 2,380,000 francs ($476,000) in 1816 and 5,575,000 francs ($1,115,000) in 1829.

The capital city after 1826 possessed its own public transportation system. Beginning in 1829 the Omnibus Company had about a hundred vehicles which transported about thirty thousand people each day at a uniform fare of five cents (five *sous*). Its success brought out a number of competing enterprises whose carriages were named Favorites, Diligentes, Carolines, Ecossaises, Béarnaises, Dames Blanches, Citadines, Batignolliennes, etc. All of these others, together, carried almost as many passengers as the Omnibus Company. This new city transport service raised a storm of protests from the cab drivers, who had previously had a veritable monopoly of carrying passengers. In 1826 there were in Paris about 2,100 cabs (*fiacres* and *cabriolets*) which were hired either by the trip—1.50 francs (30 cents) anywhere within the walls—or by the hour at 2.25 francs (45 cents) per hour for hacks and 1.50 francs per hour for cabriolets. It was also popular to have recourse to cab rental services where they were rented by the day for from fifteen to thirty francs (three to six dollars). The number of private carriages was much higher, more than nine thousand in 1826. Lastly, at all the Paris tollgates were found some post-chaises, called *"coucous,"* all sorts of carriages, which took from fifteen to twenty thousand passengers per day for distances of up to forty leagues from the capital.

The mail-coaches and stagecoaches of the messagerie services could only carry small parcels. The heavy merchandise which could not use the coastal trade nor the inland waterways had to depend on the use of wagons (*roulage*). There was nothing more diverse than the means, the organization, and the rates of this heavy transport service. It extended from the powerful company with its central offices in Paris and branches in the provinces and its many horses, down to the individual peasant who, in the idle winter season, offered his horse and oxen for haulage service. In certain regions, pack mules and pack horses were used, or merchandise was loaded in wicker baskets on the sides of these draft animals. Wines were sometimes carried in half-casks (*portoirs*) on both sides of these animals. Even human porter service was used. The average price for ordinary wagon cartage kept going down during the Restoration: 1.25 francs (25 cents) per league-ton in 1818 to .93 francs (18.6 cents) in 1829. The wagon-drivers (*rouliers*) did not usually use the relay services and drove only in daytime, making only about twenty-four miles a day. Under the Restoration, however, a fast wagon service was inaugurated which used relays for almost uninterrupted trucking and made from forty-two to fifty-four miles in each twenty-four hours. But the high price for this kind of transport limited it obviously to luxury goods.

When it is realized that in 1818 it still cost 1.66 francs (thirty-three cents) per league-ton to transport Saint-Etienne coal by road up to the Loire River, one can understand how an archaic transport system paralyzed the development of the French economy.

### Railroads and Water Transportation

It was precisely this need to open up the coal and iron complex of Saint-Etienne that was to lead to the establishment of the first French railroads. As early as 1818 a mining engineer, Gabriel de Gallois, had pointed out the services furnished by railways in England. The initiative for such a railway in France is credited to Louis Beaunier, director of the Saint-Etienne School of Miners. Supported by a group of Paris capitalists and by some industrialists of the Saint-Etienne region, he obtained from the government, in February 1823, the first concession for the construction of a railway connecting Andrézieux on the Loire to Pont-de-l'Ane on the Furens. This line of 12.3 miles was opened in June 1827 and had cost 1,783,000 francs ($356,600). But in July 1826, Mme la Dauphine (the Duchess of Angoulême), visiting the region, attended a memorable experiment on the section already completed—a horse, running at a trot, pulled five cars loaded with ten tons of coal amid the applause of an enthusiastic crowd. Such was the modest beginning of an invention which was going to revolutionize the French economy. No one at that time suspected its importance; to the most forward-looking the railway appeared to be just a simple successor to canals, to be used in regions where the terrain did not permit the construction of inland waterways. They had no idea that it could be used for anything else than transporting ore over short distances. As to the method of moving these cars, it was done by a variety of means along the line: horses on the level and on gentle slopes, fixed steam engines pulling the cars up the steep ramps by means of a system of cables, and lastly on the downgrade letting the cars coast down under the control of brakes. Engineer Girard argued in favor of horse power over steam power in these words: "While locomotive machines can only be run at the ever-rising cost of a diminishing fuel supply, animal power will continue to find in the inevitable changes of the seasons its inexhaustible source of life and strength."

The success of this first enterprise, which brought about an appreciable reduction in coal transportation costs, encouraged other local attempts in the same region. One after another concessions for other freight railways were given: from Saint-Etienne to Lyons (1826), from Andrézieux to Roanne (1828), from Epinal to the Bourgogne Canal (1830). None of these lines began hauling before 1830. A few days before the downfall of Charles X, Baron Capelle, minister of public works, authorized a preliminary study of a railroad from Paris to Orleans. It was the harbinger of a new era.

Until that time should come, France, following England's example, thought she had found, in a better arrangement and use of her inland waterways, the right answer to the transport problems arising during the early years of the industrial revolution. Some water channels were used at that time which today no longer carry any traffic. The mileage of the river network in navigational use in 1830 amounted to about five thousand as compared to the present 2,700. The Isère River, for example, was practically the only outlet for heavy industry and agriculture in the Grenoble area, and, as in the Old Regime, the

Loire River was the main export artery from Orleans to the sea in spite of the obstacles along its course. Along the rivers Seine, Saône, and Garonne, and the Two-Seas Canal (from the Garonne to the Mediterranean), the passengers and mail boats were pulled by horse teams, which were changed at certain points just as were the stagecoaches on the royal highways. On the Two-Seas Canal travelers could make the trip from Toulouse to Béziers in thirty-six hours. On the Rhone there were huge barges from fifteen to twenty-five yards long which floated down, each one by itself, and then were pulled slowly back up the river against the current in trains of from five to twenty barges by prodigious teams of from forty to eighty horses. It was the attractive Saône River which had the first regular steamboat service from 1822 on, after having served as a trial stream for the celebrated experiments of the Marquis of Jouffray d'Abbans. The Seine River saw its first steamboat in 1828 as did the lower Loire, from Nantes to Angers, and naturally the Gironde. On the Rhone a steamboat in 1829 succeeded in going from Arles to Lyons in seven days instead of in the forty days required by the big horse towing teams.

All these natural waterways were constantly inspected and improved; yet the big governmental effort was for canals. Even in 1820 their total mileage did not exceed 435 miles. Two laws of August 5, 1821 and August 14, 1822 authorized the inauguration of a vast co-ordinated construction program of fifteen new canals, representing a total of 1,480 miles with 1,085 locks. It was a long-range project which was not completed until 1845. Yet, even under the Restoration they had already dug 555 miles of canals and spent 188 million francs ($37,600,000). This amount had been furnished mainly by bond issues and the rest from the royal treasury and by the concession companies, who were to share the operating profits with the state. Among these new lines, the most remarkable were the Rhone-to-Rhine Canal and the one through Burgundy with its famous tunnel running through a mountain for two miles which was practically finished in 1830.

## Communications

The postal communications were obviously limited by the slowness and drawbacks of transportation. Although, in Paris, the mail service in 1828 was delivering 43,000 letters a day, the mail service in the departments, by contrast, was very defective. Only 1,780 communes, out of a total of 37,367, had post offices. The other communes had to send paid messengers to fetch their mail from the nearest post office. A law of June 3, 1829 provided that after April 1, 1830 the postal administration would furnish postmen to collect and distribute mail, at least every other day, in all the communes of France. "This service," Chabrol declared proudly, "will be the most active of its kind that has ever been devised and executed." Contrary to the present usage, the cost of sending letters and other mail was paid by the receiver rather than by the sender, and the rates were determined by weight and distance. The minimum was twenty centimes (four cents) for a letter of 7.5 grams (.26 ounces), sent a distance of twenty-four miles—the equivalent in today's values of fifty centimes (ten cents). A plain letter from Paris to Marseilles cost then 1.10 francs (22 cents), the equivalent of today's two to three francs (forty to sixty cents). The rate for newspapers and magazines was uniform regardless of distance beyond the department: five centimes (one cent) per page of thirty square decimeters (46.6 square inches) outside the department and 2.5 centimes (.5 cents) within the department. In 1826 the daily mail leaving Paris amounted to 36,000 letters, sixty thousand papers and magazines, and ten thousand items of miscellaneous printed matter. The transmission of thought like that of goods was therefore at a much smaller quantity and slower pace than today. In 1826 it took Paris ten days to receive a reply from Marseilles —more than it would take today to correspond with Australia!

In this thick wall which distance erected against communications there was one lone crack, but a very tiny one as to practical effects— the aerial telegraph invented by Chappe during the Revolution. The sight of these big creaking arms going up and down on the top of steeples and towers might make us smile today, but it should not be forgotten that this antediluvian equipment produced astounding results in those times. For example, in April 1829, the news of the election of Pope Pius VIII, which arrived at Toulon from Rome at 4:00 A.M., was known in Paris eight hours later. In 1814 there were only four such telegraphic lines connecting Paris with Boulogne, Strasbourg, Brest, and Lyons. The Lyons line was extended to Toulon in 1821, and in the following year a line was hastily set up to Bayonne in preparation for the military intervention in Spain. The principal weakness of the Chappe system was that it could not operate at night or in foggy weather, and the messages obviously had to be very brief.

Such as it was, however, it was a valuable system, and the government jealously reserved its use to itself. The rest of French society had to be satisfied with the speed of stagecoaches and canal-boats.

More than any other factor, the slowness and difficulty of transportation and communication characterize the material civilization of this period and explain its archaic appearance. From the economists' point of view the great French Revolution was almost an insignificant period, and Restoration France was nearer to that of Louis XV than that of Napoleon III.

With the exception of a few privileged sectors of production, such as those of metallurgy, cotton, and silk, France was still in a condition of local economies. Each region lived more or less unto itself, producing all that was necessary for its daily consumption. Consequently, there were astonishing variations in prices from one region to another; famine could be sweeping over one province while others had an abundance. Industry was not concentrated and kept its artisan character and its diverse procedures and formulas. The provincial traditions survived vigorously in the outward style of living, in dress, in customs, and in language. France presented a picture of a less active and less unified way of life, but also a more peaceful and especially an infinitely more varied one than that of today.

## Agricultural Backwardness and Progress

This picture of French life applied particularly to the agricultural economy on which depended, in 1826, seventy-two per cent of Frenchmen and which furnished the country three-fourths of its annual income. At that time there were vineyards in the vicinity of Paris, and even, unbelievable as it may seem, right in Paris. On the other hand the Alpine peasants and those of other mountain regions persisted in growing cereals at altitudes where the return was as low as it was risky. Flax was cultivated in forty departments and hemp in fifty-seven, many small domestic manufacturers wanting to avoid buying the textiles they needed. Dye plants almost unknown today, such as madder, woad, yellow-weed, and saffron, were still important crops. The prices of agricultural products were extremely variable from one region to another: thus, in December 1827, the average price of a hectoliter of wheat was quoted as 14.18 francs ($2.84) in Ille-et-Vilaine when it was 30.95 francs ($6.19) in the Vaucluse; and, in one region alone, unusual weather conditions could bring considerably more differences in harvests from one year to another. For example, in the Haut-Rhin a hectoliter of wheat fell from 81.69 francs ($16.34) in June 1817 to 27.47 francs ($5.49) in June 1818.

Farming methods remained for the most part those of the preceding century. The old plow with the wooden moldboard was still the only type known to most peasants, and in some places, because of a lack of draft animals, the soil was turned by spade or hoe. Here and there some restrictive customs of the Old Regime still persisted: community grape and wheat harvesting (*bans de vendange*), common pastures, and obligatory field rotation of crops (*servitude d'assolements*). In fact some continued the traditional practice of keeping one field out of three fallow for a year, in the south even for two years. This shows that fertilizers were scarce; they had only the manure of their farm animals, and, near the cities, powdered night-soil (*"poudrette"*), the evil-smelling residue of the city cesspools. To use lime to sweeten the strongly acid soils was a luxury for only a few enlightened large landowners.

The government continued to consider its role in national agriculture from the point of view of the problem of subsistence, as in the days of Turgot. It never wearied of having its scribes draw up long lists of crop predictions and compile market quotations, but the only way it knew to encourage agriculture was to keep prices up by protective tariffs, which, alas, did not succeed either. As for undertaking great projects of draining swamps or clearing land, as for introducing new species and promoting new methods which would increase production, the government considered that such things were not its business. Its principle remained that formulated by Chaptal, Napoleon's former minister: "An enlightened government ought to limit itself to encouraging production and leave it entirely to private enterprise, which alone can apply the encouragement to activity, foresight, and enlightenment." Only in one instance, under Decazes in 1819, did the minister of the interior depart from this inertia; a council of agriculture was set up, which was to have correspondents in every department, instructed to promote good farming methods. They sent out missions here and there to buy good breeding animals and to study new and useful crops. But once Decazes was out, the budget for agriculture was reduced from year to year. In 1828 it was down to the ridiculous figure of 2,131,000 francs ($426,200). About nine-tenths of this was to be used as welfare aid to farmers hit by disaster; the rest was used to support stingily the veterinary schools in Alfort, Toulouse, and Lyons, two royal sheep farms, remaining from the six in existence in 1822, and one or two tree nurseries.

Nevertheless, the government showed itself capable of decisive action when it came to saving the remnants of the splendid French forest domains, which had for the last thirty years suffered terrible pillage, reducing its size to 16.5 million acres from a previous 21.5 in 1789. The Restoration itself had at first made the situation worse by proceeding to sell large areas of national forests under the pressure of financial necessity. In addition it had inadvisedly reassigned the administration of forests to that of the domains, which meant turning over to the grasping policy of the revenue service a treasure of national wealth which had to be conserved to avoid upsetting the balance of the water flow and the erosion of mountain soil. Not until 1820 did the government come to realize that it had made a mistake. Then the Forest Service recovered its autonomy, and a committee prepared a code of forest legislation which replaced the confused piecemeal legislation of the various governments since the Old Regime. Thenceforth there was less effort to increase the value of the products than to prepare for the future by reforestation and conservation programs. The men of the Forest Service were given wide powers, and their training was to be improved by a school of forestry founded at Nancy in 1824.

It is well known that in England the large estates had been the means of progress in scientific agriculture. In France the breaking up of estates by the sale of national lands and by the inheritance laws increased from year to year. The land tax rolls in 1815 showed 10,083,000 land assessments; in 1834 there were 10,896,000, representing 123,360,000 separate small holdings. The large estates, however, were not as nonexistent as these figures would lead us to believe. According to a contemporary estimate, out of 111,870,000 acres of agricultural property in 1815, 47,500,000 belonged to estates averaging 2200 acres. Land still seemed to be a preferred investment for the bourgeois fortune gained in commerce and banking. For example, the banker, Laffitte, purchased near Breteuil a large domain including two very large farming estates and 18,750 acres of forest land. But most of the purchasers, following the example of the former owners, had only one ambition and that was to obtain over the years an assured income from their lands. To accomplish this, the most practical way was to split up these large estates into small lease-holds, so that even the large estates were reduced down to the dimensions of small units of production whose small-scale farming did not permit expensive improvements.

In this somber picture, however, a few streaks of light appear. All was not stagnation and neglect. The peasant had been freed from feudal dues and unfair taxation by the Revolution. Now, protected by a paternalistic and unharassing government, he saw the possibility of working without the fear of seeing his son, his animals, and his crops requisitioned by the military. So he threw himself into his work and little by little increased the acreage of his cultivated lands by reclaiming moors and enclosing former common lands—it was by sweat rather than by science. In Picardy, for example, from 1821 to 1833 over 17,550 acres of wasteland had been cleared as compared to 3,655 between 1792 and 1821. Local agricultural societies studied and taught improved methods. Everywhere the sickle was given up in favor of the long-handled scythe. Here and there some of the large landowners undertook a regular campaign for modernizing farming. They were, like the Duke of La Rochefoucauld-Liancourt, a few great nobles who had been followers of the physiocratic ideas of the eighteenth century—agriculturists who had the laudable ambition to see France rival England, like Mathieu de Dombasle, author of a *Manuel du cultivateur* (*Farmer's Manual*) and publisher of the *Annales de l'Agriculture,* applying his theories on his model farm at Roville in the department of Meurthe. There were also some former army leaders who found in agriculture an outlet for their energies which could no longer be used on the battlefields. Such a one was Marmont, Duke of Ragusa and son-in-law of the banker Perregaux, who sank more than 700,000 francs—in today's franc value 2 to 3 million— ($140,000 or in today's dollar value $400,000 to $600,000) in more-or-less successful improvements on his estates in the Châtillonnais. Or, read the victory bulletin written by Colonel Bugeaud in 1823 from his Perigordian domains:

> The area where I live was cultivated by the alternate fallow field system, that is that only half the land was sowed to crops each year. The other half was plowed four times without any crops, except for a few patches of potatoes and buckwheat. Sowed hayfields were totally unknown; and the few livestock farmers had were fed hay exclusively. A more barbarous farming can not be imagined. I worked by might and main to change all this on my lands and to advocate better principles among my neighbors. I had to overcome old habits, sarcastic comments, prejudices, and even saucy remarks from my tenants. But I overcame all obstacles, and today I am a quoted authority. My livestock have doubled, and my earnings soon will too. My lands are covered with beautiful squares of cultivated forage, such as Dutch clover, annual clover, vetch, rye, radish, maize, buckwheat, etc. I have 1800 plow-days (*journaux*) of land on just one estate, without counting the woods. These are worked by thirteen families, amounting to a total of 106 people. I also have twelve male and female servants to process

my share of the production. . . . Add to that 80 oxen, 50 cows, 10 mares, and 500 sheep, and you will see that I have enough for a right good battalion.

## Farm Products and Fluctuations

Northern and eastern France had made more progress than the south and center. There crop rotation and seeded hayfields were making rapid headway. Taken all together the statistics of sown fields revealed not only an overall increase, but also a relative gain of rich cereals like wheat over the secondary cereals.* The average yield of wheat went up from 10.25 hectoliters for the years 1815–1819 to 11.77 for the years 1826–1830. Potato raising was increasing enormously in all regions. Beet-sugar production, almost discontinued in 1815, had recovered to the figure of six thousand tons as compared with eleven hundred tons in about 1814. Wine growing had also expanded; in 1829 it covered 4,982,500 acres, or, 1,095,000 more than in 1789. It furnished over the years an average annual yield of 770,000 gallons of wine, and the beverage tax, which brought in eighty-two million francs ($16,400,000) per year before 1820, tallied up to more than a hundred million francs (twenty million dollars) in 1830.

The main purpose of cattle-raising remained, as in the eighteenth century, that of furnishing the farmer with plowing and draft animals as well as with manure. Nevertheless, beef livestock increased appreciably— 6,971,000 head in 1812, according to Chaptal, and 9,130,000 head in 1830, according to the *Statistique de la France*. By contrast, horse-breeding remained almost stationary—2,280,000 in 1812 and 2,453,000 in 1829, according to Moreau de Jonnès. And it appeared insufficient for the country's needs, since, in the years 1829 and 1830, sixteen hundred and eighteen hundred horses were imported from the Netherlands, Switzerland, and Germany. The quality of this livestock left much to be de-

* TABLE OF CEREALS

|  | Area Sown (acres) | |
|---|---|---|
|  | 1815 | 1830 |
| Wheat | 11,477,500 | 12,527,500 |
| Mixed wheat & rye | 2,290,000 | 2,175,000 |
| Rye | 6,432,500 | 2,742,500 |
| Barley | 2,680,000 | 3,237,500 |
| Buckwheat | 1,635,000 | 1,647,500 |
| Millet & maize | 1,352,500 | 1,452,500 |
| Oats | 6,245,000 | 6,900,000 |
| Potatoes | 1,395,000 | 2,007,500 (1835) |

sired: the best strains had been decimated by the Napoleonic wars, the state stud-farms accounted only for about one-third of the annual foals, and furthermore, these stud-farms, run by former officers who were obsessed with raising English and Arab saddle horses, used stallions which were too light to furnish good draft horses needed by agriculture and heavy transport.

Sheep raising had been disappointing.* It is known that, since the end of Louis XVI's reign, there had been an attempt to introduce into France the Spanish merino sheep, producers of fine wool. Louis XVIII's government discontinued such importations; yet the movement had made such headway that the merinos continued to be popular until about 1820. In that year there was a slump in fleece prices, and the merino raisers discovered that merinos did not have a very good sale as meat animals. From then on, sheep-raisers went over to English breeds, such as the Leicesters and Southdowns, which were especially bred for their meat.

In 1818, the industrialist Ternaux, a manufacturer of cashmere shawls, succeeded in having imported into France a flock of a hundred Tibetan goats, purchased in Russia. Decazes used state funds to procure them and settled them in the region of Perpignan. But these animals could not adjust themselves to the new climate, and by 1829 none had survived. Ternaux' political friends accused the Ultra-Royalist government of having deliberately let these poor liberal goats die out!

Silk culture, stimulated by the increase in the Lyonnaise silk manufacturing, underwent an extraordinary boom. In all the departments around Lyons, mulberry trees began to spread at the expense of walnut trees, of borders of oaks, and even of food crops. In the Isère, for example, the number of mulberry trees went up from 454,000 to 602,-000 between 1814 and 1832, and they even tried to raise silkworms in the region of Paris. As a whole, the production of French raw silk increased from 308,000 kilograms in 1815 to 688,000 in 1830.

One would have a very wrong idea of the progress in agriculture in this period if it was presented by a gradually and continuously rising curve. The real situation was more complex, for farming had its ups and downs, mainly reflected by cereal production. Whenever this production declined, wheat prices shot up sharply, which allowed wheat growers to compensate for their smaller crops, stabilize land prices, and encourage

* Still, it is difficult to believe that the number of sheep had fallen from 35,187,-000 in 1812 to 29,130,000 in 1830. The first figure, given by Chaptal, was probably too high; it probably referred to the more extensive Empire territory as it was in 1812 (including the Low Countries, Luxemburg, the Rhineland, northwest Germany, and western Italy).

wheat planting, but which also inflicted on consumers in general such high prices that it reduced their buying power and produced a slump in all the other sectors of production, agricultural as well as industrial. On the other hand, when wheat crops were good, the large supply brought a collapse of the market, and wheat producers saw their margin of profit reduced. With loud cries they called for a protective tariff and tried to reduce crop acreage. Such was the sad fate of farmers that poor crops or good crops were equally bad for them, and they always had something to complain about.

The harvests of 1814 and 1815 had been so good that the government authorized rather generous grain exportations. But the foreign occupation and its requisitions used up the surplus. An unusually rainy and cold summer ruined the 1816 harvest; the average price of a hectoliter of wheat, which had been 19.53 francs ($3.91) in 1815, went up to thirty-four francs ($6.80) in December 1816 and 46.50 francs ($9.30) in May 1817, in certain departments the price even went over eighty francs (sixteen dollars). The price of bread followed this same catastrophic curve, going up here and there to one franc (twenty cents) or 1.25 francs (twenty-five cents) a pound. People in certain villages in the northeast no longer had anything to eat except grass and roots, and even bark from trees. Under these conditions bread riots were seen to break out again as under the Old Regime. There were attacks on wheat convoys, pillaging of markets and bakeries, and raids on isolated farms. Troops had to intervene, and there were some people killed and wounded.

The government found itself forced to take action in spite of its determination not to interfere in the economic life of the country. Molé described its consternation:

> M. de Richelieu lost sleep over this and was visibly getting thinner. Lainé wore himself out in vain efforts and saw, much to his sorrow, the bad situation get worse in spite of all he could do to relieve it. Corvetto groaned over what all this cost the Treasury. Pasquier, believing he possessed an immense experience . . . because the people of Paris had almost died of starvation when he was prefect of police, held forth every day . . . and could only explain, by what he called *the fumbling of M. Lainé*, the failure of his own advice which had been followed exactly. Decazes played his usual role, claiming for himself the honor of success, when there was any, and blaming his colleagues whenever things went wrong.

At least the people of Paris did not die of starvation; a bread price adjustment fund, made up of nineteen million francs ($3,800,000) from the national government and five million francs (a million dollars) from the city, was created to cover bakers' losses when they were required to sell bread at thirty-one centimes (six cents) a pound. The government also bought seventy million francs (fourteen million dollars) worth of wheat from Russia and elsewhere, which they threw on different markets at a loss, and it gave 5,705,000 francs ($1,141,000) of subsidies to importers, opened charity workshops, and encouraged the growing of potatoes. Everywhere the prefects mobilized local resources as well as private charity, and the royal family set a worthy example. In all, the food crisis cost the Treasury more than forty-nine million francs ($9,800,000), and it has been estimated that just the rise in the price of bread itself had drawn on the national revenue an additional expense of 1,729,000,-000 francs ($345,800,000). From this it is easily understood how the food crisis unleashed a general crisis in the whole economy.

But hardly had the situation been readjusted in regard to food supply than a contrary unbalance began to develop. In 1819 the average price of wheat was quoted at 18.42 francs ($3.68) a hectoliter at a time when it was believed that twenty francs (four dollars) was the minimum price to the French farmer for making wheat raising profitable. To make things worse, Russian wheat was arriving in Marseilles, where it was being sold at fifteen and thirteen francs ($3.00 and $2.60) a hectoliter, as one deputy put it, "blockading French wheat in its granaries." Come, they cried, give us tariffs and customs barriers! They did not realize that foreign importations as a whole represented only a minute proportion of the national wheat production, three per cent in 1818, and that it could not move very far inland. They rejected the idea that the lowering of bread prices was good for the poorer classes. The most liberal industrialists themselves proclaimed the belief that the high price of bread forced the worker to work better and faster and stimulated his zeal. From Left to Right the deputies agreed on establishing an adjustable scale of tariff rates, automatically raising rates on foreign wheat in proportion to the rise in domestic prices (July 1819), and this system was further intensified in 1820 and 1821 until French foreign purchases were practically ended. But the wheat growers did not benefit by this because the anticipation of high prices led to increased acreage devoted to cereals and a continuing decline in price—17.79 francs ($3.58) for a hectoliter of wheat in 1821, 16.22 francs ($3.24) in 1824, and 15.85 francs ($3.17) in 1826. "France is raising too much," groaned Deputy Sirieys de Mayrinhac.

What protective tariffs had not succeeded in doing, weather conditions accomplished in 1828. In that year, long summer rains damaged the crops, and, in the course of the following winter, freezing weather paralyzed river traffic. As in 1817 the country was faced with local famines, and again food riots broke out. Yet, the situation was not as serious as during the previous crisis. The government did not have to intervene directly; the application of the protective tariffs was automatically suspended; imports quickly supplied the demands for cereals; the average price of wheat did not exceed 21.55 francs ($4.31); and the wheat growers only made limited profits.

On the whole it appears then that, up to 1830, French agriculture went through a difficult period when the margin of realized profits— when they existed at all—were not sufficient to permit the large investments necessary to increase appreciably the productivity of the soil. Hence the relative stagnation portrayed above. No doubt the hardest hit were the large landowners, who were compelled to lower their terms at each period of lease renewals and often had to forego collecting any rent from their tenants. The tenants were also to suffer, since they were required to fulfill contracts negotiated under more favorable circumstances. The wages of farm labors continued to decline, which did not prevent, in certain cases, their real purchasing power from improving. The least unfortunate, no doubt, were the small farm-owners, for whom the sale of wheat, produced in small quantities, had only a slight effect in a local economy tuned largely to family self-sufficiency. As more than half of the land belonged to them, French agriculture was in the end to survive this crisis more easily than neighboring countries, similarly affected by the general slump in prices. Finally we can discern in this crisis itself the beginnings of progress, the first signs of which have already been noticed and which were to become more apparent under the July Monarchy. The large landowners now saw that tariff protection was powerless to guarantee them a profit, which they then began to seek by an improvement in their agricultural methods. When we realize that since the seventeenth century the known yields per acre had undergone practically no change, that the production averages came by and large from farming where the majority was still resistant to any new methods, the upward trend which can be noted, however small it may be, reflects great individual effort, and it takes on the appearance of the initial reverberations of a profound revolution.

## Artisan Industry

The persistence of structures and archaic methods, the appearance of new forms, such is likewise the picture presented by industry in this same period.

Under this general term of industry lies a reality very different from what this term evokes in our twentieth-century minds, and here again an effort of the imagination is required to fill in its concrete aspects. The transformation of rural products began in the rural economy itself, in the thousands of little family workshops in which, as in the Middle Ages, spinning wheels and distaffs turned and weavers plied their shuttles on rudimentary looms. Every village and small town had its cabinet-makers, dyers, wheelwrights, smiths, etc., who were also farmers at the same time. The agricultural and industrial activity dovetailed to such an extent that it is totally impossible to use statistics to verify the number of men in industry as compared to those in farming. In the same way, in the city, industrial activity often became mixed with commerce, with the artisan shopkeeper selling his own products.

The rural domestic industry was encouraged by the clothier system. The clothier was a big merchant who distributed the raw material to hundreds of worker-peasants and then picked up the products which they had manufactured according to his specifications. When necessary, the clothier sold, rented, or loaned the required machines or tools. So industry existed in a sort of nebulous state over vast regions which later were to become purely agricultural. Around Vimoutiers, twenty thousand weavers wove cretonnes, and in the Aube an equal number of looms and stocking-frames were found in the hosiery industry of Troyes. Likewise Rouen, Saint-Quentin, Lyons, Cambrai, and Nancy were centers of industrial "nebulae." This form of work was not limited to textiles. Around Rugles, in the Eure, there were 3,500 nail-makers and 2,500 pin-makers; the locksmiths of Vimeu, numbering three thousand, furnished two-thirds of the locks in the capital; in the arrondissement of Mézières there were five thousand nail-makers working at home, etc.

One step higher, the rural workers grouped themselves around a few machines, in small workshops, called *"pacus"* in the North, and went from farm work to shop work according to the seasons. Dispersion was again the general rule here, even where the workers were completely uprooted from their previous locations. It could not be otherwise when the motive force commonly employed was the water-wheel and when the industrial fuel was wood. Coal-mining, carried on by many little enterprises with archaic methods, grew slowly: 1 million tons in 1814, 1.5 million in 1826 —of which 560,000 came from the Loire region. The northern fields, in spite of the prosperity of Anzin, did not produce that much. The metallurgical industries sought therefore the forest areas, and, if they wanted to avoid an early exhaustion of fuel, they had to disperse their blast-furnaces. The edge-tool and textile industries lined the favorable streams. Thus the little Bolbec River, in Normandy, turned twenty-seven mills, twenty-nine cloth print shops, twenty-two cloth-bleaching establishments, sixteen red dyeing mills, and eighteen other miscellaneous industries. The factory, in the modern sense of the term, with its masses of workers concentrated in a small space, was still a rare phenomenon. The Ziegler workshops at Guebwiller employed three thousand workers, men and women; the forges and mines of Fourchambault in the Allier, 2,500; the Saint-Gobain establishments in the Aisne, three thousand. But these figures remained very exceptional.

Moreover, the financial resources of these small businesses were not sufficient to permit them to develop larger enterprises. The owners were, in a majority of cases, former merchants who had moved from commerce to manufacturing, very often by the intermediary step of being clothiers of an area or circuit, or again possibly former overseers, who were self-made men coming up from the artisan class and whose starting capital had been furnished by some bourgeois who were looking for places to make advantageous investments. The enterprise remained essentially a family one. Even a capitalist-type company, like that of the Anzin mines, was jealously kept in the control of some thirty families. The small factory was managed like a farm, which was expected to average a good income over the years. The obsession for unlimited production, the urge toward indefinite growth, which seem to be an internal law of our modern capitalist enterprises, were unknown in those days, for these factories were dependent on raw materials and markets which were obviously restricted within very narrow limits by the lack of good means of transportation.

The dependence of industry on transportation facilities shows up clearly if a map of the density of industrial establishments is compared with one showing the lines of transportation. The departments north of the Loire—with the exception of the Brittany peninsula—were incomparably better endowed with good transportation, and the industrial zone followed exactly the courses of the Garonne and the Rhone and then spread out all along the Mediterranean coast.

Finally, the transportation situation explains the astonishing differences found in industrial prices from one region to another, just as with agricultural prices. In April 1826 a ton of pig-iron cost 150 francs (thirty dollars) in Champagne, 265 francs (fifty-three dollars) in Berry, and three hundred francs (sixty dollars) in Franche-Comté. This then explains how the most archaic modes of production could coexist along with the most modern and scientific. While the Paris region already possessed an active chemical industry, Agricol Perdiguier was able to see the winegrowers, in the little wine-producing towns of Languedoc, obtain copper sulphate by spreading the pressed pulp of grapes over copper sheets and scraping off the residue.

## The Mechanization of Textiles

Machines were introduced slowly and unevenly. They encountered all sorts of obstacles: the high cost of machines which often had to be purchased in England, faulty construction and poor material used in making French machines, and the lack of skilled workers to run and repair them. They had to bring over workers from England, and by 1824 there were thirteen to fourteen hundred English specialists in France. Lastly, if many small employers were opposed to improvements, workers were even more hostile. In their minds, machines were diabolic inventions to deprive them of jobs or to reduce their wages. Here and there riots broke out when an employer tried to introduce some new mechanism.

Wherever industries were mechanized, the machines were still, more often than not, run by water power, by horse power on a wheel, or even by manpower. The steam engine, still called the "fire pump," was an object of curiosity early in the Restoration just as it had been in 1789. By 1830 there were only 572 in all France. In 1818, there had been no more than two hundred.

The government was not disinterested in industrial progress, but it refused to intervene directly to encourage it. For the believers in the prevailing philosophy of laissez-faire (economic liberalism), Colbert's state manufacturing establishment was a monstrosity. All they asked of the government was that it protect national industries by high tariffs, as it did for agriculture; and the large landholders, whose forests supplied fuel for the blast-furnaces, were in full agreement with the industrialists. In 1820 an abrupt rise in duties on steel was passed by just one vote less than unanimity in a chamber otherwise violently divided along party lines. In all fairness it must be said that the government did encourage inventors and industrialists by arranging expositions in Paris in 1819, 1823, and 1827. The *Conservatoire national des Arts et Métiers* (National Conservatory of Arts and Crafts), reorganized in 1819, gave technical courses. But private initiative founded the *École spéciale de Commerce et d'Industrie* in 1820, the *École centrale des Arts et Manufactures* in 1828, and other professional schools. There were still other private associations like the *Société d'encouragement pour l'Industrie nationale* and the *Société industrielle de Mulhouse*.

The group of textile industries turned out to be by far the most important in numbers employed and the value of its annual production—820 million francs ($164,000,000) was the estimate for 1828. Here was also where the most rapid transformations were made. By the end of the Restoration, machinery and concentrated industry had taken over cotton spinning. Around the spinning mills of the Nord, of Alsace, and of Normandy, grew up the first modern industrial agglomerations. But the thread thus produced was still woven largely in family workshops. There resulted from this an unbalanced situation in production and employment. While in 1827 spinning employed two hundred thousand workers, weaving required 450,000 and still absorbed only a part of the spinning production, the rest having to be used by the trimming and hosiery industries, etc. Yet in 1822 the first experiments in machine weaving were made in Alsace, and by 1830 there were in the Haut-Rhin two thousand power looms as against twenty thousand hand looms. All together, the cotton industry seemed to have tripled its production in fifteen years, since raw cotton imports went up from twenty-four million pounds in 1816 to sixty-two million in 1829. The result was that the prices of calico, percale, and muslin in 1830 were a third or a fourth lower than they were in 1816.

The wool industry still surpassed the cotton industry as far as weight of raw material used was concerned—96 million pounds in 1825—but its technical advance was slower. If machine spinning clearly predominated for carded wool, handwork maintained itself in combing; and weaving was in great measure still done in the small rural workshops. The principal wool centers were still in the Norman towns of Elbeuf and Louviers and in the Northeast at Rheims and Sedan. Of the raw wool used, French flocks supplied eighty per cent. Merino wool, used by the manufactures of high-grade woolen cloth, gave to French cloth, according to a contemporary English economist, "a luster and delicateness of weave that the material of no other country can equal."

As to the manufactures of linen and burlap, they held to the old hand methods and were stagnating or even declining, especially in Brittany.

Lyons was more than ever the silk capital. Led by an enterprising group of employers who welcomed new ideas, the Lyons industries experienced uninterrupted growth in spite of its vulnerability to depressions. While there were only seven thousand looms in use in 1817, there would be 26,000 in 1825 and 42,000 in 1832. The final process, weaving, was still done by hand, and the Jacquard loom, improved by Breton, made possible an admirable variety of designs. The great mass of *"Canuts"* (silk-weavers) still worked in the city of Lyons itself, in the high buildings of the Croix-Rousse section, but the owners had already shown a tendency to seek more docile labor in the surrounding countryside. By a reverse process from what we saw in other branches of the textile industry, the silk industry, at least for weaving, tended toward dispersion rather than concentration. By 1825 one-third of the looms were already outside the city. In the whole Rhone region, which furnished the raw silk for Lyons, the throwing and spinning processes advanced rapidly and became mechanized.

## Metallurgical Industries

The French metallurgical industries were still far behind those of Great Britain. In 1828 there were still 130 Catalonian forges from which iron was obtained directly by an archaic process, and in 1830 there were only twenty-nine blast-furnaces using coke in contrast to 379 continuing to use charcoal. The latter were then still supplying eighty-six per cent of the national production. Nevertheless, recent studies require that one apply some corrections to the traditional picture of a French metallurgy imprisoned in its old routines by the selfish blindness of its ironmasters. On the contrary it seems that certain ones, and not the least conspicuous —the Wendel firm for example—made every effort to introduce the latest British processes. Protective tariffs may have encouraged technical stagnation here and there, but it also gave some capitalists the incentive to expand and modernize on a large scale. The last ten years of the Restoration witnessed the appearance of large mining and metallurgical complexes, such as those of Fourchambault, Châtillon (established by Marmont), Decazeville (sponsored by the former minister of Louis XVIII), and Alais (by Soult). Concentrations of small pre-existing firms began to take form under the leadership of some Parisian capitalists: the Boigues, former wood merchants, undertook to concentrate the forges of Berry and the Nivernais, introducing reverberatory furnaces, rolling mills, and steam blowers. The banker, Milleret, united under his control his Loire mines with his Dauphiné iron works.

These efforts bore fruit: the total production of pig-iron moved up from 114,000 tons in 1818 to 220,000 tons in 1828. The average price of forged iron was brought down from 550 francs ($110) per ton in 1825 to 450 francs (ninety dollars) in 1830. The small metal industries—edged tools, cutlery, and hardware—succeeded in throwing on the market an ever-increasing amount of low-priced goods, resulting, for example, in making the table knife no longer a privilege of the leisure classes. In 1817 France still produced only 72,000 scythes and had to import some; ten years later the one factory of Garrigou in Toulouse alone turned out

120,000 and national production was able to meet a considerably in-creased demand. The Schlumbergers and the Koechlins, Alsatian textile magnates, began to set up for themselves the machines they needed.

## French Commerce

During the debates on the finance bill of 1822 M. de Saint-Cricq, director of customs, declared that the government's doctrine in matters of commercial exchanges was "to buy as little as possible from others and to sell them as much as possible." And he was only giving expression to the general opinion, as found, for example, a few years later in the writings of the economist, Moreau de Jonnès, who could hardly be sus-pected of having an excessive love for the principles of the Old Regime. Thus both public opinion and the government, who had adopted the laissez-faire principles of Gournay and Adam Smith for the domestic economy, were still following Colbert's mercantilism in matters of inter-national commercial policy.

"To buy as little as possible," that was relatively easy to accomplish. All one had to do was systematically strangle imports from abroad by protective tariffs; and that was exactly what all Restoration governments did—no matter what their political coloration—with the support of over-whelming majorities in the chamber. The liberal (*laissez-faire*) indus-trialists, who would have protested loudly if the government had had the audacity to intervene in the least degree in the question of labor con-ditions which they imposed on their workers or in the selling prices of their goods, were the first ones to insist, in the name of national interest, that international commerce should be put under the most rigid controls. Leave them alone, yes, but don't let anything in.

The tariff restrictions on foreign wheat and iron have already been discussed above. Most other imported products were, one after another, subjected to crushing tariff rates: woolens, cotton goods, linens, hemp goods, dyes, all sorts of fabrics, hops, oils, tallow, livestock, etc. As to colonial commerce, so flourishing under the Old Regime, it suffered heavily from the loss of Santo Domingo. It could not recover in the re-maining colonies without the strict reapplication of the "closed colonial system," again a return to the purest Colbert mercantilism. The mother country would purchase all colonial exports, and the colonist would pur-chase only from her all the manufactured goods needed for their pro-duction and their everyday living. Furthermore, all their commerce, in either direction, had to be carried in French ships.

No sooner had England returned Martinique, Guadeloupe, and Île

Bourbon to France, than the colonists demanded an arrangement which would guarantee them a monopoly of the French sugar market. The government agreed to their request by imposing brutally discriminatory tariffs against foreign sugar. The same was to be done for coffee, cocoa, quinine, and spices. In return the colonists were not to establish industries, not even sugar refineries. Nevertheless, it was to prove impossible to maintain such a tight archaic system; smuggling and commercial interloping found opportunities to make sensational profits. When the liberated Spanish colonies asked for the right to trade with the French Antilles, the hope of opening the South American and Mexican markets to French industry finally persuaded the French government to allow a breach in the system of exclusive trade. An ordinance of 1826 admitted a limited amount of foreign merchandise into colonial ports.

In France herself the enforcement of the system was not to be without its loopholes. The enormous differences between domestic and foreign prices of certain commodities encouraged large-scale smuggling across all the national boundaries. On occasion the government was forced to wink at these practices in order to avoid ruining certain home industries. For example, the muslin industries, which kept the town of Tarare alive, required a specially fine thread which could not be produced in France; so all its raw material was furnished by a perfectly organized smuggling service to which the customs service indulgently closed its eyes.

"To buy the least possible"—but, if they also wanted "to sell as much as possible," they certainly had to permit industries to obtain the raw materials which French agriculture did not produce in sufficient quantities. This was the case in textiles, such as woolens, silk, and especially cotton. An ingenious compromise was concocted to satisfy the opposing demands of industrialists and farmers. The purchasers of foreign raw wool, silk, and cotton continued to pay the high tariffs when they imported them, but they were reimbursed by an export rebate when they shipped out their finished goods. The domestic prices did not benefit by this rebate, and the practice amounted to what we call dumping today.

Another more serious but quite predictable inconvenience of the protectionist policy was soon to appear. The countries, whose products were thus hit, in a short time began to retaliate with similar tariffs against French goods. England, Russia, Sweden, the United States, and the Netherlands imposed very high tariff rates on French wines. France's wine exports, which had exceeded 52,631,000 gallons between 1815 and 1819, fell to 25,631,000 gallons between 1820 and 1824. The winegrowers, especially those of Burgundy, who suffered most, complained bitterly about the avidity of the ironmasters who had provoked these reprisals by iron-exporting countries. The sugar refiners attacked the closed colonial system:

> Under the present system [wrote Alexandre de Laborde] it is not the colonies which belong to the mother country, but it is the mother country which is made dependent on the colony. It is not the 20,000 inhabitants which supply themselves from the protecting power, but rather it is this power which gives up all the other markets in order to consume only the products of these 20,000 inhabitants and to pay them a third more than what it would cost them elsewhere.

And there were also other complaints about protectionism: cotton manufacturers protested against the excessive prices for machines demanded by the metallurgists; the Lyons silk firms wanted at the same time free importation of raw silk from Italy and the East and the prohibition of the importation of British silks; and the chambers of commerce of France's big ports stressed the stagnation of maritime trade. In many cases French ships were obliged to return half empty or with ballast. Opinion began to be uneasy and to have doubts about the beauty of M. de Saint-Cricq's system. The fall of Villèle, who had made himself the stubborn and zealous promoter of this protectionist policy, appeared to herald its end. The chamber in 1828 inserted in its address to the king some free-trade passages: "The first need of commerce and industry is freedom. Anything which unnecessarily obstructs the smooth functioning of our relations hurts commerce and indirectly affects even more remote interests." An investigative committee was instructed to plan on an eventual revision of commercial legislation. But the combined interests of the large landholders and the industrialists, who dominated the electorate and hence the chamber, were too solidly entrenched. The free-trade trend was soon stifled in the parliamentary committee, and the high-tariff system was continued.

What was its effect on French foreign commerce in general? This is hard to determine exactly. No doubt the official customs statistics show a slight increase during the Restoration, but it is possible to question this, as Charléty has done so positively. The values attributed to goods in trade were completely arbitrary, much lower than the real prices for imports, and these evaluations were made according to price scales which fluctuated from year to year. Furthermore, up to 1826, statistics did not distinguish between special and general commerce, that is, they did not distinguish between transit imports and imports staying in France or French-made exports.

To obtain some idea of business growth, it is necessary to approach the question indirectly by considering the amount of revenue collected by the export and import customs. Yet these reveal an almost stagnant condition, if one considers the progressive tariff increases on some products and the rebates allowed to exporters:

|  | 1821 | 1825 | 1829 |
|---|---|---|---|
| Duties on imports | 69,913,000 fr. | 86,993,000 | 99,633,000 |
| Duties on exports | 2,671,000 | 7,683,000 | 1,394,000 |
| Duties on navigation | 1,738,000 | 1,546,000 | 2,154,000 |
| Total | 74,322,000 | 90,220,000 | 103,181,000 |

In the present state of work in economic history, it is even impossible to have an exact idea of the direction of trade balances. One can only suspect that they were more often unfavorable. Even the customs statistics showed this for the year 1830.

What were these imports and exports? If one can believe the official figures, the raw material for industry in 1825 represented sixty-seven per cent of the value of imports. In order of importance they were: cotton, raw silk, industrial oil, copper, wool, indigo, raw hides, coal, hemp and linen threads, lead, potassium, cochineal. Agricultural products amounted to about twenty-one per cent: sugar, coffee, livestock, olive oil, timber, tobacco, cheese, spices, citrus fruits. Manufactured goods, principally fabrics and machines, amounted to only twelve per cent. As to exports, manufactured goods came to sixty-nine per cent and agricultural goods to thirty-one per cent. Among the former, silk goods were far ahead, then followed the other fabrics—linens, cottons, and woolens. Leather goods, textile fabrics, paper, china and glassware, wearing apparel, books and engravings, jewelry, clocks and watches.

France's customers in 1825 were, in order of importance: the United States, England, the Netherlands, Spain, and Germany; her principal furnishers were: the Netherlands, Sardinia, the United States, England, and Germany. One-third of her commerce was by land, the rest by sea. The stagnation of French foreign commerce is confirmed by the figures of French ship tonnage devoted to this trade: 335,000 tons in 1820 and 340,000 in 1830. This little-changed situation is all the more striking because in the same period the coastal trade increased from 1,334,000 to 2,373,000 tons. The special statistics of the ports do not distinguish between foreign and coastal trade; and thus it can be explained why Rouen seemed, by the trade figures, to be far ahead of Marseilles and Bordeaux. It must also be said that the small size of oceangoing ships of that day—the largest did not exceed eight hundred tons—allowed them easily to ascend the Seine River. We easily see by these statistics that port activity was more dispersed than it is today. Abbeville, Saint-Malo, Bayonne, Perpignan, and Montpellier still had a sizeable shipping business. But the movement toward concentration, so characteristic of the contemporary period, was already beginning. Only the ports of Marseilles, Le Havre, Bordeaux, and Cherbourg were growing, while others were stationary or declining. Finally it must be noted that, although the tonnage sailing under the French flag remained stationary, foreign navigation grew steadily: 354,000 tons in 1820 and 669,000 in 1830, the latter representing double the French tonnage. The complaints of the French shipbuilders can therefore be easily understood.

As to domestic commerce it naturally eludes all statistical evaluation. Yet, one is led to believe that, in spite of the material difficulties growing out of poor transportation facilities, it developed more satisfactorily than foreign commerce. The growth in the coastal trade, noted above, is one indication of this, among others. The ports, the big cities, and Paris especially, acted like high-pressure air-pumps, communicating to the surrounding regions a business activity unknown in such vast areas as the Breton northwest or the Massif Central, which continued to move at an almost medieval pace. Also one has the feeling, without being able to put one's finger on the causes or the aspects of the phenomenon, that there were changes in the traditional flow of domestic commerce. For example at Beaucaire, whose annual fair had been for centuries the great center for business transactions in the Mediterranean south, the number of transactions declined from 29,590,000 to 16,622,000 between 1819 and 1829.

## Banking and Finance

It is only in the money market, that is, in the organization of banking and credit, that it is possible to have any exact figures.

The French economy, as indeed that of the other countries of the civilized West, suffered at that time from a real shortage of coins. The total of specie in circulation was estimated, in January 1828, as 2,713,-000,000 francs ($542,600,000), which was 700,000,000 francs ($140,000,000) more than in 1814. When one considers the fact that during this same year of 1828 the annual revenue amounted to eight billion francs ($1,600,000,000), one can realize how inadequate this monetary fund was to lubricate properly the economy of the country, especially since this metallic money was not easily transported. Paper money was of little help in remedying the situation. The Bank of France issued only paper bills of one-thousand or five-hundred franc denominations (two-hundred or one-hundred dollars) and these bills circulated only in Paris. In the departments, they were not even accepted by the tax collectors, and they were discounted from one to two per cent. The total of these bills was 153 million francs ($30,600,000) in 1820 and 223 million francs ($44,600,000) in 1830. In some provincial cities like Rouen, Bordeaux, and Nantes, there were some note-issuing banks, but their notes were limited entirely to local use.

Under these conditions the fiduciary circulation of commercial paper— bills of exchange, bank drafts, and promisory notes—should and in fact did come into use to make up for the lack of currency and its inadequate circulation. The total of commercial paper held by the Bank of France— which, by the way, had no provincial branches—rose from 393 million francs ($78,600,000) in 1816 to 828 million francs ($41,200,000) in 1815 to 617 million francs ($123,400,000) in 1830.

The handling of commercial paper seemed to be about the only banking activity. The practice of savings and checking accounts was almost unknown. Private individuals usually entrusted their capital savings to their notaries. As for making loans to new commercial or industrial businesses, the banks would not take such risks. Indeed, they were in no position to do it. In general these were small family businesses, and more often than not the banker was also a merchant in his own right.

If some big bankers, like Jacques Laffitte or the Périer brothers, became interested in industrial enterprises, they used their own funds rather than those of their clients. Laffitte, who was very much ahead of his time, proposed in 1825 the founding of a *Société commanditaire de l'industrie* (Joint Stock Industrial Bank) with a capital of a hundred million francs (twenty million dollars); but the plan failed because of the lack of government support and the financial crisis of 1825, although half of the capital had already been subscribed.

The very multiplication of banks was an indication of their small size: in Paris in 1826 there were no less than two hundred private banks, and in the provinces it was generally the big merchants and shipbuilders who served as bankers. Over this financial community reigned what was called the *Haute Banque parisienne* (the great Paris banking community) —a dozen banking houses, almost all founded before 1815, those of the Mallets, the Delleserts, the Hottinguers, the Thurets, the Laffittes, the Périers, the Baguenaults, and the Lapanouses, powerful because of their wide network of connections and the positions held by their leaders on the board of regents of the Bank of France. They still refused to admit to the board James de Rothschild, who, however, far outstripped them with his immense fortune. In 1824 his capital alone had already reached thirty-three million francs ($6,600,000) while his nearest rival, Laffitte, did not command more than six million francs ($1,200,000).

It was extremely difficult to find any fresh capital. In the provinces it was the notaries, the capitalists enriched by trade or by dealing in national lands, who served as moneylenders. Often operating secretly, they took advantage of their position by demanding usurious rates of interest. No loan could be obtained for much less than eight per cent and often the interest was higher. The usurer was a stock character in novel and play; Balzac had only to look around among his contemporaries to produce the hideous characters of the Rigous, the Grandets, and the Gobsecks.

The system of joint-stock companies, such as defined by the Commercial Code of 1807, was not conducive to the mobilization of capital. In order to found a joint-stock company by the sale of shares, a government permit was required, which was only granted after deliberation in the council of state. So, between 1815 and 1829, only ninety-six stock companies were founded. The most used form was the collective liability company in which each one of the members accepted responsibility for all the eventual principal invested. Such companies, requiring complete confidence among their participants, obviously remained limited to three or four individuals. They could only attract a limited amount of capital, and they were short-lived because the death of one of the members automatically brought a dissolution of the company. They were only just beginning to discover the possibilities of limited liability companies which would later be able to circumvent the laws on stock companies.

The denominations of the shares which made up the capitalization of the few stock companies (*sociétés anonymes*) were so large—one thousand to ten thousand francs (two hundred to two thousand dollars)— that only the very large fortunes could afford to purchase them. A share of stock then did not fluctuate much and was seldom traded but remained a family possession which was religiously transmitted from father to son like a rental property or a landed estate. Under such conditions most of these shares were not quoted on the Bourse (the stock market). The total number of issues registered on the Paris Bourse was only thirteen in 1820, and thirty-eight in 1830. Even these were French public bonds, foreign government bonds shares of the Bank of France, of some insurance companies, and of canal-construction and canal-management companies. In fact these last issues changed hands very seldom, and it was almost exclusively in government bonds that speculation and fluctuations appeared. Just outside the jurisdiction of the official stock market, which was reserved to the Company of Stock Brokers (*Compagnie des agents de change*), there developed, more or less by tolerance, over-the-counter trading (*la coulisse*), which dealt with issues not admitted to the exchange and with futures operations forbidden by law.

Trading in stocks and bonds would therefore have been rather easy, if the very high rate of brokerage fees had not limited it to a minority of capitalists, who did large-scale trading and toward whom public opinion, furthermore, showed a distinct hostility. As to the small stockholders who never dreamed for an instant of selling their hard-earned holdings, they were not interested in the capital gains of their shares but rather in a regular income from dividends. Besides, these small holders were not numerous—only 189,000 in 1829, and almost all of them Parisians. In short, personal wealth did not represent, to Frenchmen, a comparable value to that of landed wealth, the basis for social respectability and political influence, and the banking system was unable to mobilize the resources of small savings for the use of industry. In this case, as in others, they had made no progress beyond the Old Regime.

The relative stagnation of business was not peculiar to France. In fact it seemed that the entire Western World had entered, around 1817, a cycle of depression, characterized by a slow decline in prices, following upon a steady rise which had taken place during the second third of the eighteenth century. But, along with this, France had suffered from several secondary economic crises. First there was, as we have seen, a food shortage in 1817, which was reflected in a temporary decline in buying power for the mass of consumers. To this was added a financial and stock-market crisis brought on by overspeculation in the liberation loans. There followed from this a period of slump for industrial and commercial enterprises. Business did not begin to pick up until near the end of 1822. Thereafter France enjoyed a real prosperity for several years. All the barometers of economic life were rising: building activity, rising city tolls (*octrois*), and increases in indirect taxes. The year 1825 marked a veritable high point: in Paris, building was increasing at a feverish rate; the city toll records showed the importation of 75,000 cubic yards of building stone as compared to 27,000 in 1816.

But the year 1826 again ushered in a series of difficult years—at first it was a financial and commercial crisis. France felt the effects of a still more severe crisis in the English economy, which obliged Great Britain to restrict her purchases on the Continent. The flow of British aristocratic travelers, dispensers of guineas, took a sharp drop, as can be seen by the returns from the tax on entering foreign carriages—381,000 francs ($76,200) in 1825 and 75,000 (fifteen thousand dollars) in 1827. On top of this came, in 1828, a new food shortage; industry and commerce, in turn, suffered from the general decrease in agricultural income, which brought increasing business failures in its wake. It seemed as if the depression would never end; indeed, it did last until 1832. Without going so far as to claim a cause-and-effect relationship, one can not fail to notice some synchronization between the economic fluctuations and the main periods of the political life of the Restoration. The eclipse of the "constitutional" policy of Richelieu and Decazes coincided with the economic crisis of 1817 to 1818; the success of the Ultra-Royalist government at the end of the reign of Louis XVIII corresponded with a period of prosperity; and the decline in strength and popularity of the Villèle ministry came with the return of hard times. Lastly it can not be denied that the general economic uneasiness may have had some connection with that atmosphere of discontent and restlessness which led to the revolution of 1830.

Out of all of this economic discussion, one would be led to conclude that—contrary to the generally accepted view—the Restoration was not a period of material prosperity for France. While we are compelled to come to this conclusion on the basis of modern criteria, contemporaries of that period, who had experienced, one after the other, the restrictions of the Old Regime, the disorders of the Revolution, and the devastations of wars and invasions, could rightly consider that they had never seen better times. There is no doubt at all that the French nation, next after England, was the richest and most progressive in the world. Certainly, when one compares the economic life of the Restoration with the prodigious strides of today, it seems scanty and stagnant; but the local isolation imposed by poor means of transportation could not allow it to be otherwise.

What could the government have done about it? No doubt it could not have let down the tariff barriers without bringing ruin to certain categories of producers, but it could have loosened up a bit on import restrictions. It could have employed a larger share of the government revenues to improve the transportation system, taken a more direct interest in technical education, and showed more initiative in agricultural improvements and in the modernization of heavy industries. Paralyzed by the shortsighted attitude of a privileged electorate, more than by the prevalent laissez-faire theories, and perhaps obsessed by the memory of the financial catastrophe which unleashed the Revolution, the government seemed to have hypnotized itself into a policy of niggardly appropriations, low taxes, and restricted borrowing. The stinginess of Louis

XVIII and Villèle led to the same results as did the extravagance of Calonne and Necker—that is, sacrificing the future to the interest of the present. Seen from this angle, the widely touted financial policy of the Restoration does not appear to have been very successful.

It is undeniable, however, that France became richer during the Restoration—slowly, but certainly surely. There is no want of evidence. Here are some random indications: from 1816 to 1828 income from indirect taxes increased from 140 million francs (twenty-eight million dollars) to 212 million ($42,400,000); the number of licensed businesses increased from 847,000 to 1,101,000 between 1817 and 1829, as compared with the previous fifteen years with only 56,000 new businesses; luxury industries showed real prosperity—goldsmiths used twice as much gold and silver in 1825 as in 1818; building construction went up and up—in Paris 2,671 new houses between 1817 and 1827, representing a present capital outlay of from five hundred to eight hundred million francs (a hundred to a hundred and sixty million dollars); in all of France, 1,246,000 new buildings between 1818 and 1831; the gold balance increased to 938,152,000 francs ($187,630,400) in ingots and coins between 1821 and 1830, which would have made Colbert leap for joy in his grave! Finally French savings increased to the point that they were ready to be invested abroad. It is estimated that 525 million francs ($105,000,000) were used for this purpose, mainly in loans to foreign governments.

Because the period of Louis XVIII and Charles X came before the railroad age and, in spite of early signs, before the industrial revolution, it is more closely associated with the Old Regime, of which it is, in a way, the last flowering. It remains, however, to its credit that, coming after troublous times, it brought a much-needed period of calm to permit the French nation to recover from exhaustion. These fifteen years, so wanting in spectacular accomplishments, were years of convalescence, consolidation, and maturation, on which would be built the foundations of future expansion. In a word, here so really appropriate, these were years of restoration.

# 15

❧ ❧ ❧ ❧ ❧

# Social Life

## French Demography

THIRTY million Frenchmen in 1815—32,400,000 in 1830. Every year for fifteen years the population of the kingdom increased from 160,000 to 245,000 subjects. The record number of births was reached in 1826— 992,000, at a rate of 318 for each ten thousand. This is a far higher rate than the 183 for each ten thousand in 1959. At the 1826 rate, if it had been maintained, France would now have almost seventy million inhabitants! In this respect, as in that of the economy, Restoration France was an extension of the Old Regime, but even here appeared the heralds of a new day. After 1829 the birth rate fell below three hundred for each ten thousand and would not go up again.

Yet men married later than they do today, more often between the ages of thirty and forty-five, but they married maidens much younger than themselves. More children were born, four was the average for a household, but, since birth control was a common practice in a bourgeoisie that was desperately anxious to rise on the social scale, it must be supposed that families of six to eight children were common. Thus the losses caused by the Empire wars were quickly made good.

The map of birth rates shows a striking difference from that of today. The lowest rate—one birth for every forty-five inhabitants—was then in the Calvados where today it has gone up to being the fourth among French departments in births; while the highest rate—one for every twenty-five inhabitants—was located in the Loire department, which today is only twenty-fifth in births.

One can also well believe that the distribution of population was itself somewhat different from what it is today, although no one, up to now, has tried to prepare a map for this period of our concern. One fact is that the rural areas had more population; a contemporary computation gave only twenty-one per cent of the total population in towns of over one thousand five hundred souls. The French nation therefore still remained, in large part, a country of rural inhabitants. Charles Pouthas showed that the rural areas were never again to be so heavily populated as in this first half of the nineteenth century. Calvados, for example, which had 442,000 people in 1954, had 492,000 in 1824. Lot, between these same dates, went down from 275,000 to 147,000; Ardèche from 304,000 to 249,000; and Haute-Marne from 233,000 to 197,000. Only three cities had more than a hundred thousand souls: Paris, Lyons (131,000), and Marseilles (115,000); and five had more than fifty thousand: Bordeaux (89,000), Rouen (86,000), Nantes (68,-000), Lille (64,000), and Toulouse (52,000). What is more, in all these cities, the population figures seemed to remain unchanging.

Only Paris showed an appreciable gain in population: 622,000 in 1811, 713,000 in 1818, and more than 800,000 by 1830.* Two-thirds of this increase is accounted for by the influx of people from the departments: in 1833 Bertillon estimated that out of a hundred persons dying in Paris only fifty were born there. The admirable works on historical demography by Louis Chevalier enabled him to make maps of the departments from which the emigration went. These show that the influx came from the nearby regions to the north, east, and southeast of the capital. Paris had no attraction to the departments south of the Loire except in Creuse and Cantal. Once again we are led to notice the influence of transportation on the life of the nation. It is not without some political significance that the Paris population came almost entirely from the north and east, traditionally oriented toward the parties of the Left by their experience in municipal local elections and by their defensive reflex against foreign countries.

The social history of France in the early nineteenth century is no longer that *"terra incognita"* that it would have appeared to be a few years ago. Yet, the admirable studies, which have opened large cracks in the wall of ignorance, remain too local in their subject matter to permit valid conclusions for the social picture of the country as a whole. The few observations of a general nature to be presented below will only be given as hypotheses from provincial studies.

The first thing which stands out without contradiction is that the French nation, at the beginning of the nineteenth century, was appreciably younger than it is today. In the age pyramid of 1826 those under

* The figure of 785,000 given by the census of 1831 is no doubt erroneous, as Louis Chevalier has demonstrated.

forty were sixty-seven per cent as compared with fifty-seven per cent a century later. This means that, if there was still a high birth rate, there was also a high mortality rate. The life expectancy of the average Frenchman, which is now more than sixty-four, was only thirty-six in 1826, and a great deal lower among those of the less fortunate classes. The real decline in the death rate since the beginning of the nineteenth century, thanks to medical progress and especially to better nutrition, had only contributed to the pyramid bulge for the earlier ages, because the older generations, those before the Revolution, had to pay their tribute to death at the much heavier rate of the Old Regime. Moreau de Jonnès found that the annual death rate declined to ten out of 395 as compared to ten out of 255 in 1776.

## Youth's Frustrations

Consequently after 1827 Frenchmen who were twenty years old in 1789, and who could have longed for the return of the Old Regime or tolerated its abuses, represented only one-ninth of the nation; and at that date, one-fourth of those who had lived during the Empire had already died. One has to take this sort of layer-peeling of society into consideration if one wants to understand the rapid changes in public opinion between the reign of Louis XVIII and that of Charles X. The young people who became so enthusiastic over the liberty in 1830 could understand neither the lassitude which caused their fathers to acquiesce in the imperial despotism nor the relief that Frenchmen felt upon the return of the Bourbons along with peace in Europe. The political disputes which had excited the preceding generations left them cold. With what scorn the young Montalivet in 1827 spoke of "those old men, laden with their past of hostile antecedents . . . survivors of the Emigration (exile), the Anarchy, and the Despotism."

In the electorate itself the numerical majority moved over in 1825 to those who had not reached twenty in 1789. But Article 38 of the Charter, by fixing the age of forty as the minimum for deputies, continued to deny positions of power to the representatives of the younger generation. There was here an element of unbalance and discontent. In 1828 the Genevan, James Fazy, just then becoming known in Paris, published a pamphlet entitled *De la gérontocratie, ou de l'abus de la sagesse des vieillards dans le gouvernement de la France* (*On Gerontocracy, or the Abuse of the Wisdom of Old Men in the Government of France*). According to Fazy, it might be noted in passing, anyone over forty was an old man. "They have reduced France down," he said, "to seven thousand or eight thousand asthmatic, gouty, paralytic eligible candidates with enfeebled faculties . . . and do they think they can find steady decisions appropriate to the needs of the times out of these ruins of a stormy age in the past . . . ?"

Politics was not the only area where youthful ambitions felt themselves to be blocked by officeholders of a previous generation. A very obvious congestion likewise existed in the liberal professions and in administrative careers. Here was the real complaint of the age (*mal du siècle*) from which the youth of 1830 suffered.

For over thirty years all the political events had conspired with the biological laws to bring about this result. The Revolution, the Empire, and even the Restoration had suddenly brought into administrative and command positions a generation of relatively young men; the promotions which they had subsequently received naturally resulted in delays for appointment and promotions for those who came afterward because once in a position a man tends to hang on to it. For example the proportion of prefects over the age of fifty went from fifteen per cent in 1818 up to fifty-five per cent in 1830. The government's policy of financial retrenchment leading to a reduction in the number of government employees, the appointment preferences shown to court and clerical favorites, both of these practices limited still more the possibilities of breaking into the green fields of career opportunities. On the other hand, if there were less jobs available, there were always many more applicants. The Revolution had made government jobs open to every one, even to the sons of workmen and peasants, and the nobles themselves avidly sought jobs which they would have blushed to accept under the Old Regime. The educational system of those times ignored the economic needs of the kingdom; stressing the literary and theoretical, it turned young students in the direction toward law, administration, and the liberal professions. The business professions were haughtily scorned: industry? they left that to "the metallic aristocracy"; banking? to the "divided slaves"; commerce? to the "market morons" and to the "calicoes." To confer a grocer's license, to them, meant to certify someone's stupidity. The great Ampère himself, dreaming of seeing his son, Jean-Jacques, attain immortality, advised him to compose some great poem and exhorted him to learn English, not as an anxious father would today because it would be the commercial language, but because it would enable him to read Byron in the original!

Thanks to this fine educational system, the youth of 1830 was therefore bulging with lawyers without cases, doctors without patients, sons of workers and peasants whose studies had incapacitated them for manual labor without opening the way to their preferred careers, bourgeois young men furious at having to mark time in waiting rooms or seeing themselves hopelessly relegated to subordinate administrative positions. It was only too natural that they would therefore blame the regime for their disgrace, that they would look upon it as the result of the revival of noble privilege and the Congregation's secret maneuvers.

## Physical Weaknesses

There is also reason to believe that the French population was rather different physically from what it is today. It had not yet undergone that massive infusion of foreign blood which has profoundly transformed her ethnic characteristics since the close of the nineteenth century. It was noticeable that most of the common people described by Balzac and Eugène Sue were blond. One needs only to be reminded that in 1851, that is, after the influx of refugees of the 1848 revolutions in Europe, there were still only 380,000 foreigners in France, and almost all of them grouped together in frontier regions or in the big cities. The diet and hygiene of Frenchmen were also very different from what they were to be in the twentieth century. The difficulties of transportation, particularly south of the Loire, supported a smaller and less sturdy breed of men, as the records of the draft boards show in dramatic statistics. Out of 1,033,422 draftees examined from 1818 to 1826, a total of 380,213 had to be rejected because they had not attained the required height of five feet, one and a half inches. For every thousand recruits accepted from 1825 to 1829 they had to exempt 765 others for various deformities and physical incapacities other than insufficient height—192 for "weak constitutions," forty-two for ringworm and scrofula, twenty for loss of teeth, eighteen for goiter, etc. In spite of this selective process, in the French army in 1825 only forty-five per cent of the men were over five feet, five inches in height, while, since 1900, the average height of all adult Frenchmen has been five feet, five.

One can understand then the discouraging remark of Fiévée, prefect of Nièvre, as he came out of a draft board meeting in 1813: "There are certain groups of monkeys in which we would find something less hideous than in this collection of 361 Frenchmen!"

One could easily imagine, on the basis of some Pantagruelian menus, that Frenchmen in these earlier days ate better than those of today. That was true for a very small minority of privileged people, who could afford to pay for the luxury of gout and apoplectic strokes, but the people in general were less well fed than they are now. Moreau de

Jonnès estimated in 1831 that the average consumption of meat was thirty-six pounds a year per man. In Paris, according to the toll tax (*octrois*) records, it was 86 pounds. It is true that averages have little meaning; but here is a typical worker's budget drawn up for the Anzin mines; one is astounded to see that a family of six persons is not expected to consume in one year more than sixty pounds of meat, twenty pounds of butter, a hundred quarts of milk, a hundred eggs, and ten pounds of sugar. The basic food was bread: 2,120 pounds a year, or about one pound per person per day. In Dijon, a city in the heart of the wine country, the lower classes usually had to be content with bad weak beer. It was the same situation for the rural lower classes; there is plenty of evidence that meat was a rarity, and white bread was a special treat reserved for holidays or fed only to children.

As to sanitation, one example will suffice: it was found in another typical budget, one worked out by the office of the prefect of the Seine for the average Parisian. So, how many baths did Prefect Chabrol permit to his Parisian fellow-citizens? Two a year! And one of these was to be taken in summer in the river! If the subject were not too nauseating, a lot could be said about the garbage collection service and on the scarcity of, or to be more exact, the nonexistence of those comfort stations to which a great Roman emperor (Vespasian) gave his name and which our century considers indispensable.

The good old times! How disagreeably surprised some people would be who, believing sentimental legends, had their wish fulfilled to go back to those olden days!

## Illiteracy, Crime, and Immorality

If we turn from the body to the mind, comparisons are harder to make, and on this point one can only be guided by individual examples which may not be representative of the whole. Thus, Frenchmen of 1830 appear to have been more spontaneous than our contemporaries, more accessible to enthusiasm, more credulous, more gay, more relaxed, more carefree, simpler in their tastes, more stable, more sociable, more courteous—in other words, more contented with life. One gains this impression from the memoirs, correspondence, newspapers, and the pictures of this period. But it would be very difficult to find positive proofs of all this.

Yet, indirectly, certain statistics give us some terms of comparison. There are, for example, once again some data from the draft boards. Thanks to their records, we know that in general among the young men of the 1829 contingent only forty-one per cent knew how to read and write as against fifty-one per cent who were completely illiterate; and this proportion represented an appreciable improvement over the situation found at the beginning of the Restoration. If one considers that the generations growing up during the Revolution and Empire were for the most part neglected, if one considers that the education of girls was even more neglected than that of boys, one can easily believe that, without exaggeration, more than three-fourths of Frenchmen were illiterate. A serious estimate in 1830 by the *Société de Statistique universelle* of Paris puts the proportion up to even five-sevenths.

It is easy to understand, then, the influence that the parish priests could exercise from their pulpits, and, on another level, the influence of the conversations in cabarets and at the markets, without mentioning popular songs which, like the catechisms, were the only things learned by heart.

Less well-fed and much less educated than Frenchmen of 1950, those of 1830 were, on the other hand, more balanced and, on the whole, happier. At least we assume this from the statistics on suicide and insanity, two categories easily verified in any period. From 1826 to 1830 the average annual number of suicides was 1,827, or fifty to each million of inhabitants. In 1946 there was 4,321, or 106 for each million. In 1830 there were in France about thirty thousand insane persons, in 1950, eighty thousand. Here again the proportion doubles—a rather striking coincidence. May not the worshipers of the good old times have been right after all?

The statistics on crime are no less suggestive, although obviously it is necessary to take into account the ever-increasing activity of the repressive police service as well as the increase in the types of crimes as defined by law. But, after all, a murder is a murder, and a theft, a theft, and people in those days were no more inclined than we are, probably less inclined, to let themselves be robbed and murdered with impunity. What then do the statistics tell us from the records of the assizes courts? They show that during the years 1826 to 1830 there were an annual average of 589 cases of voluntary homicide and 305 cases of rape and indecent assault. The corresponding figure for the years 1934–1938 (annual average) were respectively 402 and 274. From 1826 to 1830 the correctional courts handed down a yearly average of 12,576 convictions for petty thefts; from 1934 to 1938, 44,638. We are led to conclude that, if the people of the Restoration period allowed themselves to be carried away more easily by passion, their sense of justice and propriety was sounder than that of modern Frenchmen.

The secret domain of family and sexual morality is not exempt from the revelations of statistics, and social history should not disregard this subject. One gains the impression that Restoration society was held to an unrelenting austerity by the combined influence of church and state. Yet, is it realized that, in Paris alone in 1824, 163 houses of prostitution (only eighteen less than in 1945 for the whole Seine department) were open for business with licenses issued by Prefect of Police Delavau, a pious Congregationist? In that same year of 1824 there were 2,653 prostitutes properly registered at the prefecture and given periodic medical examinations, and it is estimated that there were five or six times this number of clandestine girls plying their trade in disreputable hotels or even outdoors in unbuilt areas of the capital or just outside the city's gates. Only in 1829, under the Polignac ministry, did Prefect of Police Mangin decide to launch a campaign against the more noticeable scandals. He required that the proprietors of these too-accommodating hotels take out licenses as houses of prostitution or stop their irregular business. A regulation of May 1, 1830 forbade every category of prostitute to appear on the streets. The hostile reaction aroused by these measures among the procurers and clients of these ladies is shown by the astonishing number of protesting brochures published on that occasion. The resentment which Mangin brought down on himself among the turbulent elements of students, soldiers, and workers probably was not unrelated to the ardor of their feelings against him during the July days (Revolution of July 1930). So here was a "moral" factor of which the victors of the Three Glorious Days did not boast!

The birth records reveal other departures from morality. From 1824 to 1830 there were born on the average each year seventy thousand illegitimate children, to which no doubt should be added the great majority of foundlings, of which there were around 33,000. In Paris, if we are to believe Dupin, every third child was illegitimate. It may then be concluded that Frenchmen of 1830 were not much more virtuous than those of today.

## The Family

And yet the Restoration appears as an epoch when the family virtues, even if they suffered a few twists, were honored more than in many other periods. There was a natural social reaction after the war years, when husbands and sons had been taken out of the home, and within the favorable atmosphere of a regime which liked to boast of a paternal and familial character. The king was thought of as a father, in contrast to the pitiless master that the emperor had been. "Long Live Our Father from Ghent!" (*Vive notre père de Gand!*) was chanted somewhat sillily in July 1815. Later it was to be the birth of the "miracle child," the Duke of Bordeaux, whose cradle was a symbol of hope for the regime. A favorite hymn in official ceremonies was: "Where can one be happier than at home amongst one's own?"

Naturally, too, the religious revival among the upper classes, which took pains to renounce the skepticism of the eighteenth century, contributed to this state of mind. By 1816 the Chambre Introuvable had outlawed divorce, which had been permitted in the Napoleonic Code. Charles de Rémusat was to remark in 1827: "Fidelity has ceased to be ridiculous, and lawful love, foolish."

It does not seem that the Revolution had relaxed the bonds of family solidarity. The father's authority remained just as absolute, and marriages were still, more often than not, arranged by the parents without consulting the parties concerned. It was this way from the top to the bottom of the social scale. Sebastian Commissaire, son of a small rural artisan, recounted: "My father was excessively severe. When he gave a command, you had to obey him instantly or he would beat you soon after the command. . . . He believed he had a right to beat his wife and children without anyone questioning it. . . . I remember having seen these ideas shared by a large number of workingmen." The *Mémoires* of Agricol Perdiguier have the same ring: "My father was severe; often we were in fear and trembling in his presence. All he had to say was one word, and we would all take wing to obey him."

The civil code kept the wife dependent on her husband, but foreigners noticed with some astonishment the real influence she exerted. In the little business shops, like the Birotteaus and the Matifats, it was the bourgeois wife who controlled the till. The English traveller, John Scott, humorously described the interior of a Paris café:

> Madame was enthroned in all her majesty at the counter, welcoming clients with a nod or a smile, following closely the coming and going of the waiters, and making them toe the mark. As to the man of the house, he was relegated to the kitchen, and, if perchance he dared to show his white cap in the dining room, he heard himself scolded in such a despotic tone that he did not have a chance to get angry: "Hey, my good man! What do you think you're doing here? Come on, get out! Quick with you!". . . and out he goes.

Another traveller, Morris Birbeck, saw at Louviers a woman run a textile business with competence and good discipline. In Paris women were even seen driving post-chaises (*"coucous"*).

The Countess of Agoult recalls women of high society: "If young, they reigned by their beauty; if old, they gained respect by their experience and retained precedence in the family circle, the privilege to say what they pleased, and to banish and to pardon. They passed sovereignly on delicate questions of propriety and personal honor." The symbol of the position of the married woman, and her inviolable refuge, was the boudoir, the best located and best furnished room in the house. Feminine influence was all-powerful when it came to obtaining a position or a favor in the government. In the ministerial antechambers the elegant lady applicants were always received ahead of the less fortunate men who had been waiting for hours, and the old marquise with a haughty shrill voice would confound clerks and ushers by her air of self-assurance.

## Social Classes

Was French society, as the theory of the Civil Code would have it, "a dust of equal and disconnected atoms"? No, of course not. In addition to family ties, which survived all the Revolutionary upheavals, there still existed numerous principles of distinction and identification which distributed the mass of Frenchmen into classes or social groups. More than today, outward signs, like costumes and language, differentiated them.

The social distinctions of the Old Regime, founded on juridical principles, no longer existed; but it was easier to remove them from legal codes than from custom, and they continued to mark off distinct groups. Money was another factor in social discrimination; its importance was reinforced by the fact that, by the constitution, it became the basis of political power. The three-hundred-franc (sixty-dollar) voters and the thousand-franc (two-hundred-dollar) candidates formed a new privileged class in the nation. A deputy from the Gironde wrote to Villèle in 1827: "The basis of all our laws is wealth; the condition of all distinction is gold; the reward pursued by everyone is riches. So it is to the altars of fortune, and to them alone, that sacrifices are made today by that part of the nation which wants to amount to something." There was also a third social distinction which was superimposed on the two preceding ones—one's occupation. With the common people of Paris, it was noticed, it was one's trade more than one's fortune which made close relations among individuals and families. Certain professions, such as the clergy, the military, and the civil service, were clear-cut as distinctive groups, and again, within each of these groups, hierarchy created many subdivisions. But there were others where the distinguishing lines were very vague. For example, in what category would we put a banker engaging in big commercial ventures or financing an industrial enterprise; or the merchant directing a line of domestic manufactures; or the military man or civil servant continuing to supervise the affairs of his landed estates; or the small artisan selling his own products; or finally the peasant carrying on domestic spinning or taking up carting or peddling for part of the year?

Three other factors also contributed to the confused picture. First, there was politics: in the upper classes, liberal people did not mingle with the royalist crowd. A man like La Fayette, for example, who was a nobleman, an émigré, and a wealthy landowner, found himself cut off from his own class because of his political connections; and inversely some wealthy royalist bourgeois, such as the banker Jauge, joined the social circle of the exclusive Saint-Germain district. Second, Paris society was different from provincial society, and from one province to another the principles of social distinction varied a great deal. Last, the Revolution and Empire set off at all levels of society a general movement of class advancement which rapidly moved individuals and families up the social ladder by wealth and professions. In pre-Revolutionary France the usual rule was for the son to follow the father's profession; now the children wanted to rise above the parental status, and the parents made the greatest possible sacrifices to see their children's ambitions realized, ambitions which they themselves had had to forego. Louis Veuillot recounts a naive dialogue between his parents, which curiously reminds us of the reveries of the young Julien Sorel: "My poor Marianne," the father said, "you are crazy. Did anyone ever hear of workers' children becoming notaries?" "Why not?" she replied, "Napoleon started as a corporal and became an emperor." Imaginary or real, this simple scene explains the deep sense of attachment that the masses had to the memory of the Emperor and illustrates the great social revolution of the nineteenth century.

When all is said and done, in this society of infinitely varied and changing aspects, if we except those employed in church and state, whom we shall discuss later, we really find only two classes whose distinctive features can possibly be defined in terms both precise and general enough to be applied to all France—the nobility and the industrial workers. And should we include the bourgeoisie? Certainly it existed, and its hour of complete triumph was already at hand, but how could one define its limits in a society in which it was growing rapidly out of all the elements unassociated with manual labor? How could one describe the bourgeoisie without going into detail about the various professions? And the scale of social considerations varied a great deal from province to province. That was still truer for the rural classes. To cite only two of the more recent and remarkable studies of rural history, what did the winegrowers of the Côte d'Or (studied by Robert Laurent) have in common with the peasants of the Vivarais (described by Pierre Bozon)? Besides, among the peasantry progress was so slow that our period of fifteen years reveals no characteristic that was not just as true for the end of the eighteenth century as it was for the years leading up to 1850.

## The Nobility

The Charter recognized the existence of a nobility: "The old nobility will resume its titles; the new will keep its own; the king may make new nobles at his pleasure, but he only gives them their ranks and honors without any exemption from the taxes and duties of citizens" (Art. 71). In addition, the establishment of a chamber of peers, organizing an aristocratic power side by side with royal power and the national elective representation, seemed to promise to the nobility a political influence even more regular and more effective than it had enjoyed under the absolute monarchy. However, this influence was only in appearance. One has only to realize the difference between the noble chambers of the old Estates-General, which were really representative of the nobles of the realm who had elected them, and this chamber of peers, chosen entirely by royal authority, which could also appoint commoners if it pleased.

The Ordinance of August 19, 1815, instituting the heredity of the peerage and a sort of hierarchy of titles within the upper house, assured this body at least a kind of supplementary independence without, at the same time, making it any more representative.

We no longer have, or do not yet have, an aristocracy [said Royer-Collard in February 1816], we must wait for time to make it. The aristocratic power created by the Charter is still only a fiction; it rests solely on the virtues, the courage, and the intelligence of the men to whom it is confided. It will not become a reality until it becomes the faithful expression of a definitely recognized superiority.

What superiority? Of intelligence and of culture? But one cannot will that. Of authority connected with a government post? But no one dreamed of starting again what Napoleon had attempted—a sort of noble rank coming with government office. Of services rendered to the country? But the heredity of the peerage severely limited access by this route. What remained then, was superiority in wealth, the basis of political power as defined by the Charter for the electoral system. Landed wealth, especially, appeared to be the kind to give the aristocracy its required status, and it was in this direction that it was oriented, while trying to palliate the effects of the equal distribution of inheritances as provided in the Civil Code.

An Ordinance of August 25, 1817 provided that no one would be appointed to the chamber of peers unless he had previously set up an entailed estate (*majorat*)—that is, a piece of inalienable, indivisible, and unconfiscatable property, to pass to the eldest son along with the title of peer. The value of the entailed estate should vary according to the hierarchy of titles: furnish for dukes an income of thirty thousand francs (six thousand dollars); for counts, one of twenty thousand francs (five thousand dollars); and for viscounts and barons, one of ten thousand francs (two thousand dollars).

Eventually they tried to extend these provisions to the nobility in general. The titles of nobility granted by the king would only be passed on to the sons on the condition that an entailed estate would be provided that would bring an income of ten thousand francs (two thousand dollars) for a marquis, and of five thousand francs (a thousand dollars) for a viscount (February 10, 1824). But these conditions were still too high for the great majority of the nobles with such large families. In 1826, only 307 entailed estates were set up outside the peerage. Of this number 105 dated from the Empire (new nobility). According to its supporters, the famous successions law, proposed in 1826, was expected to remedy this situation, but we will see that it was rejected by the chamber of peers itself.

The noble families, who no longer enjoyed the king's gifts and bounties to help them maintain their rank, now made concerted raids on the government's budget, trying to obtain priorities for all salaried positions, even those which the members of the old aristocracy would not have thought it possible to accept without degrading themselves. Thus numerous gentlemen were seen to become police officers, justices of the peace, tax collectors, tax receivers, comptrollers, ministerial employees, road surveyors, even postmasters. The Ecole Polytechnique (for civil engineers) admitted sons of noble families in greater numbers than it would later under the July Monarchy—seventy as compared to forty-seven. For the first and last time in modern French history, the prestige deriving from birth and family name became associated with political and administrative position. Of 164 prefects appointed under the Restoration, 118 were Old Regime nobles, and of the 536 subprefects and secretaries general of prefectures 219 were also of the old nobility. Government service, for want of very intelligent and qualified persons, at least gained a class of civil servants of exceptional integrity, accustomed to put the honor of serving ahead of material interests. In spite of the vituperations of the opposition against the "fat bellies" of the majority cabinet and in spite of the portrait that a certain novel of Balzac could give, there were never so few political-financial scandals as during this period. In all these fifteen years, among all the prefects and subprefects, only two cases have been found of dismissal for dishonesty.

On the other hand this did not work well for the interests of the bourgeoisie, who saw themselves frustrated from preserving one of the principal results of the Revolution (jobs given according to ability). Their disappointed hopes cried out against the "feudal reaction," and one must see in this one of the principal causes for the unpopularity of the Restoration among those of the middle class.

From this situation comes, too, the importance of the irritating question of titles of nobility—a question that is hard to understand today. The old aristocracy held very few titles which had been given by royal warrant or letters patent in the ordinary way; its members, when they did not take a lordly title connected with their landed estates, called themselves "knights" or "squires." Upon the return of the king they therefore found themselves, from the point of view of title, at a great disadvantage beside the Empire nobles all of whose titles were given by official act. "The old nobility reassumes its former titles" said the Charter, but most of the nobles by birth, who were only children in 1789, had never borne titles! By common consent, they "reassumed," then, titles chosen as they pleased, only the title of duke remained reserved for a formal grant by the king. A certain number of nobles took the precaution of having these new titles regularized by new letters patent; but, because the formalities to follow were complicated and the chancellery fees were high, most of them dispensed with the formalities and were contented to be marquises, counts, viscounts, or barons by the grace of their own assertion. These were what were called "courtesy titles."

This concern to assume a rank which lacked a juridical basis gave henceforth to the particle *de* an importance and meaning that it had not had during the Old Regime. There was not a Dubois or a Dupont but who for advancement in his career, wanted to be called Dupont or Dubois *de* something or other. Some were fortunate enough, like the minister Decazes, to be able to produce the precious particle by just a space between syllables (Monsieur De Cazes)! It can be imagined how much deceit and ridiculous posing was involved in this race for noble distinction. The parents of the great Balzac, as fine commoners as one could find, after marrying their daughter to a Monsieur *de*———, thought they should have two different sets of announcements printed: one in which they called themselves *de* Balzac according to the usage of the circle into which their daughter was entering, and another, with just plain Balzac, according to the usage of their old friends who might have been amused at the new pretentions of the family. This little incident is not only piquant but is also more revealing of the spirit of a society than any long treatise could be.

## Labor

The exact number of manufacturing workers is very difficult to ascertain. One statistic of 1820 asserts that 4,300,000 persons worked in industry as compared to 22,251,000 in other occupations, but this is based on families and not on individuals. Besides, as we have already seen, many farmers spent part of their time in manufacturing. Another indication is found in the statistics of the draft boards, which on the average reported 228 "industrials" as compared to 516 farmers out of every thousand recruits.

The living conditions of workers were very different as between craft workers, factory workers, and farmer-artisans in the country. The last group had one advantage over the others in living at home and obtaining cheaper subsistence. Yet their wages went down steadily because of the pitiless competition of the big concentrations of industrial factories, which eventually brought an end to domestic manufacturing. For example the muslin workers of the Tarare region, who earned, in 1820, from 40 to 45 sous (cents) a day, were only earning 28 to 30 sous fifteen years later. In 1815 the prices paid in Rouen for a dozen handkerchiefs varied according to size from five to thirty francs (one to six dollars); they fell to 1.5 francs and 4.5 francs (thirty and ninety cents). Besides, the living conditions of this category of workers were very different from one region to another, like the conditions of the peasantry to which they continued to belong.

The urban craft workers formed the aristocracy of the laboring classes and retained the traditional artisan structure so favorable to the encouragement of the best human qualities. The working day was certainly long; but, since its length was generally determined by that of daylight, the long winter evenings afforded some leisure. Also they usually observed time off for meals from 9:00 to 10:00 and 2:00 to 3:00, and lastly they benefitted by the Sabbath day of rest and the religious and guild holidays. The companions (travelling workers) usually boarded and roomed with their employers; or, if they were members of a compagnon-nage (union of travelling workers), they roomed with young men of their own age in a "mother" hostel where a family atmosphere prevailed. Their wages were usually enough to assure them an honest and comfort-able living; in Paris in 1820 they were five francs (a dollar) a day for a locksmith, 4.5 francs (ninety cents) for a roofer, 3.50 francs (seventy cents) for a stone-cutter, and 3.25 francs (sixty-five cents) for a carpen-ter. At these wage rates we find in Paris, from settlements of estates, some workers who were able to amass a little capital in government bonds, in private loans, or in town and rural real estate.

During nonworking hours the artisan gave much attention to his dress, and nothing in his exterior appearance distinguished him from his employer or the lower bourgeoisie. The blouse, which was later claimed to be the symbolic dress of a worker, was actually of peasant origin and was only introduced into working circles with the influx of workers up-rooted from the country by the attraction of factory employment. Some trades had traditional costumes, such as the silk-weavers of Lyons who wore a light blue coat, yellowish trousers, a shirt with a high starched collar, a white tie, blue stockings, and a balloon-style hat. All workers attached great importance to their hair style, and untidiness was severely frowned upon. Some wore earrings or trinkets representing the tools of their trade. Their amusements were simple and respectable: bowling, cards, fishing trips, songs, theater, guild balls, even lectures, because some of them had a veritable hunger for culture. Perdiguier tells that at Bordeaux the companions in the evening met in a room where one of them would read to the rest the tragedies of Racine, Ducis, Piron, and Voltaire. "We liked sad and terrible plays especially; the more deaths there were at the end of the tragedy the more sublime, magnificent, and perfect we thought it was." He himself had also read the *Discourse on Universal History* by Bossuet, *Henriade, Jerusalem Delivered,* etc.

Among the workers, trade unionism was strong, and this was another sign of life. In spite of the Le Chapelier Law of the Revolution (forbid-ding trade associations) some trade organizations survived with their elected officials, rulers, monopolies, and mutual aid institutions—such as the porters and caulkers of Marseilles, the "harness-makers' brigade" of Lille, and the market-porters of Paris. Mutual aid societies were numer-ous: 160 in Paris in 1823, thirty-four in Marseilles in 1821, 113 in Lille in 1830. Legislation permitted these societies, and those who began to be troubled by the social question were not slow in seeing them as a panacea. The Paris Philanthropic Society, which brought together the bourgeois and representatives of the professions, undertook the role of acting as a link between them, of encouraging these societies, and of gaining them the goodwill of public officials.

Too ephemeral, too restricted in their membership, and too well watched by the government, these mutual aid societies could not play an effective role in the defense of labor interests. In 1828 an owner of a silk workshop, named Pierre Charnier, a Catholic and good royalist, set up among the silk-weavers of Lyons an association which could be considered for the workers of that time as the nearest approach to modern unions. Called the Society of Mutual Duty, it was supposed to function as a society not only for social security and relief but also for resistance against declining wages. The form of a secret society had been adopted in order to evade the police, and, in order to remain within the letter of the law, it was subdivided into groups of twenty members each. In both its organization and the attitude of its founders, it was a sort of anti-Masonic and anti-Charbonnerie movement aimed at countering bourgeois liberalism by its ceremonies and charities. Yet Charnier's organization was not to become very important until after 1830.

## The Compagnonnages

The principal workers' organizations were the compagnonnages, which existed in the following trades: shoe-makers, leather-workers, chamois-dressers, tanners, curriers, hatters, barrel-makers, wheelwrights, locksmiths, tinsmiths, carpenters, joiners, and stone-cutters. Agricol Perdiguier estimated the number of their active members to be about a hundred thousand, a minority of all the workers, but also an elite which set the tone for the rest. Although without any legal status, these compagnonnages were tolerated by the authorities, who recognized that it was impossible to abolish them. The artisan employers, in contrast to the old guild masters, tolerated their activities very willingly because these associations guaranteed qualified, well-behaved, and steady employees.

The most successful and best known of the practices of the compagnonnages was the famous "tour of France," thanks to which young men could improve their skills and at the same time acquire invaluable experience in knowing men and in seeing their country. Every society, or Duty (*Devoir*), had its chain of hostels called "Mothers," where the young companions found board and room under the best conditions. They also served as the meeting-place or *cayenne* for the local society. When a companion arrived, the roller (*rouleur*) of that particular week undertook to find him a job. If no job was available, he could choose to move on to another city, and in that case each member of the *cayenne* gave him a franc for the expenses of his journey. Or, if he decided to stay, then it was up to the longest-lingering worker in the Duty to give him his job and move on himself. The older companions exercised a stern supervision over the conduct of their fellow-members; every case of improper language or untidiness was punished by fines. Woe to the blackguard (*brûleur*) who skipped out without paying his debts; thenceforth he would find the hostels closed to him and little access to jobs. Before leaving a town, a member had to undergo the conferment of a release (*levage d'acquit*), a short ceremony in which the employer and the companions, in the presence of the roller, formally declared that they had settled with each other. During his long voyages, the young artisan moved up in the ranks of the compagnonnage: from trainee (*aspirant*) he would move up to accepted companion and then to finished companion. On the occasion of being accepted by traditional rites, he received a name by which he would then be known in the association. Nothing could be more delightful or suggestive than these pseudonyms: Vivarais-Contented-Heart, Poitevin-Unlocker-of-Hearts, Agenais-the-Faithful, Toulousain-Brotherly-Love, etc.

All was not perfect in these compagnonnages; the older members treated the trainees too severely, the fines were often used to pay for drinking parties, and the movement especially was splintered into many different branches, or Duties, which opposed each other with hates as ferocious as they were inept. Stuffers, Devourers, Surly Dogs, Passing Companions, Foreign Companions, Liberty Foxes, all clashed in bloody fights, which required police intervention and discredited the institution. When the Stuffers replaced the Devourers in a workshop, or vice versa, the newcomers burned sulphur, resin, or incense, sprinkled vinegar and eau de Cologne on the tools, all to fumigate the place and sterilize the tools.

These excesses, however, did not prevent these workers from being good Christians or from esteeming it a point of honor to observe the trade's holidays by going to mass in a procession in which they carried the signs of their trade—flowing ribbons in hats or buttonholes, embroidered shoulder belts, or tall canes covered with ribbons. In certain associations the companion was expected to take communion on his acceptance day. The picturesque details of these customs can be found in the memoirs and documentary works of the admirable Agricol Perdiguier, Avignonnais-the-Virtue, who undertook to devote his life to purging the institution of all its faults and extending its benefits throughout the working classes.

Although he was finally to fail in his noble design, he contributed power-fully to the survival of the compagnonnages and furnished an appealing image of one of the finest types of men, who did honor to their class and their times.

## The Suffering of Factory Labor

This failure of Perduguier was fatal. The compagnonnages, born among the craft workers, were not adaptable to the new laboring classes growing out of the emerging factory industries. In turning from the former to the latter one gets the horrible impression of entering a dark universe where the people, dehumanized, ground down with poverty, are no longer individuals but nameless larvae in a hopeless mass. The factory worker became a slave to a crude machine, designed with no concern for the rest, health, or safety of its operator. The long work day, endur-able in the family workshop, where variable and creative work was in-volved, became stupefying when associated with the rigorous discipline of the same mechanical motion and in a locale reeking of machines and concentrations of men.

Villermé describes the appearance of these miserable groups which he saw in Alsace:

> One should see them arriving each morning and leaving each eve-ning. Among them are a multitude of thin, pale women, walking bare-foot in the mud and, without umbrellas, putting their aprons or outer skirts over their heads in the rain to protect their faces or neck, and a still larger number of children, just as dirty and wan, clad in rags made greasy by the oil from the looms which dripped on them while they worked. These little ones, better protected from the rain by this waterproofing of their clothes, were not carrying, like the women, their daily lunch baskets on their arms, but instead each clasped in his hand or hid underneath his jacket, as best he could, a piece of bread which was supposed to sustain him until he went home that night.

It seems as if a fatal combination of circumstances continually de-pressed wages. A deputy estimated in 1830 that, in all the trades, wages had declined on an average of twenty-two per cent since 1800, at the same time that the prices of consumer goods had increased by sixty per cent. In fact Simiand's studies tend to prove that the decline in wages dated rather from 1820 and that, before that time, their general move-ment had been upward. In any case it is certain that in 1830 the Lyons silk weavers earned only a third of their 1810 wages. The economist

Dupin estimated that in 1827 the average annual wage of a worker varied between 387 and 492 francs (seventy-seven and ninety-eight dollars). In the Nord, daily wages were found to be from 1.50 to three francs (thirty to sixty cents) for men and from .50 to 1.25 francs (ten to twenty-five cents) for women. In the Haut-Rhin, from 1.50 to 2.50 francs (thirty to fifty cents) for weavers and from .25 to .50 francs (five to ten cents) for women and children. How could they subsist on such wages? The Rouen worker, Noiret, assures us—and he can well be believed—that with every imaginable economy it was impossible to get enough to eat for less than one franc a day. The economist Bigot de Morogues calculated that the minimum living wage for a family of three was 860 francs ($172) a year, and Dr. Guépin in Nantes considered that a worker earning less than six hundred francs ($120) a year was in dire poverty. How numerous they would have been if this had been the criterion for poverty! The least layoff or the shortest of illnesses would plunge the worker well below this minimum living wage which he hardly expected to attain by working every day of the year.

The number of those in dire need increased frightfully in the departments where the large industrial factories began to appear. In 1828, out of 224,000 workers in the Nord, 163,000 had to be helped by welfare agencies; in that same year there were 80,000 in the Pas-de-Calais and 63,000 in the Seine department. Villeneuve-Bargemont, the perfect of the Nord, described the slums in which the unfortunate of the suburbs of Lille stagnated: ". . . narrow, low underground cellars, without water or light where the most disgusting filth prevailed and where father, mother, children, and sometimes even adult brothers and sisters slept on the same pallet." Such living conditions were conducive to the worst moral and physical decadence. The children were especially the victims of them, with thin and deformed bodies and premature vices. As a means of supplementing their inadequate wages, the young working girls resorted to prostitution—which was called "the fifth quarter of their working day." Among the men alcoholism was the only escape from monotony, and they became so addicted to it that often on Mondays the factories remained closed because the workers were not in a condition to return to work after their Sunday drinking bouts.

Acknowledging and deploring these horrible conditions, the local authorities still felt powerless to do anything because their hands were tied by the laws passed by the Revolution and adopted without change by the Restoration. If a prefect dared to move toward establishing a minimum wage, he would find himself disavowed and reprimanded by the minister of interior. Official doctrine forbade the government from tampering with the "freedom of working." The workers did not have the right to take their defense into their own hands; "combinations" and strikes were forbidden to them, and Napoleonic legislation put them under strict surveillance. They had to carry a record book (*livret*) given them by the police, without which they could not quit their job or find other employment. Finally, the scales of justice were different for employers than for workers; in case of a dispute over wages "the master was to be believed on his word," while the worker was expected to furnish evidence. The Penal Code punished worker combinations with prison sentences, while employer combinations brought only penalties or fines. The worker had to resort to the courts to obtain any arrears of pay, but the employer could always collect on the workers' debts by just withholding sums from their weekly wage. The arbitration boards, which were supposed to play the role in industry of justices of the peace, were composed of a majority of employers; and the workers were only represented by foremen and skilled workers.

It is obvious that, under such conditions, combinations and strikes were rare. From 1815 to 1830 there were only 125 strikes, all of them very limited as to length of time and number of workers involved. It was also noticeable that almost all of them took place among the skilled trades, which were less impoverished but more advanced in ideas. As Villermé observed, the flock of machine slaves was too weak and too stupified by poverty even to conceive of revolting. But could it not be that they reflected the resigned passiveness of the rural workers from whose midst they came?

The liberal party, which furnished docile workers to its wealthy voters, fitted very well into this iniquitous regime. The protests arose rather from the Right, and were prompted as much by hate for the new industrial aristocracy as by Christian charity. But these protesters at first had no other remedy to propose than the resurrection of the old guilds or a utopian return to the land. It would only be at the very end of the Restoration that the Viscount of Villeneuve-Bargemont, prefect in the Loire-Inférieure and later in the Nord, would elaborate the principles of a new Christian social policy, based on an extensive investigation of the conditions created by the rise of the industrial revolution. As to socialist reformers, we shall encounter them further on.

Meanwhile, it was the public welfare agencies with their hospitals and relief offices, and also private charities, which cared for these pitiful outcasts of society. Their histories, if they were written, would show, we believe, that the wealthy privileged classes were not as callous toward working-class suffering as is generally thought, but they had not yet come to the realization that these bad conditions were far too acute for much to come from the meager funds donated by individual contributions. No other period in history had been richer in all sorts of charities; and, fashion coming to the aid of religion, there was no woman of high society but who considered it an honor to have "her poor." Just one item of statistics is sufficient to characterize the change in attitude in this regard which came about after 1815: under the Empire the average annual giving or bequeathing to orphanages and hospitals was one million francs ($200,000); between 1814 and 1830 this average rose to three million ($600,000).

## Daily Life in Paris

It would be very interesting to end this study of French society at the time of the Restoration by describing its usual round of work and play, its thousands of little material or sentimental nothings which made up the course of its daily life in the variety of relationships which constitute social life in its fullest meaning. But this would require a volume by itself. Here we can give only a few glimpses, chosen from among those which carry a more general significance or which are more useful in contrasting the difference in mentality between Frenchmen then and now.

"France in the nineteenth century," Balzac said, "was divided into two big zones: Paris and the provinces. . . . Formerly Paris was the first among provincial cities, and the royal court stood above the city. Now Paris and the royal court are one, and the provinces and the city are one." And in fact, since Paris has become the center of a rigidly centralized government, the capital has taken on such a moral and intellectual predominance over all the other cities, and made such material progress, that one feels himself to be living in another world, moving by another rhythm. Today, the ease of travelling and the custom of summer vacations multiply human contacts between Paris and the provinces. But in the old days, although the people of the provinces came to Paris for education, business, or politics, Parisians were almost totally ignorant of the provinces and never left the city, except for the residents of the Faubourg Saint-Germain, who spent their vacations in their châteaux.

Among the provincials in Paris an exception must be made of the numerous students in the university and higher schools. Abruptly freed from the influence of their local environments, much more completely separated from their families than they are today—as much because of travel difficulties as because of the school schedule, which provided almost no vacations—the crowd of uprooted youth formed a very special world of its own with its peculiar customs, slang, meeting places, and entertainments. Young people of very different status and background became conscious of their solidarity and power, before returning to their original or adopted class compartments on attaining the age of thirty or on obtaining the desired appointment. Easily aroused and loud in their demonstrations, they constituted an ideal audience for the flattering attentions of authors, journalists, and politicians. We have seen them at work in the disturbances of 1820; we will encounter them again in 1830.

The capital itself was very different from what we know today in its outward appearance and in its very atmosphere, which industrial and home chimneys had not yet polluted with coal smoke. An English traveller in 1814 exclaimed over "the unusual transparency through which all objects seem to be set off with such astounding clarity," on the limpidity of the waters of the Seine, "a crystalline green in color," on the whiteness of the quays and monuments. The pictures of the time also confirm these impressions. The city was still surrounded by the toll wall of the farmers-general (old collectors of indirect taxes) with its thirty-two access points still guarded by troops. Out beyond were the semi-rural communes (townships), and Balzac, living at Passy, was to have the feeling of being as far from the center of the capital as does today's suburbanite.

One can hardly imagine the appearance of Paris streets before the time of Haussmann (the great transforming prefect of the mid-nineteenth century). Narrow and winding, they were paved with big, badly joined blocks of sandstone. The plan was that the water would drain from the two sides of the street toward a gutter in the middle where the householders threw their daily garbage and night soil indiscriminately, except in front of their own doors. Before the arrival of the heavy street-cleaning carts, this filthy refuse was scattered about by dogs and rag-pickers, and crushed and spread around by passing carriages. The home toilets also emptied into these streets by more or less corroded pipes. If the droppings of the thousands of horses in the traffic are added to all this, it will be easily understood why there were such complaints by contemporaries about the dirtiness of the public streets, the pestilential odors they exhaled in summer, and the mud that had to be splashed through in winter. How could people avoid this mess? There were no sidewalks, and only a few began to be built under Charles X. To dodge the carriages, pedestrians had to jump on the protective jutting cornerstones or seek refuge in entrances to buildings. As to street lighting, it was the same system used under Louis XV—oil lamps suspended over the middle of the street.

It was only at the end of the Restoration that they made the first experiments with gas lighting in the Place du Carrousel and in the shopping streets, which, themselves, date from that period. Store windows were also much more rare and much smaller, the displays were not skillfully arranged. The ancestors of our department stores, which were then called "novelty stores" or "omnia," bore such names as "Sicilian Vespers," "Unchaperoned Girl," "Plowman Soldier," "Two Maggots," "Little Saint Thomas," "Day Laborer," "Little Sailor," etc. One of the larger of these stores was the "Three Quarters," founded in 1829 and located in the lower floors of only two residential buildings.

The social differentiations among the various sections of town were not as marked as they are today. Instead of being on a geographically horizontal basis, distinctions were, one might say, vertical. The various classes were distinguished by the various floors of the buildings—the higher the class and the rents, the lower the floor in a day when elevators were unknown. Thus, in a residential building on Place Vendôme, one of the best locations, the second floor was rented for six hundred francs ($120) a month and the attic apartments for forty (eight dollars); elsewhere the rents paid by the lower classes might run from fifty to four hundred francs (ten to eighty dollars) *a year*. By this vertical arrangement, the most diverse social classes met each other on the stairs, and the rich bourgeois on the second floor, not being able to ignore the poverty which existed up under the mansard roofs, was more readily inclined to give aid. Nevertheless, the rapid rise in rents (twenty-five per cent between 1817 and 1827) began to drive the less fortunate out beyond the city walls—the early stage in the development of suburbs. But, until this move became more general, it was in the oldest central sections of the city that the lowest level of the proletariat piled up hideously, swollen in numbers by the castoffs from the provinces. The failure of house construction to keep up with this influx resulted in an unwholesome condition which revealed itself in a frightening way by the rising incidence of crime and a higher death rate. Villermé discovered in 1824 that on a certain unhealthy street of old Paris the death-rate was four and a half times higher than in the well ventilated houses of the Île Saint-Louis. In these slums swarmed an humanity on the outer fringe of society. Sociologists, journalists, and writers of fiction became aware of the existence of these "dangerous classes" which would raise serious problems after 1830. Eugène Sue was soon to write that "the barbarians are in our midst."

The most noticeably different section of Paris from the social point of view was the Faubourg Saint-Germain (south of the Seine and toward the southwest of the city) with its elegant residences protected from the noisy streets by courtyards and portals often guarded by a doorman. Only one business street, Rue du Bac, traversed this section. However, more than a material community, the Faubourg Saint-Germain represented a social group, that of the upper nobility, and its influence was never greater nor its life more brilliant than in this period. Here it was, and not at the royal court of the Tuileries, that the center of social life was found.

The royal court, now descended from its Versailles empyrean, and almost submerged in the great capital city, had lost a great deal of its prestige and radiance. A worthy Nantes priest, visiting Paris in 1827, noted indignantly the indifference of Parisians toward their princes: "A dog falling into the Seine would attract more curiosity than the royal family taking a drive through Paris." There are many reasons for this royal eclipse, and first of all was the new financial system obviously limiting the ceremonial expenses. The king's annual civil list, permanently appropriated at the beginning of each reign, had been set at thirty million francs (six million dollars) for Louis XVIII and at twenty-five million (five million dollars) for Charles X, plus 7 million ($1,400,000) for the princes: about eight million ($1,600,000) also came from the royal domains. But on such a budget the king had to meet the extraordinary payroll of the companies of the royal guard and maintain the royal castles. A large part of it was absorbed by pensions granted to old household retainers, to victims of the Revolution, to artists and men of letters; and, as to charities, princely generosity was supposed to be boundless. Lastly, the civil list also maintained the royal manufactures, the furniture repository, the Louvre Museum, the Opera, etc. What was left then for the royal court itself? In the last years of the Restoration the expenses of the civil house hold amounted to 1,600,000 francs ($320,-000) a year, that of the royal stables to a little over two million ($400,-000).

Even had they been able, neither Louis XVIII nor Charles X wished or could afford to return to the pomp of Versailles (in the pre-Revolutionary palace, south of Paris). The main enjoyment of the gouty king was conversation with an intimate circle of guests, that of Charles X was hunting. Both were old men, preferring peace and quiet, and their previous wandering life in exile had accustomed them to a fairly simple life. Under Louis XVIII, circumstances more often imposed a social reserve: the foreign occupation, the mourning for the Duke of Berry, and later the failing health of the king himself. The accession of Charles X was to revive life at the court a little; there were the usual receptions, weekly "circles," hunting parties at Rambouillet and Compiègne, and public suppers; but the presence of the Duchess of Angoulême, cold and morose, imposed a certain constraint and people were downright bored at the palace. Courtiers felt duty-bound to attend court but left as soon as possible to spend the rest of the evening in a salon of the Faubourg. Only the Duchess of Berry, when she took over her apartment in the Pavillon de Marsan (north wing of the Tuileries Palace) after the accession of Charles X, was able to attract some life and gaiety. In February 1829 she gave a big costume ball, reminiscent of the court of Francis II; but the very notoriety of this little social event underlines its exceptional character.

In another way, too, the center of social life was no longer in the Tuileries but was in the Paris salons. In this period the latter developed a charm, an activity, and a political and literary influence unknown in subsequent regimes.

> Conversation had returned [remarked Lamartine] along with liberty and leisure. . . . The constitutional regime, by its continual topics of party controversy, by its guaranteed freedom of opinion . . . , by the very novelty of a free regime in a country which had undergone ten years of enforced silence, accelerated more than at any other time in our history that expression of ideas and that steady and lively murmur in Parisian society.

The outward simplicity which prevailed at receptions enabled everybody to hold them more often. For example, at a ball given by the Countess of Flavigny, the buffet set out the following menu: a bouillon, rice-milk, and milk of almonds. The orchestra was composed of a piano, a violin, and a fife. When they were not dancing, the guests sat at card tables and engaged in the quiet pleasures of bezique, piquet, bouillotte, reversi, or whist, and the stakes were very modest. At the end of the evening a few refreshments were passed. Every important personage received twice a week, beginning with the ministers and deputies.

All these social gatherings did not really deserve the name of *salon* in the sense given to it in literary history. In the salon as properly conceived, it is the conversation, and not card games or dancing, which is the principal attraction. There has to be a certain continuity which establishes for it a reputation and style, a certain community of tastes and ideas among its habitués, and finally, as an essential factor, the mistress of the house must give evidence of a very special authority to group her circle of friends and direct the conversation. Politics being the principal subject, along with literature, it is easy to imagine that these salons were characterized especially by their political color. Thus, in the Faubourg Saint-Germain, the Princess de la Trémoille reigned over the Ultra-Royalist people; the Duchess of Broglie, succeeding her mother, Madame de Staël, was the rallying point for the Doctrinaires; and also very influential was the Duchess of Duras at whose home men of all political shades on the Right met with men of letters. As to Madame Récamier's salon, it was a little chapel completely consecrated to the cult of the god Chateaubriand.

Opposite this noble Faubourg was its powerful rival, the Chaussée d'Antin quarter, the fief of the big bankers, where liberalism dominated. Laffitte was its unquestioned king, and the newly rich luxury which he liked to display contrasted with the simplicity of the aristocratic salons. His daughter having married the young Prince de la Moskowa, son of Marshal Ney, his house was the crucible in which were fused the liberalism and Bonapartism which opposed the Bourbon regime. The other great liberal leaders, such as Casimir Périer, Benjamin Delessert, and Ternaux, were just as hospitable, but their salons lacked the necessary feminine authority. This, however, was found at Madame Davilliers', daughter and wife of big industrialists, at Madame de Rumford's where the spirit of the eighteenth-century Encyclopedists still survived, and at the Countess Baraguay d'Hilliers' where the "old mustaches" of the Empire met together. Among the more definitely literary salons were those of Etienne Delécluze, on Rue des Petits-Champs, frequented by Beyle, Mérimée, and Jean-Jacques Ampère; that of Madame Ancelot, quiet meeting-place of the classical and romantic schools; and finally that of the good Nodier at the Arsenal.

> I never saw so much spirit anywhere else [Madame Ancelot said]. Painters, poets, musicians, who formed the underpinning of society, were left to all their individual eccentricities and filled the salon with loud and lively words. They sang, danced, and recited verses. . . .

A few rich foreigners living in Paris also opened salons which benefited from the favorable advantage furnished by curiosity and the fact that political opponents could meet there on neutral territory. "In Paris," General de Castellane wrote of those days, "to attract the best company to one's home, one only had to have two qualifications: be a foreigner and have money." Thus, among the Russians were Princess Bagration, Prince Tufiakin, high liver in whose house one might chance to meet women of questionable virtue, and Madame Swetchine, who, on the other hand, recruited her guests from the most religious people. Countess Apponyi, wife of the Austrian ambassador, inaugurated dancing mornings and musical evenings. Still more numerous were the English salons, introducing into France the "party"—for example those of Lady Holland, a great admirer of Napoleon; of Lady Morgan, an eccentric woman whose works on France overflowed with naive infatuation; of Lady Aldborough, a raucous woman whose salty remarks even made the men blush; of Lady Bessington; of Lady Oxford; and of many others. Very numerous were the English who came over every year to spend a few weeks or months in France—more than twenty thousand in 1821. Some came over to establish residence, in order to take advantage of the lower cost of living and to avoid taxes at home. The cities along the Channel coast, especially Caen, had regular British colonies, very much valued by the local population for the money they brought to business.

All this social activity went on from autumn until spring, because in summer the Faubourg society retired to their châteaux. The Countess d'Agoult defined the annual rhythm this way: "Six months of château, six months of Paris, the ball to the carnival, the concert, and the lenten sermons, marriages after Easter, very little theater, no traveling, cardplaying at all times."

We can obtain a clear idea of what the peaceful and wholesome château life, so restful after the Paris hustle and bustle, was like from a series of drawings by Eugène Lami which amount to a sort of illustrated reporting. The morning was spent in the library, writing endless letters and teaching the children. The mistress of the château made it a point to visit the tenants, so she is shown in riding dress, seated in the modest cottage, the object of respect on the part of the abashed peasants standing before her. Naturally there were constant exchanges of visits among neighboring châteaux residents, who sometimes arrived unannounced in the midst of a billiard game. The big daily event was the arrival of the mail: the women concentrated on reading long missives from their friends who were just as idle as they, while the men gathered around the master of the château to hear him read aloud the latest Paris newspaper, a reading no doubt spiced with running comments. Other distractions were short excursions in which they stopped to make sketches of some picturesque corner, and hunting in all its forms. In the evening, gathered around a big table with its single lamp, women working on their embroidery were captivated by a story read by an amiable old gentleman, while in the shadows the tired hunters dozed beside their dogs. Such was the easy life of high society, whose principal business seemed to be organizing their leisure time. It must be added that it was relieved of all material concerns by numerous servants—the Paris census of 1831 listed fifty thousand servants out of a population of 750,000 inhabitants.

As for the lower bourgeoisie, the class of subordinate civil servants, small shop keepers, and artisans, things were very different—hard work from dawn to dusk. Yet in Paris there were many idle people—some living on small investments, state pensioners, foreigners, provincial favor-seekers, rural landowners who preferred the city while living on the income from their lands. Early in the afternoons all those without much room at home filled up the cafés, the reading rooms, the dance halls, and the little theaters. The favorite gathering-places were the Palais-Royal, the center of the less respectable amusements, with its battalions of prostitutes; the gambling houses where life savings were lost playing biribi, craps, and roulette; and also the boulevards with their crowded shops, their buffoons, and their entertainers of all kinds. As for the Champs-Elysées, it was dangerous to go there at night, and it was only on Sunday that the big crowds went there on their way to the Bois de Boulogne. The workers and people with small incomes also frequented the roadside inns just outside the city gates, where wine cost less than that on which the toll had been paid. Here they could bowl, shoot darts, sing, and learn new songs. Singing was popular in those days; there were even some singing societies, sort of clubs where one could try out one's repertoire. Some of them actually developed some literary reputation, like the *Caveau Moderne* (*Modern Cellar*), run by Desaugiers, and later the *Diners du Vaudeville* and the *Soupers de Momus*.

## Daily Life in the Provinces

In contrast to the bright and animated life of the capital, how dull—especially for young people—was the life of the little provincial cities! "It was," wrote Lamartine, in speaking of life in Mâcon, "routine and narrow, like living in a monastery, where the cloisters had been extended to the proportions of a small town." So it also appeared in the novels of Balzac. His small towns were peopled with rejected old maids, miserly bachelors, semi-failures, all leading almost vegetable lives in a monotonous round of repetitive movements. Youth was stifled in an atmosphere of continual spying, scandal, and spiteful gossip. The standards of morality were severe, at least in appearance, and conservative conformity allowed for no originality. Social distinctions and political cliques were known for their unrelenting rigidity, and, for lack of more elevating diversions, the least incident gave rise to ridiculously exaggerated factions. Balzac observed that "in Paris men are systems, in the provinces systems become men."

In truth the picture appears too black to be true, and one must realize that Balzac's provinces did not go beyond Bordeaux and Angoulême. Lyons, Marseilles, Toulouse, and Bordeaux had a rather brilliant social life. Intellectual life appeared in the flowering of local learned societies. A listing in 1832 showed 297 of them. One must avoid the illusion of treating all provinces alike. France, still so varied in her life today, was much more so at the beginning of the twentieth century. The imperfections in her system of communications maintained many different stages of civilization in her various departments. While the people in the ports of Bordeaux or Nantes already knew all the refinements of British material civilization, people in some isolated rural areas were still living as the Gauls did back before the Romans. There was as much difference between the rich Norman farmer and the miserable share-cropper of the Cantal as there was between the opulent banker of Paris and the needy artisan. Beside Balzac's peasants, nearer to being animals than men, one could place the farmer encountered by Etienne de Jouy, near Pézenas, who had a physics laboratory in his house and whose wife read Sophocles in the original Greek. What caused these differences—it must be repeated—was the practical impossibility of moving about. Balzac put into the mouth of good old Fourchon these words which explain the condition of the peasant:

> To leave home you must have as many *écus* [one equals 60 cents] as you have villages [to traverse], and there are not many Fourchons who have enough to visit six villages; . . . so we have nothing better to do than stay in our communes, where we are bedded down like so many sheep by the force of circumstances, just as we had been previously by the manor lords.

In the twentieth century the peasant is usually just a farmer, making all his income from crops and livestock. Formerly, however, in almost all rural communities they worked also at some manufacturing on the side. And one thing that is too often overlooked is that the farming class furnished most of the inland transportation by lending their horses, wagons, and workers. By this they garnered considerable extra profits in cash and produce, profits which the coming of the railroads was to transfer to the coal mines, the machine factories, large industry, and a whole new class of railroad maintenance crews and experts, all of them city dwellers.

This transfer of the peasants' commercial work to the city explains, as much as the transfer of industrial work, the flight from the rural areas which was so apparent in the second half of the century.

Except for this general picture of the provinces under the Restoration, their other aspects, especially those of the rural provinces, were so varied that any summary description leaves an obviously false impression. This diversity appeared outwardly in peasant costumes whose picturesque colors enchanted travellers; it also appeared in the various provincial dialects which were exclusively used by several million Frenchmen in Brittany, Flanders, Alsace, and in all the south. Right up to the suburbs of Bordeaux, according to Perdiguier, there could be found families who spoke no French. For the Provençals the Northerners, whom they scornfully called "Francos," were like foreigners; and, on the other hand, the rare Parisian who adventured into the Mediterranean south, found himself just as much in a foreign land as would a modern Frenchman who landed in an Arab city. "When I arrived in Avignon," wrote Mérimée in 1834, "it seemed as if I had just left France . . . language, costumes, appearance of the country, all seemed strange to anyone from central France. I thought I was in the midst of a Spanish city. . . ."

This deep-seated diversity of the French nation can be seen in the least apparent aspects of life, which are only revealed by those same statistics used earlier in this chapter as to the height of young army recruits. The draft board of the Haute-Vienne had to reject 818 out of every thousand, while in the Doubs they rejected only 73 per thousand. As to education, they found eighty-one per cent illiterate in the Corrèze and only seventeen per cent in the Jura. While the number of draft dodgers rose to 130 for each thousand in the Cantal, eight departments had only one per thousand.

We have already seen the differences in birthrate from one region to another, differences not much wider than those of today. More striking are the differences in statistics of illegitimate births and foundlings, from which we can infer moral behavior. When the department of the Seine (Paris) had 313 illegitimate births per thousand births, in the Rhone there were 142, in the Haute-Saône 119, while in the Ille-et-Vilaine there were only twenty. As to foundlings, they averaged 67 per thousand in the Bouches-du-Rhône, while the average was only one per thousand for all other departments, including the Haute-Saône which had headed the list of declared illegitimate births. Is this not an indication of completely different mental and social attitudes? As to suicide the Haute-Loire listed one suicide per year per 163,000 inhabitants, while the Oise had one per 5,460, or over twenty-nine times more, not to mention the Seine, where they counted one per 3,632 inhabitants. Court statistics also give us some astounding data: here, for example, are the number of civil suits tried by the courts of first instance from 1820 to 1830—in the appeals district of Nîmes there was one trial for every fifteen inhabitants, while in the district of Rennes it was one for every ninety-five, or over six times less. As to crimes against property and persons, tried in the assize courts from 1828 to 1832 there were over three times as many in the Seine-Inférieure (one for 2,782 inhabitants) as in the Ain (one for 9,394).

From whatever angle we look at it, the French nation during the Restoration appears to have been infinitely more varied than today, still retaining in its social structure the distinctions of the Old Regime, on which were superimposed the new distinctions based on economic life. It also retained, and much more markedly, the differences of mentality and customs connected with provincial peculiarities which had been respected by the old royal government. The process of unification was, nevertheless, moving on apace; and, while awaiting a transportation revolution which would complete this unification, it had to be promoted by the state apparatus, rigidly uniform and centralized, thrown over France by Napoleon like a steel net, and retained in all its parts by the Restoration and all successive regimes.

# 16

❧ ❧ ❧ ❧ ❧

## *Political Life*

### *Royal Powers and the Ministries*

WHEN we endeavored to recall the economic life of Restoration France, we pointed out—as a source of inevitable errors in perspective—the persistence of the same names for places which have undergone great subsequent changes. The same thing must also be true for institutions. The familiar terms of ministry, chamber of deputies, prefecture, party, etc., all represent today things rather different from what they were then.

First of all, it requires some effort to conceive of a political structure where the authority does not come from below, from the sovereign people, but from above, from a monarch, providential depository of a power granted by God himself. Certainly there were already, in the days of the Restoration, many men who did not believe in divine right; but, for the mass of people, royal majesty was still surrounded with a religious prestige which commanded an obedience and a respect of a kind not to be found again after 1830. The existence of representatives of the nation, the restrictions imposed by the Charter on the good pleasure of the king, could not change the fundamental orientation of the system: the monarchy of Louis XVIII and Charles X was a constitutional monarchy, not a parliamentary monarchy.

This can be seen especially in the position of the ministers: if in practice they assumed the duties of government, it was as representatives of the king and not as representatives of the nation. Royer-Collard explained it thus in February 1816:

> The day when the government exists only by the majority in the chamber, the day when it will be established in fact that the chamber can overthrow the king's ministers and can impose on him their own

ministers which are not his, in that day it will be not only the end of our Charter but also the end of royalty . . . in that day we'll be a republic!

The conditions under which the various ministries were dissolved under the Restoration illustrates this theory. Some, like that of Talleyrand in 1815 and that of Villèle in January 1828, resigned before facing a hostile chamber; others, like the ministry of Richelieu in 1818 and that of Dessolles in 1819, fell apart because of internal dissensions; still others were dismissed on the king's initiative—for example, Martignac in August 1829. So there was no ministerial responsibility in the sense we understand it today.

In this system the respective roles of king and ministers depended entirely on the circumstances of time and persons. Nothing would have prevented Louis XVIII from exercising in 1814 all the governmental functions as actively as Louis XIV or Napoleon, and he seemed at first to have the inclination to do it. But his natural indolence, his infirmities, his ignorance of administrative details, were very soon to confine him to a role more like that of an irresponsible constitutional monarch. It is interesting to find in his own handwriting, in a letter addressed to Decazes on January 20, 1819, his ideas on the division of functions between himself and his minister:

> It is my will which should do everything. Responsible ministers tell the king: "Here is our opinion." The king replies: "This is what I want done." If the ministers, after thinking it over, believe they would not be risking too much to follow this view, they will follow it. If not, they will declare that they can not. Then the king will give in, if he thinks he can not do without his ministers. In the contrary case he will find new ones.

Charles X's conception of royal power was not fundamentally different from his brother's.

> I should prefer to saw wood [he said] than to be king under the conditions of the kings of England. In England the ministers govern, so they must be responsible. In France it is the king who governs, he consults the chambers, he takes into serious consideration their advice and remonstrances, but, when he is not convinced, his will has to be carried out.

In contrast to his brother, however, he tried to control the actions of his ministers down to the smallest detail, and it certainly seemed that, in doing this, he was inspired less by a natural inclination to exercise authority than by a strict conception of his duty.

Under these circumstances the role of the president of the council (prime minister) was not exactly the same under the two reigns, and governmental practice took various forms. During the first Restoration the official ministers holding portfolios found themselves subordinated to a council, composed of princes of the blood and of a certain number of ministers of state, before which they were called to present their reports. This heavy machinery had soon shown itself to be an obstacle to getting things done, and each minister had gotten the habit of dealing with important questions of his department in private interviews with the king. It was certainly necessary, from time to time, to call together inter-ministerial conferences, but all that took place at irregular intervals and without there being a definite cabinet as an integral team. The faults in this system were so obvious that Louis XVIII had decided, on his re-turn from Ghent, to confide authority to a real cabinet whose unity of action would be assured by a president of the council. Such was the Talleyrand ministry and such were those which followed. Again in 1820 the king wrote Decazes: "If the Duke (of Richelieu) returns, he himself must choose his colleagues: it is not the king who is the keystone, it is the president of the council." An ordinance of April 19, 1817 had specified the composition and forms of cabinet councils; as to the privy council of 1814 it had been retained in principle, but was never convened. The title of minister of state became a sort of sinecure, a consolation prize given to resigning ministers or to disappointed seekers of cabinet posts; it brought an income of ten thousand francs (two thousand dollars). In 1830 there were no less than fifty-seven ministers of state, a budgetary scandal which the liberal opposition would justifiably denounce and which the July Monarchy would abolish.

Molé described in very spicy terms the council sessions in Richelieu's time:

> The council of ministers met three times a week, Monday and Fri-day at its president's home and Wednesday with the king. . . . It con-vened at one o'clock; we were all usually on time, except Decazes who arrived an hour, sometimes two hours, late, carrying under his arm the red portfolio . . . which he had the habit of sending daily to the king. It started out by waiting for Decazes for a half hour or forty-five min-utes, while the members told little stories. Then Richelieu would become impatient, turn his chair around to the table, and open the session. Each minister brought to the council all the current business and important nominations of his department. The keeper of the seal [minister of jus-

tice] would lead off; his business was very brief. It was while he was speaking that Decazes entered with a worried, nonchalant, absent-minded look, without apologizing, and sat down next to me. Then Decazes opened his portfolio, drew out his police reports, passing them on to M. de Richelieu, and then began to write or read without paying any attention to what was being said. M. de Richelieu, for his part, read the police reports [in silence], and the minister whose turn it was to report spoke to deaf ears, until, wanting to have some decision, he begged in a discouraged tone that the president and the favorite would deign to give him just a moment's attention. When I became convinced that it was always going to be this way, I did the same as the others and only listened when something interested me. Most of the time I walked around the room; Gouvion went to sleep, M. de Richelieu and Decazes read or wrote, Pasquier warmed himself at the fire, and Lainé was the only one to listen because of his pedantic conscience, but became angry because he felt obliged to do it; and Corvetto, who had known, as I also had, different ways of dealing with state business, experienced an impatience which was revealed by his most subtle sallies and by sly glances cast in my direction.

When Louis XVIII presided, he spoke little, but, as unquestioned master, he summarized the discussions with an admirable clarity of conception and a selection of terms in which one could surmise that they came from a prepared speech, learned by heart in advance. At the end of his reign, Chateaubriand recalled, "His Majesty often dozed off in council meeting, and with good reason; if he did not go to sleep, he told funny stories. He had an admirable talent for mimicry, which did not amuse M. de Villèle who wanted to get down to business." During the long administration of Villèle, the council met very often, almost daily in certain periods, but, it seems, not on a fixed day. More assured by a long term in power, and by the complete confidence of Charles X, Villèle worked more and more often with the king in private and no longer consulted his colleagues except as a matter of form. The notion of ministerial solidarity, so well-established under the second ministry of Richelieu, also lost its force, and more than once changes were made in appointments to one or more individual portfolios without causing any downfall of the cabinet as a whole.

Once Villèle was gone, the distinction between royal and ministerial power was practically to disappear. Charles X claimed that he himself exercised the functions of head of the government, and, for two years there was no one holding the title of president of the council. When the ministers met without the king, the keeper of the seal opened the meeting. In the long run, however, the king realized the inconvenience of this practice of no prime minister; not only did it not permit a sufficient co-ordination of business as a whole, but it made it difficult to conciliate it with the theory of royal irresponsibility. The *Gazette de France,* announcing in November 1829 the re-establishment of the presidency of the council in favor of Polignac, commented on this decision in these terms:

> The president of the council is in reality the king, since to him alone belongs the executive and administrative power. But the person of the king is inviolable, sacred, and irresponsible. So it is necessary, when it should please a member of the opposition to go to the tribune to hurl an epithet against the system of government, that the sally he utters should find a target that is not for us a sacred one.

What a naive precaution was this paper screen whose artificial character writers still are careful to emphasize!

In fact, as one might guess, this stratagem did not do away with the confusion over the division of authority, and the absolute subservience of the new president of the council continued to leave to the king the role of head of the government. Baron d'Haussez has sketched a picture of the council sessions of this second reign which is in no way inferior to that of Molé quoted above:

> The council met four times a week [wrote d'Haussez]. On Tuesday and Saturday the meetings, starting promptly at four o'clock and running on to eleven, or sometimes to midnight, took place at the residence of each minister in turn. The work was interrupted for one hour for dinner. . . . The discussion was carried on in a very polite and friendly manner. . . . Generally it took the form of a running conversation. . . . On Wednesdays and Sundays the meetings were at the palace, where the king presided and the Dauphin [the heir to the throne] attended. Each minister brought up the business he had to submit to His Majesty and presented the ordinances needing his signature. Then they took up other questions not connected with the previous reports. The king joined in the discussion, with good common sense, a knowledge of the questions, and especially great care not to affect the debating by giving his opinion the appearance of a final decision. . . . The council proceedings also had their amusing side. Each of the ministers had some peculiar quirk of behavior which began to appear at moments when their close attention was not absolutely required. The king would cut up paper with strange shapes and carefully carried away his finished work at the end of the session. The Dauphin would leaf through the military almanac on which he would note in pencil the transfer of [military] assignments, the list of which the minister of war, after going over these

notations, would make up and resubmit to him. Otherwise the Dauphin took very little part in the discussions, hardly ever broke into them except to make some brief remarks, and too often introducing them with some such apologetic phrase as: "Perhaps what I'm going to say is crazy, but you won't pay any attention to it anyway." Messieurs de Polignac and de Montbel covered the notebooks in front of them with pen sketches. M. de Chabrol spent his time stabbing wax sticks with a stiletto, with some pricking of his fingers when the wax broke off. . . . If someone happened to go to sleep, the king would laugh and tell the others not to wake the sleeper, or, if he did want him awakened, would have his snuff-box passed to him.

No doubt in other times and in other regimes, business may have been handled less casually and more efficiently, but where could anyone find ministers who could sketch such pretty little scenes for the history books?

One last characteristic of the governments of the Restoration was the small number of ministerial departments. At first there were only seven: foreign affairs, justice, interior, finance, war, navy, and police. Then, when they did away with the department of police by putting it under the interior, because they considered it, as Chateaubriand said, "a monster born in the Revolutionary mire by mating anarchy with depotism," there were only six. In 1820 Richelieu asked for the re-establishment of the ministry of the royal household, left vacant by the resignation of Blacas in 1815, but Louis XVIII supported the idea with great repugnance, rightly feeling that the administration of his civil list should remain above political disputes. Yet, since the president of the council this time did not want to take over foreign affairs and had added three ministers without portfolios to his team, this second Richelieu ministry, including eleven Excellencies, had the largest number for this period. When Villèle added foreign affairs to the presidency of the council, they again came back to seven in number.

The reign of Charles X was to be marked by a greater instability in the assignment of duties. First came, in August 1824, the creation of the ministry of ecclesiastical affairs and public instruction, which was to be separated into two in 1828. The ministry of the royal household passed out of existence in 1827, when its minister, the Duke of Doudeauville, offered his resignation; its functions were carried out until the end of the reign by an "intendant of the civil list." Early in 1828 they established a ministry of commerce and manufactures and tried to detach from the war ministry the administration of its personnel, which was entrusted to the Duke of Angoulême; but this lasted only a few days. Under Polignac, public instruction went back under ecclesiastic affairs, the ministry of interior took back commerce, but, on the other hand, in May 1830 they were to take public works away from the interior and raise it to a separate ministry.

No doubt the functions of ministries were not as heavy as they are today, but, nevertheless, the ministers could not bear their burdens alone, especially since they also had to appear before parliament. An ordinance of 1816 allowed them to be assisted by undersecretaries of state, but this practice was hardly used after 1822. Certain general directories practically amounted to regular "little ministries," for example: that of fine arts, annexed to the royal household; those of customs and waters and forests, under finance. And in the cases of postal service, brought back under finance, and police, coming under the interior, the nature of their functions gave them real political importance.

The ministers could still be aided by the council of state which had been divided into sections or committees corresponding to the different ministerial departments and located in the very buildings of these respective ministries. The council of state itself was only the shadow of what it had been under Napoleon. The legitimacy of its existence was vigorously challenged. The royalists looked on this Bonapartist creation with a jaundiced eye; and the liberal opposition objected that it did not have a constitutional existence in the framework defined by the Charter. It seemed to be an underhanded way by which the executive branch tried to take over judicial functions, reserved in principle for an independent magistracy, and also to take over legislative functions reserved for the chambers. During the whole period of the Restoration it was the subject of endless controversy, and the council of state only managed to survive by restricting itself to the field of administration. The size and composition of its membership varied frequently. In 1826, for example, it included thirty councillors, forty masters of petitions, and thirty auditors; but in addition to this personnel, which represented the "ordinary service," they had dreamed up—as a sop to vanity—an "extraordinary service," which gave them a chance to adorn some eighty high officials of the central and departmental offices with additional dignities and certain rights of precedence.

## Central and Local Administrations

When one leafs through the *Almanach Royal* of those times, one gains the impression of a rather simple governmental machine well adapted to its role, one very much like that set up by the first consul, but deprived of the adventitious appendages and artificial nooks and corners which the emperor had added to facilitate the exercise of his arbitrary despotism. The small number of civil servants which directed these administrative departments and the rigid economy which watched over expenditures offers a striking contrast to the situation with which we are familiar today. In 1830 the total number of persons who, under one heading or another, drew their salaries from the government budget was 647,000. If you omit 245,000 on pensions, 47,000 clergymen, 236,000 soldiers and sailors, there remain, in all, 119,000 government employees in all the civil services (compare with 962,000 on April 1, 1950). The total number of employees in the ministries in Paris did not exceed five thousand; the ministry of finance, numerically the largest, with all the related administrative services, had by itself three thousand; but foreign affairs was contented with eighty-eight employees, justice with eighty-seven, and public instruction seventy-one. In a budget of 1,095 million francs (219 million dollars) in 1830, the total provided for salaries for all categories amounted to 292 million ($58,400,000). Deduct from it all that is appropriated for the clergy, army, and navy, and there is left 150 million (thirty million dollars) for the cost of the administrative services, or a little more than thirteen per cent of government expenditures.

That did not prevent the people of those days from groaning as much as we do under the intolerable burden of the bureaucracy. "Everywhere enormous salaries," shouted a deputy, "immense office expenses, armies of clerks, all overload the treasury and are insulting to the public poverty! Penpushers continue to crush the state and load down the administration!" As today, they complained bitterly about red tape and the slowness and fussiness of bureaucrats. Just as today, Frenchmen took revenge by ridiculing the masters they had chosen: the novel by Balzac, *The Employees,* and the satirical works of d'Imbert, less well known but just as amusing, are worthy prototypes of those of Courteline.

I knew an office [d'Imbert wrote] with a staff of seven people. The senior clerk took lessons on the violin, and, taking advantage of the sound-proof isolation of his private office practiced without interruption during office hours; the assistant senior clerk studied his English lessons; of the two writers of documents, one penciled caricatures and the other arranged vaudeville skits for special occasions; the order clerk made cardboard objects; the delivery boy made embroidery patterns; and the office boy made coats and pants. A petitioner came in on business and was greeted by a loud "I have no time for you," which was repeated up the line like a military command. . . . So [this office] was considered to be the busiest in the administration.

Naturally all the personnel was masculine, and the need to write everything by hand made good penmanship an indispensable art for those who sought promotion. Offices were open without interruption from nine in the morning until four in the afternoon, a working schedule explained as much by the need to avoid the costs of artificial lighting as it was by the difficulty of employees to travel home for the noon meal. Some brought cold lunches with them to eat in the office; others had a hot dish brought up by the house-porter (*concierge*) of the ministry, who also furnished restaurant services; more fortunate ones slipped out at about noon to go to a neighboring restaurant, with nothing but their hats left behind to show that they were on the job. It is told that a certain minister, making a tour of inspection in his offices at that critical hour, found three hundred hats and not one employee.

If the public complained about the bureaucracy, the employees for their part had complaints to make about their working conditions. Salaries were very low: twelve hundred francs ($240) a year on the average. Some starting salaries were as low as 800 francs ($160). At the age of thirty a lower employee might get eighteen hundred francs ($360), and six thousand (twelve hundred dollars) at the end of his career. How did they manage to subsist, especially when they had a family to support? Most of them had to find extra outside jobs: one was associated with a merchant whose books he kept, another gave private lessons or taught courses; this one was a member of a theater orchestra, another one turned out cheap vaudeville skits, melodramas, and short stories.

What was most irritating to these bureaucratic plebeians was the ostentatious contrast existing between their misery and the large salaries received by those in the higher echelons: a minister received 150,000 francs (thirty thousand dollars) a year, without counting his expense fund of 25,000 francs (five thousand dollars) for a first-class residence, a ministry director received forty thousand (eight thousand dollars), a prefect twenty to thirty thousand (four to six thousand dollars), a councillor of state sixteen thousand ($3,200). Thus between the highest and lowest echelons there were differential ratios of 1 to between 100 and 150. Besides, there was no hope for the lower-ranking employees to rise to the higher echelons where riches and respectability were found. There were no rules for promotion; it depended on political and parliamentary influence and court recommendations, with no counterweight other than nepotism and the favoritism of administrative directors. Lastly there was not even the assurance of tenure in these jobs; with each ministerial change, with each budget debate, came salary reductions, staff contractions, which meant the dismissal of hundreds of poor wretches, offered as sacrifices to the economy god. Villèle, for example, succeeded in reducing the staff of his ministry from 4,502 to 2,137; and in fifteen years the governments of the Restoration abolished four thousand tax collectors.

The consequences of this state of things were inevitable: if the Restoration had, in general, a corps of higher officials remarkable less for competence than for a high professional sense of duty and scrupulous honesty, the lower-level jobs could attract and retain only mediocre or unqualified people. It is from this period that dates, in France, the unflattering reputation of Mr. Bureaucrat (*M. Lebureau*).

If one is to believe Balzac, the situation of a government employee in the provinces, if not more lucrative, was nevertheless more enviable. The cost of living was lower, the working conditions not as bad, and the position of representing the central government brought him a respect not enjoyed by the Parisian civil servant. Perhaps this may be accounted for, in part, by the fact that the government employee in the provinces enjoyed better tenure and that they were almost all men from the area in which they worked. As under the Old Regime, the provinces furnished their own administrators and judges; the subprefects were almost always chosen from among the leading families of the department or district; only the prefects, like the earlier intendants, came from elsewhere. But they often stayed on one assignment long enough to become identified with the interests of the locality. In many ways the prefects of the Restoration were the worthy successors of the great intendants of the eighteenth century, and Stendhal noted, in his *Mémoires d'un touriste,* that their successors in the July Monarchy (1830–1848) caused the people of the departments to regret their departure. They functioned with the same frugal appropriations as the central offices; often, to keep up the style of their rank, they drew on their own wealth or went into debt. In 1816 the large prefecture of the Calvados carried on its work with twenty-six office employees, plus five hired helpers (*salariés*) for cleaning and maintenance. Administrative costs amounted to 46,000 francs ($9,600), including salaries.

Although in principle the prefects were just as obligated as those of today to report all their official acts to the central government, the slowness of communications gave them a freedom of initiative and, consequently, a great deal more personal authority. Especially in matters of public order, they had to make some very serious decisions on their own. In the departments their authority had no checks except those of the military commander and the bishop, and in the administrative realm it was absolute. The general councillors (representatives on the general council of the department, similar to a county council) and the district councillors were practically appointed by the prefects, since the central government merely ratified their nominees. Therefore these councils during their brief annual sessions could hardly do more than approve the proposals of the prefect concerning appropriations and make some recommendations. As to the cities and townships, they were also under the control of the prefect's authority which appointed the members of their councils and their mayors. The fact that the officials of cities of over five thousand inhabitants were appointed by royal ordinance (thus by the central government) made no difference, since the initial nominations themselves came from the prefecture.

Thus nothing had been changed from the rigid centralization established by the Consulate, and Louis XVIII enjoyed in fact an administrative power more absolute and efficient than Louis XIV himself. Of course it was no more in conformity with the practice of the ancient monarchy than with the principles of the constitutional monarchy established by the Charter. So, during the entire Restoration, they spoke of administrative reform which would revive local initiative by decentralization. Unfortunately the problem always ran into party politics and never came to anything. In the beginning of the Restoration the promoters of decentralization were from the Right, hoping to revive the old generalities (fiscal and civil administrative districts) and provincial assemblies. The liberals, who took their stand behind royal prerogative, became defenders of centralization, aided naturally by the old officials of the Empire, who occupied key positions until 1820. Then, when the royalists came into power in 1822, the positions were reversed. Villèle, who had been in 1816 the most ardent defender of local rights, was careful to utilize the means of controlling elections which the Napoleonic administrative system gave him. Decentralization and local rights then became, in reverse, the battle horse of the liberal opposition. Martignac was going to attempt early in 1829 to obtain some results in the direction of local autonomy by bills which turned back election arrangements to the town and departmental councils. We shall see how they were torpedoed.

In fact, while the parties debated the question of local self-government by speeches, the ministerial bureaucracy was left free to pursue silently by circulars its control over local resources, and it all ended up, in the excellent phrase of M. Pouthas (French historian), by the provinces finding themselves in 1830 "under a more effective centralizing yoke, now regularized, than they had been in 1814 when it was considered arbitrary."

## Public Finance

In all the administrative accomplishment of the Restoration there was no aspect more justly praised than that of finances. Everything was managed as if the officials of the period had been obsessed by the recollection of the budgetary disorder and financial crisis which had triggered the downfall of the old monarchy and as if they had set to work, as a consequence, to give the restored monarchy a solid foundation with an irreproachable financial system. But credit must also be given to the severe restraint exercised by a chamber elected by a taxpaying suffrage, that is by those who shouldered the principal burden of taxation.

The early ministers of finance in the Restoration, Baron Louis and Count Corvetto, had the job of liquidating the disastrous situation bequeathed by the Empire and of fulfilling the enormous exactions imposed by the war indemnity and the foreign occupation. The rigid economy in domestic expenditures, the retention of the excise taxes (*droits réunis*) in spite of the promises given by the Count of Artois, withholdings from the salaries of government officials, massive sales of national forests, a forced loan of a hundred million (twenty million dollars) from the richest taxpayers—all of these expedients would not have sufficed to bridge the gap. By making the heroic decision of honoring all the debts of the preceding regimes, Baron Louis revived the credit of the French government and enabled it to find a way to borrow the necessary sums for its liberation from the occupation.

Once this was accomplished, they could begin to think about setting the budget on a more normal basis. The great artisan of this work was Villèle, aided by Count d'Audiffret, director of the general office of accounts (like the United States Bureau of the Budget). It is impossible here to go into details, admirable as they might be but too technical, of the great ordinances from 1822 to 1827 which literally founded the first modern system of public finance. The results, as far as the budget was concerned, can be summarized in four words—unity, speciality, annuity, and sincerity. Henceforth, all the expenditures and receipts of the state, from whatever sources, were to be recorded according to uniform rules of accounting in all the services and brought together in a single document—the finance law. No hidden receipts, no extraordinary funds, no supplementary budgets, no expenditures were left to the discretion of officials. Appropriations would no longer be voted as a lump sum for each ministry but by detailed sections, with transfers from one to another forbidden after passage. The budget would have to be voted before the beginning of the fiscal year and without any recourse to the procedure of providing for "provisional twelfths." All the expenses anticipated in the budget for the fiscal year should be decreed and paid before September 30 of the following year, so that the definite accounts, determined on December 31, could serve as a base for drawing up the next budget. All appropriations which had not been expended by September 30 would be automatically cancelled, and it would be necessary to get them approved again. Lastly, all government expenses, all administration of funds, would be set up according to exact rules for clarity and with receipts and enclosures. The entire report would be submitted to the independent scrutiny of the Court of Accounts, which in turn would prepare it for the scrutiny of parliament and public opinion. "In no time in history, and in no other country," read the preamble of the ordinance of July 9, 1826, "would an administration have submitted itself to such a difficult ordeal, if it was not the best guarantee of its principles and of the correctness of its action." And Villèle could say with just pride: "Now it is impossible for us to have a dishonest man as minister of finance."

Even after the liquidation of the consequences of the war had relieved the pressure on the treasury, the most rigid control did not cease to be exercised in all parts of the administration. Villèle alone made annual economies of thirty million (six million dollars) in the various services of his ministry of finance. In spite of that—and if we omit the budgets of 1815 to 1818, laden with the extraordinary burdens of indemnity and occupation—the total of expenditures and receipts continued to increase slowly, as was normal indeed for a country whose population and economic production was steadily growing. From 1819 to 1829 the budget went up from 896 to 1,104 million ($179,200,000 to $220,800-000); only three times, in 1823, 1825, and 1827 did it have a deficit. In the first of those years it was because of the expedition to Spain; in the second, because of the indemnification to the émigrés; and in 1827, because of the economic crisis. But, thanks to the prudence and skill of Villèle, this last budget of 1827 was the only one to end up finally as a deficit in the books.

There were no substantial changes in the tax system. The four direct taxes in force since the Directory were kept: the land tax based on the net income from landed property; the personal and chattel property tax, which was based, after 1820, on the rent value of houses; the door and window tax; and the licenses imposed on commercial and industrial businesses. The income from these was improved by the establishment of a single roll, common to the four taxes, by the application of a uniform method of operational forms for those in charge, by the reduction in the number of tax collectors, etc. The completion of land surveys was speeded up: from 1821 to 1830 the number of communes surveyed went up from 11,000 to 21,000, and many inequities of taxation were thereby corrected.

What explanation is there then for the fact that the income from direct taxes, which was 390 million ($78 million dollars) in 1819, fell to 329 million ($65,800,000) in 1829? It was because, on several occasions, the ministers of finance had lowered the rates of land taxes; in all these reductions amounted to 92 million ($18,400,000). The over-all increase in receipts therefore came almost entirely from indirect taxes, and this in spite of reductions in some of these. This increase, which the Count of Chabrol, the last Restoration minister of finance, figured to be 212 million ($42,400,000), was then entirely the result of national economic growth.

As a final result, the policy of order and prudence restored public credit. When Richelieu in 1817 had to negotiate loans for the liberation of the territory, he could find takers only at the rate of 52.50 francs ($10.50) for government bonds with a nominal value of a hundred francs (twenty dollars). A new issue at five per cent in 1821 was taken up by Paris bankers at 85.50; by 1824 the five per cent bonds had gone up to and over par. This was what made it possible for Villèle to plan his big refinancing operation of the government bonds of 1824 and 1825. Unfortunately their realization was obstructed by politics and passion, as we will have occasion to explain below. In the end the public debt was represented by three kinds of issues: five per cent, four-and-a-half per cent, and three per cent; in 1830 these issues were quoted respectively at 109, 108, and 85 francs.

They could have taken advantage of these high quotations to borrow more money, but they avoided that as much as possible in order not to burden the budget with additional annual interest charges. In 1815 the public debt required annual interest payments amounting to 63,307,-000 francs ($12,661,400). The various loans made to liberate France and liquidate the liabilities of the Empire and the Hundred Days raised the interest on the public debt to 143 million francs ($28,600,000). There-after it did not increase more than 45 million (nine million dollars). But, since the amortization fund had already repurchased and wiped out sixteen million ($3,200,000) of this and the refinancing of loans carried out by Villèle had reduced it again by 31 million ($6,200,000), the public debt by the end of the Restoration period totaled only 204 million francs ($40,800,000); and the amortization fund, which contained 38 million ($7,600,000) of it, was capable of continuing its regular and early extinction.

The only criticism which might be made of this financial policy was its very perfection. We see it suggested by Chabrol himself at the end of his famous report of 1830 which explained the broad outlines of these accomplishments: "It is certainly prudent to avoid excessive expenditures, but it is no less wise to replace sterile savings by expenditures which could increase the resources of the Treasury and of individual citizens." This appeal to productive investments was to be heard and acted upon by later regimes, but without these years of austerity and prudence, would the credit of the state have been able to entice out of French savings those floods of investment capital which stimulated the economic life of the country during the rest of the nineteenth century?

## Army, Navy, and Colonies

Among the governmental expenditures, those for military purposes constituted a higher proportion than one would ordinarily think for so peaceful a regime: 214,366,000 francs ($42,873,200) in 1829, or about twenty-one per cent of the total budget, for a theoretical force of 225,000 men and 47,000 horses.

Right after the events of 1815 the reorganization of the army had posed some difficult problems; Marshal Gouvion-Saint-Cyr laid down its basic plan in the course of his brief tenure of the war ministry from July to September 1815. His plan was original, breaking with the tradition of the imperial army without, at the same time, returning to that of the Old Regime. The infantry was set up mainly into eighty-six departmental legions, each one recruiting its men in its own department and consisting of a number of battalions according to the number of volunteer recruits it could obtain. The same system was used for cavalry regiments except that some departments were combined into double districts with forty-seven regiments in all. In moving closer to the system of a national army, they thought they were destroying the old esprit de corps of the imperial army units.

The efforts of Marshal Clarke, who was war minister from September 1815 to September 1817, were directed principally to the organization of a royal guard, an elite force, which was intended to provide for the safety of the regime. It was composed of eight infantry regiments—two of them Swiss—eight cavalry regiments, and three artillery regiments, or a total of 1,160 officers and 25,000 men. The officers had a rank and title one grade higher than the corresponding one in the army; and the pay scale for men and officers up through the rank of captain was half again that of the regular army—for higher-ranking officers, it was one-fourth. Their uniforms were particularly distinguished: for the infantry, for example, it was a royal blue coat with white buttons and buttonholes, their trousers of blue wool for winter and of white linen for summer; the insignia, the folded trim, the braid, the epaulettes, varied in color according to the unit and the specialty; for headdress they wore high fur hats with a white plume. The uniforms of the different cavalry regiments—horse grenadiers, cuirassiers, light cavalry, lancers, hussars—presented even more color and variety. The most characteristic was that of the cuirassiers with their long boots over white trousers, their cuirasses of polished steel and their helmets of black chenille with a white plume, also worn by the dragoons. The different corps of the royal guard were quartered near Paris and came in, in turn, to mount guard at the royal châteaux for three months at a time, along with five companies of the royal life guards of the king's military establishment.

However, the royal guard having drained off the best elements, the rest of the army stagnated in a sorry state; on January 1, 1817 the total personnel of the French armed services did not exceed 117,000 men. A military career no longer attracted enough volunteers to attain the permitted size, and the oversupply of officers whom they had tried to transfer, no less than the arbitrary way they chose commanders—which smacked of politics—discouraged all hope of advancement. By 1829 captains and lieutenants were found who were over fifty years of age. Even before Richelieu had achieved the liberation of the territory, Gouvion-Saint-Cyr undertook to endow France with an army worthy of her rank as a great power. This was the objective of the law of March 12, 1818, which caused hot debates in the chambers. The manner of recruiting, the organization of the reserves, and promotions—these were the three problems with which the law tried to deal. (See above, p. 147.)

A few weeks before leaving the war ministry, Gouvion-Saint-Cyr had the king sign an ordinance putting an end to departmental legions made up of local recruits. Experience had shown that this system did not work. The attraction of the military services and the aptitude of recruits differing sharply from one region to another, commanders were faced with very unequal units—some were almost skeletal while others were overcrowded, some had strong and intelligent men while others had dull and gawky subhumans. The addition of new recruits furnished by conscription was to make it possible to fuse all elements in the army into a more homogeneous mass. So the departmental legions gave way to a national system of sixty regiments of line infantry and twenty of light infantry, which were designated, as during the Empire, by numbers. The same was also done with the cavalry. The overcrowded units were split up, while the smaller ones were combined to form uniform regiments made up of three battalions.

The expedition to Spain in 1823 served as a tryout for the new royal army. The more active foreign policy which Chateaubriand claimed to be carrying out, as well as the maintenance of a corps of occupation beyond the Pyrenees, required an increase in the armed forces, and the law of June 5, 1824 provided for it. On the one hand, the upper limit of the permanent army was raised from 240,000 to 400,000 men and that of the annual call-up from forty thousand to sixty thousand; on the other hand, the legal term of service for all military personnel was set at eight years. In fact, as before, they were never to take in more than a part of the draftees chosen by lot, and the size of the army was never to exceed much beyond 250,000 men. The reason for extending the term of active service was to produce a professional army, firmly controlled by its commanders. They were returning in fact to the Napoleonic conception, to the praetorian army, as if they might now have feared that they were coming too close to a national army. "The soldier must learn to like army life," said Count Curial, Inspector General of Infantry; "the marshal's baton must be given time enough to emerge from the knapsack." As to the marshal's baton, it was a sour joke, considering how promotions were made; but, as to developing a liking for the army, it was only too true that after six or eight years of barrack life the young uprooted peasant, trained to a life of idleness and passive obedience, was no longer fit for anything else but to lead a soldier's life. All he could do when his term of service was over was to sign up again or, better yet, try to sell himself as a substitute for a draftee, which brought him an extra seven hundred francs ($140). Every bourgeois, or even artisan, or rich farmer family was ready to pay such a price; and thus the draft only affected the poorest of peasants and workers. So the army became, as Alfred de Vigny called it, "a nation within a nation."

The upper-class officers did not make a career in the army; out of 4,499 first lieutenants appointed in all the services from 1821 to 1831, only 1,952 were graduated from the military schools; the others were former noncommissioned officers who had been promoted to officer rank. A large number of young royalists or former officers of royal armies, who had sought epaulettes in the early days of the Restoration, became disgusted rather quickly with a career from which they obtained neither a good income nor public esteem, and resignations were numerous every year. To fill these vacancies, they called on the former imperial officers, those famous half-pay officers, who served the king just as loyally as they had the emperor, in spite of a tenacious legend to the contrary.

These fifteen years of the Restoration, so peaceful by contrast with those of preceding regimes, were nonetheless not years of stagnation for the army. The three expeditions—to Spain in 1823, to the Morea (Peloponnesus) in 1828, and to Algeria in 1830—were all of them successes. Important efforts were made to improve the technical competence of the officer corps. In 1818 the general staff corps for officers and the general staff training school were created; and in February 1828 was founded the Superior War Council made up of three marshals and twelve lieutenant generals. The artillery service, which had hardly undergone any improvement since the time of Gribeauval, was given, after 1823, new, more mobile weapons which were to remain in use until 1853. An ordinance of 1817 set up an army quartermaster's corps.

The navy, even more than the army, had had to suffer from the consequences of defeat. In 1814 it had had to turn over all its ships anchored in North Sea ports, which meant almost half of Napoleon's fleet; those left to France were in such a bad state that by 1819 there were only thirty-one out of seventy still afloat. The purge of 1815 removed four hundred experienced officers to make room for former émigrés, who were often not very qualified. Lastly, the scrimping economic policy reduced the naval part of the budget to just enough to save it from extinction. Even as late as 1818 it did not exceed 43,200,000 francs ($8,640,000). A change for the better did not come until December 1818 with the arrival at the naval ministry of Baron Portal, who brought to the naval and colonial policy of France the ambitious views of Bordeaux' big merchants. The naval budget was rapidly increased to 65 million (thirteen million dollars) in 1821, and even to eighty million (sixteen million dollars) in 1828. They went to work seriously to replenish equipment and personnel. The main influence behind all this was the Admiralty Council, set up in 1824, whose competency fortunately made up for the deficiencies of the minister imposed on the navy by politics.

A committee on naval construction, organized in 1820, approved new types of ships; its principal innovations were the so-called "wall-sided ships" (*murailles droites*) for ships of the line, a design which allowed a better arrangement of naval guns, and a reinforcement of the masts. The calibres of guns were standardized, and Commander Paixhans perfected the explosive shell, which in a very short time was to spell the end of wooden battleships. "In certain ways," a specialist in maritime history wrote, "there is a greater distance between the fleet of 1835 and that of the First Empire than there had been between the latter and the ships of the Sun-King (Louis XIV)." In 1830 the French royal navy consisted of thirty-five ships of the line in excellent condition, forty frigates, and 209 miscellaneous craft, with crews amounting to about twenty thousand men. The stagnation of foreign commerce had severely restricted voluntary naval enlistments; it became necessary to have recourse to the draft to fill out the crews with marine infantry and naval gunners. The education of future naval officers was provided first, on the theoretical side, at the Royal Naval College of Angoulême, and later completed by periods of practical training aboard training corvettes.

The glorious role played by the French navy at the Battle of Navarino in 1827 marked its revival by revealing dramatically the excellence of its equipment and the quality of its crews. The preparation and the flawless execution of the transportation and landing of the expeditionary corps at Algiers gained no less an honor for it.

The administration of the colonies was also assigned to the naval ministry. The treaties of 1814 and 1815 had restored to France her colonial possessions as of January 1, 1792, except for Tobago and Santa Lucia in the Antilles and Île de France (Mauritius) in the Indian Ocean; but her finest gem, Santo Domingo, remained under the control of the Negro republic founded in 1804. The treaties of Paris gave France the right to re-establish her authority on that western half of the island which previously had belonged to her, and the royal government, harassed by the loud complaints of the former colonists, thought seriously of doing so on several occasions. However, its reconquest by force of arms seemed too difficult, especially because of the open hostility of England and the United States. Villèle, taking a realistic approach, opened secret negotiations which were concluded in 1825. The king, to save face, "granted" independence to his erstwhile insurrectionists, and, in exchange, the Republic of Haiti promised to pay a sum of 150 million francs (thirty million dollars) to indemnify the former colonists. It also granted very favorable terms to French commerce. This quite reasonable settlement raised a storm of protest among the former colonists, and it was one of the principal criticisms of the extreme Right opposition to the Villèle government.

As to the other colonial possessions—Guadeloupe and Martinique, French Guiana, Saint-Pierre and Miquelon, the posts in Senegal, Île Bourbon, and the Indian factories—France had great difficulty in retaking possession of them because England, who occupied them, used them as a lever to force compliance with the financial clauses of the treaties of 1815. They had tried, in 1814, to re-establish in the colonies the entire administrative machinery of the Old Regime. But, under the stress of experience, and after a long period of groping, they settled on a system which combined the traditions of the old days with the practice in the mother country. Power was concentrated in the hands of a military governor representing the king; he was assisted by a director general of the interior for the civil administration, by an adjutant general for military administration, and by a procurator general to watch over the courts, which were set up in line with those at home. A privy council, composed of officials and two notables of the colony, was a sort of council of state for the governor; and then there was a general council, meeting twice a year, like those in the French departments, which had a consultative role in budgetary matters.

The productive part of these colonial possessions did not exceed 5,000 square kilometers (1,930 square miles), less than the area of a French department. The crops which had formerly brought wealth to the Antilles—such as cotton, indigo, coffee, and tobacco—now felt the competition of new producing areas in the two American continents. The cane sugar crop was compromised by the raising of sugar beets in Europe; and, most important of all, the prohibition of the slave trade deprived the colonists of their necessary labor supply. Since the old colonies were declining because of slave labor shortages, could they not remedy the situation by removing the lucrative crop production to places where labor could be found? This idea led to a few attempts at agricultural colonization in places which up to then had only been occupied as trading posts and naval stations. The most determined effort was made in Senegal, where, for ten years, they tried to expand French domination along the shores of the river and to found large plantations. In the end, in 1826, the whole scheme was abandoned, and they returned strictly to the system of trading posts. At least the contacts made with the Sudanese tribes and the repeated explorations in the back country paved the way for future conquests.

In Madagascar, where the French had settled at Sainte-Marie, Fort-Dauphin, and Tintingue, their attempt to expand out from these points ran into armed resistance from the sovereign Hovas, supported by England. An attempt at European colonization in French Guiana failed miserably in 1824, as had previous attempts, because of the pestilential climate. Elsewhere, the government encouraged the unsuccessful efforts of the Bordeaux shipowners to establish regular trade with Annam. The

Pacific islands were explored by Bougainville and Dumont d'Urville with the idea of setting up a naval station in that area.

All of this was overshadowed, obviously, by the conquest of Algiers, which was to open for France the doors to a new empire.

## The People and the Legislature

Although all Frenchmen were affected in one way or another by the administrative action of the government, politics in the narrow sense remained outside the purview of the masses, and their political activities, to which history gave too-exclusive attention, in fact only concerned the upper level of the nation. To become convinced of this fact, one only has to remember the high proportion of illiterates, the communication difficulties, and the isolation in which most of the rural communities lived. Here are two previously unpublished pieces of evidence which confirm the above general statements. The first is written by the Swedish ambassador, Count Gustaf Löwenhielm, who reported from Marseilles in August 1819 to his cousin, Palmstierna:

> No one talks politics. . . . There are some agitators, but they are not very successful. Exhaustion and self-interest guarantee peace and quiet. Also the people in the provinces are far from understanding the fundamental laws, and consequently do not give them much attention. Some of the main results of the Revolution remain in their hearts: equality before the law, etc., but for the rest they don't care. They don't even know what liberty is. They are so in the habit of obeying, and one must include the inertia of things as they are.

The other piece of evidence is a report of an observer sent into the provinces by the English ambassador in August 1822. Although he was hostile to the Ultra-Royalist government, he was struck by the appearance of security and prosperity which refuted the accounts in the Paris papers.

> Nothing [he wrote] appears less like a suffering people. . . . Outside the cities, papers are not read very much, and political discussions are almost unknown. They neither like nor hate the government. They have little interest in its activity, and they don't feel its heavy hand either for good or ill. One might say that things run on their own steam with no one getting involved in them. . . .

Since all the local councils were appointed by the central government, politics came to life in the cities and provinces only on the eve of a national parliamentary election or at the time of a special event, such as a political visit or a sensational political trial. Parties in the local communities were made up of a circle of a few friends, and all of one party could be contained in one salon or one coffee house. "Today," wrote Benjamin Constant in 1824, "only in the capital do you find a nation." Only in Paris did political fighting have an important place in the concerns of the leisure class and spread down to all levels of the population, and even this activity died down between parliamentary sessions.

The chamber of peers, although it was superior in dignity to that of the deputies and although it might participate as an equal in the legislative process, managed only rarely to assert any ascendancy in political affairs or move into the limelight of public opinion. "True it is," remarked Polignac, "it sits on the second floor and the chamber of deputies on the first; but the latter can be heard in the streets, while the former's voice trails off into thin air." The cause was easy to find. First of all, its sessions were not public, and the *Moniteur* only published a pale résumé of them. But, more important, what authority could the opinion of an assembly claim when it was chosen entirely by the executive branch? No doubt theory would have it that it was the voice and the seedbed of a new aristocracy, the gathering place of all the great of the nation. But in fact what did they find? The chamber of peers was made up of the sedimentary strata of all the political systems which France had tried and rejected one after another during the last quarter of a century: great names of the Old Regime; Vendean émigrés; royal conspirators; moderate republicans of the Directory; administrators, soldiers, and courtiers of the Empire; and protégés of Talleyrand, Decazes, and Villèle. What sort of governmental doctrine or political direction could be found in such a motley collection?

The first appointments of peers made by Louis XVIII in 1814 and 1815 were inspired by a real attempt to join the eminent people of the new France with those of the old monarchy. But soon the needs of partisan politics got the upper hand. Hardly had the upper house showed signs of independence when its opposition was diluted by an infusion of new elements chosen less for their individual merits than for the support which could be expected from them. Decazes set the precedent for this by his "batch" of peers made in March 1819. Villèle was to follow his example and even go beyond him in 1827 when he appointed 76 peers with one fell blow. The other promotions to the peers made in little batches during the preceding and following years seemed like consolation prizes or political small change given out as part of ministerial deals. Someone said the upper house had become the "Old Soldier's Home" (*l'Hôpital des Invalides*) of the ministry, and *Figaro,* in a parody on the Charter, wrote under Article 24: "Any minister removed from office by demand of the nation will automatically and by right be raised to the peerage." On the eve of the revolution of 1830 the peerage consisted of 384 members instead of the 210 of 1815, but, of this number, forty-six had not taken their seats because either they were not yet twenty-five years of age or they had not yet been officially sworn in.

When one compares the age and wealth requirements for membership in the two houses, one finds the paradox of the upper house, supposedly designed to moderate legislation, generally made up of younger and less wealthy men than the forty-year-olds of the lower house who had to qualify by being thousand-franc direct tax-payers. These latter, holding seats by election and not drawing any legislative salary, were in a stronger and more independent position than the peers, whose dignity came from the good pleasure of the king and continued to be dependent on him by the big pensions attached to their appointment—thirty thousand francs (six thousand dollars) for the former senators of the Empire and twelve thousand ($2,400) for the others.

The chamber of deputies was therefore incontestably the center and pivot of political life. There and there alone the great goals which divided the nation—or at least its cultivated elite—were found to be clearly represented by men and parties. Only there could they freely express themselves before the country. The nation knew no other conflicts than those involving their elections, and their debates were the principal topics of newspaper discussions.

The number of deputies, after having been 402 in 1815, had been reduced to 262 by the ordinance of September 5, 1816. The electoral law of 1820 raised it again to 430. A thorough and definitive study of the parliamentary members of the Restoration has not yet been made. The number of members who had played a role in the Revolution and Empire was larger than usually supposed: 54 in the Revolution and 291 in the Empire. Naturally the old and new nobility were prominent in its membership; never less than forty per cent, the proportion rose to fifty-eight per cent in the chamber of 1821. Since there was no restriction against a deputy holding an administrative office, the various governments did not fail to take advantage of this to build up a majority in the chamber either by running one of their administrative officials for a seat in the chamber or by appointing a deputy, already elected, to a lucrative post in the government. That was why Martignac chose at one stroke twenty-eight councillors of state and three masters of petitions from among members of the majority. Even prefects were seen to divide their time—the Lord only knows how!—between parliamentary sessions and the administration of their departments. In the last chamber of the Restoration the proportion of officeholders rose to 38.5 per cent; in other respects large landholders were 41.5 per cent, economic professions represented 14.8 per cent, and the liberal professions only 5.2 per cent.

The material appearance of the chamber, and the rules which prescribed the procedures of its sessions and legislative work, were quite different from what they are today in the national assembly. The hall was the same one which had been hastily erected in 1797 for the council of five hundred: very plain Greco-Roman design whose appearance was made more austere by the great stones' remaining uncovered; the president's tribune, made of marble, was located in a sort of contrived apse in the middle of the right wall of the back. The seats, sloping up, were arranged, as today, in a semicircle and the Right and Left were designated in relation to the president's chair in front of them. The heating was furnished by pipes installed beneath the mosaic floor, and the lighting came from chandeliers which could be lowered, when necessary, from openings cut in the glassed double ceiling; but the sessions never went beyond five or six o'clock in the evening. This hall, prototype of so many parliamentary halls built since then, was torn down in 1829, and, for the session of 1829 to 1830, a temporary wooden hall was built in the gardens of the Bourbon Palace, while work continued on the one to replace it, which would not be ready until in 1832.

While there were no legislative salaries, the deputies were a great deal more assiduous during the sessions than they are today, not only because they had a lofty conception of their duty but also because their voting was strictly an individual matter. It must be admitted too that they were less overburdened with outside work and that the sessions lasted only six months, beginning at the end of the year, in November or December, sometimes even in January, and ending in July at the latest, sometimes sooner. The session was opened by a speech from the throne, delivered by the king before a joint session of the two houses, in which the sovereign briefly reported on all current questions and announced the principal legislative measures which would be proposed for parliamentary consideration. The two houses replied with addresses whose wording was carefully weighed, debated in secret sessions, and sometimes containing advice and criticisms conveyed in the most respectful forms—as we have seen, for example, in the address of 1821.

There were no specialized standing committees as today, but at the beginning of the session the chamber was divided into multipurpose "bureaux" chosen by lot. Bills were examined simultaneously by all the bureaux and were not brought to the floor until two-thirds of the bureaux had studied them and appointed a general reporter. The various clauses of bills, like all current business, were decided by a standing vote, with right to a recheck, but the final acceptance of the whole law was always decided by a secret vote. As their names were called, the deputies filed up to the tribune, and put a white ball in the box for *yes* or a black one for *no*. The balls that were not used were put in a second box as a recheck on the result. When the Ultra-Royalists were in the opposition, the black balls—which they always found to be the same number in all the votes—were called "the heir-apparent's plums" (*"les prunes de Monsieur"*).

At that time there were no parties, or organized groups, with chairman, party committees, and party discipline. Instead, outside the chamber, and completely unofficially, there were rallying points—certain salons where deputies of similar ideas congregated to exchange their views and plan their tactics. Such a salon for the Ultra-Royalist party, which supported Villèle, was the "Piet meetings"; others were that of the Duchess of Broglie for the doctrinaires; that of Laffitte for the liberals; and that of Ternaux for the Left-Center. Still, the dividing lines of the parties remained more or less indistinct, and the freedom of voting was so complete that the outcome of a vote on a bill could never be predicted with any certainty. A speech which provoked an incident on the floor of the house could have a decisive influence on the voting, and this uncertainty constituted an element of keen interest in the parliamentary game.

When we go back over the minutes of the parliamentary debates, we are struck by the earnestness, dignity, and loftiness of mind which prevailed within the legislative halls. "The Charter," Thiers affirmed, "had transformed the forum of the ancients into a hall of decent people." No doubt there were a few stormy sessions; no doubt some stenographers less able or more discreet than those of today did not record all the interruptions or all the mistakes in the French language caused by the excitement; and no doubt it was the current practice of the deputies to correct afterwards the record of their remarks, even to have inserted in the record some speeches they had never delivered. Yet, just the same, it can be said that never in France had parliamentary eloquence achieved such a high quality. Most of the deputies would have felt that they were lacking respect for the chamber if they had not brought to the tribune speeches carefully prepared and written out; and they listened patiently and courteously to long dissertations on public law, political economy, history, or even philosophy. Rare were those, like Benjamin Constant, who dared to extemporize, and any such inclinations were discouraged by rules which frowned upon speaking from one's seat and expected one not to mount the tribune without wearing the deputy's garb, which was royal blue with white buttons and embroidered silver *fleurs de lys* around the collar and cuffs.

## The Press and Elections

Nor did the debates in the chamber ever have more coverage in the press and a more profound influence on public opinion—one speech by Royer-Collard had, they say, a million copies reprinted. From the fact that there were legal restrictions always limiting to a certain extent the freedom of expression for journalists, the parliamentary tribune was almost the only place where opinions hostile to the government could be freely aired, and the authorities had no way of stopping newspapers from reporting the debates. The principal papers of various parties have already been discussed above, and the history of the different regulations imposed on papers and periodicals is shown to be intimately connected with political fluctuations. What needs to be discussed in further detail here is the physical appearance of the newspapers of the Restoration: only four pages of a size about half that of present newspapers, no big headlines, two or three columns of small type covering foreign news, French news, minutes of parliamentary debates or judicial proceedings. Political editorial articles (*leaders*) were never signed, unless just by initials; literary news and criticism of plays commanded much space, but no advertising, no serial short stories, no scandal sheets, perhaps a few human-interest items (*faits divers*). The newspapers were intended for serious readers who had time to read them from beginning to end.

They were also intended for a well-to-do public. As there was no sale of single copies, one had to obtain newspapers by subscription; but the subscription prices were high: for example, 72 francs ($14.40) a year for the *Quotidienne* in 1824. So the circulation remained very small; the *Journal des Débats* and the *Constitutionnel*, the two largest papers of the period, never exceeded twenty thousand subscribers; most of the others remained below five thousand. In 1826 the fourteen political papers in the capital had a total of 65,000 subscribers in the country at large. They did, however, have a much larger circle of readers, because often several people joined together for one subscription, and, in Paris as well as in the principal provincial cities, there were reading rooms and coffee houses where, for a modest fee, one could read regularly one's favorite paper. In spite of all this, it is certain that newspaper reading, like all other political activities, remained the privilege of a minority; in 1826 Dupin estimated that there was one subscriber for every 427 Frenchmen.

How, then, did newspapers make ends meet? Casimir Périer, on the occasion of the debates on the press law of 1827, gave a glimpse into the budget of the *Constitutionnel*: the gross receipts, coming from twenty thousand subscriptions in 1826, amounted to 1,373,976 francs ($274,-795). Out of this sum the stamp tax, imposed by the government, alone took 450,000 francs (ninety thousand dollars), and the delivery costs took another 102,000 francs ($20,400), while all the others—editorial and administrative expenses, etc.—amounted to 394,000 francs ($78,800), leaving an annual net profit of 375,000 francs ($75,000) to be divided among about ten shareholders—such was the lucrative business, one can see, of taking issue with government and church! But the papers with a small circulation survived only through the interested generosity of some rich patron or of some political party, more often by government subsidies. Thus in 1826 everyone knew that the *Drapeau blanc* belonged to the minister of foreign affairs, the *Etoile* to the keeper of the seal, the *Journal de Paris* to the minister of finance, the *Gazette de France* to the minister of interior, and all of them more or less directly to M. de Villèle, president of the council. Under these conditions only those with very large circulations could boast of real independence, and this reputation strengthened their position by attracting subscribers who became disgusted with the poorly disguised servility of the ministerial press. In 1826 all the government newspapers together did not have more than fourteen thousand subscribers, to 49,000 for the opposition papers.

One newspaper, in the last years of the Restoration, carved a special niche for itself; initiated by Jouffroy, edited by Paul Dubois, the *Globe* was in theory not a political paper, and its editorial staff included a number of literary men and philosophers along with some doctrinaires. Remaining aloof from political strife, in the sphere of pure ideas, it handed out haughty criticisms and sarcastic observations to both the Left and the Right. For many years it was the voice and spiritual guide of the young intellectuals, and its influence transcended national boundaries— Goethe admitted that its "stern, bold, profound, and prophetic" articles gave him much to ponder.

The provincial press, which saw a brief moment of activity under the liberal regime of the laws of 1819, soon fell back to almost nothing. The departmental paper—when there was one—was only a small sheet, composed more often in the offices of the prefecture; in it were found the official acts and announcements, some local news, some literary essays, and, for political news, some extracts from Paris papers. In the later years of the Restoration, there appeared in a few big provincial cities like Lyons, Lille, Marseilles, Bordeaux, etc., some papers of a certain opinion, generally financed by the opposition.

But, once again, there can be no political life in the provinces except as it is connected with that in the capital, and only the legislative elections gave political parties the chance to assert themselves and oppose each other.

The number of voters reminds us that political participation remained the privilege of a small minority. The bitterness of the excluded intellectuals emerges from this notation inserted in January 1824 by a faithful royalist, Pierre-Sébastien Laurentie, in his *Journal intime:*

> The list of Paris voters has just been published. All of them are butchers, stone-masons, apartment landlords, bakers, grocers, or people of such professions. . . . What a pity! If I had a license as a stocking merchant, I would be a voter. But I'm not, because I am only an inspector general of education!

The Charter made money the touchstone of political responsibility by setting three hundred francs (sixty dollars) of annual direct taxes as the voting requirement. The voting population was thus made up of some ninety thousand voters, more or less at different times. In other words, there was about one voter for every one hundred Frenchmen who had reached their majority. Half of the departmental electoral colleges did not have more than twelve hundred voters; the extremes were the Seine department with ten to twelve thousand, and Corsica with only forty. In the latter case, a deputy could have been elected by twenty-eight votes. The electoral law of 1820, providing for a double vote, set a privilege within a privilege, by providing that the one-fourth highest taxpayers should form departmental or grand colleges. The number of these upper voters went as high as 22,445 in July 1830.

The requirements for legislative candidates were not only a thousand-franc (two-hundred-dollar) direct tax but also one of age (forty years), which made for an even more restricted participation—16,052 in 1817 and 14,548 in 1828. This reduction of eligible candidates is explained by the deliberate reduction of taxes by the government in order to make it impossible for some opponents to run for office. It therefore happened that in some departments there were only about ten men eligible to run, and among them there were some who were not too anxious to run for an office which would keep them in the capital for six months without any monetary compensation.

The first big job for those who managed elections was to find candidates; and here began some more or less fraudulent maneuvers. The question of residence was not too difficult; one's legal residence could be transferred to any department in which one paid even a minimal tax. The thousand-franc tax requirement was harder to evade. One of the favorite methods of evasion was for the candidate to make a fictitious purchase of taxable property. At the same time the notary would draw up a secret counter-deed which would nullify the sale. In some cases the voters of a party were so attracted to a candidate that they would take up a subscription to purchase for him the required taxable property. The liberal voters did this for Dupont de l'Eure in 1824, and the royalists did the same for Berryer in 1830. They also manipulated the professional license system. All one had to do was to ask for a professional license which might cost the direct tax requirement. For example, to become a candidate, a retired general took out a license as a surveyor.

When it came to drawing up the list of voters, the administration had all the advantages, because this was the job of the prefect. It was customary to eliminate opposition voters either by lowering their taxes, or dragging out the registration procedures, or just simply by forgetting to write down the voter's name on the list. To pad the government party's list, on the other hand, they quite often included the names of ineligible voters. To avoid loud protests, the lists were posted at the last moment, or they were printed without being in alphabetical order, posted in a remote place and up so high on the wall that a ladder would be needed to read it. In Paris there was a bit of gerrymandering where the opponents were all grouped in one section so as to leave little opposition to the government candidates in the other sections.

These fraudulent practices were more difficult after the passage of the law of 1828 on the drawing up of voter lists, but government pressures still remained. Government officials felt the full weight of these pressures. The keeper of the seal (minister of justice), Peyronnet, for example, expressed himself in these terms in his circular of January 20, 1824:

> The government gives out jobs only to those who will serve and support it. . . . If the official refuses to perform the services expected of him, he betrays his trust and voluntarily breaks the agreement concerning the objective or the conditions of his job. The government no longer owes anything to anyone who does not in turn fulfill his obligation.

In what nice phrases these thoughts were expressed! For the nonjob-holding voters they used other arguments, as witness the prefect of the Aisne, who was writing to the voters of Laon:

> The fate of your district, and of your district seat, is in your hands. From the party you choose will come your prosperity or decline. Make a choice offensive to royal majesty and you lose forever the favors of a just and paternal government, which is necessarily severe when it is outraged.

Necessarily the candidate had to carry on his campaign by visits, individual promises, and dinners. Campaign meetings were prohibited by law; and the custom of distributing printed pre-election statements on issues came into use only very late. Even by 1818, such a statement was indignantly denounced by the *Conservateur* as it stigmatized "the demagogic effrontery with which a candidate has prostituted himself for the votes of a certain part of the electorate."

Government influence continued to be felt right into the operations of the elections themselves. The president of the electoral college himself ran as an official candidate, and this royal designation conferred on him a certain prestige in the eyes of men for whom the cult of monarchy was a sort of religion. In opening the session on the first day, he alone had the right to make an address, which would be the only speech delivered in the election campaign. Also he was in a position to keep a check on how people voted. Of course the secret ballot was guaranteed in theory; but, since it was not obligatory, the supporters of the official candidate, government officials or others, generally were careful to vote openly in order to be sure to qualify for his favors. After that, whoever cast a secret ballot branded himself, by that very act, an opponent of the administration. Furthermore, the number of voters were so limited that it was often possible for the tellers to recognize handwritings. The president of the electoral college of Jonzac in February 1824, wrote triumphantly to the minister of the interior: "All the voters cast open ballots in my presence . . . the most horrible liberals wrote their choice under my gaze in favor of the royalist candidates."

The voting went on over a period of several days. On the morning of the first day, after the president had appointed a temporary staff (*bureau*) of election clerks, they would proceed to the election of the permanent staff. This vote was a real show of strength for those party members who were present at the opening. Every voter, before voting for the first time, took the usual oath, and every voting session was to remain open for at least six hours. When we realize the difficulties of travel, we are not surprised that certain voters did not take the trouble to attend the college meetings, especially after the electoral law of 1817 was in force, when the elections had to be held in the departmental capital. At this time the absentees numbered about one third; after 1820 the percentage of absentees was still from ten to twenty per cent. On the second day, if they did not have to have more balloting for the permanent staff, the real voting for candidates could begin. Because every party list had to contain as many candidates as there were deputies to be elected in the department, no one could be elected on the first voting unless he received a majority of ballots cast and at least a total equal to a third of all registered voters. This last requirement more than once allowed a minority to prevent an election of its opponent by a massive abstention. If, after the first round, there were still parliamentary seats to be filled, the voting had to be concentrated on those who had received the highest totals in the earlier round, and the winners were those who obtained a plurality of votes.

In general, except in the south in 1815, the elections were orderly and quiet; however hot the political passions became, the campaign was conducted among gentlemen.

Taking place under such procedures, the elections obviously could not reflect opinions in the provinces, and any political map of France based on them would reveal some astonishing anomalies. That is why so well-known a royalist department as the Vendée could send liberal deputies like Manuel to the chamber. They represented a bourgeois minority which was that much more virulent in opposition to the monarchy because it remembered the Revolutionary days when its cities had been besieged by the Chouan tidal wave from the country regions. The principal differences that would be found in the political maps of France between 1825 and 1960 would be, first, in the northeastern provinces, formerly considered leftist strongholds and, secondly, in those in the Aquitaine, Languedoc, and Provençal south which then showed as much devotion to the white flag as they do now to the red. But, lacking data for detailed analyses, which universal suffrage alone could furnish, one is obliged to limit oneself to vague, over-all comparisons.

What, then, characterizes the political life of Restoration France in general, is first of all the stability of institutions, thanks to which, for fifteen years, France was able to undergo an apprenticeship in constitutional government, permitting the nation to have a real participation in political affairs. However restricted was this participation, the Charter of

Louis XVIII showed itself definitely more helpful in leading up to a really democratic and parliamentary regime than the utopian and stillborn constitutions of the Revolutionary period. For the first time parties faced each other freely in a parliamentary arena and in a framework of institutions which guaranteed to the minority party, lacking the advantages of power, at least the satisfaction of criticizing their victorious opponent without fearing prison or scaffold.

A second characteristic was the narrowness of this political activity, which was limited to a very small minority of the privileged rich. No doubt the condition of society and contingencies of an economic sort did not yet permit a conscious participation of the lower classes in political life, but one cannot avoid feeling that the arbitrary restrictions imposed by the system of a high taxpaying suffrage were singularly petty and unfair. It should be noted at this point that the liberal bourgeoisie, the so-called friend of the people, was more opposed than the royalists to the extension of the suffrage. Undoubtedly the royalists made a big mistake, once they were in power in 1822, in not carrying out the ideas of a more liberal suffrage which they had advocated when they were in the opposition.

Similar, and just as serious, was their mistake in accepting Bonaparte's system of extreme centralization, which they themselves had denounced as baneful between 1815 and 1820. The legitimate monarchy had nothing to gain from pandering to a bourgeoisie which was jealously guarding its uncertain gains. Neither did it have anything to gain from concentrating all the political life of the country in its one capital city. The revolution of 1830, prepared by the taxpaying voters of the opposition, but precipitated by the Paris insurrection in a generally passive France, was to be the punishment for such heedlessness.

# 17

✤ ✤ ✤ ✤ ✤

# Religious Life

## Religion and the Restored Monarchy

"WHEN Dagobert rebuilt Saint-Denis, he cast his jewels and his most cherished possessions into its foundations. Let us cast likewise religion and justice into the foundations of our new temple." Vivid imagery, medieval retrospect: in these strokes of the pen we recognize the hand of Chateaubriand. He was expressing by this sentence, written in 1816, the general feeling among royalists—that the monarchy would be religious or it would not be. This was a very different attitude from that of those who, in the eighteenth century, had tried to regenerate the old monarchical institution by rationalizing in the manner of the Encyclopedists to make it into an "enlightened depotism."

This revolution in monarchist doctrine has been most often attributed to the movement of ideas which had developed among the émigrés. Under the combined influence of the purifying ordeal of exile and the great thinkers like Joseph de Maistre and Bonald, the frivolous and Voltairian nobles of the Old Regime had understood that, by associating themselves with attacks against religion by the *philosophes,* they had undermined the foundations of the political order of which they had been the beneficiaries. Certainly there is a great deal of truth in this traditional thesis, and one could cite as proof numerous individual cases, among which that of the Count of Artois himself. However, one should not assign too great an importance to the ideas of the émigrés. The works of Maistre and Bonald remained practically unknown in France before 1815, and, if the émigrés were obliged to adjust themselves to the new France in setting up the new political order, it would be hard to imagine that they could have imposed their ideas in just the one sphere of religion. In fact it seems that the new accent given to the religious character of

300

the monarchy resulted from a whole combination of factors. It gave expression to a movement of opinion issuing from the very depths of the nation as well as from émigré circles. Furthermore, it was a part of a larger movement of a Europe-wide trend of thought, of which the so-called Holy Alliance was one manifestation among many. It was the Revolution itself which renewed the somewhat loosened ties between throne and altar, when it attacked the church at the same time that it struck at the monarchy. First came the heroic Vendeans who were shedding their blood for God and king at the same time that the émigrés at Coblenz were still reading Voltaire. Later it was Bonaparte, when he proclaimed by the Concordat with the pope that religion was necessary to preserve order in society and when he appealed to the pope to give his new monarchy the aura of sanctity. He also contributed to welding the church's cause to that of the Bourbons when he imprisoned the pope and persecuted the faithful clergy. His final defeat was to appear as if spiritual forces were taking revenge upon material forces.

The Revolution had tried to dechristianize France and had ended in anarchy; the Empire had tried to force religion into the service of the state and had degenerated into tyranny. The "Very Christian King" (Louis XVIII) owed it to himself, on the other hand, to put the state at the service of the church. If his power came from on high, was it not logical to conclude that his main obligation was to lead his subjects to God? "The throne of Saint Louis without the religion of Saint Louis is an absurd supposition" (Chateaubriand). Besides, the king's interest coincided with his duty since, by following this line, he assured divine protection for his throne and the unqualified support of a clergy which could direct the lower classes. To follow such a line of reasoning, one did not have to read Maistre or Bonald, one need not have fled from France; the secret society of the Knights of the Faith, which was certainly the most representative institution of this new ideal, was born right in France and through the initiative of a young man who had not left the country. It was the young men of the generation of Ferdinand de Bertier and Alexis de Noailles who furnished the main membership not only of the Knights of the Faith but also of the Congregation and of the Chambre Introuvable.

Lastly, one must take into account the new intellectual climate of the period, which represented a reaction against the rationalism of the eighteenth century. German thought was abandoning the marvels of the *Aufklärung* (Enlightenment) and turning to God again by the obscure routes of romanticism and mysticism. In France *Le Génie du Christianisme* opened the door to an apology for feeling and beauty. "My conviction came from within my heart," wrote Chateaubriand. "I wept and found faith." Romanticism, in its early stages, concealed its turbulence of individualistic anarchy beneath the mask of a cult for the medieval past, where the monarchy of Saint Louis, feudal society, and the church of Saint Bernard were all associated together in nostalgic admiration.

As "the cornerstone of legitimacy," religion then took its place at the top of the list in the program of the restored monarchy. If it was solely the job of the church to recover souls, the civil government could at least lend the clergy the material means for action which it needed, as well as the moral support of its authority. Louis XVIII showed in various ways how he took pains to assert, right from the time of his return in 1814, his new religious policy: Catholicism declared the state religion by the Constitutional Charter; ordinance of June 10, 1814 encouraging gifts to ecclesiastical institutions; ordinance of October 5 permitting bishops to open an ecclesiastical school in each department, exempt from university control; law of December 18 on the observance of Sabbath and religious holy days; etc. But the big event, the foundation of the work of religious restoration, was to be the abrogation of the Napoleonic Concordat of 1801 and the return to that of 1516. Louis XVIII had never pardoned Pius VII for having momentarily lent the support of the church to the "Usurper," and the bishops of that time who had refused to submit to the decision of the pope were considered to be the only ones worthy of his confidence. Their influence was to be all-powerful in the nine-man ecclesiastical committee which replaced the ministry of worship in 1814 and which was the source for all the religious policy of the First Restoration.

So there arrived in Rome on July 22, 1814 the former Bishop of Saint-Malo, Mgr. Cortois de Pressigny, appointed as ambassador of the king to the Holy See. His instructions, as drawn up by Talleyrand, required him to ask the pope for the nullifying of all the acts "exacted from his weakness" since 1800, in particular the Concordat of 1801. The old dioceses were to be re-established, the episcopate to be completely renovated, and, to carry out this program, the pope was to dispatch a legate to Paris with full powers to negotiate. Pius VII would not have been sorry to see the end of the Concordat of 1801, which he had only accepted in order to end the schism and fend off an exceptional, almost desperate, situation. He especially wanted to see nullified the Organic Articles, which had been attached to the Concordat by a unilateral act of the first consul and which were so contrary to the religious liberties demanded by the church. But he did not want to make his own past record look bad and accept the role of repenting his guilt which the French king's demands seemed to imply. To re-establish the old dioceses would be fine, but the pope, for his part, thought he had a right to demand an act of submission from the bishops who had refused him obedience in 1801 and from the former constitutional clergy whose position had not been clarified and who had been able to defy him with the support of the imperial government. He also was worried about the maintenance, as announced by the Charter, of Revolutionary laws which were, on a number of points, contrary to ecclesiastical law.

The negotiations, undertaken in a tone of mutual recrimination, dragged on slowly. Jaucourt, who substituted for Talleyrand during the latter's attendance at Vienna, thought it advisable to dilute the royal wine with a little water; he sent Jules de Polignac to Rome with instructions which were more conciliatory and respectful in their phraseology. Napoleon's return in 1815 naturally was to bring an end to the whole affair. It was taken up again with some success only in the spring of 1816, when Cortois de Pressigny was replaced in Rome by the Count of Blacas. Richelieu had recommended to him not to insist on a formal disavowal of the Concordat of 1801, and, in the meantime, the king had obtained a collective act of submission from the surviving bishops among those who had refused to submit their resignation in 1801, by promising them places in the reconstituted church. Cardinal Consalvi, the papal secretary of state, finally gave his approval to a convention whose wording satisfied the susceptibilities of the Holy See by merely stipulating that the Concordat of 1801 "ceased to be in effect"; the Organic Articles were abolished; "a suitable number" of the old dioceses would be re-established by common accord; those which had been set up in 1801 would be retained, as well as their bishops "with a few exceptions based on legitimate and serious causes"; finally, the material independence of these bishoprics would be assured by an endowment of property or state bonds.

Agreement seemed to be complete, and the pontifical chancellery was busying itself with the composition of the bulls and briefs necessary for the promulgation of the accord, when the king, on receiving the reports from Blacas, insisted on inserting in the act of ratification a reservation stating that it was not his intention to "undermine the liberties of the Gallican Church or to weaken the wise regulations which the kings, his predecessors, had made, at different times, against the Ultramontane claims." Straightway the pope also refused to ratify it. Blacas and Consalvi had to go back to work on more negotiations. The resulting new accord of June 1817 was nearly the same as the previous one. The pope had agreed to adding to the clause which abolished the Organic Articles these restrictive words: "as far as they are contrary to the doctrine and laws of the church"; for his part, the king, in a separate note, declared that the oath of fidelity required by the Charter for ecclesiastical officials "would not in any way affect the dogmas or laws of the church . . . that it only related to civil affairs."

The pope quickly ratified the treaty as amended, and by July 17 he published the bull which established forty-two new French dioceses. On the following day, in consistory, three French cardinals and thirty-four new bishops, nominated by the king, were approved.

This haste and publicity by the Holy See was easily understood: the final accord constituted for him a great success; but they were to be the cause of its undoing. The negotiations, as was proper in well-conducted diplomacy, had been carried on in the greatest secrecy, to such an extent that even the cabinet members, except Richelieu and Lainé, had no knowledge of their nature. Therefore great was their surprise and that of public opinion when the text of that bull became known in France. According to the traditional form of pontifical acts, the act was presented as coming from the "full and free authority" of the pope; it was supposedly he himself, and not the King of France, who "assigned" the promised endowments to the new bishoprics. The old Gallican blood boiled up, and the opposition found support in that faction in the cabinet which leaned at that time toward the Left, mainly Decazes and Pasquier. They demonstrated to Richelieu that the right of the king to sign treaties with the approval of the chamber did not apply in the present case, since this act modified the text of the Concordat of 1801, which had become the law of the state; that it involved the interior organization of the kingdom and it required budgetary appropriations. The president let himself be convinced by the legal arguments of his colleagues, and it was decided to present to the chamber, not the text of the treaty signed by Blacas, but a law worded in such a way as to give every appeasement to Gallican opinion. Article I said that the king alone appointed the bishops "by virtue of the inherent right of the crown"; Article V required the approval of chamber and king of any pontifical acts affecting the Church of France; Article XI asserted the maintenance of the "maxims, franchises, and liberties of the Gallican Church," of the laws and regulations on ecclesiastical matters, that is, of the Organic Articles. Thus, the government of the king, after having signed and ratified a treaty with the Holy See, completely deformed its spirit and tenor by a unilateral act. This was just what Bonaparte had done.

The pope appeared deeply offended by these proceedings. The discussions on the government's bill in the parliamentary committees dragged on in the midst of the excitement of public opinion sustained by a flood of pamphlets. By its own fault the government found itself in a most embarrassing position. The Left, on which the majority of that period depended, still refused to vote for a bill that it thought was favorable to the church; and the Right, whose votes could have made up for this defection, became indignant over the subjection which the bill seemed to impose on the clergy. One of the rightist members, the Count of Marcellus, Knight of the Faith, wrote directly to Pius VII to ask advice as to what stand he should take. The pope replied with a brief in which he declared the government bill entirely unacceptable. Under these conditions, the government gave up the plan of reporting the bill to the chambers. But, in the meantime, they were floundering around in complete confusion. Since the new ecclesiastical districting, defined by the pontifical bull of July 1817, had not been agreed upon by the civil authorities and the old system had ceased being in force in the eyes of the church, no one knew any longer where the dioceses began and ended. The thirty-four new bishops appointed by the pope, on the recommendation of the king, found themselves without dioceses; and, on the other hand, there were other dioceses which had two bishops at the same time.

They sent off to the Holy See the son of the former minister of ecclesiastical affairs, Portalis, then a member of the council of state, to see if he could reach an agreement. Pius VII and Consalvi refused to accept any change in the treaty of 1817. They said it had been negotiated at the request of the king, and it had been signed, ratified, and published. If the French government now found that it was powerless to enforce it, the only thing to do was to go along with what existed before—that is, the Concordat of 1801. That was what they had to be resigned to do. The pope declared that the old system of fifty dioceses should be maintained and the former bishops confirmed in their jurisdiction. As for the king, he promised, in accord with the Holy See, gradually to increase the number of French dioceses up to a total of eighty, just as fast as the necessary funds for their endowment were available through the lapse of ecclesiastical pensions. This promise, at least, was carried out faithfully, thanks to the changes taking place in domestic politics after February 1820. In October 1822, the thirty new dioceses which had been planned were set up, and there were henceforth in France eighty bishoprics whose boundaries, corresponding to those of the departments, were almost the same as they are today.

## The Secular and Regular Clergy

The reorganization of the ecclesiastical personnel had not waited upon that of the territorial jurisdictions. By 1820 there were only twenty-six prelates left out of the Napoleonic episcopacy, and only nine in 1830, among whom were two former constitutional bishops who had given proof of their repentance: they were Montault des Isles at Angers and Belmas at Cambrai. Most of the others disappeared from the scene by death; a few had, more or less voluntarily, turned in their resignations in 1815, like Mgr. de Barral, Archbishop of Tours, who had compromised himself by his servility to Napoleon and by his celebration of the solemn mass of the Champ-de-Mai in June 1815.

The Restoration was therefore able to supply itself rather rapidly with an episcopacy entirely devoted to the monarchy. Contrary to what is generally said, it was not chosen entirely from the old nobility. Out of ninety-six new bishops there were at least twenty "commoners." Nonetheless, the intention was evident of "scouring out" the episcopacy, as it seems Mgr. de Quélen called it. The extreme example of the Abbé-Duke of Rohan-Chabot was characteristic of this state of mind. Born in 1788, he was, under the Empire, one of the pillars of the Congregation; the tragic death of his young wife, Armandine de Sérent, from burns suffered in an accident, led him to enter the seminary of Saint-Sulpice in 1819. Hardly had he been ordained as a priest when he was appointed honorary canon and vicar general of Paris; in 1828, at the age of forty, he was made Archbishop of Besançon and in July was made cardinal. His family name, his ostentatious devotion to the monarchy, his good looks, and his salon connections seemed to be sufficient qualifications for such favors. The intellectual gifts and the pastoral abilities of this fashionable prelate were, however, weak, as Stendhal caricatured him in the person of the Bishop of Agde in his *Le Rouge et le Noir.* "To be gracefully decked out in rich lace," Sainte-Beuve wrote, "was for him an occasion of satisfaction and triumph. He would stand a long time before his mirror, trying it on." And Chateaubriand had this comment: "His pious locks, fresh from the curling-irons, gave him the elegant look of a martyr. He would preach at dusk, in shadowy pulpits, before devout women, taking care to light his pale face in half-tones, like a painting, with the help of two or three candles artistically placed."

Fortunately, all Restoration bishops were not of this type, and at the other extreme could be cited, for example, Mgr. Devie, former seminary president, as remarkable for his doctrinal studies as for his pastoral zeal and administrative ability. His long episcopate, from 1823 to 1852, was to have a lasting effect on the diocese of Belley. In most of France this Restoration episcopacy differed appreciably from that of the Old Regime. Its morals were irreproachable, generally it remained in residence, assiduously if not too intelligently devoting itself to the duties of its office. The income of fifteen thousand francs (three thousand dollars) allotted to each bishop by the state budget—25,000 (five thousand dollars) for archbishops—only allowed them a very modest style of living. "In all good truth," the nuncio Macchi wrote in 1826, "one can say that France never had more edifying and virtuous pastors." But he added: "One could only wish that they were more learned and better read." As much from tradition as because of the difficulties of travel, the bishop appeared to be isolated from his flock and his clergy, from whom he was separated by his little ecclesiastical court and the aura of respect and adulation surrounding all his appearances, much more than by the walls of his episcopal palace. Nothing could have been more mediocre than those pastoral letters in which abounded, with repetitive bemoaning of the "evils of the times," all of the pathos of the waning eighteenth century and the vague and abstract battle of words behind which lurked an ignorance of realities and an inability to become adapted to the needs of a new society.

Yet, on one crucial matter—that of recruiting new clergymen—the episcopacy of the Restoration did not fail in its task. By its own sustained efforts, and, it must also be said, thanks to the effective support coming from the government, it succeeded in a few years in remedying a situation which appeared in 1814 to be extremely critical.

In that year the clergy numbered about 36,000 priests, hardly half the total in 1789; 3,345 chapels out of 23,000 had no regular priest, and, in the country as a whole, according to the bishops, fifteen or sixteen thousand more priests were required to care for religious needs satisfactorily. Prospects for the future were even more discouraging when the age of this clergy was considered. Hardly eighteen per cent of the clergy was under fifty years of age, and only four per cent were younger than forty. "If things keep going as they are," Chateaubriand could write in 1816, "twenty years from now there will be only enough priests in France to remind us that once upon a time there had been altars for worship." From 1790 until 1800, ecclesiastical recruiting had practically come to a standstill, and under the Empire the annual number of ordinations held to between 350 and five hundred, in contrast to five to six thousand under the Old Regime. The bishops had great difficulty supporting financially the seminary and the single ecclesiastical school they were allowed to have in each diocese. Young men tended to avoid the priesthood as much because of the subordinate and humiliating position of priests under the Concordat as because of the meager salaries provided by the budget of the ministry of worship. For the senior parish priest it was between a thousand and fifteen hundred francs (two and three hundred dollars) a year; for assistant priests it was between 350 and five hundred (seventy and a hundred dollars), and still less for vicars and chaplains, whose incomes were left to the parsimonious discretion of the communes (townships). Many parishes had no presbytery (parish house), and in many places the priests, in order to keep alive, had to appeal to the charity of their parishioners or spend part of their time on outside work. The prefect of the Basses-Pyrénées wrote in 1815: "The dignity of the priesthood has fallen so low that in several villages the local priest is nothing more than the commercial broker for all business deals, a sort of commissioner, a little more educated than other villagers, whom they could pay so much a day to consult a lawyer, see the procurator, or report back on public opinion in the nearby town."

The royal government made every effort to improve the material welfare of the clergy. By a series of decisions, made gradually as budget possibilities warranted it, the different ecclesiastical salaries were increased; for example, those of the assistant priests, who made up the most numerous class of priests employed in the ministry, increased in 1827 to nine hundred and a thousand francs ($180 and two hundred dollars). At the same time considerable sums were spent on the construction and furnishing of seminaries, on the endowment of scholarships in these schools, and on the construction of new churches. The budget for worship for the country at large went up from twelve million ($2,400,000) in 1815 to 33 million ($6,600,000) in 1830. It was not long before the results of these efforts were being felt, in actual numbers: the number of large seminaries, in line with that of new dioceses, went up from fifty to eighty; that of the ecclesiastical schools (little seminaries) from fifty-three to 144; the enrollment in the large seminaries more than doubled, reaching 13,257 students in 1830. The number of ordinations increased every year: 910 in 1815, 1,405 in 1820, 1,620 in 1825, 2,357 in 1830. Under the influence of this infusion of young blood, the average age of the clergy went down: in 1830 the proportion of sexagenarians was brought down to thirty-two per cent from forty-two per cent in 1814. Finally, while under the Empire and again quite early in the Restoration the number of deaths among priests exceeded that of ordinations, after 1825 the situation had so reversed itself that in 1830 there were 4,655 more priests on duty than in 1814.

But how good was this new clergy? That is more difficult to determine. The quality of recruits could reflect the means employed to enlist them. All the young priests of that time were not, certainly, Julien Sorels, but it would be very astonishing if the attraction of an improved situation and of a career favored by the state with new attention would not have brought into the rank of the clergy a certain number of dubious recruits.

Lamennais wrote his brother in 1815: "Ambition and politics are every-thing, religion nothing, or almost nothing. Paris is the center of the vilest intrigues; religious jobs now are like government jobs. Everyone is seek-ing an important station in life, and that is all religion amounts to."

However it may be, one thing is certain: the clergy lacked homoge-neity. The dividing years of the Revolution and Empire widened the gulf between generations. It was a commonplace of the literature of the period to contrast the old priest of the Old Regime, wearing knee-breeches, powdering his hair like hoarfrost, but revealing a cultivated and broad-minded outlook, with the young priest, a product of the hothouse semi-naries of the Restoration, with a shaved head under his square cap, shabby manners, and affected austerity, making up for his ignorance by an out-and-out fanaticism. Naturally the former was faithful to the good old maxims of the Gallican Church, while the latter embraced with en-thusiasm the Ultramontane doctrines of M. de Lamennais. The older generation was itself profoundly divided by the lingering feeling about old quarrels. The juring clergy, in spite of all their honorable amends, remained stamped with a sort of flaw which deprived them of all hope of advancement; and in the other direction those favoring the "Little Church," those who would not recognize the Concordat of 1801, per-severed in their insubordination toward the pope. There were still about a hundred of these in 1820. Lastly, and here a serious matter in a time of exceptional intellectual effervescence, the clergy appeared to be clearly deficient from the point of view of humane or even religious learning. "Formerly," wrote Lamennais in 1828, "the clergy was the leading group in society for its learning. Never, for many, many centuries, has the clergy, taken as a whole, been so ignorant as it is today, and never, how-ever, has real learning been more necessary."

Surely it is understandable that priests trained during the Revolution lacked the time and indispensable means for a thorough education. But, just the same, the seminaries had been reopened for a long time. What were they doing in them? The spirit then predominating in the training of the clergy was that of the Society of Saint-Sulpice. We get an idea of it in the advice given in 1825 by the superior of the famous society, M. Mollevaut, to one of his students who had just been appointed a professor in the large seminary of Le Mans: "Beware of new ideas, holding firm to the traditions of the Church Fathers. Be fearful about encouraging the spirit of curiosity which is deadly for acts of thanksgiving; remember that a large majority of your students are destined to serve in the country among our good peasants and in that light consider what will be most use-ful to them." The seminary libraries, pillaged during the Revolution, had not been resupplied with the missing books, and the professors themselves had often received only an improvised training; their textbooks were still those of the eighteenth century. The bishops, pressed by needs for new personnel, shortened much too excessively the training period of their charges, and very often the seminarians were taken out of their classes to fill positions of proctors or professors in the little seminaries.

The weakness of the clergy in the area of learning left the leadership to laymen in elaborating the doctrine of the new order. The current Church Fathers were Joseph de Maistre, Louis de Bonald, and even Chateaubriand. It was a layman, Michel Picot, who edited the most widely circulated ecclesiastical newspaper of the time, the *Ami de la Religion et du Roi.*

Lamennais was the only ecclesiastic whose voice, emerging from the general mediocrity, made itself heard in the public at large, but his extreme statements made him suspect to part of the clergy, especially to the episcopacy, whom he attacked in reckless terms. This little man with a sickly appearance had come from Chateaubriand's part of the country (Brittany), and like him he had received the gift of expressing himself in a language at times poetic and tender, at other times striking and prophetic, illuminated with lightning flashes, but also very often marked by strident notes of exasperated passion and of polemical tartness. "He would raise the dead" was what the unsympathetic Frayssinous said of him. His heart, tortured with scruples, had caused him to enter the rank of the clergy in 1815 under the influence of his brother, Jean-Marie, an apostle with a more balanced temperament. His *Essai sur l'indifférence en matière de Religion,* published in 1817, suddenly raised him to the first rank of celebrated literary writers, and thenceforth his pen knew no rest. He collaborated with the *Conservateur* and the *Drapeau Blanc,* and he founded and directed successively the *Défenseur* and the *Mémorial catholique.*

His apologetics broke boldly with the underlying premise of past philosophical constructions from Aristotle to Descartes—that is, the belief in the value of individual reason and in its ability to arrive at truth. For Lammenais, on the contrary, only collective thought, or as he said, common sense, which is expressed through universal consent, presented all the guarantees of infallibility, because here one finds the reflection of the original revelation from God. "By the very nature of things," he said, "to isolate oneself is to doubt; the intelligent being only preserves itself in the midst of society." This original revelation had transmitted itself through all the wanderings of polytheism until the moment when Christ came to give it its pure and supreme expression of which the Catholic

Church is now the guarantor. From this derived the pre-eminent role which he attributed in modern society to the papacy, whose immense transformation he perceived. "No pope, no church; no church, no Christianity; no Christianity, no religion—no society; hence the life of European nations has found its source, its only source, in the papal power."

This passage is found in his work entitled *De la religion considérée dans ses rapports avec l'ordre politique et civil* (1825), which was a diatribe against the Gallicanism professed by the bishops of France, and in particular by the minister of ecclesiastical affairs, Mgr. Frayssinous. It was, he said, democracy introduced into the church, an assault on its divine constitution, a work soiled with schism and heresy, which ended up by putting spiritual power in abject dependence upon political power. The episcopate reacted at once; fourteen prelates meeting in Paris—cardinals, archbishops, and bishops—addressed a letter to the king in which they protested their loyalty to the principle of the separation of powers and the independence of the state in temporal matters. Solicited by Frayssinous, all the other bishops, except four, added their approval. Lamennais, haled before the correctional police court, was sentenced to a fine and the seizure of his book.

Soon after this, he began to carry out a big project aimed at the regeneration of the French clergy. With the help of his brother and his first two disciples, Gerbet and Rohrbacher, he founded a society for the purpose of re-establishing the authority of the Holy See in the hearts of men, to spread the new philosophy of common sense and to create a new body of Catholic doctrine, covering all branches of learning. This Congregation of St. Peter, as it was called, set up in 1829 its novitiate and its school at Malestroit, in the Morbihan, while those disciples who did not intend to take religious vows or who were feeling their way remained grouped around their master at his estate of La Chênaie.

At this juncture Lamennais' political thought had changed drastically. As an Ultra-Royalist at the beginning of the Restoration, and even a member of the Knights of the Faith, if we are to believe certain statements, he therefore considered the Charter as "a basically Revolutionary disease with which they had innoculated the monarchy to encompass its death." Now, embittered by the stern action taken against him by the government, he urged Catholics to separate their cause from that of the monarchy and join the inescapable movement drawing peoples toward liberty. Such was the theme of his last work, published shortly after the downfall of Charles X, entitled *Des progrès de la Révolution et la guerre contre l'Église* (*On the Progress Made Against the Church by the Revolution and War*).

Lamennais' influence, combatted by the episcopate, spread rapidly in the clergy, especially in Brittany. The priests adhered to it the more readily because they could see in the re-enforcement of the authority of the Holy See in France the only counterweight to the despotic power of the bishops over them as provided by the Concordat.

Parallel to the reconstitution of the diocesan clergy was that of the religious congregations. The Revolution had abolished the religious orders in France; but the Emperor had tolerated, even protected, women's orders, at least those he thought to be "useful," such as the nursing and teaching societies. But the men's orders remained outlawed, except for three missionary societies—the Lazarists, the Foreign Missions, and the Mission of the Holy Spirit—which were officially recognized, and two others—the Sulpicians and the Brothers of Christian Schools—which were merely tolerated.

The monarchy's program of religious restoration obviously presupposed a regime more favorable to religious orders, but the persistence of the parliamentary and Gallican tradition, combined with rationalist prejudices, were to prevent even the most reactionary governments from furnishing a very definite juridical base for the different forms of religious life. An early law on January 2, 1817 laid down that only legally authorized religious associations could acquire property. This was an indirect way of saying that some unauthorized societies might possibly exist but just barely be tolerated. The government tried to do more for them in 1824 when it proposed a bill tending to give it the right to authorize new congregations by a simple royal ordinance, but the chamber of peers rejected it. Thereafter they tried to do something for women's congregations, which raised less opposition; the law of May 24, 1825 gave the government the right to authorize, by a simple administrative decision, new women's convents, which could henceforth receive gifts and legacies.

Under this benevolent regime the convents increased with astonishing rapidity: 1,829 convents and 12,400 nuns in 1815; and fifteen years later, 2,875 convents and 25,000 nuns; and the statistics still could not include innumerable parareligious organizations, communities still in a trial stage, and contemplative communities which had not dared or had not decided to take advantage of the new law to come out of the semi-hiding in which they had been living since 1790. One might wish, by name or example, to give illustrations of the burgeoning of religious orders which brought forth during the nineteenth century cohorts of saintly women, with headdresses of every sort and color, whose obvious bad style generally makes it now possible to surmise the date of their origin. But this would be a history which has not yet been written. At present it is even impossible to say how many diverse congregations were founded in this period; with all the fusions, the interconnections, the duplication of names, the splits, the most expert authority would have to disqualify himself.

The history of these foundations is almost always the same, and, to understand their disconcerting multiplicity in the face of identical needs, one must always remember the isolation of various provinces from one another. A pious girl, either spontaneously or by the advice of a priest, would choose to devote herself to the education of children or to work among the sick or the poor. Soon she would enlist some companions who were attracted by her example. The mistress of the local château would lend her moral and financial support, the local priest would encourage or block their efforts. A Jesuit confessor would be lurking in the background; soon its foundation became more definite, a house was bought, His Grace the Bishop came into the picture. To obtain his approval, they had to have rules, a costume, a responsible mother superior, a name, a patron saint, and a novitiate. All this crystallized little by little, and one fine day they were ready to seek the authorization of the Holy See and the government—a new religious order was born.

As for men's religious houses, it is even more difficult to give exact numbers, because most of them lived on the fringes of the law, and their members appeared to be plain secular priests. The three missionary congregations authorized under the Empire were the only ones to receive legal authorization; seven other societies of teaching brothers or teaching clergy were also recognized as associations of public utility. But it was just by plain toleration by public officials that the Sulpicians and the Brothers of Christian Schools were continued and that such orders as the Marists of P. Colin, the Oblates of the Immaculate Mary of Abbé de Mazenod, the Fathers of the Sacred Heart of Father Coindre, the Marianists of Father Chaminade, etc., were founded and successfully maintained. Some old orders timidly came out of hiding: the Chartreux of the Grande Chartreuse, the Capuchins of Marseilles, the Trappists at La Grande Trappe and at La Meilleraye, and especially the Jesuits whose importance and influence were exaggerated by liberal politicians way out of proportion to their real membership. In fact this famous Society had a hard time reconstituting itself in France; in 1828, at the time action was again taken against it, as will be seen below, the Jesuits had a membership of only 456, including students, novices, and brother coadjutors.

## Religious Activities of Laymen

Outside the secular clergy and the orders of the regular clergy, the church in this period benefited from the activities of an impressive number of lay organizations and charities, which in many ways resembled the present-day movement of Catholic action. It was something rather new to see this direct and deliberate lay intervention in a field which still seemed reserved for the clergy, and one has to search back to the famous Society of the Blessed Sacrament of the seventeenth century to find a comparable activity. It was not thought of as just an expedient intended to fill in for the numerical insufficiency of the clergy; but to certain zealous Christians it seemed to be required by the new social and political conditions. "I am convinced," Ferdinand de Bertier, the founder of the Knights of the Faith, wrote in 1820, "that priests can no longer be the most effective apostles." This phrase contains an even deeper meaning.

We have already mentioned this man and his organization; but it was more a political than a religious society, even though the founder had originally intended to make it a sort of lay religious order, like the Knights of Malta. But the institution, more and more involved in political and parliamentary struggles, had finally become little more than a sort of rival society to that of Freemasonry, with all the inherent pettiness of such secret societies.

The real stimulator of most of the nationwide lay charities was the famous Congregation to which also belonged many Knights of the Faith. Founded in 1801 by a former Jesuit, Father Bourdier-Delpuits, it had had to discontinue its meetings in 1809. It quickly started up again in 1814, and another Jesuit, Father Ronsin, became its spiritual leader. Yet its leadership remained one of laymen; and it was put under the control of a "prefect" and his assistants, elected each year. Its total membership was over a thousand, but many were only temporary members, such as students, for example, who became inactive once they returned home to the provinces after completing their studies. There were also so-called "honorary" members, such as bishops and other ecclesiastics, like the nuncio himself, who certainly did not very often participate in the society's activities. Its assemblies were held every other Sunday at seven-thirty in the morning in a place made available by the seminary of Foreign Missions. Here they listened first to a lecture on the lives of the saints, to a roll call, to practical advice from Father Ronsin, and to a reading of a list of new members. After that came the mass, attended by all, communion for all, a prayer of thanksgiving, a sermon, and a common prayer read aloud.

The Paris Congregation was not the only one. At Bordeaux, Father Chaminade had founded very active Congregations, which anticipated very closely the "specialized movements" of the recent Catholic Action, with its separate organizations for men, women, and young people. The Lyons Congregation, founded in 1802, insisted on complete secrecy. Its founder and leader was a merchant, Benoît Coste, who, because of his zeal for all charities, was to earn the enviable title of "First Christian of the Diocese." These Bordeaux and Lyons Congregations were independent of the Paris organization. Yet most later provincial Congregations, about sixty, were affiliated with Paris in order to benefit from its spiritual privileges. Some were organized in colleges and in small seminaries, and one military Congregation was founded by a captain of the royal guard.

Almost all the cities in the south had their brotherhoods of white, gray, black, blue, etc. penitents—all of them were at one and the same time pious brotherhoods and mutual aid societies; but their activities were completely local and traditional, and, if there is any truth to the old saying "drink like a brother of charity," then religion could at times have served as a simple pretext for jolly social foregathering. The new Congregations, though, were to lead to all sorts of charitable and religious programs. The Society for Good Works represented, in a sense, the active side of the Congregation and was divided into three sections, devoted to hospitals, chimney-sweeps, and prisoners. The Society for Good Studies was the earliest attempt at student study circles and provided a meeting-place, a library, and organized lectures on religious and general cultural subjects. The Catholic Society for Good Books had been established in 1824 to counter the too-obvious efforts of the antireligious press. By the end of 1826 it had eight thousand subscribers and had distributed 800,000 volumes. The Association of Saint Joseph, founded in 1822 by Abbé Lowenbrück, with the support of Lamennais, was intended to find jobs for workers in Christian workshops, to furnish lodging for them until a job was found, and to give them a meeting place, in off-hours, where they could have wholesome distractions, training in improved craft skills, etc. This charitable program, sponsored by the royal court and financially supported by the Faubourg Saint-Germain (the aristocratic quarter of Paris), had in its membership over a thousand industrialists and merchants and seven thousand workers. The Congregationists were also found on the committees of a lot of less-known charities founded or re-established in this period: the Society for Orphan Apprentices, the Society for the Training of Christian Schoolmasters, the Society of the Friends of Children, the Institution for Blind Youths, Aid for the Uncomplaining Poor, the Society for Imprisoned Debtors, etc.

The largest and most lasting of these charities fostered by the Congregations was no doubt the Society for the Propagation of the Faith. They may argue over who was its real founder—Benoît Coste or Pauline Jaricot—but what is certain is that it was a purely lay charity in the beginning. Later its administration was provided by two central councils sitting in Paris and Lyons, "topped" by a superior council, presided over by the Grand Almoner, Cardinal de Croy, who supervised the distribution of funds raised by the councils. The society was to count in 1830 over fifty thousand members under just the northern council, with receipts amounting to 128,000 francs ($25,600). Its local organization by tens and hundreds strangely ressembled the *Charbonnerie*. Also the Liberals liked to become very excited about it, seeing in it one of the instruments of Jesuit domination in French society.

The Association for the Defense of the Catholic Religion, founded in 1828, at a time when the Liberal Party unleashed an assault against the Jesuits and the small seminaries, devoted itself to promoting the publication of writings favorable to Catholicism, to setting in motion judicial action to check the campaign of calumnies against the clergy, to defending religious charities, and to encouraging advanced ecclesiastical courses. Eleven peers of France were on its council as well as deputies, general officers, and members of the Institut. It was not to come up to the hopes that Lamennais had had in it, who complained that the Association was behind the publication of the magazine, *Le Correspondant,* which competed with the one he published, *Le Mémorial.*

The Revolution of 1830 was to bring about the discontinuance of most of these charitable enterprises by dispersing their members; but it could not undo the fact that in their ranks a whole Christian elite had enjoyed the experience of serving the church and the poorer classes. It is here that is found the origin of the early Catholic social movement, which, in spite of many intervening ups and downs, has survived to the present time.

Catholicism, the state religion—was it really, as the letter of the Concordat of 1801 claimed, "the religion of the majority of Frenchmen"? Yes, it certainly was, if we consider the number of baptized Christians. But as to practicing Catholics, concrete and detailed studies which would be necessary to give an authoritative answer are lacking. Only two things seem incontrovertible: that the religious situation differed greatly from province to province; and that in general religious instruction and worship had undergone, since the Old Regime, a very appreciable decline.

There is too much evidence of various kinds to prove this last statement, besides the usual lamentations of episcopal circulars and of preachers on the "impiety of the century." It was the opinion also of Baron de Saint-Chamans, former prefect and councillor of state, who wrote in 1826: "From what I have seen in Paris I think I can say truthfully that in France hardly five men out of one hundred go to church even on Easter. . . . In all the great schools, with students from the best French families, out of four hundred there are hardly fifteen or twenty who fulfill this duty, and even here evasively and inconspicuously." And again here is the opinion of the nuncio, Mgr. Macchi, who in that same year of 1826, described the situation to which his functions and his six years in France lent authority. "More than half the nation," he wrote, "is in complete ignorance of its Christian duties and is plunged into indifference. In Paris hardly an eighth of the people go to church, and one can wonder whether there are as many as ten thousand men in the capital who practice their religion."

The support of the government, the numerical increase of the clergy, the multiplication of religious societies and lay charities, all of these could only indirectly prepare for the necessary revival. The two great remedies on which the Church of France counted to regain that society which it was losing were the education of its youth and, for adults, missionary work.

## Education

As early as 1814 numerous voices had been raised to denounce the baneful influence of the Napoleonic University—those schools, said Chateaubriand, "where, summoned by the sound of drums, children become irreligious, debauched, and scornful of domestic virtues." Lamennais was later to give shocking examples of the impiety and immorality which predominated in the state institutions, "seminaries of atheism and vestibules to Hell." "Better no education if education does not become again a part of the ministry of worship," Abbé Liautard wrote in 1814, and it was only the difficulty of replacing the university staff from top to bottom which prevented the rightist royalists, when they were in power in 1815, from doing away with "the legitimate daughter of Buonaparte." At least, the University monopoly, so absolute under the Empire, was dismantled in such a way that there could be re-established a purely ecclesiastical secondary school system on the fringe of the state school system —small seminaries attended, in spite of regulations, by a large number of students not studying for the priesthood; clerical schools set up by parish priests for a small number of children; full-fledged colleges, enabled by the Ordinance of February 27, 1821 to confer the same degrees as royal colleges; mixed colleges, growing out of a fusion of a communal college and an ecclesiastical school, whose principal and professors were chosen by the bishop.

When the Right came back into power in 1821, the clergy found itself in a position to infiltrate and take over the University system itself.

Henceforth they no longer demanded its abolition and thought of nothing better than settling down comfortably in the captured fortress. The functions of Grand Master of the University, which since 1814 had been taken over by a committee of six members, were re-established for Mgr. Frayssinous, who became in 1824 the minister of ecclesiastical affairs and public instruction. The combination of these two titles was an accomplishment in itself. Frayssinous resolutely harnessed himself to the task of purging the University and of using it for the purpose of the moral and religious re-education of French youth. "The bases of a college education," read the Ordinance of February 27, 1821, "are religion, monarchy, legitimacy, and the Charter." The bishops were given the right of supervision over the royal colleges in their dioceses. Frayssinous eliminated little by little the professors whose tendencies were antireligious, and he replaced them mostly with ecclesiastics, especially in the more important posts, as those of rectors of academies, headmasters of royal colleges, and professors of philosophy. In 1827, for example, out of eighty-eight professors of philosophy in royal colleges, sixty-six were priests; and in 1828 out of 309 principals of communal colleges, 139 were ecclesiastics. In general it is possible to estimate at almost one-third the proportion of churchmen in the University at the end of the Restoration.

The purely religious education was given by chaplains endowed with great authority; but in other things nothing was neglected in putting a religious imprint on all education; opening prayer, daily mass, monthly compulsory confession, etc. That such methods, applied with a heavy hand, may often have had a result contrary to that intended seems very plausible, especially in the case of children from families hostile to the clergy. But that the state religion was taught in state schools was quite in line with the logic of the system.

In the area of primary or popular education, the church had plenty of elbow-room. In fact the elementary schools did not come under the supervision of the University, but were at the discretion of the communes. From the beginning of the Restoration, the clergy was called upon by the government to join in the organization of primary education. An Ordinance of February 29, 1816 created canton school boards, chaired by the priest of the canton seat and given charge of the communal schools. Every school teacher, before receiving his certificate from the rector of the Academy, was to present a certificate of good conduct signed by his local priest and mayor. Later on in 1824 the right to issue teaching certificates was given to a committee of six members, three clergymen and three laymen, presided over by a delegate from the bishop, or even by the bishop himself for schools not financed by the communes. Besides, the Brothers of Christian Schools and the members of authorized religious orders could be called to teach in communal schools without any certificate other than the bishop's permission and the assignment from their superiors.

So the education of the common people was very definitely under the control of the church; but the latter no longer had, as under the Old Regime, the necessary funds to undertake this whole job of educating the lower classes. Since the state continued to be uninterested in this, as it had previously been under the Empire, the financial cost fell entirely to the local commune (township) governments, and these disliked taking any steps to raise money for this purpose. Elementary education, when it was not provided under religious auspices, remained therefore subject to the most pitiful neglect. In the eyes of most of the mayors the best teachers were the cheapest ones. Martin Nadaud recounts in his *Mémoires* the types of schoolmasters to which he was subjected during his childhood. First, there was an old churchwarden of a neighboring village who taught him two hours a day; then came a qualified teacher assigned in his Limousin village by a good parish priest. But this arrangement did not last, and the successor to the capable teacher was a poor devil who could not keep discipline in the classroom. So they sent young Nadaud to a neighboring village where an eccentric misanthrope agreed to teach reading and writing to a few pupils. Finally his "education" was completed by a former officer of the imperial army "who drank one glass of brandy after another." It was common practice for former officers and noncommissioned officers, with nothing else to turn to, to become school teachers; and one can imagine that in addition to the letters of the alphabet these fine army men could well have taught their young pupils many other less respectable things. In 1829 there were still 13,984 communes out of 38,132 which had no schools; and attendance in all boys schools amounted to only 1,372,000, and these still only in the winter months—in summer it fell to 681,000.

This sad situation explains the momentary popularity enjoyed by the mutual teaching method introduced in England by Lancaster and brought over to France in 1814. Using the older boys as monitors for the others, the system helped, they thought, to spread the rudiments of knowledge faster and at less expense. This method, whose promise was to be belied by experience, had nothing in itself either favorable or deterimental to religious education; but, in fact, seeing that it had been originally sponsored by Carnot during the Hundred Days, that it came from a Protestant country, that its French promoters were liberal politicians, organized in a Society for the Encouragement of Elementary Education, party politics took over a controversy which should have remained purely on a pedagogical level. The Right and the clergy forbade simultaneous instruction practiced by the Brothers of Christian Schools and denounced Lancastrian schools as centers of moral corruption and republican inspiration, while the liberals maintained that the clerical opposition to this method had no other reason than to slow down "the progress of enlightenment" and to impose its yoke on the people by keeping them in abject ignorance. In spite of their efforts there would be in 1829 not more than 829 mutual schools in the whole country, in comparison to 1500 in 1821.

## Revival Missions

Still more passionate were the controversies aroused by mission revivals, an approach on which the clergy and royalists counted to bring back the lower classes to Christianity. The effort was not new, and as early as in the eighteenth century teams of missionaries, inspired by such strong and original personalities as Grignion de Montfort and Brydaine, had attracted vast audiences. But twenty years of interruption were to make the renewal of mission revivals look like an innovation; and especially since, up to then, no one had carried on this work so systematically and vigorously. As soon as the king had returned, a missionary society was set up under the name of Priests of the Missions of France; its founder and leader was a Bordeaux priest, Abbé Jean-Baptiste Rauzan, and his principal collaborator was Abbé de Forbin-Janson, the future Bishop of Nancy. The Missionaries of France had their headquarters on the Mont-Valérien, site of an ancient pilgrimage. Other societies soon took up the same work: the Jesuits, the Lazarists, the Montfortains, new congregations like those of the Priests of the Sacred Heart of Father Coudrin, the Oblates of Mary Immaculate of Father de Mazenod (who evangelized principally the southern provinces), and several other diocesan societies, to say nothing of independent revivalists and parish priests who occasionally gave a helping hand to the visiting revival missionaries.

Nothing was spared to make the visit of a revival missionary group a sensational event which would jolt the unbelievers and renew the spiritual life of the faithful. Upon arrival the missionaries invited all local officials to a grand opening ceremony, generally presided over by the bishop, often including a procession through the city streets. Then began the regular revival meetings, whose schedules were arranged in such a way that all categories of people could attend without interfering with their work hours. There were always very early morning sessions for the workers and evening meetings lasting as long as two hours with hymns, practical talks, dialogue lectures, and evening services of the Blessed

Sacrament. From this they went on to separate retreats for different categories of faithful, revival sermons in the religious houses, in the hospitals, in the prisons, etc. Because they rightly believed that they had to reach the common people by sensational and emotional appeals, because they had to set in motion a reaction against a long tradition of fear of public ridicule, growing out of the Voltairian eighteenth century and twenty years of official impiety, the revival missionaries put great emphasis on spectacular ceremonies: making amends for private wrongs and forgiveness of injuries, solemn reparation for public crimes—a ceremony which sometimes took place on the very spot where the Revolutionary scaffold had previously been set up—renewal of baptismal vows, consecration to the Blessed Virgin, procession to the cemetery where the preacher happened to speak on Hell and death—holding a skull in his hand—general communion, and finally the raising of the cross, which was the crowning act of the mission and for which the revivalists had no qualms about mobilizing for a whole day the civil and military officials and all the people of a town.

It is impossible to doubt that these revival missions, more often than not, produced the desired effects—that is, a stirring up of public opinion, a renewal of Christian feeling in the souls of the faithful, a reconciliation of numerous Christians who had been shunning the sacraments because of a conciousness of their errors. The impressive numbers of general communions, the activity of the missionaries at the confessionals, the manifestations of enthusiasm and affection toward them on their departure, these were all unmistakable signs of success. In Marseilles in 1820, the faithful literally fought among themselves to get seats in the churches. But, having said this, one must also admit that the revivalists exposed themselves to criticism by their excessive language, their tactlessness, their overuse of public ceremonies, their moral pressure on local officials and, through them, on the people, to compel them to take part in the demonstrations. The most serious complaint that can be leveled at them is that they mixed politics and religion by preaching on all occasions loyalty to the regime, by presenting it as an essential part of their creed, and having the people sing the popular song:

> Long Live France,
> Long Live the King!
> Forever in France,
> The Bourbons and the Faith!

Such emphases could justly arouse the anger of the liberals and turn against the missions the very ones whom they were out to convert. No doubt, the revival missionaries were merely reflecting the ideas of many of their contemporaries when they thought that the religion of Saint Louis and the monarchy of Saint Louis were inseparable; but this mixing of the two really could only be harmful to the church.

## Throne and Altar

At this point we encounter one of the most discussed aspects of the history of the Restoration—that is, the mixing of spiritual with temporal affairs; the use by the church of political means to impose its teachings and, conversely, the use by the state of the church's influence to impose a political regime. In essence this was nothing new, and it is well-known how rigorously was applied in both Catholic and Protestant countries in the seventeenth century the principle of *cujus regio ejus religio* (ruler's religion prevails). Even in the eighteenth century the mutual support given by throne and altar and the interference by the political authorities, by the parliaments especially, in religious affairs seemed so normal that there were only rare protests. Why were they to cause such uneasiness and let loose such an anti-religious reaction after 1815?

No doubt it all arises from the political, social, and moral changes brought about in France by the Revolution and the Empire. In earlier times the union of throne and altar resulted from an age-old tradition of which it was, in a sense, the natural and unquestioned outgrowth. The great mass of the nation accepted Catholicism just as it accepted monarchy, not conceiving of any other form of political or moral life. The clergy, sure of its own power, showed itself to be just that much more tolerant and moderate in its demands as it felt stronger and more in-dependent of the state, thanks to its own wealth. The attitude of the state in favor of religion was likewise tempered by the general anarchy, by the skepticism of the cabinet ministers and the ruling classes; and the Gallican parlement judges vigorously repressed any sign of independence on the part of the bishops.

Conditions were entirely different in 1815. Twenty-five years of lay predominance had distinctly separated state and church and on the other hand had tightened the ties between the French bishops and the Holy See. In his system Napoleon had always left religion in a reduced and subordinate position which would not cause offense to unbelievers. When the union of throne and altar reappeared in 1815, it took on a more systematic and deliberate character which made it look like a combat weapon. It had the appearance of something entirely new in a society which no longer remembered its earlier existence. Thanks to the efficiency deriving from Napoleon's administrative setup, which now was serving the church instead of restricting it, the latter assumed a course, a general appearance, and an overwhelming force lacking in the weak sinews of the old monarchy. The state was no longer, as before, in the hands of skeptic leaders hostile to religion, but, at least after 1821, in those of an aristocracy which considered itself dutybound, no matter how, to impose its religious convictions on the rest of the nation.

If the government was consistent in favoring with all its might the religion which the constitution proclaimed as the state religion, the unbelievers, who, it is said, represented a good part of the nation, could consider, for their part, that these efforts were a violation of the freedom of thought guaranteed by that same constitution and an abuse of power by both state and church. The clergy itself, in its effort to regain control, evinced the fanatical ardor of the weak which had endured persecution and now were not too sure of their new-found power. Deprived, by the Revolution, of its organization and endowed income which formerly had given it a certain independence, this clergy was to have unrestrained recourse to the secular arm without realizing that every service it received restricted its freedom of action and bound it hand and foot not only to a regime but to a political party.

Whole books could be written on instances of the clergy's abuse of its power, of administrative coercion in religious matters, and of incautious statements unerringly noted and challenged by the liberal press. Even if some of these incidents were greatly exaggerated or pure inventions, there still were enough cases to make a very unedifying picture. What astonishes us most today is that there were some clergymen who were still not satisfied and complained bitterly of the "weakness" of the government. The Cardinal of Clermont-Tonnerre, Archbishop of Toulouse, was quite serious when he wrote to a close friend in 1825: "We have much reason for sorrow over the condition of the church and the little inclination to help religion on the part of those who govern us." And a year later: "The foes of righteousness would soon be silenced if they were made to feel the force of governmental authority."

This same Cardinal-Archbishop of Toulouse, at the end of 1823, had caused a great outcry by publishing in a pastoral letter what he considered to be the legitimate demands of the church: revision of the civil code to bring it in line with canon law; the return to the clergy of the right to register births, deaths, and wills; the re-establishment of synods and provincial councils, of religious (non-working) holidays that had been discontinued by the Concordat, ecclesiastical courts, religious orders, clerical endowments to guarantee the financial independence of the clergy;

the reorganization of cathedral chapters; and the abolition of the Organic Articles. The government was so little inclined to move in these directions that it turned this pastoral letter over to the council of state and obtained from it a decree which suppressed the letter as one bearing the stamp of illegality.

Yet the opposition would not cease to denounce the clergy's interference and the submission of the government to its orders. Later on we will discuss that campaign which was to arouse so violently a part of public opinion against the monarchy and the church. Here we will merely give a concluding opinion about it. It is thought and generally said that this "clerical" policy of the Restoration was really just as bad for the altar as it was for the throne, and people refer to the Revolution of 1830 as justification for condemning the very principle behind it. But, first of all, they forget that that Revolution was a purely political accident and that it might have been possible to avoid it. They forget, too, that this antireligious movement had not originated during the Restoration but had gone back to a trend of thought already very strong at the end of the eighteenth century. In any case opponents of the church would have appeared on the scene and would have found reasons to complain.

On the other side of the ledger from the provocation of an anticlerical movement by the religious policy of the Restoration, there could be and should be credited to that policy the rapid recovery of the material possessions of the Church of France, the thousands of reopened or newly built churches, the springing up of hundreds of religious houses and a variety of charities, innumerable conversions achieved by the revival missions, and especially the rejuvenation of the ranks of the clergy— all of these were results which could not have been accomplished without the protection and help of the government and which were to continue to make their influence felt long after the echoes of the polemics of 1830 had died away. Without these fifteen years of reconstruction and reconquest by the Church of France, would it have been able to maintain and develop its works of charity and religious faith to the extent that it did in the nineteenth century?

## Protestants and Jews

An account of the religious life in Restoration France would be incomplete without mention of the Protestant and Jewish faiths.

In 1815 there were less than 500,000 Protestants, although there are certain statistics which claim that they were three times that number. These exaggerated claims are due to the fact that the Organic Articles of 1802 set at six thousand the necessary number of members to establish a "consistorial church" which could apply for government contributions. It is only natural that the pastors tried to qualify for these government payments by using every pretext to swell the membership statistics of their flocks.

The Protestants of Alsace, almost half of all the French Protestants, adhered to the Augsburg Confession; and the Protestants of the old principality of Montbéliard, now included in the departments of Doubs and Haute-Saône, were also Lutherans. The Calvinists of the French Reformed Church were much more scattered; they were found in some forty departments and did not form compact communities except in the Gard, the Ardèche, and the region of Montauban.

These Protestants had been for so long mistreated by the monarchy that they found it difficult to throw off their persecution complex. They were always ready to attribute the most evil intentions to the royal government and the Catholic Church. Nevertheless, they had no good reason to complain since the "persecution" which hurt them most was only the requirement that they decorate their houses when Catholic processions went by. The explosion of anti-Protestant violence which accompanied the White Terror in the south was limited to the Gard and was exclusively the result of a popular movement rather than government action. Indeed, the local officials did all they could to stop this outbreak and to guarantee the Protestants security and real equality under the civil law. Still, since they were held to be, in general, more favorable to liberal ideas, they were less well treated after 1822 than they had been under Decazes' government. Behind a façade of impartiality, which scrupulously respected the rights of religious minorities, these latter could sense a distrust and dislike on the part of rightist governments. This governmental attitude is noticeable enough in a letter by Frayssinous in 1827 to his colleague, the minister of interior, in which he indicated "the grave consequences of giving too much protection to a form of worship opposed to the state religion."

In spite of this, Protestants carved out finer and more imposing niches in Restoration government and society than they had occupied since the time of Henry IV. The royalists could not forget the support given to their cause by Protestant nobles who fought side by side with them in the ranks of the émigrés, by the Bordeaux merchants who joined in the demonstrations of March 12, 1814, by the Boissy d'Anglases and the Jaucourts who had been co-workers with Talleyrand in April 1814. The chamber of peers had six Protestants; and the higher ranks of the army, of the navy, of the administration, and of the judgeships were largely open to the Reformers, as were also those of the University. One has only to cite the names of Guizot and of Cuvier, who was for a time even president of the committee on public instruction before becoming director of reformed religions in the interior ministry. Protestant theology had its schools at Strasbourg and Montauban. Parisian high society had Protestant salons—those of Albertine de Staël, the Duchess of Broglie, and of her brother Auguste; of Stapfer, former representative in Paris of the Helvetic Confederation; of Mme de Gasparin; of the Delabordes; of the banker Delessert, etc. Again in Paris the Protestants found privileged positions in high finance, with the banking houses of the Perregaux and the Hottinguers. In Alsace the Koechlins and the Dollfusses were in the forefront of technical and social progress in the textile industries. From all over Europe men came to admire the accomplishments of Pastor Oberlin who had transformed morally and materially the impoverished inhabitants of the Vosges valley at Ban-de-la-Roche by his educational and religious programs.

Just as in Catholicism, the Reformed confessions also underwent a great intellectual and spiritual fermentation in this period. The pietist "Revival" movement, introduced from Switzerland by Henry Pyt, Ami Bost, and Felix Neff, and from England by Charles Cook, rekindled their earlier fervor as a reaction against the rationalist moralism of the eighteenth century. They encountered the opposition of liberal Protestants, led by Pastor Samuel Vincent of Nîmes, and these controversies led to a deeper understanding of doctrine. The Protestants had their newspapers, their schools, and their lay action groups. Corresponding to the Catholic charities under the auspices of the Congregations, were the Bible Society, founded in 1818, the Society of Evangelical Missions, the Society of Christian Morals, the Society for the Encouragement of Primary Education, fostered by Guizot, and the Religious Tracts Society, which published books and magazines.

As a whole, then, for French Protestantism as for the Catholic Church, it was in the course of these fifteen years of the Restoration that the foundations were laid for the rewarding accomplishments of the nineteenth century.

The Jews numbered about sixty thousand, divided into three principal groups, presenting rather different social characteristics. Those of the Comtat-Venaissin, descendants of those who had been attracted to the area by the protection afforded them by the Avignon papacy, devoted themselves particularly to the small artisan trades. Those of Bayonne and Bordeaux, coming from Portugal, were already well-assimilated and had been able to find an important place among the big merchants. The Jews of the German rite, concentrated in Alsace, kept much more to their ancestral customs; their professions of second-hand dealer, peddler, and pawnbroker caused them to be disliked by the people and distrusted by local officials. It was during the Restoration that the last legal barriers were removed which separated them from the rest of the nation. Napoleon, while giving a legal status to the Israelite religion in 1808, had, from the civil law point of view, kept the Jews living in the eastern provinces under an exceptional regime, which was to last for ten years as a trial period. In 1818 this period ended and, since the royal government did not return to the earlier discriminations, the Jews of Alsace were juridically on the same footing as all other Frenchmen. From the social point of view the arrival of the Rothschilds in Paris and the services they rendered to the finance ministers and to numerous highly placed people were to open the way to their coreligionists and to themselves for the winning of advantageous positions in the economic and political life of the country.

# 18
✤ ✤ ✤ ✤ ✤

# *Intellectual Life*

## *The Reawakening*

ONE day in 1812, just before Napoleon left for his Russian campaign, the members of all sections of the Institut de France were received in a body at the Tuileries. The emperor, seeing the poet Lemercier in the group, asked him abruptly: "Well, Lemercier, when are you going to write us a beautiful tragedy?" "I am waiting, Sire," was the academician's dry retort. Many others, voluntarily or under compulsion, had done the same thing in those days when, according to Lamartine's expression, "the geometric men were the only ones who had the floor." For all French thinkers, the fall of the Empire seemed like a deliverance of the mind, a chance to reforge the chain of intellectual progress broken by the Revolution. The grave Guizot, fifty years later, used phrases pulsating with juvenile enthusiasm to recall his impression of 1814: "Then it was that the first of the freedoms, intellectual freedom, regained its vitality and power. It is said that in the North, after a long and dreary winter, spring comes forth all of a sudden and the burgeoning life of nature puts in an appearance on every hand in all its lavishness and beauty. Who can help remembering the great intellectual movement which took wing and spread rapidly during the Restoration? The human mind, previously absorbed or constricted by the rude tasks of war, regained its free and unrestrained activity. Poetry, philosophy, history, moral and literary criticism, all types of intellectual effort received a new and bold impulse."

Several others, among them writers who were later to become famous, expressed the same impression in similar words. "It was a blind impatience to live," said Edgar Quinet, "a feverish waiting, a premature aspiration for things to come, a sort of intoxication of reawakened thought, an unappeased thirst of the soul after years in the desert of

328

Empire. All of that, combined with a consuming desire to produce, to create, to accomplish something in the midst of a still empty world." That the Restoration was, in contrast to the Empire, a period of intense intellectual production was later proven by cold statistics compiled by Count Daru, one of those "geometrical men" for whom Lamartine was to have so much scorn. While in 1812, over the whole territory of the Great Empire, 4,648 works were published, totaling 72 million full-printed sheets, in 1825, in the more restricted France with its 1815 boundaries, French publications amounted to 7,542 works, with a total of 128 million full-printed sheets, or the equivalent of thirteen or fourteen million volumes. No doubt many of these books were reprints of eighteenth-century authors, but these figures are, nevertheless, significant, especially when we realize that three-fourths of all Frenchmen were illiterate. If we consider periodicals, which were not included in the above figures, the contrast between the Empire and the Restoration becomes even more marked: 238 titles for the former and 2,278 for the latter. Of course, many of the periodicals were short-lived, but they comprised a big category of printed material to be added to that of books—one which Daru estimated to run to 21,660,000 sheets for the year 1825.

The history of the big organs of public opinion is rather well known, and literary criticism has also been interested in the history of certain papers which played a role in the evolution of romanticism. But what is known today of those hundreds of little publications which glowed for a few months before falling back again into oblivion? It is in these that the most lively expression of that intellectual fermentation of the time—with its so strongly marked characteristics of individualism, almost of anarchy—would be found. In fact there was no one directive center, no arbiter of taste—rather, there were so many of them that they cancelled themselves out by their very multiplicity. The salons, the academies, the College of France, the faculties, the big schools, the provincial learned soiceties—who regained for a few years an activity they would no longer know when the capital centralized all the country's resources—the literary societies, the lecture societies like the Athenaeum and the Society of Good Literature, and even reading rooms, circles, editorial rooms, and literary cafés—all of these constituted such a numerous and varied reading public that an author no longer knew, as before, to whom to turn, to what trend to conform. Henceforth the writer, if he was Chateaubriand or Stendhal, could only consult his own genius; if he was a Lamothe-Langon or a Jouy, he would aim at the lowest, he would take his inspiration and style from the *Constitutionnel,* whose twenty thousand subscribers inspired a jaundiced color to all the tribe of needy scribblers.

But here we are touching that vague dividing line where literature comes close to the provender market!

Three factors explain the rapidity and the extensiveness of this intellectual revival after 1815: freedom of expression, peace, and foreign contacts.

The liberal protests against the press control of the Restoration have obscured the undeniable fact that, with the exception of the early days of the Revolution, thought in France had never before been able to express itself with such impunity. The prepublication censorship which at times reined in the political press, generally did not affect the purely literary periodicals. In any case the authors of books were restrained only by the the fear of being prosecuted in the courts for having exceeded the bounds of decency.

Peace was naturally to bring back toward intellectual activity the national energies channeled for the last twenty-five years in revolutionary and military enterprises. It was an unaccustomed experience for a whole generation to have the country plunged suddenly into an interval of peace and quiet. Literature, the sciences, and the arts provided a diversion for unemployed administrators, demobilized officers, and young men kept out of politics by the tax requirement. "Those were the days," said Augustin Thierry, "when there was a generation of young and devoted men whose ambition could find an outlet only in a literary career, when there was a passion for a literary revival, associated by public opinion with the honors and popularity of the political opposition. The profession of a teacher was raised to the rank of social power; on him were lavished ovations and civic crowns."

The post-1815 French intellectual revival owed a great deal, however, to the great disturbances of the preceding era, even if this result did not show up immediately. Until the end of the eighteenth century cultural exchanges between France and other countries only involved a minority of aristocrats, literary men, and artists; besides, it was in a sense a one-way street—French culture, in its haughty superiority, spread itself generously but deigned to receive very little. However, the Revolutionary disturbances had scattered to all the countries of Europe and even across the ocean an early wave of Frenchmen who would not otherwise have left home; and these émigrés, mostly noblemen and priests, represented an elite who were in a position to profit to the fullest from this sojourn in the midst of such a different society. They were to bring back to France by the first years of the new century a whole collection of new ideas which, little by little, were to make their influence felt, as M. Baldensperger has so well demonstrated. A second wave, numerically stronger but geographically less widespread, and especially less capable of profiting by these contacts, was made up of the returning Revolutionary and Imperial armies. Another, a much less important third wave, that of the post-1815 Bonapartist emigration, would cast small groups upon the shores of the Near East and the Americas, but without much visible contribution to French culture back in France.

In 1814 and 1815, by an opposite movement, it was Europe which poured into France: first of all a military invasion, obviously not very favorable to cultural relations, indeed arousing some contrary nationalist reactions; then later a peaceful invasion of thousands of tourists, Englishmen and foreigners of all nationalities, attracted by the congeniality and prestige of Paris, "the most desirable haven in the universe for the scholar, the writer, and studious man," as Lady Morgan wrote at the time. And Frenchmen, too, when their humiliating memory of defeat and occupation had faded, began to open their eyes to those foreigners who had ceased to be enemies any longer. They rediscovered that England whose parliamentary institutions their grandfathers had envied, and they admired now its industrial growth, its commercial prosperity, and its technical advance. As M. Pierre Reboul said in such an excellent comparison, England would be for Restoration Frenchmen what the United States was in 1945, the country with "vistas of the future life." It must be added that England was to be the great shepherd, guiding French literature into the paths of romanticism—Shakespeare, Byron, Sir Walter Scott, inexhaustible sources of inspiration for the theater, lyric poetry, and the contemporary French novel. They were also to rediscover the road to Italy, a land of beauty and love, a fountain of music and picturesque fantasy. Thanks to the union of Bourbon thrones, a friendly Spain was to welcome French travellers again and was to furnish romanticism its contribution of local color and wild passion. Finally, Mme de Staël was to introduce Frenchmen to Germany, "the metaphysical nation par excellence," inhabited by conscientious scholars, profound philosophers, sensitive and religious poets, and virtuous and orderly citizens. Curiosity would turn them even to America—to its Indians, dear to Chateaubriand and whom the works of James Fenimore Cooper were to bring to life in new and more realistic colors, and also to its genuinely republican institutions, the ideal of La Fayette and of the liberals, a haven for those prescribed by the Bourbon regime. A former consul of the United States in France, Daniel Warden, then settled in Paris, was to make himself a promoter of cultural exchanges between the two countries by publishing, in 1820, a *Statistical, Historical, and Political Description of the United States* in five volumes.

Thus it was that the French mind, regaining its power and its universal outlook at the very moment when the material strength of the country was undergoing a decline, was to win some less notable but more durable triumphs than those of her armies. It would be impossible to try to draw up in a few pages even a summary list of these accomplishments. All that can be undertaken is to indicate, in a few broad strokes, the main directions and to pin onto this outline some names, titles, and characteristic traits.

An enlargement, in all directions, of the fields of knowledge; some original and fruitful concepts of the reform of human society; the creation of a new esthetics in literature and the arts—such seem to have been the acquisitions of French culture in the course of these fifteen years of peaceful labor.

## The Sciences

A young American, George Ticknor, who went over to Europe to complete his education, wrote back in 1817 to his illustrious protector, Thomas Jefferson, his first impressions of the intellectual life of Paris: in all respects of erudition, of literary and historical culture, he found nothing there which approached what he had seen in Germany and England. But, he added, in the field of the sciences there was nothing in the whole world that could rival the phalanx of scholars who at that time held seats in the Academy of Sciences. However strange this notion might appear to Frenchmen today, Paris was then, in the opinion of cultivated circles, less a capital of the letters and arts than that of the scientific displines. It was in this area, at least, that the Revolution and Empire had not allowed intellectual activity to decline, and it is only fair to note that the scientific advances realized under the Restoration only continued and crowned those of the preceding period. The Ecole Polytechnique, steadily draining off the best minds of the country, forcing them into an intensive mathematical preparation, set a salutary example and contributed to an elaboration of the highest standards. In fact, what was so striking among the learned men of the day was the admirable effectiveness of their mathematical culture, which made it possible for them to formulate with little difficulty, in a common language, the very diverse phenomena of experimental physics, astronomy, and chemistry. From here they rose almost effortlessly into the realm of philosophical generalizations; more than that, it seemed that it was for them an irresistible necessity.

One great name, however, stood out in the field of pure mathematics, that of Augustin Cauchy (1789–1837), a professor at the Ecole Polytechnique and the Collège de France, a Congregationist and ardent royalist, who was to go into exile in 1830 to be with Charles X. His studies practically founded infinitesimal calculus, but in other respects there was no important aspect of mathematics which was not dealt with by him in the twenty-seven quarto volumes of his complete works.

The physical sciences had the appearance of an army of forest clearers on the march, pushing back the frontiers of the unknown all along the line by their attacks; and there were more than twenty names which should be cited along with Fourier, Laplace, Gay-Lussac, Arago, Poisson, Biot, and Girard. From this legion three bold innovators stood out— Fresnel, Ampère, and Carnot—who by inspired intuitions opened the way in three different directions to all the science of the nineteenth century by making deep breaches in current conceptions.

Augustin Fresnel, a young engineer in the Bridge and Road Service, was dismissed during the Hundred Days for having taken a stand against the emperor. Back at home with his parents in Mathieu (Calvados), he made use of his idle hours by studying the problem of light interference. The new theory which he developed out of this destroyed the Newtonian concept of the emission of light particles and created the wave theory. This was an unusually bold position to take, and, when he presented his conclusions to the Academy of Sciences in 1819, the members of the committee were very prejudiced against him. They had to accept his views, however, when they saw his irrefutable demonstration, and soon Fresnel was admitted as a member in their midst. On the basis of this first discovery he succeeded in explaining easily all the optical phenomena then known. During his lifetime he saw a practical application of his studies: the adoption by lighthouses of stepped-up lenses, still in use and often called Fresnel lenses.

André-Marie Ampère (1775–1836) is the very type of scientist for a Horatio Alger novel: a delightfully naive soul, legendary absent-mindedness, complete self-effacement, great discoveries produced in a makeshift laboratory with rudimentary instruments made by himself. And yet today wherever that vital fluid of modern life, electricity, flows, millions of machines, large and small, obey laws formulated for them, over a century ago, by this unusual man. His researches in various fields had already brought him fame when in 1820 his attention was attracted to an experiment done by the Dane, Oersted: a magnetic needle changing direction under the influence of an electric current coming from a Volta battery. Ampère concluded from this that magnetism and electricity were the same thing, and after just a few weeks of experimentation and computations he figured out the laws of electromagnetism, the properties of electrically charged solenoids (coil-windings), and the principles of the electric magnet and of the telegraph, and calculated their mathematical formulas. One of his successors, the English physicist Maxwell, indicated his place in the history of science by calling him "the Newton of electricity."

A still more astonishing homage is read in a work of another British scholar, a contemporary of Maxwell, Lord Kelvin, who said: "In all the areas of the sciences there is nothing greater than the accomplishments of Sadi Carnot." What had he done, this son of the great Carnot, this lonely and sad young man, who was to die in 1832 at the age of thirty-six? He had written only one paper of about one hundred pages, published at his own expense in very few copies, and never submitted to any academy, any learned society, or any journal. But this work founded thermodynamics at one stroke by freeing physics from the traditional notion that heat was a special fluid. "Heat," wrote Carnot, "is nothing more than motive force, or rather nothing more than movement changing its form. It is movement among the particles of substances. Wherever there is a destruction of motive force, there is a simultaneous production of heat to an exactly proportional amount. Reciprocally wherever there is a destruction of heat, there is a simultaneous production of motive force. . . ." The young scientist also gave the mathematical formulas of these laws. Their practical results in that century called "the age of steam" are easy to guess.

Chemistry did not produce such revolutionary discoveries, in spite of the remarkable work of Gay-Lussac on the analysis of organic substances and that of Chevreul on fatty substances.

Neither did the natural sciences lend themselves to sensational discoveries. Progress here was to be in unparalleled efforts at description, classification, and especially synthesis. Three powerful but contrasting personalities stand out from the crowd of the emulators and collaborators. Jean-Baptiste de Monet, Chevalier de Lamarck (1744–1829), was carrying on an encyclopedic work, begun under the auspices of Buffon in the reign of Louis XVI. From 1815 to 1822 he published his monumental *Histoire naturelle des animaux sans vertèbres* (*Natural History of Invertebrate Animals*), and in 1820 his *Système analytique des connaissances positives de l'homme* (*Analytical System of Positive Knowledge of Man*). Heir to the "philosophic" spirit of the eighteenth century, he formulated the earliest of the bold hypotheses on the evolution of human beings and on the origin of man, that Darwin was to take up later. Etienne Geoffroy Saint-Hilaire (1772–1844) was interested especially in mammals and reptiles. He perceived the importance of embryology for the interpretation of the anatomy of adult animals and began the systematic study of monster anomalies—teratology. Of a generalizing and systematic mind, he presented in his *Philosophie anatomique* a grandiose conception of the unity of the animal kingdom which incorporated in a more moderate way the evolutionary transformism of Lamarck.

It was with this last idea that his friend Georges Cuvier (1769–1832) took issue. He had been a long-time secretary of the Academy of Sciences, a member of the French Academy, the council of state, and the royal council for public instruction, etc. On the head of this successful man all the regimes had showered honors, which he definitely merited. He enjoyed a kind of supremacy in the scientific world by the abundance and clarity of his works and by his ability as an initiator and organizer. All of zoology, and still more of paleontology, which can almost be considered his creation, would retain the imprint of his guidance during the nineteenth century. The history of the skeleton of prehistoric animals entirely reconstructed from just one bone illustrates his reputation of infallibility. It was this famous man who entered the arena to combat the evolutionary transformism of Geoffroy Saint-Hilaire. In his opinion the organization of each of the animal forms was the one the Creator had assigned to it in order to permit it to live in conditions determined by a strict general finality. Behind the theories of his opponent, this fervent Protestant disclosed a dangerous pantheism and a perfidious attack on the Bible, whose complete concordance with the teachings of geology he had taken pains to show in his *Discourse on the Revolutions of the Globe* (1821). The controversy went on between 1825 and 1829 in their publications and finally came out in public in the Academy of Sciences, stirring the intellectual world in France and abroad. In fact it now became much more than a quarrel between scientists; it was a confrontation of two different philosophical conceptions of creation, as well as two scientific methods: that of a prudent and rigorous analytical mind and that of intuition and a synthesizing imagination. With Geoffroy, the latter approach had gone further than the positive findings of the time would permit, and in the end Cuvier felled his adversary under the weight of his impeccable learning. As a result of the outcome of this memorable debate, "fixism" prevailed for many years in French science, and evolutionary transformism was to come back only after changing its nationality and name.

At this time medicine also had its supreme pontiff in the person of Broussais (1772–1838), professor at the Val-de-Grâce School. His astonishing authority came as much from his gift of speech and his power of invective as from the value of his works, and he won the acceptance of the strange theory in pathology which attributed all diseases to the irritation of tissues, and he cared not a whit whether his patients, systematically starved and bled white, died like flies! Fortunately at the same time some great minds brought honor to French medicine: Orfila, the creator of toxicology; Dupuytren, an incomparable surgeon, Récamier, who constituted gynecology as a specialty; and finally Laënnec, one of the finest examples of his profession. Thanks to the invention of the stethoscope, he was able to accomplish a decisive step in the method of listening in the diagnosis of heart and lung diseases, before he himself succumbed in 1826 to tuberculosis contracted in the service of science and of mankind. The founding in 1829 of the *Annales d'Hygiène publique et de Médecine légale* reflected the activity of a remarkable group of scientists who stood at the intersection of preventive medicine, sociology, and philanthropy: Halle, Fodéré, Villermé, Bigot de Morogue, Parent-Duchâtelet, and others. Carried away with statistical research, and very much ahead of their time in this regard, they had the noble ambition of understanding nature and the mechanism of social ills in order to equip the administration with ways to remedy them.

## Geographical Sciences

The curiosity of naturalists was one of the principal reasons behind the numerous voyages of exploration which launched Frenchmen of that day out in every direction on the trade routes of the world. The royal government, the Société de Géographie of Paris, the Muséum d'histoire naturelle, and several other learned societies encouraged and financed explorers and helped them in publishing the results of their discoveries. Geology, geography, ethnography, linguistics, botany, and zoology all profited from this by enlarging their horizons in all directions, and an abundant travel literature brought to the man in the street the wonders of exoticism and the pleasant sense of imagined travels abroad.

The spirit of adventure was admirably embodied in René Caillé. Humble son of a Niort baker, he was fascinated by reports of a fabulous city, Timbuktu, the forbidden town which no European was allowed to enter. At the price of many years of patient approach maneuvers, suffering, and danger, Caillé finally in April 1828 succeeded in seeing the city which his dreams had represented to him as being resplendent with all the treasures of the African continent. Alas, all he found was a miserable collection of mud houses, in the midst of an immense arid area. It made no difference, France gave a triumphal welcome to this hero just the same.

At this same time the flora of North America was being studied by Alexander Lesueur, and the countries of South America were being covered by Alcide d'Orbigny and several others. The royal navy, encouraged by the leading merchants of Bordeaux, undertook to reconnoiter the Pacific Ocean in all directions. These were the great voyages of circumnavigation of the "Uranie," by Louis de Freycinet (1817–1820); of the "Coquille," by Duperré (1824–1825); of the "Thetis," by Bougainville (1824–1826); and especially of the "Astrolabe," by Dumont d'Urville (1826–1829). This last explorer, covering 25,000 leagues (about 62,500 miles), brought back sixteen hundred plants, nine hundred mineral samples, maps, and many other things of inestimable value for a knowledge of the peoples of the South Pacific. In addition he had found the wreckage of La Pérouse's ships, which had been lost in storms forty years before on the reefs of Vanikoro in the New Hebrides.

The Near East had been popularized by Chateaubriand and still more so after 1820 by the Greek war for independence. Firmin-Didot, Forbin, Marcellus, Laborde, and others, would try to repeat their own *Itinéraire* and follow the footsteps of Childe Harold. Others were to push on much farther, in the footsteps of Alexander the Great, into central Asia, and in 1828, Victor Jacquemont, a friend of Stendhal, would leave to visit the Indies.

Orientalism was not just a traveler's preoccupation or an artistic and literary fad; it was also a research science with Paris as its uncontested world center. Of the thirteen nonscientific chairs in the Collège de France, six were devoted to oriental languages. Abel Rémusat published his *Éléments de grammaire chinoise* in 1822 and brought a knowledge of Far Eastern literature into the West. Eugène Burnouf discovered the secret of the ancient languages of Persia and the Indies. Silvestre de Sacy published an Arab *Chrestomathie* and an Arab *Anthologie grammaticale,* and directed the *Ecole spéciale des langues orientales,* established by the government. Along with Rémusat he also founded the *Journal asiatique* in 1822.

Also the French had had, after Bonaparte's expedition, a sort of monopoly on Egyptology. Jean-François Champollion, extracting the secrets of the hieroglyphics, opened in 1822 a whole new province for ancient history. The generosity of Charles X was to permit him in the next few years to arrange in the Louvre one of the finest galleries of Egyptian antiquities.

## History

The years of the Restoration coincided in France with the birth of modern historical consciousness. This was such an important step in the evolution of human thought that we should pause here for an instant in order to try to sort out the causes leading to the maturation of this progress at this precise moment in time.

In the preceding centuries historical evolution, in its social aspects, took place so slowly that the movement could not be sensed by those immersed in it. The purely political events—such as wars, diplomacy, court intrigues—were not noticed by the mass of common people. And yet, after 1789, prodigious changes had suddenly stirred them down to their lowest levels. The breathless success of these political changes forced contemporary minds to consider the relations of cause and effect. They transposed the marble images inherited from Greco-Roman antiquity into terms of blood and iron. Marathon was now Valmy, Sulla was Robespierre, and Caesar was Napoleon. History leaped from dusty books and took them by the throat. Edgar Quinet wrote:

> The great invasions of 1814 and 1815 had left in my memory a crowd of impressions and scenes through which I tended to evaluate everything. The downfall of a world had been my earliest education. I became interested in everything in the past which could show some resemblance to these immense human changes which for the first time had struck me so forcibly. Thanks to this analogy, history, previously insufferable, became a living thing instead of the dead thing she had been to me before. . . . I too, in 1814 and 1815, had heard the hammer of Attila resound in our countrysides. I had seen again and again the Goths and the Visigoths; yesterday once more they were arriving with their heads wreathed with green boughs, like the walking woods in Macbeth's dream.

One can sense, too, throughout this passage, another circumstance favoring a return to the past. It was romanticism with its search for strange colors and emotions, with this same longing for the far-off places which impelled the Caillés toward the discovery of distant worlds. Behold how historical vocations were born. A pale and nervous child discovered the magic of the past among the medieval sculptures of the Museum of French Monuments in Paris. Later he wrote:

> I can still remember the emotion stirring my heart when, as a small boy, I went in beneath those dark vaulted arches and gazed upon those

pale faces, when I was going and searching. What, I know not. The life of those distant times, no doubt, and the genius of its age.

This child was Michelet. At about the same time, at the College of Blois, another young boy had just come upon *Les Martyrs* of Chateaubriand. Carried away with enthusiasm, he paced back and forth within the cloisters. As his footsteps resounded on the pavement, he repeated aloud the hymn of the Franks: "Pharamond! Pharamond! We have fought with swords!" This schoolboy was named Augustin Thierry.

A third favorable factor was the reawakening of political life with its parliamentary battles and the open clash of doctrines. The parties involved in the struggles, compelled to persuade rather than guillotine, had to search for arguments from the recent past. As a matter of fact political passion could be just as dangerous to history as it was useful, which was also true of the love potion of romanticism.

Fortunately circumstances offered more solid bases for a sound development of history. The Revolutionary interval had brought out for use by the erudite a mass of parchments and papers which had up to then been jealously guarded by administrative offices, religious houses, and families, either because the claims or rights which they were intended to substantiate no longer existed or because they had become useless in the work of administrative offices set up under a new system. Already carelessness and ignorance, as well as Revolutionary fanaticism, had destroyed a goodly portion of this national heritage, but the royal government made an effort to rescue what survived the shipwreck. An ordinance of 1821 founded the Ecole des Chartes (School of Paleography) and put it under the supervision of the Academy of Inscriptions and Belles-Lettres, and here twelve young men were to learn "to read divers manuscripts and explain the French dialects of the Middle Ages." It is amusing today, when we know the immense services rendered by that institution, to recall the sarcastic remarks about it from the liberal opposition, which claimed to see in its establishment a measure of feudal reaction. Béranger lashed out against it with a song entitled *L'Enfant de bonne maison* (*Child of a Good Family*):

> Sole arbiters
> Of the seal of titles
> Charter-keepers, bestow upon me honor.
> I am a bastard of a great noble lord,
> I am a bastard of a great noble lord,
> From your flourishing scholarship,
> I expect parchments and coats of arms.

All liberals, fortunately, were not so basely demagogic; the more intelligent among them understood full well the support their ideas could find in the serious study of the institutions of ancient France. Thus it was that Guizot launched a great new collection of *Mémoires relatifs à l'histoire de France* and another *Documents relatifs à l'histoire d'Angleterre*. At this very same time the ex-Conventional Daunou, dismissed in 1816 as director of the royal archives, was giving a series of well-attended lectures at the Collège de France on historical methods.

History in all its forms had, then, in these years an unexampled vogue. It cropped out everywhere—in political discussions, in the tracts of social reformers, in the pleadings of lawyers, in novels, in drama, in poetry, and in painting. If, as they said, the annual total number of works published in France almost doubled between 1812 and 1825, historical works more than tripled (from 306 to 1,073). And what happy times, when readers and publishers could digest without a frown a history of France in thirty-one volumes, like the one Sismondi published in 1821! The public was particularly eager for memoirs, and this preference, coinciding with the urge of numerous people to justify their conduct in the preceding years, rolled up fortunes for the publishers. When there were not enough authentic memoirs, clever scribblers, like the prolific Lamothe-Langon, produced endless *Secret Memoirs,* filled with piquant "revelations" and racy anecdotes. The *Magasin Pittoresque* (*Picturesque Storehouse*), launched in 1830, promised "history for all pocketbooks" at two cents a copy.

All of this immense output—not counting the documentary publications—is today out-of-date, not only because history in our time is more exacting on matters of documentation and critique but also because most of these authors were "involved" in the political struggles of their times and were trying especially to illustrate their preconceived theses. Only as works of art can we now admire a few of them.

Outside of Michelet, whose talent did not come to full maturity until after 1830, the greatest of these artists of the period was no doubt Augustin Thierry. His great work, *Récits des temps mérovingiens* (*Accounts from Merovingian Times*), was not to appear until later, but he had given a token of his talent for reproducing the spirit of past times in 1825 in his *Histoire de la conquête de l'Angleterre par les Normands* in which could be seen the influence of Sir Walter Scott. In it could also be seen, transplanted across the channel, the false but appealing thesis on which his concept of the history of France was based: that is, the insurmountable antagonism of a conquered people—the Gauls—toward a conquering people—the Franks—persisting over the centuries through the struggles of their respective descendants, the Third Estate (commoners) and the nobility. His *Lettres sur l'histoire de France,* published first in installments in the *Censeur Européen* and then collected in a book in 1827, affected to enhance, through highly colored episodes of medieval communal uprisings, the movement of a people toward a free and democratic government.

Prosper de Barante, a peer of France and an unemployed administrator since the fall of his patron, Decazes, was a lonely aristocrat amid a cohort of bourgeois historians. Seeking only to please the salons, he was a wonderful success with his *Histoire des ducs de Bourgogne,* a brilliant mosaic skillfully fitted together with extracts from the chronicles of a period rich in picturesque accounts. Further, the writer had been able to retain, in his style of adaptation, that trace of conventional archaism whose affected prettiness was to enrapture the gentle maidens.

The two works, both entitled *Histoire de la Révolution française,* published at almost the same time by Thiers (1823–1827) and by Mignet (1824), were in contrast politically inspired. Both authors were writing apologies of the Revolution in a period when official historiography was retaining only its most hideous and most disastrous aspects. Mignet said: "When a reform has become necessary and the right moment for its accomplishment has arrived, nothing can stop it and everything promotes it." Thiers explained: "The internal resistance led to the sovereignty of the multitude, and the outside aggression to military domination." With their tons of printed pages all the apologists of the Revolution will not say much more than this. The political passion inspiring these works also made them a success; neither their historical nor literary value could justify it. Their accounts, based solely on official records and a few memoirs, dealt with superficial facts. The underlying social struggles, the administrative transformations, ideas and customs, the aspects of the Revolution in the provinces, all that had escaped the attention of Thiers and Mignet.

Taken altogether, one can discover only one serious historical work for this period, that of François Guizot. Politics and administration had absorbed him until July 1820, and his temporary political disgrace was to furnish him the occasion for an admirable intellectual maturation. Certainly, like the others, he had his political preoccupations, and his historical works in the beginning aimed at showing that the representative constitutional regime was the final goal of centuries of striving. As he advanced in his work, he rose to a more noble concept of his role as a historian and professor, rejecting the stratagems used by his colleagues to win applause. Among the three "Greats" who then dominated the liberal arts at the Sorbonne—Guizot, Cousin, Villemain—the first was the best "teacher," according to Legouvé. Guizot's lectures, he added, had a "solidity, a seriousness, heightened by his fine, grave voice." Above all, Guizot, following the example of the German historians whom he admired, taught his students to have recourse to sources, critical discussions of them, and bibliography. He showed a realization, unusual in his day, of the complexity of historical phenomena and of the value of economic and spiritual aspects of civilization. Thus this Protestant was to bring to light the role of the church in the Middle Ages and in terms that Bonald would not have gainsaid. His *Histoire du gouvernement représentatif en Europe* and his *Essais sur l'histoire de France* were still rather strongly imbued with political predilections which had made him choose these subjects as themes for his courses in 1820 and 1822. For this he was punished by the temporary suppression of his teaching, and yet his *Histoire de la Révolution d'Angleterre*, the result of his forced retirement, already rose to a higher level of objectivity. And, when he was able to take up his teaching again in 1828 and write successively his *Histoire de la civilisation en Europe* and his *Histoire de la civilisation en France* (from the fall of the Roman Empire to 1789), he brought to them all his distinguished historical talents.

## The Social Sciences

The general feeling of this whole generation was that the main purpose of history, and especially contemporary history, was to contribute to political reflection, and the same factors account for the revival of political and sociological literature. Yet, up to 1814, this field of thought had suffered more than any others the effects of the repressive regime. As in 1789, the nation was giddy with the rediscovered pleasure of reasoning on affairs of state and on social reforms. Political, economic, and social thought spread in a torrential flood of hundreds of tracts, thousands of brochures and pamphlets, and tens of thousands of speeches and articles. Politics contaminated more or less all fields of thinking with the deplorable result that the success of literary works, and especially of plays, was often proportionate to the allusions which political parties could find in them. Science itself was not immune to the clashes in the forum; the success of the medical theories of Broussais, for example, is explained in part by the fact that they brought water to the liberal mill by their materialistic philosophical postulates.

It is not easy to introduce some orderly arrangement within this massive production. Hardly do you think you have discerned some great "schools" of thought than you discover influences and unexpected connections between theories apparently alien to each other, or, on the other hand, you find complete incompatibility between systems which at first sight had seemed associated. Philosophical, religious, political, social, and economic conceptions gave, by their infinitely varied ingredients and articulations, compounds whose complexity could only be expressed by analytical formulas similar to those used in organic chemistry.

Three principal schools are usually recognized in the field of pure political thought, corresponding to three attitudes which could be taken toward the Restoration regime. There was the liberal school, with its devotion to the immortal principles of 1789, which rejected the regime; there was the Catholic traditionalist school, which claimed to be forging a new ideological framework within the reactionary efforts of the Ultra-Royalist party; finally there was the doctrinaire or constitutional school, which tried to conciliate the past and the present and believed they had found in the Charter of 1814 the basis of the necessary compromise. Each of these schools adhered to a definite philosophical system: the first, to the Ideologues, heirs of the Encyclopedists of the eighteenth century; the second to the Catholic faith; and the third to eclecticism.

But this subdividing, however satisfying it may appear, is far from covering the entire field of thought in that period. On the fringe of this framework were also those who refused to be involved in the current political fights, which they considered out-of-date, and who claimed to be inaugurating a new social order founded on a new science; and there were others who chose as the principal objects of their meditation the economic and social imperatives of the emerging industrial era. For all these latter thinkers the dividing lines were far from coinciding with those in the fields of politics and philosophy. Thus the thought of Auguste Comte and that of Saint-Simon reveal affinities as much with the Ideologues as with the theocrats such as Joseph de Maistre.

Yet, for lack of anything better, and not forgetting the artificial character of this classification, we shall resign ourselves to following the schema indicated above for the exploration of these doctrines.

## The Ideologues

The "Ideologues" adhered to the dominant principles of the philosophy of the preceding century: sensualism, deism or atheism, faith in reason and progress, individualism; but their productivity seemed exhausted. Cabanis had died in 1818. Volney was to live until 1820 and Garat until 1833; but the former went over to linguistic studies, and the latter, after being expelled from the Institut and retiring to the country, returned to the practice of religion to the great scandal of his friends. The principal representative of this school, who had dominated the Institut in the early years of the century, was Destutt de Tracy (1754–1836). His *Eléments d'Idéologie* were reprinted in 1824 and his *Commentaire sur l'Esprit des Lois de Montesquieu*, published first in the United States, came out in Paris in 1819. Faithful in psychology to the sensualist empiricism of Condillac, in politics Destutt de Tracy believed in "a democracy of enlightened reason" and wanted a government which would assure the greatest possible individual liberty. The serious-minded Daunou for his part demanded the "necessary freedoms" of man and citizen in his *Essai sur les garanties individuelles* (1818).

One would be mistaken, we believe, if one minimized the influence of this trend of materialist thought—deist or atheist—on the thinking of the period. Although it had not produced many new works, it was nourished by innumerable reprintings of eighteenth-century authors. One report from the bookstore trade estimated that from 1817 to 1824 there had been published 1,598,000 volumes of the works of Voltaire and 492,000 volumes of those of Rousseau; in the same period Volney's *Les Ruines* went through eleven reprintings, and the works of Helvetius, Diderot, Raynal, Saint-Lambert, Condorcet, and Holbach had a similar vogue. Ideology had furnished a simple philosophy accessible to all those opposed to a state religion. It had penetrated the economic thought of Jean-Baptiste Say and the social thought of Saint-Simon and Auguste Comte and also, naturally, the eclectic school. It inspired the scientific theories of Lamarck and Broussais, and in the field of literature it had been the religion of the whole Voltairian school. By its doctrine of analysis of sensations it infused new blood into the psychological novel and fashioned, among other things, the genius of Stendhal. It gave birth to a literary genre, that of the "Physiologies," the first of which in time (1825) was that of Brillat-Savarin, the *Physiologie du goût* (*Physiology of Taste*), a masterpiece of humor and finesse. So then in politics, at least, all the adherents of liberalism—even those who repudiated atheism—owed to Ideology the fundamental postulates of their systems: the sacred character of the rights of man, faith in free reason, the belief that the state should serve the welfare of individuals.

The most complete, clearest, and most long-lasting of these theorists of liberalism was without doubt Benjamin Constant de Rebecque, that astonishing Proteus of intelligence and sentiment who could cause women to suffer while adoring them, who could serve Napoleon in 1815 after having covered him with insults, who could write the subtlest and tenderest psychological novel, *Adolphe*, and reveal himself in journalism as a cruel and dazzling polemicist, who could live as a skeptic, lend his talent to the most violent anticlerical policy, and devote a lifetime to a major five-volume work on religion. His political thought is found in his *Cours de politique constitutionnelle* (*Lectures on Constitutional Politics*), which is nothing more than a collection of his previous works inspired by current situations (1818–1820). The basis of his system was popular sovereignty, and liberty was considered the highest guarantee of all the other natural rights. To assure their protection against the excesses of democracy, he wanted to have a parliamentary monarchy on the English model, in which the wealthier citizens alone would have the right to vote. As to economic matters, in line with the views of Adam Smith, he opposed any state intervention.

Among the crowd of second-rate writers who sold the liberal doctrine to the general public, one must cite Paul-Louis Courier, a refined Hellenist and one of the greatest pamphleteers of all time. Rarely had more bad faith and more baseness of thought been clothed with a more Attic style, with a more stinging irony, or with a greater mastery of smutty and slanderous suggestiveness.

## The Catholic and Royalist School

The Catholic and royalist school, still called traditionalist, theocratic, or Ultramontane, furnished if not the most original at least certainly the most characteristic contribution to the period of the Restoration. It was in a sense its projection on the intellectual level. "Legitimate kings have been restored to their thrones," wrote Haller in 1816, "we are also going to enthrone legitimate learning, which serves the Sovereign Master and whose truth the whole universe confirms." More than any other current of thought, it really constituted a school, thanks to the fundamental unity furnished to its diverse voices by their common acceptance of the principles of Catholicism. It also presented a more European character, having been born in émigré circles in touch with German philosophers and the antirevolutionary influence of Burke.

Thus it was a Savoyard nobleman, Count Joseph de Maistre (1753–1821), who laid the cornerstone of the reactionary edifice in his *Considérations sur la France,* published in Lausanne in 1795. It is true that he had hardly lived in France and had died by 1821, but his work was unquestionably a part of French Restoration thought because of the enormous influence it exerted on it. His two major works, *Du Pape* (*On the Pope*) and *Les soirées de Saint-Pétersbourg* (*St. Petersburg Evenings*), were published in 1819 and 1821. He found unforgettable expressions for crushing human pride, reason, atheist philosophy, and the principles of the French Revolution. For him the only salvation was in a return to a monarchical regime, the natural emanation of the providential social order; and as he recognized no other legitimate sovereignty than that which issued from God, the temporal princes, in his system, were subordinated to the pope, God's representative on earth.

With less splendor of expression and less prophetic insights, but with greater depth, more rigorous logic, and greater abundance, Viscount de Bonald (1754–1840) was to express the same ideas. "Is it possible," Maistre wrote him in 1818, "that nature may have amused itself by stretching two cords as perfectly in tune as your mind and mine?" It was also during the emigration that Bonald wrote his first work, *Théorie du pouvoir politique et religieux dans la société civile* (*Theory of Political and Religious Power in Civil Society*) (1796). Back in France at the end of the Directory, he published one after another his *Essai analytique sur les lois naturelles de l'ordre social* (*Analytical Essay on the Natural Laws of the Social Order*) (1800), *Du divorce* (*On Divorce*) (1801), and *La législation primitive* (1802). After this he became silent, in spite of Napoleon's favor, which elevated him to the council of the University. The Restoration brought him again to the front of the stage; as deputy, and then as peer of France in 1823, he was in these bodies the oracle of the Ultra-Royalist party. But he also collaborated with several periodicals, wrote occasional brochures, and published two other great works: *Recherches philosophiques sur les premiers objets des connaissances morales* (*Philosophical Researches on the First Objects of Moral Understanding*) (1818), and *Démonstration philosophique du principe constitutif de la société* (*A Philosophical Demonstration of the Constitutive Principle of Society*) (1828). In Bonald's system, the individual is given even less consideration than with Joseph de Maistre. "Man exists only for society," he wrote, "society shapes him only for itself." And again: "In society there are no rights, there are only duties." The pretension of a man to set himself up as a legislator for society was just as untenable as would be his attempt to add to his own weight. The constitution of society, whether religious or political, was derived necessarily from its nature. The state, as Bonald conceived of it, was of a patriarchal type: one grand family, made up of several domestic societies obeying common laws. The monarch had the right to intervene in the material and moral life of the cells of which his people were composed. He should do "little for men's pleasures, enough for their needs, everything for their virtues." The author of such an austere formula for government could hardly hope to receive much popularity. He did not seek it and did not possess it, leaving to others the concern for captivating public opinion.

Among the latter Chateaubriand and Lamennais stood out in the first rank. With the coming of the Restoration the author of *Le génie du Christianisme* (Chateaubriand) had descended to the political arena, and his writing had become that of a journalist and pamphleteer—but with what genius, what striking superiority over his pale confederates! This part of his work suffers today from a general lack of understanding of the circumstances which inspired it, but, to those who know, it is still able to arouse a shiver of admiration such as one feels on seeing the decisive thrust by the matador after a series of brilliant passes. But there are better things than these controversial works. *La monarchie selon la Charte* (*The Monarchy According to the Charter*), published in September 1816 for the defense of the Chambre Introuvable, contained a complete program of government, at the same time monarchical, religious, and parliamentary.

The personality and work of Lamennais have been discussed in the preceding chapter. It is obvious that he should be considered, at least before 1828, as one of the representatives of the theocratic school, and he, more than any other, deserved to be given that designation. His literary genius and his polemical ardor were to assure him a wide stratum of readers which Bonald's metaphysical dissertations did not reach.

If, in gauging authors, we only considered the influence they had on their times, we could pass over in silence the work of Pierre-Simon Ballanche (1776–1847), who was known only to a limited circle of friends. But today he appears as the most original and perhaps the most arresting of the writers of that school. He was as flexible as Bonald was rigid, as open to opposing ideas as Maistre was walled in by his prejudices. The very title of his major work raised many eyebrows—*Essai de palingénésie sociale* (*Essay on Social Regeneration*) (1827–1829); but if we are willing to go deeply into it, we find in it original and sometimes prophetic views, expressed in poetic language.

Finally should be mentioned the considerable work of Louis de Haller, a Bernese by birth and a Protestant convert to Catholicism, who settled in France and who even obtained a position in the French foreign ministry. His *Restauration de la science politique* was first published in German, appeared in a French edition in 1824, and attracted many readers.

## The Eclectics

Between the materialism of the ideological school and Catholic theology, the last years of the Empire had seen emerge, with the government's benediction, a curious attempt to create a spiritualist philosophy founded on psychological observation and reason. Its initiators in the imperial university had been Laromiguière, a disciple of Condillac and an amiable and eloquent professor, and Royer-Collard, whose system was inspired by that of the Scotchman, Thomas Reid. It was going to fall to Victor Cousin, who in 1815 had succeeded Royer-Collard in his chair of philosophy, to give this sort of philosophical "third force" its most finished and most popular expression. The eighteenth century, he said, had been the age of destruction; the nineteenth should be that of intelligent rehabilitation. "It is for this century to find, in a deeper analysis of the mind, the principle of the future, and, using the accumulated debris, to erect finally an edifice that reason can accept." "What I recommend is an enlightened eclecticism, which, judging all schools with equity and even with sympathy, would borrow from them what was true and reject what was false." But by what criteria would they make the distinctions between the true and the false? It was all very simple; the new philosophy had to defend the sound, noble, generous ideas which did not undermine religion or the social order. Thus it would be based on the eternal axioms of "The True, the Beautiful, and the Good"—the exact title of his later book in 1854. The success of this system, in spite of its obvious weakness, is explained not only by the fact that it answered a need of the moment but also by the extraordinary talent with which its author explained it in his lectures at the Sorbonne from 1815 to 1821, and again after 1827. Taine called him "the most admirable tragedian of the century." We can also see how this way of envisaging philosophy was to turn the French school toward the history of doctrines rather than toward independent research.

This spiritualist school, however, produced at that time two remarkable minds turned toward introspective research—Maine de Biran (1766–1824) and Jouffroy (1796–1842). "He is the teacher of us all," Royer-Collard said of the first one; but his deep, refined, and often sad analyses were not to be published until after his death. As to Jouffroy, professor at the normal school, "a convert" from Christianity to skepticism, he continued to seek salvation under a different name, applying all philosophy to the problem of human destiny.

The aim of Victor Cousin was not more purely philosophical than that of the two schools between which he tried to trace a middle way. It involved finding a spiritual basis for that constitutional or Doctrinaire party which claimed it was also trying to find a middle course between the monarchical tradition and the principles of 1789, thus reflecting the aspirations of the tax-qualified bourgeois voters.

Royer-Collard, the unquestioned leader of the Doctrinaires, has left no systematic exposition of his political thought, and we have to look for it in his parliamentary speeches, collected and elucidated later by his disciple Barante. For him, sovereignty did not reside in the people, nor solely in the king, but in all the independent authorities taken together, which had been the products of historical evolution: the king, the hereditary peerage, and the elective chamber. The latter was not the mouthpiece of the nation, but that of a category of interests, the interests of citizens rich enough to be worthy of participation in political activity. Even Guizot recognized *de jure* sovereignty only in reason; as to *de facto* sovereignty, it was to be distributed among those qualified as they emerged and asserted themselves in the course of the progress of society.

The respective success of each of these three schools of thought was closely tied to that of the political parties. The debates around the program of the Chambre Introuvable gave the first impulse to the Catholic and royalist school; the constitutional government of Decazes took its inspiration from Doctrinaire theories, or, rather, the latter was born from the need to justify this constitutional approach. The royalist return to power in 1822 momentarily re-established the preponderance of Bonald's school, but it was soon weakened by the defection of Chateaubriand, whose personal vengeance thrust him into the arms of the liberals and by the defection of Lamennais, who was raising the standard of integral Ultramontanism against the Gallican Catholicism of Frayssinous. Liberalism regained its strength under the Martignac ministry, and the Doctrinaires, accepting its alliance, brought about the downfall of the royalist and religious system at the same time as that of the regime with which it was identified.

## The Economists

In contrast to the men we have already considered, the thought of the theoreticians who remain to be discussed owe little to the political circumstances of the times.

Economic liberalism, accepted without question by all the parties, found its best interpreter in the person of Jean-Baptiste Say from Lyons (1767–1832). Not only did he clarify the doctrine of Adam Smith, but he completed it on some important points and introduced into the study of economics an objective and descriptive method resembling that of the natural sciences. "As head of a government," he said, "you are already doing a lot of good if you do nothing bad." And Decazes seemed to approve his views by establishing a chair of "industrial economy" for him at the Conservatoire des Arts et Métiers (Conservatory of Arts and Crafts).

It is easy to understand how the liberals and even the Doctrinaires may not have distinguished economic liberalism from political liberalism, but it is more difficult to understand today how statesmen on the right could adjust themselves to such an ideal, especially when at that very time a doctrine much more in conformity with the spirit of a Christian monarchy was making an appearance. The *Nouveaux principes d'économie politique* of Sismondi had been published in 1819. The author vigorously denounced the evils of free competition, which led to working-class misery, and the inhuman characteristic of an economic system which was exclusively preoccupied with increased production without concern for its just distribution.

> It is not the manufacturer's profits which constitute the national interest; it is the benefit that manufacturing spreads among all classes who engage in it. . . . If the administration was to choose the advantage of one of the classes of the nation over that of the others, it should be precisely the day laborers that it should favor. By assuring their welfare the great mass of the nation would prosper.

This same humane and Christian note was to be found among the precursors of social Catholicism, the best-known of whom, Alban de Villeneuve-Bargemont, had been able to observe, as prefect of the department of Nord, the horrible abuses of the industrial system.

These reformers, while calling for state intervention in economic affairs, did not call into question the traditional structure of society. They did not threaten property rights, and they remained adherents to Christianity.

The views of Saint-Simon, on the other hand, opened the way for a revolutionary reorganization of the whole social and even moral edifice. Nothing was so strange as the career and personality of this nobleman who had served in the fight for American independence, had jumped into the Revolutionary torrent, had amassed and then lost a large fortune in it by speculating on national lands, then suddenly transformed himself into a needy intellectual, and died in the role of messiah of a new religion. From 1814 to 1825, the date of his death, he proclaimed his message in a mass of disparate writings, among which were three periodicals successively founded by him: *l'Industrie, le Politique, l'Organisateur*. In his opinion, the method which had enabled the physical sciences to establish a set of general laws could be used to discover for the social order analogous laws which could be effectively applied for the welfare of humanity. He showed how, in contemporary society, industry embodied the productive and creative forces, while the political power remained in the hands of the military and the landed proprietors, whose real ability no longer existed. To get the political power into the hands of the productive class was the solution of the future. The new society would have no idle, and the new Christianity—a religion of brotherhood and love—would replace feudal Catholicism. The eminence of Saint-Simon came not so much from his personal influence on his time, which was almost null, nor from his ideas themselves, which were too confused and contradistory to be generally accepted by the public; rather it came from the fact that his magnetic personality and the bold richness of his thought gave rise to two powerful currents of thought which ran through the whole nineteenth century—socialism and positivism. After Saint-Simon's death his disciples organized a sort of religious sect under the leadership of an old Carbonaro, Bazard, and of a former Polytechnique graduate, Enfantin. In their *Exposition de la doctrine saint-simonienne* they gave a systematic appearance to the master's doctrine, which modified it in certain respects. The abolition of property and inheritance would prepare the way for the establishment of the new society, in which there would no longer be any exploitation of man by man. It would be governed by a hierarchy of industrialists, scholars, and priests, and it would have as its fundamental law: "To each man according to his abilities; to each ability according to its productivity." The extravagances of Enfantin were to lead, some years later, to the dissolution of the sect, but several of its members were to play an important role in the economic development of the country, particularly in the introduction of railroads.

The more purely philosophical aspect of Saint-Simon's thought was to be developed by Auguste Comte, who was his secretary and close collaborator from 1817 to 1824. The history of Comte's positivism really does not belong to the Restoration, but we can not forget that his *Système de politique positive* was published in its original form as early as 1822 and that it was in November 1829 that Comte began to bring out his *Cours de philosophie positive*.

Charles Fourier (1772–1837), did not enjoy during his lifetime the notoriety of Saint-Simon. This small business clerk, self-taught and withdrawn, pursued by himself his inner dream, and his works, published at his own expense, had scarcely any readers. Their strange style and their baroque composition tended to disconcert their readers. At the beginning of his chapters one could read such headings as these: Pre-lude, Cis-lude, Citer-Pause, Trans-appendice, Ulter-logue, Postalable, etc. The ideal world which he dreamed up reminds one of modern surrealist paintings because of his hallucinatory details and the luxuriance of his phantas-magoria. "The societal order," or "the universal harmony," which he invented, would result from a minute listing of all the human inclinations and passions which were 810 in number. All one would need to do would be to give them free play to see a real order emerging from them, generating well-being. The basic element of this liberating order would be the "phalanx," grouping 1,620 men and women together, representing every variety of character so that each one would find among the common useful employments the one most conforming to his own preferences. They would live together in a "phalanstery," a sort of garden-city, where no government would be needed, so perfect would be the adaptation of the individual desires to the general interest. Some of Fourier's predictions are amusing, as when he describes the world trans-figured by the work of a harmonious society: oceans transformed into lemonade, cruised by convoys of ships pulled by domesticated whales, man prolonging his life to the age of 144, eating seven meals a day, deserts made fertile and cultivated by tamed lions, etc. Others of his works seem prophetic: the digging of canals through Suez and Panama, the use of "magnetism" as an industrial energy, news transmission by starry relays, etc. In certain respects Fourier looked like a theoretician of anarchy; but his penetrating criticism of the liberal, capitalist regime, as well as certain of his views on production, commerce, co-operative activ-ities, education, and the role of women in society, have, for the most part, been taken over by socialist schools of thought.

"The French Revolution," wrote M. Gouhier, "had been too deeply felt as a spiritual experience not to impose a Restoration spiritual problem." The whole nineteenth century, and even our own, has not exhausted the richness of the infinitely varied responses which were proposed for this problem in the course of these years of prodigious intellectual fermentation.

## Romanticism versus Classicism

Yet it is very doubtful whether contemporaries would have had a realization of this intellectual greatness of their time. If we could have polled them on what they thought had been their greatest accomplishment, they probably would have answered: the triumph of romanticism over classicism.

The romantic revolution, we know, was not a French monopoly; it had already come to dominate England and Germany when it won out in France. We know, too, that it was not entirely a product of the Restoration: many of its characteristic works would appear only after 1830. And, besides, its foundations had been laid by the end of the eighteenth century. Under the Empire it had had brilliant precursors in the persons of Chateaubriand and Mme de Staël. Still it was unquestionably between the years 1820 and 1830 that romantic esthetics succeeded in moving out of the old forms to which most of the literary and artistic productions had conformed up to that time.

Let us try to understand the delayed yet rapid character of the revolution in taste then taking place. First we must underline the circumstances recalled at the beginning of this chapter and indicating the general revival of intellectual activity after 1815. But also, why did romanticism achieve its breakthrough only in the last years of the Restoration? First of all, it was only after 1820 that foreign influences, such as those of Byron, Sir Walter Scott, Schiller, Goethe, and others, had been able fully to impress themselves upon France. In the early years of the Restoration national pride, crushed by defeat and occupation, considered it to be a sort of treason to admire foreign literary productions. So it was that Mme de Staël was castigated for her enthusiastic book on Germany, and the first attempt of an English troupe to present a Shakespeare play to a Parisian audience in 1822 ran up against a "patriotic" uproar. Wasn't it true that this good-for-nothing Shakespeare was one of Wellington's aides-de-camp? Yet the same year, 1821, would see the translation of Schiller's plays by Barante, a new edition of those of Shakespeare by Letourneur, and the first volume of the collection of foreign dramatic masterpieces published by Ladvocat.

Another element in the explanation of the shift to romanticism would be the emeregence during these years of a new generation unacquainted with the modes of thought and expression of the eighteenth century. We have already noted this in its social context, and we can add that this generation—trained in a period when its system of education was in complete disarray, was, less than others, impregnated with the spirit of earlier ones—had, in a sense, to train itself. The dissolution of the old society was also effective in weakening the old criteria of literary taste. The new reading public, more plebeian, less cultivated, more steeped in the daily spectacle of Revolutionary tragedies and military exploits, was asking for new and violent emotions. One young colonel remarked to Stendhal: "It seems to me, after the Russian campaign, that *Iphigénie en Aulide* is no longer such a beautiful tragedy."

Finally the impact of political influences is undeniable. Romanticism was essentially a revolt against an established order. But, until 1820, the established order was Louis XVIII, an avowed follower of classicism; the French Academy, composed of veterans who had made their literary reputations under the old school; a government which favored the rationalist and liberal ideology. The opposition, on the other hand, was Chateaubriand, Lamennais, and the *Conservateur*. From 1820 on, the royalist party was sailing before the wind, it was taking over the government, the aging Louis XVIII was ceding his place to his brother—in effect, a new era was dawning. The romanticists, who at that time were allied to the extreme Right, were swept up by this wave, they were able to make use of it to breach the wall erected against them, up to then, by a hostile coalition of social and political forces. Once done, and gradually as the new royalist administration took on, with Villèle, the extremely realistic and "mathematical" appearance of the preceding governments, the romanticists were going to abandon this alliance, which was basically an unnatural one, and find themselves free to link their cause with those who had become the opponents of the established order —the new liberal generation.

Here is, perhaps, one of the essential facts of the time which could throw much light on the spiritual failure of the Restoration, that sort of desertion by public opinion of which it was the victim in its later years and which left it, so to speak, high and dry on the rocks of 1830. So let us follow briefly the romanticist battle in its chronological course.

The early years of the Restoration found classicism solidly established in the fortresses of the Academy and the University, dominating public opinion unopposed. Facing it, romanticism had no rules, theories, leaders, or models. Indeed, everywhere, it was a puzzle as to what meaning should be given to the word introduced into France by Mme de Staël. Even in 1823 Victor Hugo would say that he "does not know what was meant by the classical and romantic style." Yet, in general, *romantic* designated everything which wandered from the literary traditions of the seventeenth and eighteenth centuries. It was on this count that it looked like a menace to the national heritage and drew upon itself the ridicule and scorn of the recognized critics.

A typical representative of classical poetry at that time was Népomucène Lemercier. This great man had analyzed *Athalie* from twenty-six different points of view and determined that Racine had satisfied the required conditions in all twenty-six. So *Athalie* was a perfect tragedy, and to make another equally good tragedy, all one had to do was to apply the twenty-six infallible recipes! In like manner *Tartuffe* revealed twenty-three rules for comedy, and that of the *Iliade,* twenty-four for the epic. Uniting precept with example, Lemercier wrote twenty-two tragedies (*Agamemnon, Camille, Charlemagne, Christophe Colomb, Charles VI,* etc., etc.) and five epics, one of which was a *Mérovéïde* in fourteen songs and an *Atlantiade* in six thousand verses. And how many others were there like him in those days who thought they could attain immortality by spinning out thousands of purring Alexandrine verses and who were quickly buried in the oblivion of the dust of just one generation: Raynouard, Arnaud, Etienne, Andrieux, Duval, Picard, Lemontey, Jouy, Dupaty, Moreau, Tissot, Viennet. . . .

Scrupulously faithful to the *Art poétique* and to the conventions of the "noble" style, the real poet of those days, to speak of cider and cheese, felt obliged to say "the liquor of apples" and "the milk product hardened in the wicker baskets"; a rain storm became "the unchecked urn of the Hyades." "You had to have," said Lamartine, "a mythological dictionary under your pillow if you wanted to dream up verses."

And it is to this very Lamartine that the glory goes for having freed French poetry from this tyrannical predilection for pagan antiquity and for having furnished the first model of a personal and religious lyricism, penetrated with a feeling for nature. His *Méditations poétiques,* published in 1820, aroused a commotion such as the literary world had not seen since *Le Génie du Christianisme.* "Today one cannot imagine," wrote Sainte-Beuve, ". . . what enthusiasm, what transports there were among those of our age for the first verses of Lamartine . . . we felt there the shock of a revelation; a new sun was rising and was already warming us with its rays." In the classical camp there was, on the contrary, consternation and horror. Legouvé related that a friend of Andrieux, permanent secretary of the Academy, found him at home, pacing back and forth in his study like a madman; in his hand was a copy of the *Méditations* which he was tearing apart. "Oh, you whimperer," he cried, "may you lament your fate! You are as a withered and consumptive leaf! What do I care? *The Dying Poet! The Dying Poet!* Well, drop dead, you animal. You shall not be the first!" Andrieux could fume all he wished, the hole had been made in the dike and through it would burst a thousand melancholy and ardent Renés. In the front rank of these was soon to appear Victor-Marie Hugo, the "sublime child," whose earliest *Odes* were going to be published in 1822.

## Literature and Politics

This early romanticism was royalist and Catholic. Like the traditionalists they repudiated the cult of pagan antiquity which had excited the imagination of the republicans of the Revolution and had adorned the

Empire with the wonders of Rome; like them they turned toward the Christian Middle Ages in order to find in them an ideal more suitable to the national spirit; like them they also hated Voltaire and the skeptical irony of the eighteenth century; and finally, like them, they found followers in aristocratic circles who, because of their emigration experience and their support of the Holy Alliance, more willingly welcomed foreign influences than did liberal circles, imbued with Jacobin and Bonapartist nationalism. "The new literature," declared Victor Hugo in 1824, "is the expression of the religious and monarchical society which would emerge from so much of the old debris and from so many of the recent ruins." And Ulric Guttinguer was to say: "To be romantic is to sing about one's country, one's affections, one's customs, and one's God."

The liberals, on the other hand, for whom Voltaire was the law and the prophets, vehemently denounced those "saturnalia of literature." The *Constitutionnel* stigmatized Hugo and his friends, who, in an effort to produce something different, took the liberty "of outraging good taste, of insulting reason, of descending to the most disgusting trivialities, or of losing themselves in the limitless regions of the absurd." One faction of the royalists, especially those who belonged to the older generations, were also just as alarmed by these assaults on what was for them the legacy of the France of Louis XIV. The joint efforts of these and the liberals came to a climax in April 1824 with a solemn excommunication, fulminated in the name of the French Academy by Auger in a session attended by the entire Institut. "Do we have to wait, then," he cried, "until the sect of romanticism . . . goes so far as to put in question all our rules, insult our great literary works, and pervert by an illegitimate success that mass of opinions which can always be turned in any direction?" The University also entered the dispute through the voice of Frayssinous; at the general awarding of prizes (the main commencement), in August 1824, he delivered an attack against the romanticists, who only enjoy "what is false, bizarre, and nebulous." From all sides, by journals, songs, and pamphlets, the innovators were made to look ridiculous. The *Muse française,* which had been a romantic magazine in 1823 and 1824, was abandoned by one of its founders, Soumet, who aspired to membership in the Academy; it was to go out of circulation and its group had no other rallying point than the hospitable salon of Charles Nodier, librarian of the Arsenal. Victor Hugo himself felt he had to speak out in support of the sound rules of language:

> It is well understood [he wrote] that liberty does not mean anarchy,
> that originality cannot be made an excuse for bad usage; the more

they disdain rhetoric, the more reason to respect grammar. They should dethrone Aristotle only to make Vaugelas prevail.

This relative moderation was not to last long. The above quotation was written in October 1826; one year later, in December 1827, in his *Préface de Cromwell,* Victor Hugo raised the standard of revolt: "Authors have the right to be daring, to venture, to create, to invent their own style, and to control their own grammar." What was it that had happened to Hugo in the meantime? First of all, romantic works were flooding the bookstalls, crushing their mediocre opponents by their "illegitimate successes." In 1824 appeared the *Eloa* of Vigny and the *Nouvelles Odes* of Hugo, in 1825 the *Théâtre de Clara Gazul* by Mérimée and *Racine et Shakespeare* by Stendhal, and in 1826 *Bug-Jargal* by Hugo and *Cinq-Mars* and *Poèmes antiques et modernes* by Vigny. In the course of these years English romantic literature, the novels of Sir Walter Scott in particular, had invaded France, and in July 1827 new performances of Shakespeare by English actors had had a huge success.

Besides this, a real reversal of alliances had taken place; romanticism had deserted the royalist camp in favor of the liberal opposition. Why and how? The Villèle government, by its commonplace tone and its political jobbery, had disappointed the hopes of the Catholic and idealistic extreme Right; it had persecuted Ultramontanism in the person of Lamennais, poetic genius in the person of Chateaubriand, and freedom of thought by its clumsy attempt in 1827 to bridle the press. It had succeeded in making royalism appear to be just as opposed to the aspirations of the new generation as Napoleonic despotism had been in 1814. A new breed of liberals had arisen; encouraged by the *Globe,* it repudiated all old patterns, those of the Revolution as well as of the Old Regime. Between the two oppositions of Right and Left Chateaubriand bridged the gap, and the struggle for Greek independence furnished a common cause for contest and enthusiasm, permitting the aspirations toward freedom to be united with the defence of Christianity and the military tradition. Hugo sensed from what direction the wind blew, from which side came the most applause. His *Hymne à la Colonne* of February 1827 is the indication that he had made his choice. The royal government, which had heaped honors and pensions upon him, had not yet perceived his shift. The decisive break would come with the appearance of *Marion Delorme.* The government, in spite of its favors toward the poet, would not be able to authorize the performance of a play in which the King of France was portrayed as a melancholy idiot and Richelieu as his evil genius. Hugo would reject disdainfully the pecuniary compensation that was offered him, and from that time forward it was open war. He was eventually to proclaim his new political allegiance in his preface to *Hernani:*

> Romanticism . . . taken as a whole. . . . is only liberalism in literature. Literary liberalism will be no less popular than political liberalism. Liberty in art and liberty in society, those are the same goals to which all consistent and logical minds should march in step. The *ultras* of all kinds, classical or monarchical, will be working in vain if they try to restore the Old Regime unchanged. . . . Liberty's every step will tumble whatever structure they will have begun to build.

With *Hernani* also triumphed, needless to say, the romantic drama. This was a decisive victory if we realize the social importance of the theater in that day. The success of lyric or epic poetry could only be measured in bookstore sales or in salon conversation; only in the theater did the author confront his public, and the spectators, excited by the gathering, showed their feelings in violent ways. A significant coincidence was that the French Academy tardily in April 1830 seemed to ratify the public's verdict by admitting Lamartine to be numbered among the Immortals.

What were the results of this esthetic revolution for French literature? If it be said that it destroyed the old rules of poetry, mixed up literary forms which had been recognized as distinct since the eighteenth century, proposed new sources of inspiration, and modified the language, nothing new is added to what has already been said. But how can more be said without going beyond the scope of this book? Especially how could one do justice in a few lines to such differing geniuses as Vigny and Béranger, Alexandre Dumas and Eugène Scribe, Sainte-Beuve and Villemain, Stendhal and Balzac? So one must leave to literary history the inventory of these riches. Yet, without them, one would have only an incomplete view of the Restoration, a mutilated view precisely because it was the principal concern of many Frenchmen of that time and because today it gives us a closer glimpse into their emotions and interests.

## The Fine Arts and Music

The creative renewal of the French spirit in this period is found in the field of the arts. It is true that architecture suffered from the parsimonious financial policy of the various governments; and it was no longer a question of the monarchy, restricted by a civil list, building new palaces when it could hardly save from ruin those of the Old Regime which it had inherited. Their main concern would be in finishing—slowly, very slowly—certain constructions initiated by previous governments: the new façade of Versailles begun by Gabriel, the Madeleine, the Arc de Triomphe de l'Étoile. In the few new buildings—the expiatory chapel, the churches of Notre-Dame-de-Lorette and of Saint-Vincent-de-Paul—the neoclassical formulas of the eighteenth century still dominated. The false-Gothic style would not make its appearance until the end of Charles X's reign, and then principally in the ornamentation of private houses, in furniture, and in the minor arts. Viollet-le-Duc would only be sixteen years old in 1830.

Sculpture also resisted romantic influences. The great master of the day was Baron Bosio, whose whole ambition was to imitate Canova. Pradier was beginning, under his auspices, his long career of fondness for feminine beauty, which led him from harem nymphs on up to his lewd creations of the Second Empire. Rude came back to France in 1827, after a voluntary exile in Belgium to be with David, but it would not be until after 1830 that he would give free rein to the fire of his temperament. David d'Angers made many sharp sculptured portraits of his contemporaries; but when he undertook more ambitious subjects, he remained faithful, to an absurd degree, to the pseudo-classical canons, representing, for example, General Foy, the great liberal orator, at the tribune of the chamber in the noble and simple costume of Archimedes stepping from his bath!

Only painting exposed itself to the new gusts at that time revolutionizing literature. The point of departure was the same: a classicism transfixed in an idolatrous respect for conventional antiquity; an academism wearing itself out in the pursuit of a "beau idéal," which the permanent secretary of the Academy of Fine Arts, Quatremère de Quincy, defined as "a compound being of which observation and science, imagination and sentiment, make up its parts." David, although in exile, still was the law. The academic rewards, the officials contracts, and the public favor still went to those who could represent Greek and Roman heroes exhibiting their bloodless plaster nudities in the plastic poses of the official repertory of emotions. Only the delicate Prud'hon, disdained by the others, saved something of the voluptuous fantasy of Watteau and Fragonard in his misty mythologies.

The three principal students of David—Girodet, Gros, and Gérard (the three G's)—would continue to produce according to his prescriptions. Still, the need to satisfy official requests would oblige them to condescend more often to abandon antiquity and dress up their human subjects. Gros painted Louis XVIII's departure in March 1815 and the embarkation of the Duchess of Angoulême at Bordeaux, Gérard the entrance into Paris of Henri IV and the coronation of Charles X, and Girodet the portraits of Bonchamps and of Cathelineau—all with the same zeal and academic correctness that they had used to illustrate the Napoleonic epic. However, the Middle Ages invaded painting: in the exposition halls of 1819 the Jeanne d'Arcs, the Saint Louis, the Merovingians, and the troubadours dethroned the Epaminondases and the Dianas. This same historical and purely thematic romanticism was to inspire the tireless brush of Ary Scheffer and those of Delaroche, Horace Vernet, and Léopold Robert. Religious subjects also became more frequent because of requests by the churches, which were attempting to repair the damage done in the Revolutionary period.

The renewal was to come elsewhere. In that very exposition hall of 1819 a dark and tragic canvas was to sound a striking note of realism across the classical and medieval bric-a-brac: it was the *Radeau de la Méduse* by Géricault. Unfortunately this precursor of the Courbets and Manets was going to die prematurely in 1824, a victim of his passion for horses, which he loved to paint. Ingres, also, in his own way, had first combatted Davidian classicalism in the name of truth. He repudiated the notion of ideal beauty, revolted against the superstition of antiquity, introduced the Orient into painting, and sketched the features of his contemporaries with an infallible pencil. Yet, his emphasis on style—like that of the Raphael school—his worship of the beauty of forms, and, above all, perhaps, his quarrel with Delacroix, were going to make him the rallying point of the routed Davidian school. His *Apothéose d'Homère*, unveiled in 1827, assured his fame.

Romanticism, with all that it contained of passion, audacity, and freedom of expression, was truly incarnated by Eugene Delacroix. His three great canvases of the time, *La Barque du Dante*, *Les Massacres de Chio* (1824), and *La Mort de Sardanapale* (1827), revealed a new world of feelings and colors. The classicists emitted cries of horror. "We do not know which to criticize more in it," wrote the *Gazette de France* about *Les Massacres de Chio*, "whether the overwhelming naiveté of all those slaughterings, or the still more barbarous way in which M. Delacroix sketched them without regard for the proportions of the design."

Devéria, whose *Naissance d'Henri IV* (*Birth of Henry IV*), exhibited in 1827, was greeted with enthusiasm by the romanticists, was not to fulfill his promise later on; while Corot, modestly beginning his career this same year of 1827 with a few Roman landscapes, was going to lead a productive line of French nineteenth-century landscape painters. The examples of Constable and Bonington, no less than romantic inspiration, successfully brought French painting back to a feeling for nature, so completely absent from classical studios.

The history of art must finally take account of the appearance of a new process, that of lithography, more flexible and economical than copper engraving. Without speaking of the stimulus it gave to the industrial production of engravings and popular cartoons, this new method was ennobled by the works of Devéria, Celestin Nanteuil, and Tony Johanot. Also thanks to it, the illustrated book had a renewed success. Nobody paid any attention to the strange experiment of a certain M. Niepce (Nicéphore) who had succeeded in 1822 in developing the first photographic image on a sensitive plate.

What Delacroix had been for painting—that is, an isolated and much criticized genius but elevated by posterity above all his detractors—Berlioz was to be for music, and in a still more noticeable way. Without him France would hardly have been exposed to the musical revival except through foreigners. Weber, with his *Der Freischütz* (1824), and Rossini, with his *Guillaume Tell* (1829), were received with enthusiasm at the Paris Opera. To tell the truth, pure music did not have very many followers in France. With the exception of the theater, they only cared for old-fashioned singing or tasteless ballads. The popular musicians, such as Auber, Boïeldieu, and Hérold, remained faithful to the forms of Méhul and Cherubini who dominated the Conservatory. The romantic picturesque came into musical drama only through its libretto subjects; in that way *La Dame Blanche,* Boïeldieu's greatest success (1825), received its inspiration from Sir Walter Scott.

Nothing in all of this heralded the frantic genius which came to light by a mass performed at Saint-Roch. Unleashing "floods of sinister vibrations," according to his own words, Hector Berlioz tried to shock the "Philistines" of the Conservatory. Public incomprehension, which he defied, did not stop him from producing. In 1828 came his overtures of the *Francs-Juges* and of *Waverley,* and in 1830 the essential pieces which were to become the *Symphonie fantastique* and the *Damnation de Faust.* There is no better way of describing the impression produced by this music than by quoting the author himself about the overture of the *Francs-Juges:*

The day of the concert this introduction produced an effect of astonishment and dismay difficult to describe. I was standing next to the kettledrummer, who was clinging tightly to one of my arms and could not refrain from shouting convulsively at intervals: "It's superb! It's sublime, my dear man. . . . It's frightening. It can make one go out of his mind!" With my other arm I was yanking crazily on a tuft of my own hair. Forgetting it was my own piece, I was ready to scream: "How monstrous, colossal, horrible!"

By his life, his writings, as much as by his music, Berlioz remains one of the most complete incarnations of the romantic soul.

To the eyes of military history, all bedazzled by the exploits of the Empire, the Restoration may look like a period of decline. Liberal history, a victim of its own antimonarchical prejudices, may depict it as an age of obscurantism. It is not certain that even today Frenchmen have a sufficient realization of the real greatness of the period which produced both works and men as diverse and as influential as Fresnel and Ampère, as Lamarck and Cuvier, as Burnouf and Champollion, as Benjamin Constant and Bonald, as Lamennais and Chateaubriand, as Victor Hugo and Lamartine, as Delacroix and Berlioz.

By their combined efforts, France resumed in just a few years that intellectual and moral leadership that she had held since the seventeenth century and which her fit of military imperialism had caused her to lose. And this development came about all the more easily because the circumstances precluded any thought of political hegemony. Paris again became the meeting-place of all those in Europe who were interested in things of the mind. Goethe, in his old age at Weimar, waited impatiently for the arrival of the *Globe,* the only paper which gave him "something to think about," and Mazzini, in all his wanderings, never wanted to leave behind his collection of magazines published in Paris under the Restoration.

Let us hope that contemporary historians, leaving aside their old prejudices, will be willing to accept the conclusion that one of the most perceptive historians of the contemporary Italian school, the late Adolfo Omodeo, furnishes us. According to him:

> The great transformation—by which the cultivated man of the nineteenth century, so profoundly differentiated from that of the eighteenth century by his moral sensitivity, by his active participation, by that great new faith of Europeans in progress, by his ability to consider reality in historical perspective . . . and to give a development to this vision of the world in a new scientific context and in a new political order—that was the work of French thought between 1814 and 1830.

PART
# IV
✤ ✤ ✤ ✤ ✤

*The Reign of Charles X*

# 19

❧ ❧ ❧ ❧ ❧

# Villèle and the Defeat of Reaction

## The New King and the New Reign

THE steady rain falling on that day of September 27, 1824 did not prevent the Parisian crowds from warmly acclaiming their new king, Charles X, when he made his joyous entrance into the capital. What a change in appearance for royal majesty! Instead of a fat man carried around like an idol in a chair or open carriage, one could now admire an elegent monarch, still young in looks, riding on an Arabian steed decked with silver trappings. In his sixty-seventh year Charles X still retained his supreme ease of manners and friendly informality which had previously made him the spoiled child of the Versailles Court and the prince charming of the ladies. A long face framed in short white sideburns, large brown eyes with an almost childish look, and a large protruding lower lip gave him the air of somewhat sheepish benevolence, and yet of some distinction. Mme de Boigne, not noted for her partiality for Charles X, admitted: "I have never seen anybody have so completely the attitude, forms, bearing, and language of the court, so desirable in a prince." In contrast to Louis XVIII, who had admirers and favorites but no friends, Charles X evoked in his inner circle a sentimental, almost feudal devotion. "When he said 'Good Morning,'" one of them wrote, "his voice seemed to come so from the heart, he had such a gentle way of greeting, that it was impossible not to be moved by it." One example of his warm-hearted nature: The Viscount of Vaudreuil, after receiving a dressing-down, wrote him a rather strong letter of protest, reminding him that he had been serving him for thirty years. The prince's note had this reply: "You old fool, stop talking about your thirty years of friendship. Tomorrow it will be thirty-four years that I have known and loved you!"

It is more difficult to say exactly what was beneath this amiable exterior. A very mediocre intellectual baggage in any case—his early education had been scandalously neglected, and later on he had not bothered much about completing it. Less intelligent than his brother (Louis XVIII), no doubt he was not as much lacking in ability as is generally thought. Pasquier, just as prejudiced against him as was his good friend, Mme de Boigne, reported that he had once had an occasion to attend a council meeting presided over by the king: "I was at that time impressed by the intelligent way Charles X discerned the principal points in the discussion and by his ability to sum them up. The habit of presiding over the council and of listening to the discussions must have singularly matured his mind." Other confirmatory impressions could be cited on this point. The king also had fine moral qualities: a high sense of his state duty, which made him devote almost all his time to government affairs; a strong desire to preserve the greatness and welfare of his country; a simplicity in taste which made him refuse any sumptuous expenditure for himself, combined with an almost excessive generosity toward others. "He had considered his civil list," said La Rochefoucauld, "as a sort of loan which, borrowed from the nation for the purpose of its grandeur, was to be repaid by state luxury, magnificence, and services." Finally he retained a perfect dignity in his private life. Since that day in 1804 when he knelt by the deathbed of his last mistress, Mme de Polastron, and swore to devote all to God, he had faithfully and scrupulously kept his word. His somewhat narrow and formalistic devotion was nevertheless indulgent toward the backslidings of others, and he never frowned upon those who did not share his religious convictions.

So what prevented this excellent man from becoming a good king? Perhaps one thing was that he did not ascend the throne at a time when ordinary qualities would have been enough. It can even be seen that his virtues, as well as his weaknesses, were to hurt him, because, had he been more of a skeptic, more of a playboy, less a devotee of his kingly duty, in other words, more like his royal English contemporaries, he would not have encountered the conflicts which brought him to ruin. If he was to plunge head down into the fight, it was because he was stubbornly faithful to a conception of royal prerogative which was incompatible with a parliamentary regime. One day when one of his ministers cited the example of England to convince him of the necessity of having a majority in the two houses, he replied with vigor, "That's true, but in England the houses defined the role of the king, and here the king defined the role of the houses." In other words, his major fault appears to have been a radical inability, not only to accept, but even to understand the point of view of the new generations of Frenchmen brought up during the Revolution.

The other faults for which he can be blamed—and no doubt rightly—make up a curiously contradictory portrait. Thus he is represented as set in his opinions and at the same time easy to influence; as too frank in his remarks, too careless in the choice of his confidants, and at the same time possessed of a conspiratorial frame of mind and given to secret intrigues. It is certain, in any case, that the influences of court and church were to have in his reign more apparent importance than under Louis XVIII, and that was to be detrimental to the moral authority of the crown.

To these influences can already be attributed Villèle's ministerial shake-up a few days before the death of Louis XVIII. The Duke of Doudeauville had been appointed minister of the royal household in the place of Lauriston, who was compensated by a marshal's baton; Sosthènes de La Rochefoucauld, son of the new minister, found himself in charge of the bureau of Fine Arts and Letters, which was set up out of the many duties belonging to his father's ministry and was to give him the privilege, long coveted by this intriguing busybody, of working directly with the king. The Bishop of Hermopolis, Mgr. Frayssinous, grand master of the University since 1821, had become minister of ecclesiastical affairs and public instruction. Foreign affairs, remaining without an appointee since the disgrace of Chateaubriand, had been given to Baron de Damas, hitherto minister of war; the insignificance of these ministerial appointees, as inexperienced as possible in administrative affairs, was to allow the president of the council to continue to manage them. Clermont-Tonnerre went from the navy to the war ministry, and to fill the former post, Villèle called upon Count Chabrol de Crouzol, a former prefect and a former director general of lands and registries. "A good man, stiff as a post," Frénilly wrote of him, "and one under whose iron exterior lurked the mildness of a sheep and the weakness of a child." And it could be added: particularly an incorrigible weakness for ministerial office.

This last appointment showed Villèle's tendency to find support from the Right-Center to compensate for the growing opposition which he was encountering from the extreme Right. The same policy was even more noticeable in his reshuffling of personnel in the council of state and in the second level of ministerial appointments. Several men of the Right who had spoken or written against the ministry during the last session lost their administrative posts, which only increased their irritation and that of their friends. The president of the council had had the shrewdness to have the responsibility for these various measures assumed by the now-defunct king. The new reign could then be opened in a general atmosphere of satisfaction and hopefulness; the ministry could rightly congratulate itself on having assured the best of situations for a new reign which, it had been believed a few years before, would bring with it a fatal crisis for the regime.

Charles X, for his part, did all he could to insure favorable public opinion. Right after Louis XVIII's death he told a delegation from the two houses about his determination to observe the Charter faithfully; he granted a wide amnesty to political offenders; and finally, over the objections of Villèle, he decided on lifting the censorship. Promptly the liberal press itself intoned praises for the new king. For several days it was all a cloudless idyl between Charles X and his people.

The generous character of the monarch was shown in another more remarkable way in regard to his cousin, the Duke of Orleans. Louis XVIII distrusted him and had firmly maintained a distance between the older and younger branches of the Bourbon family. Charles X, on the contrary, was profuse in his favors. The duke received the title of royal highness, as did his children and his sister, Mme Adelaide; the young Duke of Chartres was appointed a colonel of a regiment of hussars; and finally the king had an article inserted in the law on the civil list which gave legal sanction to the restoration to the older prince of the remainder of the immense appanage of Philippe-Egalité (his father). We now know how the Orleans prince was to show his gratitude in 1830.

The truce was not to last long. The first disappointment inflicted by the king on his temporary panegyrists was his retention of the Villèle cabinet. On the Right and Left, the enemies of the president of the council had only raised their voices in praise of the king in order to bring down the ministers. "There existed a unique situation in the history of monarchies," Chateaubriand wrote, "the general and complete acquiescence in the new reign, alongside the general and complete opposition to the ministry." Do away with the ministry, and everything would be fine. But why should Charles X get rid of Villèle? Had he not put together this ministry himself? And since then had this man disqualified himself at all? Instead, were they not indebted to him for the way he managed the transition from one reign to the other? And who could replace this precious Villèle who had a ready reply for everybody? And how could one find a way to bolster a viable new combination of such contradictory programs as those of the Right and the Left? So Villèle stayed on, transferring to the new reign the store of resentments with which he had laden the preceding one in its last years.

And it would not be long before he would increase the weight of this burden. On December 2 an ordinance was issued retiring all general officers who, having reached the age limit, had not been on active duty since 1823. Nothing was more normal or justified from the financial point of view. But it was found that the 250 men involved were almost all former officers of the Empire. The liberal press, which had found similar measures just fine when taken by Gouvion-Saint-Cyr a few years before against émigré officers, now cried out in sharp indignation: What! So that's the happy accession gift from the new king to the glorious remnants of the Imperial armies! And for this they choose that date of December 2, the anniversary of Austerlitz. Poor Charles X, all upset by this explosion, did all he could to make up for the blunder by issuing numerous individual exceptions, but it only served to nullify the financial benefits of the measure without repairing the moral damage.

## The Indemnification Bill

The opposition did not fail to class this act along with the bill for the indemnification of the émigrés, which the government was drawing up at the same time and which, in fact, was announced in the speech from the throne at the opening of the parliamentary session on December 22.

Because this measure was presented chronologically at the beginning of the reign of Charles X, it has often been interpreted as an obvious sign of the blind spirit of reaction that they attributed to the new king, as the first departure from the prudent and conciliatory policy of Louis XVIII, as the first concession made by Villèle to the wishes of the Ultra-Royalist majority of the Chambre Retrouvée. Nothing is further from the truth. In fact, this bill corresponded to one of the dearest ideas of Louis XVIII, and it was only because of financial difficulties that its recommendation had been postponed. Villèle himself had not needed to be prodded on this point; the efforts that he had made in the session of 1824 to create the indispensable financial conditions for it, and his irritation at the opposition of the chamber of peers, are proof of it.

In fact, what was involved was not just the interests, certainly very justified, of a category of unfortunate Frenchmen, but, in addition, one of the gravest problems facing the Restoration monarchy—that is, the enormous and awful question of the nationalized lands. A radical solution—and one that could be justified in law—would have been to nullify all the land confiscations of the Revolution and return the estates to their original owners, with the understanding that the new owners, who had purchased the land in good faith, would be indemnified in one way or another. But they were afraid that this would unleash a civil war, and, besides, Louis XVIII had closed this way of escape by proclaiming, on his return to France, the irrevocable character of the Revolutionary property transfers. Another solution might have been to leave it to time, hoping that it would eventually bring an end to the demands of some and calm the alarms of others. But a just consideration for the interests of the dynasty, and indeed for national interests, was not going to permit a resort to such a lazy solution. Louis XVIII in 1814 may very well have bowed to an imperious necessity, but he had always deeply regretted having seemed to trample underfoot the rights of his faithful at the very time he was winning back his own, thanks in part to their devotion. After all, had they not been punished for responding to his call? Could one discourage, even exasperate, those who had been naturally the best supporters of the throne? And what would become of the principle of legitimacy, what would become of Christian and natural morality if property rights were disregarded? With 1814 the injustice of the confiscations had been recognized, since the restitution of the unsold nationalized lands had been decided upon. Could they very well abandon these less-favored landowners just because they had not been as lucky?

To these considerations of principle were added more practical ones. The former landowners could not easily resign themselves to their losses, and the complaints they voiced, often supported by the clergy, stamped these nationalized lands with a sort of moral condemnation which made it hard to sell them and so reduced their value to some extent. Lastly, as long as their situation remained in doubt, the new owners would be uneasy and could not rally wholeheartedly to the regime. By having the old owners accept an indemnity, the ministry would bring an end to their demands, erase all distinctions between nationalized lands and other lands, let the lands return to their normal values, reassure the new holders, open to them the way to a sincere rally to the regime, and thus deprive the enemies of the monarchy of their most likely followers.

The only valid objection which could be raised against this great measure of monarchical and national interest was the difficulty of finding the necessary money without ruining the finances of the government which they had taken such pains to restore. As a result of preliminary investigations the total value of these properties for which they were proposing indemnification did not amount to less than one billion francs. Villèle had brought all the resources of his practical genius to bear on the solution of this problem, and by early 1824 thought he had found a way to do it by refinancing the state bonds. It was an operation of which no one today challenges the legality and which has been resorted to more than once; but at that time it was a rather new thing, and many, not understanding it very well, were even to look upon it as a sort of dishonest transaction. Ever since the consolidation of the public debt under the

Directory, it was represented by hundred-franc bonds at five per cent interest. But in 1824 the quotation of these bonds, which had never gone higher than ninety (in 1807), had risen to par and even above par. Investors were then willing to pay more than a hundred francs for an annual dividend of five francs; which meant that the real money return, as determined by the law of supply and demand, was less than five per cent. Under such conditions there was no reason for the government to assure investors a rate of return detrimental to the taxpayers. It would therefore offer them the following alternative: either they would agree to the government's repurchase of their bonds at a hundred francs (and this was not unfair because more often they had bought them at a lower rate) or, if they wanted to continue to be holders of government bonds, they would be given three per cent bonds at a reduced quotation of seventy-five francs for a bond of a hundred francs face value, or an actual dividend rate of four per cent. Considering the large number of these bonds then in circulation, the budgetary savings on this transaction through lower interest costs would amount to about thirty million francs (six million dollars). This saving came to just about the amount needed to pay three per cent on a billion-franc (200 million dollar) bond issue, and it would be such a bond issue which Villèle proposed to distribute to the émigrés in compensation for their lost lands.

This solution, however clever it was from a financial point of view, involved a serious political inconvenience; that is, it made the old bondholders, mainly Paris bourgeois people, pay to the émigrés the debts owed them by the Revolution and the Monarchy. It was pointed out that these bondholders, mostly people of modest income, did not care much about receiving a premium on their capital investments and only noticed one thing—that their annual dividends were going to be reduced one-fifth. For this reason as well as for others of a more technical nature, the bill providing for the bond conversions had encountered strong opposition in the chamber of deputies and finally had been voted down in the chamber of peers on June 3, 1824 (see Chapter Sixteen).

Villèle had learned his lesson from this setback, and, in the session of 1825, he adopted another strategy aimed at separating the technical from the political aspects of the operation. First he would have the two houses approve the principles of the indemnity and the method of its distribution; after which they could not refuse the financial stipulations to provide the necessary funds.

The first debate therefore began in February 1825 on the bill to create, for the benefit of the former owners of nationalized lands, a billion francs of government bonds bearing three per cent interest. As can be expected, the discussion was long and stormy, and from the halls of the chambers the disputes spilled out over the whole country through the newspapers and a flood of pamphlets. The defenders of the Revolution clashed violently with those of the emigration, rekindling passions which it had been hoped could be extinguished. The speakers on the far Right, La Bourdonnaye in particular, went so far as even to bring in question Article IX of the Charter, which had declared the sale of the nationalized lands to be irrevocable. Louis XVIII, one of them said, had no more right to dispose of émigré property than the émigrés had to dispose of his crown. They tried, by amendments, to give the measure the character of a restitution in strict justice. The Left tried to discredit the bill by emphasizing that too many deputies were personally interested in its passage. Forgetting that a great many Frenchmen had only left their country to save their own lives, they condemned the whole emigration movement during the Revolution as a crime. To these bad Frenchmen they did not owe any compensation because the confiscation had been a just punishment. Thus to them the indemnity would be a fine imposed on France in favor of those who had betrayed her and an insult to the army which, at the same time, they were putting on short allowance.

> Have they the right to punish a whole nation [exclaimed Deputy Méchin] until it has been proven that freedom from land tenure obligations, equality before the law, equality in taxation, and freedom of religion and thought are not appreciable possessions in themselves? Should 29 million Frenchmen have to pay for wanting what 50 thousand spurned?

In the end the Indemnification Law, after a few minor amendments by the chamber of peers, was passed by the chamber of deputies by a vote of 221 to 130.

Although the debate on financing the law was less heated, it was nonetheless intense. But Villèle's bills were finally accepted. Instead of obtaining the needed annual thirty million (six million dollars) from the conversion of government bonds, the minister of finance had provided for a more complex system. Half of the sum was to be furnished by an amortization fund; the other half was to come from the anticipated excess of yields from budgetary collections, particularly from the tax on transactions. In addition, he combined with this a new optional conversion of the five per cent bonds to $4\frac{1}{2}$ per cent. It is impossible here to follow the technical details of all these operations. In the end, according to the account of M. Gain, author of a definitive thesis on the subject, the indemnity for the émigrés was to cost France 25,995,000 francs ($5,199,-000) of government annual dividends at three per cent, representing bonds worth a face value of 866,510,000 ($173,302,000) and, in the light of the average quotation of this issue which in fact remained much below par, worth a real value of about 630 million francs (126 million dollars). So they fell somewhat short of that legendary estimate of a billion francs.

Given the prosperous condition of the country, the treasury easily supported this increase in the public debt. But did this settlement have the hoped-for results? Not entirely. The nationalized lands, freed from the moral mortgage which had depreciated their values, now rose in price, but the increased receipts on the transaction tax did not come up to their expectations. The indemnity did not permit the émigrés to receive back their landed fortunes. As a result of the circumstances of inheritance, there were about seventy thousand eligible for indemnity, and the average share for each one was about 1,377 francs ($275.40) of annual dividend, or 45,000 francs (nine thousand dollars) of bonds at face value, much less in actual fact. Besides, the real individual indemnity was, for the most part far below this average because of some big compensations, such as, for example, that of the Duke of Orleans, which amounted to 12,704,-000 francs ($2,540,800) of bonds. Nevertheless the main result was accomplished: after 1825 there was no longer two kinds of property, two kinds of landowners; there was no longer any material barrier to a real national reconciliation.

Unfortunately, this latter development depended still very much on emotional factors, and on this score the debate on the Indemnification Law was for the moment to widen the gulf between Frenchmen who profited by the Revolution and those who suffered from it. The ministry also did not come off scot-free. Most of the beneficiaries of the indemnification were not appreciative of a compensation they judged to be much lower than what they had lost. The liberal opposition could add to their arsenal the theme of the poor little bondholders fleeced for the benefit of the greedy nobles:

> . . . Sad day, when your dark three per cents
> To dismayed bondholders appeared as a threat
> Disdaining the pain of an outraged France
> And scorning the cries of a rebellious Bourse.

Villéle also lost some of his reputation for cleverness in the partial failure of his financial combinations; and the apparently excessive advantages he offered to the bankers who supported him—Rothschild in particular—made it possible to accuse him of collusion with the world of high finance and to cast undeserved doubts upon his own disinterestedness.

## Two Religious Laws

While the deputies were considering the Indemnification Bill, the chamber of peers was presented with two bills on purely religious matters, one concerning the legal status of congregations (religious orders), the other on sacrilege. There is no doubt that Villèle, in proposing these measures, was motivated less by personal conviction than by the necessity of showing deference to the feelings of the king and to the demands of that part of his majority which was inspired by the ideals of the Knights of the Faith and which amounted to about a hundred votes in the chamber. The reporter of the first of these bills in the chamber of peers was none other than Mathieu de Montmorency himself, the Grand Master of the secret society.

The Concordat of 1801 did not provide for religious orders; yet they had been able to take advantage of the sympathetic toleration of the various governments of the Restoration to re-establish themselves (see Chapter Seventeen). Nevertheless, the absence of legal status caused practical inconveniences. Not enjoying the rights of a corporation, they could only acquire real estate or government bonds through a third party, nor could they receive gifts or bequests. A law passed in January 1817 provided that religious orders could acquire property only if authorized by a legislative act. Did it not practically paralyze the re-establishment of religious orders to require each new foundation to submit to the slow and public parliamentary procedure?

By the month of July 1824 the government had presented to the chamber of peers a bill which gave the king the authority to give legal recognition to these religious orders—and the benefit of the law of 1817—by a simple ordinance approved by the council of state. This bill had been rejected by a majority in the peers, made up not only of a more numerous liberal and Voltairian faction than in the elective chamber since the 1819 batch of appointees, but also of faithful Catholics of the Gallican parliamentary tradition, obsessed by a fear of the Jesuits.

The new bill, presented to the upper house early in 1825, took these fears into account by providing that its terms applied only to women's religious communities. Besides, the freedom of action intended for them was surrounded by restrictive precautions: all property transactions carried out in the name of the religious order should have a ministerial authorization and no nun could give to her religious community more than one-fourth of her personal property.

This still did not seem enough for those who feared that the principle involved in the bill would soon permit its benefits to be extended to men's orders. A brochure by Lamennais, published at the same time, had frankly proclaimed this intention. So the chamber adopted an amendment, proposed by Pasquier, which limited the advantages of the proposed new system to the orders existing on January 1, 1825 and their new houses. As to those to be formed in the future, as well as for all men's religious orders, they could only acquire corporative status by special legislation. Charles X was so upset by this semi-defeat that he wanted to withdraw the bill, but he finally became resigned to it as a lesser evil. It was in this spirit too that it was passed in the chamber of deputies, in spite of the disappointment of the majority. Lamennais was so exasperated that he wrote that the law was going to make "a class of pariahs" out of those in religious orders.

Nor had this same Lamennais failed to pour his dose of extremist passion into the much more important debate which came on next in the chamber of peers on the bill against sacrileges. The motive first brought forward was the disturbing number of thefts of sacred vessels from churches: 538 in four years. However, it was impossible to be fooled by this stated reason. What the majority of the chamber wanted was, as the keeper of the seal said, "a necessary expiation after so many years of indifference and impiety"; it was the first fulfillment of a wish expressed by Bonald: "The Revolution which began by a declaration of the rights of man will end with a declaration of the rights of God." It would be the first breach in the Concordat system which made the church and state two allied but distinct authorities.

> The Catholic religion [wrote Lamennais] ought to be considered true and the others false. It ought to be a part of the country's constitution and thence spread to political and civil institutions.
> Otherwise the state professes indifference toward religion, it exiles God by its laws, it is atheistic.

The bill established a scale of crimes and penalties according to whether the profanation was committed on sacred vessels containing no consecrated elements, on vessels containing the consecrated host, or on the host itself. In the first case the punishment should be forced labor for life; in the second case the death penalty; and in the third case, as in those of parricides, the severing of a hand before the beheading. These provisions, terrible at first sight, were in fact made inoperative by the conditions written into the bill. To be an act of sacrilege, it would, by definition, have to be committed "voluntarily, publicly, and out of hate or scorn for religion." But where had anyone seen such a theft committed "publicly" in a church? And how could it be proved that the deed had been perpetrated "voluntarily, out of hate or scorn for religion?"

This inconsistency was emphasized by the orators of the opposition, especially by Chateaubriand, who said: "The religion which I presented for the veneration of men is a religion of peace which likes to pardon rather than punish, which wins its victories by mercy, and only needs scaffolds for the triumph of its martyrs." The Duke of Broglie expressed the alarm that Protestants might feel over the precedent that could be introduced:

> The freedom of religion relies on the great maxim that among all those questions which divide consciences . . . the legislator will remain, not indifferent, but neutral. Violate this maxim just once, draw the sword just once in support of a purely theological truth, and then the principle of intolerance of consciences, the principle of persecution looms beside you.

On the other side of the argument Bonald, driven by his pitiless logic, uttered some shocking words:

> They object to the death penalty for sacrilege. Let's dare to proclaim here some powerful truths. If the good people owe their lives to society through service, the evil ones owe their lives as examples. Yes, religion commands man to pardon, but requires government to punish. . . . And, besides, by punishing sacrilege, what is done if it is not to send the offender before his natural judge?

Finally a majority of peers were found who would accept the fundamental argument invoked by the reporter, Breteuil: "In order to succeed in having laws respected, we must begin by having religion respected." And the government's bill was passed 127 to 92 with just one change, requested indeed by Bonald, that, instead of the punishment of parricides, honorable amends should be substituted.

In the debates in the chamber of deputies the point of view of the intransigent Catholics were expressed by the deputy of Ille-et-Vilaine, Duplessis de Grénédan, who protested against the ineffectiveness of the law. What would the chamber say, he asked, if it was proposed to punish regicide only if it was committed *voluntarily, publicly, and by hate or scorn of royalty?* The great event in the debates was the speech of Royer-Collard against the bill.

> Not only does it introduce into our legislation a new crime [said the orator] but, what is more extraordinary, it creates a new principle of criminality, a new class of crimes called supernatural. . . . Thus the law again calls into question both religion and civil society, their nature, their purpose, and their respective independence. . . . Are governments the successors to the apostles? They have not received from on high the mission of declaring what is true in matters of religion and what is not.

If dogma was to be embodied into law, he went on, there was no reason to stop here, and we would soon have an absolute theocracy in which the priest would be king. This great fragment of eloquence was unable to change the fate of the bill, which was passed by a vote of 210 to ninety-five; but by its tremendous reverberations outside the chamber it succeeded in making the bill lose favor in public opinion.

As it was easy to predict, the conditions restricting the definition of the crime were so unrealizable that the law was never carried out. Its authors took satisfaction from the thought of having made a striking demonstration in favor of their religion; but how little did they realize that, in associating altars with scaffolds in the process, they were reviving against religion the most baneful memories of the Inquisition!

## A King Is Crowned

From that time forward, in all that the king and his government did in favor of the state religion, people insisted on seeing only the frightening signs of the mysterious and growing influence of ecclesiastical society on civil society. This malicious interpretation was to prevail notably in the case of the coronation of Charles X, which took place on May 29, 1825, immediately after the adjournment of the session of parliament.

Its inspiration, however, was predominantly political; it was in accord with the logic of the regime which had undertaken the task of "rejoining the links in the chain of time." Could the Most Christian King show himself less concerned than Napoleon had been about having his reign consecrated religiously? The coronation of the king had been stipulated in Article LXXIV of the Charter, and Louis XVIII himself at the opening of the session of 1819 had publicly announced his intention of receiving the royal anointing. Although his infirmities had finally obliged him to give up the idea, his successor had no reason for omitting it. The ceremony in Rheims, permitting the whole nation to participate together in a manifestation of monarchical fervor, would mark, by the brilliance of its display, that France finally had emerged from the withdrawal imposed on her by her misfortunes; it would be an act of faith in the grandeur of her new destinies.

That was why nothing was spared to give it the greatest possible splendor. Precautions were also taken not to alarm certain categories of Frenchmen. The Archbishop of Rheims explained, in a pastoral letter, that the royal power had its source in the hereditary right even prior to the coronation; the wording of the oath to be taken by the king had been changed so as to include a mention of the Charter; and such impressions as spoke of the extinction of heresy, which could have offended Protestants, had been removed. Furthermore, in the ceremony they gave a prominent role to representatives of the new France: the marshals Moncey, Soult, Mortier, and Jourdan had been assigned the honors of carrying the insignia of royal power—the sword of the high constable, the scepter, the hand of justice, and the crown. Finally, in addition to a very extensive amnesty for political offenders there was added, for all categories of meritorious service, a generous shower of decorations, cordons, titles, pensions, etc. The ministers, whose job it was to draw up the lists of these awards, had the rare elegance to exclude themselves as well as the members of their families.

The king made his entry into Rheims early in the afternoon of May 28. The immense gilded top of the coronation coach passed first under an almost continuous vault of triumphal arches and flowery streamers which began about a league out of town. From the city's gate to the cathedral the streets were covered with sand and strewn with flowers; the house fronts were hung with tapestries and garlands, "all Parisian in the windows and all Rhemish on the roofs." According to custom the king attended vesper services and a solemn *Te Deum,* and heard a sermon delivered by Cardinal de la Fare, the same one who had preached at the opening of the Estates General of 1789.

On May 29, at the first break of dawn, the crowd of invited officials converged on the old basilica now all hung inside with velvet and silk, shining with chandeliers of candles whose flames reflected in sparkles from the fringes of gold and silver. The royal procession made its entry shortly before eight, preceded by halberdiers in Henry IV gala costumes. The king was dressed in white silk, embroidered in gold, wearing on his head a cap bedecked with plumes and diamonds. First he took the prescribed oaths and received the spurs and sword. After a long prayer, during which he prostrated himself full-length, the archbishop performed the ritual of seven anointings; and then the royal robes and insignia were bestowed upon him. Finally, the archbishop, with the aid of the two highest princes of the blood, placed the crown upon his head. The clergyman's thrice-repeated shout of *Vivat Rex in aeternum* unleashed a joyous roar—the spectators taking up the shout at the top of their lungs. The clergy sang the *Te Deum,* accompanied by the resounding organs and the blaring trumpets, women wept and waved their handkerchiefs, the cathedral doors opened to admit the packed crowds outside, and, beneath the vaulted arches, doves, released at this tense moment, flitted frightened among the clouds of incense. Outside, the guns boomed upon the ramparts, and on the city's squares the troops fired musket salvos. All the bells rang out full peal; in the streets the people shouted themselves hoarse with their acclaims and scrambled for the silver medals which the heralds-at-arms threw out by the fistsful. "The aging Universe dreams of a new golden age reborn," Lamartine was to write.

But all the efforts of official poets, all the celebrations organized by the government, were not to succeed in the end in arousing in the rest of the country the same enthusiasm as in Rheims. The changes in the details of the ceremonies could not surmount the essential fact, only perceived by the general public—this was the resurrection of the Old Regime in one of its most archaic forms and one most charged with religious significance. When the king made his solemn return to Paris on June 6, everybody noted the relative coolness of the people, which contrasted painfully with the exuberance of his welcome the preceding September.

The demogogic pen of Béranger translated this sentiment in his famous song, *Crowning Charles the Simple:*

> At the feet of prelates stitched in gold
> Charles went to his confession.
> They dressed 'im, and kissed 'im, and oiled 'im up,
> Then, to the tunes of sacred hymns,
> He placed his hand on the Bible.
> His confessor told 'im: "Swear!
> Rome, the party here concerned,
> Rises anew from an oath thus sworn."

## An Anticlerical Campaign

This verse is only one example among thousands of the tone assumed at that time by the antireligious controversy. The extent, the violence, and ingeniousness of the attacks, the readiness with which they were greeted—all of these present, as we look back upon it, a disconcerting and even a somewhat humiliating picture for the honor of the French intellectuals.

It is rather difficult to explain it in a satisfactory way. It is not enough just to say it was a normal reaction against the clergy's excessive pretensions and abuses of power, against the mistakes of a regime which used religion for politics as much as politics for religion. The disproportion remains too evident between the real peril and the almost hysterical violence of the counterattack. We are therefore led to suspect that it involved a deliberate scheme of the liberal opposition, and certain admissions uttered later on confirm this explanation. The enemies of the regime, smashed by the elections of 1824, had had to acknowledge that their direct attacks against the dynasty had failed. Charles X having solemnly sworn to respect the Charter and the problem of the nationalized lands having been settled, the main economic and social results of the Revolution had been assured, and there no longer remained any clearcut political questions capable of arousing the passions of the masses. Under such conditions the only recourse left to the opposition was to appeal to the very sensitive attachment of Frenchmen for freedom of thought and expression, to call up the specter of clerical domination aiming at oppressing mind and conscience. Such a line of attack had all sorts of advantages: it made it possible for them to undermine the regime while continually protesting their loyalty to king and Charter; it could even ally itself with a certain respect for religion whose cause was separated from that of its imprudent ministers. It tickled national sensitiveness by appearing to be a defense of the liberties of the venerable Gallican church against Roman interference; and finally it furnished a way to divide the victorious royalists, because, if part of them equated the defense of altar with that of throne, others among them remained faithful to the Voltairian spirit or the parliamentary Gallicanism of the eighteenth century.

With this orientation the campaign made amazing progress in the course of the years between 1825 and 1830, using every means to influence opinion, such as cartoons, songs, satirical poems, pamphlets, plays, newspapers, coffee house remarks, and public demonstrations. Coins were circulated on which Charles X was represented in Jesuit garb and Louis XVIII as a clerical canon. A society made a generous distribution of the works of Voltaire, Rousseau, and other irreligious authors of the eighteenth century. Disturbances were organized by students in the churches where revivalist missionaries were preaching; they hurled firecrackers and stink bombs at them and poured ink in the holy water fonts. In Lyons, Rouen, and Brest such incidents degenerated into regular riots which had to be put down by troops. The play *Tartuffe,* in demand everywhere, furnished occasions for antireligious demonstrations. It was also their good luck when some famous man died such as Talma, who had refused the last rites and could be taken to the cemetery in a triumphal procession without a church service but with the customary funeral oration by a prominent liberal at the graveside.

Some themes, some favorite subjects supplied this concert. First of all, it was the intolerance of the clergy, which gave them a chance on every occasion to recall the Inquisition, Galileo, the Saint-Bartholomew massacre, and the dragoonings of Louis XIV. The *Constitutionnel* had a special column in which it reported innumerable little incidents, some real, some exaggerated, and others even simply invented. Such accounts told of Protestant children taken from their parents and put in Catholic institutions, of excitable girls entering convents against their fathers' will but in obedience to their confessors, of sacraments refused, of Protestants and Jansenists persecuted, of teachers dismissed on the request of the parish priests, of confession slips required of poor people and workers, of books burned as impious, of students expelled from colleges for not having shown enough devotion, of false miracles revealed, of ridiculous practices. But they were always careful to present all of these in such a vague way that no verification or denial could be made.

Also cautiously—for fear of libel suits—they insinuated doubts about the morals of the clergy. Here is a typical example taken from the *Constitutionnel:* "Brother Redon [a Lazarist missionary] who was director of singing at Crouy, had first tried out ten-year-old girls but their voices broke; then he tried out fifteen-year-olds, but their voices were not yet developed enough; now he has those aged eighteen and seems to be quite satisfied." The *Frondeur,* reviewing the crimes of the previous week, called its article "a weekly sketch of the moral example given to us by all those who follow the Jesuitical ethics."

Ultramontanism (Roman predominance) was another popular theme, and the exaggerations of Lamennais never failed to raise the hackles of the Gallicans. One of the latter, the lawyer Dupin, hit upon this famous remark in 1825: "Our present-day Pharisees are devising our tortures. Feel the slashes of the sword whose hilt is at Rome and whose point strikes in all directions!"

The theme of clerical influence in the government crystalized in about 1825 in the myth of the Congregation and a priest party. They were imagined to be a secret society, spreading everywhere its network of affiliated local units and aiming at the destruction of the Charter and its replacement by a theocracy. "It has jobs, funds, awards," wrote Alexis Dumesnil, "everything is lavished on those who express a desire to join;

they seduce and corrupt right up to the steps of the throne." In the provinces the Congregation was accused of forming an inner circle to threaten the judges, commanders, prefects, and mayors. In Paris it was claimed that it dominated the ministry and the court, and in the chamber its members totaled about a hundred. The legend could seem to be easily substantiated because the Congregation was very much alive (see Chapter Seventeen). That they might attribute a political influence to it is rather natural if one recalls the existence of the Knights of the Faith and the fact that several of the society's leaders were known as members of the Congregation.

Nothing contributed more toward creating this confusion than the pamphlet published at the end of February 1826 under the curious title of *Mémoire à consulter sur un système religieux et politique tendant à renverser la religion, la société et le trône* (*Memoir to Be Consulted on a Religious and Political System Tending to Overturn Religion, Society, and Throne*). The author was the Count of Montlosier, an old Auvergnat gentleman, known up to then as a pillar of aristocratic reaction. That such a personage threw himself into the anticlerical campaign showed the effectiveness of the new liberal tactics. So, disregarding his antecedents, they showered him with their bouquets, acclaimed him as the "Tirésias of Auvergne," and contrived to make every possible use of this new ally. The "system" revealed by Montlosier had four aspects: the Congregation, the Jesuits, Ultramontanism, and priestly meddling.

The public excitement aroused by this pamphlet and by others caused the minister of ecclesiastical affairs, Mgr. Frayssinous, to make a public statement on the religious policy of the government. In May 1826, in a long speech, he tried to destroy the myths created by this propaganda by using some facts. How could they claim, for example, that the education of youth had been turned over to the Jesuits when they only directed seven small seminaries out of a total of one hundred, and besides that there were eighty-six royal colleges, sixty communal colleges, and eight hundred private schools where there was not a shadow of a Jesuit? No matter, they only remembered one passage in his speech—that was where he had acknowledged the existence of the Congregation and especially of the Jesuits, whose presence had been illegal in France since the reign of Louis XV.

Henceforth the fire of the anticlerical controversy concentrated especially on the Jesuits. Anything religious which could arouse their distrust was attributed to the Jesuits, such as revival missions, congregations, brotherhoods, the Society for the Propagation of the Faith, Ultramontanism, sentimental devotions, etc. Laymen devoted to the church were called "Jesuits in short coats," devout women and nuns were called "Jesuitesses." The *Journal des Débats* asserted that "the ministry had only one object in mind, the re-establishment of an order (Jesuit) whose stormy career is bracketed between the Jean Châtel pyramid and the Damiens scaffold, an order whose clamors resounded among the factious clamors of the Sixteen, the groans of the dragoonings, and the orgies of Mme du Barry." Stendhal wrote in May 1826: "One would think today that the genius of the nation had nothing else to do but make fun of the Jesuits." Along this line they did not hesitate to circulate the most enormous absurdities. They printed that at Montrouge, at the novitiate of the Company, the young Jesuits were taught to stab the enemies of their order, that they gathered arms for a new Saint-Bartholomew of patriots, and that they practiced firing cannon underground! Montlosier followed up his first success by issuing in July 1826 a *Dénonciation aux cours royales relativement au système religieux et politique* (*Report to the Royal Courts on the Religious and Political System*), already pointed out in his *Mémoire à Consulter,* and then by a *Pétition à la Chambre des Pairs* on the same subject, which led the judiciary and the upper house to declare the illegality of the Jesuits in France.

Béranger issued his famous song on the "Reverend Fathers":

> Men in black, whence come you forth?
> We issue from the nether world,
> Half foxes and half wolves.
> Our rules are a mystery,
> We're the sons of Loyola.
> You know why they exiled us,
> Now we're back, and you'd better be quiet!
> And see that your children go to our schools.
>
> . . . . . . . . . . . . . .
>
> A pope abolished us
> And he died of the colic.
> A pope re-established us,
> And of his bones we'll make relics.
>
> . . . . . . . . . . . . . .
>
> Our missionaries are all
> Traveling salesmen promoting our business.
> The Capuchins are our Cossacks,
> They're training to take over Paris.
>
> . . . . . . . . . . . . . .
>
> And now acknowledge us
> To souls already seduced.
>
> . . . . . . . . . . . . . .

We are, we are the Jesuits!
Frenchmen, may you all tremble,
as we bless you!

Charles X, much grieved, witnessed this outpouring so incompre-
hensible to him. The more religion was attacked, the more he thought
he should show his devotion openly. So, when the Jubilee of 1825 was
extended to France in 1826 and the Archbishop of Paris had called for
public processions, the king insisted on joining them on foot, a candle
in his hands, surrounded by his family and representatives of the governmental branches. Since he was dressed in violet, the color of mourning for the kings of France, it gave birth to the rumor that he had been
ordained as a bishop and said Mass secretly in the Tuileries!

## The Bills on Primogeniture and Press

Extremely unpopular with public opinion and hopelessly on the defensive on the religious questions, the ministry encountered in the session
of 1826 other serious defeats on political and parliamentary questions.

The royalist majority in the chamber of deputies had pushed the
government to propose a bill to modify the provisions of the civil code
on the subject of inheritances in such a way as to check the trend toward
the endless splitting up of large estates and thus to consolidate the position
of the rural aristocracy. It was this very idea which had inspired Napoleon
to favor the institution of entailed properties. According to the code, the
father of a family had the right to increase the share of one of his children by bequeathing to him a legal extra share (*préciput légal*) or dis-
posable share (*quotité disponible*); but, in actual fact, very few people
made use of this option. All the government's bill did was to reverse the
optional provisions of the code. Henceforth, to have an equal distribution
of the father's property among his children, he would have to provide for
it specifically in his will or else the extra share would go automatically
to his oldest son. In a word, optional before, inequality became the general rule, and equality, no longer automatic, became optional. This was
as far as the bill went, which the opposition was to portray as a return
to the right of primogeniture. Its application was further limited by the
fact that its provisions were only supposed to apply to landed property
paying at least three hundred francs (sixty dollars) in direct taxes, that
is, to about eighty thousand families out of a national total of six million.

In other words the ministry, by this halfway bill, hoped to ingratiate
itself with two opposite attitudes: to satisfy the formal wishes of a part

of its majority and mollify the opposition that it sensed coming from public opinion. The angry public reaction was way beyond its anticipation. Newspapers and pamphlets denounced this in frightful terms as a return to the Old Regime, as a barefaced assault upon modern society. The *Constitutionnel* explained with a straight face that the bill had been inspired by the Jesuits who wanted to fill up the religious houses with younger sons and daughters who would have to enter because of a lack of any other way of subsisting.

The bill was presented first in the chamber of peers where it was the occasion for a long and important debate, from March 11 to April 8, 1826. The more talented men of the opposition—Molé, Pasquier, Roy, Barante, Decazes, Siméon, and Cornudet—lined up all the conceivable arguments against this change in the civil code. The final blow was struck by the Duke of Broglie, who raised the level of the debate by attacking less the rather harmless provisions of the bill than the intentions behind it.

> This law [he said], is not a law, but a declaration of principles . . . a manifesto against the present state of society. . . . The right of primogeniture is the foundation of inequality of status, it is privilege, pure, absolute, undisguised, and unrelieved. . . . It is inequality of status for its own sake. . . . What is here under consideration is a social and political revolution, a revolution against the Revolution, which took place here in France forty years ago.

The upper house finally defeated the bill by 120 to 94. This decision was greeted with extraordinary enthusiasm; the liberal press thanked the peers for having saved France from an "antisocial" law. In the streets there were noisy demonstrations, illuminations, and firecrackers as if celebrating the news of a great victory.

For two years the government had found itself under fire from an ever livelier and disloyal controversy, and all its efforts to contain these attacks had been ineffective. Indeed it was practically disarmed: it did not dare reimpose censorship—besides, the king would not hear of it. The great papers of the opposition were not for sale. The 43,000 subscribers of the liberal press plus the six thousand of the papers of the rightist counteropposition crushed by their very weight the fourteen thousand subscribers that the government press could barely muster. The judges, especially, who could have constrained the publicists toward more moderation by convictions *post factum,* let themselves be influenced, by their desire to play for popularity, to show a systematic indulgence toward journalists. Thus, when the government, at the end of 1825, had preferred charges in the royal court in Paris against the *Constitutionnel* and the *Courrier français* for attacks on the state religion, the court had acquitted the two papers on grounds tantamount to a slap at the government, and this had greatly increased the audacity of the opposition. It was to avoid a similar embarrassment that they had decided not to prosecute the Montlosier pamphlet.

After the legislative setbacks in 1826 it appeared difficult to govern indefinitely against the dominant opinion of the press and the people of Paris. The king, his ministers, and their majority in the chamber could well have come to the conclusion that they had taken the wrong road and that it was time to change their policies. But the way they saw it— and is it surprising?—the opposition was wrong, and if opinion supported it, this opinion had been corrupted by the lies in the press.

So if the papers were the cause of all this trouble, if censorship was not wanted, if existing laws were not sufficient to make them behave, then there should be a new law. Villèle was doing the same as the bad doctor who treated the fever without trying to cure its organic causes.

The bill presented to the chamber of deputies on December 29, 1826 by the keeper of the seal, Peyronnet, was drawn up in two parts, because they wanted to deal with not only papers but also pamphlets and brochures of all kinds which were as harmful as, or more so than, the papers themselves.

All non-newspaper publications were to be deposited at the book control office at least five days before printer's release; in this way the police could have them seized if they seemed subversive. Besides, those writings of less than five printed sheets—the most dangerous they thought—would have to pay a one-franc (twenty cent) stamp for the first sheet, plus ten centimes (two cents) for each subsequent sheet. Finally all infractions were to be severely punished, the least irregularity bringing a fine of three thousand francs (six hundred dollars) and the confiscation of the whole edition.

As to newspapers and other periodicals, the tax would be ten centimes (two cents) for every sheet of thirty square centimeters and one centime (.2 cents) for every additional square decimeter. No periodical paper or magazine could be founded without an advanced declaration of the identity of its owners, whose names should be printed at the top of each number, and joint ownership could not be more than five persons. The law, having a retroactive effect, would give the existing periodicals thirty days to comply. The penalties in the previous law for press infractions would be considerably increased, and the prosecutions would be henceforth against the owners themselves and no longer against the editors who had previously shielded them.

At the very announcement of these Draconian provisions, Casimir Périer cried out: "Better to propose just one article suppressing printing in France in favor of Belgium!" The entire opposition, of both Left and Right, exploded in indignant protests. Lamennais (right) called the bill "a unique monument of hypocrisy and tyranny." And Chateaubriand called it a "vandal law." The printers and booksellers of Paris, among others that of the *Moniteur,* published a petition claiming that inevitable ruin of all publishing houses and great distress for hundreds of families would result. The French Academy itself, on the proposal of Lacretelle and Michaud, voted a protest appeal to the king. The keeper of the seal tried to defend his proposal in an article in the *Moniteur;* by an unbelievable blunder he called it a "law of justice and love." The opposition pounced on the expression, and it was to serve henceforth as an ironic designation of the bill.

The general protest from public opinion intimidated the government majority in the chamber, and the committee appointed by it amended the bill seriously, easing its fiscal aspect and softening the originally planned regulations on almost all points. But that diminished not at all the ardor of the opposition, and the debate between February 13 and March 12 was to remain in the parliamentary annals as one of the most memorable of that day. All of the arguments for or against freedom of the press were brought out and repeated over and over again by forty-six different opposition orators and the thirty-two government supporters. In this flood of eloquence they were to remember especially the speech of Royer-Collard, which can still be considered as one of the high points of eloquence even today.

> According to the thinking in the law [he said with haughty sarcasm] there was an oversight on the great day of creation by letting man out, free and intelligent, into the universe; from this issued evil and error. A higher wisdom comes to repair the mistakes of Providence, restrict his imprudent liberality, and render a wisely mutilated humanity the service of raising it finally to the happy innocence of brutes! . . . Intellectual progress comes not just from books. Originating in a free environment, it thrives on work, wealth, and leisure; urban concentrations and travel facilities sustain it. To subjugate men, you must disperse and impoverish them; poverty is the guarantee of ignorance. Believe me, you must reduce the population, send men from industry back to the soil, burn the factories, fill in the canals, plow under the main roads. If you don't do all that, you will have done nothing. If the plow does not turn under the whole of civilization, what is left will be enough to undo all your efforts.

Along with this majestic harangue, to be fair, we should present the point of view of the government. We find it in a peroration of the keeper of the seal (minister of justice), which certainly was not unworthy of that of his adversary. Benjamin Constant had just imagined what he would do if, as a minister, he had had the intention of stifling the press.

> I also wonder [said Peyronnet] what I myself would do if I had decided to prepare and bring on gradually new agitations in my country. Here is just what I would do. Not daring at first to attack the throne openly, I would attack religion, on which the throne is supported; I would make it look as if it were superstitious, ambitious, and oppressive. Intolerant and persecuting just toward it alone, I would reproach it with lacking tolerance and charity; I would call up old quarrels that are no longer understood. . . . If I saw some men around the throne, if not outstanding for their services, at least deserving of goodwill in principle and of the esteem of good people, I would want them to lose that good-will and that esteem so that their courage would become at least powerless. If I did not succeed in tiring them out or making them falter, I would shower them with disgust and I would beat them down with injustices. If the country was prosperous, I would talk of nothing but distress; if the people were making a comfortable living, I would prove to them that they were poverty-stricken. I would teach the people how to throw off the restraints of the law; I would bring them around to the point of view, in the words of another speaker, that resistance can become a sort of point of honor. And when I would have done all of that, Gentlemen, what do you think of it? Would it be time to bring such activities to a halt? Do we always have to heed those who would say: "Let them say and do as they please!"

Galvanized by these words, the majority closed its ranks around the ministry and passed the law by a vote of 233 to 134. If it is recalled that in April 1824 this same chamber had only twenty outright leftist opponents, it can be easily seen how much ground had been lost since. What was perhaps even more serious, the two oppositions of the extreme Right and the Left had used the same arguments, and the debates had created a sort of solidarity among their representatives.

When the bill was later sent to the chamber of peers, the latter appointed a committee made up of men opposed to it, and they began to turn the bill upside down. Seeing this, the government resigned itself to the withdrawal of the bill. Once again there was general rejoicing; and once again the ministry and its majority had aroused animosity of opinion against itself without obtaining the least concrete result in return.

## Trouble with the Paris National Guard

Some days later the king had the opportunity to see this for himself. At the suggestion of Marshal Oudinot, commander of the Paris National Guard, Charles X had decided to review the capital's militia, something he had not done since his accession. His ministers, who had not been consulted, were apprehensive lest there might be hostile manifestations. Nevertheless, the papers having announced the coming event, they felt to avoid the ordeal would be an admission of weakness. Every precaution was taken for the safety of the sovereign, even the opposition papers gave out the word to remain calm.

So on the scheduled day, April 29, the king proceeded to the Champs-de-Mars where, awaiting him, were twenty thousand national guardsmen, drawn up in battle formation before an immense crowd of spectators. There was plenty of cheering, but in the ranks of some legions, along with cries of *Long Live the King!* were others such as *Long Live Freedom of the Press! Long Live the Charter! Down with the Ministers! Down with the Jesuits!* Once the king turned his horse toward one man, who had broken ranks to be heard better, and told him sternly: "I came here to receive homage and not lectures." In spite of it all, since he had feared it would be much worse, the king left with a feeling of relief. One legion of the national guard, on its way back from the review, passed in front of the ministry of finance and loudly jeered the prime minister. Villèle, furious, persuaded the king to take immediate and exemplary measures in order to safeguard his dignity. That very evening an ordinance was issued dissolving the whole Paris national guard, and during the night all their duty posts were taken over by troops of the regular army.

Certainly they could not let the insolent incident go unnoticed, but it was a clumsy mistake to punish the whole corps for the actions of a few—whose number amounted to only five per cent according to the best estimates. For all of those who had gone to the expense of buying new outfits for the review, it meant a considerable financial loss; but especially the dissolution was an official indication to the whole Paris bourgeoisie that it was considered to be among the enemies of the regime. Certain ministers had seen this implication and had protested against the clumsy harshness of the measure, but Villèle refused to listen. The Duke of Doudeauville, minister of the royal household, resigned rather than be associated with such a stupid action. Here and there, in the Paris store windows, could be seen national guard uniforms with signs reading: "Uniform for sale—without weapons." In fact the weapons were to find a ready use—at the end of July 1830.

## The Downfall of the Villèle Ministry

The parliamentary session of 1827 closed on June 22 in an atmosphere of irritation and general uneasiness. Two days later censorship was reimposed. It was the government's reply to the chamber of peers' refusal to pass the press bill. Bonald, appointed as chairman of the press surveillance council, justified the measure in these words: "Censorship is a sanitary precaution to protect society from the contagion of false doctrines, just like measures taken to prevent the spread of the plague."

Chateaubriand promptly announced the founding of a Society of Friends of the Freedom of the Press, which was to receive funds from both the liberal opposition and the extreme Right counteropposition and fill the void of enforced silence on the newspapers by a whole series of brochures. He exhorted all the enemies of the ministry to take advantage of a law, just passed, which allowed the voters to check the voting lists whose composition had up to then been left largely to the arbitrary action of the prefects. For this special task another society was formed with the title of God Helps Those Who Help Themselves, and Guizot was its organizer. In a few months it succeeded in restoring fifteen thousand names to the voting lists.

In fact it seemed to everybody that the ministry was at the end of the road and that it could with difficulty face another session without taking some extreme measures. Castellane noted in his *Journal,* on October 1, 1827: "M. de Villèle has just as many supporters as the plague would have if it distributed pensions." The liberal opposition had more than regained the ground lost between 1820 and 1824. Above all, the royalists, so strongly united when they were in the opposition, were now deeply divided. The counteropposition from the Right, originally made up of a few disappointed ambitious men, like La Bourdonnaye, was gradually reinforced by various elements. In the chamber of deputies up to 1825 the Knights of the Faith "banner" had maintained a certain cohesion on the Right, but early in 1826 the founders of the society, Montmorency and Bertier, unhappy with the way Villèle was using it, had decided on its dissolution. After this the frittering away of the rightist majority went on at a faster rate, and its results were seen in the vote on the press law. No doubt it would have been possible for Villèle to disarm some of these opponents by giving them government positions where they would have obviously learned to behave or by simply buying them off. Several times the question of recalling Mathieu de Montmorency to the ministry came up, but Villèle would not have it, and he had adroitly maneuvered to sidetrack him by appointing him as tutor to the Duke of Bordeaux early in 1826. But Montmorency was to die suddenly in March of the same year. Instead of looking for support from strong and independent men, Villèle always seemed to be constricting the moral bases of his power by eliminating or alienating anyone of any distinction. His resentments were shown in petty persecutions, and his clever finesse often degenerated into duplicity. His foreign policy, devoid of grandeur, humiliated national pride, making it appear as if France were being taken in tow by England. Even his reputation as a financier was shaken: the economic crisis, by decreasing the tax collections, caused a budget deficit of 38 million ($7,600,000) in 1827 and compromised the success of his too-ingenious schemes for handling government bonds. At court they openly criticized him, and the king, to whom they repeatedly asserted that the unpopularity of his minister was hurting the crown, began to lose that confidence that he had previously had in the resourcefulness of his "dear Villèle."

Under the circumstances, the more dignified and at the same time shrewder decision for the ministry would have been to retire voluntarily and leave to its opposition the job of producing the experimental proof of their inability of governing any better than it could. But Villèle—and should he be blamed for a weakness so common to statesmen?—hung on to power, sincerely convincing himself that he was irreplaceable, and he was encouraged in this by his job-holders, who had everything to lose by a change. The king allowed himself to be easily convinced that a change in his government while it was under fire would be a confession of weakness on his part. There was nothing to gain, he thought, from making concessions to the "factions"; only unflinching firmness on his part could "force them to make some." A trip he made in the north in September, in the course of which the people could not have given him a better welcome, confirmed him in the idea that he was strong enough to hold out against a misled opposition, and he finally determined to uphold Villèle against all comers.

Every imaginable measure was to encounter the opposition of the chamber of peers—as experience had proved. So it was especially necessary to change its majority, as Decazes had done in 1819. But where else could they find new peers except among the loyal deputies of the majority? They would then have to fill these vacated seats, about forty, at least, through by-elections. Yet time seemed to be working in favor of the opposition; would it not be better to take it by surprise and try to obtain another favorable majority in a new legislature with a seven-year term? Villèle perhaps also calculated that, faced with a strengthened liberal opposition, the dissident royalists would feel obliged to soft-pedal their old resentments and rally around the throne—and the ministry.

The *Moniteur* of November 6, 1827 published three ordinances. The first appointed seventy-six new peers, among whom were forty deputies and five archbishops: "the Congregation's honors list" was what it was called. The second dissolved the chamber and called for new elections on November 17 and 24. The third lifted the censorship, as the law of 1822 required for election periods.

This coup did not take the opposition by surprise. Everywhere the election committees were on the job, and the God Helps Those Who Help Themselves society showed the voters how to get around the prefects' maneuvers. The Right and Left opposition in many places presented the same slate of candidates. The district colleges, voting first on November 17, gave 195 seats to the opposition and only eighty-three to the government; in Paris the number of liberal votes increased from 3,522 of 1824 to 6,500 out of a total of 7,800 voters. The government, now thoroughly frightened, tried to make a last-minute deal with the rightist opponents. The street celebrations in the capital, at first just good-natured, degenerated into violence when certain hot-headed elements began to break the windows of those who did not illuminate. A few barricades were erected in the poorer sections of the center of the city and the troops had to intervene, causing a few people to be killed and wounded. The Liberals, in an effort to disavow their own responsibility, claimed that these disturbances were maneuvers by the "priest party," in an effort to scare voters in the second round of elections. The big (departmental) colleges, more conservative, gave 110 seats to the government and some fifty to the opposition. In the end, at first sight, the new chamber was to show only 150 to 180 Villèle royalists against an almost equal number of liberals and about sixty to eighty counteropposition royalists.

A ministerial change was inevitable, unless they wanted to depart from the constitution. Charles X had decided on having a new government as early as December 6, but it was delayed for another month by the difficulty in finding a workable combination. Each one of the three main groups—independent royalists, Villèlists, and leftists—were subdivided into two or three shades of opinion, and intrigues and negotiations went on and on in a confusion which added to the hesitations of the king. Villèle took advantage of the delays to sound out all the parties in the hope of staying in power in spite of everything. Finally, for lack of a better solution, he settled for the formation of a team of second-rate men who would continue his policy, but he was very disappointed when the prospective appointees, on being approached, made as a condition of their acceptance the elevation of Villèle to the peerage, that is, his exile from active politics. The *Moniteur* of January 5, 1828 announced the names of the new ministry, and Villèle went into retirement filled with bitterness.

Certainly he did not deserve the insults heaped upon him by the hatred of the opposition, and posterity has done justice to his administrative talents. There remains just the same, on his debit side, one undeniable fact: the position of the monarchy, excellent in 1824, had become a subject of concern in 1827. No doubt he was not the only one to be blamed for this unpopularity; but, after all, he had been the helmsman, and the confidence the king had continued to give him was anything but an extenuating circumstance. Outside of the faux-pas which have already been noted, there are three fundamental mistakes which explain his downfall. The first was lending his support to certain reactionary measures demanded by a part of his majority, measures which he himself considered to be baneful. With a little more directness and a little less fondness for power he could have forced them to make a choice between his resignation or their submission. The second mistake was not finding ways to prevent the split within the royalist group. A little more magnanimity and a few jobs given to the right people would at least have been able to attenuate the seriousness of the split. The third mistake was to minimize the force of ideas and feelings, to have confused good politics with good administration, to have thought that to govern all he had to do was to see that he had the support of the constitution, the king, and the chamber and to have neglected to court that power which is sovereign in a representative system—public opinion.

# 20

✣ ✣ ✣ ✣ ✣

# *Foreign Policy, 1824-1829*

THE foreign policy of the Villèle government had also contributed much to his unpopularity and furnished the opposition some of its most strident themes of complaint. We have already seen that Chateaubriand had wanted France to play an active and prominent role, flattering to national pride, even to the extent of opening itself to criticism by its audacity. Villèle, from a love of peace as much as from faint-heartedness, was to bring back foreign policy into the paths of mediocrity and passivity.

His fundamental conceptions of policy are found rather well expressed in a letter he wrote in 1827 to Polignac, then France's ambassador to London:

> We are not strong enough either to challenge England on the sea or to take on the formidable alliance now dominating the continent. What should we do in such a situation? Defend our honor and safety against all comers if they ever tried to assail them; but give up any pretension of imposing on others orders which we are not in a position to enforce. . . . With this kind of conduct, uninspiring but safe, maintain as long as possible the general peace of which we have such need. . . .

In fact this prudence, under the existing circumstances, was going to take on all the aspects of a willing submission to the dictates of British policy, directed since the death of Castlereagh in 1822 by the imperious George Canning.

## *England, the Spanish Colonies, and Portugal*

France's intervention in Spain had been carried out over the protests of England. Canning had immediately taken advantage of the fall of Chateaubriand to chalk up a few points of his own. The logic of the Alliance system, with which France had become associated, would require that the European governments lend their assistance to the King of Spain in order to restore to his authority the Spanish-American colonies which had declared their independence. But the government of the United States had clearly indicated in December 1823 by the Monroe Doctrine that it would not tolerate an intervention of this kind. Chateaubriand, in consultation with Russia, had tried to find a solution which would give Spain some satisfaction in principle and avoid letting the new states pass under the exclusive influence of the Anglo-Saxon powers. Villèle hastened to give short shrift to the plans of the tsar and Metternich by declaring on June 18, 1824 that he would in no wise give France's support to the policy of the Great Alliance. Thenceforth, sure of France's neutrality, Canning officially recognized the new republics, thereby giving them England's moral and financial support and obtaining in return the possibility of a British monopoly of this vast South American market.

Villèle's pacifism was also exploited fully by Canning in the affairs of Portugal. In this country there was also a liberal faction opposing an absolutist group led by the crown prince Dom Miguel. The attempt of this prince to impose his will on his weak father, John VI, had failed in April 1824. Besides, Portugal had not been able to prevent Brazil's declaration of independence under the scepter of the oldest son of the king, Dom Pedro, who had remained in Rio when John VI had returned to Europe. Early in 1824 the French ambassador, Hyde de Neuville, had offered John VI the support of French occupation troops in Spain, which would have allowed the king to send his own army to Brazil. The followers of Dom Miguel hoped very much to take advantage of this to overthrow the constitutional government, and, profiting by the sympathetic attitude of the absolutist Spanish government, they were already infiltrating across the border into Portugal and fomenting disorders there.

Canning reacted vigorously. He let Villèle know that the entrance of French troops into Portugal would be considered a *casus belli* by England, and at the same time, basing his policy on old alliance treaties, he announced the dispatch of a corps of English troops to Portugal. Villèle once more showed his desire for peace by recalling Hyde de Neuville (in December 1824), and under pressure from England John VI recognized the independence of Brazil in May 1825. The death of the old king in March 1826 could have reversed the whole situation. England intervened between Lisbon and Rio, and Dom Pedro, Emperor of Brazil, renounced his rights to the Portuguese throne in favor of his eldest daughter, Dona Maria, who was to marry her uncle, Dom Miguel, when she became of marriageable age. In the meantime—she was only seven years old!—her aunt would be regent. Dom Miguel, impatient to take the throne, began his intrigues, supported by Ferdinand VII of Spain and the French ambassador, the Marquis of Moustier. Canning went to Paris and saw Villèle, persuading him to send severe instructions to Moustier. Nevertheless the Miguelist filibustering forces, organized in Spain, crossed the border at the end of November. Villèle immediately recalled his ambassador, and Canning sent to Lisbon ten thousand men whose very presence would make the absolutist plans fail.

The English minister proudly trumpeted his triumph in a speech delivered in December 1826 in the house of commons:

> Contemplating Spain . . . I resolved that if France had Spain, it should not be Spain "with the Indies" [colonies]. I called the New World into existence to redress the balance of the Old. . . . While I leave France to carry her burden . . . , I know that if . . . this country enters a war . . . she will see under her banners . . . all the discontented and restless spirits of the age, all those who—whether justly or unjustly—are dissatisfied with the present state of their own countries. . . . There exists a power to be wielded by Great Britain more tremendous than was perhaps ever yet brought into action. . . . The situation of this country may be compared to that of the Ruler of the Winds.
> ". . . *Celsa sedet Aeolus arce*
> *Sceptra tenens . . .*"
> ("Aeolus sits in his lofty citadel, holding his sceptre . . . [*Aeneid*, 1:56-57].")

This undisguised appeal to the liberal and national forces which were simmering in Europe aroused the greatest irritation in the cabinets of the Alliance. In France people remembered especially the insulting remarks about her. "Never has France been so grievously outraged," wrote the *Quotidienne*. "M. Canning has tried to tarnish the glory of our arms, and yet M. de Villèle is his ally, M. de Villèle remains silent." Chateaubriand in the chamber of peers answered Canning's attack in splendid and haughty terms. As for Villèle, he limited himself to having Baron de Damas read a rather colorless declaration in which he recognized England's right to intervene in Portugal. Canning, who was very fearful of a Paris reaction, was astounded at such submissiveness: "Damas is a saint, and Villèle an angel," he wrote to his ambassador without a smile.

## The Powers and the Greek Insurrection

In the Portuguese affair Villèle was opposed only by the rightist opposition because the liberals were happy to see a defeat inflicted upon the absolutist parties of the peninsula. On the other hand, in the Greek question the leftist opposition came out against Villèle's policy from the start, and it was only somewhat later that it was to be joined on the issue by the counteropposition on the Right.

The Greeks had risen up in March 1821 against the sultan's domination, and their first clash had succeeded in driving out or massacring the Turkish garrisons in the Peloponnesus and Attica. But these successes had not been followed up. Divisions among the Greeks, the intervention of the Egyptian army, and the nonintervention of the European powers were to leave them by 1826 in desperate straits. The Greek executive council, which had been set up in 1822 under the presidency of Alexander Mavrocordato, was dominated by religious and bourgeois elements; it was the focus of the ever-growing hostility of the rude mountain fighters of the Peloponnesus and of the Aegean pirates, who more often were waging their own war, holding for ransom friend and foe alike. The rivalry between the two parties, which was to grow into a veritable fratricidal war, paralyzed the Greek resistance against the Turkish counteroffensive. Sultan Mahmoud had appealed to his powerful vassal, the Pasha of Egypt, Mohammed Ali, who had organized, with the help of French officers in his service, a European type of army, with good artillery, and an excellent navy. In July 1824 an Egyptian army, commanded by Ibrahim Pasha, the eldest son of Mohammed Ali and a brilliant warrior, landed in Crete and took the island, which had been offered by the sultan as his reward. Then in March 1825 Ibrahim invaded the Morea (Peloponnesus), established its base of operations at Navarino, took over Tripolitsa, and began to ravage the countryside systematically, tracking down the guerrillas with mobile columns and deporting and killing the helpless civilians. At the same time a powerful Turkish army, commanded by Reshid Pasha, attacked the mainland of Greece and laid siege to Missolonghi. The fall of this citadel in April 1826, after a heroic defence, seemed to sound the knell of Greek independence.

Up to this point the European powers had remained practically motionless in the face of the unrolling drama. Tsar Alexander, the natural protector of the Orthodox Christians of the Balkans, was restrained in his inclination to intervene by his fear of encouraging European revolutionary movements and by the opposition of Metternich. As for England, she was just as anxious to keep good relations with Constantinople as to avoid any Russian intervention into the Balkans.

And France? Certainly, as a great Mediterranean power, she could not remain indifferent to events. But up to 1824 the combination of foreign and domestic problems had completely militated against any action in the area. From 1822 to 1824, as we have seen, Spanish affairs had absorbed all her attention, and her absolute need to have Russian and Austrian support had obliged her to conform to their views in the Near East. Furthermore, the liberal party having ardently embraced the cause of the insurgents—for reasons not exclusively humanitarian—the royalist government, which had just had to contend with the dangerous attempts of the Charbonnerie at home, were naturally inclined to consider the revolt of the Greeks as one case of a vast liberal and national movement agitating Germany, Italy, and Spain at the same time.

Only in 1824, once the Spanish affair was settled, did the Near Eastern question finally become the top problem in French diplomacy—that is, it was up to Villèle to determine his attitude. But he did not lack good reasons for inclining toward a prudent hands-off policy, preferred by his bookkeeper mentality, so averse to crusading. If he gave in on the Spanish expedition, it was because he was pushed into it at sword's point by his own party; but in this case this same party, in spite of more and more voices raised in favor of the Greeks, remained hostile to the insurgent cause until 1824. The reports which he received from the Near East from his ambassadors, consuls, and naval officers presented the Greeks in an unfavorable light. They persecuted Catholics while the Turks showed special regard for them; they gave themselves over to just as abominable cruelties as their adversaries, sometimes committed against their own fellow-countrymen; they committed numerous acts of piracy to the detriment of French commerce. To come to the aid of the Greeks, were they ready to alienate the traditional friendship of Turkey and compromise the privileged position that the Capitulation arrangements guaranteed to France's representatives in the Levantine ports of call? Would not England take advantage of this to elbow France out and inflict a defeat on her in the Mediterranean? Lastly, the intervention of the Pasha of Egypt introduced a new and important factor into the affair. Mohammed Ali acted as if he were a supporter of France and appeared to certain people—in particular France's consul-general in Egypt, the active Drovetti—as destined one day to succeed Mahmoud, who had no descendants. Mohammed Ali reigning in Constantinople! What a prospect for France—the Ottoman Empire modernizing itself with the help of her engineers, soldiers, and administrators, would become a sort of French protectorate! Looked at from this seductive viewpoint, the Greek affair could appear as a disagreeable interruption which must be handled without compromising future possibilities.

Such were the reasons which could justify Villèle's neutrality policy up to 1827. His nonintervention decision was shown in two main circumstances. Early in 1824 Tsar Alexander had proposed a plan which would have had the effect of dividing Greece into three autonomous principalities under the distant sovereignty of the sultan. Austria and England, both basically very opposed to this plan which would permit Russia to extend her influence in the Balkans, nevertheless agreed to discuss it. Two conferences therefore took place in Saint Petersburg in June 1824 and February 1825. The delaying tactics of Metternich and Canning were favored by Villèle, and he adopted them as his own. The Greeks themselves did not want to hear of a division of their country, and finally Russia's proposal was buried with all the honors of diplomacy. Alexander, not wanting to break up the European alliance which had been the great idea of his reign, did not insist on it.

In April 1825 a few pro-Greek Frenchmen got the idea, along with a group of Greek leaders, of offering the Greek throne to the Duke of Nemours, the second son of the Duke of Orleans. This would be an effective way, they thought, of persuading France to do something for Greece's independence. Emissaries were therefore sent both to Villèle and to the Duke of Orleans. Villèle would have nothing to do with it, and the Duke of Orleans, who no doubt would have benefitted by the plan, was also obliged to decline the offer.

The Greeks then put all their hopes on England. They appointed as commander of their fleet an English officer, Admiral Cochrane, who had spontaneously offered his services, and they sent a deputation to Canning to ask him to take their country under his protection. Canning, anxious to keep in the good graces of the sultan, officially disassociated himself; but he began to work on a mediation which, by calling a new state into existence, as he had done in South America, would permit him to install England's influence solidly in the Balkans and would constitute a temporary dam against Russian ambitions in the Eastern Mediterranean.

One unforeseen change spoiled this great plan: Tsar Alexander died in December 1825, and his brother and successor, Nicholas I, decided immediately on energetic action without any longer having concern for the European concert. Consequently, early in 1826 the Greek affair entered a new active phase, triggering power rivalries in the Mediterranean. France could no longer remain aloof without abdicating her role as a great nation.

Conditions had also changed at home. The philhellenic movement, at first confined to liberal circles, had, by 1824, won the support of the right-wing royalists. Religion, politics, humanitarian sentiments, the literary movement, all had contributed to it. Catholics, like Montmorency and Bonald, could not stand seeing Christian people massacred by the Mussulmans. "It is the Vendée of Christianity," said the Duchess of Duras. Philanthropists were becoming indignant at the inconsistency of a government which condemned the slave trade and stood with folded arms while the Turks sold off their Greek captives by the thousands. The liberals accused Villèle of conniving with Metternich to let a heroic people be crushed while fighting for their freedom, and the counteropposition royalists found in this an occasion to denounce once more the abject timidity of a minister who was sacrificing national honor and having France trail around behind England. Writers and artists of the classical school were aroused by the misfortunes of the homeland of Homer, Pericles, and Phidias, while the romanticists waxed enthusiastic about the folklore of modern Greece as revealed by Fauriel, shuddered at the Massacre of Chios as painted by Delacroix, and mourned for Byron, their favorite poet, who had died at Missolonghi. If one were to assess this literary philhellenism, it would include almost all the illustrious names of the period.

Chateaubriand, the prince of letters, undertook himself to lead the movement; his *Note sur la Grèce* (1825), a stirring speech in the chamber of peers in May 1826, and a preface to a new edition of his *Itinéraire* in 1827, launched even more urgent appeals in favor of the martyred people. Under his presidency a society was formed with the name of *Société philanthropique pour l'assistance aux Grecs,* which included men from the Right, like Fitz-James, and men from the Left, like La Fayette and Laffitte. This committee collected money, published propaganda brochures, and sent food, clothing, and weapons. They recruited and sent out volunteers and even had ships built for the insurgents.

Villèle, too unsentimental, could not understand any of this enthusiasm. "Money does not like cannon fire," he was to jot down in his notebook after the Battle of Navarino. His minister of foreign affairs, the inept Damas, had the misfortune of uttering a phrase in his speech in the chamber of deputies in these words: "It is not the interest of this or that locality that governments should consider, but the common interest of all peoples." Greece a *locality!* Thus, for the minister, the sacred land of Attica, the homeland of Socrates, of Plato, of Demosthenes was only a *locality!* It caused a big storm among the opposition.

Charles X, a warm-hearted man, was won over by the general emotion in spite of Villèle, and he made a very firm declaration that he would not allow this heroic people to be annihilated. Thus, when the decided action of Russia made the great powers abandon their hesitations, French opinion was ready to support armed intervention, and under this pressure the government, at first timid, was to become gradually more involved until it was finally to take charge of the diplomatic operations.

Yet, as long as Villèle was at the helm, France would continue more or less to follow in England's wake and would try especially to prevent hostilities; but after January 1828 the new ministry would give a more active and more honorable impulse to French policy.

Big diplomatic moves began in the month of March 1826 when Tsar Nicholas sent an ultimatum to the Turks. As a matter of fact it only involved Russia's demand for the evacuation of the Rumanian provinces, provided for by the Treaty of 1812. Yet, it was obvious that once war broke out, Muscovite troops would not stop at the Danube, and the tsar would be in a position to dictate a solution to the Greek problem. Canning, wishing to avoid this unilateral action, sent Wellington to Saint Petersburg. From these conversations emerged, on April 4, 1826, a protocol which provided for an Anglo-Russian mediation between the sultan and his subjects in revolt. France had not been consulted or informed in advance; she thus felt she had been treated as a negligible quantity. Villèle raised a protest. Canning, quite willing to give ear to this complaint—because French support could be useful in restraining Russia—proposed that Villèle adhere to the Convention of April 4, 1826. To remove the appearance of humiliating inequality which this step might imply in regard to France, it was understood that this document would be replaced by a new treaty to be drawn up with the collaboration of France.

In the meantime, this great-power collaboration intimidated the sultan, and in October 1826 he decided to give in to the Russians on the Rumanian question by the Convention of Ackerman. But this in no way involved the fate of Greece. England, Russia, and France insisted upon a written reply to their mediation proposals. This move came at just the worst time: the Acropolis of Athens, the last citadel of the Greeks had fallen into the hands of the Turks. The sultan replied by a haughty note in which he absolutely rejected any foreign intervention in a purely domestic conflict. It involved nothing more, according to the very principles of the European Alliance, than bringing insurgent subjects back to obedience to their legitimate sovereign.

## Armed Intervention by the Powers

From this time forward it was necessary to think in terms of the use of force. The three powers accepted that prospect by the Treaty of Lon-

don, signed on June 6, 1827. It was not yet a question of actually declaring war on the Porte, but of only imposing a mediation on it and a
preliminary suspension of hostilities. Villèle and Canning both hoped for
a peaceful solution and a halting of the Russian armies, but events were
to frustrate this scheme.

Because of the long distances the governments had had to give rather
broad instructions to their fleet commanders in the Mediterranean, whose
delicate task it was to enforce a truce. Admiral de Rigny, commander of
the French fleet, was to play a preponderant role as a result of his long-
established cordial relations with Ibrahim Pasha. He tried to come to an
understanding with him to institute the desired armistice in spite of the
sultan. Ibrahim, who himself had cause to complain about the Turks,
agreed to stop fighting while he asked for new instructions from both
Constantinople and Alexandria. But the Turks would listen to nothing,
and their troops continued their devastations and massacres in the Morea.
Then the three admirals had a meeting and decided to make a demonstration before Navarino to force the Turkish and Egyptian fleets to lift
anchor and return to their bases, which would paralyze their land armies
and deprive them of the necessary supplies to carry on their operations.

So on October 20 the allied squadrons, under the supreme command
of Admiral Codrington, appeared at the entrance of the port of Navarino
where they found the Muslim fleets concentrated along with a multitude
of transports. In principle no one wanted an engagement, but there is
no doubt that the European officers, especially the French, hoped for an
incident which would give them a chance to distinguish themselves. This
was not lacking; shots fired on the English emissaries and on the French
flagship, "Sirène," unleashed a confused and murderous battle. Ships,
hemmed in close together, fired point blank at each other. Although the
Muslims were superior in number—64 ships to 26 allied—they were
quickly struck down by the precision and rapidity of the fire from their
Western adversaries. In two hours the Ottoman fleet was annihilated. The
French squadron suffered only forty-three dead and 117 wounded.

This event seriously modified the situation, but without getting a hair's
breadth closer to a solution of the Greek problem. The Turco-Egyptian
army, isolated in the Morea, was at the mercy of the allied naval blockade; and the Greeks were again more hopeful. But the sultan, indignant
at what he considered to be an unjustifiable attack, was even less than
ever ready to listen to a peaceful settlement, while the Russians, given
a good pretext, were preparing for a large-scale war.

England, on the contrary, was more than ever opposed to hostilities.
An important change had just come in her government; George Canning

had died early in August, and his successors, Goderich and Wellington, lacking imagination, clung stubbornly to the traditional policy of the integrity of the Ottoman Empire. Wellington called the victory at Navarino "a fatal accident," in accord on this with Metternich, for whom it was "a terrible catastrophe."

By the end of 1827 it all seemed to be leading to an Anglo-Russian conflict which could escalate into a general war in which the fate of the poor Greeks could very well be forgotten. It was therefore fortunate for them and for Europe that France at this moment abandoned the immobility to which she had been held by Villèle and took bold and reasonable initiatives of her own which were going to make it possible to save Greece as well as the general peace.

The credit goes, in the first place, to Count de la Ferronnays, who had received the portfolio of foreign affairs in the new ministry appointed early in January 1828. To be fair, it should be added that he had the unreserved support of Charles X, who was anxious to restore France to her rank as a great nation. "France," he said one day, "when it is a question . . . of rendering a great service to a people cruelly oppressed, does not ask anyone else's advice. So, whether England wants to or not, we are going to liberate Greece." La Ferronnays, a former ambassador to St. Petersburg, also had the confidence of the tsar and knew how to play this trump to avoid an open rupture between England and Russia.

In April 1828, Nicholas I, taking note of the fact that the Treaty of Ackerman had not been carried out, declared war on the sultan and moved his troops into Moldavia. British opinion became aroused, and the English government re-enforced its Mediterranean squadrons in a menacing gesture. La Ferronnays and his ambassador in London, Polignac, did all they could to convince the English that they could not stop the Russians from overexploiting the situation unless they associated themselves with the Russian's move to some extent. It was in a sense the Canning policy in reverse—London was now following the lead of Paris. France proposed a division of the zones of operations: the Russians in the northern Balkans, the Anglo-French forces in the Mediterranean. But Wellington balked; he did not want any English action against Turkey at any price. Then La Ferronnays boldly proposed that France might take the responsibility for all the military operations—England could limit herself to furnishing the transport services. The English did not like this either. Not only did they not want to do anything themselves, but they did not want anyone else to make up for their default. La Ferronnays let them know that, if need be, France would do without England's consent, and they finally gave in, with the most obvious ill humor.

Without any more delay the government of Charles X organized a small expeditionary corps of fifteen thousand men, commanded by General Maison. It was landed on the Morea early in September 1828; its mission was to obtain the withdrawal of the Egyptian forces by friendly agreement as much as possible. In fact, thanks to the good relations between Rigny and Ibrahim, things were arranged with a minimum of bloodshed. Maison, on good advice, was careful to make it possible for Ibrahim to save face. Between the two generals it was an assault of polite and chivalrous courtesies. For Turkish leaders, who pretended to put up a token resistance in some of the citadels, they let them have a little face-saving display of gunpowder indispensable for relieving them from the effects of the anger of their Lord. The French officers wanted very much to cross the Isthmus of Corinth and liberate Athens, but the government of the king, anxious to get along with England, forbade them to do so. With the Morea they had a sufficient hostage to impose the solution of her choice on all parties concerned.

And, in fact, in the conferences which took place—first in Poros at the end of 1828, and later in London early in 1829—it was France's point of view which won out on the principal question in dispute—the definition of the frontiers of independent Greece. The new state was to enjoy an autonomous status, under the nominal suzerainty of the sultan, but under the real authority of a Christian prince. The protocol of this accord was signed on March 22, 1829.

But the question was not settled at this point. The Turks, who had not participated in these negotiations, obstinately refused to agree to the results. The Russian troops, halted at the Danube in the fall of 1828, resumed their operations in the spring of 1829. When they arrived at the gates of Constantinople in the last days of August, the sultan finally resigned himself to accepting the terms of his conquerors. The Treaty of Adrianople, signed on September 14, 1829, settled the status of the Rumanian provinces and of Serbia according to the wishes of the tsar. As to the Greek question, which always remained secondary according to the priorities of Nicholas I, Turkey accepted in their entirety the terms of the accord of the preceding March 22.

Thus modern Greece was born. The heroism of its people and the weight of Russian arms had no doubt been the principal factors leading to its independence; but the France of Charles X, by its successful intervention at just the right time, had avoided a European crisis and facilitated the reasonable and humane solution which prevailed. This success, unsullied by any selfish motives, cast new luster on France's diplomacy and betokened her readmission to the ranks of the great powers.

# 21

✤ ✤ ✤ ✤ ✤

# The Martignac Ministry

## The New Ministers and Their Difficulties

COLORLESS, weak, and unhomogeneous, the new ministerial team, called to power early in 1828, reflected in its composition the difficulties and compromises which had presided over its birth. It included two members of the preceding government, Mgr. Frayssinous, minister of ecclesiastical affairs, and Chabrol, naval minister. Others also connected with the previous ministry, in which they had faithfully served in lower positions, were: Martignac, former director of state lands and registries, appointed as minister of interior; Saint-Cricq, former director of customs, for whom was created a new ministry of commerce and manufactures; and General de Caux, raised to the rank of minister while continuing the administration of the war ministry. Questions concerning military personnel were to remain, in fact, entirely in the hands of the Dauphin (the heir to the throne), who, in any case, had been in the council. The new foreign minister, Count de la Ferronnays, was a career diplomat without any apparent political affiliation, having lived in St. Petersburg since 1819. The chivalrous generosity of his character and his former intimate friendship with the Duke of Berry were to assure him the confidence of the king and the possibility of giving, as we have seen, a new and successful direction to foreign policy. Count Roy returned to the finance ministry which he had once before successfully managed during Richelieu's second ministry. This great bourgeois leader, raised to the nobility by the Restoration after he had made his fortune during the Revolution—a fortune estimated at forty million francs (eight million dollars)—was in no sense a liberal, but he had often opposed the financial policies of Villèle in the chamber of peers. Hence his appointment could appear to be a concession to the opposition. It was the same in the case of Portalis, appointed as keeper of the seal (minister of justice). This son of Napoleon's minister of worship, a Gallican like his father, had won the favor of the leftist press by coming out against the Jesuits in his report to the chamber of peers in January 1827 on the Montlosier petition. Besides, this expert and subtle jurist, this pursuer of Jesuits, had the benign and plump appearance of the popular idea of a parish priest.

In other words this was what we would call today a ministry of technicians with a Left-center orientation. No one was designated as prime minister, either because the king still hoped to bring Villèle back into the government, or because he harbored a desire to exercise a more active control over policy, or else because he simply had not found a man with sufficient moral authority. In any case Martignac, a former Bordeaux lawyer, and the only real orator for the ministry, was to become its regular spokesman in the two houses and to end by being considered the head of the government. By his strong points as well as by his weaknesses, he was indeed a rather good personification of the ministry as a whole.

> He was [said Barante] a man of a gentle, easygoing, and friendly character, and with unquestioned ability. His language was clear, elegant, easy to understand, persuasive and pleasing. . . . One was charmed by the way he spoke or read. . . . In his youth he was in Berlin, when Siéyès was ambassador there. He has composed songs and vaudeville shows, and as a result of these talents his manner was more like that of a secretary of embassy and writer than of a lawyer. As to a point of view, he had no convictions, but was softened by unconcern and idleness. He was a libertine, associating rather publicly in society with actresses and dancers, which diminished a little the respect which his talents deserved . . .

The formation of the ministry did not bring to an end the political confusion from which it had sprung, and it took some time before it found its stride. The king's concept was that a change in personnel meant in no way a change in policy. When the ministers came to take their customary oath of office, he told them: "I must say to you that I am sorry to lose M. de Villèle; the public misjudged him; his system was mine, and I hope you will do your best to conform to it yourselves." During the early months of 1828, Charles X was indeed to carry on an almost daily correspondence with Villèle, consulting him on all the details of public affairs. The public suspected this. "The main actor," wrote the *Constitutionnel,* "has left the stage only to take refuge in the prompter's box."

The role that Charles X tried to impose on his ministry was not only humiliating and false, it was untenable from the parliamentary point of view. If he was going to try to continue Villèle without Villèle, he could not count on the support of the latter's opponents of Right and Left, which now, combined, had a majority in the chamber. It was not even certain that he would have the votes of old Villèlists. It was absolutely essential, then, to find a way of enlarging the parliamentary base of the ministry on the Right and Left.

The first move of the ministers was to ask the king for permission to approach Chateaubriand, who laid down as conditions for his support the appointment of Royer-Collard to the ministry, jobs for Bertin de Vaux and Salvandy, and 500,000 francs ($100,000) for the *Journal des Débats*. These demands appeared unacceptable. Then they turned to the extreme Right and proposed to give the naval ministry to La Bourdonnaye. The ambitious orator of the counteropposition was strongly tempted to accept, but he did not dare commit himself without consulting his friends. These in turn gave him to understand that they also wanted jobs and favors. The ministry was not inclined to grant these demands, and La Bourdonnaye had to decline the offer much against his own inclinations.

As the next best thing they tried to calm public opinion by a few concessions. Some of Villèle's henchmen were sacrificed, among whom were Franchet d'Esperey, director of the general police service, whose position was abolished; his friend Delavau, Paris prefect of police, who was considered a tool of the Congregation, was replaced by Debelleyme, royal procurator in the Paris court of first instance. The king restored three Academicians to their places—Michaud, Lacretelle, and Villemain—who had previously been dismissed for having taken the initiative of protesting against the "law of justice and love." The latter, as well as Guizot and Cousin, was allowed to give courses again at the Sorbonne. A commission was appointed on January 22 to "examine what measures were needed to carry out the laws of the kingdom on teaching in the church's secondary schools." Finally, and still more significant, an ordinance of February 10 detached public instruction from the ministry of ecclesiastical affairs, and this new portfolio was given to a layman, the former judge Lefebvre de Vatimesnil.

However, the king had opened the parliamentary session on February 5. The voting for the officials of the chamber of deputies revealed the confusion of the parties. The first ballot for choosing the president put La Bourdonnaye at the top of the list; but the final run-off vote gave it to a man on the Left. Between the two votes the Left had negotiated an agreement with a faction of the extreme Right which rejected any reconciliation with Villèlists. This group of about thirty men followed Chateaubriand and recognized the deputy Agier as their leader. Because of this situation these thirty "defection" votes—as they were called—held, in spite of their small number, the balance of power in determining the parliamentary majority. The king immediately gave a satisfaction to the coalition which was beginning to take shape by appointing Royer-Collard as president of the chamber.

The Agier "defection" joined the Left again in the phrasing of the reply to the king and inserted a sentence which called the Villèle government "a deplorable system." Charles X was so offended by this that for a moment he thought of refusing to hear it read. Chabrol and Frayssinous did not think they could stay in the ministry with a chamber condemning so strongly a government to which they had belonged. Their resignations seemed to Martignac to be a good occasion to rally the important votes from the "defection." First the naval ministry was offered to Chateaubriand, who spurned it with a kick—to him this position was too far inferior to the one he had lost in 1824. However, he did consent to make his peace with the government and bring the *Journal des Débats* over to its support. At his request the naval ministry was given to his old friend, Hyde de Neuville, former ambassador to Washington and Lisbon, who, like him, had combined a militant Ultra-Royalist past with certain liberal tendencies. Chateaubriand was himself to accept the embassy in Rome as a token of his reconciliation. As to ecclesiastical affairs, it was given (March 4) to Mgr. Feutrier, Bishop of Beauvais, a conciliatory, amiable, and worldly prelate, who was known as an enemy of the Jesuits.

From then on the parliamentary situation was a little clearer. The Left, re-enforced still more by by-elections which took place on April 20 for forty seats, found itself in a position to impose its program on the ministry, but on the condition of having the support of the "defection," which was to keep its demands within certain limits. The opposition was represented by the Villèlist Right; and it was to be joined by the faction of the old rightist counteropposition which was following La Bourdonnaye, about thirty deputies in all. Partly because of thwarted ambition, partly from loyalty to principle, they were going to refuse to associate themselves with the measures proposed by the Left, and they were to move closer to their previous adversaries. Parleys even took place between Villèle and La Bourdonnaye, and the latter on several occasions defended the conduct of the previous government.

All of this did not make the government's position any more comfortable. Put together by the king himself as a derivative of the Villèle ministry, it was gradually forced, in order to prolong its very life, to renounce its origin and rely on the Left. But it could not entirely satisfy the Left without losing the king's confidence. The king, disappointed in this unforeseen turn of events, decided to wait and see what would happen. He withdrew into an attitude of neutrality and ostensible indifference, while hoping that the increasing demands of the Left might forge again the union of all the rightist elements.

## Changes in the Election and Press Laws

The domestic policy of the Martignac government was then to be a series of concessions to the Left, but made so hesitantly and grudgingly that these measures, which alienated the king and irritated the Right, were not even going to win over the Left completely.

As the first bone to gnaw on, Martignac offered the chamber a bill which changed the existing provisions on drawing up the voting lists. The idea was to do away with the abusive practices of the prefectural administrations, practices of which numerous examples were to be revealed by the verification of election credentials at the beginning of the session. Henceforth the voting lists were to be permanent. Drawn up on the first of January each year, they were to be posted in every commune. The name of each voter was to be accompanied by the sum of his taxes and a detailed list of the places where he paid them. Any complaints about inclusions or exclusions on the lists were to be presented to the prefectural council. Any citizen on the electoral list would have the right to ask for third parties' inclusions or exclusions, and tax collectors were to be obliged to release extracts from the tax rolls and certificates were to be asked of them in support of such complaints. The chamber had a provision added that would permit an appeal to the royal courts against a decision by the prefectural council. The Right protested in vain that the bill legalized the removal of the legitimate influence of the government in favor of the electoral committees, that it corrected an abuse by resorting to a usurpation and removed a scandal by igniting a civil war. The Villèlist paper, the *Gazette de France,* moaned: "It is the enactment of the democratic principle, the permanent enrolling and recruiting of the militia of revolutions."

After revision of the electoral system came that of the press. On April 14, Portalis presented a bill which reflected the wishes expressed by certain members of the opposition during the previous year in the discussion of Peyronnet's clumsy bill. They removed three of the principal instruments of repression which Villèle had found in the law of 1822: the right to reimpose censorship between parliamentary sessions; the requirement for advanced approval, replaced by a simple declaration; and finally the prosecution for the tendency of ideas. At first the chamber and the press greeted the bill favorably, but soon they discovered other provisions in the bill which cancelled out the announced concessions. There would be a responsible director required to be chosen from among the owners of each paper, a much higher financial deposit would be extended to literary journals as well, and the fines would be made heavier. The correctional courts would continue to have sole jurisdiction over press law infractions, and besides, they would have the right to suspend for three months any paper guilty of a second offense. The extreme Left, with Benjamin Constant at its head, and the extreme Right for different reasons, opposed Portalis' bill. Martignac's eloquence and a sensational speech by Chateaubriand in the chamber of peers succeeded in saving it, and it was finally passed with amendments which reduced the deposits and fines. This was the fifth law imposed on the press since 1815!

## Ordinances on the Small Seminaries

It could be seen, in the discussion of the press law, how mixed was the majority which had appeared at the beginning of the session. The Left itself was divided in its voting. Only one thing could preserve an appearance of cohesion, and that was hatred of Villèle. Very appropriately a deputy of the extreme Left, Labbey de Pompières, on June 14 drew up a proposal to indict the previous ministers. Villèle's own friends joined in this demand—it was the best way to counter the blow—and an investigating committee was designated. Naturally it was not going to amount to anything; but the threat it caused to hang over the head of the former president of the council was to be an obstacle to his eventual return to power, and the agitation aroused against him helped maintain the precarious union of the Left with the "defectionists." That was why, in spite of the too obvious outcome, they were careful to drag out the work of the investigating committee until the end of the session.

Labbey de Pompières' proposal had also served as a way to get the king to sign the ordinances of June 16 on the small seminaries. It was the end result of the campaign carried on for years by the liberals against the Jesuits and against the clergy's control of education. From the beginning of the year the ministry had launched a move in this direction by appointing an investigating committee and then by removing public instruction from the ministry of ecclesiastical affairs. A third step was the ordinance of April 21, 1828 which took away from bishops some of the power over primary schools given to them in April 1824. Henceforth, the duty of supervising belonged to a departmental committee on which would be three ecclesiastics and six other members chosen by the prefect and the rector of the academy.

This bill was passed with little fanfare. What aroused public opinion was the fate of the houses of secondary education run by the Jesuits. The latter, taking advantage of the privilege of bishops to open small seminaries exempt from state supervision, had founded under this label regular secondary colleges which enrolled children from upper-class families. The one at Saint-Acheul, near Amiens, especially famous and well filled, had eight hundred students in 1827. It was known that Mgr. Frayssinous had publicly admitted in 1826 the existence of these Jesuit houses and that the chamber of peers in 1827 had solemnly pointed out the illegality of this situation. Portalis, who had been the reporter of the resolution in this case, was determined to set things straight. The committee he had appointed in January 1828 had not brought in a report until the following May. It had shown that out of 126 ecclesiastical schools properly authorized there were fifty-four which had evaded unduly the supervision of the University, and it proposed various measures to end the abuse of admitting to the small seminaries students who had not the least intention of entering holy orders. On the question of the Jesuits the committee was divided, but the majority of its members (five against four) claimed that the bishops had the right to call on any one they pleased to direct their small seminaries. The Jesuits, it said, had been chosen by them as individuals and not as members of a society not recognized by law. This declaration aroused the fury of the Left, and its dissatisfaction was shown in the debate on the press law.

The ministry, fearing it might be put in a minority, decided on making a major concession to liberal opinion and submitted the texts of two ordinances to the king. According to the terms of the first one, countersigned by the keeper of the seal, ecclesiastical schools which were not genuine small seminaries, or which were run "by persons belonging to a religious order not legally established in France," would henceforth come under the supervision of the University; and in the future no one could exercise any teaching function until he signed an affidavit that he did not belong to an unauthorized religious order. The second ordinance, presented by the minister of ecclesiastical affairs, regulated the system of small seminaries in such a way as to prevent the bishops from using them as camouflaged secondary colleges: the over-all number of students were not to exceed twenty thousand, a number large enough to allow the normal recruiting of new clergy; the ecclesiastical schools could only receive resident students, and those over fourteen years of age would, after two years of attendance, have to wear clerical garb; the appointment of professors was to be approved by the minister. Finally, to compensate for the financial loss caused by the exclusion of a category of students, the government would set aside a sum of 1,200,000 francs ($240,000) for use as scholarships in the small seminaries.

Would the conscience of the king permit him to take the responsibility for such measures? He hesitated for a long while, consulted Frayssinous and even Father Ronsin, the provincial of the Jesuits. Obviously his refusal would force him to replace his ministers. But by whom? Finally he gave in, to avoid a dangerous crisis. The ordinances, signed on June 16, appeared the next day in the *Moniteur*. The Left was exultant: "The scepter of the Inquisition is broken!" cried the *Journal des Débats.* In the other camp explosions of fury exceeded all bounds. The *Gazette de France* wrote: "Revolution has triumphed . . . all that is needed now is to go through with the restoration of the Republic and the erection of altars to the Goddess of Reason."

> Go on and applaud, you tribe of impious and sacreligious [said the *Quotidienne*], you factious writers, go on, applaud! Behold a priest giving you the sanctuary, and a magistrate giving you the power. You wanted the episcopate in chains, and they sacrificed it. Yea, even more, they hold it in such contempt that they offer it a few pieces of silver in advance in payment for a baseness on which they count with certainty.

Portalis and Feutrier were compared to Diocletian, Julian the Apostate, and Saint-Just.

The Jesuits, accustomed to bending before the storm, submitted without protest and scattered into small residences where they could continue to carry on other ministrations. But the episcopate, stirred by the rightist press, put up a strong fight. A committee of seven bishops, headed by the Archbishop of Paris, drew up a protest which was signed by seventy prelates. In this document they rejected the principal provisions of the ordinance intended to be imposed on them as subversive to the freedom of the church and, in closing, said that "they [the bishops] would simply say, with all due respect, as had the apostles before them: *non possumus.*" However, Charles X, upset by this open challenge, had sent a secret emissary to the pope to ask for his support, and the foreign ministry, for its part, had the chargé d'affaires take steps in Rome. Leo XII said that the ordinances did not violate episcopal rights, and he sent word to the bishops "that they should put their confidence in the manifest piety and wisdom of their king in the way the ordinances would be executed and walk in accord with the throne." Charles X engaged his close collaborator, Mgr. de Latil, Archbishop of Rheims, to work on each of his colleagues individually. Most of them gave in. Yet there were a few who still refused to furnish the documents requested by the ministry. Clermont-Tonnerre, Cardinal Archbishop of Toulouse, replied in these haughty words: "Monsignor, the motto of my family, given to it by Callistus II in 1120 is this—*Etiamsi omnes, ego non* (even if everyone else [does], I won't). This is also the motto of my conscience. I have the honor to be, etc." For this insolence he was forbidden to appear at court.

In the end the government had come out on top, and it showed itself to be rather lenient in making use of its victory. For example it did not demand from the seminary professors the written declaration required by the ordinance.

### The Left Against the King

If the ministry thought it could obtain the unqualified good-will of the Left by these measures, it was woefully mistaken. The parliamentary session had hardly ended early in August when the liberal press resumed its attacks against the "weakness" of the government and put forward new demands. "M. de Martignac is a man of words," said the *Figaro,* "but he is not a man to keep his word." They especially complained of the fact that the administration was still filled with Villèle men; so in the various departments continued this "deplorable system" and the "reign of the Congregation." The ministers would have liked to have had the king come out frankly for or against the policy they were following. So they addressed an important memoir to him to explain to him how they had been compelled by the parliamentary situation to seek support from the Left; what they had been trying to do was to rally the two centers of Left and Right around a frankly constitutional program. If the king wanted to change the emphasis, he would have to dissolve the chamber; but it was certain that new elections would only strengthen the Left. And then? "Then," they concluded prophetically, "Your Majesty would only have this double alternative left—either of lowering your august head before the chamber or of having recourse to the constitution-making power which the Charter had forever taken from you, and that could be hazardously invoked again only by plunging France into new revolutions in which the crown of Saint-Louis would disappear entirely."

Charles X was less than ever inclined to bend before parliament. Early in September he had made an official trip through the eastern provinces where liberal opinions predominated in the bourgeoisie; everywhere he had been greeted by a show of enthusiasm and affection. Instead of giving the ministry credit for a policy which had undoubtedly contributed to this rise in popularity, the king came to the conclusion that he would have the support of the people and the army whenever he wanted to shake off the parliamentary yoke. A remark escaped his lips in the presence of Martignac that if he had known what he had just now learned about the real feeling of the people, he would not have agreed to certain things.

So when the ministry asked his approval of a reshuffling of the upper administrative personnel, which the leftist press was demanding, Charles X would only agree to the sacrifice of nine Villèlist prefects and four councillors of state. When these changes were announced on November 14, the *Courrier français* called them "a sad miscarriage of the hopes aroused by the ministers' promises." However, even more than the legislative measures, these dismissals made it now absolutely impossible to bring about any reconciliation between the ministry and the Villèlist Right.

Already the Martignac government and its policy were just about repudiated in the mind of the king, and from 1828 on, he was thinking of going into reverse. To do that, he would have to find a new majority and new men. He could count on the chamber of peers where Villèle had swamped the old imperialist and constitutional majority under a flood of rightist elements drawn from the "Chambre Retrouvée" of 1824. In the chamber of deputies itself it was not impossible to find a rightist majority if they succeeded in bringing about a union of the Villèlists with the Right-Center and all the factions of the old counteropposition. Ravez, the former president of the chamber, guaranteed this. To effect this regrouping it would be necessary to retain some Right-Center men—Martignac among others—whose tactful ways rather pleased the king, and to add to them men from the Right and the extreme Right, like La Bourdonnaye and Ravez. The key man on this team would be Polignac. It had become an obsession with Charles X to bring his "dear Jules" to power, a man who alone was capable of understanding and achieving his conception of monarchical government. A few years earlier he had thought of him as being rather mediocre. "Poor old Jules, he is so incompetent," he had said at that time; but it was Villèle who, fearing him as a rival, had taken it upon himself to inculcate this idea. However, Polignac had done a good job as ambassador in London, and La Ferronnays, more appreciative, had gone out of his way to stress his good points. He did not want to turn over his own position of foreign minister to him, but he recognized the advantage of having in the ministry a man who really had the confidence of the monarch. The other ministers in fact could not but realize that they did not have it, and that lack was the government's great weakness.

An unforeseen situation forced the king to unveil his scheme prematurely, which brought about its failure—temporarily. La Ferronnays became seriously ill early in January 1829, and it was necessary to find a replacement for him. The ministers proposed that Charles X call in Chateaubriand. The king refused and confided the interim tenure of the vacant portfolio to Portalis and secretly called Polignac back to Paris and summoned Ravez. When he announced his intention of having these two men occupy seats in the council, the ministers protested that they could not agree in any case to accept Polignac. "What?" the Dauphin asked Martignac, "doesn't the king have the right to choose a minister?" "He can choose nine," he replied, "and we can do nothing but submit to it." The king, irritated by this, was beginning to think of doing just that, and when Polignac arrived in the capital on January 21 or 22, he was asked to form a new ministry without more ado. The ambassador had intermittent talks with all sorts of people, while the liberal press, alerted by his sudden return, unleashed on him a furious volley of attacks. But there was not enough time to form a viable combination. The opening of the parliamentary session had been announced for January 27. The king could not any more present to the chamber a ministry still in the process of being formed than he could a ministry about to be condemned; so he decided to deny the rumors of a ministerial change by officially ordering Polignac back to his post. Nevertheless, before obeying, the crestfallen aspirant gave a great speech in the chamber of peers in which he protested his attachment to the Charter and to parliamentary institutions. As for the foreign ministry, it remained provisionally in the hands of Portalis.

## The Defeat of Administrative Reform

The ministers had had a chance to see, through these false maneuvers, how weak their position was in respect to the throne. Would they at least succeed in keeping parliament on their side? One of the conditions raised by the Left before assuring its own support was a promise of administrative reform, which had been talked about ever since the coming of the Restoration without one move being made in that direction. Was it normal, in a regime which associated the representatives of the country in the direction of the state, to deny them the least share in local administration? Was it not contrary to the spirit of the Old Regime as well as to that of the constitutional monarchy to maintain unchanged the centralizing straightjacket imposed on France by Bonaparte? Villèle, after having denounced the anomaly when he was in the opposition, made unscrupulous use of it once he got in power. Now the Left attached that much more importance to dismantling this organization in which it saw so many instruments of the "deplorable system" perpetrating themselves—prefects, subprefects, and mayors. It was much more anxious now to see the electorate intervene in local affairs as it saw the menace of royal dictatorship loom on the horizon. Elected departmental councils could eventually furnish the basis for resistance to arbitrary government. For the same reason Charles X was in no great haste to introduce politics and electoral campaigns on the local level. However, Martignac was committed to do something about it at the very outset of his administration. On February 28, 1828 a commission had been set up to make proposals for administrative reform. It had on it only men who were hostile to liberal ideas, and so the proposals it drew up and presented to the chamber on February 9, 1829 as the main course for the session were way below the hopes of the Left. Martignac could not have been unaware of it; but it was the maximum concession he could wring from the king, and he tried to disarm his critics by a brilliant defence of the proposals, full of fine liberal statements. One glance at the provisions of the bill was unfortunately enough to show up its fallacious character. First, administrative centralization was continued at all levels: prefects, subprefects, and mayors were all still to be appointed by the central government.

"For someone else to pick the minister's agents . . ." explained Martignac, "and then at the same time call him responsible for the acts of those forced upon him would be an inconsistency and an injustice . . ." The authority of the local councils was not to be increased; they were to remain purely consultative and the administrative supervision by the central government in financial matters was even going to be increased. The only notable concession dealt with the selection of the members of the municipal, district, and departmental councils; they were to be elected instead of appointed by the government. But here again the conservative timidity of the bill was obvious. They had arranged for a complicated scheme which amounted to reserving the right to vote and run for office to a small number of notables and rich land-owners. Thus, in the villages, in elections for municipal councillors there were to be only thirty voters for every five hundred inhabitants, and in the cities still fewer. For the elections of general (departmental) councils the proportion was one voter for every thousand inhabitants.

Naturally the Left protested against the inadequacy of these provisions and prepared to overhaul them by many amendments. Martignac had divided his reform into two distinct bills: one on communal (municipal) administration and one on departmental administration. The first one, better prepared, caused few objections and seemed headed for quick adoption; but the second one encountered the strongest possible criticisms in the committee sessions. The committee's reporter, Sébastiani, pointed out that under the proposed system it would end up with the paradoxical situation of electing the general councils by less than forty thousand voters while the voters qualified to vote in elections for the chamber of deputies would amount to twice as many.

The battle began on the order of priority for the consideration of the two bills. The government was naturally desirous of having the communal bill discussed first, because it hoped to have a favorable decision on this part. But the Left, foreseeing that the session would be too short to pass both parts of the reform, wanted to begin by the departmental bill so as to hasten the expulsion of Villèle men from the general councils. The Right seized upon this occasion to inflict a defeat on the ministry. When, in line with its principles, it ought to have done all it could to block departmental reform, it voted with the Left to give it priority. The Right knew that the king was not going to tolerate any important amendments to the ministerial bill and that he would withdraw the whole reform rather than consent to it. And that was what happened. On April 8 they debated an amendment which would have done away with district councils (between those of department and commune). In spite of the supplications of the ministers, the Left and Left-Center determined to vote to support it. If the rest of the chamber had voted against it, the amendment could have been defeated, but on the final count the Right, which had sat silent and scornful during the oratorical debates, obstinately remained in their seats. By this tactical abstention the government lost and the amendment won. Immediately Martignac and Portalis left the hall to take the news to the king. "I told you so," the king observed with satisfaction, "there's no way of getting along with those people. It is time we stopped trying." A few moments later the two ministers returned to the deliberations and read a royal ordinance which just simply withdrew the two bills. The Right was

exultant; it had obtained its desired result. The Left, crestfallen, realized it had been outmaneuvered by its opponents. For having demanded
too much, it had lost even the little that the king was willing to concede
to it, and, besides, it had brought on the final blow to a ministry which
it did not like, but which, nevertheless, had made an effort to give it as
much satisfaction as the king would permit.

After that, everybody seemed to think that the ministry's days were
numbered. Martignac, now disillusioned, declared among his close friends:
"We do what we can. But all we can do is lead the monarchy back
to the bottom of the stairs, while the others would throw it out the
window." The king, who had by now become completely convinced
that he would dismiss the ministry, found it preferable to keep it until
the end of the session in order to let it do the job of getting the budget
passed. After that, he thought, its successors would be relieved of that
indispensable formality, and they could use the interval of the parliamentary vacation to consolidate themselves before facing the chamber.

## The Fall of Martignac

One last ministerial change in the month of May made obvious the
king's intention of doing nothing to infuse new blood into the condemned team. They had to find someone to be foreign minister. Charles
X still refused to call in Chateaubriand. Portalis agreed to accept the
portfolio, but on the understanding that, when he left the ministry, he
would be given the lifetime position of president of the court of cassation.
By a precaution worthy of a lawyer he even asked to have the ordinance
for his future appointment signed with the date left blank! As to
Portalis' former post of keeper of the seal (justice), that was given
to Bourdeau, a deputy of the Left-Center who had been since January
carrying out the duties of under-secretary of state for justice.

So things were arranged and the king, untroubled, could concern
himself with the formation of a ministry to his liking. To safeguard the
secrecy of the negotiations, he used the former Paris deputy, Ferdinand
de Bertier, who had been one of the most prominent members of the
counteropposition in the chamber of 1824. This man had kept on
good terms with a great many deputies, and his role as creator and
activator of the now-defunct secret society of the Knights of the Faith
assured him in political circles of wider influence and means of accomplishing things than anyone realized. Villèle had punished him for
his opposition by dismissing him from the council of state; but Martignac
had reappointed him, and he had taken advantage of the position to

regain the confidence of the king and suggest to him in secret interviews a whole plan of action. It was understood that the two pillars of the future ministry would be Polignac and La Bourdonnaye and that they would include people from all factions of the Right, even those of the "defection."

As soon as the session ended, Polignac, who had been kept informed of the negotiations through Bertier, arrived in Paris and contacted the king and La Bourdonnaye. The predominant influence of the latter made it necessary to exclude men from the Right-Center, like Lainé and Decazes, whom Polignac would have liked to bring in. He also had poor Bertier excluded as too "congregationist," after the latter had done so much to bring him into power. The list of ministers was drawn up on August 8, and the *Moniteur* of the ninth finally brought an end to public uncertainty by announcing the formation of the new government.

The Martignac experiment—a government both monarchist and liberal—had therefore failed. Can we even call it an experiment? In that case it would have had to have been undertaken as such and carried out from beginning to end with a minimum of good will and good faith. For Charles X the ministry of January 1828 had been at the outset only an expedient made necessary by Villèle's retreat, and the liberal orientation, imposed on Martignac by the parliamentary situation, had never had the king's approval. Among the liberals there were no doubt a certain number of men who were ready to accept the monarchy, but on conditions which required changes that would deprive it of its traditional meaning. Impatient to attain their objective, they let themselves be carried along too easily by the extremists. They could not forget their old resentments, and they could not overcome the king's feelings nor reassure that important segment of society which saw in them harbingers of revolution. In the end the ministry, adhering to no doctrine, and concerned mainly with staying in office, was contented to tack back and forth between the king and liberal opinion without being able to dominate either one.

The final upshot was that, in spite of a kind of truce that it had established after the fall of Villèle, the Martignac ministry left the regime in a worse state than that in which it found it. It had not succeeded in setting up in parliament a centrist and moderate majority, whose elements did nevertheless exist, and its weakness, leaving to the king a most obvious responsibility for his government, exposed the crown to the direct shock of unpopularity, which Villèle, at least, had drawn off onto his own head.

# 22

⚜ ⚜ ⚜ ⚜ ⚜

# The Polignac Ministry

## The New Ministers

THE idea of the king and his secret advisors had been to form a ministry which could bring together all shades of the Right with the purposes of stopping the spread of liberalism and of making a monarchical interpretation of the Charter prevail. But the lack of psychology which was shown in their choice of men, their incompetency and their poor judgment, as well as their unexpected defections, ended in that paradoxical result of presenting to the public a ministerial team most likely to disturb and irritate it and at the same time the least likely to cope with the seriousness of the situation by intelligent and energetic action.

Jules de Polignac, who was its standard-bearer rather than its real leader, had already accumulated an exceptional number of causes for his unpopularity. Son of the former favorite of Marie Antoinette on whom the pamphleteers of the time had pounced, émigré, Ultra-Royalist, prince by the grace of the Holy See, congregationist, husband of an Englishwoman, and himself an Anglophile—there are few men in French history who have been so universally disliked. Some have resented him because of his blind devotion to monarchy; others have not been able to forgive him for having ruined the cause which he was appointed to defend. A recent biography, based upon the unpublished family archives, brings a few retouches to his traditional image, which was a little too oversimplified in its blackness. In this work Polignac appears as an estimable individual, sensitive and wary, a perfect man of the world, having an agreeable and even charming approach, sincerely religious, with an enlightened religion, without any of that visionary exaltation which was attributed to him on the basis of some questionable evidence. He had endured with admirable courage all sorts of tribulations, especially a seemingly endless captivity. In fact, compromised in the Cadoudal plot in 1802, he had been condemned to two years of prison, but Napoleon had arbitrarily kept him under arrest until early in 1814. It is suspected that certain aspects of his personality are due in large part to this long imprisonment—that sort of propensity to live in a dream world, that inability to get down to realities, that tendency toward dissimulation even toward his best friends, that lofty melancholy—all of these, curiously, were traits which are also found in another illustrious product of prison life, Napoleon III. Two other character deficiencies are likewise to be noted—an extraordinary stubbornness and an imperturbable confidence in himself.

In spite of all this, Polignac's rise to power surprised no one. It had been expected for a long time. The assignments of La Bourdonnaye to the ministry of interior and of Bourmont to the war ministry were more unexpected and more shocking in the eyes of the public. In its opinion, the first incarnated the royalist reaction of 1815 in all its most odious and violent aspects. "The very name of this man [La Bourdonnaye] was enough to wrench a cry of terror from France," wrote the *Journal des Débats*. In the chamber he had made a speciality of using the most intransigent language, and no minister had been found worthy of pity from him. In contrast to Polignac, he affected great scorn for the Congregation and the clergy. Besides, this man was not pleasing in attitude and appearance, if we can believe the image of him depicted by one of his colleagues:

> A sad face, a hard look which he excelled in giving it, piercing eyes, insolently fixed on his questioner, eyebrows arched in a perpetual frown, a mouth habitually twisted by a laugh more nasty than evil . . . jerky, inattentive, disdainful conversation, which livens up only when it becomes ungracious and annoying.

The choice of Bourmont, the responsibility for which was credited to the poor judgment of the Duke of Angoulême, appeared to be even more ill-advised. No doubt he was a capable military man, a man of decision, but not to speak of his past Chouan activities, his name was detested by all of those who remained sentimentally attached to the glorious memories of the Empire. On the eve of Waterloo he had deserted the imperial army, and it was claimed that information furnished by him to the enemy enabled it to win the victory. This was not true, but traitors are always necessary to salve the self-esteem of the vanquished. They also held against him his crucial testimony in the trial of Marshal Ney.

Compared to this champion bogyman, the other ministers looked more like supernumeraries. Charles X would have liked to retain

Martignac and Roy, but they absolutely refused to be associated with a combination schemed up behind their backs and so obviously destined to antagonize public opinion. Because of this, they lost one more means of wooing the Right-Center. At least the Villèlist group was well represented by Chabrol, who agreed to take the finance ministry, and also by a newcomer, the Count of Montbel, who had succeeded Villèle as mayor of Toulouse and who was completely devoted to the former council president. They assigned him the ministry of ecclesiastical affairs and public instruction, which were again brought together under one man. The choice of Courvoisier for the ministry of justice was an example of their clumsy attempt to widen the parliamentary support of the new ministry toward the Left. He was a judge who had, as a deputy from 1816 to 1824, fought in the ranks of the Left-Center; but he had a queer mentality, even perhaps a little unbalanced, illustrated by his sudden conversion from Voltairianism to fanatical Catholicism. As a symptomatic and disturbing indication, he tried to interpret the events of his time by the Book of Revelation! Finally the king had wanted to embellish his government with a ray of military glory by calling in Admiral de Rigny, the victor of Navarino. He was the nephew of Baron Louis, the former finance minister under Decazes—which tells us to what political opinion he belonged and also how vain it was to hope that they could get him to join such a crew. That Charles X and Polignac could think they could announce his appointment without even asking his consent shows how little they realized the niceties of political integrity. When, to their great surprise and great displeasure, Rigny declined the appointment, they fell back on a devoted administrator without any special competence, Baron d'Haussez, who was a career prefect. He was to turn out to be an energetic and able statesman. Unfortunately his status as a newcomer in politics and the slightly secondary character of his ministry confined him to a subordinate role, especially at the beginning.

## Press Hostility and Government Fumbling

The immediate outcry of the press against the ministry exceeded in violence their worst fears, and the king himself did not escape attack. A few examples will indicate the tone of the reaction. This was what the *Globe* said, a paper which prided itself on being objective:

> In our simple-mindedness we could not believe that they were up to schemes still more stupid than they are reprehensible. Had we then forgotten that there is a place where whim and prejudice, stubbornness and

thoughtlessness predominate; a place where the hardest and most striking lessons are neither heeded nor understood; a place where history
tells us that coups d'états, which arouse nations and carry off dynasties,
are so often decided between going hunting and going to confession?
This place is the court. From here, and from here alone, came the
new ministry. Intrigue prepared it, the good pleasure of the king formed
it. His accession has split France in two—the court on one side, the nation on the other.

And the *Journal des Débats:*

So here again is broken that tie of love and confidence which bound
people and monarch together. So here again we have the court with its
old resentments, the emigration with its old prejudices, the clergy with
its hatred of liberty, which are coming to thrust themselves between
France and her king. What she has won by forty years of toil and
pain they take away; what she rejects with all the strength of her
will . . . they impose on her by force. What perfidious counsels could
have misled Charles X and hurled him into a new career of disorder
right at that time of life when an atmosphere of peace and quiet is the
first requirement for his happiness? Luckless France! Luckless king!
[August 10]. Coblenz, Waterloo, 1815! these are the three people in
the ministry. . . . No matter how you squeeze or wring this ministry,
all that drips out is humiliation, misfortune, and danger [August 15].

In another key, the satirical *Figaro* published on August 10 a number
bordered in black. In a series of imaginary small news items it recounted
the plans attributed to the ministry: arbitrary imprisonments (*lettres de
cachets*), compulsory registration of arbitrary laws (*lits de justice*), forgotten men doomed to life imprisonment (*oubliettes*), feudal rights, criminal substitutes (*lieutenants criminels*), bailiffs and seneschals, in brief,
the whole panoply of medieval institutions. You would gather from this
paper that Polignac was preparing to rebuild the Bastille, to abolish the
metric system, to turn the country over to the Jesuits and Capuchins.
And this last piece of insolence was aimed at the king: "M. Roux, head
surgeon of the Charity Hospital, is about to perform a cataract operation
on an illustrious personage." This pamphlet was such a success that some
copies were sold for as much as ten francs (two dollars) a piece.

In the provinces loud liberal protests appeared on the occasion of a
voyage that La Fayette made in the southeast. Everywhere he was greeted
by triumphal receptions. At Grenoble he was presented a wreath of silver
oak leaves "as an emblem of the force that the Grenoblois, like him,
would be able to summon to uphold their rights and the constitution."

And at Lyons he was welcomed by an escort of five-hundred horsemen and eulogized like a sovereign. At this same time the Dauphin, visiting Normandy, was given a completely cool reception.

A more disquieting sign, a certain number of people still holding public office—some councillors of state, diplomats, the prefect of police Debelleyme, and others—were going to hand in their resignations in order not to link their future with such an unpopular team. The most serious of these defections was that of Chateaubriand, although at first he had shown himself favorable to the idea of a Polignac ministry combining all shades of the Right. At the time it was organized, he was taking the waters at Cauterets, and he certainly did not discourage the advances made to him by the ministry; basically he wanted to keep that Roman embassy, which furnished him a happy and dignified retirement. But when he returned to the capital, he was besieged by his friends who had already taken their position. They told him that his popularity would be finished if he sided with Polignac. With a heavy heart he also sent in his resignation. By this one act all of the plans carefully made at the end of the preceding session fell to the ground, plans by which the ministry was supposed theoretically to constitute a favorable majority in the chamber. In fact, to achieve the indispensable number, it was necessary to include not only the old counteropposition, represented by La Bourdonnaye, not only the Villèlist right, represented by Montbel, not only the doubtful Right-Center, but also the small group of the disaffection, such as Agier, Hyde de Neuville, and their consorts. These latter not having been represented in the ministry, only Chateaubriand could have stopped them from going over to the opposition.

## Government Decline and Liberal Growth

Under these conditions it was absolutely impossible to count on governing constitutionally—that is, with the support of the chamber. From then on, it would have been necessary to act with vigor and speed and immediately carry out that coup d'état which everybody expected. But, instead of doing that, the government wasted six full months in almost complete political inertia, weakening itself by internal divisions, emboldening its adversaries by its hesitations, and discouraging its supporters by its inaction. We are told of this dialogue between Polignac and Michaud, the editor of the Ultra-Royalist paper, the *Quotidienne*.

> "We are not going to spring a coup d'état."
> "I am sorry to hear that."

"And why?"

"Because, having only men who want a coup d'état for you, if you don't have one, you'll have no supporters left."

Polignac, in fact, was in no wise the votary of absolutism that the opposition press painted him for public opinion. His sojourn in England had transformed him into a sincere believer in a liberal and representative regime, firmly kept in line by a strong royal prerogative and a strong aristocracy. All that could not be done, he thought, within the framework of the Charter. The *Moniteur* of September 17 published a sort of ministerial manifesto in which could be read the passage: "Unless they have lost all common sense, the ministers could not even conceive of the idea of breaking the Charter and substituting the rule of ordinances for the rule of law." The other ministers had no more ideas or resolution than Polignac. Montbel wrote to Villèle on August 12 about his own defeatist feelings: "People cannot have confidence in us because we do not have confidence in ourselves. No precedents, no aptitude for political affairs, no influence over an opinion that is inclined favorably toward the ministers which may have to be called upon. A Hercules would be needed to manage all that."

La Bourdonnaye, on the other hand, was, at least in what he said, an advocate of the forceful approach. They attributed to him some sinister remarks, such as this: "One can govern easily enough with gallows and prostitutes." Yet, he did not do anything either, and his arrival in the ministry had not even been marked by those dismissals and changes in the personnel of the prefectures which people had expected. Having arrived at the height of his ambition, the great demolisher had quickly revealed himself to be completely devoid of administrative ability. A quarrelsome fellow, "a masculine shrew," he became just as unbearable to his colleagues. No doubt La Bourdonnaye himself realized the falsity of his position and looked for a chance to pull out of the game. He found his opportunity in the question of the presidency of the council. At the time the ministry was being formed, he had insisted on the condition that there be no president. Chabrol and d'Haussez seized on this as a way to eliminate their troublesome colleague. Pretending not to know of this condition, they asked, on November 17, for the re-establishment of the presidency in favor of Polignac. As they expected, La Bourdonnaye handed in his resignation. He was to receive as compensation the title of minister of state with a pension of twelve thousand francs ($2,400) and the promise of a peerage. To cover his defeat with an honorable pretext, he declared: "When I am staking my head, I want to hold the cards."

Montbel would have liked to use this occasion to bring Villèle back into the government; but Polignac did not want to share with anyone the glory of saving the monarchy, and Villèle was too shrewd to be compromised in a game that was going so poorly. Finally Montbel himself took the ministry of the interior, and, to fill his place, they sought out the procurator general of Lyons, Guernon-Ranville, about whom not much was known, except that he was a good royalist and a good speaker.

Polignac hoped that the elimination of the man of 1815 would reassure opinion as to the purity of his constitutional intentions. However, the liberal press only concluded that the ministry, if it was a little less *prévôtal* (arbitrary), would be a little more Jesuit. And this press redoubled its audacity, encouraged by the tolerance of the judges, who acquitted one out of every two journalist offenders whom the government brought to trial.

The resistance began to organize itself in various forms. The society God Helps Those Who Help Themselves reactivated its election committees and formed some new ones. The *Journal du Commerce* spread the idea of having an association of those who would refuse to pay taxes in case the government tried to set up a budget without the consent of the chamber. In Paris, under the leadership of La Fayette, it brought together all the leaders of the opposition, and it spread into fifteen departments. In January 1830 a republican society was organized among the students of Paris, whose newspaper was the *Jeune France,* founded by Armand Marrast. This group, to tell the truth, was not very large or influential. Much more dangerous to the government was the Orleanist party which was beginning to take shape under the very cautious inspiration of Talleyrand. Thanks to his secret patronage, a new paper, the *National,* was founded, whose great supplier of funds was Jacques Laffitte, the liberal banker and the great business manager for the Duke of Orleans. Its editors were Armand Carrel, Thiers, and Mignet; they did all they could to spread the idea that the constitutional regime desired by the nation was incompatible with the maintenance of the throne of the elder branch of the Bourbons. To preserve liberty, revolution was not even necessary; all one had to do was to carry out the Charter faithfully and, in order to do that, to replace a monarch blindly following the path of the Old Regime by another who understood his times. In other words, all Frenchmen needed to do was to imitate what the English had done in 1688:

> All had gone off then with the greatest calm. There was a family replaced by another family. . . . James II was dethroned, because he

loved what his people rejected. . . . England was so unrevolutionary at that time that, respecting as much as she could the ancient law, she chose the family most closely related to the fallen prince.

This was speaking rather clearly!

The extreme rightist press, furthermore, rather imprudently fed the liberal flames by pulling out all the stops in their exaltation of the king as the source of constitutional authority. It was already commenting on Article XIV of the Charter, finding in it the right of the sovereign to seize, in critical circumstances, dictatorial power. The ministry, for its part, continued to play dead. "The ministry is very decided," the *Globe* remarked sarcastically, "but it doesn't know for what." In fact Polignac and his colleagues were very much absorbed by the preparation of the expedition to Algiers (see below). As to the domestic situation, they whipped up some more or less unrealistic plans without succeeding in taking a very definite line of conduct. All their cleverness was reduced, in the last analysis, to delaying the opening of the parliamentary session until the beginning of March. They were going to present to it only the budget and a bill for big public works which would be financed by a new conversion of government bonds.

## The Parliamentary Showdown

The wording of the speech from the throne was weighed minutely in the council of ministers. The two houses met in joint session on March 2, 1830 to hear it. After the usual review of the foreign situation and the announcement of the public works to be proposed to parliament, Charles X added in a much louder voice:

> The Charter has placed the public freedoms under the safeguard of the rights of my crown. These rights are sacred, and my duty to my people is to transmit them intact to my successors. Peers of France, deputies of the departments, I do not doubt your collaboration in carrying out the good that I want to do. You will spurn with scorn the perfidious insinuations that malice is trying to promote. If unfriendly maneuvers raise obstacles against my government such as I do not wish to foresee, I would find the strength to overcome them in my determination to maintain public order, in the just confidence of Frenchmen, and in the love that they have always shown for their king.

What would be the reaction of the two houses to this menacing attitude? The reply (*adresse*) of the chamber of peers remained vague and moderate, in spite of a biting speech by Chateaubriand. The chamber of deputies showed what would be the attitude of the majority by electing Royer-Collard and Casimir Périer, in that order, as candidates for the presidency (speakership). With the support of the Left-Center and the "defection" the Left was then going to be in a position to bring the ministry down, and, in fact, the committee on the reply was entirely composed of opposition deputies. Royer-Collard intervened in the composition of the proposed reply to assure himself of a form suited to the gravity of the warning that was going to be given to the king. The floor discussions were the occasion for a great debate where two constitutional concepts, two interpretations of the Charter, clashed. Also were seen to make their appearance for the first time two of the greatest parliamentary figures of the century—Guizot and Berryer.

The point of view of the opposition was clearly stated by Sébastiani: "The crown's appointments should necessarily be given to men who inspire enough confidence to rally the support of the chambers around the administration. . . . When the councillors of the crown do not enjoy this confidence, so necessary for the operation and strength of the government, their duty is to resign their offices." To which Guernon-Ranville, in the name of the government, replied that the king could not bow to the will of the chamber without renouncing the prerogatives and independence of the executive branch as defined in the Charter.

> The ministers are the king's appointees, representing the views of the government. . . . How can that strange reversal of ideas be admitted whose result would be to tie down the head of state to what is the freest thing in the world—confidence . . . ? On that day when the crown would allow itself to be thus dominated by the two houses, on that day when such injunctions could be made and received, the constitutional monarchy would have ceased to exist, soon we would no longer have either throne, or Charter, or chamber. . . . The most violent anarchy . . . would again begin its aberrations.

In spite of his efforts, the committee proposal was passed by a vote of 221 to 181. It should be noted that a shift of thirty votes—those of the "defection"—would have been enough to reverse this result.

> The Charter [so read the chamber's reply] . . . guarantees, as a right, the intervention of the country in the deliberations on questions of public interests. . . . It makes the permanent accord of the political views of your government with the wishes of your people the indispensable condition for the steady advance of public affairs. Sire, our loyalty,

our devotion forces us to tell you that this accord does not exist. An unjust distrust of the feelings and thoughts of France is today the fundamental attitude of the administration. Your people are distressed by this because it is an affront to them; they are alarmed by it because it is a threat to their liberties.

And the text ended by a respectful appeal to the prerogative of the king that he might re-establish harmony among the various branches of his government by changing his ministry.

No one seriously expected the king to obey this injunction, and the dissolution which would bring the conflict back to the voting public appeared to everybody as the logical outcome of this first encounter. The opposition was not afraid of new elections, certain as it was of winning additional seats. Yet, in the ministry Guernon-Ranville and d'Haussez asked them not to be so hasty in taking such a step just on an unfavorable vote on a nonsubstantive issue; they ought to prove more clearly to the country that the opposition would be responsible for the dissolution. Would they not be in a better position to start the fight if, for example, the chamber refused to approve the budget or the funds for the Algiers expedition? Besides, d'Haussez boasted that he could garner forty additional votes if they were willing to pay the price. But Charles X firmly rejected the idea of having recourse to corrupt means, as Decazes and Villèle had done and as the governments of Louis-Philippe were to do systematically.

## Dissolution and New Elections

The dissolution of the chamber having been agreed upon in principle, it would have been wiser to have new elections immediately so as not to give the opposition time to organize. But here once again the fateful irresolution of the government got the upper hand. An ordinance of March 19 provided for calling the new parliamentary session on the following September 1, a half measure which would allow the ministry to choose a propitious moment for new elections. But what would be that moment? First they thought of putting it off as long as possible. This would give them time to revise the voting lists and make available, in case of need, the troops of the African expeditionary corps, which would have completed its job. But, Villèle, when consulted by the king, convinced him of the necessity to end the provisional financial situation as soon as possible. Very probably the former president of the council, encouraged by advances made to him by a group of deputies of the Center, was hoping to return to power and was in a hurry to see the end of that chamber which had voted to indict him and with which he could not in all decency collaborate. Therefore, on May 16, the royal ordinance appeared which announced the dissolution of the chamber and called for the meeting of the electoral colleges for June 23 and July 3.

Then came a third question: suppose the elections again gave a majority against the ministry, what would they do? The ministers had been considering this possibility since the end of April. Polignac spoke of having recourse to Article XIV of the Charter to use the ordinance power to modify the election system and the press restrictions. But Courvoisier and Chabrol said they were unalterably opposed to this and decided to resign rather than give their consent. This disagreement within the ministry came very near to precipitating its complete dissolution, each minister—except Polignac—going in turn to offer his resignation to the king. After four weeks of intrigues and comedies Charles X and Polignac succeeded in patching up their team as best they could. Courvoisier was replaced by Chantelauze, president of the Royal Court of Grenoble; good old Montbel, the ministry's jack-of-all-trades, agreed to take over finance from Chabrol and so left the interior to Peyronnet, the former keeper of the seal, still just as bullying and sure of himself. The king counted a great deal on the energy of this man to direct the elections, but his return to office only irritated public opinion some more by adding to the unpopularity of Polignac that of one of the most criticized men in the Villèle ministry. Finally, the directorship of public works was detached from the interior and became a separate ministry for Baron Capelle, the ex-prefect of Seine-et-Oise. He was known as an expert master cook when it came to election dishes.

On both sides eager preparations were made for the battle. All shades of the opposition, from the republicans on the Left to the center monarchists and the "defection," combined their forces with the goal of re-electing the 221 deputies who had voted for the reply. Their newspapers gave them a vocal outlet up and down the scale, and the election committees of the society God Helps Those Who Help Themselves mobilized all their resources to assure the maximum voter participation. The governmental press replied by stressing the royal prerogative as Decazes had done in 1816. The *Drapeau Blanc* went so far as to claim that any voter who cast his ballot for a candidate designated by the king as disqualified for the legislature would be guilty of a misdemeanor. The bishops, at the deliberate request of the government, sent out pastoral letters to recommend government candidates, and the ministers used to the fullest all the ordinary means of political pressure: circulars to public officials, promises, threats, dismissals from office. The king himself did not hesitate to take sides and descend into the arena. He issued on June 14 a proclamation which was to be published in all the communes.

> To maintain the Constitutional Charter and the institutions it has founded, has been, and always will be, the object of all my efforts. But to attain this aim, I must exercise freely, and have respected, the sacred rights which are the attributes of my crown. . . . The nature of the government would be altered if culpable attacks weakened my prerogatives. . . . Voters, hurry and go to your colleges . . . may you all rally around the same flag! It is your King who is asking you to do this; it is your father who is calling upon you. Do your duty and I'll do mine.

At the last minute the ministry had recourse to a maneuver which it justified by the pretext that the royal courts, swamped by the large number of voter listing appeals, had not been able to hear them all. So, in the Seine department and in nineteen others where the opposition was stronger, the voting was adjourned to the thirteenth and nineteenth of July. In this way they thought they could avoid the bad examples that the anticipated defeats in the district colleges would give to the departmental colleges, and on the other hand they could influence the undecided voters of these twenty departments by the news of ministerial victories which they hoped to gain in the remaining departments. As a result, the voting period, with all the turmoil which necessarily goes with it, was to drag on for almost a month.

The final result gave 274 seats to the opposition, against 143 for the ministry, and 11 undecided or unfilled. Of the 221 who voted for the reply, 202 were re-elected. The defeat was sweeping and unequivocal, and, because of the imprudence of the king and his councillors, the blow, instead of striking at just the responsible ministry, fell with full force upon the crown itself. Seemingly all was not yet lost for the dynasty and the regime. The opposition deputies, quite satisfied with their victory at the polls, were entirely disposed to be magnanimous and spare the old king's amour-propre; they were even ready to accept almost any ministry as long as there was a new one. Certain deputies, like Casimir Périer and Sébastiani, even made advances to Polignac with the proposal that he stay in a new government if the king would appoint them too. The perspective of a violent revolution, of a popular uprising, horrified these well-to-do bourgeois.

But the idea of making an orderly retreat or of surrendering was not considered for a moment by Charles X and Polignac. In their feudal simplicity they saw only one thing: they were attacked and they must fight without a backward step. By courage alone right would triumph! Their firm decision was fortified by the brilliant victory won at just that time by their foreign policy, with the capture of Algiers, which was known in Paris on July 9.

## Polignac, Russia, and the Great Plan

     La Ferronnays' Near Eastern policy had brought about a Franco-Russian rapprochement and had, at the same time, loosened France's bonds with England, whom Villèle had taken such pains to placate. The arrival of "my lord" Polignac in the foreign ministry was generally interpreted to be the sign of a new reversal of policy. Had he not been, in London, the active agent of a Franco-British entente? Were they not saying that Wellington had favored the formation of his government? "His taking of office," wrote Metternich, "will be a thunderclap to the Russian cabinet." And the *Journal des Débats* declared: "The French cabinet, tied hand and foot, has been turned over to England."

They were forgetting that France's foreign policy was now being directed by the king as much as by his minister and that personal sympathies could not prevail against permanent interests. Moreover, Polignac was to use his intimate knowledge of British leaders the better to defeat them.

Hardly had he taken office when he made an approach to the ambassador of the tsar to assure him that the basis of French policy would always be the Russian alliance. Besides, this corresponded to a constant tendency in the Ultra-Royalist party and, since 1824, in that of the counteropposition. Richelieu, Montmorency, and Chateaubriand had in turn made this the pivot of their diplomacy. We have already seen how Chateaubriand had at one point considered using it to obtain a revision of the treaties of 1815 along the Rhine frontier. What a triumph it would be for the monarchy if it could wipe out the humiliation which hung over the Restoration! And what a counterthrust it would be to the leftist parties, which had made this issue their rallying cry!

Polignac set to work immediately to try to transform this mirage into reality. In the month of August 1829 the Muscovite armies were advancing almost unopposed upon Constantinople. Was not the Ottoman Empire going to crumble? France's ambassador to Saint Petersburg, the Duke of Mortemart, asked for some guidance on what he should do in such an eventuality. Polignac's reply, dated September 4, constituted one of the most hair-raising documents in French diplomacy, and one might think one was dreaming when told that it had been thoroughly considered in a cabinet meeting. Envisioning the possible collapse of the Turkish Empire, Polignac said that France should come to an agreement with Russia and Prussia to impose a general revision of the map of Europe. Austria, isolated on the continent, could not oppose the combined determination of the three powers, and they would obtain her adherence by offering her a tempting slice of the cake— Serbia and Bosnia. Russia would receive the Rumanian provinces and a good slice of Asia Minor on the Armenian border. Egypt would become independent, and the caliphate could be transferred to Mohammed Ali. Greece would form a great independent Christian state, comprising all Greek-inhabited territories in Europe and Asia with Constantinople as its capital. France would not ask for anything in the Near East, but as compensation she would demand the dissolution of the Netherlands, which was already under way in the serious domestic quarrels then going on. Belgium would go to France and Holland to Prussia. As for King William—nothing more simple, he would go to Constantinople to reign over the revived Byzantine Empire. England would obviously oppose any such arrangement, but what could she do against a united continental Europe? The Austrians and Russians, moving into the Mediterranean, would have every interest in uniting their fleets to that of France to break the naval preponderance of the English, and likewise Prussia would become a sea power by the acquisition of Holland. Such was Polignac's "Great Plan," whose highly chimerical character it is hardly necessary to emphasize.

In fact, they only sent it to Mortemart as a general background for conversation in case the tsar brought up the question of the dismemberment of the Ottoman Empire. But this contingency was not to materialize: when the ambassador received these papers, the peace of Adrianople had just been signed. Therefore he did not have to make use of it. How would the tsar have entertained such proposals? Mortemart's attempt to sound him out a few weeks later gives us some idea. Austria having submitted a partition plan for European Turkey, the French ambassador insinuated that in that case France would want compensations on her northern frontier; and immediately Nicholas I interrupted him by saying that it was unthinkable. Thus Polignac's "Great Plan" evaporated before it had even the least beginning of materialization. He finally had to return to the more modest and more practical policy of La Ferronnays, in which spirit the Greek affair was settled.

England, full of ill-humor against an arrangement which had been practically imposed by Russia and France, still caused many difficulties over the boundaries to be given to the new state and the choice of its sovereign. There is little use in going into the details of these negotiations here. Concessions were made on both sides, and the agreement finally reached on November 30, 1829, was consigned to a protocol signed on February 9, 1830. Greece was not made quite as large as France and Russia had wanted her to be at first; but she was completely independent of the sultan, and the crown of the new state was to be offered to Prince Leopold of Saxe-Coburg, son-in-law of the King of England.

## The Expedition to Algiers

The conquest of Algiers, which is entirely the accomplishment of the Polignac ministry, appears in certain respects to be the corollary of Near Eastern affairs. In any case it proceeds from the same intentions and methods: that is, from an enterprising and firm policy relying on Russia and tipped slightly in the direction of concern for the general interests of Europe; from a policy of prestige, looking less to augmenting the material powers of France than to re-enforcing her moral position before Europe and that of the monarchy before the nation.

The origins of the conflict were distant and complex. For a long time the Western powers were trying to bring a halt to Algerian piracy. In 1819, following the Congress of Aix-la-Chapelle, France and England had agreed to a joint protest to the Dey of Algiers, Hussein. The latter had paid no attention to it, but the irritation which it had caused him had led him to give a more unfriendly twist to two pending matters between him and France—the question of African concessions and that of the Bacri and Busnach loans. Since the beginning of the sixteenth century, France had possessed, along the North African coast, some trading posts called "concessions," which enjoyed a monopoly of the trade with the interior as well as of the coral fishing. Naturally the wars of the Revolution and the Empire interrupted these activities. In 1817 the Dey of Algiers had agreed to renew the privileges of the concessions in return for an annual payment of sixty thousand francs (twelve thousand dollars). Immediately after the joint protest of 1819, in one jump he tried to raise it to 214,000 francs ($42,800), and he increased his petty annoyances toward French administrators.

At the same time Hussein brought up claims in another direction. The Directory had made large purchases of wheat from a firm of Leghorn Jews, Bacri and Busnach, who enjoyed a privileged position in the commerce of the Algiers Regency. The profits they claimed to make from it were so scandalously high that Bonaparte refused to pay them. The Restoration examined their claims like all the other French debts of the preceding twenty years, and, in 1820, the government decided to pay them seven million francs ($1,400,000) instead of the fourteen million ($2,800,000) which they were demanding. The dey, who had, on his own part, loaned 250,000 francs (fifty thousand dollars) to Bacri and Busnach, imperiously requested that the French government turn over to him the sums granted to the Jewish merchants. Naturally, it refused to agree to a procedure so contrary to French laws. Hussein made Deval, the French consul, responsible for the refusal and asked for his recall, which was also refused. On April 30, 1827, when Deval had come for a courtesy audience, Hussein upbraided him for having conspired with the Jews to frustrate him; carried away by his anger, he hit the consul three times with the handle of his fly-swisher.

At the news of this insult France sent six war vessels to demand reparations. Upon the haughty refusal of the dey, the French squadron took on board Deval and all Frenchmen residing in the Algiers Regency and began a blockade of the port. This measure turned out to be ineffective; they could stop all Algerians from leaving, but they could not stop ships flying other flags. Clermont-Tonnerre, minister of war in the Villèle government, proposed a punitive expedition, supported by the landing of troops. But Villèle would not hear of it. Besides, at this moment the naval forces were necessary in the Eastern Mediterranean, and a part of the army was still required in Spain. For similar reasons—the expedition in Greece—the Martignac government did not find itself able to act forcefully, and La Ferronnays, engaged in a delicate diplomatic game between Russia and England, wanted to avoid any diplomatic friction. Nevertheless, it was decided to make a new attempt to obtain from the dey some minimal satisfaction which could be displayed as an honorable conclusion to the dispute. Ship's Captain La Bretonnière was sent to see the dey, but Hussein, encouraged by the English representative, gave an arrogant refusal to talk. Moreover, the parley ship, the "Provence," was fired on eighty times as it left the port (August 3, 1829).

The news of this attack reached Paris right at the time that Polignac was assuming office. In spite of his desire to bolster the prestige of his government by some successes in foreign policy, he was to hesitate a rather long time before undertaking an armed intervention. Perhaps he thought he could gain a lot more from his "Great Plan"; more likely he had in mind another solution no less fantastic. Mohammed Ali, Pasha of Egypt, offered himself to the French government as the executor of its great designs. He boasted that he could settle France's accounts with Hussein provided they helped him by advancing him twenty million francs (four million dollars) and gave him four ships of the line to support his ground forces, which he claimed he could lead to Algeria through Tripolitania and Tunisia. Polignac thought it was an excellent idea. In this way they would not be committing the armies of the King of France against an adversary unworthy of them, and the affair would be settled between Muslims, which would avoid any risk of a holy war against Christians in the East. Charles X and d'Haussez balked at the idea of letting Egypt have French vessels, and Bourmont succeeded, not without difficulty, in having Polignac understand the practical impossibility of moving an army of forty thousand men across a desert three thousand kilometers (1860 miles) wide. It could be suspected that the astute pasha, by this scheme, was mainly looking for a chance to increase for his own benefit both his fleet and his treasure.

On January 31, 1830 the council of ministers then rallied to the principle of direct intervention in North Africa, and a few days later preparations were started. Militarily the enterprise was full of dangers; "Algiers the Well-Guarded," Algiers which had held out against Charles V and against eleven Christian expeditions, had the reputation for being unassailable. The best minds in the admiralty council raised all sorts of technical objections, and they had all possible difficulties finding an admiral who was willing to risk his reputation on such an enterprise. Duperré, who finally accepted without enthusiasm, declared that the expedition could not be ready before the spring of 1831. Fortunately the king found in d'Haussez a man capable of prodding these very timid warriors. His contagious enthusiasm and his organizing talent worked miracles. In three months all was in readiness at Toulon—103 warships, 350 transport ships, 27,000 sailors, 37,000 soldiers, eighty-three siege pieces, and an enormous quantity of supplies and equipment.

It must be said in justice to Polignac that he was to assure the diplomatic preparation with the same good results. A circular of March 12 announced France's intentions to the powers. "Our aim [he said] is humanitarian. We are seeking, in addition to satisfaction for our own grievances, the abolition of the enslavement of Christians, the destruction of piracy, and the end of humiliating tributes that the European states are having to pay to the Regency." And he promised that France would consult with its allies when it came to establishing a new order of things in North Africa. The tsar gave a most cordial reception to this communication, and his attitude helped to obtain the assent of Prussia and Austria. On the contrary, England reacted strongly, and it was probably only the fact that Wellington's government was then having domestic difficulties which prevented it from having recourse to force. At least on the diplomatic side no protest and no means of direct or indirect pressure was spared by England to prevent France from carrying out her plan. By repeated and urgent interventions, in London to the French ambassador as well as in Paris to the king's foreign minister, Lord Aberdeen, the foreign secretary, tried to obtain a written commitment to the effect that France would limit herself to a punitive expedition and would not try to hold on to her conquest permanently. Polignac adroitly evaded the question by suggesting that England could be satisfied by the general assurances furnished to all the powers. To give a special assurance to one of the powers would cause the expedition to lose its character of international interest which it was intended to preserve. Wellington, exasperated, declared that Polignac was "one of the most clever and most dishonest of men." His ambassador, Lord Stuart, tried intimidation on the minister d'Haussez, which elicited the sharp reply:

> My Lord, I have never permitted a threatening tone to be used toward me, even as an individual; I will allow it even less toward the government of which I am a member. I have already said that I do not want to deal with this question diplomatically; you will now find this out by the words which I am going to employ: France doesn't give a damn about England.

Charles X, with more royal dignity, stopped Stuart's protests by saying: "Mr. Ambassador, all I can do for your government is not to listen to what I have just heard."

Opposition also came from home. As at the time of the expedition to Spain, the liberals could not endure the prospect of success for the detested government, and their partisan passions stifled their patriotism. If one were to believe them, the expedition was a folly, a crime. Just look! The necessary expenditures have been appropriated without the previous consent of the two houses! "There's the real insult that France must feel," wrote the *Journal des Débats,* "much more than the fan slap of a barbarian on the cheek of a foolhardy man." The liberal press did not even hesitate to publish confidential information on the forces assembled and on debarkation plans—a deed which could have had most fatal consequences with any other adversary.

But no more than in 1823 did this uproar prevail against the fighting man's joy of getting out of his barracks and having a chance to distinguish himself. And it was in an atmosphere of enthusiasm that the departure of the expeditionary corps took place from May 25 to 27.

The chief command was given to Bourmont who yearned to wipe out by a national triumph the bad reputation attached to his name. As a precaution he had in his portfolio a royal ordinance which put under his authority Duperré, an officer whose ill-will inspired some mistrust. In fact the latter showed excessive caution. As they were arriving in view of the African coasts on May 30, the winds seemed contrary; therefore he turned the whole fleet toward Palma de Majorca. Yet, in fact, the site chosen for the debarkation was protected from the east winds, and he could have made the landings without any serious difficulties. The ten days lost in waiting at Majorca only served to tire and fret the troops and to permit the Dey of Algiers to assemble his naval units.

The winds having finally changed, they set sail on June 10; and once again Duperré wanted to delay. Finally Bourmont had to exercise his authority, and on the morning of June 14 the debarkation began in the Bay of Sidi-Ferruch, twenty kilometers (12.4 miles) west of Algiers. The landing operation was to require four days, delayed not so much by the sporadic attacks of enemy units as by a storm which rose on the night of the fifteenth and for a moment threatened disaster. Finally on the nineteenth Hussein's army attacked in force. It was commanded by the Agha Ibrahim, son-in-law of Hussein, and contained about fifty to sixty thousand men. The French army, smaller in size but better armed and commanded, had little difficulty in warding off the impetuous assault of the Arab cavalry, and, going over to the offensive, it captured the enemy artillery and the plateau of Staouëli where Ibrahim had made his camp. Bourmont, however, was unable to follow up this success because he had to wait for his supplies to catch up, especially for his siege guns, delayed in Majorca by Duperré's orders. The advance could be resumed only by June 24, and the French columns moved forward only with great difficulty, relentlessly harassed by the horsemen of the Algerian army. On the evening of the twenty-ninth the trench was completed in front of Fort Empereur, a key position dominating by its elevation of 214 meters (702 feet) the city and the Kasbah. The siege artillery, once in place, began its work of destruction on the morning of July 4. A few hours later the defenders of the fort abandoned their battered walls, blowing up their powder magazine.

The dey asked for Bourmont's conditions, and the commander-in-chief dictated the terms of surrender: the French would occupy the city; the dey would keep his property and be free to retire wherever he wished, as would be his Turkish mercenaries; the freedom, property, and religion of the inhabitants would be respected. On July 5 the French flag was hoisted over the Kasbah and the Algiers forts. "Twenty days were all that were required," said Bourmont proudly in his proclamation to his troops, "for the destruction of a state whose existence had harrassed

Europe for over three centuries." Rarely had a conquest so weighted with consequences cost so little. The 48 million francs ($9,600,000) found in the dey's treasury was to cover, and more, the cost of the expedition. The army casualties amounted to 415 killed and 2,160 wounded.

In any other country under any other circumstances the news of this brilliant success would have aroused the enthusiasm of the nation and aroused its gratitude toward the monarch and government who had made it possible. But public opinion, blinded by the internal struggle, did not give any credit for this. In the elections, minister d'Haussez's candidacy failed in nine departments. As for the king—before he took his leave, however, Charles X rendered a last service to France. The future fate of the conquest remained in suspense for some days. About July 20 the king decided that Algiers would be kept in any case. To the written requests for explanations, presented by the British ambassador, Charles X replied in his own hand: "In taking Algiers I considered only France's dignity, in keeping it or returning it, I shall consider only her interests."

The continuous ill-will of England and her Paris representative was to hang heavily—certainly not decisively, but appreciably just the same— over the drama of the later July days (see next chapter).

From still another point of view, the successful taking of Algiers was to be fatal for Charles X. It stiffened, in fact, his determination to resist at all costs the will of the electorate. The liberals had predicted, even openly hoped for, the failure of the expedition. Why could not their predictions and their threats be countered at home by that same firmness that had triumphed in North Africa? Would not the great majority of the nation, who had been able to appreciate in the latter case the beneficent fairness of the king's views, accept his political decisions? The Archbishop of Paris, Mgr. Quélen, encouraged him; he wrote in his pastoral letter calling for a *Te Deum* of thanksgiving: "Three weeks were enough to humiliate and reduce the superb Muslims to the weakness of a child. Thus may the enemies of our lord and king be treated always and everywhere; thus may be confounded all those who dare to rise up against him!"

# 23

⚜ ⚜ ⚜ ⚜ ⚜

# The Overthrow of Charles X

## Preparing the Overthrow

THE election results in the district colleges were known on June 29, and the council of ministers had to consider what it should do next in the face of an inevitable defeat. The ministers found themselves in agreement on feeling justified in having recourse to Article XIV of the Charter, permitting the king to issue ordinances in emergencies. But in what way would they use it? In the next few days Polignac and Chantelauze proposed various plans which were discarded as impractical. Finally on July 6 they all agreed on three measures suggested by Peyronnet: dissolve the new chamber as soon as the election returns were in, have a new legislature elected according to a new electoral system, and suspend the freedom of the press. The king approved this program and gave the following justification for his decision:

> The revolutionary spirit survives in its entirety among the men of the Left. In attacking the ministry it is really royalty that they resent, it is the monarchical system that they want to reverse. Unfortunately, Gentlemen, I have more experience on this point than you, who were not old enough to have seen the Revolution. I remember what happened then: the first retreat that my hapless brother made led to his downfall. . . . They pretend that they are only angry at you, they say to me: "Dismiss your ministers and we will come to an understanding." . . . I will not dismiss you; first of all, Gentlemen, because I have an affection for you all and because I give you my full confidence, but also because, if I gave in to their demands this time, they would eventually treat us like they treated my brother. . . .

As a result, Peyronnet was given the job of preparing the texts of the ordinances. Those he brought in on July 10 were discussed in detail by his colleagues during the next few days. Finally on the twenty-fourth the definitive version was adopted. Guernon-Ranville and d'Haussez had fought against the proposed measures right up to the end. The former contended, as in March, that they ought first to put the new chamber to the test; the latter criticized the proposed electoral system; and both apprehended a popular explosion and doubted the effectiveness of the precautions taken by Polignac, who was acting as the war minister in the absence of Bourmont. Yet the prefect of police, Mangin, appeared to be full of confidence: "No matter what you do, the people of Paris will not stir. Go ahead boldly, I'll stake my head on Paris, I'll see to her." Finally the two opponents gave in to the views of the majority in the council; the more the peril seemed great, the more they felt bound by honor to stand by their king and colleagues on the eve of the decisive showdown.

### The Four Ordinances

On the following day, July 25, Charles X called his ministers together at Saint-Cloud after Mass. He had them read to him the prepared texts twice, then turning to his son, he asked:

"You have heard this?"

"Yes, father."

"What do you think of it?"

"When the danger is inevitable, you must meet it head on. We either win or lose."

"Is this your opinion, Gentlemen?" the king asked, glancing around the table.

"Yes, Sire," d'Haussez replied, "we are agreed on the ends, but not on the means." Here he elaborated his objections.

"So you don't want to sign?" the king asked.

"I'll sign, Sire, because I would consider it a crime to abandon the monarchy and the king under such circumstances. . . ."

"Then," Guernon-Ranville tells us, "Charles X fell into a deep spell of reflection; for several minutes he held his head in his hand and his pen poised two inches above the paper. Whereupon he said: 'The more I think of it the more I am convinced that it is impossible to do otherwise.' And he signed. . . . After that we all countersigned in profound silence. . . . Before retiring Charles X spoke again: 'Here are some great measures! We shall have to have a lot of courage and firmness to make them succeed. I count on you, you can count on me. Our cause is one. For us all it is life or death.' "

All of this took place in great secrecy, since Charles X and Polignac, especially, were convinced that the element of surprise was indispensable to the success of the operation. Thus, to deceive the opposition even more, they went so far as to send the deputies letters of summons for the opening of the parliamentary session, and Polignac appeared openly to be working on the speech from the throne. This could also explain why no military precaution had been taken: they wanted to avoid giving themselves away by any troop movements. Because of this, the government, to counter any uprising, would only have available the ordinary forces of the Paris garrison, about twelve thousand men, plus thirteen hundred life-guards. Many of the officers were back home in the departments where they had gone to vote. Only at eleven o'clock at night did Chantelauze hand over the texts to Sauvo, editor-in-chief of the *Moniteur*, with an order to print them in the next day's edition.

"What do you think of them?" asked Montbel, who was also present, after giving him time to look them over.

"God save the King and France," this good man replied. "Gentlemen, I am fifty-seven, I have seen all the days of the Revolution and I draw back in profound terror!"

The texts of the ordinances were preceded by a report to the king, or a justification, which Chantelauze had composed. It was especially a vigorous denunciation of the excesses of the press:

A fierce attack, dishonest and passionate, full of scandal and hate . . . is stirring up among us an ever-growing fermentation and could lead us by degrees back to barbarism. . . . The facts, when they are not entirely invented, come to the knowledge of several million readers only in shortened and twisted form, mutilated in the most odious way. . . . Against so many wrongs, law and justice are both reduced to admitting their powerlessness. . . . [Chantelauze goes on to justify their recourse to exceptional measures.] We are no longer under the ordinary conditions of representative government. A turbulent democracy is tending to substitute itself for legitimate authority. It obtains the majority of the elections by means of its newspapers and the help of its numerous affiliations. It has paralyzed . . . the regular exercise of the most essential prerogative of the crown. . . . By this very fact the constitution of the state is violated. The right as well as the duty of guaranteeing its maintenance is the essential attribute of sovereignty. . . .

Then followed the four ordinances, described here in abbreviated form.

*First.* The present press system is suspended. Henceforth no paper or periodical and no brochure of less than twenty pages may appear without authorization.

*Second.* The king, "being informed of the maneuvers practiced in several places in the kingdom to deceive and mislead the voters during the recent voting in the electoral colleges," declares the dissolution of the newly elected chamber.

*Third.* The number of deputies is put back to 258. The chamber is elected for five years, with one-fifth elected each year. The deputies are to be elected in the departmental colleges, composed of the one-fourth highest voting taxpayers. As to the district colleges, their role will be limited, as in 1815, to nominating candidates for the consideration of the departmental voters. To determine the voter and candidate tax qualifications, only land taxes and the assessments of personal and movable property will be counted. Business licenses and door and window taxes are excluded from the computation.

*Fourth.* The electoral colleges are called to meet on September 6 and 13, and the session of the chamber will open on the twenty-eighth of the same month.

Only the third ordinance calls for some commentary. It made, in fact, the most obvious change in the political system. It also gives one a chance to recognize the sense—or rather the lack of sense—which prevailed in the counsels of the king. Since they wanted to counter the tax-paying bourgeoisie which made up the electorate, it no doubt would have been good politics to seek support among the lower strata of the nation. There the prestige of royalty, the love of peace and quiet, the force of inertia, and the combined influence of the landed aristocracy and the clergy could have, perhaps, procured for the throne that confidence and backing that the majority of the enlightened class had withheld. The more dictatorial a regime is, the more it needs the support of the uneducated masses. They had seen it in 1799 and were to see it again in 1851. This was the point of view stressed by Guernon-Ranville, and he was quite in the tradition of absolute monarchy, which had only broken the power of the aristocracy by, we might say, passing over this class to obtain the backing of the bourgeoisie. Now that the latter in turn had become the obstacle, Charles X could have tried the same operation again, only one notch lower. Doing this, he would have pulled the rug out from under the liberals. There was nothing these people dreaded so much, as can be seen in the curious article in the *National,* published on July 22, in which the author accused the government of throwing itself in the arms of the lower classes in order to break the opposition of the high tax-paying electorate. Unfortunately for the monarchy, Charles X and Polignac had chosen the opposite path—instead of enlarging the electorate they had tried to restrict it still further. The last election had given a slight advantage to the government in the departmental colleges, and so they gave them the exclusive right to elect the deputies. Furthermore, in the electorate in general, the industrial and commercial element was more favorable to liberalism; consequently they tried to eliminate it by excluding business license taxes from the tax total of three hundred francs (sixty dollars) and a thousand francs (two hundred dollars) required for voter and candidate eligibility. To what extent would such an arrangement have attained the desired effect? M. Jean Vidalenc has computed it for the Eure department. Out of 1,122 registered voters in 1830, Polignac's ordinance would have disqualified ninety-three of them, among which would have been only seven landed proprietors as contrasted with twenty-four merchants, twenty-three manufacturers, six innkeepers, five tanners, etc.

## The July Revolution

The *Moniteur* came out on July 26 a little later than usual, toward 11 o'clock in the morning. Then the storm broke. Let us now try to give a blow by blow account of the events.

### Monday, July 26

—At the same time that the royal ordinances were being published, an order from the prefect of police forbade the printing of newspapers without prescribed authorization.

*Afternoon.*—The editors of the principal opposition papers met at the home of lawyer Dupin along with other liberal lawyers. They agreed that the ordinances were illegal, and that they did not have to be obeyed.

—The journalists transferred their meeting to the office of the *National* and decided that they would publish their papers the next day in spite of the prefectural order.

—On Thiers' suggestion, they drew up and signed, forty-four of them, a protest couched in the following terms:

> Legal rule is interrupted; that of force is beginning. . . . Obedience ceases to be a duty. . . . It is not for us to tell the illegally dissolved chamber what its duties are, but we can urge it, in the name of

France, to stand on its obvious rights and resist with all its strength the violation of the laws. . . .

In the course of the afternoon and evening this manifesto was printed and distributed in the cafés and on the streets.

—Industrialists and merchants, assembled at the City Hall for the election of the commercial court, decided they would close their workshops on the following day. Thus their workers would be in the streets and available for the agitators.

—At the Bourse government bonds fell four points.

*Evening.*—Fifteen deputies, meeting at Alexandre de Laborde's, decided that they were not in sufficient numbers to take any initiative and that they would meet again at Casimir Périer's the next day at about 3:00 P.M.

—Some gatherings of printing workers and students began to assemble around the Bourse and the Palais-Royal, crying "Long Live the Charter! Down with the ministers!" The windows of the finance ministry were stoned.

—The theaters and popular dance-halls were full as usual.

*11:00* P.M. *Saint-Cloud.*—The king returned from Rambouillet where he had spent the day hunting with his son.


*Tuesday, July 27*

—The night had been calm.

—The *National, Temps,* and *Globe,* were published without authorization and contained the journalists' protest. The *Constitutionnel* and the *Journal des Débats* abstained. The royalist papers, authorized, exulted in lyric terms on the triumph of the king over the factions.

—The prefect of police ordered the seizure of the presses of the recalcitrant papers. At the *Temps* printing office, on rue Richelieu, its doors had been barricaded, and several hours were required before the police commissioner found a locksmith who was willing to force open the locks for the breaking up of the presses.

—Warrants were issued for the arrest of the journalists who had been signers of the protest. But they were not carried out.

—In the streets the agitation grew. The students in the republican societies tried to call out the workers who were left unemployed by the closing of the shops. They began to break the signs bearing the royal coat of arms. Some gun shops were pillaged.

*—11:30* A.M. Marshal Marmont, Duke of Ragusa, who was commander-in-chief of the royal guard on duty for this trimester, was called to see the king.

> Marshal [the king said to him], I understand that there are disturbances in Paris. You will go there and take command of the troops. You will have all gatherings dispersed, and if, as I hope, all is quiet by evening, you will come back to Saint-Cloud for the night. On your arrival you will report to M. de Polignac.

*—12:30* P.M. Polignac handed Marmont the ordinance, dated July 25, which gave him supreme command of the troops in the Paris garrison. It may be noted that this choice was one which would irritate opinion because it recalled the "betrayal" of 1814. Besides, the marshal criticized the ordinances and only accepted the assignment against his best judgment and with a concern not to add to the load of unpopularity which weighed upon him. He set up his headquarters at the general-staff office of the guard, on the Place du Carrousel, but as nothing had been provided in advance by Polignac, he had to spend several hours in assembling his troops and dispatching them to their stations.

*—3:00* P.M. The deputies, assembled to the number of thirty at Casimir Périer's, refused to support an insurrectional resistance. They assigned Guizot to prepare the text of a protest against the ordinances.

—The gendarmerie (constabulary) charged the gathering crowds around the Palais-Royal and the foreign ministry on the Boulevard des Capucines.

*—About 3:00* P.M. The first insurgent was killed.

*—5:00* P.M. Marmont had the principal strategic points of the capital occupied. There was little resistance to this. Only two barricades were raised around the Palais-Royal. A few were killed and wounded. The guard post at the Bourse was burned.

—The ministers decided to declare a state of siege in Paris, which would give full powers to Marmont.

*—9:00* P.M. The agitation died down, and the troops were ordered back to barracks.

—A group of extreme-Left voters formed twelve district (*arrondissement*) committees, with the duty of organizing an insurrection. Most members were former Charbonniers.

*Wednesday, July 28*

—At dawn the insurrection began to take shape in the workers' sections of the city. A mixed crowd of workers, national guardsmen, young university students, and former soldiers gathered in the streets, forced the surrender of isolated military stations, cut down trees, pulled up paving stones, built barricades, and hoisted the tricolor flag to the cries of "Down with the Bourbons! Long Live the Republic! Long Live the Emperor!" They took over the Arsenal, the powder magazine of the Salpêtrière, and the military supply depot. The City Hall and Notre Dame Cathedral were occupied. The tocsin was sounding continuously.

—*8:00* A.M. Marmont wrote the king: "This is no longer a riot, it is a revolution. It is urgent that Your Majesty resort to some means of pacification. The honor of the crown can still be saved. Tomorrow perhaps will be too late. . . ."

—*12:00 Noon.* The marshal, having received no answer, decided to carry out the plan drawn up during the morning by the general staff. Four columns were to fan out and occupy the four principal points of the revolting districts and clear out the big arteries as they passed. The leaders had orders to hold their fire as much as possible. In the withering heat, the progress was slow and difficult. The soldiers knocked down the barricades rather easily, but the insurgents, fleeing into the houses and to the roofs, kept up a murderous fusillade and hurled various missiles at their adversaries.

—The deputies met again at Audry de Puyravault's. For the first time La Fayette and Laffitte were present, returning hastily from the country. They still refused to depart from legal action and only adopted the protest text composed by Guizot. They decided to send a five-man delegation to Marmont, made up of Périer, Laffitte, Mauguin, and Generals Gérard and Mouton.

—*3:00* P.M. Admitted into Marmont's office, the deputies asked him to bring the bloodshed to an end. If he could persuade the king to withdraw the ordinances and dismiss his ministers, they could, on their side, try to stop the popular uprising. Marmont replied that he could not, on his own, stop the battle and that it was not up to him to propose political measures so long as the revolters did not lay down their arms. Polignac, who was holding continuous council meetings in the next room, refused to receive the commissioners. When they told him that certain units of the regular army were fraternizing with the people, he replied, "All right then, fire on the troops!"

—*5:00* P.M. Marmont's columns had reached their objectives: the Bastille Square, City Hall, Innocents Market, Place des Victoires, and the Madeleine. But behind them the barricades were thrown up again. Each of his units were isolated from each other without supplies, and they began to run out of ammunition.

—The deputies rejoined their colleagues in another place. The party of conciliation was discouraged. They decided to remove from the protest their expressions of attachment to the king. Casimir Périer shouted: "After what the people have begun, should we have to risk our heads ten times, we are dishonored if we don't stick with them!" Laffitte came forward with the idea of appealing to the Duke of Orleans, who had retired to Neuilly and was not accessible.

—Marmont, anticipating an order from the king, decided to call in his dispersed troops and concentrate them around the Louvre and Tuileries. "This position is unassailable," he told the ministers, "I can hold out against all Paris for two weeks, if necessary, and we will have time to call in additional troops." The movement of concentrating the troops ran into the same difficulties as there had been in dispersing them. Some detachments of regular troops laid down their arms and joined the insurgents. When the concentration had been completed they found that the royal forces had lost 2,500 men, killed, wounded, prisoners, and especially deserters. Only then did they give orders to send in regiments of the royal guard from the garrisons in Beauvais, Orleans, Rouen, and Caen.

—At Saint-Cloud, from where they could hear the sound of fighting, the king affected the appearance of confident calmness and held his usual card game.

### Thursday, July 29

—The recall of the royal troops and the defection of the regulars gave a great impetus to the insurrection. The mass of the population seemed now to be joining in, and, in the morning six thousand barricades had transformed all the sections of the center and east into one vast entrenched camp.

—Former officers of the empire and students of the Ecole Polytechnique organized insurgent troops and maneuvered them so as to overwhelm the Louvre from the left bank of the Seine. They assailed some important positions, such as the Palais-Bourbon and the Swiss barracks on Rue de Babylone.

—Marmont persuaded the ministers to go to Saint-Cloud to advise the king themselves to withdraw the ordinances and to arrange a change in government.

—The Fifth and Fifty-Third regiments of regulars, who were occupying the Place Vendôme, defected. To replace them Marmont was obliged to draw upon the royal guard and the Swiss guard who were defending the royal palaces. A misunderstanding during this shift left undefended the façade of the Louvre facing Saint-Germain l'Auxerrois, and the insurgents took advantage of this to infiltrate into the galleries by climbing in the windows and then suddenly firing on the Swiss in the inner courtyard. Seized with panic, they fled and carried along with them in their flight the troops of the guard which were waiting in the Tuileries Gardens. Marmont could only try to regroup them on the Champs-Elysées, and, to avoid encirclement, had them fall back to the Étoile city gate.

—Talleyrand, from his window, at the corner of Rue Saint-Florentin, saw this débacle. He drew out his watch and said: "At five minutes after noon, the elder branch of the Bourbons ceased to reign."

—Early in the afternoon the capital was entirely in the hands of the insurgents, and fighting had ended. They were to learn later that it had cost about two hundred killed and eight hundred wounded among the royal troops and eighteen hundred killed and 4500 wounded on the other side.

—The deputies, assembled toward noon at Laffitte's, finally decided to assume the direction of the movement to prevent it from being taken over by the republicans. La Fayette received the command of the Paris National Guard and General Gérard that of the regular troops. A city committee was formed: it was composed of Laffitte, Casimir Périer, General Mouton, Schonen, and Audry de Puyravault. It would be installed at the City Hall around 4:00 P.M. La Fayette, conducted in a triumphal procession, went on ahead.

*Saint-Cloud.*—Toward the end of the morning the king had received Sémonville, d'Argout, and Vitrolles, peers of France, who had begged him to form a ministry of conciliation with the Duke of Mortemart, a peer sympathetic to the liberals.

—*1:30* P.M. Opening of a council meeting with the ministers recently arrived from Paris. During their discussion they learned of the taking of the Louvre and the rout of the royal troops. They began to doubt Marmont's loyalty, the supreme command was given to the Duke of Angoulême. The latter now ordered the Duke of Ragusa to bring the loyal troops to Saint-Cloud.

—The ministers approve the retraction of the ordinances. Charles X finally said:

Here I am in the same position of my unfortunate brother in 1792. The only advantage I have over him is that I did not have to suffer so long. In three days all will be finished for the monarchy. As for the monarch, he will suffer the same fate. Since I have to, I am going to summon the Duke of Mortemart and send him to Paris. I pity him for having obtained the confidence of my enemies.

—The king received Mortemart and agreed to let him form a ministry with Casimir Périer and Gérard.

—*6:00* P.M. Sémonville, Vitrolles, and d'Argout left for Paris to carry the news of the king's concessions. They had a hard time getting to the City Hall. The city committee listened to them unsympathetically and sent them over to the deputies meeting at Laffitte's.

—*8:00* P.M. D'Argout arrived alone, but, as he brought no official document, Laffitte used it as an excuse for delaying any decision.

—The Paris newspapers reappeared in the evening, and rejoiced at the victory of the people. In the night the coach companies had coaches leave on all routes, flying the tricolor flag, which would bring to the departments the news of events.

### Friday, July 30

*Saint-Cloud.*—The king went to bed without signing the documents giving official approval to his concessions, and Mortemart was therefore waiting with hands tied. About 2:30 in the morning Vitrolles and d'Argout were back and insisting on the urgency of Mortemart's presence in Paris. The king, awakened, agreed to have the ordinances drawn up and signed. It was only at about seven o'clock that Mortemart could leave Saint-Cloud.

*Paris.*—On the walls was spread an anonymous proclamation, the work of Thiers and Mignet:

> Charles X can no longer enter Paris. He has caused the people's blood to be shed.
>
> The Republic would expose us to awful divisions and would embroil us with Europe.
>
> The Duke of Orleans is a prince devoted to the cause of the Revolution.
>
> . . . . . . . . . . . . . . . . . . . . . . . .
>
> The Duke of Orleans carried the tricolor flag in battle. Only the Duke of Orleans can carry it again. We want no other one.
>
> The Duke of Orleans has taken his position: he accepts the Charter as we have always wanted it to be.
>
> It is from the French people that he will take his crown.

—Mortemart, arrived in Paris with great difficulty, went furtively to the Luxemburg Palace. Some peers, who were there, dissuaded him from going to the City Hall. One of them volunteered to carry the royal ordinances to La Fayette. The reading of it was accompanied by jeers. The city committee forbade the *Moniteur* to publish them, and Mortemart found no printer who dared to do it.

—Thiers, sent to Neuilly by Laffitte and Sébastiani did not find the Duke of Orleans, who had hidden himself at Le Raincy. He explained the situation to the Duchess of Orleans and to Mme Adelaide, the prince's sister, and the latter vouched for her brother's acceptance and sent him a message to have him return to Neuilly.

—*Noon.* About sixty deputies assembled in the Palais-Bourbon under the presidency of Laffitte. After a long discussion they decided to invite the Duke of Orleans to come to Paris to exercise the functions of lieutenant-general of the realm, a solution which was said to have been suggested by Talleyrand.

—The foreign diplomats got together to decide what attitude they should take. Should they go to Rambouillet to bring the support of Europe to the sovereign, or should they stay in Paris and thereby recognize the *de facto* government? In spite of the efforts of the representatives of the Holy See, Sweden, and Naples, the second possibility won out.

—The city committee, which now called itself "the provisional government," issued a proclamation:

> Charles X has ceased to reign over France. Not being able to forget the origin of his authority, he has always been considered as the enemy of our country and of its liberties, which he could not understand. After he had surreptitiously attacked our institutions by every means which hypocrisy and fraud furnished him . . . he had decided to drown them in the blood of Frenchmen. Thanks to your heroism, the crimes of his power are over. . . . You will have a government which owes its origins to you . . . all classes have the same rights, these rights are guaranteed.

—The republicans urged La Fayette to hold a plebiscite and, before any decision on the form of government, to get a statement of guarantees and democratic reforms accepted. They wanted to proclaim a republic at noon on the following day.

—*Neuilly, 9:00* P.M. The Duke of Orleans received the emissaries from the chamber of deputies. On Talleyrand's advice he decided to go to Paris.

—*11:30* P.M. The Duke of Orleans arrived at the Palais-Royal.

*Saturday, July 31*

—*Saint-Cloud. 3:00* A.M. More and more defections were taking place among royal troops. Marmont, fearing for the safety of the royal family, urgently advised that they move out to the Trianon. The departure took place immediately.

—*Paris.* At the same time the Duke of Mortemart was secretly being received by the Duke of Orleans, who had asked to see him. "Duke of Mortemart," exclaimed the prince, "if you see the king before I do, tell him they brought me back to Paris under duress, but I will be torn to pieces rather than let them put the crown on my head."

—*6:00* A.M. La Fayette refused the presidency of the republic, offered to him by the insurrectionary leaders, and rallied in principle to the Orleanist solution.

—*8:00* A.M. The Duke of Orleans received a deputation from the chamber which came to offer him officially the lieutenant-generalship of the realm. After a moment's reflection, he accepted.

—The chamber acknowledged this decision and drew up a proclamation to announce it to the country. The deputies went in a body to the Palais-Royal to present it to the prince. An exchange of speeches.

—*2:00* P.M. The Duke of Orleans, escorted by the deputies and some national guardsmen, went to the City Hall. He was received with hostility by the crowd assembled in the square. But La Fayette greeted him cordially, appeared with him on the balcony, and embraced him in the folds of the tricolor flag. Then popular acclamation finally sanctioned the new power. The republic was set aside.

—La Fayette returned the visit by going to the Palais-Royal: "What the people need today," he said, "is a popular throne, surrounded by republican institutions."

—*4:00* P.M. The unrest of the Versailles populace made Charles X decide not to stay at the Trianon and to continue on to Rambouillet, where he arrived at about 10:00 P.M.


*Sunday, August 1*

—*Paris.* The city committee resigned its powers into the hands of the Duke of Orleans. The latter appointed provisional ministers and convoked the chambers for August 3.

—The victorious people rested and rejoiced.

—*Rambouillet.* The Duchess of Angoulême, coming from Vichy, rejoined her family. The king still had twelve thousand faithful troops and forty cannon. Certain ones urged him to go with them to the western provinces to organize there the resistance to the Paris revolution.

—Charles X himself decided to appoint the Duke of Orleans as lieutenant-general. Thus the monarchical principle would be saved.

### Monday, August 2

—*1:00* A.M. This ordinance was delivered to the Duke of Orleans.

—*6:00* A.M. The king received his reply: the prince declared that he held his power from the representatives of the people and that he could not accept another investiture.

—*Noon.* The king assembled a family council. He decided to abdicate in favor of his grandson. Here is his letter to the Duke of Orleans:

> My cousin, I am deeply grieved by the ills which afflict or could threaten my people, for not having sought a way to prevent them. I have therefore come to the decision to abdicate my crown in favor of my grandson, the Duke of Bordeaux. The Dauphin, sharing my sentiments, also renounces his rights. In your capacity as lieutenant-general of the realm you will therefore have the accession of Henry V to the crown proclaimed. You will also have all the measures taken to arrange the forms of government during the minority of the new king. . . .

—The Duchess of Berry wanted to go to Paris to have her son recognized by the lieutenant-general and the authorities. Charles X absolutely refused to let her.

—*10:00* P.M. Four commissioners, sent by the Duke of Orleans with the mission of persuading Charles X to leave and of guaranteeing him a safe-conduct, arrived in Rambouillet. "Safe-conduct," asked the king, "what is that for? I don't need any. I am surrounded by a faithful army. I have made my intentions known to the lieutenant-general and I will only leave Rambouillet as they conform to them."

—*11:00* P.M. The act of abdication was handed to the Duke of Orleans. He replied that the document would be communicated to the chambers, which alone had the authority to decide what action should be taken on it.

### Tuesday, August 3

—*4:00* A.M. The commissioners, returning from Rambouillet, woke the Duke of Orleans: "Monseigneur, the attitude of Charles X appears hostile. It is urgent to strike a decisive blow to frighten him."

—La Fayette was therefore ordered to organize a corps of national guardsmen to make a demonstration on Rambouillet. To the sound of drums which beat out the call to arms, a multitude of volunteers joined them.

—*Noon.* Brandishing a miscellany of weapons, a disorganized throng got underway, piled into all sorts of requisitioned vehicles. "A rout in reverse," one contemporary called it.

—*1:00* P.M. The Duke of Orleans went to the Palais Bourbon to open the session of the chambers, in the presence of 240 deputies and sixty peers. His speech announced the abdication of Charles X and of his son, without alluding to the Duke of Bordeaux. He defended his conduct and announced a modification of the Charter and the program of his future government.

—*8:00* P.M. The Paris "army" arrived three leagues from Rambouillet. Odilon Barrot, General Maison, and the lawyer Schonen had gone ahead of the column. Admitted to the presence of Charles X, they begged him to avoid a bloody encounter. At first the king appeared determined to resist. He took General Maison aside and asked him: "You are a military man, consequently incapable of lying. How many are there?"

—"Sire, I haven't counted them. There must be sixty to eighty thousand." And he insisted again on the danger of the situation.

—"All right, I'm leaving," the king finally said.

But, Maison, heaped with honors and money by Charles X, Maison had lied. "They" were no more than fifteen to twenty thousand whom a few cannon shot would have scattered "like a flock of sparrows." But could this shedding of blood have changed at all the fate of the monarchy?

In the night, Charles X, surrounded by the remnants of his court and troops, moved on to Maintenon. This was the end.

### Reflections on the Events

When one considers the lamentable drama as a whole, one is amazed at the repeated mistakes committed at each step of the way. After the reply of the 221, Charles X could have changed ministries without compromising the dignity of the crown. Having chosen to take the dispute to the electorate, he could have bowed in good faith to the verdict, and that attitude no doubt would have rallied the support of his opponents of good faith. The coup d'état which he preferred to try could have succeeded if it had been accompanied by relatively easy military and police precautions. On the first day of the insurrection, he could still have saved his throne by withdrawing the ordinances and by confiding the authority to a Casimir Périer, for example. Finally, if his abdication had come three days earlier, he could have thwarted the Orleanist intrigue. Instead of this, at every point Charles X had been wrongly inspired, ill advised, and badly served. Everything he did had made the situation worse; all his parrying had hit back an instant too late.

In other words, it appears that this revolution was not at all inevitable. The electorate undoubtedly rejected Polignac and the interpretation that the king tried to give to the Charter, but it did not hold it against the dynasty or even against the person of Charles X. The voters especially were not desirous of making a new revolution. The attitude of the deputies in Paris in the course of the July days was significant, and they rallied around the Orleanist solution because it permitted as much as possible the limiting of the consequences of an uprising which had broken out and spread without their participation.

Could the Duke of Orleans have gotten Henry V accepted? Perhaps. In any case, it does not seem plausible that he would have seriously envisioned or attempted it, and there is still no proof that this solution, so satisfactory from many points of view, would have been impractical. What he chose instead, even though it lasted eighteen years, was really to turn out to be not much more viable.

Charles X, having lost everything, had nothing else to do but leave the scene; but at least the slow majestic pace of his departure was to cast upon the sunset of the old monarchy a final and melancholy glow of greatness.

At Maintenon the royal guard and the remaining faithful troops were released from duty; only the life-guards, about a thousand men, were to accompany the king as far as Cherbourg, where he embarked. Through Dreux, Laigle, Argentan, Vire, Saint-Lô, and Valognes, "the funeral procession of monarchy" slowly traversed a Normandy decked out in all the splendor of a beautiful summer; the people, now hostile, now sympathetic, watched him pass with respect. The commissioners of the new government did what they could with delicacy to humor the feelings of the old king and to avoid a clash between the life-guards with the white cockades and the national guardsmen with the tricolored cockades. They were also to take discreet precautions against a last-minute attempt to depart from the agreed route.

At Valognes, on August 15, took place a final ceremony. The life-guards handed over their flags to the king. "Gentlemen," the king told them, "I accept these standards. You have preserved them unsullied. I hope a day will come when my grandson will have the joy of restoring them to you."

The next day, at about ten o'clock, the king, who had changed from his uniform to civilian dress, entered his carriage for the last leg of his journey. The procession avoided crossing the city of Cherbourg, where royalist demonstrations were feared, and it arrived at about one forty-five at the pier where were awaiting it two American ships, the *Great Britain* and the *Charles Carroll,* leased by the government. The famous explorer, Dumond d'Urville, accepted the task of conducting the royal family to England. The port was full of ships flying the tricolor, but the last wish of the king was respected—he was to sail under his own banner, the white flag. The quays, the ramparts, and the nearby houses were covered with immense, but silent, crowds. The life-guards stood in formation, facing the sea; the king said his farewells and courteously thanked the commissioners for their good offices. Standing on deck, he waved for the last time to his faithful followers, now in tears. At a quarter past two the departure signal was given.

Who was the real loser—the nation, which at that hour thought it was victorious; or the obstinate old man who was leaving these shores for good? The latter was giving up the most glorious throne of the finest kingdom in Europe; the former was depriving itself of a principle of political authority, of national unity, and of social stability, the equivalent of which it was never again able to recapture. After a hundred and thirty years of revolutions and wars, of dictatorial or anarchical governments, France can today estimate the irreparable seriousness of the wound which she inflicted upon herself by her eviction of Charles X, and she beholds with nostalgic envy her great neighbor across the Channel who had the wisdom to reconcile monarchical tradition with the inevitable democratic evolution.

# Epilogue

As we come to the end of this account, we inevitably face the question of whether the Restoration was a viable regime for France. The Revolution of 1830 appears, at first sight, to prove that it was not. But this is a bad argument, because that revolution, it has been shown, was an entirely avoidable accident. The congenital weakness of the Restoration was that it grew out of a compromise, having been, as Balzac wrote, "a period of continual compromises between men, between things, and between accomplished facts on the one hand and those looming on the horizon on the other"—or, if you will, between the new society, forged by the Revolution and Empire, and the old society, going back to feudal, monarchical, aristocratic, and religious times. All compromises are not necessarily bound to fail; the one presented by the Charter system was reasonable, acceptable to the greatest number, and compatible with the needs of the moment and with the degree of political education in the nation. To consolidate itself, the Restoration only needed time and also a certain flexibility which would allow it to evolve imperceptibly. And the text of the Charter, by its obscurities on certain important points, offered that margin of uncertainty which made necessary adjustments possible. The Anglo-Saxon spirit would have adjusted to it; but the French spirit, with its logical insistence, demanded uncompromisingly and immediately a clarification of all salutary contradictions. Charles X, by clearly raising the question of royal prerogative, put his finger on the critical point and provoked the catastrophe.

He was wrong in believing that the crown, by surrendering to the nation a part of its powers, could no longer be of use to it; he was wrong in giving up his role of supreme arbiter for that of party leader; he was wrong in letting himself be blinded by his memories of the Revolution and in confusing liberalism with anarchy; he was wrong in clashing head-on with public opinion when there was no way of silencing it; he was wrong in looking like the enemy of liberty when the tradition of his family as well as the state of the nation repudiated despotism.

Yet, the errors and deficiencies of the monarch are not alone responsible for the failure of the regime. There must also be included the resentments and fears of the survivors of the old aristocracy, the imprudence and blindness of a part of the clergy, and finally the mediocrity of the statesmen: Talleyrand, intelligent but venal and cynical; Richelieu, unselfish but unstable and inexperienced; Decazes, audacious but superficial and unreliable; Villèle, solid but narrow-minded and resentful; Martignac, witty but opportunistic and flighty; and Polignac, devoted but obtuse and utopian. Not one of them had the qualities of a great minister who could have dominated the princes, elicited the support of the nation's elite, and given a life-saving dynamism to the regime.

Nor were his adversaries themselves without reproach. "There are two wise attitudes indispensable to free peoples," wrote Guizot. "One is not to believe instantly the first impressions the free press gives them and all the rumors whispered in their ears. The other is to know how to accept and tolerate the imperfections and weaknesses of their rulers, kings, or ministers, when good principles and good results generally prevail in their government." The Frenchmen who attacked the Restoration and provoked the revolution of 1830 lacked these two wise qualities. If there were people on the extreme Right who did not accept the required compromises, there were just as many on the extreme Left. The obtuse violence of their attacks, the bad faith and boldness of their calumnies were just the kind to propel Charles X into the ill-fated fight in which he engaged. On them, as well as on the luckless monarch, rests the responsibility for the misfortunes of France in the nineteenth century.

The Bourbons therefore did not succeed in consolidating the regime of the Restoration and in healing the wounds of the Revolution. At least, their fifteen-year rule procured a salutary respite for France, which even seemed like one of the happiest periods in her history. "It would take centuries for most of the people of Europe to attain the same degree of happiness that France enjoyed under Charles X." Stendhal was saying this in 1829. And when an objective assessment is made of the period, one can certainly say he was right.

No doubt France had never been better administered, with more honesty up and down the hierarchical scale, with more respect for laws and regulations, with more concern for the rights of citizens, and with less misappropriation of the public funds. Has anyone ever seen a time like this one, when the only financial scandal that the opposition found to denounce was the isolated instance of Minister Peyronnet when he exceeded the 179,000 franc ($35,800) appropriation allotted for the necessary transformations in the ministry building.

French finances had never been so successfully handled, and the wise regulations drawn up by Villèle supported them during the entire nineteenth century. Until 1870 the army thrived on the principles laid down by Gouvion-Saint-Cyr in 1818, and the navy likewise flourished on the technical innovations of the Restoration until the coming of the age of steam. It was also in this period that the present functions of the council of state began to take shape and the tradition of the integrity and independence of judges was firmly established.

Under the Restoration, France had been able to serve her apprenticeship in a parliamentary regime and obtain her political education. For the first time parties were able freely to challenge each other's points of view, and from this peaceful clash emerged political theories and rules of procedure. In those days they still believed in the worth of ideas, and, if violent passions erupted, at least they did not know sordid conflicts of interests and lobby intrigues.

The pre-machine-age economy attained its ultimate perfection, and, if later progress made it look stagnant by comparison, it offered to the individual a place on the human scale and a security conducive to the development of his spiritual gifts. Its society also presented a happy balance between social mobility and the stability of social stratifications. It recovered its moral equilibrium after revolutionary convulsions and the heady intoxications of the conquering Empire. From all of this resulted an atmosphere eminently favorable to intellectual efforts, and France reassumed her pre-eminence in the fields of science, letters, and arts.

In the area of foreign policy the government of the Bourbons committed almost no mistakes and took full advantage of the disastrous situation bequeathed by the Empire. In a few short years the humiliating consequences of defeat had been liquidated, and France had regained in Europe the rank to which her residue of real power had qualified her. On at least three occasions she had been able to assert the independence and efficacy of her arms and her diplomacy: when she intervened in Spain in 1823, when she contributed to Greek independence, and finally when she conquered Algiers, in spite of England, and thereby founded a new colonial empire.

Because all this had been accomplished under a dynasty which had been thrown out, under a regime which they never wanted to see again, it was necessary for a long time to minimize it, to ignore it, and distort it. It was necessary to show up the errors and petty deeds, from which no regime had been exempt, much less those regimes coming after that of Charles X. History today ought to be able to rise above outworn resentments and fears and subscribe to the judgment that Ernest Renan had already pronounced a hundred years ago: "The Restoration set in motion the true development of France in the nineteenth century and remains endeared to all those of lofty thoughts."

# Bibliography

THERE is no systematic and satisfactory bibliography of the Restoration. A good orientation is given by M. Jacques Droz in volume IX of the CLIO collection: *L'Époque contemporaine—I: Restaurations et Révolutions* (2d edition 1963). The *Bibliographie annuelle de l'histoire de France,* edited by Mme Albert-Samuel, and supplied with excellent indexes, furnishes most detailed listings for the years 1953 and following. The titles which will be found below constitute only a summary bibliography, the selection of which was based mainly on the two criteria of importance and recency. It was not thought possible to list all the magazine articles used in this work, although they may have often contributed valuable information. I should like to thank particularly MM. Daniel Resnick and Nicholas Richardson who permitted me to use their then-unpublished works devoted respectively to the White Terror and to the prefects of the Restoration. I have also made use of unpublished documents found in French and foreign archives, and I apologize to the specialists for not having been able, because of the character of the original French edition, to indicate the origin and extent of use of these sources.

Furthermore, in this English edition, I am adding a few more items in English and other foreign languages. An old, but still helpful bibliography of the Restoration under English auspices is volume X (1907), *The Restoration* of the first edition of *The Cambridge Modern History,* especially for France (see pp. 791–795). Also very useful are the bibliographies in the volume of the Langer series, *Reaction and Revolution,* by Frederick B. Artz. The author has taken pains to update these bibliographies for each new printing.

## Printed Sources

### 1. Documentary Collections

DUVERGIER, *Collection complète des lois, décrets, ordonnances, règlements et avis du Conseil d'État* (generally one volume a year).
*Archives parlementaires.* . . . Series II, 1800–1860.

### 2. Pamphlets and Occasional Writings

The Restoration produced a very large quantity of these. Their titles will be found in the *Catalogue d'Histoire de France* of the Bibliothèque Nationale, vol. III and XI (supplement).

### 3. Newspapers and Periodicals

The main ones are listed in E. HATIN, *Bibliographie historique et critique de la presse périodique en France* (1866). But this work contains numerous errors and shows many omissions, especially concerning those periodicals published irregularly.

### 4. Iconography and Songs

The series *Histoire de France* of the print-room of the Bibliothèque Nationale is rich in materials concerning the Restoration, but other series and collections should also be consulted, especially the Vinck Collection, for which there is a printed catalogue; volume V, dealing with the Restoration, was compiled by Anne-Marie ROSSET. An excellent selection of songs is found in the collection by Pierre BARBIER and France VERNILLAT: *Histoire de France par les chansons*, vol. VI: *La Restauration* (1958).

### 5. Memoirs and Correspondence

These are extremely numerous for this period. Listed here are some of the more useful ones.
ABRANTÈS (Duchesse d'): *Mémoires sur la Restauration* . . . , 6 vol., 1835–1836.
AGOULT (Comtesse d'): *Mes Souvenirs, 1806–1833,* 1877.
APPONYI (Comte Rodolphe): *Vingt-cinq ans à Paris,* vol. I: *1826–1830,* 1913.
BARANTE (Prosper de): *Souvenirs du baron de Barante* . . . , 8 vol., 1890–1897.
BASSANVILLE (Comtesse de): *Les Salons d'autrefois, souvenirs intimes* . . . , 4 vol., 1862–1866.
BEUGNOT (Jacques-Claude): *Mémoires du comte Beugnot* . . . , 2 vol., 1866.
BOIGNE (Comtesse de): *Récits d'une tante* . . . , 5 vol., 1921–1923.
BROGLIE (Victor de): *Souvenirs du feu duc de Broglie* . . . , 4 vol., 1886.
CASTELLANE (Maréchal de): *Journal* . . . , 5 vol., 1895–1897.
CASTLEREAGH (Viscount): *Correspondence, dispatches and other papers* . . . , Third series, *1813–1822.* 4 vol., 1848–1853.
CHATEAUBRIAND: *Mémoires d'outre-tombe.* (The new centenary edition compiled by Maurice Levaillant is now the only valuable one.)
CHATEAUBRIAND: *Correspondance générale,* edited by Louis Thomas, 5 vol., 1912–1924. (Unfinished and most incomplete. A new and better edition is in preparation under the auspices of the Société Chateaubriand.)
DELÉCLUZE (Étienne): *Souvenirs de soixante années,* 1862.
FERRAND (Comte): *Mémoires* . . . , 1897.

FRÉNILLY (Baron de): *Souvenirs* . . . , 1908.
GUERNON-RANVILLE (Comte de): *Journal d'un ministre* . . . , 1873.
GUIZOT (François): *Mémoires pour servir à l'histoire de mon temps*, vol. I, 1858. (An English edition 1858.)
HAUSSEZ (Baron d'): *Mémoires* . . . , 2 vol., 1896–1897.
HAUSSONVILLE (Comte d'): *Ma jeunesse, 1814–1830*, 1865.
HUGO (Victor): *Choses vues.*
LAMBRUSCHINI (Cardinal): *La mia nunziatura di Francia*, 1934.
LAMENNAIS: *Œuvres posthumes* . . . , *correspondance, publiée par E. Forgues,* 1859.
LAMENNAIS: *Œuvres inédites. Correspondance, publiée par A. Blaize,* 2 vol., 1866.
LAMENNAIS: *Correspondance inédite entre Lamennais et le baron de Vitrolles,* 1866.
    (In addition to these collections there are a great number of partial publications of Lamennais correspondence.)
LEGOUVÉ (E.): *Soixante ans de souvenirs*, n.d.
METTERNICH: *Mémoires, documents et écrits divers;* 8 vol., 1880–1884.
MOLÉ: *Le comte Molé . . . sa vie, ses mémoires,* 6 vol., 1922–1930.
PASQUIER: *Histoire de mon temps* . . . , 6 vol., 1893–1896.
PERDIGUIER (Agricol): *Mémoires d'un compagnon*, 1914.
POLOVTSOV: *Correspondance diplomatique des ambassadeurs et ministres de Russie en France* . . . , *de 1814 à 1830,* 3 vol., 1901–1907.
PONTMARTIN (Vicomte de): *Mes Mémoires*, 2 vol., 1885.
RAGUSE (Maréchal Marmont, duc de): *Mémoires*, 9 vol., 1857.
REISET (Vicomte de): *Souvenirs*, 3 vol., 1901–1902.
RÉMUSAT (Charles de): *Correspondance de M. de Rémusat pendant les premières années de la Restauration* . . . , 6 vol., 1883–1886.
RÉMUSAT (Charles de): *Mémoires de ma vie*, vol. I and II, 1958–1959.
RICHELIEU: *Lettres du duc de Richelieu au marquis d'Osmond, 1816–1818*, 1939.
ROCHECHOUART (Général de): *Souvenirs sur la Révolution, l'Empire et la Restauration*, 1933. English edition in 1920.
SAINT-CHAMANS (Général, comte de): *Mémoires*, 1896.
SALABERRY (Comte de): *Souvenirs politiques* . . . , 1900.
SERRE (Comte de): *Correspondance* . . . , 7 vol., 1876–1882.
STENDHAL: *Courrier anglais*, 5 vol., 1935.
VIDOCQ: *Mémoires de V., chef de la police de sûreté,* 1828–1829.
VIENNET: *Journal de Viennet, témoin de trois règnes,* 1955.
VILLÈLE (Comte de): *Mémoires et correspondance* . . . , 5 vol., 1887–1890.
VITROLLES (Baron de): *Mémoires et relations politiques*, 3 vol., 1883–1884.
WELLINGTON: *Supplementary despatches, correspondence and memoranda, 1797–1818,* 12 vol., 1858–1865.
WELLINGTON: *Despatches, correspondence and memoranda, 1819–1829,* 5 vol., 1867–1873.

## General Works

Some of the old histories of the Restoration are still useful, either because their authors were personally involved in the events, or because they cite documents now difficult to find. They are those of CAPEFIGUE (1831–1833), 10 vol.; DU-

VERGIER DE HAURANNE, under the title of *Histoire du gouvernement parlementaire en France* (1857–1872), 10 vol.; VAULABELLE (1857), 8 vol.; VIEL-CASTEL (1860–1878), 20 vol.

Among the more recent histories, one should consult: CHARLÉTY (Sébastien): *La Restauration* (vol. IV of *Histoire de France contemporaine*, edited by E. Lavisse), 1921.

LA GORCE (Pierre de): *Louis XVIII, Charles X*, 2 vol., 1926–1928.
ARTZ (Frederick B.): *France under the Bourbon Restoration*, 1931.

And especially the courses given in the Sorbonne by Professor Charles POUTHAS: *Histoire politique de la Restauration, La Politique étrangère de la Monarchie constitutionnelle*. Published in the form of offset copies by the Centre de Documentation Universitaire, they constitute together the most solid and impartial account of the Restoration period.

Two works in English

HALL (J. R.): *The Bourbon Restoration*, 1909. (Largely obsolete.)
LEYS (M. D. R.): *Between two empires. A history of French politicians and people between 1814 and 1848*, 1955. (Summary but excellent.)

The history of the period has been examined for certain special topics.

THUREAU-DANGIN (P.): *Royalistes et républicains*, 1874.
THUREAU-DANGIN (P.): *Le Parti libéral sous la Restauration*, 1876.
WEILL (Georges): *Histoire du parti républicain en France de 1814 à 1870*, 1910.
MARION (M.): *Histoire financière de la France . . .*, vol. IV and V, 1925–1928.
RENOUVIN (Pierre): *Histoire des relations internationales*, vol. V: *Le XIXe siècle. I. De 1815 à 1871*, 1954.
HAMMER (Karl): *Die französische Diplomatie der Restauration und Deutschland, 1814–1830*, 1963.
PONTEIL (Félix): *Les institutions de la France de 1815 à 1870*, 1966.
PLANEMATZ (J.): *Revolutionary movements in France, 1815–1871*, 1952.
RICHARDSON (Nicholas): *The French prefectural corps, 1814–1830* (1966).

There are few serious works on local history outside of the following:

MOULARD (J.): *Le comte Camille de Tournon, préfet de la Gironde, 1815–1822.* 2 vol., 1932.
CONTAMINE (H.): *Metz et la Moselle de 1814 à 1870*, 2 vol., 1932.
VIDALENC (J.): *Le département de l'Eure sous la Monarchie constitutionnelle*, 1952.
LEUILLOT (P.): *La première Restauration et les Cent-Jours en Alsace*, 1958.
LEUILLOT (P.): *L'Alsace au début du XIXe siècle*, 3 vol., 1959–1961.

## Biographies

Biographies are very numerous, yet we still lack reliable works on several important political figures such as Richelieu, Blacas, and Decazes. Here are some of the more important and useful ones:

JOINVILLE (P. de): *L'armateur Balguerie-Stuttenberg et son œuvre*, 1914.

ALMÉRAS (Ch.): *Odilon Barrot, avocat et homme politique*, 1950.

LUCAS-DUBRETON: *Béranger*, 1934.

LUCAS-DUBRETON: *La duchesse de Berry*, 1935.

LACOMBE (Ch. de): *Vie de Berryer*, vol. I, 1894.

BERTIER DE SAUVIGNY (G. de): *Le comte Ferdinand de Bertier et l'énigme de la Congrégation*, 1948.

BEAU DE LOMÉNIE (Em.): *La carrière politique de Chateaubriand*, 2 vol., 1929.

ROUSSET (Camille): *Un ministre de la Restauration, le marquis de Clermont-Tonnerre*, 1885.

BOTTENHEIM (J.): *Corvetto et son œuvre . . .* , 1941.

LANGERON (R.): *Decazes, ministre du roi*, 1960.

BASCHET (R.): *E. J. Delécluze, témoin de son temps*, 1942.

ZIEGLER (P.): *The duchess of Dino*, 1962.

PERRET (Edouard): *La dernière favorite des rois de France, la comtesse du Cayla*, 1937.

MADELIN (L.): *Fouché*, 1900.

GARNIER (A.): *Frayssinous*, 1925.

POUTHAS (Ch.): *Guizot pendant la Restauration*, 1923.

PERCEVAL (E. de): *Un adversaire de Napoléon, le vicomte Lainé*, 1926.

GIGNOUX (C.-J.): *La vie du baron Louis*, 1928.

SAINT-MARC (Pierre de): *Le maréchal Marmont . . .* , 1957.

WOLFF (Otto): *Die Geschäfte des Herrn Ouvrard*, 1933.

BRIQUET (J.): *Agricol Perdiguier*, 1955.

NICOULLAUD (Ch.): *Casimir Périer, député de l'opposition*, 1894.

PERCEVAL (E. de): *Un condamné de haute-cour, le comte de Peyronnet*, 1930.

ROBIN-HARMEL (P.): *Le prince Jules de Polignac*, 2 vol., 1940–1950.

GERVAIN (Mme de): *Un ministre de la Marine, le baron Portal*, 1888.

WIECLAWIK (L. de): *Alphonse Rabbe dans la mêlée politique et littéraire de la Restauration*, 1963.

HERRIOT (E.): *Madame Récamier et ses amis*, 1904.

COX (Cynthia): *Talleyrand's successor. The life of Armand-Emmanuel, duke of Richelieu*, 1958.

LANGERON (R.): *Royer-Collard*, 1956.

COMBES DE PATRIS: *Le comte de Serre*, 1932.

LACOUR-GAYET (G.): *Talleyrand*, 3 vol., 1928–1931.

FOURCASSIÉ (J.): *Villèle*, 1954.

See also the other biographies listed in the sections on religious and intellectual life.

## Special Topics

The Fall of the Empire (Chapters I and II)

HOUSSAYE (H.): *1814*, 1888.

BENAERTS (L.): *Les commissaires extraordinaires de Napoléon en 1814 . . .* , 1915.

THIRY (J.): *La chute de Napoléon Ier*, 2 vol., 1938–1939.

MADELIN (L.): *Histoire du Consulat et de l'Empire*, vol. XIV, 1951.

See also the biographies listed above of Talleyrand (chapters XXIV–XXVIII) and F. de Bertier (chapters III–V).

### The First Restoration (Chapters III, IV, and V)

HOUSSAYE (H.): *1815*, vol. I, 1893.

FIRMIN-DIDOT (G.): . . . *La France en 1815 d'après les rapports inédits du comte Anglès*, 1897.

DUPUIS (Charles): *Le ministère de Talleyrand en 1814*, 2 vol., 1920.

THIRY (J.): *La première Restauration*, 1941.

MADELIN (L.): *Histoire du Consulat et de l'Empire*, vol. XV, 1952.

SIMON (Pierre): *L'élaboration de la Charte constitutionnelle de 1814*, 1906.

### The Congress of Vienna (Chapter VI)

PALLAIN (G.): *Correspondance inédite du prince de Talleyrand et du roi Louis XVIII pendant le congrès de Vienne* . . . 1881.

WEBSTER (Sir Charles): *The foreign policy of Castlereagh*, 1931.

WEBSTER (Sir Charles): *The congress of Vienna*, 1934.

NICHOLSON (Harold): *The congress of Vienna*, 1946.

GRIEWANK (K.): *Der wiener Kongress und die europäische Restauration, 1814–1815*, 1955.

KISSINGER (H.): *A World restored, 1812–1822*, 1955.

### The Hundred Days and the Second Restoration (Chapter VII)

HOUSSAYE (H.): *1815*, vol. II and III.

THIRY (J.): *Le vol de l'Aigle*, 1942.

THIRY (J.): *Les Cent-Jours*, 1943.

THIRY (J.): *Waterloo*, 1943.

MADELIN (L.): *Histoire du Consulat et de l'Empire*, vol. XVI, 1954.

PONTEIL (F.): *La chute de Napoléon Ier et la crise française de 1814–1815*, 1943.

LE GALLO (E.): *Les Cent-Jours. Essai sur l'histoire intérieure de la France depuis le retour de l'île d'Elbe jusqu'à la nouvelle de Waterloo*, 1924.

GRAND (Roger): *La chouannerie de 1815*, 1942.

FLEISCHMAN (Théo): *Louis XVIII et les émigrés français à Gand pendant les Cent-Jours*, 1953.

See also the biographies of Fouché, by MADELIN (chapters XXIII–XXVI) and of F. de Bertier, by BERTIER DE SAUVIGNY (chapter VI).

### The Reign of Louis XVIII (Chapters VIII to XIII)

LUCAS-DUBRETON: *Louis XVIII*, 1925.

DAUDET (E.): *Louis XVIII et le duc Decazes*, 1899.

ANDRÉ (R.): *L'occupation de la France par les alliés en 1815*, 1924.

DAUDET (E.): *La Terreur blanche*, 2d ed., 1906.

KURTZ (Harold): *The trial of Marshal Ney*, 1957.

DUMOLARD (Henry): *La Terreur blanche dans l'Isère. Jean-Paul Didier et la conspiration de Grenoble*, 1930.

CISTERNES (R. de): *Le duc de Richelieu. Son action aux conférences d'Aix-la-*

*Chapelle. Sa retraite du pouvoir,* 1898.
LUCAS-DUBRETON: *Louvel le régicide,* 1923.
RESNICK (Daniel): *The White Terror and the political reaction after Waterloo,* 1966.
GUILLON (E.): *Les complots militaires sous la Restauration* . . . , 1895.
LUCAS-DUBRETON: *Le culte de Napoléon, 1815–1848,* 1960.
ŒCHSLIN (J.-J.): *Le mouvement ultra-royaliste sous la Restauration,* 1960.
BERTIER DE SAUVIGNY (G. de): "Metternich et Decazes, d'après leur correspondance inédite," *Études d'Histoire moderne et contemporaine,* vol. V.
RAIN (P.): *L'Europe et la Restauration des Bourbons, 1814–1818,* 1908.
BERTIER DE SAUVIGNY (G. de): *France and the european alliance. The private correspondence between Metternich and Richelieu,* 1958.
BOURQUIN (M.): *Histoire de la Sainte-Alliance,* 1954.
SCHROEDER (Paul W.): *Metternich's diplomacy at its zenith, 1820–1823,* 1962.
TEMPERLEY (H.): *The foreign policy of Canning, 1822–1827,* 1925.
ROBERTSON (W. S.): *France and Latin-American independence,* 1939.
GRANDMAISON (G. de): *L'expédition française d'Espagne en 1823,* 1928.

Economic Life (Chapter XIV)

SÉE (H.): *Histoire économique de la France,* vol. II, 1951.
CLOUGH (Shepard B.): *France. A History of national economics, 1789–1939,* 1939.
CLAPHAM (J. H.): *The economic development of France and Germany, 1815–1914,* 1936.
CHABERT (A.): *Essai sur les mouvements des revenus et de l'activité économique en France de 1798 à 1820,* 2 vol. 1945–1949.
CAMERON (Rondo E.): *France and the economic development of Europe, 1800–1914,* 1961.
CAVAILLÈS (H.): *La route française* . . . , 1946.
GRAS (L.-J.): *Histoire des premiers chemins de fer français,* 1924.

Statistical data for agriculture is to be found in:

TOUTAIN (J.-C.): *Histoire quantitative de l'économie française,* vol. I–II: *Le produit de l'agriculture française de 1700 à 1958.*

But there is no good general survey of French agriculture for the early XIXth century. Numerous studies on agricultural history have been published in journals, and devoted either to single provinces or departments, or to some special crops. Here are a few examples:

LAURENT (R.): *L'agriculture en Côte-d'Or pendant la première moitié du XIXe siècle,* 1931.
VIDALENC (J.): "L'agriculture dans les départements normands à la fin du Premier Empire," *Annales de Normandie,* 1957.
VIDALENC (J.): "Notes sur la vigne en France, de 1789 à la fin de la Restauration," *Annales de la Faculté d'Aix,* vol. XXIX (1954).
CASTELLAN (G.): "Fourrages et bovins dans l'économie rurale de la Restauration," *Revue d'Histoire économique et sociale,* 1960.

A great deal may also be found in some recent important studies on social history or human geography, such as:

ROUCHON (U.): *La vie paysanne dans la Haute-Loire*, 3 vol., 1933–1941.
CHEVALIER (Michel): *La vie humaine dans les Pyrénées ariégeoises*, 1956.
LAURENT (R.): *Les vignerons de la Côte-d'Or au XIXe siècle*, 2 vol., 1958.
BOZON (Pierre): *La vie rurale en Vivarais*, 1961.

For the conditions of industry and banking there are more comprehensive historical studies:

DUNHAM (A. L.): *Industrial revolution in France, 1815–1848*, 1955.
GILLE (Bertrand): *Recherches sur la formation de la grande entreprise capitaliste (1815–1848)*, 1959.
LÉON (Pierre): *La naissance de la grande industrie en Dauphiné*, 1954.
SÉDILLOT (R.): *La maison de Wendel* . . . , 1958.
BARKER (Richard J.): "French entrepreneurship during the Restoration . . . the Anzin mining company," *Journal of Economic History*, 1961.
GILLE (Bertrand): *La banque et le crédit en France de 1815 à 1848*.

Social Life (Chapter XV)

WEILL (G.): *La France sous la Monarchie constitutionnelle*, 1912.
POUTHAS (Ch.-H.): *La population française pendant la première moitié du XIXe siècle*, 1956.
CHEVALIER (Louis): *La formation de la population parisienne au XIXe siècle*, 1950.
GUERRY (André-M.): *Essai sur la statistique morale de la France*, 1836.
MARCEAU (Félicien): *Balzac et son monde*, 1955.
PRADALIÉ (G.): *Balzac historien. La société de la Restauration*, 1955.
BATJIN (N.): *Histoire de la noblesse en France depuis 1789*, 1862.
LHOMME (J.): *La grande bourgeoisie au pouvoir*, 1960.
DAUMARD (A.): *La bourgeoisie parisienne de 1815 à 1848*, 1963.
CHALMIN (P.): *L'Officier français de 1815 à 1870*, 1957.
VIDALENC (J.): *Les Demi-Solde. Étude d'une catégorie sociale*, 1957.
BOURGIN (H. et G.): *Les patrons, les ouvriers, l'Etat. Le régime de l'industrie en France de 1814 à 1830*, 3 vol., 1912–1941.
PAILLAT (Paul): *La vie et la condition ouvrière sous la Restauration*. (Unpublished essay which the author kindly allowed me to use.)
BURNAND (R.): *La vie quotidienne en France sous la Restauration*, 1943.
ALMÉRAS (H. d'): *La vie parisienne sous la Restauration*, 1910.
BERTAUT (J.): *Le faubourg Saint-Germain sous l'Empire et la Restauration*, 1949.
CHEVALIER (Louis): *Classes laborieuses et classes dangereuses*, 1958.
BLANCHARD (M.): *La campagne et ses habitants dans l'œuvre d'Honoré de Balzac*, 1931.
TOLEDANO (A.-D.): *La vie de famille sous la Restauration et la Monarchie de Juillet*, 1943.
CAMP (Wesley D.): *Marriage and the family in France since the Revolution*, 1961.
DENIEL (R.): *Une image de la famille et de la société sous la Restauration*, 1965.
PARENT-DUCHATELET (Dr.): *De la prostitution dans la ville de Paris*, 3rd ed. 1857.

Political Life (Chapter XVI)

BASTID (P.): *Les Institutions politiques de la Monarchie parlementaire*, 1954.
COLLINS (Irene): *The Government and the newspaper press in France, 1814–1881*, 1959.
MARQUANT (R.): *Thiers et le baron Cotta*, 1959. (Useful for the secret dealings of the opposition press.)
LEDRÉ (Charles): *La Presse à l'assaut de la Monarchie, 1815–1848*, 1961.
ARTZ (Fr. B.): "The electoral system in France under the Bourbon Restoration," *J. of Mod. History*, 1929.
CAMPBELL (P.): *French electoral systems and elections, 1789–1957*, 1958.
MONNET (C.): *Histoire de l'administration provinciale, départementale et communale en France*, 1885.
LEPOINTE (G.): *Histoire des insitutions du droit public français au XIXe siècle*, 1953.
CHABROL (Comte Chr.): *Rapport au Roi sur l'administration des Finances*, 1830.
AUDIFFRET (Fl.-L. d'): *Système financier de la France*, 1840.
MONTEILHET (J.): *Les institutions militaires de la France, 1814–1924*, 1926.
TITEUX (E.): *Histoire de la maison militaire du roi de 1814 à 1830*, 1889.
GIRARD (L.): *La Garde nationale, 1814–1871*, 1964.
CHEVALIER (Capitaine de vaisseau): *Histoire de la marine française de 1815 à 1870*, 1900.
SCHEFER (Chr.): *La France moderne et le problème colonial*, 1838.

Religious Life (Chapter XVII)

POUTHAS (Ch.): *L'Eglise de France sous la monarchie constitutionnelle*, 1961; (mimeographed lecture courses).
PHILIPPS (G. S.): *The Church in France, 1789–1848*, 1928.
DANSETTE (A.): *Histoire religieuse de la France contemporaine*, 2d ed., vol. I, 1951. (An English translation in 1967.)
LATREILLE (A.) et RÉMOND (R.): *Histoire du catholicisme en France*, vol. III: *La période contemporaine*, 1962.

The histories of dioceses and religious orders are much too numerous to be listed here. We can regret, though, that there are not more of them like the two following:

GENEVRAY (P.): *L'Administration et la vie ecclésiastique dans le grand diocèse de Toulouse . . . sous la Restauration*, 1941.
FAUGERAS (M.): *Le diocèse de Nantes sous la Monarchie censitaire, 1813–1822–1849*, 1964.

Very numerous also are the biographies of bishops and founders of religious societies. Some of the more recent ones are outstanding for the breadth of conception and soundness of factual content:

SEVRIN (E.): *Mgr. Clausel de Montals, évêque de Chartres*, 2 vol., 1955.
LIMOUZIN-LAMOTHE (R.): *Monseigneur de Quélen, archevêque de Paris*, 2 vol., 1955–1957.
LEFLON (J.): *Eugène de Mazenod*, 3 vol., 1957–1965.

The essential figure of Lamennais continues to bring out a flow of studies since the basic book by:

DUINE (F.): *Lamennais, sa vie, ses idées, ses ouvrages*, 1922.

The bibliography given by the same author (*Essai de bibliographie de Félicité-Robert de Lamennais*, 1923) can be brought up to date by the following three important books:

DERRÉ (J.-R.): *Lamennais, ses amis et le mouvement des idées à l'époque romantique (1824–1834)*, 1962.
VERRUCCI (Guido): *Félicité de Lamennais*, 1963.
LE GUILLOU (L.): *L'évolution de la pensée religieuse de Félicité de Lamennais*, 1966.

On educational questions:

LOUIS-GRIMAUD: *Histoire de la liberté d'enseignement en France*, vol. V: *La Restauration*, 1950.
GONTARD (M.): *L'enseignement primaire en France de la Révolution à la loi Guizot*, 1959.

One should also see the biography of Frayssinous listed above. Also there is a dissertation in progress by R. TRONCHOT on the Lancasterian schools in France (*L'enseignement mutuel en France, 1815–1830*).

Two important problems have been the subjects of studies which can be called definitive:

SEVRIN (E.): *Les missions religieuses en France sous la Restauration*, 2 vol., 1948–1959.
BILLAUD (A.): *La Petite Eglise dans la Vendée et les Deux-Sèvres, 1800–1830*, 1961.

On Protestants and Jews:

MAURY (L.): *Le réveil religieux dans l'Eglise réformée à Genève et en France, 1810–1850*, 1892.
BENOIT (J.-P.): *Oberlin pasteur d'hommes*, 1955.
ROBERT (Daniel): *Les Eglises réformées en France, 1800–1830*, 1961.
LUCIEN-BRUN (H.): *Etude historique sur la condition des Israélites en France depuis 1789*, 2d ed., 1901.

Intellectual Life (Chapter XVIII)

OMODEO (A.): *La cultura francese nell'età della Restaurazione*, 1946.

On France's cultural relations with other countries, the fullest bibliographical indications are found in:

BALDENSPERGER and WERNER: *Bibliography of comparative literature*, 1950.

Also should be added some important dissertations recently defended:

MONCHOUX (A.): *L'Allemagne devant les lettres françaises de 1814 à 1835*, 1951.
REBOUL (P.): *Le mythe anglais dans la littérature française sous la Restauration*, 1962.
RÉMOND (R.): *Les États-Unis devant l'opinion française, 1815–1852*, 2 vol., 1963.

Science

CAULLERY (M.): *La Science française depuis le XVIIe siècle*, 1948.
GUIART (J.): *Histoire de la médecine française*, 1947.
ACKERKNECHT (E. H.): "Hygiene in France, 1818–1848" in *Bulletin of the History of Medicine*, 1948. (Very important.)
FAIVRE (J.-P.): *L'Expansion française dans le Pacifique, 1800–1842*, 1953.

History

JULLIAN (C.): *Extraits des historiens français du XIXe siècle. Introduction*, 7th ed., 1913.
STADLER (P.): "Politik und Geschichtschreibung in der französischen Restauration, 1814–1830," *Historische Zeitschrift*, 1955.
MELLON (Stanley): *The political uses of history. A study of historians in the French Restoration*, 1958.
ENGEL-JANOSI (Fr.): *Four studies in French romantic historical writing*, 1954.

Philosophy

PICAVET (F.): *Les idéologues*, 1891.
BOAS (G.): *French philosophies of the romantic period*, 1964.
CRESSON (A.): *Les courants de la pensée philosophique française*, 1927.
GOUHIER (H.): *La jeunesse d'Auguste Comte et la formation du positivisme*, 2 vol., 1933–1941.

Political and social ideas

MAYER (J. P.): *Political thought in France from the Revolution to the Fourth Republic*, 2d ed., 1949.
LEROY (M.): *Histoire des idées sociales en France*. Vol. II: *De Babeuf à Tocqueville*, 1950.
BAGGE (D.): *Les idées politiques en France sous la Restauration*, 1952.
SOLTAU (R.): *French political thought in the 19th century*, 1959.
MURET (T.): *French royalist doctrines since the Revolution*, 1933.
HUDSON (N. E.): *Ultra-Royalism and the French Restoration*, 1936.
RÉMOND (R.): *The Right Wing in France from 1815 to De Gaulle*, 1966.
MENCZER (B.): *Catholic political thought*, 1962.
DUROSELLE (J.-B.): *Les débuts du catholicisme social en France*, 1950.
CAPPADOCIA (E.): "The nature of French Liberalism during the Restoration," *Canadian Hist. Ass. Rep.*, 1961.
STARZINGER (V. E.): *Middlingness: Juste Milieu political theory in France and England, 1815–1848*, 1965.
CHARLÉTY (S.): *Histoire du Saint-Simonisme*, 1931.
BOUGLÉ (Ch.): *Socialisme français . . .* , 1933.
MANUEL (F.): *The new world of Henri Saint-Simon*, 1956.
IGGERS (G. G.): *Cult of authority, political philosophy of the Saint-Simonians*, 1958.
MANUEL (F.): *The prophets of Paris*, 1962.
EVANS (D. O.): *Social romanticism in France*, 1951.

Economic theories

GIDE (Ch.) et RIST (Ch.): *Histoire des idées économiques,* 7th ed., 1947.
REYNAUD (P. L.): *Jean-Baptiste Say,* 1953.

Literature

Since we cannot give here listings on literature, the reader is referred to these specialized bibliographies:

LANSON (G.): *Manuel bibliographique de la littérature française,* 1931.
THIEME (H. P.): *Bibliographie de la littérature française de 1800 à 1836,* 3 vol., 1933.
TALVART et PLACE: *Bibliographie des auteurs modernes de langue française,* 1928 and following, still incomplete.

For the point of view of our treatment, the most important book is still:

MARSAN (J.): *La bataille romantique,* 1912.

In English

FINCH (M. B.) and PEERS (E. A.): *Origins of French romanticism,* 1920.
CLEMENT (N. H.): *Romanticism in France,* 1939.
GEORGE (A. J.): *The development of French romanticism,* 1955.

Arts

HAUTECŒUR (L.): *Histoire de l'architecture classique en France,* Vol. VI: *La Restauration et la Monarchie de Juillet,* 1955.
LUC-BENOIST: *La sculpture française,* 1945.
ROSENTHAL (L.): *La peinture romantique. Essai sur l'évolution de la peinture française de 1815 à 1830,* 1900.
FRIEDLAENDER (W.): *David to Delacroix,* 1952.
ROBIQUET (J.): *L'art et le goût sous la Restauration,* 1928.
BOUCHOT (H.): *Le luxe français. La Restauration,* 1893.
LOCKE (A. W.): *Music and the Romantic movement in France,* 1920.
LAFORET (C.): *La vie musicale aux temps romantiques,* 1929.
EINSTEIN (A.): *Music in the romantic era,* 1947.
BARZUN (J.): *Berlioz and the romantic century,* 2 vol., 1950.

The Reign of Charles X (Chapters XIX to XXIII)

LUCAS-DUBRETON: *Charles X,* new edition 1963.
VIVENT (J.): *Charles X, dernier roi de France et de Navarre,* 1958.
GAIN (A.): *La Restauration et les biens des émigrés,* 2 vol., 1929.
GARNIER (J.-P.): *Le sacre de Charles X et l'opinion publique en 1825,* 1927.
LESPAGNON (J.-H.): *La loi du sacrilège,* 1935.
DAUDET (E.): *Le ministère de M. de Martignac,* 1875.
GARNIER (A.): *Les ordonnances du 16 juin 1828,* 1929.
RADER (D. L.): "The Breton Association and the press," *French Hist. Studies,* II, 1961.

Foreign affairs

CRAWLEY (C. W.): *The question of Greek independence*, 1930.
CANAT (R.): *L'Hellénisme des romantiques*, 1951.
DOUIN (D.): *Navarin*, 1927.
PURYEAR (Y.): *France and the Levant, from the Bourbon Restauration to the peace of Kutiah*, 1941.
JULIEN (Ch.-A.): *Histoire de l'Algérie contemporaine*, Vol. I: *Conquête et colonisation*, 1964. (Contains a most thorough bibliography.)

Revolution of 1830

MAAG (Dr. A.): *Geschichte der schweizer Truppen in französischen Diensten während der Restauration und Julie Revolution, 1816–1830*, 1899. (Contains precise details.)
DAUDET (E.): *La révolution de 1830 . . .* , 1907.
GIRARD (G.): *Les trois glorieuses*, 1929.
WEILL (G.): "La révolution de Juillet dans les départements," *Revue d'Histoire Moderne*, 1931.
PINKNEY (D. H.): "A new look at the French Revolution of 1830," *Review of Politics*, 1961.
CONTAMINE (H.): "Le Convoi funèbre de la monarchie à travers la Normandie," *Normannia*, 1938.

# Index